# Where to Wear 2005

## THE INSIDER'S GUIDE TO NEW YORK SHOPPING

Fairchild & Gallagher
NEW YORK • LONDON

PUBLISHERS
Jill Fairchild, Gerri Gallagher & Julie Craik

EDITOR
Greg Zinman

WRITERS
Kara Alaimo, Balint Bognar,
Shane Cisneros, Andrew Der,
Kimberly Donato, Allyson Drucker,
Nicole Goldberg, Kelly Mills,
Naomi Nevitt, Krishna Patel,
Antonia Santangelo

PREVIOUS WRITERS
Jami Attenberg, Jenna Gallagher,
Catherine Townsend, Greg Zinman

COPY EDITOR
John Graham

FACT CHECKER
Hamish Anderson

DESIGN/PRODUCTION ARTIST
Jeff Baker

COVER DESIGN
Richard Chapman

DISTRIBUTION, SALES AND MARKETING

The Julie Craik Consultancy

Where to Wear, New York, 2005 Edition
ISBN 0-9715544-3-9

Manhattan maps © 2000 Eureka Cartography
Original design and Manhattan maps
courtesy of Graphic Image, Inc.

Printed and bound in United Kingdom

# Table of Contents

# Introduction

Dear New York Shopper,

Welcome to *Where to Wear*, the world's most detailed and authoritative directory of clothing and accessory stores. *Where to Wear* annually updates its collection of global guides, making your travels through the world's fashion cities a breeze. We pioneered in 1999 with *Where to Wear New York*, and we have since added London, Los Angeles, Paris, San Francisco and Italy, which includes Florence, Milan and Rome.

The 2005 edition of *Where to Wear New York* has all the information you'll need to look and feel great. We describe nearly 1,000 different clothing and accessories stores, ranging from the global celebrity names of Madison Avenue and SoHo to out-of-the-way treasure-houses. *Where to Wear* shows visitors where to begin and New Yorkers where to go next. If you want the best vintage value or the brightest bikini, you'll find them using *Where to Wear*.

*Where to Wear* is the only shopping guide written by a team of professional fashion journalists. We have our fingers on the pulse of the ever-changing fashion world. We've tromped through each and every store to discover what's fabulous, functional, frumpy, fancy or frightful in them this season. We tell you what the store and its merchandise are all about and who its target customer is, and we list the address, phone number and opening hours. We've marked those stores that merit special consideration with a star ( ⭐ ), and occasionally we have something sweet (or not so sweet) to say about the staff's helpfulness or attitude. Please let us know if you disagree.

And to make your life even simpler we have included ten pages of user-friendly maps and two separate indexes grouping the stores both by category and by location. Shopping has never been easier! In addition, you'll find the best addresses for beauty treatments, fitness studios, day spas, couture dry cleaners, shoe repair shops, specialty stores (for beads, ribbons, etc) and much else.

Life is not all shopping, of course, so you will also find a list of in-store restaurants and other delightful lunch spots. It's an eclectic list, chosen by our experts for your fun and convenience.

So rev up your credit card and get going, and make sure to keep *W2W* in your handbag, briefcase or backpack.

—Jill Fairchild, Gerri Gallagher & Julie Craik

p.s. We love feedback! Please e-mail us on wheretowear@aol.com or uk@wheretowear.com

**Jill Fairchild Melhado**, daughter of fashion world legend and *W* magazine founder John Fairchild, worked as an intern at *Glamour* magazine, *GQ* and *Vogue*. Ms Fairchild has also worked for Ailes Communications, a television production company, and in the late Eighties she founded and ran her own accessories company.

**Gerri Gallagher** is a Condé Nast editor who has lived in Europe for 15 years. She was the managing editor of Fairchild Publication's *W Europe* from 1990 to 1993 and is currently associate editor of *Tatler* magazine in London.

**Julie Craik**, *Where to Wear* partner and director of sales, marketing and distribution has worked in publishing for 20 years. Before joining *Where to Wear* she was associate publisher of *Tatler* magazine and had previously worked for the National Magazine Company.

# Where to Wear 2005

## Best Picks

## Size Conversion Chart

## Best Picks

Here are our particular favourites
(marked ★ in the Directory)

**If money were no object...**

37=1
Alexander McQueen
Asprey
Barneys

Balenciaga
Basso Furs
Bergdorf Goodman
Bottega Veneta

Brioni
Burberry
Celine
Chanel

Chloé
Christian Louboutin
Comme des Garçons
Dolce & Gabbana

Domenico Vacca
Dunhill
Emanuel Ungaro
Eres

Gucci
Helmut Lang
Hermès

Hot Toddie
Jeffrey
Jimmy Choo
J.Mendel

Keni Valenti
Kirna Zabête
Linda Dresner
Louis Vuitton

Manolo Blahnik
Marc Jacobs
Marni
Michael Kors

Missoni
Prada
Pucci
Ralph Lauren

Resurrection Vintage
Seize sur Vingt (16/20)
Tod's
Vera Wang

Versace
Yohji Yamamoto
YSL

**Because we're worth it—
for instant cheer on a rainy day...**

99X
Bond 07
Borealis
Calypso

Cantaloup
Castor & Pollux
Erica Tanov
Geraldine

Jamin Puech
Kid Robot
Le Corset
La Petite Coquette

Lunettes et Chocolat
Malatesta
Marc by Marc Jacobs
Mayle

Me & Ro
Pucci
Selima Optique
Shop

Some Odd Rubies
Tory by TRB
Tracy Feith

## Show-stoppers—
### these stores have to be seen to be believed...

Alexander McQueen
Asprey
Balenciaga

Bergdorf Goodman
Carlos Miele
Catherine Malandrino

Christian Dior
Diesel
Donna Karan

Geminola
Helmut Lang
Hermès

Jeffrey
Kirna Zabête
Louis Vuitton

Prada
Stella McCartney
Tiffany & Co

## Great style, fantastic prices...

30 Vandam
Amarcord Vintage Fashion
Beacon's Closet

Century 21
Darling
Hootie Couture

Ina
Pearl River Mart
Slang Betty

Sorelle Firenze
Tokio 7

## Pitter-patter of tiny feet...

Au Chat Botté
Cadeau
La Layette
Liz Lange Maternity

Mommy Chic
Pumpkin Maternity
Veronique Maternity

## ...and for the kids themselves

Baby Bird
Bombalulus
Bonpoint
Calypso Enfant

City Cricket
Gap Baby/Kids
Great Feet

Greenstones & Cie
Gymboree
Jacadi

Julian and Sara
Just for Tykes
Koh's Kids

La Petite Etoile
Lilliput/SoHo Kids
Magic Windows
Morris Bros

Old Navy
Oilily
OshKosh B'Gosh

Peanutbutter & Jane
Peter Elliot (Kids)
Petit Bateau

Ralph Lauren Baby
Yoya
Z' Baby Co

3

**Ever-reliable...**

American Apparel
Ann Taylor
Banana Republic
Barneys

Bergdorf Goodman
Brooks Brothers
Century 21
Coach

Earl Jean
Eileen Fisher
Gap
Henri Bendel

J.Crew
Jeffrey
Lord & Taylor
Old Navy

**If we could take the whole shop home...**

Alife
Asprey
Hermès
Jeffrey
Kirna Zabête

Marc Jacobs
Miu Miu
Some Odd Rubies
Tracy Feith

**Service with a smile —
the most helpful people in town...**

Addison on Madison
Bagutta
Blades Board and Skate
Brioni

Brooks Brothers
Chanel
Christian Dior

Darling
Denimaxx
Eastern Mountain Sports

H.Herzfeld
Henri Bendel
Hervé Léger

Jane
Jeffrey
Keiko
Malia Mills

Paragon
Pookie & Sebastian
Ralph Lauren

Saint Laurie
Swiss Army
Super Runners Shop

Turnbull & Asser
Yves Saint Laurent
  Rive Gauche

# Clothing & Shoe Size Equivalents

### Children's Clothing

| American | 3 | 4 | 5 | 6 | 6X |
|---|---|---|---|---|---|
| Continental | 98 | 104 | 110 | 116 | 122 |
| British | 18 | 20 | 22 | 24 | 26 |

### Children's Shoes

| American | 8 | 9 | 10 | 11 | 12 | 12 | 1 | 2 | 3 |
|---|---|---|---|---|---|---|---|---|---|
| Continental | 24 | 25 | 27 | 28 | 29 | 30 | 32 | 33 | 34 |
| British | 7 | 8 | 9 | 10 | 11 | 12 | 13 | 1 | 2 |

### Ladies' Coats, Dresses, Skirts

| American | 3 | 5 | 7 | 9 | 11 | 12 | 13 | 14 | 15 |
|---|---|---|---|---|---|---|---|---|---|
| Continental | 36 | 38 | 38 | 40 | 40 | 42 | 42 | 44 | 44 |
| British | 8 | 10 | 11 | 12 | 13 | 14 | 15 | 16 | 17 |

### Ladies' Blouses and Sweaters

| American | 10 | 12 | 14 | 16 | 18 | 20 |
|---|---|---|---|---|---|---|
| Continental | 38 | 40 | 42 | 44 | 46 | 48 |
| British | 32 | 34 | 36 | 38 | 40 | 42 |

### Ladies' Hosiery

| American | 8 | 8.5 | 9 | 9.5 | 10 | 10.5 |
|---|---|---|---|---|---|---|
| Continental | 1 | 2 | 3 | 4 | 5 | 6 |
| British | 8 | 8.5 | 9 | 9.5 | 10 | 10.5 |

### Ladies' Shoes

| American | 5 | 6 | 7 | 8 | 9 | 10 |
|---|---|---|---|---|---|---|
| Continental | 36 | 37 | 38 | 39 | 40 | 41 |
| British | 3.5 | 4.5 | 5.5 | 6.5 | 7.5 | 8.5 |

### Men's Suits

| American | 34 | 36 | 38 | 40 | 42 | 44 | 46 | 48 |
|---|---|---|---|---|---|---|---|---|
| Continental | 44 | 46 | 48 | 50 | 52 | 54 | 56 | 58 |
| British | 34 | 36 | 38 | 40 | 42 | 44 | 46 | 48 |

### Men's Shirts

| American | 14 | 15 | 15.5 | 16 | 16.5 | 17 | 17.5 | 18 |
|---|---|---|---|---|---|---|---|---|
| Continental | 37 | 38 | 39 | 41 | 42 | 43 | 44 | 45 |
| British | 14 | 15 | 15.5 | 16 | 16 | 17 | 17.5 | 18 |

### Men's Shoes

| American | 7 | 8 | 9 | 10 | 11 | 12 | 13 |
|---|---|---|---|---|---|---|---|
| Continental | 39.5 | 41 | 42 | 43 | 44.5 | 46 | 47 |
| British | 6 | 7 | 8 | 9 | 10 | 11 | 12 |

# Alphabetical Store Directory

## ★ 37=1

Designer Jean Yu's clients are 'women who can discern the small and subtle nuances'. Maybe that's why most are willing to pay upwards of $300 for a pair of panties. Not that 37=1 is just lingerie, it's more like a couture atelier in the Vionnet mold. And although Yu's chic made-to-measure pieces and garter belts are worth the trip alone (lingerie here has no elastic and is made from the most delicate silks, secured with subtle hooks), she also dreams up beautifully constructed silk dresses with a slightly decadent Twenties bent. In a word, extraordinary.

*Luxury*                                             *Amex/MC/V*

**SoHo**                                        **(212) 226-0067**
37 Crosby Street                             btw Broome/Grand
NYC 10012                     Tues-Sun 12-6 (and by appointment)

## A Atelier

Packed with threads from hot designers such as Ann Demeulemeester, Thomas Engel Hart and Dirk Schonberger, A Atelier comes off like the highest-fashion mini mall. The small store is filled with sleek and slender shirts, jackets and well-cut pants for those New Yorkers looking to distinguish themselves from the rest of the fashion crowd.

*Moderate*                                           *Amex/MC/V*

**SoHo**                                        **(212) 941-8435**
125 Crosby Street                                     at Prince
NYC 10012                     Mon-Fri 11-7, Sat 12-7, Sun 12-6

## AB Apollo Braun

'I am one of the few designers who does not want to work with Gisele because I love to offer something new', says owner, fashion designer and former gossip columnist Apollo Braun, gesturing to the walls papered with spreads from *Paper* and *I-D* magazines. To that end he's created a mecca for downtown hipsters in search of one-of-a-kind accessories and deconstructed T-shirts from his own line as well as other up-and-coming and mostly local designers. Britney Spears and Nicole Kidman have both stopped by to pick up slogan shirts like 'Madonna is My Mother' while browsing the leather, fur and rhinestone accessories. Don't miss the $29 sale rack.

*Moderate*                                           *Amex/MC/V*

**East Village**                                    **(no phone)**
119 East 8th Street                          btw First/Avenue A
NYC 10003                                           Daily 12-10

**Lower East Side**                             **(212) 726-8075**
193 Orchard Street                         btw Houston/Prince
NYC 10002                                          Daily 12-10

## Abercrombie & Fitch

Known for its risqué catalog, occasionally naughty logo T-shirts and fresh-faced, outdoorsy American style,

Abercrombie & Fitch trades in affordable, sexy and athletic looks. Stamped with the ubiquitous A&F logo, the chain offers a wide selection of pants (cargo, denim, and parachute), shorts (including the bright ones for surfers), tees, sweaters, knits and outerwear. Also on the agenda are a slew of accessories (from adjustable caps to belts and flip-flops), intimates, tanks, halter tops and swimsuits. Abercrombie & Fitch has something for everyone in the fraternity—oops, family—from preppy striped polos to snappy tote bags. *abercrombie.com*

*Affordable*                                              *Amex/MC/V*

**Lower Manhattan/Tribeca**                    **(212) 809-9000**
199 Water Street                          at South Street Seaport
NYC 10038                                      Daily 10-9 (Sun 11-8)

## ABH Design

A lovely, quiet, space to take in exotic scarves, handcrafted jewelry and eccentric home accents. Owned by movie costume designer Aude Bronson Howard, ABH Designs specializes in custom napkins and tablecloths with specialty fabrics from India and Italy. Bejeweled flip-flops, pointy striped slippers, silk scarves and robes in rich greens and orange reveal a Far Eastern influence on Howard's goods, while quilted paisley jackets and floppy sunhats offer stylish updates on homey comfort. ABH Designs has a slew of celebrity/socialite clients (but they're too demure to name names) who swear by the store's candles, place mats, evening wraps, towels and everything an Upper East Side woman could possible need for herself or her glamorous home.

*Expensive*                                              *Amex/MC/V*

**Upper East Side**                               **(212) 249-2276**
401 East 76th Street                                    at First Ave
NYC 10021                                        Mon-Sat 11-6:30

## a.Cheng

A tour of duty at Tommy Hilfiger gave designer Alice Cheng the savvy—and commercial sense—she needed to open her own shop. Cheng's collection is pretty and delicate enough to appeal to the softer side of any professional. Best buys: her signature shirt dress as well as skirts, pants dressed up with decorative waistbands, jackets, silk print tops and feminine button-down shirts. *achengshop.com*

*Expensive*                                              *Amex/MC/V*

**East Village**                                  **(212) 979-7324**
443 East 9th Street                           btw First/Avenue A
NYC 10009                          Daily 11:30-8 (Sat-Sun 11:30-7)

## Active Wearhouse

Hit up your inner hip-hop hottie—or at least just dress like one—at this store nestled in the heart of Broadway. Choose from the latest offerings in urban clothing, from beloved labels like Rocawear, Phat Farm and Babyphat. And don't forget to check out Active Wearhouse's larger-than-life collection of kicks from all the major sneaker brands like Puma, Nike and Adidas in the basement. *activewearhousenyc.com*

*Affordable*                                    *Amex/MC/V*

**SoHo**                                     **(212) 965-2284**
580 Broadway                         btw Broome/Spring
NYC 10012                   Mon-Sat 9-9, Sun 10-8

## Add accessories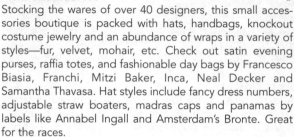

Stocking the wares of over 40 designers, this small accessories boutique is packed with hats, handbags, knockout costume jewelry and an abundance of wraps in a variety of styles—fur, velvet, mohair, etc. Check out satin evening purses, raffia totes, and fashionable day bags by Francesco Biasia, Franchi, Mitzi Baker, Inca, Neal Decker and Samantha Thavasa. Hat styles include fancy dress numbers, adjustable straw boaters, madras caps and panamas by labels like Annabel Ingall and Amsterdam's Bronte. Great for the races.

*Affordable*                                      *Amex/MC/V*

**SoHo**                                      **(212) 539-1439**
461 West Broadway                 btw Houston/Prince
NYC 10012                                Daily 11-8

## Addison on Madison

No it's not on Madison any more because the lease ran out, but no matter—this is the place for the man who hates shopping. A far cry from the stuffy darkness and wood paneling of traditional men's departments, this bright, uncluttered office space will outfit you with your choice from over 400 different A on M styles in Italian cotton or silk. They provide on-site tailoring, custom sleeve lengths, and custom-made shirts. Short on time? Request a set of fabric swatches by mail. Accessories include neckties, bow ties, pocket squares and cufflinks.

*Affordable to moderate*                          *Amex/MC/V*

**Midtown East**                            **(212) 308-2660**
29 West 57th Street (9th floor)         btw Fifth/Sixth Ave
NYC 10019                                Mon-Fri 10-6

## A Détacher

Owner/designer Monika Kowalska's collection, with its high-concept Japanese sensibility, is, in her words, 'art fashion for adults'. The result is a clean, minimalist line of constructed but feminine dresses, pants, skirts, blouses and more. Kowalska uses linear cuts (not form-fitting) and a basic color palette of black, white and gray, as well as some prints. Head to the back of the shop for handbag designer Dillen's fantastic, Hermès-like, made-to-order accessories. Also amuse yourself with a quirky collection of housewares— everything in the store is for sale, you just have to ask…

*Moderate*                                       *Amex/MC/V*

**Nolita**     **(212) 625-3380**
262 Mott Street     btw Houston/Prince
NYC 10012     Tues-Sat 12-7, Sun 1-6

## Adidas

With the coolest three stripes in the sports world, Adidas has had a firm hold on everyone from athletes to the style set for over 80 years. And it just keeps getting better. Its Originals store in SoHo befits the ideal Adidas consumer—garage-style layout with a DJ spinning in the back. Hipsters head here for the newly reinvented and super-hip Originals line. Shiny polyester tracksuits beloved by the artists and athletes alike, limited-edition sneakers, casualwear—the whole world of retro Adidas is here for you. Too cool for school.     *adidas.com*

*Affordable*     *Amex/MC/V*

**SoHo**     **(212) 777-2001**
136 Wooster Street     btw Houston/Prince
NYC 10012     Daily 11-7 (Sun 12-5)

## Aerosoles

As comfortable as ever, Aerosoles' sporty, cushiony footwear is now looking much hipper than you might remember. You'll find a full range of styles, from business casual to sporty weekend—all on the company's famous orthopedically correct soles. Many knee-high winter boots, stiletto sandals, and loafers are under $60.     *aerosoles.com*

*Affordable*     *Amex/MC/V*

**Harlem**     **(212) 665-5353**
2913 Broadway     btw 113/114th St
NYC 10025     Mon-Sat 9:30-8, Sun 11-6

**Upper East Side**     **(212) 987-9483**
150 East 86th Street     btw Lexington/Third Ave
NYC 10028     Mon-Fri 9-8, Sat 10-8, Sun 11-7

**Upper East Side**     **(212) 751-6372**
1155 Second Avenue     at 61st St
NYC 10021     Mon-Sat 9:30-8, Sun 12-6:30

**Upper West Side**     **(212) 865-4934**
2649 Broadway     btw 100/101st St
NYC 10025     Mon-Sat 9:30-8, Sun 11-6

**Upper West Side**     **(212) 579-8659**
310 Columbus Avenue     btw 74/75th St
NYC 10023     Mon-Sat 9-8, Sun 11-6

**Midtown East**     **(212) 755-0683**
709 Lexington Avenue     btw 57/58th St
NYC 10022     Mon-Sat 9-9, Sun 10-7

**Midtown East**     **(212) 370-0094**
137 East 42nd Street     btw Lexington/Third Ave
NYC 10017     Mon-Fri 8-8, Sat 10-8, Sun 11-6

**Midtown West**     **(212) 563-0610**
36 West 34th Street     btw Fifth/Sixth Ave
NYC 10001     Mon-Fri 8-9, Sat 9:30-9, Sun 11-7

**Midtown West**                    **(212) 307-6465**
1250 Avenue of the Americas                    at 51st St
NYC 10112              Mon-Fri 9-9, Sat 10-8, Sun 11-6

**Flatiron**                    **(646) 486-2826**
168 Fifth Avenue                    btw 21/22nd St
NYC 10010              Mon-Sat 9:30-8, Sun 11-6

**NoHo**                    **(212) 358-7855**
63 East 8th Street        btw Broadway/University Place
NYC 10003                    (opening hours as above)

**Lower Manhattan**                    **(212) 577-9298**
18 John Street (lobby level)        btw Broadway/Nassau
NYC 10038                    Mon-Sat 10-7

**Lower Manhattan**                    **(212) 608-4980**
206 Front Street            at South Street Seaport
NYC 10038        Mon-Wed 10-8, Thurs-Sat 10-9, Sun 11-8

## Agent Provocateur 👤

Welcome to the underworld. No one has given designer lingerie such a kick in the pants as Agent Provocateur, the masters of kinky chic. London's most exclusive lingerie label, started almost a decade ago by Vivienne Westwood's son Joe Corré and wife Serena Rees, perfectly marries shameless eroticism and naughty exhibitionism—which is probably why their little nothings are craved by every supermodel and superstar on the planet. This SoHo store is a chic retail bordello with a comely staff in baby-pink uniforms (think Fifties beautician/diner waitress/nurse)—a world of equally naughty, retro-inspired knickers. It's the perfect place to dispatch your boyfriend to pick up the signature lingerie (which also includes elegant silk and lace numbers), Swarovski-crystal-studded collars and cuffs, Forties peep-toe heels, or perhaps a bottle of AP's saucy fragrance. Sexy with a capital S.        *agentprovocateur.com*

*Expensive*                    *Amex/MC/V*

**SoHo**                    **(212) 965-0229**
133 Mercer Street                    btw Prince/Spring
NYC 10012                    Mon-Sat 11-7, Sun 12-6

## agnès b. 👤

Effortlessly stylish women have long shopped at agnès b. to snare some Parisian bon ton (fashionability without trendiness). The classic and clever ready-to-wear collection offers pants, jackets, sweaters, suits and skirts that are simple, chic and feminine—and some of the best T-shirts around. New and very cool is Madame B's collaboration with boxing label Everlast, b.Everlast, elegant urban streetwear like hooded sweatshirts and tanks.        *agnesb.fr*

*Expensive*                    *Amex/MC/V*

**Upper East Side**                    **(212) 570-9333**
1063 Madison Avenue                    btw 80/81st St
NYC 10028                    Mon-Sat 11-7, Sun 12-6

**Flatiron**                    **(212) 741-2585**
13 East 16th Street        btw Fifth Ave/Union Square West
NYC 10003                    (opening hours as above)

| | |
|---|---|
| **SoHo** | **(212) 925-4649** |
| 103 Greene Street | btw Prince/Spring |
| NYC 10012 | Daily 11-7 |

## agnès b. homme 🕴

Agnès b. homme caters to the suave and preppy men of the world seeking classic looks with that particular Parisian edge. Choose from a ready-to-wear collection of suits, dress pants, shirts, khakis and jeans—all up, a one-stop foolproof wardrobe. It's clean-cut clothes with covetable French elegance. Sizes run small.          *agnesb.fr*

*Expensive*                                         *Amex/MC/V*

| | |
|---|---|
| **SoHo** | **(212) 431-4339** |
| 79 Greene Street | btw Spring/Broome |
| NYC 10012 | Daily 11-7 |

## Aldo 🕴👩

Calling all twentysomethings: this is your funky footwear home. Shop for streety looks like Cher-worthy platforms, wedges, rubber or wooden soles, boots, sassy stilettos and sandals in bursts of raspberry pink, purple, blue and orange (black and white, too, if you insist). Affordably priced footwear with attitude to spare.          *aldoshoes.com*

*Affordable*                                         *Amex/MC/V*

| | |
|---|---|
| **Upper East Side** | **(212) 828-3725** |
| 157 East 86th Street | btw Lexington/Third Ave |
| NYC 10028 | Mon-Wed 10-8, Thurs-Sat 10-9, Sun 12-7 |

| | |
|---|---|
| **Midtown East** | **(212) 832-1692** |
| 730 Lexington Avenue | btw 58/59th St |
| NYC 10022 | Mon-Sat 10-9, Sun 11-7 |

| | |
|---|---|
| **Midtown West** | **(212) 594-6255** |
| 15 West 34th Street | btw Sixth/Seventh Ave |
| NYC 10001 | Mon-Sat 10-9, Sun 11-8 |

| | |
|---|---|
| **Flatiron** | **(212) 229-9865** |
| 97 Fifth Avenue | at 17th St |
| NYC 10003 | Mon-Wed 10-8, Thurs-Sat 10-9, Sun 12-7 |

| | |
|---|---|
| **NoHo** | **(212) 982-0958** |
| 700 Broadway | at East 4th St |
| NYC 10003 | Mon-Sat 11-9, Sun 11-8 |

| | |
|---|---|
| **SoHo** | **(212) 226-7974** |
| 579 Broadway | btw Houston/Prince |
| NYC 10012 | Mon-Wed 10-8, Thurs-Sat 10-9, Sun 11-7 |

## Alex 👩

Alex helps women look fabulous with the least bit of effort. Casual chic has never looked or felt so good as with the super-soft, super-flattering tees by Majestic that you'll find here, and don't miss great shirts and dresses by C+C California and gotta-have-'em jeans by Paper Denim and Cloth. Find a few colorful pieces among the mainly neutral-toned color palette, and you'll be set for a stylish weekend.

*Expensive*                                         *Amex/MC/V*

**Nolita**                                           **(212) 343-0567**
268 Elizabeth Street                          btw Houston/Prince
NYC 10012                                                Daily 11-7

## ★ Alexander McQueen

Fashion's dark prince, who once again stunned audiences with his runway homage—complete with dancing models—to *They Shoot Horses, Don't They?* has established himself as a bona-fide international brand, following backing by fashion powerhouse Gucci. After opening his first store in Tokyo, McQueen's New York outpost, in the über-fashionable Meatpacking District, is a deliberate trip into the recesses of his mind. 'It's supposed to be a spaceship environment, so everything hovers. It's very ethereal,' he says. The single-floor store showcases the majority of McQueen's women's collection: sinuous suits, sharp pants, his signature leather corsetry, death-defying shoes (six-inch stilettos) and logo sunglasses.                 *alexandermcqueen.com*

*Luxury*                                                 *Amex/MC/V*

**Chelsea**                                         **(212) 645-1797**
417 West 14th Street                btw Washington/Ninth Ave
NYC 10014                        Mon-Sat 11-7, Sun 12:30-6

## Alexandre de Paris

Having trouble finding a barrette? Well, this is the best option you will ever find in New York City. You'll find bows, banana clips, headbands, small veils, pins, scrunchies, combs—and all handmade to perfection. A private line of hairbrushes and mirrors is also available. Simply put, this Paris-based store will have your hair looking as beautiful as your ensemble.

*Expensive*                                             *Amex/MC/V*

**Upper East Side**                              **(212) 717-2122**
971 Madison Avenue                        btw 75/76th St
NYC 10021                                           Mon-Sat 10-6

## Alexandros Furs

Choose from a collection of quality avant-garde and classic fur coats—from sporty fox to luxurious chinchilla, mink, sable or lynx. Alongside the house label, they design and carry the luxe line Ekso. Other outerwear includes cashmere overcoats and reversibles. Alexandros also offers storage, cleaning and remodeling.

*Luxury*                                             *Amex/MC/V*

**Midtown East**                                  **(212) 702-0744**
5 East 59th Street (2nd floor)        btw Fifth/Madison Ave
NYC 10022                           Mon-Fri 10-6, Sat 10-5
                                       (closed Saturdays in summer)

**Chelsea**                                         **(212) 967-1222**
213 West 28th Street                 btw Seventh/Eighth Ave
NYC 10001                                         Mon-Sat 10-6
                                   (also Sundays, October-February)

## Alexia Crawford Accessories

A tiny boutique packed to the rafters with accessories. Dress up a dull outfit with one of Crawford's delicate jewelry designs, or opt for a silky diaphanous scarf or shawl with matching evening bag. Styles run from young and trendy to classic and sophisticated. Great prices. *shopalexiacrawford.com*

*Moderate* *Amex/MC/V*

**SoHo** **(212) 473-9703**
199 Prince Street btw Sullivan/MacDougal
NYC 10012 Mon-Thurs 11-7, Fri-Sat 11-8, Sun 12-6

## Alfred Dunhill

Think of an English gentleman's club for the Jude Law set. Offering British suits and sportswear that's sexy, not stuffy, the Dunhill line balances high style with functionality. The accessories, leather goods and jewelry are all crafted with a certain theme or time period in mind, like the smooth red leather of the Cricket line or the old-world elegance of the Tradition collection. Pyromaniacs and avid smokers alike will never put down Dunhill's celebrated luxury lighters. Saunter up to the Club level on the second floor and enjoy the humidor and a bespoke tailoring service. *dunhill.com*

*Expensive* *Amex/MC/V*

**Midtown East** **(212) 753-9292**
711 Fifth Avenue btw 55/56th St
NYC 10022 Mon-Sat 10-6:30 (Thurs 10-7), Sun 12-5

## Alice Underground

Take a trip into Alice's world and discover a vast selection of secondhand clothing and other serendipitous goodies. Shop for vintage looks from the Fifties to the Nineties, including reconditioned vintage leather, dresses, sweaters, saucy lingerie, shoes, retro scarves and jewelry. Don't overlook the bargain bins in the back stuffed with a random selection of merchandise. All up, it's the place to go for that Kenny Rogers T-shirt you've always wanted.

*Affordable to moderate* *Amex/MC/V*

**SoHo** **(212) 431-9067**
481 Broadway btw Broome/Grand
NYC 10013 Daily 11-7:30

## Alicia Mugetti

Alicia Mugetti, who designs fancy duds for opera, theater and film, specializes in romantic damsel dresses designed in rich velvets and crushed satins. Find them in beautiful colors and feminine, floor-length silhouettes. It's lush fabrics and Renaissance looks—all very Knights of the Round Table (or the princesses they woo, anyway). *aliciamugetti.com*

*Expensive* *Amex/MC/V*

**Upper East Side** **(212) 794-6186**
999 Madison Avenue btw 77/78th St
NYC 10021 Mon-Sat 10-6

## Alife

Get Alife! An eclectic, defiantly downtown mix of footwear, clothing, graffiti paraphernalia (i.e. loose, comfy hip-hop wear), design books and the ever-vital stuffed animals. Check out a skateboard designed by graffiti guru ESPO, Rogan jeans, local designer tees, silk-screened sweatshirts, shirts, industrial accessories and edgy shoes ranging from modern-looking sneaks by Ritefoot and Converse. Every two months they feature progressive installations by up-and-coming artists. *alifenyc.com*

*Expensive* *Amex/MC/V*

**Lower East Side** **(646) 654-0628**
178 Orchard Street btw Houston/Stanton
NYC 10002 Tues-Sun 12-7

## ★ Alife Rivington Club

Confirming the Lower East Side's new status as the sneaker capital of the world, along comes Alife Rivington Club, looking like a cross between a Savile Row tailor and Athlete's Foot. Find obscure and dead cool limited-edition sneakers back-lit and reverently displayed in cherrywood cases. Look out for classic retro Adidas and contemplate your next sneaker addition from the gorgeous Italian leather couch that lines an entire wall of the store. Of course, shoes this cool cost a bundle—think of it as the club's membership dues. *alifenyc.com*

*Expensive* *Amex/MC/V*

**Lower East Side** **(212) 375-8128**
158 Rivington Street btw Clinton/Suffolk
NYC 10002 Tues-Sun 12-7

## Alixandre

Run by three generations of the Schulman family, Alixandre delivers honest, reliable and knowledgeable service as well as an outstanding selection of fur coats. Find top quality shearlings, broadtails, minks and sables from Oscar de la Renta. Alixandre also offers superior cleaning, storage, remodeling and alteration services. Appointments suggested between Memorial Day and Labor Day. *alixandrefurs.com*

*Expensive* *Amex/MC/V*

**Midtown West** **(212) 736-5550**
150 West 30th Street btw Sixth/Seventh
NYC 10001 Mon-Fri 9-5, Sat 9-1:30
(appointments suggested)

## Allan & Suzi

The eccentric, self-proclaimed 'Home of Retro Fashion', Allan & Suzi sell new and vintage consignment garb from all the industry heavyweights (Gucci, Prada, Versace, Pucci, Cavalli, to name only a few) and relative newcomers like Zac Posen. Specializing in shoes, especially of the platform variety, and eveningwear, where the motto seems to be The More Sequins, The Better, owners Allan Pollack and Suzi

Kandel are sure to please any Elton John or Vanna White in waiting. With trademark style, Kandel claims that the opening of a second location in New Jersey has set off New York's 'pilgrimage to Asbury Park'.    *allanandsuzi.net*

*Expensive*                                              *Amex/MC/V*

**Upper West Side**                          **(212) 724-7445**
416 Amsterdam Avenue                              at 80th St
NYC 10024                                        Daily 12-7

**New Jersey**                               **(732) 988-7372**
711 Cookman Avenue            Thurs-Sat 11-5, Sun 12-5
Asbury Park
NJ 07712

## Allen Edmonds

For over 75 years, the customer has come first at Allen Edmonds. Find over 200 styles of dress and corporate classics, from casual weekend shoes to fashion-forward lifestyle footwear. Great care has gone into obtaining the perfect balance between quality and price.

                                800-235-2348  *allenedmonds.com*

*Moderate*                                              *Amex/MC/V*

**Midtown East**                             **(212) 308-8305**
551 Madison Avenue                          btw 55/56th St
NYC 10022                    Mon-Fri 9-7, Sat 9-6, Sun 12-5

**Midtown East**                             **(212) 682-3144**
24 East 44th Street                  btw Fifth/Madison Ave
NYC 10017                         (opening hours as above)

## Allure Lingerie

A super-sweet neighborhood lingerie shop, featuring brands like Only Hearts, Hanky Panky, Hanro, Wolford, Lejaby, Pluto and Cosabella (for the thong lover in all of us). Find a great selection of seamless bras, panties and thongs, as well as hosiery by DKNY and Wolford. Robes and slippers are also available.

*Moderate*                                              *Amex/MC/V*

**Upper East Side**                          **(212) 860-7871**
1324 Lexington Avenue                        btw 88/89th St
NYC 10128                         Mon-Fri 11-7, Sat 11-6

## Alpana Bawa

Alpana Bawa's signature is vibrantly colored pieces with brave geometric and floral patterns. They also stock accessories in hand-embroidered wool, silk, cotton or nylon. Look for A by Alpana for equally vivid and adventurous casualwear. The Bawa line includes a collection of colorful cotton men's shirts, embellished with prints and embroidery, as well as jackets and pants favored by out-there actor types like Willem Dafoe.    *alpanabawa.com*

*Moderate*                                              *Amex/MC/V*

**SoHo**                                     **(212) 965-0559**
41 Grand Street                btw West Broadway/Thompson
NYC 10013                    Mon-Fri 11-7, Sat 12-7, Sun 12-6

## Alskling

Alskling, a small Swedish dress boutique who's name means 'darling' in its mother tongue, offers clothing for women and girls who prefer May flowers to April showers. In addition to their signature line of slip and sundresses in an array of prints from punchy polka dots to pretty posies, Alskling offers a variety of super-girly garments like camisole tops and flouncy skirts that make every day feel like spring has finally sprung.

*Moderate*                                              *Amex/MC/V*

**Upper West Side**                              **(212) 787-7066**
228 Columbus Avenue                            btw 70/71st St
NYC 10023                                            Daily 11-7

## Amarcord Vintage Fashion

This airy shop sells vintage clothing lovingly handpicked by owners Patti Bordoni and Marco Liotta. These passionate Italian expatriates collect many of their pieces direct from Europe through word-of-mouth and top-secret sources. Find both non-designer prized pieces, as well as winning looks by Cacharel, Gucci, Roberto Cavalli, you name it. Everything is in great condition (especially the classic hand-bags) and attractively priced. Unlike so many other vintage emporiums they only pick the best, and they color code them too.                              *amarcordvintagefashion.com*

*Expensive*                                             *Amex/MC/V*

**East Village (women only)**                  **(212) 614-7133**
84 East 7th Street                              btw First/Second Ave
NYC 10003                                      Tues-Sun 12:30-7:30

**Williamsburg**                                **(718) 963-4001**
223 Bedford Avenue                    btw North 4th/North 5th St
Brooklyn 11211                                         Daily 1-8

## ★ American Apparel

Sexy, simple, perfect. Surrounded by the photo exhibits, hip music and beautiful sales staff at American Apparel, you would never guess that this rising star of a company stands nearly alone in the garment industry in its commitment to socially-conscious manufacturing and labor practices. AA's 'sweatshop-free' goods are made in downtown L.A. with organic, pesticide-free materials; workers are paid competitive wages and have access to free English language classes held in the L.A. workshop. If the politics don't motivate you, the great fits, stylish colors and reasonable prices—qualities helping make the label a preferred choice for rock bands' tour tees—certainly will. Best bets are flattering basics like solid-colored tees, pants, sweats and skirts, most of which can be had for under $40. Also find comfy loungewear, hot underwear, trendy tanks, cute kids' clothing and a small selection of art and photography books for sale. If it sounds too good to be true, just get in line—you'll be glad you did.                                    *americanapparel.net*

*Affordable*                                            *Amex/MC/V*

**NoHo**    **(646) 383-2257**
712 Broadway    at Washington Place
NYC 10003    Mon-Fri 10-8, Sat 10-10, Sun 11-8

**Lower East Side**    **(212) 598-4600**
183 East Houston Street    at Orchard St
NYC 10002    Mon-Thurs 11-10, Fri-Sat 11-12, Sun 12-9

**West Village**    **(646) 336-6515**
373 6th Avenue    at Waverly
NYC 10014    Daily 11-9 (Sun 11-8)

# American Girl Place    ♀

Return to the valley of the dolls. The place to be up to about age 12 is clearly American Girl. Find storybook dolls from different eras of American history, or contemporary figures with their own pom-poms and yoga mats. If your daughter wishes to feel especially close to her doll, you can buy toy-and-toddler matching outfits. If you get tired of playing, afternoon tea is served at the in-house café and performances of American Girl Revue run nightly at the store's theater. Don't forget to stop by the hair salon to update your doll's 'do', too.    800-845-0005  *americangirlplace.com*

*Moderate*    *Amex/MC/V*

**Fifth Avenue**    **(212) 317-2220**
609 Fifth Avenue    at 49th St
NYC 10017    Mon-Wed 10-7, Thurs-Fri 10-9
    Sat 9-9, Sun 9-7

# Amsale    ♀

Fed up with puffy wedding cake bridal gowns, Amsale Aberra took matters into her own hands—and designed her own. Today she is the leading vendor of couture bridal gowns in department stores, as well as the largest bridal salon on Madison Avenue. Known for timeless, classic elegance, the collection features both elaborate hand-beaded gowns with Swarovski crystals and simple column dresses. Prices run from $3,000 to approximately $15,000, with a six-month delivery. Don't miss the Evening collection, which glistens with glamour and sophistication. Looks include cocktail dresses, suits, satin coats, silk ballgowns, slinky long dresses and fabulous tuxedo jacket and pant ensembles.    *amsale.com*

*Luxury*    *Amex/MC/V*

**Midtown East**    **(212) 583-1700**
625 Madison Avenue (mezzanine)    btw 58/59th St
NYC 10022    Tues-Sat 10-6 (Thurs 10-7) (by appointment)

# Amy Chan    ♀

Fashion girls make the pilgrimage here for the adventurously edited collection of pieces from over 40 young, edgy designers like Cigana, RTN and Mara Hoffman. The progressive retailer even hosts an occasional open house for new names to show their wares. The result? You'll be guaranteed to find something no one else has (which, in fashion, is vital). Chan's handbags are known for their luxurious fabrics and detailed exotic handcrafting. Among them is her signature mosaic bag, where small acrylic tiles are heat-sealed onto colorful pinstripes, floral motifs, denim or other fabrics.                                                                    amychan.com

*Expensive*                                                                    *Amex/MC/V*

**Nolita**                                                          **(212) 966-3417**
247 Mulberry Street                              btw Prince/Spring
NYC 10012                                                          Daily 12-7

## Amy Downs Hats at YU                                    👨 👩

Amy Downs is one of New York's most creative milliners; her style is deliberately and eclectically downtown. Shop for headwear with names like Twister or Happy Family, or choose from a collection of polar fleece and wool hats, straw sunhats, funky felts, fun fake furs, bold berets, wool ski hats and more.

*Moderate*                                                                    *Amex/MC/V*

**Lower East Side**                                            **(212) 979-9370**
151 Ludlow Street                                  btw Stanton/Rivington
NYC 10002                                          Wed-Sat 12-7, Sun 12-6

## Andy's Chee Pees                                    👨 👨

A vintage store for style swingers in search of fun one-of-a-kind fashion hits. Find collectible denim, swing clothes from the Forties and Fifties, biker and bomber jackets, jeans, old police leather jackets, Hawaiian shirts, a complete line of unisex Dickies in bold, bright colors, party wigs, vintage jewelry and more. For the 18-35 crowd desperate for some nostalgia—or something eye-catching to wear to a costume party.                                                 andyscheepees.com

*Affordable*                                                                    *Amex/MC/V*

**NoHo**                                                          **(212) 420-5980**
691 Broadway                                                  btw 3/4th St
NYC 10012                                          Mon-Sat 11-9, Sun 12-8

## Angelo Lambrou                                          👩

Celebrities from Goldie Hawn to Salma Hayek look to Angelo Lambrou for modern, sexy clothing. Inspired by art and design from all over the world, this Botswana native creates ethereal silk dresses and beaded tops that are both edgy and timeless. From couture bridal dresses to ready-to-wear evening attire, Lambrou's designs are bias-cut for a perfectly flattering fit. Lambrou himself puts shoppers at ease with his warm, gregarious personality.                                                 angelolambrou.com

*Luxury*                                                                    *Amex/MC/V*

**East Village**                                              **(212) 460-9870**
96 East 7th Street                                  btw First/Avenue A
NYC 10009                                                    Tues-Sun 1-8

## Anik                                                          👩

Talk about a wide range of options—Anik has everything from careerwear to sportswear for both moms and daughters. The store's broad assortment includes Alice & Trixie dresses, Duca d'Andrea suits, Malika cashmere sweaters and Moncler baseball jackets. The best part of Anik is a sale section in the back of the shop, where you're bound to find something worth more than what you'll pay. Prices range from $40 for a Splendid tee to $500 silk dresses. *aniknyc.com*

*Moderate to expensive*                                  *Amex/MC/V*

**Upper East Side**                                  **(212) 861-9840**
1355 Third Avenue                                  btw 77/78th St
NYC 10021                                  Daily 11-8 (Sun 11-7)

**Upper East Side**                                  **(212) 249-2417**
1122 Madison Avenue                                  btw 83/84th St
NYC 10028                                  Mon-Sat 10-8, Sun 11-7

## Anna

One of New York's best kept secrets, this is the kind of boutique that fashion-obsessed East Village girls wish they could keep to themselves. Sorry, we have to spread the love. Owner/designer Kathy Kemp sells her collection of addictive striped wrap dresses with ribbons and girlish double-layered skirts, plus carefully chosen, complementary vintage pieces in the sale bin (always $20). The look is feminine and fantastically offbeat, and no item costs more than $360.

*Moderate*                                  *Amex/MC/V*

**East Village**                                  **(212) 358-0195**
150 East 3rd Street                                  btw Avenue A/B
NYC 10009                                  Mon-Sat 1-8, Sun 1-7

## Anna Sui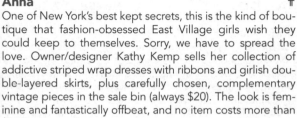

Purple, purple everywhere. At the heart of every Anna Sui collection comes 'the celebration of the nouvelle hippy'. Her SoHo treasure trove is inspired by a myriad of decades, but the Sixties and Seventies are clearly the favorites. The store is decorated with vintage-style posters from bands such as 311, Foo Fighters and The Doors. Choose Sui's head-to-toe collection: dresses, skirts tossed with crocheted pieces, romantic blouses, chunky coats, sexy denim, patchwork and even dainty underwear. Devotees include Britney Spears, Madonna and all of Anna's many model friends. Accessories include fanciful decorative shoes, handbags, jewelry, cute-goth make-up, and fragrances. *annasui.com*

*Expensive*                                  *Amex/MC/V*

**SoHo**                                  **(212) 941-8406**
113 Greene Street                                  btw Prince/Spring
NYC 10012                                  Mon-Sat 11:30-7, Sun 12-6

## Anne Fontaine

Brazil-born and Paris-based designer Anne Fontaine's New York boutiques are visions in white—white shelves, white carpet, white walls. Not that this should come as a surprise, as the designer's sole obsession is perfecting the white shirt. Fontaine displays roughly 100 variations on this wardrobe staple, using ruching, lace, flowers made of fabric, mother-of-pearl buttons, strong tailoring and a variety of materials—from stretchy cotton to poplin to organza appliqué—to turn plain into perfection. *annefontaine.com*

*Expensive*                                    *Amex/MC/V*

**SoHo**                                    **(212) 343-3154**
93 Greene Street                        btw Prince/Spring
NYC 10012                              Mon-Sat 11-7, Sun 12-6

**Fifth Avenue**                          **(212) 489-1554**
610 Fifth Avenue                            btw 50/51st St
NYC 10020                    Mon-Fri 10-7, Sat 11-6, Sun 12-5

**SoHo**                                    **(212) 343-3154**
93 Greene Street                        btw Prince/Spring
NYC 10012                              Mon-Sat 11-7, Sun 12-6

## Anne Klein

Established and elegant, Anne Klein has been dressing women for more than 30 years. But the brand upped the ante of late, positioning itself as a fashion-oriented collection rather than simply a career-driven bridge line. Modern looks and clean-cut styles permeate the Anne Klein label— think simple pieces like silk jersey tops and taffeta pants— plus the sportier AK Anne Klein line. The signature lion's head logo is in evidence, both on accessories and in the store's dramatic decor. *anneklein.com*

*Moderate*                                     *Amex/MC/V*

**SoHo**                                    **(212) 965-9499**
417 West Broadway                      btw Prince/Spring
NYC 10012          Mon-Wed 10-7, Thurs-Sat 10-8, Sun 12-7

## Annelore

Frustrated by mass-produced clothing that can be seen on every fifth girl riding the subway, designer Juliana Cho has created a line of original, hand-sewn and impeccably tailored pieces for women. Cho employs a tailor, seamstresses and a cobbler to transform her handpicked European fabrics and leathers into timeless feminine pieces. The cuts are flawless, and include intricate details like hand-painted glass buttons. Annelore's limited-edition pieces have drawn a loyal following from clothes-horses like Helena Christensen and Gretchen Mol.

*Expensive*                                    *Amex/MC/V*

**West Village**                          **(212) 255-5574**
636 Hudson Street                            at Horatio
NYC 10014                    Tues-Fri 12-7, Sat-Sun 12-6

## Annika Inez

A fab little secret on the Upper East Side, Annika is a destination for chic beaded jewelry made by Swedish store owner Annika Salame, using vintage beads from the Thirties to the Seventies. The store is simple and uncluttered, all the better to display this small collection which also includes coconut-bead charm bracelets, acrylic-bead and cork cuffs, semi-precious necklaces, minimalist sterling silver earrings and Danish knitwear designers. Great for gifts—or just for spoiling yourself.     *annikainez.com*

*Affordable*                                          *Amex/MC/V*

**Upper East Side**                    **(212) 717-9644**
243 East 78th Street              btw Second/Third Ave
NYC 10021                    Daily 11-7 (Thurs-Fri 12-8)

## Ann Taylor

Gone forever are the days when Ann Taylor catered solely to young professionals. The new version encompasses everyone from corporate women to chic urbanites of all ages. Find suits and separates for the office, sportswear for weekends and understated cocktail dresses for evening. In addition, shop a terrific selection of private-label shoes, an extensive petite section, and some winning accessories.

800 677-0300  *anntaylor.com*

*Affordable*                                          *Amex/MC/V*

**Upper East Side**                    **(212) 988-8930**
1055 Madison Avenue                       at 80th St
NYC 10028              Mon-Fri 10-8, Sat 10-6, Sun 12-6

**Upper East Side**                    **(212) 832-9114**
645 Madison Avenue                        at 60th St
NYC 10022              Mon-Fri 10-8, Sat 10-7, Sun 12-6

**Upper East Side**                    **(212) 861-3392**
1320 Third Avenue                      btw 75/76th St
NYC 10021              Mon-Fri 10-8, Sat 10-6, Sun 12-6

**Upper West Side**                    **(212) 721-3130**
2380 Broadway                             at 87th St
NYC 10024                     Mon-Sat 10-8, Sun 12-6

**Upper West Side**                    **(212) 873-7344**
2015-17 Broadway                          at 69th St
NYC 10023                     Mon-Sat 10-8, Sun 12-6

**Midtown East**                       **(212) 308-5333**
850 Third Avenue                          at 52nd St
NYC 10022              Mon-Fri 10-8, Sat 11-6, Sun 12-5

**Midtown East**                       **(212) 949-0008**
330 Madison Avenue                        at 43rd St
NYC 10017               Mon-Fri 9-8, Sat 10-7, Sun 12-5

**Midtown West**                       **(212) 642-4340**
1166 Sixth Avenue                         at 46th St
NYC 10036               Mon-Fri 9-8, Sat 10-7, Sun 12-6

**Fifth Avenue**                       **(212) 922-3621**
575 Fifth Avenue                       btw 46/47th St
NYC 10017              Mon-Fri 10-8, Sat 10-7, Sun 11-6

**Flatiron**                           **(212) 253-1445**
149 Fifth Avenue                          at 21st St
NYC 10010                     Mon-Sat 10-8, Sun 12-6

**Lower Manhattan**                    **(212) 945-1991**
225 Liberty Street            at World Financial Center
NYC 10281              Mon-Fri 9-7, Sat 11-5, Sun 12-5

| **Lower Manhattan** | **(212) 480-4100** |
|---|---|
| 4 Fulton Street | at South Street Seaport |
| NYC 10038 | Daily 10-8 (Sun 10-7) |

## Ann Taylor Loft  👤

If you like to dress up with Ann Taylor during the week, then you'll probably enjoy relaxing in Ann Taylor Loft on weekends. Taylorphiles shop here for casual basics like sweater sets, pants, cotton and silk shirts, dresses—all up, laid-back and practical pieces at lower price points than the signature line. This year's collection includes a versatile array of accessories: sunglasses, necklaces, stockings, shoes and hats, as well as new items like watches and umbrellas. *anntaylorloft.com*

*Moderate*                                              *Amex/MC/V*

| **Midtown West** | **(212) 244-8926** |
|---|---|
| 35 West 34th Street | btw Fifth/Sixth Ave |
| NYC 10001 | Mon-Sat 10-9, Sun 11-7 |

| **Upper East Side** | **(212) 472-7281** |
|---|---|
| 1492 Third Avenue | at 84th St |
| NYC 10028 | Mon-Sat 10-9, Sun 11-6 |

| **Midtown West** | **(212) 398-1078** |
|---|---|
| 1290 Sixth Avenue | at 52nd St |
| NYC 10104 | Mon-Sat 9-9, Sun 11-6 |

| **Upper East Side** | **(212) 772-9952** |
|---|---|
| 1155 Third Avenue | btw 67/68th St |
| NYC 10021 | Mon-Sat 10-8, Sun 11-7 |

| **Midtown East** | **(212) 883-8766** |
|---|---|
| 150 East 42nd Street | at Lexington Ave |
| NYC 10017 | Mon-Fri 9-9, Sat 10-8, Sun 11-6 |

| **Midtown East** | **(212) 308-1129** |
|---|---|
| 488 Madison Avenue | at 52nd St |
| NYC 10022 | Mon-Fri 9-8, Sat 10-7, Sun 10-6 |

| **NoHo** | **(646) 602-1582** |
|---|---|
| 770 Broadway | btw 8/9th St |
| NYC 10003 | Mon-Sat 10-9, Sun 12-6 |

| **SoHo** | **(212) 625-0427** |
|---|---|
| 560 Broadway | btw Prince/Spring |
| NYC 10012 | Mon-Sat 10-8, Sun 12-6 |

| **Tribeca** | **(212) 809-1435** |
|---|---|
| 2 Broadway | btw Beaver/Stone |
| NYC 10004 | Mon-Fri 8-7 |

## Anthony T Kirby  👤👤

Here we have the essential haberdashery for clients such as *Vanity Fair*'s Graydon Carter and his fashionable peers. Make an appointment with Anthony T for custom-made neckwear and debonair accessories. His new gray flannel trouser collection for men has garnered raves, and his canvas totes are perfect for getting around town or for a day off at the beach. Also find a selection of English bench-made shoes for men and women. *anthonykirby.com*

*Expensive*                                    *Amex/MC/V*
**(by appointment only)**                  **(718) 783-2570**

# Anthropologie

The grown up sibling of Urban Outfitters, this massive store has a Parisian flea market feel and is packed with an eclectic selection of apparel and home furnishings aimed at a slightly more sophisticated customer. Labels include in-house designers Odille, Elevenses and Louie, as well as La Cosa, Nanette Lepore, Plenty, Ruth and Marimekko. There is also a vast selection of affordable housewares from antique-style tableware to luxurious provencal bath lotions and potions.          800-309-2500  *anthropologie.com*

*Moderate*                                        *Amex/MC/V*
**SoHo**                                       **(212) 343-7070**
375 West Broadway                           btw Spring/Broome
NYC 10012                                  Daily 11-8 (Sun 11-6)

**Flatiron**                                   **(212) 627-5885**
85 Fifth Avenue                                      at 16th St
NYC 10003                             Mon-Sat 10-8, Sun 11-7

# Antoin

This is a reliable neighborhood store packed with hip shoes. Although you won't come across any heavy-hitter designer labels, you're still guaranteed to find lots of designer looks like stilettos, fashionable mules and everything in between. Names include Petra, Rinaldi, Enzo Burini, Martini Osvaldo, Varo Mariani di Foffo and Via Condotti alongside Antoin's house label.

*Moderate*                                        *Amex/MC/V*
**Upper East Side**                            **(212) 249-6703**
1110 Lexington Avenue                          btw 77/78th St
NYC 10021                    Mon-Fri 9-8, Sat 10-8, Sun 11-7

# Anya Hindmarch

This quirky London handbag designer turns out sophisticated and witty collections of Italian-crafted designs. Choose from classics in scratch-resistant, luxurious leathers, evening numbers in couture satins and velvets, and cotton or silk bags with playful, vintage photographic images of dogs, cats and ladies lying on the beach. Resort bags are printed with kitsch maps of the Hamptons or Mustique. Each bag carries (stamped or hand-sewn) a dainty bow logo. The fashion crowd are still carrying the personalized bags, complete with photos of their own choosing. Pay $210-$250 for print bags and $400-$1,400 for leather handbags. Small leather goods, jewelry, wallets, travel and make-up bags are also available.        *anyahindmarch.com*

*Moderate to expensive*                            *Amex/MC/V*
**Upper East Side**                            **(212) 750-3974**
29 East 60th Street                        btw Madison/Park Ave
NYC 10022                                       Mon-Sat 10-7

**SoHo**
115 Greene Street
NYC 10012

(212) 343-8147
btw Prince/Spring
Mon-Sat 11-7, Sun 12-6

## The Apartment

This hip space blazed a new trend through the retail scene: store as reality entertainment, where the customers (and occasionally models) play the role of performer/observer and the shop and merchandise become the stage and props. As one would expect, The Apartment's primary focus is on groovy furniture, kitchen equipment and bathroom fixtures; however, cutting-edge clothing and accessories from Trash A Porter, Alice Roi and the Apartment T-shirt line can be found among the housewares. *theapt.com*

*Moderate*                                    *Amex/MC/V*

**SoHo**
101 Crosby Street
NYC 10012

(212) 219-3661
btw Prince/Spring
Wed-Sat 12-7, Sun 12-6
(Mon-Tues by appointment)

## ★ A.P.C.

A.P.C., an abbreviation for Atelier de Production et Creations, is a favorite among fashion insiders seeking urban basics that are cool without trying. Owner/designer Jean Touitou produces a trendy yet casual collection of lightweight dress shirts, comfy sweaters, cool sweatshirts, chinos, and outerwear along with some of the coolest jeans (approximately $109-$120) around. Accessories include sunglasses, ties, bags, limited-edition tees, CDs and shoes. Staff are super-cool, but friendly. *apc.fr*

*Moderate*                                    *Amex/MC/V*

**SoHo**
131 Mercer Street
NYC 10012

(212) 966-9685
btw Prince/Spring
Mon-Sat 11-7, Sun 12-6

## April Cornell

The Canadian-based chain boutique April Cornell offers a selection of ultra-feminine clothing, accessories and housewares that can transform even the dreariest New York winter day into a romantic countryside getaway. In addition to their large variety of dresses, straw hats and silk sleepwear, April Cornell sells children's apparel for girls ages 2-12 including delicate matching floral-printed dresses for mother and daughters. Their popular housewares collection including tea sets, table linens and bedding that appears to have been lifted from a charming traditional country home in Provence or the Cotswolds. *aprilcornell.com*

*Moderate*                                    *Amex/MC/V*

**Upper West Side**
487 Columbus Avenue
NYC 10024

(212) 799-4342
btw 83/84th St
Mon-Sat 10-8, Sun 12-6

## Arche

A super-popular family-owned French company known for comfortable, spongy leather shoes in a myriad of colors and styles. They might not be terribly refined for the grown-ups but the thick rubber soles and clunky heels—printed with everything from Klimt paintings to zebras to American flags—continue to do it for younger customers. *arche-shoes.com*

*Moderate*                                   *Amex/MC/V*

**Upper East Side**                      **(212) 439-0700**
995 Madison Avenue                          at 77th St
NYC 10021                      Mon-Fri 10-7, Sat 10-6, Sun 12-5

**Upper East Side**                      **(212) 838-1933**
1045 Third Avenue                        btw 61/62nd St
NYC 10021                          (opening hours as above)

**Midtown West**                         **(212) 262-5488**
128 West 57th Street                 btw Sixth/Seventh Ave
NYC 10019                          Mon-Fri 10-7, Sat 10-6,

**SoHo**                                 **(646) 613-8700**
123 Wooster Street                      btw Prince/Spring
NYC 10012                          Mon-Sat 10-7, Sun 12-6

**NoHo**                                 **(212) 529-4808**
10 Astor Place                      btw Broadway/Lafayette
NYC 10003                      Mon-Fri 10-7, Sat 10-6, Sun 12-5

## Arden B.

Street sensibility pervades at this overly-lit SoHo spot where the stock is finally veering away from the peasant girl look: the latest styles seem more creative and sophisticated, while still retaining their casual air. Fishnet fabrics and gauzy materials seem to be everywhere—you need to be young and/or have a great figure to pull off a lot of this stuff. Accessories like knit caps and huge belts thankfully distract one's eye from, depending on one's opinion, the either very now or very department-store decor. *ardenb.com*

*Affordable*                                 *Amex/MC/V*

**SoHo**                                 **(212) 941-5697**
532 Broadway                            btw Prince/Spring
NYC 10012                           Mon-Sat 10-8, Sun 11-7

## Arleen Bowman

Arleen Bowman's line of casual sportswear features signature two-pocket shirts in perforated suede, linen, silk, cotton and velvet, plus relaxed skirts, pants and coats. In addition, you'll find traveling suits, sweaters, dresses, T-shirts, tops and jeans from Garfield & Marks, Margaret O'Leary, Anna Moon, Cambio, Neesh, Womyn and Three Dots. Accessories include fabulous handbags, jewelry and shoes.

*Expensive*                                  *Amex/MC/V*

**West Village**                         **(212) 645-8740**
353 Bleecker                         btw West 10th/Charles
NYC 10014                           Daily 12-7 (Sunday 1-6)

## Arthur Gluck Shirtmakers

Lovely custom shirts are produced here at Arthur Gluck Shirtmakers. Choose a fabric from Gluck's stunning selection, ranging from solid broadcloth to Sea Island cotton to luxurious zendaline to silky crepe. With options like hand-sewn monograms, the shop's signature mother-of-pearl buttons, and nifty cufflinks, the possibilities for creating a unique shirt are endless. Orders are carefully prepared and take approximately one month. *shirtcreations.com*

*Moderate* *Amex/MC/V*

**Midtown West** **(212) 755-8165**
47 West 57th Street btw Fifth/Sixth Ave
NYC 10019 Mon-Thurs 9-5, Fri 9-2

## Art Fiend Foundation
Art Fiend Foundation is a not-for-profit organization pro-viding a carefully curated gallery/retail outlet for budding designers like Miyako Nakamura, Susan Cianciolo, Tess Giberson, Jodi Busby and Elisa Jiminez. Find select racks of one-of-a-kind pieces, including clothes, accessories and jewelry. Handmade treasures—from delicate skirts to tiny detailed purses—are on display here, as are photographs, paintings, books, and pretty much anything else that hap-pens to catch the foundation's fancy. A great spot to indulge in fashion's future. *artfiendfoundation.com*

*Moderate* *Amex/MC/V*

**SoHo** **(212) 420-1635**
123 Ludlow btw Rivington/Delancey
NYC 10002 Tues-Sun 1-7

## Ascot Chang
One of New York's finest shirtmakers, Ascot Chang caters to some of the world's nattiest dressers with custom-made suits and overcoats as well. Choose from 2,000 luxurious fabrics and know that your purchase will last forever. If your wallet isn't quite that flush, Chang also features off-the-rack shirts, sportcoats, blazers, pajamas and silk robes. Custom-made suits start at $1,800, shirts at $90. *ascotchang.com*

*Expensive* *Amex/MC/V*

**Midtown West** **(212) 759-3333**
7 West 57th Street btw Fifth/Sixth Ave
NYC 10019 Mon-Sat 9:30-6

## Ash Francomb
Do you love me, surfer girl? For beach bunnies or those who just want to vicariously soak some sun, this La Jolla-based retro surf paradise provides an endless summer all year round. Selling super-soft screen-printed tees of beau-tiful beaches and gnarly waves all over the globe, South American style ponchos and those Brazilian cult flip-flop Havaianas, Ash Francomb is as boss as your favorite Beach Boys record. *ashfrancomb.com*

*Moderate* *Amex/MC/V*

**SoHo** **(212) 334-3435**
35 Crosby Street btw Grand/Broome
NYC 10012 Daily 12-6

## Asprey
This iconic English brand has given itself a makeover, marrying its long-standing aristocratic, high-quality standards with an updated rock 'n' roll sensibility. And with Mick's daughter Jade Jagger designing jewelry for the esteemed brand, you know the rock is for real. The often eclectic (and always luxurious) selection includes porcelain figures, leather board games, cufflinks, tableware, pens and watches. You'll chuckle at the novelty items, covet the jewelry and gasp at the prices—all in all, not a place to miss. *asprey.com*

*Luxury*                                    *Amex/MC/V*

**Fifth Avenue**                      **(212) 688-1811**
723 Fifth Avenue                            at 56th St
NYC 10022            Mon-Sat 10-5:30 (Thurs 10-7:30)

## Assets London
A bust of colorful Ibiza energy on the Upper West Side and Tribeca, Assets London carries top European designer labels such as D&G, Cacharel and Diesel Style Lab, all looks that the most label-conscious club-hopper dreams of being decked out in. Also find a large selection of sunglasses, stockings from top brands like Wolford and why-bother underthings from the likes of Cosabella. For bored boyfriends, there's a couch and a monitor playing catwalk videos (Gisele in a swimsuit should keep their interest).

*Moderate*                                  *Amex/MC/V*

**Upper West Side**                   **(212) 874-8253**
464 Columbus Avenue                    btw 82/83rd St
NYC 10024                   Mon-Sat 11-8, Sun 12-7

**Tribeca**                           **(212) 219-8777**
152 Franklin Street                  btw Hudson/Varick
NYC 10013                             Mon-Sat 10-7

## A.Tempo
A super-girly store for that knockout party dress. A great selection features beaded and sequined evening dresses, flowing chiffon column dresses, and floor-length skirts paired with spaghetti-strap tops. Embellish your fancy outfit with coordinating accessories like beaded purses, jewelry, shawls and a ton of diamanté hair ornaments.

*Moderate*                                  *Amex/MC/V*

**Upper West Side**                   **(212) 769-0368**
290 Columbus Avenue                    btw 73/74th St
NYC 10023                   Mon-Sat 11-8, Sun 12-7

## A.Testoni
A footwear designer Bologna, A.Testoni's high-quality leather shoes are the very epitome of understatement. For men, find handmade and bench-made dress shoes, tennis shoes, colorful loafers with multiple buckles and tougher-than-you-think mandals. For women, styles run from loafers and boots to pumps and eveningwear. Check out the A.Testoni version of a slingback—so smooth. Handbags,

briefcases, scarves, ties, belts and luggage complete the offerings.                               877-testoni  *atestoni.com*

*Expensive*                                                     *Amex/MC/V*

**Fifth Avenue**                                        **(212) 223-0909**
665 Fifth Avenue                                             at 53rd St
NYC 10022                          Mon-Fri 10-7, Sat 10-6:30, Sun 12-5

## A.T.Harris Formalwear

A brilliant source for renting a tuxedo anytime, but especially for short notice and weddings, A.T.Harris takes the pain out of the penguin suit with its comfy space and speedy (but classy) service. You'll have the option of renting or buying at equally reasonable prices— expect to pay $145 to $195 for a 24-hour rental, including everything except shoes. Shirts and the necessary black-tie accoutrements are also available.                          *atharris.com*

*Moderate*                                                     *Amex/MC/V*

**Midtown East**                                        **(212) 682-6325**
11 East 44th Street                               btw Fifth/Madison Ave
NYC 10017                                 Mon-Fri 9-6 (Thurs 9-7)
                                          Sat (by appointment only) 10-4

## The Athlete's Foot

It's a bonanza of sneakers for every sport on the planet— be it yoga, tennis, running, basketball or just plain walking around. You'll find every top brand here, including Adidas, New Balance, Nike and Reebok, as well as NBA gear, although don't expect the staff to be too knowledgeable about any product. Children's sizes vary from store to store.                                   *theathletesfoot.com*

*Affordable to moderate*                                       *Amex/MC/V*

**Midtown West**                                        **(212) 391-9382**
1460 Broadway                                                at 41st St
NYC 10036                                      Mon-Sat 10-9, Sun 12-6

**Upper East Side**                                     **(212) 426-7583**
233 East 86th Street                              btw Second/Third Ave
NYC 10028                                      Mon-Sat 10-8, Sun 12-6

**Upper East Side**                                     **(212) 223-8022**
1031 Third Avenue                                            at 61st St
NYC 10021                                      Mon-Sat 10-8, Sun 11-6

**Upper West Side**                                     **(212) 961-9556**
2563 Broadway                                                at 96th St
NYC 10025                                      Mon-Sat 10-9, Sun 10-7

**Upper West Side**                                     **(212) 579-2153**
2265 Broadway                                           btw 81/82nd St
NYC 10024                                      Mon-Sat 10-8, Sun 11-6

**Midtown East**                                        **(212) 317-1920**
655 Lexington Avenue                                         at 55th St
NYC 10022                                      Mon-Sat 10-8, Sun 12-6

**Midtown East**                                        **(212) 867-4599**
41 East 42nd Street                                   at Madison Ave
NYC 10017                                      Mon-Sat 9-8, Sun 11-6:30

**Midtown West**                          **(212) 957-9461**
1668 Broadway                              btw 51/52nd St
NYC 10019                                      Daily 9-10

**Midtown West**                          **(212) 768-3195**
1568 Broadway                                  at 47th St
NYC 10036                                      Daily 9-10

**Midtown West**                          **(212) 391-9382**
1460 Broadway                                  at 41st St
NYC 10036                           Mon-Sat 10-9, Sun 11-8

**Midtown West**                          **(212) 957-9461**
46 West 34th Street                          at Sixth Ave
NYC 10001                            Mon-Sat 9-9, Sun 11-7

**NoHo**                                  **(212) 260-0360**
60 East 8th Street                           at Broadway
NYC 10003                           Mon-Sat 10-10, Sun 12-7

## Atomic Passion

Don't mess with the folks at Atomic Passion, this legendary, kitsch-heavy vintage store. 'Buy or Die' reads their business card, which also boasts a skull and crossbones in case you didn't get the message. While the eclectic mix of clothing, which includes graphic tees, Fifties dresses, Western shirts and a huge amount of shoes, handbags and sunglasses may be daunting at first, patience rewards those shoppers with time to rummage through the store's many racks. If you can see beyond the endless strands of Christmas baubles and fake fruit on the ceiling, that is…

*Moderate*                                   *Amex/MC/V*

**East Village**                          **(212) 533-0718**
430 East 9th Street                      btw First/Avenue A
NYC 10009                                       Daily 1-8

## Atrium

This marble store with denim-patched couches is an anomaly of button-downs, Seven and Miss Sixty jeans, Triple 5 Soul sweatshirts and J.Lo-style tube tops. The mix of trendy designs and streetwear includes an array of sunglasses, footwear and other accessories.         *atriumnyc.com*

*Moderate*                                   *Amex/MC/V*

**NoHo**                                  **(212) 473-9200**
644 Broadway                                  at Bleecker
NYC 10012                           Mon-Sat 10-9, Sun 11-8

## Avirex

Rappers and Red Baron wannabes get their sporty leather looks from Avirex. Since 1975, Jeff Clyman has been fashioning hides for sports legends, rock stars, actors and aviators (he's an official supplier to the U.S. Air Force). His selection of colorful collegiate jackets, motorcycle numbers, oversized baseball bombers, jeans and T-shirts (heavily logo'd with the Avirex name) are all sold here. Don't miss the encased model planes around the store.      *avirex.com*

*Moderate*                                   *Amex/MC/V*

**SoHo**
652 Broadway
NYC 10012

**(212) 254-4000**
btw Bleecker/Bond
Mon-Sat 11-7, Sun 12-6

## Avitto

In the heart of SoHo, Avitto offers footwear styles that cover all the bases. Women can choose from mules, pumps, slingbacks, evening shoes and a large boot selection; fellas can browse business and casual shoes from sandals to $800 alligator lace-ups. Labels include Gianfranco Ferré, Alberto Zago, Yoriko Powell, Avitto, Rodolfo Zengarini and Calvin Klein. *avitto.com*

*Moderate to expensive* *Amex/MC/V*

**SoHo**
424 West Broadway
NYC 10012

**(212) 219-7501**
btw Prince/Spring
Mon-Sat 10:30-9, Sun 11-8:30

## A/X Armani Exchange

This emporium caters to the logo-conscious in search of casual basics with the essential Armani insignia. Find jeans, T-shirts, pants, sweaters, jackets and outerwear that are relaxed and hip—the denim skirts are especially cool. Think of it as an upmarket Euro version of Gap. Prices are surprisingly reasonable and quality is up to the lofty Armani standards, of course. *armaniexchange.com*

*Moderate* *Amex/MC/V*

**Fifth Avenue**
645 Fifth Avenue
NYC 10022

**(212) 980-3037**
at 51st St
Mon-Sat 9:30-8, Sun 11-7

**Flatiron**
129 Fifth Avenue
NYC 10003

**(212) 254-7230**
btw 19/20th St
Mon-Sat 10-8, Sun 11-7

**SoHo**
568 Broadway
NYC 10012

**(212) 431-6000**
at Prince
(opening hours as above)

## Azaleas

Beach or bedroom, Azaleas has you covered. This adorable boutique stocks the cutest and flirtiest lingerie and swimwear around. The fabulous staff will help you navigate through the adorable goods, which range from super-flattering bikinis by Lisa Curran to coquettish underthings by Princesse Tam Tam. Other swimwear labels include Errol, Vix, and TNA. Lingerie runs the gamut from basic to stylish, functional to naughty, with brands such as Aubade, Underglam, Le Mystère and Fleur't. This is the place to shop for cheeky gifts such as Daniella Simon's 'Mommy-to-be' panties or 'Kiss the Bride' briefs. Also find a fantastically eclectic assortment of accessories such as costume jewelry, sachets, candles, and shoes. 800-775-0540 *azaleasnyc.com*

*Expensive* *Amex/MC/V*

**East Village**
223 East 10th Street
NYC 10003

**(212) 253-5484**
btw First/Second Ave
Tues-Sat 1-8, Sun 1-6

## B2Gear 👕

Keith Lewis, community mentor and founder of Youth America, came up with a wonderful idea to get children more involved in their communities—have them build their own business. B2Gear is the result: one of cheapest and coolest places for teens to shop and buy gear from other teens. Fashion-forward youngsters manage and supply the store, stocking everything from Rasta-colored tights to denim, funky jewelry, and colorfully tagged tees. Every piece has been selected and promoted by teens who know what kids want to wear. Nothing is overpriced, and a student with 50 dollars can leave with at least three new outfits for school or play. *b2gear.com*

*Affordable* *Amex/MC/V*

**Fort Greene** **(718) 643-1860**
777 Fulton Street btw South Oxford/South Portland
Brooklyn 11217 Mon-Sat 11-8, Sun 12-6

## Baby Bird 👕

Baby Bird is the perfect boutique for Park Slope princes and princesses. Parents can establish street cred at an early age with rock 'n' roll tees for baby, showcasing bands like the Flaming Lips, the Sex Pistols and Bob. Super-soft blankets and too-cute toddler kimonos (wrapped in a sushi box) are also on offer. Baby Bird smartly built a fish tank right into the front counter, so kids can gape while mom and dad make purchases. *shopbird.com*

*Moderate* *Amex/MC/V*

**Park Slope** **(718) 768-4940**
428 7th Avenue btw 14/15th St
Brooklyn 11215 Mon-Sat 10:30-6:30, Sun 12-6

## Baghouse 👕👕

This is one-stop shopping for portage needs—a huge showroom filled floor to ceiling with travel bags. There are messenger bags, rucksacks, carryalls, pouches, handbags and wallets—everything from all-weather gear by Eagle Creek to luxury suitcase sets by Tumi. It's also a great place to pick up a briefcase.

*Moderate* *Amex/MC/V*

**NoHo** **(212) 260-0940**
797 Broadway btw 10/11th St
NYC 10003 Mon-Sat 11 6:45, Sun 1-5:45

## Bagutta Life 👕👕

Moving from its former West Broadway location, Bagutta Life, a spacious SoHo boutique, boasts the crème de la crème of haute designers from both sides of the Atlantic. Snap up a D&G or John Galliano jacket. Adorn yourself in an Alaïa or Zac Posen evening dress. And if you just can't bring yourself to splurge on that decadent Dior must-have, pick up a bottle of the store's signature perfume and you will still feel like a European fashion forerunner. *baguttalife.com*

*Expensive*                                          *Amex/MC/V*
**SoHo**                                          **(212) 925-5216**
76 Greene Street                              btw Broome/Spring
NYC 10012                              Mon-Sat 11-7, Sun 12-6:20

## Bakers

In the tourist wasteland around the Empire State Building there are few clothing and shoe shops not aimed at the itinerants, but one of the oldest denizens is the shoe store Bakers. Suiting the area, its offerings are more mass than class, focusing on such labels as Steve Madden, Guess, Diesel and its own Bakers line. Designs range from ankle-wrap stilettos to sporty sneaker-pump boots—decent fashionable footwear at middle-market prices. *bakersshoe.com*

*Moderate*                                          *Amex/MC/V*
**Midtown East**                                    212 279-7016
358 Fifth Avenue                                      at 34th St
NYC 10016                          Mon-Fri 9-9, Sat 10-9, Sun 10-7

## Baldwin Formalwear

Tuxedos, black tie, white tie and tails, morning suits, shirts, neckwear, vests and cummerbunds—all a man's formalwear needs are met at Baldwin. And with class: Givenchy, Chaps Ralph Lauren, After Six, Charles Jourdan, Oscar de la Renta and Perry Ellis are just a few of the labels featured ($300 and up). Not ready to buy your own? Thousands of designer styles are available for rent ($110 and up), and you'll also find shoes by Frederico Leone. *nyctuxedos.com*

*Moderate*                                          *Amex/MC/V*
**Midtown West**                                  **(212) 867-4420**
1156 Avenue of the Americas (2nd floor)          at 45th St
NYC 10036                              Mon-Fri 9-7, Sat 10-5

## ★ Balenciaga

It's a bold move on Balenciaga's part: eschewing SoHo and the Upper East Side, they plant their flagship on Chelsea's Gallery Row. Pretentious? A bit, but with clothes this beautiful and strange they might as well be art. The space itself is a marvel of exposed distressed brick and concrete, with a flat video projection of Nicholas Ghesquière's current collection on one wall. As for the clothes, you'll feel your horizons expand as you inspect the meticulously constructed (but hot) aviator jackets, roomy drop-waist pants and shrunken knits. Superior chic, and definitely worth the out-of-the-way walk. *balenciaga.com*

*Luxury*                                            *Amex/MC/V*
**Chelsea**                                       **(212) 206-0872**
542 West 22nd Street                     btw Tenth/Eleventh Ave
NYC 10011                                  Mon-Sat 11-7, Sun 12-6

## Ballantyne Cashmere

The label tells you that Ballantyne's been making handmade cashmere goods since 1921, and it's safe to say that they've got it down to a science. You'll want to wrap your-self head-to-toe in the soft stuff, from highest-quality twin-sets to floral-print sweaters to blankets to gorgeous scarves, hats and gloves. You'll also find cashmere crews, perforated polos, and argyle patterns in this clean, elegant store. While shoppers will find the classics, they will also find fun prints, and designs decorated with bird graphics or words such as 'healthy' and 'gloss'. Make sure to pick up a 5-ply cashmere sweater for winter—you won't need a coat.

*Luxury*                                          *Amex/MC/V*

**Upper East Side**                          **(212) 988-5252**
965 Madison Avenue                       btw 75/76th St
NYC 10021                    Mon-Thurs 10-6, Fri-Sat 10-5

## Bally

In 1850 Carl Franz Bally from Switzerland was inspired by the 'subtly decorated' shoes he saw on a business trip to Paris. A successful tradition lives on in the shoes, bags, sportswear and casualwear that bear his name. The designs are sleek, from striped-handle messenger bags to signature-print vinyl satchels, and the craftsmanship is high, from sun-dried, hand-applied leather flowers on bags to the fishermen-inspired leather-and-canvas-mesh footwear.                                          *bally.com*

*Expensive*                                      *Amex/MC/V*

**Midtown East**                             **(212) 751-9082**
628 Madison Avenue                          at 59th St
NYC 10153                      Mon-Fri 10-6:30 (Thurs 10-7)
                                        Sat 10-6, Sun 12-5

## Bambini

Every child should be so lucky to be all dressed up in a jaun-ty Bambini outfit. There is everything from casual and back-to-school basics to party and dress wear. Bambini is packed with Italian brand names featuring traditional looks in pants, dresses, shirts, sweaters, tees, rompers and more. Highlights include their private-label shoes and handknit sweaters. Be sure to check out their half-yearly sales, which are legendary among the buying-for-baby set. From newborn to size 8 (some boys' suits are available up to a size 12).

*Moderate*                                       *Amex/MC/V*

**Upper East Side**                          **(212) 717-6742**
1088 Madison Avenue                        btw 81/82nd St
NYC 10021                       Daily 11-7 (Thurs-Fri 12-8)

## Banana Republic

Ah, BR. Banana Republic had a fashion show in New York last year, signifying a greater fashion focus for the one-time adventure/safari store. While the prices are still affordable, the fabrics and looks have turned to luxurious touches like silk and eyelet lace dresses, bamboo-handled suede bags, mother-of-pearl earrings and lizard sandals. Banana Republic is right for work and the mix-and-match hi/low style remains immensely popular. Men will find textured, tea-dyed shirts, mock-croc loafers, slim suits and the quintessential khakis. *bananarepublic.com*

*Affordable*                                        *Amex/MC/V*

**Fifth Avenue**                            **(212) 974-2350**
626 Fifth Avenue                                   at 50th St
NYC 10022                           Mon-Sat 10-8, Sun 11-7

**Upper East Side**                        **(212) 570-2465**
1136 Madison Avenue                        btw 84/85th St
NYC 10028                           Mon-Sat 10-7, Sun 12-6

**Upper East Side**                        **(212) 288-4279**
1110 Third Avenue                                  at 65th St
NYC 10021                           Mon-Sat 10-8, Sun 11-7

**Upper East Side**                        **(212) 360-1296**
1529 Third Avenue                                  at 86th St
NYC 10028                           Mon-Sat 10-9, Sun 11-7

**Upper West Side**                        **(212) 787-2064**
2360 Broadway                                      at 86th St
NYC 10024                           Mon-Sat 10-9, Sun 11-7

**Upper West Side**                        **(212) 873-9048**
215 Columbus Avenue                        btw 69/70th St
NYC 10023                            Mon-Fri 10-8, Sun 11-7

**Midtown East**                           **(212) 751-5570**
130 East 59th Street                       at Lexington Ave
NYC 10022             Mon-Fri 9:30-9, Sat 9:30-8, Sun 10-7

**Midtown East**                           **(212) 490-3127**
107 East 42nd Street       btw Vanderbilt/Lexington Ave
NYC 10017                      Mon-Fri 8-9, Sat 10-8, Sun 11-6

**Midtown West**                           **(212) 244-3060**
17 West 34th Street                         btw Fifth/Sixth Ave
NYC 10001                         Mon-Sat 10-8:30, Sun 11-7

**Flatiron (M)**                            **(212) 366-4691**
114 Fifth Avenue                                   at 17th St
NYC 10011                   Mon-Fri 10-9, Sat 10-8, Sun 11-7

**Flatiron (W)**                            **(212) 366-4630**
89 Fifth Avenue                                    at 16th St
NYC 10003                   Mon-Fri 10-9, Sat 10-8, Sun 11-6

**Chelsea**                                 **(212) 645-1032**
111 Eighth Avenue                           btw 15/16th St
NYC 10011         Mon-Thurs 10-9, Fri-Sat 10-8, Sun 12-7

**West Village**                            **(212) 473-9570**
205 Bleecker Street                             at Sixth Ave
NYC 10012                           Mon-Sat 10-8, Sun 11-7

**SoHo (W)**                                **(212) 925-0308**
550 Broadway                               btw Prince/Spring
NYC 10012                          (opening hours as above)

**SoHo (M)**                                **(212) 334-3034**
528 Broadway                                       at Spring
NYC 10012                          (opening hours as above)

**Lower Manhattan**                        **(212) 962-1461**
200 Vesley Street                  at World Financial Center
NYC 10285                                   Daily 8:30-7:30

## Barbara

Are you a corporate woman that lets her hair down immediately after the big meeting? If yes, you might want to consider Barami. They offer suits, co-ordinated tops, dresses
and skirts at reasonable prices—linen suits for $180 or
pleated skirts for $45, for example. They also carry denim
and plenty of casualwear. Be sure to visit the scarf and
accessory section.                                    *barami.com*

*Moderate*                                                  *MC/V*

**Midtown East**                                  **(212) 980-9333**
136 East 57th Street                           at Lexington Ave
NYC 10022                          Mon-Fri 9-9, Sat 9-8, Sun 11-7

**Midtown East**                                  **(212) 682-2550**
375 Lexington Avenue                                 at 41st St
NYC 10017                            Mon-Fri 8-7:30, Sat-Sun 11-6

**Midtown West**                                  **(212) 967-2990**
485 Seventh Avenue                              btw 36/37th St
NYC 10018                              (opening hours as above)

**Fifth Avenue**                                  **(212) 949-1000**
535 Fifth Avenue                                     at 45th St
NYC 10017                          Mon-Fri 8-8, Sat 10-7, Sun 12-6

## Barbara Bui

French-Vietnamese designer Barbara Bui's clothes are best
known for their rock 'n' roll attitude. Bui's forte is her extensive range of beautifully tailored pants, ranging from boot-
leg to man-tailored—'I always make at least three cuts of
pants, for different bodies', she says—but you can also
choose from a huge number of jackets, skirts, sweaters,
dresses, form-fitted tees (shrink-wrapped—very groovy),
outerwear and shoes. An enormous, minimalist shop
serves as a backdrop for this cool Parisian designer's
monochromatic ready-to-wear collection. Our tip: wait for
the sales, when the pricey numbers are reduced by as
much as 50%.                                      *barbarabui.fr*

*Luxury*                                              *Amex/MC/V*

**SoHo**                                          **(212) 625-1938**
115 Wooster Street                             btw Prince/Spring
NYC 10012                              Mon-Sat 11-7, Sun 12-6

## Barbara Feinman Millinery

Barbara Feinman's hats achieve that rare level of perfection
that results from old-world craftsmanship and modern
style. Beautiful fabrics (from straw to velvet) and attention
to detail have made Feinman's toppers popular with
award-winners like Marisa Tomei and Glenn Close. The
lovely fedoras, bucket shapes, newsboys and cloches are
all handmade in the back of the store. In addition to offering services like hand-blocking and custom fittings, the
boutique also carries delicate jewelry and exquisite handbags.                                            *feinmanhats.com*

*Expensive*                                                 *MC/V*

**East Village**      **(212) 358-7092**
66 East 7th Street      btw First/Second Ave
NYC 10003      Daily 12:30-8 (Sun 1-7)

## Barbara Shaum

Barbara Shaum is the haute sandal specialist, having whipped up beautiful woven versions for almost 50 years. But she has experienced something of a reinvention thanks to king of cool Calvin Klein, who once paired his men's collection with Shaum's gladiator or thong-style custom-made creations. Since then she's hit the big league, with her shoes on the fabulous feet of photographer and trendsetter Steven Meisel and designer Ralph Lauren. Prices run from $225 to $500. Belts are available, too.

*Expensive*      *Amex/MC/V*

**East Village**      **(212) 254-4250**
60 East 4th Street      btw Bowery/Second Ave
NYC 10003      Wed-Sat 1-6

## Barbour by Peter Elliot

Since 1894, J. Barbour & Sons have focused on making clothes for those weekends out of town. Famous for their commitment to quality and durability, their name is synonymous with the best of country living. A men's stowaway flyweight quilted jacket is easily packed into a pocket, and womens' tailored equestrian jackets bring grace to a long ride. Lord James Percy has joined the Barbour team and his new Northumberland range line of shooting clothing will be launched in fall 2004. It promises to be 'uncompromising in its fitness for purpose' and wearable for all seasons and disciplines (shooting and non-shooting alike). To the manor, Jeeves…      *barbour.com*

*Expensive*      *Amex/MC/V*

**Upper East Side**      **(212) 570-2600**
1047 Madison Avenue      btw 79/80th St
NYC 10021      Mon-Thurs 11-7, Fri-Sat 11-6, Sun 12-5

## Barneys New York

Oh, Barneys, hallowed be thy name. This too-chic-to-speak fashion emporium is God's gift to shopping. In addition to excellent beauty—check out the new Foundation level on the lower ground floor (get it?)—and accessories departments, it boasts seven more floors of perfectly edited and ultra-hip women's and menswear, from cute-cool Cacharel to conceptual Yohji Yamamoto. Young fashionistas head at light-speed to the seventh and eighth floor Co-op for the hippest denim, swimwear, shoes and accessories from such labels as Marc by Marc Jacobs, Theory, Joie, Juicy, Paul & Joe and a special section devoted entirely to Miu Miu shoes. Other departments include outerwear; designer shoes (from Manolos to Michel Perry); lingerie; Barneys' private label (designed by hot new designer Behnaz Sarafpour); a maternity line, aptly named Procreation; a newborn and toddler section; and Chelsea

Passage, a tabletop and gift department. Then there's a vintage section, Decades (of the renowned L.A. shop), and a fully-fledged luxury bridal salon that features over 60 unbelievably chic styles. In contrast, the men's store is an oasis of calm, where classic types can go for suits from the likes of Oxxford, Ralph Lauren, Hickey Freeman, Kilgour, Kiton and Huntsman and coolsters can choose from Armani, Dolce & Gabbana, Prada and Helmut Lang. Other departments include men's furnishings, made-to-measure suits and dress shirts, designer shoes, sportswear, rainwear, outerwear, special sizes, casualwear, formalwear, shoes and, phew, accessories. If you are nearly dropping from shopping, find sustenance at Barneys' fabulous in-store restaurant Fred's, which is an in spot for fashionistas. And did we tell you about the twice yearly warehouse sales? Legendary.                    888-222-7639  barneys.com

*Expensive*                                            *Amex/MC/V*

**Upper East Side**                        **(212) 826-8900**
660 Madison Avenue                              at 61st St
NYC 10022                    Mon-Fri 10-8, Sat 10-7, Sun 11-6

## Barneys Co-op                                    👫

This trio of trendy stores defines what it means to be fashionable in America's fashion capital. Their selection of the chicest threads, shoes and accessories by the likes of Marc by Marc Jacobs, Mayle and Theory, not to mention the definitive selection of must-wear designer jeans, makes visiting the Co-op a monthly, if not weekly, must. The Co-op plans to expand beyond the funky Chelsea and SoHo locations into the sophisticated climes of the Upper West Side with a two-level store opening in the fall of 2004.                                          barneys.com

*Expensive*                                            *Amex/MC/V*

**Chelsea**                                **(212) 593-7800**
236 West 18th Street                   btw Seventh/Eighth Ave
NYC 10011                    Mon-Fri 11-8, Sat 11-7, Sun 12-6

**SoHo (women only)**                      **(212) 965-9964**
116 Wooster Street                          btw Prince/Spring
NYC 10012                           Mon-Sat 11-7, Sun 12-6

**Upper West Side**                        **n/a at press time**
2139-2157 Broadway                          btw 75/76th St
NYC 10023                                  n/a at press time

## Barry Kieselstein-Cord                             👫

'We so often miss the beauty in things; my mission is to bring this into the world,' proclaims Barry Kieselstein-Cord. With bags featured on *Sex and the City* and jewelry worn by the Hollywood's biggest names, it's fair to say, 'mission accomplished'. From alligator earrings to diamond and platinum necklaces, you'll see why this is one of the largest designer-owned fine jewelry companies. Tom Hanks, Steven Spielberg, and Oprah are said to be Cord fans through and through, and his belts, opulent jewelry and leather-with-gold hardware handbags (examples of which

are in the Louvre and the Metropolitan) are all more than
ready for their close-ups. *kieselstein-cord.com*

*Luxury* *Amex/MC/V*
**SoHo** **(212) 529-9361**
454 West Broadway btw Houston/Prince
NYC 10012 Daily 11:30-7 (Sun 11:30-5)

## Basic Basic 🚹
Guess what you'll find here? Assuming the name didn't give
it away, you'd be right to say 'basic contemporary junior
clothing'. Choose from a great selection of tops and jeans
for tweens, as well as cute skirts, dresses and sweaters to
complete the easy-breezy assortment. Labels include Petit
Bateau, Three Dots, Juicy Couture and Mavi. *tee-zone.com*

*Affordable* *Amex/MC/V*
**NoHo** **(212) 477-5711**
710 Broadway btw Washington Place/4th St
NYC 10003 Daily 11-8 (Sunday 12-7)

## Basso Furs 🚹
Step into this light and airy store and allow yourself to be
enticed by the furrier-to-the-stars collection of perfect pelts.
The store's natural woods and limestone floors show off
Dennis Basso's sumptuous wares to their best effect, while
his white-hot client list—Hillary Clinton, Elizabeth Taylor,
Barbara Walters, Eartha Kitt, Star Jones and Patti LaBelle—
makes the goods look even better. Basso's signature sable
coats go for $25,000-$100,000, and his broadtail lamb suits
run from $15,000-$25,000. *bassofurs.com*

*Luxury* *Amex/MC/V*
**Upper East Side** **(212) 794-4500**
765 Madison Avenue btw 65/66th St
NYC 10021 Mon-Sat 10-6

## Bati 🚹
This nice neighborhood boutique has carved out a niche for
leather shoes. Carrying practical pumps, boots, flats and
sandals in both trendy and conservative styles, Bati offers a
variety of European designer brands including Enrico
Antinori, Pura Lopez and L'Autre Chose as well their own
line. For the sporty shopper, Bati also sells a variety of fashion-forward sneakers by the likes of Goya and Royal
Elastics.

*Moderate to expensive* *Amex/MC/V*
**Upper East Side** **(646) 497-0581**
1052 Third Avenue btw 62/63rd St
NYC 10021 Mon-Sat 11-7:30, Sun 12-6

**Upper West Side** **(212) 362-0244**
2151 Broadway btw 75/76th St
NYC 10024 Mon-Sat 11-8, Sun 12-7

## BBL (Baby Blue Line) 🚹
Korean designer Eunjoo Lee adds a welcome touch of
diversity to Nolita with her hip, sassy collection. Her design

philosophy: cater to all body types and make clothes comfortable and easy to wear, from sportswear to informal but romantic eveningwear. Many of her dresses, skirts and tops incorporate custom-made screen prints and unusual fabrics like crinkled viscose and silk cotton viscose. Although the clothes are well priced, the look probably won't appeal to everyone.

*Moderate*                                              *Amex/MC/V*
**Nolita**                                          **(212) 226-5866**
238 Mott Street                                    btw Prince/Spring
NYC 10012                                                Daily 12-7

## ★ BCBG Max Azria

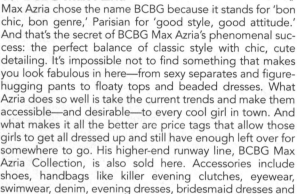

Max Azria chose the name BCBG because it stands for 'bon chic, bon genre,' Parisian for 'good style, good attitude.' And that's the secret of BCBG Max Azria's phenomenal success: the perfect balance of classic style with chic, cute detailing. It's impossible not to find something that makes you look fabulous in here—from sexy separates and figure-hugging pants to floaty tops and beaded dresses. What Azria does so well is take the current trends and make them accessible—and desirable—to every cool girl in town. And what makes it all the better are price tags that allow those girls to get all dressed up and still have enough left over for somewhere to go. His higher-end runway line, BCBG Max Azria Collection, is also sold here. Accessories include shoes, handbags like killer evening clutches, eyewear, swimwear, denim, evening dresses, bridesmaid dresses and jewelry.                                              *bcbg.com*

*Expensive*                                             *Amex/MC/V*
**Upper East Side**                                 **(212) 717-4225**
770 Madison Avenue                                       at 66th St
NYC 10021                    Mon-Sat 10-7 (Thurs 10-8), Sun 12-6

## Beacon's Closet

What a well-edited vintage store should be. Having expanded beyond its name with two locations and plenty of floorspace, Beacon's Closet includes an array of clothes—from party dresses to Western shirts—and accessories (bags, jewelry, shoes) for men and women that are carefully arranged by color, article, style and size. Unlike many thrift shops, there aren't a lot of duds in here and the look is definitely on the hipster/artsy side of the fashion scale, but you still have to pay multiple visits to make the most out of the constantly changing stock. And if you have some hip duds that you've outgrown or simply grown tired of, Beacon's Closet buys clothes every day of the week (though it's much busier at weekends).   *beaconscloset.com*

*Affordable*                                            *Amex/MC/V*
**Williamsburg**                                    **(718) 486-0816**
88 North 11th Street                                 btw Berry/Wythe
Brooklyn 11211                       Mon-Fri 12-9, Sat-Sun 11-8

**Park Slope**                                      **(718) 230-1630**
220 5th Avenue                                 btw President/Union
Brooklyn 11215                         (opening hours as above)

## Bebe

If you're a flaunt-it kinda girl, Bebe is the store for you. Its sexy pieces are heavy on the Lycra and are no doubt devilishly effective. Pants, skirts, dresses, navel-baring tops, tanks, tees and cute accessories make up the saucy collection. Only for the young, the brave...and Britney wannabes. *bebe.com*

*Moderate*                                         *Amex/MC/V*

**Upper East Side**                            **(212) 935-2444**
1127 Third Avenue                                   at 66th St
NYC 10021                    Mon-Fri 10-8, Sat 10-7, Sun 11-6

**Midtown East**                               **(212) 588-9060**
805 Third Avenue                                    at 50th St
NYC 10022                    Mon-Fri 10-8, Sat 10-7, Sun 12-6

**Flatiron**                                   **(212) 675-2323**
100 Fifth Avenue                                    at 15th St
NYC 10011                    Mon-Fri 10-8, Sat 10-7, Sun 11-6

## Behrle

Since almost everyone is in need of a new leather bustier, Carla Behrle has moved her store to bustling 34th Street, where steady clients and newcomers alike can access her creations more easily. Although she's dressed the derrieres of Jennifer Lopez, Chyna (the pro wrestler) and LeAnn Rimes, you don't have to be a celebrity to purchase these ready-to-flaunt wares. Leather pants are her forte—rocking it in every style from boot- and straight-leg to hip huggers and capris. Other sex-o-matic items include bustiers, jackets, skirts and shirts. The customer has three buying options: samples in sizes two through eight, special order (it fits, but you'd rather have it in a different color, or it needs a small alteration), and, finally, custom (any design, fit or color your heart desires). Expect a week to a month for delivery. *behrlenyc.com*

*Expensive*                                         *Amex/MC/V*

**Midtown West**                               **(212) 279-5626**
440 West 34th Street                       btw Ninth/Tenth Ave
NYC 10001                              (by appointment only)

## Belgian Shoes

Belgian shoes are distinctive, handmade loafers ('more comfort than barefoot') that continue their fine tradition as Waspy status symbols with a cult following among the 'most leisurely members of the leisure class,' according to *GQ*. Founded by Henri Bendel, the store offers an incredible range, from linen and leather to positively quirky crushed velvet. If you feel the need for a royal crest or crown (no wardrobe is complete...), they will add one just for you. Once hooked, you may end up collecting every one of their 50-plus colors. Expect to wait six months to a year for special orders, depending on how special you are. *belgianshoes.com*

*Expensive*                                         *Amex/MC/V*

**Midtown East**      **(212) 755-7372**
110 East 55th Street      btw Park/Lexington
NYC 10022      Mon-Fri 9-4:30

## Benetton

Benetton is a truly global brand that sells rainbow-colored, energetic casual clothes for men and women. Best are the sweaters in every style and color imaginable but there is also a nifty line in work suits, A-line skirts, T-shirts, jeans, wool coats, awesome swimwear, shoes and accessories. Benetton gives true meaning to the term 'lifestyle' because these are clothes purpose-built for easy living.      800-535-4491 *benetton.com*

*Moderate*      *Amex/MC/V*

**NoHo**      **(212) 533-0230**
749 Broadway      at 8th St
NYC 10003      Mon-Thurs 10-9, Fri-Sat 10-9:30, Sun 12-8

**Lower Manhattan**      **(212) 509-3999**
10 Fulton      at South Street Seaport
NYC 10038      Mon-Sat 10-9, Sun 11-8

**Fifth Avenue**      **(212) 317-2501**
597 Fifth Avenue      btw 48/49th St
NYC 10022      Mon-Fri 10-7 (Thurs 10-8), Sun 11-6

**Upper East Side**      **(212) 327-1035**
188 East 78th Street      at Third Ave
NYC 10021      Mon-Sat 10-8, Sun 12-6

**Midtown East**      **(212) 818-0449**
666 Third Avenue      at 42nd St
NYC 10017      Mon-Sat 9-8, Sun 10-6:30

**Chelsea**      **(646) 638-1086**
120 Seventh Avenue      at 17th St
NYC 10011      Mon-Sat 10-8, Sun 12-7

**SoHo**      **(212) 941-8010**
555 Broadway      btw Prince/Spring
NYC 10012      (opening hours as above)

## Ben Thylan Furs

Ben Thylan's extensive styles run the gamut from sporty to dressy. Its specialty: fur-lined or fur-trimmed water-repellent coats. These all-weather classics can be lined in any fur of your choosing, including mink, fox and sable. Cashmere, wool and camelhair coats are also available. Services include color and fashion consultations, as well as storage and cleaning.      *benthylanfurs.com*

*Expensive*      *Amex/MC/V*

**Chelsea**      **(212) 753-7700**
150 West 30th Street      btw Sixth/Seventh Ave
NYC 10001      Mon-Fri 9-5 (by appointment)

## Beretta Gallery

Clothes, accessories and accoutrements that would make James Bond proud—they're all here at Beretta. Renowned the world over for its guns, Beretta also manufactures fine hunting, sporting and weekend wear. The tweeds, lodens and cashmeres displayed beside cases of sidearms make for a sophisticated, if explosive, atmosphere. This is classic sportswear fit for a king—or a globetrotting secret agent.

*Expensive*                                          *Amex/MC/V*

**Upper East Side**                         **(212) 319-3235**
718 Madison Avenue                           btw 63/64th St
NYC 10021                                      Mon-Sat 10-6

## Bergdorf Goodman                                      ♀
Bergdorf's is the bee's knees in luxury retailing, from a first floor devoted to handbags, classic to adventurous jewelry and accessories, to six upper floors stocked with the chic to the edgy, including Chanel, Armani, YSL, Versace, Calvin Klein, Donna Karan, Valentino, Alexander McQueen and Narciso Rodriguez. The 'New Level of Beauty' is a lower-level cosmetics planet featuring exclusive beauty and skin-care treatments, fragrances, spa products, and the Buff Spa nail salon (fantastic pedicures and somewhere to rest your shopping bags). Other departments include contemporary shoes, lingerie, eveningwear, sportswear, suits, bridal, custom, couture, outerwear and a genius gift and tabletop shop. The John Barrett Hair Salon, which delivers a great blow-out, and the Susan Ciminelli Day Spa are on the ninth floor.           800-964-8619  *bergdorfgoodman.com*

*Luxury*                                             *Amex/MC/V*

**Fifth Avenue**                            **(212) 753-7300**
754 Fifth Avenue                                  at 58th St
NYC 10019              Mon-Sat 10-7 (Thurs 10-8), Sun 12-6

## Bergdorf Goodman The Men's Store                       ♂
Here is a huge, 45,000-square-foot emporium that still somehow manages to have the feeling of an intimate and exclusive gentleman's club. It might have something to do with the classic labels in stock: Turnbull & Asser, Charvet and Ferragamo shirts and ties and traditional suit collections by Oxxford, Canali, Hickey Freeman and Luciano Barbera. Not that they compromise cool: you'll also find Giorgio Armani, Jil Sander, Etro and the sex appeal of Gucci. Custom lines include Saint Andrews, Kiton, Domenico Spano and Oxxford. Mark the sales in your calendar now—they're fantastic.           800-964-8619

*Luxury*                                             *Amex/MC/V*

**Fifth Avenue**                            **(212) 339-3311**
745 Fifth Avenue                                  at 58th St
NYC 10022              Mon-Sat 10-7 (Thurs 10-8), Sun 12-6

## Berkley Girl                                           ♂
Berkley Girl is already prepping the next generation of New York style leaders with their pre-teen threads. The fun-filled store carries the latest from Puma, Betsey Johnson, Submarine and Lilly Pulitzer—all cute enough to satisfy Mom and fashionable enough to satisfy the young clothes-

horse. Accessories such as grosgrain belts, baseball caps, diaries and books make great gifts. Pick up a fashionable laundry bag for tweens heading off to camp (or boarding school); friendly, welcoming staff. Watch for a new store on the corner of 74th and 2nd coming soon.    *berkleygirl.com*

*Expensive*                                            *Amex/MC/V*

**Upper West Side**                            **(212) 877-4770**
410 Columbus Avenue                            btw 79/80th St
NYC 10024             Daily 11-6:30 (Thurs 11-7), Sun 12-6

## Bess                                                          ♀
Find exquisite designs at this serene, sensual store. Her jewelry is too elegant to be trendy and too stylish to be classic, but has a harmonious sensibility that just might make it a favorite for years to come. Long, graceful earrings and glamorous cocktail rings are standouts. Prices run from $500 to $4,500—an easily justifiable level given the mesmerizing effects of the pieces.

*Expensive*                                            *Amex/MC/V*

**Nolita**                                        **(212) 260-6740**
259 Elizabeth Street                          btw Houston/Prince
NYC 10012                                          Tues-Sun 12-7

## Best of Scotland                                      ♂ ♀
And it is. A top-floor retreat that sells Scottish cashmere sweaters at terrific prices. They carry a full range of styles for men and women, from sizes 32 to 58, at prices which average an amazing 50% below retail. Crew necks priced at $390 uptown on Madison Avenue retail for around $190, so get in here fast. Delicious cashmere overcoats, lush scarves and mufflers are also available.

*Moderate*                                            *Amex/MC/V*

**Fifth Avenue**                              **(212) 644-0415**
581 Fifth Avenue (penthouse)                    btw 47/48th St
NYC 10017                                          Mon-Sat 10-6

## Betsy Bunki Nini                                        ♀
A mouthful of a name, but worth the brouhaha, with labels like Piazza Sempione, Alberta Ferretti, Paul Smith and Rene Lezard. A pleasant mix of styles for the well put together Upper Eastsider.

*Expensive*                                            *Amex/MC/V*

**Upper East Side**                          **(212) 744-6716**
980 Lexington Avenue                            btw 71/72nd St
NYC 10021                       Mon-Sat 10:30-6 (Thurs 10:30-7)

## Betsey Johnson                                          ♀
Betsey Johnson's world is a fun, flirtatious and often completely far-out place to be. Johnson—who just celebrated her 62nd birthday and is best known for cartwheeling down the runway at the end of her shows—sells wild, sexy designs that have dazzled and shocked women for over 20 years. Her store is the perfect mirror for her worldview, with

45

pink walls, flowered wallpaper and blue tile floors. The vibrant energy isn't limited to the decor, however, as the clothes are equally sensational: signature bias-cut slip dresses, sequined shrugs, lively sundresses, and knitted car coats are standouts. Prices are never outrageous because the merchandise is always under $700. Betsey's accessories—from the amazing shoes ($190) to the street-vendor jewelry (around $40)—will spice up any outfit. A must-stop for Madison Avenue shoppers.                      *betsyjohnson.com*

*Expensive*                                                   *Amex/MC/V*

**Upper East Side**                                     **(212) 734-1257**
1060 Madison Avenue                           btw 80/81st St
NYC 10028                    Mon-Sat 11-7, Sun 12-6 (in all stores)

**SoHo**                                                **(212) 995-5046**
138 Wooster Street                           btw Houston/Prince
NYC 10012

**Upper East Side**                                     **(212) 319-7699**
251 East 60th Street                         btw Second/Third Ave
NYC 10022

**Upper West Side**                                     **(212) 362-3364**
248 Columbus Avenue                           btw 71/72nd St
NYC 10023

**SoHo**                                                **(212) 995-5046**
138 Wooster Street                           btw Houston/Prince
NYC 10012

## ★ Betwixt

Teen shopping can be hell, but Betwixt is there for you. It's a fabulous tweens lifestyle shop that totally meets the 'I wanna be cool' priorities of in-between girls. Perfect for slumber-worthy intimates, floral-print skirts, Juicy terry-cloth pants, glittery tube tops and satin tanks, while the T-shirt rack and jeans selection will cause a feeding frenzy over such bestselling labels as Diesel, Hollywood, Miss Sixty, Killer, Roxy and Itsus. A separate dress-up area does the trick for special occasions like bat mitzvahs and graduations. You may have trouble extracting your teen from the front section, though, where she'll be loading up on glittery necklaces, fuzzy pens, earrings and rhinestone-encrusted sunglasses.                                    *betwixtonline.com*

*Affordable*                                                  *Amex/MC/V*

**West Village**                                        **(212) 243-8590**
245 West 10th Street                         btw Bleecker/Hudson
NYC 10014                    Mon-Fri 11:30-6:30, Sat 11-6, Sun 12-5

## Big Drop

With an eclectic mix of young designers like Bella Freud, Karl Donoghue, Roberta Collina, Seven, Rubin Chappelle and Rebecca Taylor, Big Drop caters directly to the cool crowd. The accessories section is way underrated—be sure to check out the funky handbags.                      *bigdropnyc.com*

*Expensive*                                                   *Amex/MC/V*

**Upper East Side**              **(212) 988-3344**
1321 Third Avenue          btw 75/76th St
NYC 10021         Mon-Sat 11-8, Sun 12-7

**SoHo**              **(212) 966-4299**
174 Spring Street    btw Thompson/West Broadway
NYC 10012           Daily 11-8 (Sun 12-8)

**SoHo**              **(212) 226-9292**
425 West Broadway        btw Prince/Spring
NYC 10012              Daily 11-8

## Bio

Like to be the first to wear the Next Big Thing? Head to Bio, where you will find a rotating selection of up-and-coming labels, all on the brink of becoming fashion editor faves (and the store makes it easy for them: a short bio of each designer is included on the price tag of each item). Owner An Vu has a fabulous eye for equally fabulous pieces that are sure to start trends. A recent visit found the luxe Kulson (Lisa, formerly of Theory) collection, incredible jeans by Kasil, and the chic look of Tom K Nguyen. By the time these items hit the glossy mag pages, you can be sure that Vu will be stocking new gear for you to drool over.

*Expensive*              *Amex/MC/V*

**Nolita**              **(212) 334-3006**
29 Prince Street         btw Elizabeth/Mott
NYC 10012           Daily 12-8 (Sun 12-7)

## Billy Martins

Ride 'em, cowboy, straight to Billy Martins. This Western-themed store is the best place around for hand-crafted cowboy boots and fancy belts. Urban cowgirls and bucka-roos will also find everything from suede jackets and skirts to cowboy shirts, jewelry and belt buckles. These are high-priced statement pieces that will get you back to your Ponderosa in complete style.

800-888-8915  *billymartin.com*

*Expensive*              *Amex/MC/V*

**Upper East Side**              **(212) 861-3100**
220 East 60th Street      btw Second/Third Ave
NYC 10022     Mon-Fri 10-7, Sat 10-6, Sun 12-5

## Bis Designer Resale

Keep an eagle eye on Bis because every other day this sec-ondhand clothing and accessories store receives a delivery of designer merchandise straight from the bulging closets of well-dressed, well-heeled New Yorkers. Clever women head here for high-end European and American labels in tip-top condition—and at fabulous prices. It's not uncom-mon to spot an Armani beaded evening jacket for $300 (regular retail $1,500), an Hermès handbag for $900 ($2,600) or a Michael Kors cashmere sweater for $250 ($1,250). You'll also find the occasional vintage piece like a Pucci dress.        *bisbiz.com*

*Expensive*              *Amex/MC/V*

**Upper East Side**                    **(212) 396-2760**
1134 Madison Avenue (2nd floor)        btw 84/85th St
NYC 10028          Mon-Thurs 10-7, Fri-Sat 10-6, Sun 12-5
                                  (closed Sundays in summer)

## Bisou-Bisou

Kiss-kiss! French designer Michele Bohbot sees her clothing as being 'about a woman who is not a child, but not really a woman—she is somewhere in between.' This adds up to modern sportswear—with a hint of lace—that includes stretch pants, tight tops, dresses, skirts, shoes and accessories like cute fringed belts. Best to buy as separates to coordinate with your existing wardrobe rather than as a top-to-bottom look. Be warned: these are fashions for the young and lean.                    *bisou-bisou.com*

*Affordable*                              *Amex/MC/V*

**SoHo**                               **(212) 260-9640**
474 West Broadway                   btw Houston/Prince
NYC 10012                     Mon-Sat 11-8, Sun 12-7

## Blades Board and Skate

In-line skating is still one of the hippest sports around and nowhere can you find the requisite cool accessories better than at Blades. The selection includes skates, skateboards, snowboards and ice skates (some locations), as well as the obligatory protective gear. Top it off with matching clothing and accessories and you're ready to roll. In-line skate rentals are $20 a day with a $200 deposit. Helpful staff.                    *blades.com*

*Affordable*                              *Amex/MC/V*

**Upper East Side**                    **(212) 996-1644**
160 East 86th Street              btw Lexington/Third Ave
NYC 10028                     Mon-Sat 10-8, Sun 11-6

**Upper West Side**                    **(212) 787-3911**
120 West 72nd Street       btw Columbus/Amsterdam Ave
NYC 10023                          Daily 10-8 (Sun 10-7)

**NoHo**                               **(212) 477-7350**
659 Broadway                     btw West 3rd/Bleecker
NYC 10012                     Mon-Sat 10-9, Sun 11-7

## Blair Delmonico

Blair Delmonico incorporates Swarovski crystals into both her wedding and daywear collections for a sparkling finishing touch. The wedding collection has a wide range of looks for the bride and bridal party, while the daywear is well-suited for uptown ladies-who-lunch (almost everything's pink or pastel here)—or those who want look like they do. Look for a fabulous new store at Columbus Circle this fall, where they'll roll out a new line of Italian knits, cashmeres, sunglasses, and jet-set accessories.          *blairdelmonico.com*

*Expensive*                               *Amex/MC/V*

**Midtown West**                      **n/a at press time**
Time Warner Mall                     at Columbus Circle
NYC 20019                          n/a at press time

## Bloch

Just a hop, skip and a jump away from Lincoln Center, the 70-year-old Australian dancewear company Bloch has set up shop stateside with this chic and modern Upper West Side flagship. With their specialty bodywear including leotards, dance pants, knitwear, and footwear for ballet, jazz, tap and even hip-hop, Bloch is sure to be a pointe well taken. *blochworld.com*

*Affordable*                                                    *Amex/MC/V*

**Upper West Side**                               **(212) 579-1960**
304 Columbus Avenue                              btw 74/75th St
NYC 10023                              Mon-Sat 11-7, Sun 12-5

## Bloomingdale's

The Bloomingdale's experience is a must for any New York visitor. After all, it would be a dull tourist who didn't want to glance at Harrods on their first-ever visit to London, or at Galeries Lafayette in Paris. Yes, a stop by Bloomies is essential, but make sure you're feeling high-energy, because it can be an exhausting adventure even for the most seasoned of shoppers—the crush of people extends well past the first floor and it's all-too easy to get lost in the plus-size section when you're actually looking for shoes. But you must persist. Well into its 14th decade, the store continues to be a trendsetter, with innovative merchandising concepts and sales extravaganzas. Boulevard Four showcases the latest designer fashions for women by Armani, Calvin Klein, Chanel, Donna Karan, Ralph Lauren and others, while the contemporary selection boasts the best range in the city—Marc by Marc Jacobs, Trina Turk, Theory, Helmut Lang and William B. Men's fashions run from designer suits and formalwear to sports and casualwear from Joseph Abboud, Canali, Donna Karan, Hugo Boss and Kenneth Cole, as well as Bloomingdale's own private label. Also find one of the largest—and most intimidating—cosmetics floors and accessories departments around, as well as three floors of home furnishings and decorative accessories. An added plus are the outstanding service departments, which include personalized shopping, in-store TicketMaster, hotel delivery and a bridal registry. Shoppers suffering from low blood sugar or simply in need of some respite can choose from four in-house eateries.        800-777-0000 *bloomingdales.com*

*Affordable to expensive*                          *Amex/MC/V*

**Midtown East**                                  **(212) 705-2000**
1000 Third Ave                                   btw 59/60th St
NYC 10022                  Mon-Fri 10-8:30, Sat 10-7, Sun 11-7

## Bloomingdale's SoHo

Bloomies gone downtown. Taking cues from the cult of Barneys Co-op, this downtown version of its East Side sister features the trusted trendsetters in casualwear from

49

Juicy, Marc by Marc Jacobs, Habitual, Joie, to higher end up-and-comers like Derek Lam, Zac Posen and Matthew Williamson. The store even sells those gadgets that went from newfangled to can't-live-without in a flash, like Canon digital cameras, iPods and flat-screen TVs. Although the focus here is the women's clothes, fellows should be sure to check out the men's department in the lower level.

*Moderate to expensive*                    *Amex/MC/V*

**SoHo**                          **(212) 729-5900**
504 Broadway                     btw Spring/Broome
NYC 10012          Mon-Fri 10-9, Sat 10-8, Sun 11-7

## Blue

Greek-born designer Christina Kara sews custom cocktail dresses and bridalwear in this tiny East Village storefront. For the traditional bride, Kara has white floor-length ball-gowns fit for a fairy princess. But she also has funkier looks reflecting the hip downtown clientele—think plunging necklines and organza adornments.   *bluebridesmaids.com*

*Moderate to expensive*                    *Amex/MC/V*

**East Village**                  **(212) 228-7744**
137 Avenue A                         btw 8/9th St
NYC 10009            Daily 12-7 (Sat-Sun 12-5)

## Blue Bag

This is one of the cuter shops among the current crop of handbag boutiques in the neighborhood. Husband-and-wife team Marnie and Pascal Legrand run the design gamut from basic totes to whimsical one-offs to great looking wallets. Bags come in mixed patterns and colors in a variety of fabrics including silk, cotton and canvas. There is a constant stream of new arrivals and in summer they stock cool swim-suits, too.

*Moderate*                                 *Amex/MC/V*

**Nolita**                        **(212) 966-8566**
266 Elizabeth Street             btw Houston/Prince
NYC 10012              Mon-Sat 11-7, Sun 12-6

## Bodyhints

Sexy sophistication is this SoHo lingerie superstore's spe-cialty. Offering underpinnings from over 100 lingerie labels including favorites like On Gossamer, Swan and, of course, Cosabella, and slinky shirts and loungewear by Le Cosa and James Perse to name only a few. Add in a whole bottom floor devoted to gorgeous swimwear, and you'll see that Bodyhints makes undressing an art.   *bodyhints.com*

*Moderate*                                 *Amex/MC/V*

**SoHo**                          **(212) 777-8677**
462 West Broadway                 btw Prince/Houston
NYC 10012                           Daily 11-8

## Bohkee

A passage to India, more or less. Find handmade treasures at this lovely Upper East Side boutique. The Indian-inspired eveningwear is a standout, but don't miss the delicate jewelry, hand-embroidered blouses, and luscious pashminas. Friendly, welcoming sales staff.                    *bohkee.com*

*Moderate*                                              *Amex/MC/V*

**Upper East Side**                              **(212) 319-0707**
1077 Third Avenue                              btw 63/64th St
NYC 10021                                    Mon-Sat 10:30-7:30

## Bolton's                                                      ♀

Easy-access shopping, all over Manhattan. Head here for a selection of wardrobe staples that includes business suits, blouses, sportswear, lingerie and accessories, all at discount prices. Buyer beware: there are rarely designer finds, but you'll find some good deals nonetheless.

*Moderate*                                              *Amex/MC/V*

**Upper East Side**                              **(646) 672-9253**
175 East 96th Street                    btw Lexington/Third Ave
NYC 10128                              Mon-Fri 10-7, Sat-Sun 12-6

**Upper East Side**                              **(212) 988-7212**
1402 Second Avenue                               at 75th St
NYC 10021                            Mon-Fri 10-8 (Sat-Sun 10-6)

**Upper East Side**                              **(212) 223-3450**
787 Lexington Avenue                          btw 61/62nd St
NYC 10021              Mon-Fri 9:30-8:30, Sat 10-7, Sun 11-7

**Upper East Side**                              **(212) 722-4419**
1180 Madison Avenue                              at 86th St
NYC 10028                          Mon-Fri 10-8, Sat 10-7, Sun 12-6

**Upper East Side**                              **(212) 639-9298**
1191 Third Avenue                              btw 69/70th St
NYC 10028                              Mon-Fri 9-8, Sat-Sun 10-6

**Upper West Side**                              **(212) 362-7396**
181 Amsterdam Avenue                             at 68th St
NYC 10023                          Mon-Fri 10-7, Sat 10-6, Sun 12-5

**Midtown East**                                 **(212) 980-5587**
800 Third Avenue                                 at 51st St
NYC 10018                          Mon-Fri 9-7, Sat 10-7, Sun 11-6

**Midtown East**                                 **(646) 865-0898**
109 East 42nd Street                btw Vanderbilt/Lexington Ave
NYC 10017                            Mon-Tues 8-7, Wed-Fri 8-8
                                                     Sat-Sun 10-6

**Midtown East**                                 **(212) 684-3750**
4 East 34th Street                      btw Fifth/Madison Ave
NYC 10016                            Mon-Tues 9-7, Wed-Fri 9-8
                                              Sat 10-7, Sun 11-6

**Midtown West**                                 **(212) 935-4431**
27 West 57th Street                          btw Fifth/Sixth Ave
NYC 10019                          Mon-Fri 10-8, Sat 10-7, Sun 12-6

**Midtown West**                                 **(212) 307-5089**
1700 Broadway                                    at 54th St
NYC 10019                      Mon-Tues, Fri 9-7, Wed-Thurs 9-8
                                                     Sat-Sun 10-6

**Lower Manhattan**  (212) 385-3435
52 Duane Street  btw Lafayette/Elk
NYC 10007  Mon-Fri 8-6

**Lower Manhattan**  (212) 566-4621
253 Broadway  btw Chambers/Warren
NYC 10007  Mon-Fri 8-7, Sat-Sun 10-6

## Bombalulus

One of those great children's stores where it looks like kids were given free rein to design their own clothes. Boys explore the city wearing jackets and overalls decorated with familiar motifs like taxi cabs and fire trucks, while girls flutter about town in medieval-style princess dresses and butterfly wings. Bombalulus' flights of fancy are, for the most part, designed by the owner and priced appropriately for the seven and under clientele.  *bombalulus.com*

*Moderate*  *Amex/MC/V*

**West Village**  (212) 463-0897
101 West 10th Street  btw Greenwich/Sixth Ave
NYC 10011  Daily 11-8 (Sun 11-7)

## Bond 07 by Selima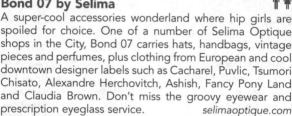

A super-cool accessories wonderland where hip girls are spoiled for choice. One of a number of Selima Optique shops in the City, Bond 07 carries hats, handbags, vintage pieces and perfumes, plus clothing from European and cool downtown designer labels such as Cacharel, Puvlic, Tsumori Chisato, Alexandre Herchovitch, Ashish, Fancy Pony Land and Claudia Brown. Don't miss the groovy eyewear and prescription eyeglass service.  *selimaoptique.com*

*Expensive*  *Amex/MC/V*

**NoHo**  (212) 677-8487
7 Bond Street  btw Broadway/Lafayette
NYC 10012  Daily 11-7 (Sunday 12-7)

## Bonne Nuit

Slightly hidden in bustling Lincoln Plaza, this crowded shop has the feel of a Left Bank pietà boutique. Delicate lingerie for women can evoke a Romantic sonnet or a rousing chanson, and is often finished with handmade details. Whether ladylike and pristine or vampy and risqué, there's something here for every trousseau. Unique children's pajamas will have them dreaming in French.

*Moderate to expensive*  *Amex/MC/V*

**Upper West Side**  (212) 489-9730
30 Lincoln Plaza  btw 62/63rd St
NYC 10023  Mon-Sat 10-9, Sun 12-7

## Bonpoint

If you're the type to play show-off with your child, the exclusive French Bonpoint is the store for you. Luxury fabrics, attention to detail and impeccable tailoring are the keys to its well-earned reputation for perfect fancy dress-up clothes—beautiful hand-smocked dresses, traditional blouses, shirts, pants, outerwear, swimwear and accessories, all at haute couture prices—maybe buy a size up, in case they outgrow of them in a month... Newborn to size 16 girls/12 boys. Could they make clothing for adults, please? *bonpoint.com*

*Expensive* *Amex/MC/V*

**Upper East Side** **(212) 722-7720**
1269 Madison Avenue at 91st St
NYC 10128 Mon-Sat 10-6 (at both stores)

**Upper East Side** **(212) 879-0900**
811 Madison Avenue at 68th St
NYC 10021

## Borealis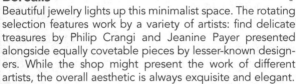
Beautiful jewelry lights up this minimalist space. The rotating selection features work by a variety of artists: find delicate treasures by Philip Crangi and Jeanine Payer presented alongside equally covetable pieces by lesser-known designers. While the shop might present the work of different artists, the overall aesthetic is always exquisite and elegant.

*Expensive* *Amex/MC/V*

**Nolita** **(917) 237-0152**
229 Elizabeth Street btw Houston/Prince
NYC 10012 Mon-Sat 12-7, Sun 1-6

## ★ Borrelli
This Neapolitan shirtmaker carries over 3,000 fabrics, and is where ageing hunks Robert Redford and Harrison Ford find their smashingly elegant attire. There is a dashing selection of ready-to-wear suits, sportcoats, leathers, cashmeres and knits. For a more luxurious purchase, custom-order handmade shirts fitted with mother-of-pearl buttons. A full women's line is imminent.

*Expensive* *Amex/MC/V*

**Upper East Side** **(212) 644-9610**
16 East 60th Street btw Madison/Fifth Ave
NYC 10022 Mon-Sat 10-7, Sun 12-6

## Bottega Veneta
Bottega Veneta has long been one of the most glamorous accessories labels in the world, and creative director Tomas Maier is holding this Italian luxury liner steady on course, continuing to turn out gorgeous *intrecciato* (woven) leather handbags, shoes and Venetian loafers. Accessories and some apparel occupy this huge, softly lit space like precious museum pieces. Men and women alike will enjoy Bottega's innovative designs that play off the suppleness of the materials, like convenient roll-up loafers and cute frog-shaped coin purses. *bottegaveneta.com*

*Expensive* *Amex/MC/V*

**Midtown East** **(212) 371-5511**
635 Madison Ave btw 59/60th St
NYC 10022 Mon-Sat 10-6 (Thurs 10-7)

## Botticelli

Located in the bustling Midtown area, Botticelli stocks Italian leather of its own design. Find classic shoes for work, casual loafers for the weekend and water-resistant boots for city puddles or country marshes. Other styles include sandals, mules, slingbacks, fur-lined loafers and fashionable boots. Also look for Francesco Biasia bags—bella! Prices run up to $595.

*Expensive*                                                    *Amex/MC/V*

**Fifth Avenue**                                      **(212) 768-1430**
522 Fifth Avenue                                         btw 43/44th St
NYC 10036                                            Mon-Sat 10-7, Sun 12-6

**Fifth Avenue**                                      **(212) 586-7421**
666 Fifth Avenue                                             at 53rd St
NYC 10103                                            Mon-Sat 10-7, Sun 11-6

**Fifth Avenue (W)**                                  **(212) 582-6313**
620 Fifth Avenue                                    at Rockefeller Center
NYC 10020                                Mon-Sat 10-7 (Thurs 10-8), Sun 11-6

## Boucher Jewelry

Celebs including Laura Dern and Courteney Cox Arquette are among those who have discovered that designer Laura Mady's tiny store is a gem (she also supplies Neiman Marcus). Browse the unusual and beautiful selection of semi-precious stones including mother-of-pearl cuffs, Peruvian opal bracelets, blue topaz drop earrings and turquoise lariats.                                     *boucherjewelry.com*

*Expensive*                                                    *Amex/MC/V*

**West Village**                                      **(212) 206-3775**
9 Ninth Avenue                                  btw Little West 12/13th St
NYC 10014                                            Tues-Sat 12-8, Sun 12-6
                                                (Monday by appointment)

## Boyd's Madison Avenue

One part high-end drugstore, one part small-scale department store, Boyd's is a one-of-kind shopping destination for luxe health and beauty products. Shop here for Mason-Pearson brushes, Manuel Canovas candles, the store's own Renoir cosmetics line and better known brands such as Clarins and Lancôme. Or just browse and find things you never knew you needed, like distortion-free make-up glasses. Also find children's toys, jewelry, lingerie and a full-service pharmacy.                    800-683-2693  *boydsnyc.com*

*Moderate*                                                     *Amex/MC/V*

**Upper East Side**                                   **(212) 838-6558**
655 Madison Avenue                                      btw 60/61st St
NYC 10021                      Mon-Fri 8:30-7:30, Sat 9:30-7, Sun 12-6

## Bra Smyth

We all know that buying a bra is never a funfest, but Bra Smyth makes it a little easier. Choose from over 1,500 styles with sizes that range from A to DDD cups. Custom fittings and alterations are their specialty. Also find a good selection of undergarments from Hanro, Lise Charmel, Aubade, Chantelle and Wacoal and swimwear by Karla Colletto and Domani. Alterations available on premises.   *brasmyth.com*

*Expensive*                                    *Amex/MC/V*

**Upper East Side**                       **(212) 772-9400**
905 Madison Avenue                      btw 72/73rd St
NYC 10021                          Mon-Sat 10-7, Sun 12-6

## Bridal Atelier
The serene, quiet atmosphere of this bridal boutique will calm the even the most anxious bride. Set in a townhouse, the store offers elegant looks from Angel Sanchez, Rivini, Monique Lhuillier and Peter Langner. Mother-of-the-bride styles are also available.

*Expensive*                                    *Amex/MC/V*

**Midtown East**                          **(212) 319-6778**
127 East 56th Street (3rd floor)    btw Park/Lexington Ave
NYC 10022                            (by appointment only)

## Brief Encounters
This boutique has a vast selection of European undergarments for all a foxy lady's lingerie lusts (gentlemen, you may come too, but by appointment only). Offering everything from sleepwear basics from Natori and The Cat's Pajamas to everyday necessities like bras, thongs, camisoles and slips by On Gossamer, DEL and Cosabella to sexy underpinnings by Lise Charme, Chantelle and Aubade, Brief Encounters have you (un)covered.

*Moderate to expensive*                        *Amex/MC/V*

**Upper West Side**                       **(212) 496-5649**
239 Columbus Avenue                        at 71st St
NYC 10023                          Mon-Sat 11-7, Sun 12-6

## Brioni
These gracious Italians have provided hand-tailored suits (off-the-rack or custom made), dress shirts, neckties, outerwear and sportswear to Donald Trump, Pierce Brosnan, Gary Cooper and Clark Gable. If you've yet to reach real estate mogul or movie star status, don't worry: everyone who sets foot in the store gets the royal treatment. Brioni's backbone lies in 11 on-premises tailors who it shares between its two men's locations. Guys wanting to enjoy the tranquility of Park Avenue Plaza should visit the 52nd Street store; power couples should head for 57th Street where the Four Seasons Hotel has looks for both men and women. Ladies looking for class and style to last a lifetime will appreciate the leather accessories, silk scarves, and blouses offsetting wool and cashmere suits.        *brioni.it*

*Luxury*                                       *Amex/MC/V*

**Midtown East**                          **(212) 376-5777**
57 & 67 East 57th Street            btw Madison/Park Ave
NYC 10022                             Mon-Sat 9:30-6

**Midtown East**
55 East 52nd Street
NYC 10022

**(212) 355-1940**
btw Madison/Park Ave
(opening hours as above)

## Brooklyn Industries

From showing borough pride with a now-ubiquitous 'Brooklyn' hoodie, to finding that perfect esoteric graphic tee to go with your thick black-framed glasses, Brooklyn Industries will help you attain that I've-lived-in-Williamsburg-for-longer-than-two-months look you've been searching for. Plenty of cool tank tees and sexy print skirts are available for gals, as are '718' baseball tees for your Brooklyn toddler. Don't forget standard-issue WB accessories like messenger bags and trucker hats. *brooklynindustries.com*

*Affordable*                                               *Amex/MC/V*

**Williamsburg**
162 Bedford Avenue
Brooklyn 11211

**(718) 486-6464**
at North 8th St
Daily 12-8 (Sun 12-8:30)

**Park Slope**
152 5th Avenue
Brooklyn 11217

**(718) 789-3447**
btw Lincoln/St John
Mon-Sat 11-8, Sun 12-8:30

**SoHo**
286 Lafayette Street
NYC 10012

**(212) 219-0862**
btw Houston/Prince
Mon-Sat 11-9, Sun 12-7

## Brooks Brothers

Brooks Brothers is so well known that its name has become an adjective, like 'he was so Brooks Brothers'. That said, the Establishment label has been subject to a series of makeovers in the last five years in an attempt to appeal to more than prep school and Ivy League types. Owner Claudio del Vecchio has now injected more of luxury flair. The Country Club men's collection, launched in 2003, incorporates luxe casual for a more sophisticated customer. It includes polos, sweaters, vests and blazers, but you'll still find basics such as suits, ties and non-iron shirts. Women have an entire department of classic suits, skirts, shirts, pants and jackets, as well as modern casualwear. The capri pants, cashmere sweater sets, T-shirts and dresses in hot, vibrant colors are a big hit. For boys over age 5, tradition dictates a trip to Brooks Brothers for that first pair of gray flannels and navy blazer. *brooksbrothers.com*

*Moderate*                                                 *Amex/MC/V*

**Midtown East**
346 Madison Avenue
NYC 10017

**(212) 682-8800**
btw 44/45th St
Mon-Sat 9-7 (Thurs 9-8), Sun 12-6

**Fifth Avenue**
666 Fifth Avenue
NYC 10103

**(212) 261-9440**
btw 52/53rd St
Mon-Fri 10-8, Sat 10-7, Sun 11-7

## Bu and the Duck

Cool name—Lord knows what it means—but Bu and the Duck sells fashionable trappings for your pampered child. Inspired by American styles of the Thirties, Susan Lane has created a clothing and toy collection that captures the innocence of children with wonderful crocheted sweaters from Peru and linen overalls. Accessories include Italian handmade shoes, delicately hand-embroidered quilts by Judy Boisson, stuffed animals and hair accessories. From newborn to eight years. *buandtheduck.com*

*Expensive*                                   *Amex/MC/V*

**Tribeca**                              **(212) 431-9226**
106 Franklin Street            btw West Broadway/Church
NYC 10013                       Mon-Sat 10-7, Sun 11-5

## Buffalo Chips USA

A specialist in handmade custom Western clothes and one of Carson Kressley's fashion finds on *Queer Eye for the Straight Guy*. Look for rocker, cowboy and biker leathers and handmade sterling and gold belt buckles. Don't forget to check out their table of bargain boots marked down 50%.

*Affordable*                                   *Amex/MC/V*

**SoHo**                                 **(212) 625-8400**
355 West Broadway                    btw Broome/Grand
NYC 10013                       Mon-Sat 11-7, Sun 12-6

## Built by Wendy

Downtown's indie girl Wendy Mullin set up shop to showcase her fun, hip and— even better—affordable clothes. This artsy lady is coolly confident with color and has just the right dose of retro chic: think cute corded canvas pants, funky blouses, edgy slogan T-shirts, plaid wool jackets and stripey tops. Mod girls, schoolgirls, cool girls…this is the place for you. Make sure you take a peek at the new men's collection, too: button-down shirts, slogan tees, and lightweight jeans with animal-print pocket lining. *builtbywendy.com*

*Moderate*                                   *Amex/MC/V*

**SoHo**                                 **(212) 925-6538**
7 Centre Market Place                btw Broome/Grand
NYC 10013                        Mon-Sat 12-7, Sun 1-6

## ★ Burberry

The British house of Burberry's signature plaid-lined trench coat (designed for 'safety on land, on air or afloat') has ruled the elements for over a century. But since its funky days—remember when the plaid became rampant everywhere from umbrellas to bikinis?—creative director Christopher Bailey has kept the tradition but added the cool. The massive Manhattan flagship is meant to showcase all that is the reborn Burberry: fantastic rainwear, of course, as well as beautiful leathers, trench-inspired dresses, great knits, better than ever accessories from bags to shoes and casualwear under the Burberry London and the more expensive Burberry Prorsum labels. For men, there are classic English suits, jackets and casualwear, plus butter-soft leathers and knits. Don't forget to browse Burberry's children's line for your tots—fantastic. The SoHo store has a younger, hipper edge, with hardwood floors and exposed ducting, and offers an edited-down selection of the collections. 800-284-8480 *burberry.com*

*Expensive*                                             *Amex/MC/V*

**Midtown East**                                  **(212) 407-7100**
9 East 57th Street                      btw Fifth/Madison Ave
NYC 10022              Mon-Fri 9:30-7, Sat 9:30-6, Sun 12-6

**SoHo**                                          **(212) 925-9300**
131 Spring Street                         btw Greene/Wooster
NYC 10012                         Mon-Sat 11-7, Sun 12-6

## Burlington Coat Factory

Burlington Coat Factory continues to grow as a chain, thanks to its unusual retail hybrid of off-price mass merchant and department store. Its motto says 'More than just great coats', so you'll also find career and sportswear, children's wear, maternity, plus sizes, shoes and baby furniture, all at discounted prices. But the coats are still the best reason to stop by. 800-444-2628 *coat.com*

*Affordable*                                            *Amex/MC/V*

**Chelsea**                                        **(212) 229-1300**
707 Sixth Avenue                                    at 23rd St
NYC 10010                            Mon-Sat 9-9, Sun 11-6

## Caché

More shopping mall than city chic, Caché is best for special-event eveningwear. Although it covers the latest trends, expect much of it to be manufactured in synthetic fabrics. Looks include spaghetti-strap dresses, tiny lacy tops and snug-fitting outfits perfect for club-hopping. A massive selection of coordinating jewelry rounds out the collection. 800-788-cache *cache.com*

*Moderate*                                             *Amex/MC/V*

**Midtown East**                                  **(212) 588-8719**
805 Third Avenue                              btw 49/50th St
NYC 10022                   Mon-Fri 10-7, Sat 10-6, Sun 12-6

## ★ Cadeau

Cadeau is an incredibly fashionable maternity brand. Why? Well, it might have to do with the fact that owners Emilia Fabricant and Chrissy Yu both worked at Barneys New York—for the beloved Co-op and as a women's designer buyer, respectively. 'The modern styles, manufactured in Italy, are about allowing a woman to be herself throughout her pregnancy without having to give up her sense of style,' Fabricant says. Hear, hear. A nice touch: the store is conveniently organized by pre-pregnancy size. *cadeaumaternity.com*

*Affordable*                                            *Amex/MC/V*

**Nolita**                                         **(212) 674-5747**
254 Elizabeth Street                      btw Houston/Prince
NYC 10012                         Mon-Sat 11-7, Sun 12-6

## Calvin Klein

Where would we all be without our Calvins? Klein reinvented American casual and continues to set the trends in slickly minimalist city pieces that strike a perfect balance between uptown polish and downtown chic. With his precise cuts and monochromatic palette (you want black, you got it) Klein is the effortless master of cool. This is the best destination for sleek-chic suits, clingy knits, shirts, dresses, skirts, relaxed sweaters and beautifully basic eveningwear. Then there are the shoes, accessories, jeans, underwear and home furnishings. All up, Calvin Heaven.          877-256-7373

*Moderate*                                    *Amex/MC/V*

**Upper East Side**                          **(212) 292-9000**
654 Madison Avenue                              at 60th St
NYC 10021          Mon-Sat 10-6 (Thurs 10-7), Sun 12-6

## Calvin Klein Underwear

You might not look like the chiseled models adorning his Times Square billboards, but Calvin Klein's underwear collection never fails to satisfy, or titillate—even when worn by mere mortals. Basic yet sexy, completely cool and comfortable, this underwear perfectly preps you for taking clothes off or putting them on. This spot marks the first Calvin Klein intimates-only boutique in the United States, and you'll love the delicate camisoles and bras in satin and lace, cotton boxers and T-shirts that you'll find here.

*Moderate*                                    *Amex/MC/V*

**SoHo**                                    **1-877-258-7646**
104 Prince Street                          btw Greene/Mercer
NYC 10012          Mon 11-8, Tues-Sat 10-8, Sun 11-7

## Calypso

From a life of growing up in the French Rivera and living in St Barths, the Hamptons and now New York City, it's easy to see where Calypso owner Christiane Celle has found inspiration for her luxurious boutiques. Never one to hide her love affair with West Indian whimsy, Celle's tropically inspired store caters to bohemians and other free spirits longing for luscious, bright, resort-ready clothing by a mixture of international designers. Bursts of pinks, blues, reds and oranges and ethnic prints dot the pleasant pastel-hued store in the form of silk sarongs, cashmere sweaters, filmy blouses, T-shirts, tiny tank tops and swimwear. And if the clothes don't immediately transport you into paradise, Mimosa, Calypso's signature scent (a blend of rose, mimosa and jasmine) will have you there in no time.                               *christiane-celle.com*

*Moderate to luxury*                          *Amex/MC/V*

**Meatpacking District**                     **(646) 638-3000**
654 Hudson Street                               at 13th St
NYC 10014          Mon-Wed 11-7, Thurs-Sat 11-8, Sun 12-8

**Upper East Side**                          **(212) 535-4100**
935 Madison Avenue                          btw 74/75th St
NYC 10021          Mon-Wed 10-6, Thurs-Sat 10-7, Sun 11-6

**SoHo**     **(212) 274-0449**
424 Broome Street     btw Crosby/Lafayette
NYC 10013     Daily 12-8 (Sun 12-6)

**Nolita**     **(212) 965-0990**
280 Mott Street     btw Houston/Prince
NYC 10012     Daily 11-7

## Calypso Bijoux

The delicate jewelry found here provides the perfect complement to the tropical-chic outfit you picked up at nearby Calypso St Barth's. Double-dipped gold and silver pieces by Heather Moria are standouts, but there are plenty of baubles here that are perfect for the beach—or for feeling like you're already there. *calypso-celle.com*

*Expensive*     *Amex/MC/V*

**Nolita**     **(212) 334-9730**
252 Mott Street     btw E. Houston/Prince
NYC 10012     Daily 11-7

## Calypso Enfant

A cuter-than-cute children's shop that carries top-of-the-line French clothing. Like the whimsical Calypso St Barths, which caters to adults, this is an outpost for spirited clothes in bursts of bright color, from bustle skirts and pants to embroidered shirts and cute accessories. You can even find your child an outfit that matches your own. For les enfants, find an adorable layette selection, irresistible sailor outfits, jumpers, pleated skirts, dresses, knits with matching hats, outerwear, shoes and accessories. Newborn to 12 years. *calypsostbarth.com*

*Moderate*     *Amex/MC/V*

**Nolita**     **(212) 966-3234**
426 Broome Street     btw Crosby/Lafayette
NYC 10012     Daily 11-7

## Calypso Homme

The male counterpart to Calypso, the store translates the same aesthetic in a thoroughly non-girly way. Think colorful shirts, knits, shorts, pants, sweaters, flip-flops and swimwear. The perfect stop for when you are heading with your gorgeous boho wife or model girlfriend to—where else?—St Barths. *calypsostbarth.com*

*Moderate*     *Amex/MC/V*

**SoHo**     **(212) 343-0450**
405 Broome Street     btw Centre/Lafayette
NYC 10013     Daily 11-7

## Camouflage

Buy these labels and you won't want to camouflage them one bit: Helmut Lang, Paul Smith, Etro, Michael Kors and John Smedley, just for starters. Casual, younger clothing melds with more sophisticated pieces. Also find outerwear, cool cashmeres and accessories.

*Expensive*     *Amex/MC/V*

**Chelsea**                                    **(212) 741-9118**
139-141 Eighth Avenue                              at 17th St
NYC 10011          Mon-Fri 12-7, Sat 11:30-6:30, Sun 12-6

## Camper

Looking for ultra-hip, immediately recognizable shoes that are scratch-resistant and equipped with light rubber soles and special linings to absorb perspiration? Look no further than Camper. This defiantly quirky Spanish shoe company is on the road to world domination. Nothing here is standard, from the five gigantic fiberglass lamps that hang above a footwear runway to the company's lofty design mission: to develop shoes so pure that every step feels as though you're walking barefoot. No stilettos here, then. The coolest styles: sneakers that look like football boots in strong color combos of black and beige.     *camper.com*

*Moderate*                                       *Amex/MC/V*
**SoHo**                                        **(212) 358-1841**
125 Prince Street                                  at Wooster
NYC 10012                              Daily 11-8 (Sun 12-6)

## ★ Cantaloup

'Downtown comes Uptown' is the rallying cry at this pink-doored oasis. Hip neighborhood girls too tired to take the train are more than pleased to stay put, what with Cantaloup's collection of cashmere, Repetto flats, hard-to-find Luella Bartley bags, Woo tanks, hottest-hot pants by Da-nang and edgy tops and clingy dresses from Australian designers Sass & Bide and Scanlan & Theodore. Don't miss the display case nestled by the checkout counter, full of flirty bracelets and funky necklaces.

*Expensive*                                      *Amex/MC/V*
**Upper East Side**                             **(212) 249-3566**
1036 Lexington Avenue                              at 74th St
NYC 10021                            Mon-Sat 11-7, Sun 12-6

## Canyon Beachwear

For a little California style, head to this store and shop for bikinis, thongs, one-pieces, tankinis and everything in between, all in the best color selection around. European and American brands include Dolce & Gabbana, Bachata by Melissa Odabash, Pin Up, TNA, Vix, Salinas, Huit, Luce di Sole, Le Tarte, Anne Cole, Calvin Klein, Delfina and Domani. Sarongs, matching cover-ups, sandals, beach hats and totes and lotions complete the amazing range. Sizes run from 0 to 22.                      *canyonbeachwear.com*

*Expensive*                                      *Amex/MC/V*
**Upper East Side**                             **(917) 432-0732**
1136 Third Avenue                             btw 66/67th St
NYC 10021                      Mon-Fri 11-8, Sat 10-7, Sun 11-6

## Capezio

Shall we dance? Well, twirl your way to Capezio, which since 1887 has caressed the feet of legendary twinkle-toes like Anna Pavlova, Fred Astaire and Bob Fosse. Today the company has expanded its horizons to cover other dancewear, including leotards, leg warmers, leggings, tights, jazz pants and knits by pro makers like Danskin, City Lights, Marika, Baltog and, of course, Capezio. They're perfect for ballerinas of all sizes and skills. Footwear includes ballet slippers, tap, jazz and toe shoes.  *capeziodance.com*

*Moderate*                                                    *Amex/MC/V*

**Upper East Side**                          **(212) 758-8833**
136 East 61st Street                   btw Park/Lexington Ave
NYC 10021                                  Mon-Sat 10-6, Sun 12-5

**Upper East Side**                          **(212) 348-7210**
1651 Third Avenue (3rd floor)                   btw 92/93rd St
NYC 10028                                  Mon-Fri 9-6, Sat 9-4

**Midtown West**                             **(212) 245-2130**
1650 Broadway (2nd floor)                            at 51st St
NYC 10019          Mon-Fri 9:30-7, Sat 9:30-6:30, Sun 11:30-5

**Midtown West**                             **(212) 586-5140**
1776 Broadway (2nd floor)                            at 57th St
NYC 10019                        Mon-Fri 10-7, Sat 10-6, Sun 12-5

**East Village**                             **(212) 254-4018**
678 Broadway                           btw Bond/Great Jones
NYC 10012                                  Mon-Sat 11-7, Sun 12-5

## Carlos Miele                                           ♂ ♀

Cutting corners in the best possible way, Sao Paolo's hottest fashion export opened his first store on the city's West Side last year, and it's a stunner. All pale green and gray curves, its Kubrick-meets-couture appearance makes it a cool place in its own right. Throw in Miele's multimedia art projects and his flamboyant, body-revealing clothes, and it feels like a very 21st-century kind of party. It's not all fun and games for Miele, though—he employs dressmakers from Rio's poorest *favelas* to help create the chiffon, silky satin, Lycra/linen and beaded crocheted looks (check out this year's abstract-print cape) that have won him an international fan base, not to mention raves from the likes of Britney and fellow countrywoman Gisele. *carlosmiele.com.br*

*Luxury*                                                      *Amex/MC/V*

**Meatpacking District**                     **(646) 336-6642**
408 West 14th Street                      btw Ninth/Tenth Ave
NYC 10014                                  Daily 11-7 (Sun 12-7)

## Carolina Herrera                                        ♀

When one thinks of Carolina Herrera, so many great words come to mind: elegance, glamour, sophistication, refinement. Regardless of seasonal trends, one can always count on gorgeous silk gowns, soft leathers, lovely fur pieces, perfectly appropriate to-the-knee skirts and immaculately cut pants. Ascend the storybook staircase to the embellished, breathtaking, embroidered wedding gowns that will enhance any bride's silhouette, while elegant organza shawls, pleated and ruffled trains, silk flow-

Directory

ers and covered buttons add the ideal finishing touches. Classic accessories include handbags, sunglasses and scarves. *carolinaherrera.com*

*Luxury* *Amex/MC/V*

**Upper East Side** **(212) 249-6552**
954 Madison Avenue at 75th St
NYC 10021 Mon-Sat 10-6

## Cashmere New York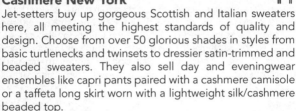

Jet-setters buy up gorgeous Scottish and Italian sweaters here, all meeting the highest standards of quality and design. Choose from over 50 glorious shades in styles from basic turtlenecks and twinsets to dressier satin-trimmed and beaded sweaters. They also sell day and eveningwear ensembles like capri pants paired with a cashmere camisole or a taffeta long skirt worn with a lightweight silk/cashmere beaded top.

*Expensive* *Amex/MC/V*

**Upper East Side** **(212) 744-3500**
1100 Madison Avenue btw 82/83rd St
NYC 10021 Mon-Sat 10-6:30

**Upper East Side** **(212) 517-3600**
1052 Lexington Avenue at 75th St
NYC 10021 Mon-Sat 10-6:30

## Castor & Pollux

A little-known jewel in the burgeoning Brooklyn style scene, Castor & Pollux offers subtle chic with an avant-garde twist. Think of Imitation of Christ's Tara Subkoff and fashion editor fave Chloe Sevigny on a non-celebrity budget, and you have the right idea. The store carries perfect summer tops and skirts from Mint and Anja Flint, Havaianas in every shade and sweatshirts and bags with Castor & Pollux's own logo, not to mention vintage and contemporary jewelry by local designers that will add panache to your outfit. A finishing touch: Italian leather bags in gold and silver that will get you noticed on and off Flatbush Avenue. *castorandpolluxstore.com*

*Moderate* *Amex/MC/V*

**North Flatbush** **(718) 398-4141**
67½ 6th Avenue at Bergen
Brooklyn 11217 Tues-Fri 12-8, Sat 11-8, Sun 11-7

## Catherine Malandrino

Flirty feminine dresses that French designer Malandrino herself says 'float around the body, making a woman feel as if she is walking in a dream,' is this beloved downtown boutique's specialty. Curve-hugging cuts and luscious luxury materials make Malandrino's designs adored by celebrities and fashionistas worldwide. A second shop in the trendier-than-thou Meatpacking District is set to open in the fall of 2004. *catherinemalandrino.com*

*Expensive* *Amex/MC/V*

**SoHo**                                      **(212) 925-6765**
468 Broome Street                                    at Greene
NYC 10013                                Mon-Sat 11-7, Sun 12-6

**Meatpacking District**                 **(n/a at press time)**
652 Hudson Street                                    at 13th St
NYC 10014                                  (n/a at press time)

## Cat Girl

This fabulous new addition to Elizabeth Street displays beautifully unique accessories. Handbags are a standout, like the exquisitely patterned clutches and sturdy leather shoulder bags inspired by Art Nouveau. Cat Girl also carries great shoes, cufflinks for men, and a small but lovely selection of home accessories. Reasonable prices mean you have no excuse not to check out this lovely, whimsical store.

*Moderate*                                          *Amex/MC/V*

**Nolita**                                    **(212) 219-1647**
167 Elizabeth Street                       btw Spring/Kenmare
NYC 10012                          Sun-Mon 12-7, Tues-Sat 11-8

## Cath Kidston

Interior designer Cath Kidston, known for her vintage-inspired housewares and accessories, brings her 10-year old Notting Hill (London) store stateside with this Nolita flagship. Her famous prints, from large flowers to Western cowboy scenes reminiscent of Fifties Americana, appear on everything from oilcloth bags and purses to ironing boards and wallpaper.                            *cathkidston.com*

*Moderate*                                                *MC/V*

**Nolita**                                    **(212) 343-0223**
201 Mulberry Street                        btw Spring/Kenmare
NYC 10012                                Mon-Sat 11-7, Sun 12-6

## Catimini

Does the image of your child outfitted head-to-toe in SpongeBob SquarePants regalia give you the willies? Catimini offers a welcome change from branding your child via Viacom. Flower prints and characters from French story-books are the preferred ornamentation on clever tops (from $36), bottoms (from $42) and coats (from $93). Six months to 10 years.                                  *catimini.com*

*Affordable*                                        *Amex/MC/V*

**Upper East Side**                           **(212) 987-0688**
1284 Madison Avenue                                at 92nd St
NYC 10128                                Mon-Sat 10-6, Sun 12-5

## Celine

Celine is the ultimate brand for uptown girls. This established French label, designed by luxe sportswear king Michael Kors, is the last word in luxurious yet casual dressing. Kors is a guru to young socialites who want their hip with a healthy dose of discretion. Styles run from cropped sporty jackets and lean pants and skirts that focus on the waist to lush fabrics like cashmere, fur and leather to sexy stilettos and extreme handbags. Celine shoes, in classic colors with witty details, are some of the best around; you'll wear them forever. Great sales, too.  *celine.com*

| | |
|---|---|
| *Luxury* | *Amex/MC/V* |
| **Upper East Side** | **(212) 486-9700** |
| 667 Madison Avenue | at 61st St |
| NYC 10022 | Mon-Sat 10-6 (Thurs 10-7) |

## ★ Century 21

Bargain hunters thank their lucky stars that Century 21 exists in such a high-priced city. Located at the edge of Ground Zero, Century 21, one of the city's cult retail destinations, came back strong after 9/11 with a refurbished interior, fresh inventory and the best prices anywhere. A polyglot mix of shoppers flocks here for heavily reduced designer clothing from Prada to Polo Sport. Check out Italian designer suits from $250 to $700, wedding dresses from $130 to $375, Polo sweaters from $40 to $70, designer outerwear from $300 to $750, and—yes!—Marc by Marc Jacobs denim and T-shirts for as little as $50. Other merchandise includes intimates, a great teens department, cosmetics, luggage, housewares, bed linens (Donna Karan, Ralph Lauren and more, all at fabulous prices), appliances and electronics. Take a deep breath and go nuts…  *c21stores.com*

| | |
|---|---|
| *Affordable* | *Amex/MC/V* |
| **Lower Manhattan** | **(212) 227-9092** |
| 22 Cortland Street | btw Church/Broadway |
| NYC 10007 | Mon-Fri 7:45-8 (Thurs 7:45-8:30) |
| | Sat 10-8, Sun 11-7 |

## Cesare Paciotti

Sex-o-matic! With their signature silver dagger logo stamped or affixed to much of their footwear, you'll never forget you're wearing a pair of Cesare Paciotti shoes. No one else will either, and that's the point. The collection showcases unapologetically sexy stiletto heels, pumps, flats and boots, with toes as pointed and sharp as the aforementioned dagger. For men, find a slightly tamer selection of shoes and boots better suited to artsy pursuits than to Wall Street.  *cesare-paciotti.com*

| | |
|---|---|
| *Luxury* | *Amex/MC/V* |
| **Upper East Side** | **(212) 452-1222** |
| 833 Madison Avenue | btw 69/70th St |
| NYC 10021 | Mon-Sat 10-6 |

## Champs

Whether it's golf, soccer, basketball, racket sports, running, billiards or the extremely athletic game of darts, Champs is happy to accommodate you. Find a large sneaker department for the whole family, as well as team logo'd jerseys and sweats. Best for boys and men.

800-991-6813  *champssports.com*

| | |
|---|---|
| *Affordable to moderate* | *Amex/MC/V* |

**Harlem**  (212) 280-0296
208 West 125th Street  at Seventh Ave
NYC 10027  Mon-Sat 10-8, Sun 11-7

**Fifth Avenue**  (212) 239-3256
1 West 34th Street  at Fifth Ave
NYC 10001  Mon-Sat 8-8:30, Sun 11-7

**Midtown West**  (212) 757-3634
1381-99 Sixth Avenue  at 56th St
NYC 10019  Mon-Sat 9-9, Sun 11-6

**Midtown West**  (212) 354-2009
5 Times Square  at Seventh Ave/42nd St
NYC 10036  Daily 8-12 (Sun 10-12)

## Chanel  ♀

Coco would be proud. Chanel's guiding light lives on in this jewel box of a store, where you'll find signature pearls and perfect tweedy suits mixed in with a dash of Karl Lagerfeld's rock 'n' roll sensibility (see the patent leather thigh-highs). Two floors stocked with make-up, perfumes, camilla pins and classic tailoring should be more than enough for any style enthusiast. And if you're not feeling properly coddled by the more than helpful sales associates, just head upstairs to the five floors of the Frédéric Fekkai spa for a little more pampering.  *chanel.com*

*Expensive*  *Amex/MC/V*

**Midtown East**  (212) 355-5050
15 East 57th Street  btw Fifth/Madison Ave
NYC 10022  Mon-Wed, Fri 10-6:30, Thurs 10-7
  Sat 10-6, Sun 12-5

**Upper East Side**  (212) 535-5505
737 Madison Avenue  at 64th St
NYC 10021  Mon-Sat 10-6

**Upper East Side**  (212) 535-5828
733 Madison Avenue  at 64th St
NYC 10021  (opening hours as above)

**SoHo**  (212) 334-0055
139 Spring Street  at Wooster
NYC 10012  Mon-Sat 11-7, Sun 12-6

## Charles Jourdan  ♀

This notable French shoe designer is perfect for that pair of 'statement' shoes. A Charles Jourdan design boasts color, sex appeal and, most importantly, high heels. Find evening shoes, chic pumps, platforms, wedges, boots, flats and sandals. Prices run from $165 to $400 (up to $600 for boots).  800-997-2717  *charles-jourdan.com*

*Moderate*  *Amex/MC/V*

**SoHo**  (212) 219-0490
155 Spring Street  at West Broadway
NYC 10012  Mon-Sat 11-7, Sun 12-6

## Charles Tyrwhitt  ♂♀

This London shirtmaker—from Jermyn Street, unbelievably elegant home of shirtmakers—is perfect for the man who is sick of staid Brooks Brothers but isn't quite ready for zany Paul Smith. Classic spread-collared shirts in fine cotton poplin are paired with silk print ties to create a crisp business look. Women will be pleased with Tyrwhitt's added attention to womenswear with his cashmere sweaters, jersey knits and tastefully tailored shirts. Handmade English shoes and boots are available, and be sure to look for the store's monthly promotions—past offerings have included 'buy two handmade shirts, get one free'. Lester Hyman, Washington insider and political and legal *éminence* who worked with John Kennedy and was John Kerry's first political mentor, swears by Charles Tyrwhitt and regularly orders from them by mail: 'The fit is perfect, the style is classy, and the price is right.' *ctshirts.com*

*Affordable to moderate* *Amex/MC/V*

**Midtown East** **(212) 286-8988**
377 Madison Avenue at 46th St
NYC 10017 Mon-Fri 10-7 (Thurs 10-8), Sat 10-6, Sun 12-5

## Cheap Jack's

It's all about sheer volume here: 12,000 square feet and three levels of vintage clothes encompassing every decade since the Thirties. There are literally thousands of jeans, disco shirts, bell-bottoms, evening dresses, sportswear (including some Boy Scouts gear), concert tees and leather jackets. Head upstairs for handbags and a fairly impressive selection of hats—just try not to go blind in the Hawaiian shirt section. *cheapjacks.com*

*Affordable* *Amex/MC/V*

**NoHo** **(212) 777-9564**
841 Broadway btw 13/14th St
NYC 10003 Mon-Sat 11-8, Sun 12-7

## Che Che

Testimonials from satisfied customers adorn the façade of this brightly lit little glass box of a shop, and it's easy to see why: Che Che represents one Hong Kong family's full-on fascination with handbags. From elegant evening clutches to fanciful sacs with hand-painted mermaids or zebras, every item is a beguiling mix of whimsy and function. Summer totes with embroidered flowers and pocketbooks shaped like fish (complete with sequined leather scales) are also guaranteed attention-grabbers, whether you're strolling on the boardwalk or sidling up to the bar. *chechenewyork.com*

*Moderate* *Amex/MC/V*

**Upper East Side** **(212) 249-0819**
1034a Lexington Avenue btw 73/74th St
NYC 10021 Mon-Fri 10:30-6, Sat 11-5

## Chelsea Girl

Owner Elisa Casas has got a Fifties thing going on, judging from this cult store which stocks a great range of sundresses in bright colors from the Twenties right through to the Seventies. Visited regularly by celeb vintage fans like Sheryl

Crow, Hilary Swank, Winona Ryder and Debra Messing, Chelsea Girl houses such labels as Yves Saint Laurent, Gucci and Valentino. Accessorize your retro look with kitschy coordinated print shoes and handbags that Lucy Ricardo would love. Be warned: Fifties dresses are best on Fifties-size waists. Breathe in. *chelsea-girl.com*

*Affordable* *Amex/MC/V*

**SoHo** **(212) 343-1658**
63 Thompson Street btw Spring/Broome
NYC 10012 Daily 12-7

## Cherry 👤👩

If you're looking for that one killer piece to top off your wardrobe, then Cherry is your store. This vintage Village shop is stocked with one-of-a-kind finds from legends like Chanel, Hermès, Versace, Pucci and Dior. Used and new pieces, from the Fifties through the Eighties, are packed everywhere, AC/DC plays on the stereo, and everything from sunglasses to scarves can be found here. Cherry's well-edited apparel is appropriate for anyone who wishes they lived in another decade. The store separates itself from other vintage boutiques with its superior selection and a nifty assortment of shoes that features never-worn vintage footwear in several different sizes. Many a fashion girl has been known to spend a week's rent on that perfect pair of boho boots.

*Expensive* *Amex/MC/V*

**West Village** **(212) 924-1410**
19 Eighth Avenue btw West 12th/Jane
NYC 10014 Daily 12-8 (Sunday 12-7)

## The Children's Place 👤

This chain's new stores have been popping up all over New York. Find lots of casual basics like jeans, T-shirts, dresses, pants, shorts, sweats, knits and accessories, all under The Children's Place label at bargain prices. Fabric and quality aren't built to last, but they'll probably out-grow them so quickly it won't matter. From newborn to size 14. *childrensplace.com*

*Affordable* *Amex/MC/V*

**Harlem** **(212) 866-9616**
428 West 125th Street btw Seventh/Eighth Ave
NYC 10027 Mon-Sat 8:30-8:30, Sun 10-6

**Upper East Side** **(212) 831-5100**
173 East 86th Street btw Lexington/Third Ave
NYC 10028 Mon-Sat 8:30-9, Sun 10-6

**Upper East Side** **(212) 717-7187**
1164 Third Avenue at 68th St
NYC 10021 Mon-Fri 8:30-8:30, Sat 9-7, Sun 10-6

**Upper West Side** **(917) 441-9807**
2187 Broadway at 77/78th St
NYC 10024 Mon-Fri 8:30-8:30, Sat 9-8, Sun 10-6

**Upper West Side** **(917) 441-2374**
2039 Broadway btw Amsterdam/70th St
NYC 10023 Mon-Sat 8:30-8:30, Sun 10-6

**Midtown West** **(212) 398-4416**
1460 Broadway btw 41/42nd St
NYC 10035 Mon-Fri 9-8, Sat 11-6, Sun 10-7

**Midtown West** **(212) 904-1190**
22 West 34th Street btw Fifth/Sixth Ave
NYC 10001 Mon-Sat 9-8, Sun 11-7

**Midtown West** **(212) 268-7696**
901 Sixth Avenue at Manhattan Mall, btw 32/33rd St
NYC 10001 Mon-Sat 8:30-8:30, Sun 11-6

**Flatiron** **(917) 305-1348**
650 Avenue of the Americas at 20th St
NYC 10011 Mon-Sat 10-7, Sun 11-6

**Flatiron** **(212) 529-2201**
36 Union Square East at 16th St
NYC 10003   Mon-Fri 10-7 (Thurs 10-8), Sat 10-5, Sun 11-5

**Lower East Side** **(212) 979-5071**
142 Delancey Street btw Norfolk/Suffolk
NYC 10002 Mon-Sat 9:30-7, Sun 11-6

## Chloé

Chloé is experiencing yet another revival under the creative
direction of Phoebe Philo. The girl has left rock chic behind
and is following her free sprit. She looks to her past for
inspiration: a fabulous (but never obvious) town-and-coun-
try aesthetic featuring mannish trousers, camel coats, cable
knits with oversized buttons, conservative blouses, razor-cut
pants and Fifties-femme dresses that give new meaning to
the word filmy. Terrific shoes and terribly popular bags complete the insouciantly glamorous look. *chloe.com*

*Luxury* *Amex/MC/V*

**Upper East Side** **(212) 717-8220**
850 Madison Avenue at 70th St
NYC 10021 Mon-Sat 10-6

## Christian Dior

Housed in the awesome glass tower designed for LVMH by
award-winning architect Christian de Portzamparc, the Dior
boutique is home to John Galliano's sexy (in a Hilton sisters
kind of way) wear. Frosted glass offsets saddlebag purses
and daringly low or high-cut dresses. Skin is always in here,
as is shockingly tight denim. Dior's sweaty, lusty fashion
shows are shown on the walls, and the fragrances, which
promise to make others equally sweaty and lusty for you,
are but an arm's reach away. The accessory-happy girl will
appreciate Dior's stilettos, watches, purses, jewelry and
fake tattoos (jeweled, and only $300-400). *dior.com*

*Luxury* *Amex/MC/V*

**Midtown East** **(212) 931-2950**
21 East 57th Street btw Fifth/Madison Ave
NYC 10022 Mon-Fri 10-7, Sat 10-6, Sun 12-6

## Christian Louboutin

Before setting up his own label, Christian Louboutin designed for Chanel, YSL and Charles Jourdan, so you know the man knows his footwear. Enter this boudoir-like boutique and you'll find yourself cooing over his line of shoes, all marked by the designer's signature red soles. 'Black soles are for widows, beige soles are for the Milanese, but red soles are for those who want to flirt and dance,' he says. Louboutin also celebrates offbeat detailing, which includes using silk fabrics from French tie manufacturers, dainty rose petals and even old postage stamps. Find mules, embroidered flats, gray-flannel spectator pumps, ponyskin boots and killer evening stilettos. His range of handbags is also wonderfully distinctive—and one you'll pay for.

*Luxury*                                              *Amex/MC/V*

**Upper East Side**                          **(212) 396-1884**
941 Madison Avenue                        btw 74/75th St
NYC 10021                                       Mon-Sat 10-6

## Christie Brothers Furs

Normally the terms 'discount' and 'luxury' are not found in the same sentence, but Christie Brothers Furs is a wonderful exception to the rule. A discount retailer of luxury fur coats with a selection of mink, shearling and Russian sable, as well as cashmere and microfiber coats which can be custom-lined and fitted with the fur of your choosing, Christie Brothers has an impressive selection. If you have an old fur in good condition, be sure to discuss trading it in against a new one. Storage facilities are available, too.

*Moderate*                                           *Amex/MC/V*

**Chelsea**                                       **(212) 736-6944**
150 West 30th Street (17th floor)    btw Sixth/Seventh Ave
NYC 10001                                Mon-Fri 8:30-6, Sat 8:30-2
                                                   (and by appointment)

## Christopher Totman

Christopher Totman melds cultures in his colorful Indian and Japanese-inspired prints, hand-loomed fabrics, circular crochets and alpaca knits. Tree-trunk table bases and a salt-water aquarium add to the natural feel of the store, which features shirts made from vintage kimonos. Also look for his trademark single-seam long skirt (the Luna skirt), gauze shirts, dresses, handknit pima cotton sweaters and more.                          *christophertotman.com*

*Expensive*                                          *Amex/MC/V*

**Nolita**                                          **(212) 925-7495**
262 Mott Street                              btw Houston/Prince
NYC 10012                                Daily 12-6:30 (Sun 12-6)

## Chrome Hearts

Every item in this ultra-luxe lifestyle store is handmade, from the soft leather couches and armchairs to the ebony and sterling silver hangers…and it's all for sale. Like it? Buy it—Chrome Hearts will restock whatever you've taken off their hands, or racks, or floors. We don't know if they've purchased the fixtures, but one-name celeb shoppers like Britney, Cher, Justin, Mick and Julia have fallen for Chrome Hearts' leather motorcycle jackets and stretch pants, executive luggage, 22k gold and sterling silver jewelry and snazzy eyewear. Chrome Hearts' commitment to excellence means they have their own woodworking and silversmith workshops, and pretty much anything you settle on should last a lifetime.                    *chromehearts.com*

*Luxury*                                              *Amex/MC/V*
**Upper East Side**                          **(212) 327-0707**
159 East 64th Street                   btw Lexington/Third Ave
NYC 10021                                          Mon-Sat 11-7

## Chuckies

Not the swankiest name, but don't be fooled: this cool boutique features a fabulous range of footwear. Find high-style shoes from Jimmy Choo, Miu Miu, Marc Jacobs and Dolce & Gabbana, to name only a few. An excellent source for fun, funky and glamorous shoes that you won't find anywhere else.

*Expensive to luxury*                                 *Amex/MC/V*
**Upper East Side**                          **(212) 593-9898**
1073 Third Avenue                               btw 63/64th St
NYC 10021                                 Mon-Fri 10:45-7:45
                                        Sat 10:45-7:30, Sun 12:30-7

## Church's English Shoes

When it comes to men's shoes, nobody does it better than the English (well, except for maybe the Italians), and Church's shoes are certainly among the best. For over 100 years they have been justly celebrated for classic, bench-made shoes. Now owned by growing fashion conglomerate Prada, Church's shoes continue to exhibit the fine materials and craftsmanship that made them famous. Find a variety of classic styles, including plain-toed oxfords, slip-ons, wingtips, loafers and moccasins. 10-12 week delivery for custom orders.                          *churchshoes.com*

*Expensive*                                          *Amex/MC/V*
**Upper East Side**                          **(212) 758-5200**
689 Madison Avenue                                  at 62nd St
NYC 10019                                          Mon-Sat 10-6

## Citishoes

Citishoes is popular with Midtown executives, as well as tourists staying at neighboring hotels. Loyal fans of the following brands will be happy with the selection of dress shoes by Alden, Church's English Shoes, Allen Edmonds, Santoni, Cole Haan and Kenneth Cole. When the work day is over, slip into casual comfort shoes by Mephisto, Ecco, Sebago or Rockport. The assortment of wide-width shoes and a professional fitting service will pacify frustrated feet, while the Crookhorn belts and Byford trouser socks might make you pick up more than you stopped in for. *citishoes.com*

*Affordable*                                              *Amex/MC/V*

**Midtown East**                               **(212) 751-3200**
445 Park Ave                                   btw 56/57th St
NYC 10022                    Mon-Fri 9:30-6:30, Sat 10:30-5:30

## City Cricket
This adorable children's shop offers an exclusive selection of merchandise with a magical appeal. Find cute knitted sweaters and one-of-a-kind handmade blankets and quilts in unusual fabrics and playful designs, plus layettes and clothing for kids up to six years old. Other items include children's indoor and outdoor furniture like upholstered wing chairs, hand-painted tables and chairs, antique wicker and bent willow twig chairs. *citycricket.com*

*Moderate*                                               *Amex/MC/V*

**West Village**                               **(212) 242-2258**
215 West 10th Street                                at Bleecker
NYC 10014                            Mon-Sat 11-7, Sun 12-5

## Clarks/Bostonian
Men head here for the selection of affordable footwear, which runs from businesswear to weekend casual. The Bostonian label offers classic lace-ups and dressy loafers, while there are sporty looks from the likes of Kenneth Cole and casual styles from such labels as Timberland, Ecco and Clarks. Women can take a break from stilettos with more-stylish-than-you-might-imagine hiking sandals and moccasin-inspired loafers. *clarksusa.com*

*Affordable*                                             *Amex/MC/V*

**Midtown East**                               **(212) 949-9545**
363 Madison Avenue                                  at 45th St
NYC 10017    Mon-Fri 9-7 (Thurs 10-8), Sat 10-6, Sun 12-6

## Classic Kicks
You can definitely get your kicks at this stylish NoHo sneaker shop, where you don't have to be an O.G. to have access to one of the city's most complete collection of classic reissues and sportswear. Hipsters and hip-hoppers alike bond over the wide selection of fresh finds by the likes of Asics, Vans, Nike, Le Coq Sportif and Fred Perry.

*Moderate*                                               *Amex/MC/V*

**NoHo**                                       **(212) 979-9514**
298 Elizabeth Street                      btw Houston/Bleecker
NYC 10012                                        Mon-Sat 12-7

## Clea Colet
This elegant boutique offers one-on-one personalized service for brides-to-be. The luxurious atmosphere creates a comfortable setting in which to browse Clea Colet's collection of glamorous bridal and eveningwear. The stunning

classic styles—which range from surprisingly come-hither columns to storybook gowns—are customized to each bride's personal style and fit. A truly memorable experience, as befitting your walk down the aisle.   *cleacolet.com*

*Expensive*                                          *Amex/MC/V*

**Upper East Side**                          **(212) 396-4608**
960 Madison Avenue                      btw 75/76th St
NYC                                    (by appointment only)

## Clifford Michael Design

The place to hit for special occasion dressing. If you're the bride, the mother-of-the-bride or just a guest, you can select your appropriate wedding attire here. When the invitation says 'black tie', doll yourself up in an elaborate gown, tuxedo, evening suit or sexy cocktail dress. Coordinating handbags and silk scarves are also available, as well as leathers and shearling outerwear.   *cliffordmichael.com*

*Expensive*                                          *Amex/MC/V*

**Upper East Side**                          **(212) 888-7665**
45 East 60th Street                   btw Madison/Park Ave
NYC 10022                   Mon-Fri 10-6:30 (Thurs 10-7), Sat 10-6

## Club Monaco

Yes, you'd rather have designer labels in your closet but let's face it, you're about maxed out on your credit cards. So let this Canadian-based company owned by Ralph Lauren come to your rescue. Club Monaco's airy store has plenty of contemporary looks: neat halter top dresses, asymmetrical striped tops and pleated skirts for women; belted white jeans and poor man's Helmut Lang-style polos and button-downs for men. The clothes may not be quite runway-class, but they are cute and the prices make them nearly risk-free. Club Monaco also has accessories and cosmetics for women.   *clubmonaco.com*

*Affordable*                                         *Amex/MC/V*

**Midtown West**                             **(212) 459-9863**
8 West 57th Street                      btw Fifth/Sixth Ave
NYC 10019                            Mon-Sat 10-8, Sun 11-6

**Upper East Side**                          **(212) 355-2949**
1111 Third Avenue                           at 65th St
NYC 10021                           Mon-Sat 10-8, Sun 12-6

**Upper West Side**                          **(212) 579-2587**
2376 Broadway                               at 87th St
NYC 10024                         (opening hours as above)

**Flatiron**                                 **(212) 352-0936**
160 Fifth Avenue                            at 21st St
NYC 10010                         (opening hours as above)

**SoHo**                                     **(212) 533-8930**
121 Prince Street                    btw Wooster/Greene
NYC 10012                            Daily 11-8 (Sun 11-7)

**SoHo**                                     **(212) 941-1511**
520 Broadway                         btw Spring/Broome
NYC 10012                         (opening hours as above)

## Coach

Coach continues to grow as an accessories brand, and the fashion crowd is proud to carry their signature totes and prance around in their cool sandals and espadrilles. Shop for briefcases, handbags, travel bags and small leather goods, manufactured in clean, chic and functional shapes. The handbag collection includes shoulder bags, sleek clutches, cotton-twill travel totes and a collection of canvas bags trimmed in leather. There are also leather jackets, wallets, belts, gloves, shoes, watches and umbrellas. 800-223-8647 *coach.com*

*Expensive* *Amex/MC/V*

**Upper East Side** **(212) 879-9391**
35 East 85th Street at Madison Ave
NYC 10028 Mon-Sat 10-8, Sun 11-6

**Midtown East** **(212) 754-0041**
595 Madison Avenue at 57th St
NYC 10022 Mon-Sat 10-9, Sun 11-6

**Midtown East** **(212) 599-4777**
342 Madison Avenue at 44th St
NYC 10017 Mon-Fri 8:30-8, Sat 10-8, Sun 11-6

**Fifth Avenue** **(212) 245-4148**
620 Fifth Avenue at 50th St
NYC 10020 Mon-Sat 10-8, Sun 11-6

**Harlem** **(212) 280-0296**
208 West 125th Street at Seventh Ave
NYC 10027 Mon-Sat 10-8, Sun 11-7

**Flatiron** **(212) 675-6403**
79 Fifth Avenue at 16th St
NYC 10003 Daily 10-7 (Sun 11-7)

**SoHo** **(212) 473-6925**
143 Prince Street at West Broadway
NYC 10012 Mon-Sat 10-8, Sun 11-6

**Lower Manhattan** **(212) 425-4350**
193 Front Street at South Street Seaport
NYC 10038 (opening hours as above)

## Cole Haan

Cole Haan delivers a brilliant footwear collection of modern classics that embrace fashion. Both sexes will find smart-looking loafers, snappy mules, driving moccasins, oxfords, sensible sandals and boots. Best buys are the fabulously comfortable sports shoes, developed with help from parent company Nike and equipped with its Nike Air technology. Coordinating accessories include classy handbags in all leathers, luggage, belts, socks and leather jackets. 800-488-2000 *colehaan.com*

*Expensive* *Amex/MC/V*

**Upper East Side** **(212) 421-8440**
667 Madison Avenue at 61st St
NYC 10021 Mon-Sat 10-7 (Thurs 10-8), Sun 12-6

**Fifth Avenue** **(212) 765-9747**
620 Fifth Avenue at 50th St
NYC 10020 (opening hours as above)

## Comme des Garçons

If you suffer from fashion's cruelest afflictions—avant-garditis and conspicuous consumption—get yourself to Comme des Garçons. Known for her high-concept designs, cult Japanese designer Rei Kawakubo's collection is long on intellectualism. Kawakubo founded Comme in 1969, and her clothes received international fame in the Eighties for their somber color palette and asymmetrical detailing. Enter the store through an aluminum tunnel into a parallel universe: an interior of white enamel-covered steel walls houses pieces from the basic to the absurd and textiles that are wondrous in color and quality. Be sure to check out Kawakubo's collaboration with English sportswear designer Fred Perry—hip tennis shirts with oversized buttons, giant zippers and funky colors that add a bit of flair to Perry's traditional stylings. Best accessory bets: her fabulous logo'd bags and wallets that look good on everyone.      *commesdesgarcons.com*

*Luxury*                                     *Amex/MC/V*

**Chelsea** **(212) 604-9200**
520 West 22nd Street btw Tenth/Eleventh Ave
NYC 10011 Tues-Sat 11-7, Sun 12-6

## Conrad's Bike Shop

Conrad's is for elite cyclists who take their sport seriously. It offers clothing, shoes, accessories, safety gear, parts and, of course, bicycles, from top brands like Seven, De Rosa and Eddy Merckx. Price points range from $1,200 to $7,000. Best for pro racing bikes.

*Expensive*                                  *Amex/MC/V*

**Midtown East** **(212) 697-6966**
25 Tudor City Place at 42nd St
NYC 10017 Mon-Sat 11-7

## Constanca Basto

Carnival! Two Brazilian designers team up to get your feet noticed. One look at their glimmering, open-toed sultry pink sandals, or the patent-leather tricolor heels, and you'll know these shoes are not for the faint of heart or the unpedicured of toe. The orange and white striped boutique, replete with enormous gilt-framed, floor-to-ceiling mirrors, will make you feel like a south-of-the-equator Cinderella as you try on pair after pair of stunning slippers perfect for work or a night on the town.      *constancabasto.com*

*Expensive*                                  *Amex/MC/V*

**West Village** **(212) 645-3233**
573 Hudson Street btw West 11th St/Bank
NYC 10014 Tues-Sat 11-7, Sun 12-6

## Copperfields New York

New York's oldest saddlery shop has been catering to English riders since 1912. There is a complete selection of riding attire (ages 4 to adult) and equipment for you and your favorite equine friend, fitted and custom riding boots, accessories, gifts and toys, as well as top-of-the line saddles by Crosby, Hermès, Excel and Pessier.    *millerharness.com*

*Expensive*                                          *Amex/MC/V*

**Flatiron**                                    **(212) 673-1400**
117 East 24th Street                      btw Park/Lexington Ave
NYC 10010                            Mon-Sat 10-6 (Thurs 10-7)

## Cose Belle

Designer Shannon McLean specializes in clean, simple designs made in luxury fabrics. Located in a penthouse showroom, Cose Belle features pants, dresses, sweaters and evening and bridal gowns. It's classic clothing with sporty elegance: you'll find everything from hip-huggers for $380 to bridal gowns starting at $2,500.    *shannonmclean.com*

*Expensive*                                          *Amex/MC/V*

**Upper East Side**                             **(212) 988-4210**
7 East 81st Street (4th floor)            btw Fifth/Madison Ave
NYC 10028                         (Mon-Fri, by appointment only)

## Costume National

Italian designer Ennio Capasa's aesthetic is a dark one: an androgynous world of lean, mean and sleek silhouettes where sexy black rules. Each collection is extremely edgy but always accessible and wearable. Capasa cuts a mean pair of pants, but the standouts are his sexy evening tops, often with cut-out backs or shoulders. This store is one of the best places in the city for a slick modern suit and killer leather pieces. Then there are his sinuous, earthy-toned shoes and kick-ass boots.    *costumenational.com*

*Expensive*                                          *Amex/MC/V*

**SoHo**                                        **(212) 431-1530**
108 Wooster Street                           btw Prince/Spring
NYC 10012                                 Mon-Sat 11-7, Sun 12-6

## Couture by Jennifer Dule

Designer Jennifer Dule specializes in women's custom tailoring for 'after five', special occasion and bridal. Bring a photograph from a magazine and she'll copy it to a T or change it to your specifications. Pants average $475, suits start at $1,800. An elaborate satin evening gown with lavish detailing will run you $3,500 plus.

*Luxury*                                              *Amex/MC/V*

**Flatiron**                                    **(212) 777-2100**
89 Fifth Avenue (4th floor)                            at 16th St
NYC 10003                                     (by appointment)

## C.P.Shades

Simple, carefree and comfortable clothing designed with down-to-earth practicality, with everything guaranteed to withstand the rigors of wash and wear. All dresses, skirts, pants and separates are made in easy-care fabrics. If comfort is key, then C.P.Shades is a must. _cpshades.com_

Moderate                                                    Amex/MC/V

**SoHo**                                              **(212) 226-4434**
154 Spring Street                    btw Wooster/West Broadway
NYC 10012                                      Daily 11-7, Sun 12-6

## CPW
The Upper West Side's best destination for downtown duds is no doubt CPW (an abbreviation for, yes, Central Park West). This 15-year-old boutique, often compared to Barneys Co-Op or Fred Segal in Los Angeles, carries the hottest up-to-the-second brands for the relaxed, west coast clothing aesthetic of flirty skirts, tiny tees, shrunken blazers and vintage belts. CPW also sells the complete range of 'it' denim lines from the likes of Chip and Pepper, True Religion, Paper Denim & Cloth and Capital.

Expensive                                                  Amex/MC/V

**Upper West Side**                                   **(212) 579-3737**
495 Amsterdam Avenue                                     at 84th St
NYC 10024                       Mon-Fri 11-7:30, Sat 11-7, Sun 12-6

## C.Ronson
Charlotte Ronson, a member of the society pages' favorite family, opened this cooler-than-cool store three years ago to showcase her hip streetwear. She's best known for her wedge-heeled espadrilles and for her cheekily named Tooshies, an underwear line. Her designs include tank tops, T-shirts and tracksuit-inspired gear, and the store also boasts Shoshanna bikinis, neon lingerie by Deborah Marquit and jewelry by various designers. The store recently moved from a shared space to a new independent location. _cronson.com_

Affordable                                                 Amex/MC/V

**Nolita**                                            **(212) 625-9074**
239 Mulberry Street                                 btw Prince/Spring
NYC 10012                                                 Daily 12-7

## Crouch & Fitzgerald
Crouch & Fitzgerald have sold first-rate leather goods since 1839. Look for pony-hair business totes in pink, yellow, and lime green, patent-leather backpacks, business accessories and Longchamp luggage in pink and blue. Crouch & Fitzgerald offer handbags and luggage from Ghurka, as well as their own line of traditional English cases for men. Beautiful jewelry boxes, too. _crouchandfitzgerald.com_

Moderate                                                   Amex/MC/V

**Midtown East**                                      **(212) 755-5888**
400 Madison Avenue                                  btw 47/48th St
NYC 10017                                       Mon-Fri 9-7, Sat 9-6

## Crunch
This hip gym chain has its own shop packed with the Crunch collection of fleece jackets, Lycra outfits, leggings,

sweats, hats, unisex jazz pants, bodywear and sportswear, perfect for working out or just posing. *crunch.com*

*Moderate* *Amex/MC/V*

**Upper West Side** **(212) 875-1902**
162 West 83rd Street    btw Columbus/Amsterdam Ave
NYC 10024    Mon-Thurs 5:30-11, Fri 5:30-10, Sat-Sun 8-9

**Midtown East** **(212) 758-3434**
1109 Second Avenue btw 58/59th St
NYC 10022    Mon-Thurs 5-11, Fri 5-10, Sat-Sun 8-9

**Midtown West** **(212) 869-7788**
144 West 38th Street    btw Seventh Ave/Broadway
NYC 10018    Mon-Fri 5:30-10, Sat-Sun 8-6

**Midtown West** **(212) 594-8050**
555 West 42nd Street at Eleventh Ave
NYC 10036    Mon-Fri 6-10, Sat-Sun 9-7

**East Village** **(212) 475-2018**
54 East 13th Street    btw Broadway/University Place
NYC 10003    Mon-Fri 6-10, Sat-Sun 8-8

**West Village** **(212) 366-3725**
152 Christopher Street at Greenwich
NYC 10014    Mon-Fri 6-11, Sat-Sun 8-8

**NoHo** **(212) 420-0507**
623 Broadway at Houston
NYC 10012    Mon-Fri 6-11, Sat 8-8, Sun 9-8

**NoHo** **(212) 614-0120**
404 Lafayette Street    btw Astor Place/East 4th St
NYC 10003    Open 24/7 from Mon 5am to Sat 9pm
Sun 8-9

## Crush ♂♀

Beloved by tweens for their impressive selection of cute Paul Frank and goth-girl Emily the Strange accessories, as well as Betsey Johnson dresses for girls, Crush is also bound to seduce their older sisters with vintage booty in excellent condition, slightly naughty knickers and way cool concert tees—the sort you shouldn't wear if you're old enough to have gone to the show. Girls of all ages will swoon over dreamy handbags. (The store has moved to Brooklyn, and opening hours were n/a at press time—check the website, or call). *crushstore.com*

*Moderate* *Amex/MC/V*

**Brooklyn** **(718) 643-6498**
231 Smith Street
Brooklyn 11231

## Cynthia Rowley ♂♀

Designer Cynthia Rowley's frilly, flirty clothes swing with unabashed girliness. Detailing emphasizes ruffles, ruching, eyelets and other retro touches and twists. Good girls will love her full-skirted dresses nipped at the waist, knits, tops with dainty detailing, print dresses and coats, while bad ones will go for her leather and sexier pieces. Rowley's frocks are guaranteed to bring out the coquette in every

woman. Don't miss the purses, shoes and sunglasses and
the rack of men's clothing in the back.    *cynthiarowley.com*

*Expensive*                                        MC/V

**West Village**                          **(212) 242-3803**
376 Bleecker Street                     btw Perry/Charles
NYC 10014                      Sun-Wed 11-7, Thurs-Sat 11-8

## Daffy's
One of New York's largest, and loudest, discount chains,
Daffy's carries clothing for the entire family with discounts up
to 80% on sportswear, outerwear, workout apparel, underwear, accessories and shoes. If you're lucky, you might even
come across a designer label like Tommy Hilfiger, Versace or
Guess. Daffy's claim their prices are so low that 'you'll be
tempted to haggle them up.'                *daffys.com*

*Affordable*                                    Amex/MC/V

**Midtown East**                          **(212) 376-4477**
125 East 57th Street              btw Park/Lexington Ave
NYC 10022               Mon-Fri 10-8, Sat 10-7, Sun 11-6

**Midtown East**                          **(212) 557-4422**
335 Madison Avenue                          at 44th St
NYC 10017                  Mon-Fri 8-8, Sat 10-6, Sun 12-6

**Midtown West**                          **(212) 736-4477**
1311 Broadway                             btw 33/34th St
NYC 10013                  Mon-Fri 10-5, Sat 10-8, Sun 11-7

**Flatiron**                              **(212) 529-4477**
111 Fifth Avenue                              at 18th St
NYC 10003                       Mon-Sat 10-9, Sun 12-7

**SoHo**                                  **(212) 334-7444**
462 Broadway                                   at Grand
NYC 10012               Mon-Thurs 10-8, Fri-Sat 10-9, Sun 12-7

## Dana Buchman
Dana Buchman offers what seem like two separate lines
catering to the executive woman in search of a professional, polished look. A comfortably stylish collection of careerwear, suits and desk-to-dinner basics are jazzed up with surprises like floor-length chiffon graphic skirts and yellow
leather jackets. Her casual line offers up chinoiserie tops
and sherbet-cool colors in flavors from raspberry to lemon.
A certain maritime influence pops up in navy blue and white
sweaters and pants, while pinstripes seem to be a favorite
print. Petite sizes also available.      *danabuchman.com*

*Moderate to expensive*                         Amex/MC/V

**Midtown East**                          **(212) 319-3257**
65 East 57th Street                 btw Madison/Park Ave
NYC 10022               Mon-Sat 10-6 (Thurs 10-8), Sun 12-5

## D&G
For many, 'sexy' can't be spelled without the letters D and
G. The bridge line of Dolce & Gabbana continues to exude
sex appeal throughout the two floors of this store's sportswear, eveningwear and casualwear. Super-tight pants, sexy

minis, distressed jeans, rugged furs, chiffon florals, lots of sheer lace, pencil-thin leathers, smart suits and VLBDs (very little black dresses) are the norm. The designers say the D&G woman 'takes incredible joy at dressing up aimed at perplexing, teasing, having fun and, of course, showing herself.' And how. Men aren't left out, though, and can choose from everything from classic Italian suits to screaming floral shirts, leather pants, jeans and logo'd T-shirts. Not for the timid. *dolcegabbana.it*

*Expensive*                                          Amex/MC/V

**SoHo**                                        **(212) 965-8000**
434 West Broadway                         btw Prince/Spring
NYC 10012   Mon-Fri 11-7 (Thurs 11-8), Sat 11-6, Sun 12-5

## Danskin
Danskin equals second skin. Check out their signature exercise, dance and activewear which include leotards, leggings, unitards, tanks, sweatpants and ballet and jazz shoes. But since you need clothes to wear on the way to ballet class, too, you can choose from Danskin's selection of fashionable streetwear such as short skirts, slim-fitted dresses and slinky tops. *danskin.com*

*Moderate*                                          Amex/MC/V

**Upper West Side**                             **(212) 724-2992**
159 Columbus Avenue                         btw 67/68th St
NYC 10023        Mon-Wed 10-8, Thurs-Sat 10-9, Sun 11-6

## Daphne
Daphne, a specialty boutique for larger-sized women, carries their own line of apparel crafted out of luxury fabrics such as silk, chiffon and cashmere that aim to flatter the figure. Carrying easy-to-coordinate separates and a sizeable selection of eclectic jewelry, including bohemian-style necklaces and chandelier earrings, Daphne sells clothing that any voluptuous diva is sure to love. *daphne1.com*

*Moderate*                                          Amex/MC/V

**Upper West Side**                             **(212) 877-5073**
467 Amsterdam Avenue                         btw 82/83rd St
NYC 10023                                   Daily 12-7 (Sun 12-6)

## Darryl's
Darryl's, an 18-year-old Upper West Side 'contemporary woman's boutique', offers day-to-day staples that aim to maximize the refined woman's wardrobe. Carrying mostly European labels like BCBG, Mica, Trina Turk, Tocca and Teen Flo, Darryl's offers a little bit of everything, from ready-for-work tailored suits to flirty dresses and casual knitwear.

*Moderate*                                          Amex/MC/V

**Upper West Side**                             **(212) 847-6677**
492 Amsterdam Avenue                         btw 83/84th St
NYC 10024                                               Daily 11-7

# Darling

Darling is oh-so dramatic and the girls are just loving it. Former Broadway costume designer Ann French Emonts Sherman has a flair for turning the spotlight on shoppers with her exquisite selection of grown-up-yet-flirty skirts, dresses, separates, jackets and fabulous lingerie. Pieces are a mix of Emonts Sherman's own designs and the talents of stylish friends such as Mary Green, as well as a vintage selection. A fun place to be a lady, Darling sweetens the shopping experience by offering wine and champagne on Thursday nights. Now that is sure to give shopaholics a buzz.

*Moderate*                                           *Amex/MC/V*

**West Village**                              **(646) 336-6966**
1 Horatio Street                                  at Eighth Ave
NYC 10014              Mon-Sat 11-8 (Thurs 11-10), Sun 12-6

# Davide Cenci

Davide Cenci's mission statement is comfort, warmth, lightness and balance. That mission is met with the clean lines and subtle color palette that characterize the Cenci aesthetic. The ready-to-wear suits, sportswear, shirts, sweaters, outerwear and accessories, plus the custom-made designs, all display luxurious fabrics and impeccable tailoring. Expect to pay for such quality: made-to-measure suits start at $2,100.                                *davidecenci.com*

*Luxury*                                             *Amex/MC/V*

**Upper East Side**                           **(212) 628-5910**
801 Madison Avenue                            btw 67/68th St
NYC 10021                     Mon-Sat 10-6:30 (Thurs 10-7:30)

# DDC Lab

DDC lab uses innovative methods to concoct seriously cool fashion-forward gear. One part pretty, one part hip, with a dash of high-tech utilitarianism, the goods range from leather-pleated minis to Teflon-treated jeans. Denim looks are the main attraction (including 18 new styles of jean), but great jackets and corduroys should not be missed. Complete your look with stylish tees and PF Flyers sneakers. The Meatpacking District store carries a higher end DDC line.                                        *ddclab.com*

*Expensive*                                          *Amex/MC/V*

**Lower East Side**                           **(212) 375-1647**
180 Orchard Street                          btw Stanton/Houston
NYC 10002                                Daily 11-7 (Sun 12-6)

**West Village**                              **(212) 414-5801**
427 West 14th Street                         btw Ninth/Tenth Ave
NYC 10014                              (opening hours as above)

# Deco Jewels

Deco's Janice Berkson travels far and wide in search of Lucite handbags from the Forties and Fifties and lovingly restores them to pristine perfection. Collectable pieces, including vintage costume jewelry and cufflinks from the Twenties to the Sixties, round out the gorgeous assortment.

*Moderate*                                          *Amex/MC/V*
**SoHo**                                          **(212) 253-1222**
131 Thompson Street                       btw Prince/Houston
NYC 10012                                    Daily 12-8 (Sun 12-7)

# Delfino

Delfino's motto is that there's a bag for every outfit (only one?) and this stylish little shop houses a selection of all sizes and shapes in eye-popping colors and wild animal textures, as well as basic leathers. Labels include Longchamp, Jack Gomme, Hervé Chapelier, Francesco Biasia, France's Bronti Bay and Mandarina Duck.                    *delfinoshop.com*

*Expensive*                                          *Amex/MC/V*
**Midtown West**                                  **(212) 956-0868**
56 West 50th Street                        at Rockefeller Center
NYC 10021              Mon-Fri 10:30-8, Sat 10:30-7, Sun 12-6

# Denimaxx

Denimaxx's sales staff will spoil you with treats from their coffee and wet bar as you frolic through three floors of fur and leather outerwear, pants, shirts, skirts, accessories, hats, purses and even housewares. Where else would you go for a fur bathing suit, Mongolian lamb pillows or a $6,000 mink bedspread? The store has even tried to accommodate animal lovers with its line of Bassoni Edwardo faux-fur coats. Be on the watch for their sales, when they discount their goods 50-70%.        *denimaxx.com*

*Moderate to luxury*                                *Amex/MC/V*
**Midtown East**                                  **(212) 207-4900**
444 Madison Avenue                          btw 49/50th St
NYC 10022                    Mon-Fri 9-6, Sat 11-6, Sun 12-5

# Dernier Cri

Owner Stacia Valle, the former tour manager for Third Eye Blind, has assembled an eclectic collection of clothes, accessories and, basically, incredibly cool stuff from designers specializing in that very thing: rocking. The store's edgy wears with a distinctly rebellious vibe are perfect for the Meatpacking District's nearby clubs. Dernier Cri's independent spirit embraces designers like Vivienne Westwood, Development, Tsubi, Circle by Mara Hoffman and Grey Ant. Also find vintage issues of *Rolling Stone*, punk T-shirts, hats by Eugenia Kim and bags by Not Rational—perfect accessories for those looking to add an offbeat spin to their wardrobe.

*Expensive*                                          *Amex/MC/V*
**Meatpacking District**                          **(212) 242-6061**
869 Washington                                  btw 13/14th St
NYC 10014                                              Daily 12-8

# Designer Loft

Ah, your wedding day—a special day that you will remember forever, and Designer Loft is here to guarantee that the memories will be happy ones. Brides-to-be will blush when they see the delicious designs available here, including Maz Chaoul, Ristarose and Kirstie Kelly. Gowns for bridesmaids and the mother of the bride are also drool-inducing. In addition to the lovely dresses, the Loft offers full wedding planner services, and their trunk shows are not to be missed.                                    *designerloftnyc.com*

*Expensive*                                              Amex/MC/V

**Midtown West**                                    **(212) 944-9013**
260 West 39th Street (suite 1101) btw Seventh/Eighth Ave
NYC 10018                                         (by appointment)

## Design in Textiles by Mary Jaeger
Melding her experience as a designer for Mary McFadden and Jack Mulqueen with her eight years in Japan studying textiles, Mary Jaeger brings a sprightly palette to her Zen-infused apparel and furnishings. Jaeger outfits clients in heavily dyed, shrunken wool shawls, capes and scarves, and makes shibori (a Japanese take on tie-dye) onesies for their children. Her home product line (which already features beautiful table runners fashioned from vintage kimonos) includes made-to-order ottomans and wall hangings.

*Expensive*                                              Amex/MC/V

**SoHo**                                            **(212) 941-5877**
51 Spring Street                            btw Lafayette/Mulberry
NYC 10012                   Mon-Fri 12:30-6:30, Sat 11-7, Sun 12-5

## Destination
After a serious designer clothes fix at Jeffrey (just one block away), make this your, er, destination for hot new accessories, from hats and shoes to handbags and jewelry from a great selection of labels. Best is an eclectic mix of jewelry (from feminine, delicate pieces to hard-core punk) by Gilbert Gilbert and Serge Thoroval and stylish handbags from labels like Jacques LeCorre.          *destinationny.net*

*Moderate*                                               Amex/MC/V

**Chelsea**                                         **(212) 727-2031**
32-36 Little West 12th Street    btw Washington/Ninth Ave
NYC 10014                                 Mon-Sat 11-8, Sun 12-7

## Detour
Wonder where young girls are getting their hip, tight-fitting outfits? Look no further—Detour features a sexy, slinky and somewhat pricey assortment of tees, jeans, skirts, dresses, leather jackets and racy ensembles perfect for club-hopping—because that's what Detour girls do.

*Affordable*                                             Amex/MC/V

**SoHo**                                            **(212) 979-6315**
472 West Broadway                            btw Houston/Prince
NYC 10012                              Daily 11-8 (in all stores)

**SoHo**                                            **(212) 966-3635**
154 Prince Street            btw West Broadway/Thompson
NYC 10012

**SoHo (M)** **(212) 219-2692**
425 West Broadway btw Prince/Spring
NYC 10012

## Diana & Jeffries

For the Charlotte York in all of us, there is Diana & Jeffries. Offering pretty pattered dresses and skirts by Tocca and Tibi, trendy jeans by Juicy Couture and Joie, shrunken tweed blazers by Nanette Lepore and delicate tanks by Cosabella, Diana & Jeffries makes every day into a walk down Park Avenue.

*Expensive* *Amex/MC/V*

**Upper East Side** **(212) 831-0531**
1310 Madison Avenue btw 92/93rd St
NYC 10128 Mon-Sat 10-7, Sun 1-7

**Upper West Side** **(212) 874-2884**
2062 Broadway btw 70/71st St
NYC 10023 Mon-Sat 11-8, Sun 1-7

## Diana Kane

Like lingerie? Sheer, lacy sweet nothings abound at Diana Kane, who sells Diane von Furstenberg's lingerie line Boudoir as well as bedroom favorites like Cosabella. Even the bathrobes are sexy here—they look and function like a wrap dress, or even a small trench. Great selection of camisoles, too. *dianakane.com*

*Moderate* *Amex/MC/V*

**Park Slope** **(718) 638-6520**
229b 5th Avenue btw Carroll/President
Brooklyn 11215 Tues-Fri 12-7, Thurs-Sat 12-8, Sun 11-6

## Diane von Furstenberg the Shop

This is your one-stop for fun, feminine and ultra-flattering fashion. Though slightly off the beaten track, it's well worth the trek: canopies suspended from the ceiling frame the central mirrors while racks of light, versatile and utterly wearable pieces—flirty ruched tops, silk shirts, bias-cut georgette and matte jersey skirts, slim-fitting Ultrasuede pants and jeans—line the walls. The wrap dress, von Furstenberg's signature creation, is continuously released in fresh, unique patterns to match the mood of each month's collection. Priced around $300, the Wrap, like everything von Furstenberg, is easy to fit, easy to wear and effortlessly chic. The lingerie in the back also offers DvF's unparalleled patterns in the same basic, true-to-size cuts, and the new make-up collection is as simple to select as it is to sport. *dvf.com*

*Expensive* *Amex/MC/V*

**West Village** **(646) 486-4800**
385 West 12th Street btw Washington/West Side H'way
NYC 10014 Mon-Fri 11-7, Sat 11-6, Sun 12-5

## Diesel

At Diesel, there's a party going on and everyone's invited. DJs spin all day at this superstore, which feels more like a club than a shop. Skaters, snowboarders and downtown coolsters will find quirky sportswear in whacked-out colors, an awesome denim selection, including 18 new styles, and Diesel's fab collection of sneakers and bags carried by club kids everywhere. Denim alert: newly svelte Chanel designer Karl Lagerfeld has designed a limited-edition collection (available only at the Denim Gallery branch)—cut on the skinny side. *diesel.com*

*Moderate*                                              *Amex/MC/V*

**NoHo**                                           **(646) 336-8552**
1 Union Square West                                     at 14th St
NYC 10003                                     Daily 11-9 (Sun 11-8)

**Upper East Side**                                **(212) 308-0055**
770 Lexington Avenue                                    at 60th St
NYC 10021                                     Mon-Sat 10-8, Sun 12-6

**SoHo (Denim Gallery)**                           **(212) 966-5593**
68 Greene Street                                 btw Spring/Broome
NYC 10012                                     Mon-Sat 11-7, Sun 12-6

## Diesel Style Lab
Diesel's high-end runway collection, Style Lab originates from the desire to 'research and experiment with style, cuts, materials and ideas,' says Diesel founder Renzo Rosso. The avant-garde sportswear—pants, jackets, shirts, sweaters, outerwear and accessories—has been given the high-tech fabric treatment, and a little bit of Diesel-style naughtiness. *dieselstylelab.com*

*Expensive*                                            *Amex/MC/V*

**SoHo**                                           **(212) 343-3863**
416 West Broadway                                 btw Prince/Spring
NYC 10012                                     Mon-Sat 11-8, Sun 12-7

## Dinosaur Designs
This Australian jewelry label launched Down Under in the late Eighties and quickly developed a cult following for its chunky resin jewelry—rings, bracelets and knockout strands of beads. Each piece is handmade in Australia. Beyond the resiny goods, the brand has expanded into strong silver pieces and housewares. Confident, colorful and cool. *dinosaurdesigns.com.au*

*Moderate*                                             *Amex/MC/V*

**Nolita**                                         **(212) 680-3523**
250 Mott Street                                  btw Houston/Prince
NYC 10012                                     Mon-Sat 11-7, Sun 12-6

## Dior Homme
Hedi Slimane's elegant but forward-looking designs for men have garnered accolades around the world, and it's easy to see why when you step into this sleek Fifth Avenue space. Everyone (women continue to sport Slimane's work) can dive into the beautifully tailored jackets and pant suits that he's known for, not to mention sleekly futuristic luggage, shoes, belts, must-have jeans, suits, accessories and

sportswear. Throw in fragrances, eyewear, shoes, and singular items like an ultra-chic, black leather iPod case, and you have one-stop Euro-lifestyle shopping. *diorhomme.com*

*Moderate to expensive*                    *Amex/MC/V*

**Midtown East**                           **(212) 421-6009**
17 East 57th Street                        btw Fifth/Madison Ave
NYC 10022                         Mon-Fri 10-7, Sat 10-6, Sun 12-6

## DKNY

Designer Donna Karan brings her spot-on vision to DKNY, her diffusion line of high-performance, affordable sportswear. The easy-to-wear clothes are infused with loads of personality, setting DKNY apart from like-minded brands. The color-coordinated collection of tops, pants, skirts, dresses and eveningwear is wonderfully fresh and fun, and distinguished by easy silhouettes and original details. Accessories include handbags and shoes. *dkny.com*

*Expensive*                                *Amex/MC/V*

**Upper East Side**                        **(212) 223-3569**
655 Madison Avenue                         at 60th Street
NYC 10021                          Mon-Sat 10-8, Sun 12-6

**SoHo**                                   **(646) 613-1100**
420 West Broadway                          btw Prince/Spring
NYC 10012                          Mon-Sat 11-8, Sun 12-7

## D/L Cerney

Being trendy can be so exhausting—and no one understands that better than husband-and-wife team Duane Cerney and Linda St John. Their antidote: a collection of classic retro-inspired clothing featuring everything from simple gabardine shirts and straight skirts to fitted shift dresses and stretch pants. It's all in natural fabrics and hand-finished, right down to the last button and stitch. Great silhouettes and colors also distinguish these clothes, from the easy sheath dresses and well-cut pants to classic button-downs. Sometimes closed Monday and Tuesday—call to check.

*Expensive*                                *MC/V*

**East Village**                           **(212) 673-7033**
13 East 7th Street                         btw Second/Third Ave
NYC 10003                                  Daily 12-8

## Do Kham

Treasures from the Himalayas are beautifully displayed in this elegant shop, where you can choose from traditional Tibetan styled dresses, skirts and tops plus a collection of richly brocaded, fur-trimmed silk hats. Check out the fabulous selection of ever-versatile pashmina shawls ($125 to $195) as well as plain or embroidered scarves, boas and handbags in a myriad of colors and fabrics.

*Moderate*                                 *Amex/MC/V*

**SoHo**                                   **(212) 966-2404**
51 Prince Street                           btw Mulberry/Lafayette
NYC 10012                                  Daily 10-8

**East Village**  (212) 358-1010
304 East 5th Street  btw First/Second Ave
NYC 10003  Daily 11-8

**NoHo**  (212) 966-2404
51 Prince Street  at Lafayette
NYC 10017  Daily 11-7

## Dolce & Gabbana

Agent provocateurs Domenico Dolce and Stefano Gabbana get sex. They really get it—and their saucy vision rules everywhere from the streets of Milan to the Hollywood red carpet. They are so in synch with what the stars want to wear that they have designed stage costumes for everyone from Madonna to Kylie Minogue, while their signature curvy, bra-strapped dresses have brought out the babe in Isabella Rossellini, Gwyneth Paltrow…every celebrity worth her *Vogue* cover. This flagship store, their largest in the world, serves up a gorgeously rich collection of men's and women's ready-to-wear as well as some couture pieces from pinstriped suits (another Dolce classic) to seductive leopard dresses. Not to mention their to-die-for accessories like silk ribbon belts and denim stilettos.  *dolcegabbana.it*

*Expensive*  *Amex/MC/V*

**Upper East Side**  (212) 249-4100
825 Madison Avenue  btw 68/69th St
NYC 10021  Mon-Sat 10-6 (Thurs 10-7)

## ★ Domenico Spano  

Calabria-born Domenico 'Mimmo' Spano has been creating extraordinary suits for tasteful gents for 'longer than he'd like to admit,' laughs a staffer. Such experience yields treasures, and these pieces will last a lifetime. The former director of custom tailoring at Bergdorf Goodman also provides a small tailoring service for women—think Katherine Hepburn's inimitable Thirties style and you've got it. This is one of the best places in the city for a wedding tuxedo, with the bespoke wool version starting at $4,200 and prices escalating, depending on threads per square inch, from there. Lack the patience (or funds) for bespoke suits but still admire the defined shoulders, tapered waists and unique color schemes that characterize Mimmo's work? He recently started his first ready-to-wear line, where his 'vintage with a modern twist' look will be made available to one and all.

*Luxury*  *Amex/MC/V*

**Midtown East**  (212) 940-2676
611 Fifth Avenue  at 50th St
NYC 10022  Mon-Sat 10-6 (Thurs 10-8)

## ★ Domenico Vacca

'The first authentic Italian boutique in the United States,' promises owner Domenico Vacca (the man behind Borrelli) of this chic slice of Milan in the heart of Midtown. Master tailor Cesare Attolini, whose father Vincenzo tailored suits for Clark Gable and the Duke of Windsor, provides movie-star glamour, while fine shirting by Finamore and hand-made belts and shoes by Stefano Bi and Andrea D'Amico complete the dapper looks. Then there's the house's signature collection of refined classic separates and suiting, lovely V-neck sweaters and brightly colored ties—all perfect for your lunch next door at Harry Cipriani.

*Luxury*                                                          *Amex/MC/V*

**Midtown East**                            **(212) 759-6333**
781 Fifth Avenue                                  btw 59/60th St
NYC 10022                              Mon-Sat 10-7, Sun 12-6

## Domseys

Domseys is still around, but sadly no longer sells clothes by the pound. With three locations in the Tri-State area, Domseys is a good stop for super-cheap used clothing and lucky finds like classic Eighties Calvin Klein jeans to pair with a military navy blazer and an 'I love Bahamas' tee. They even sell slightly (and sometimes very) worn home furnishings.

*Affordable*                                                      *Amex/MC/V*

**Brooklyn**                                   **(718) 384 6000**
431 Broadway                                            at Hewes
Brooklyn 11211                                         Daily 9-7

**Queens**                                     **(718) 386-7661**
1609 Palmetto                               btw Wycoff/Myrtle
Queens 11385                                          Daily 10-7

## Donna Karan

Discover the Donna Karan worldview at this flagship store where the clothes and the decor project the designer's calmly chic aesthetic. Karan has always designed what she herself would like to wear—distinctive yet comfortable clothing—and that's the secret of her success. This modern, streamlined style can be found on three floors of men's and women's suits, great black jackets (great black everything, actually), cozy sweaters, smart khaki trench coats, leathers and outerwear, as well as modern eveningwear. Also find home accessories to outfit the total DK-inspired lifestyle. A serene bamboo garden in the back offers a respite to weary shoppers.                                              donnakaran.com

*Luxury*                                                          *Amex/MC/V*

**Upper East Side**                          **(212) 861-1001**
819 Madison Avenue                               btw 68/69th St
NYC 10021                    Mon-Sat 10-6 (Thurs 10-7), Sun 12-5

## Dooney & Burke

Dooney & Burke's flagship offers its extensive collection of handbags, leather goods and luggage. Find a variety of fabrics and shapes, from classic, durable leather goods to more colorful, recent additions, all emblazoned with the company's logo. Be sure to look past the fabulous bags and browse the men's and women's clothing lines, which feature cashmere sweaters, hats and gloves. Also find shoes, briefcases, phone cases and even a great-looking unisex watch.   800-347-5000  *dooney.com*

*Expensive*                                          *Amex/MC/V*

**Upper East Side**                        **(212) 223-7444**
20 East 60th Street                btw Madison/Park Ave
NYC 10022                                      Mon-Sat 10-6

## Dosa

L.A.-based Dosa designer Christina Kim makes a lot of women very, very happy with clothes that have a chicly bohemian vibe. The loose, girlish pieces include silks in delicious rainbow colors, handwoven Khadi cotton, covetable cashmeres, Tibetan-inspired tops and long, wrap skirts.

*Moderate*                                          *Amex/MC/V*

**Nolita**                                    **(212) 343-0841**
271 Mulberry Street                    btw Houston/Prince
NYC 10012                            Daily 12-7 (Sun 12-6)

## Doyle & Doyle

Doyle and Doyle carry exquisite antique and estate jewelry that will seduce anyone—even those not in the market for an Art Deco diamond bracelet. Owned by two sisters from Massachusetts, the sleek space belies the friendly, welcoming service and charming atmosphere. Shop here for a range of items, from Belle Epoque engagement rings to Victorian brooches. They also carry accessories such as late 19th-century mesh purses, as well as more contemporary pieces. All the jewelry is in excellent condition and sparkles with a distinctive, unique feel. The best part? Reasonable prices, given the condition and provenance of the pieces.                                  *doyledoyle.com*

*Expensive*                                          *Amex/MC/V*

**Lower East Side**                        **(212) 677-9991**
189 Orchard Street                  btw Stanton/Houston
NYC 10002                            Tues-Sun 1-7 (Thurs 1-8)

## Dusica Dusica

Dusica Dusica shoes run the footwear gamut from sensible to sexy. The Italian label provides sultry stilettos, pumps and impressive boots as well as more functional—though equally stylish—flats, sandals and loafers. *dusicadusica.com*

*Expensive*                                          *Amex/MC/V*

**Nolita**                                    **(212) 966-9099**
4 Prince Street                      btw Bowery/Elizabeth
NYC 10012                            Daily 11-7 (Sun 12-6)

## Duty Free Apparel

Feels like a border crossing, without the hassle. Duty Free Apparel offers a fix of high-style European labels at great prices. Owner Joel Soren finds the best from across the pond and brings them to Manhattanites willing to trek to this slightly out-of-the-way space in the Garment District. Find Prada,

Gucci, Ferragamo and Armani—the best of the best—for prices slightly below retail, even for this season's styles and bags. No passport necessary. *dutyfreeapparel.com*

*Expensive* *Amex/MC/V*

**Midtown** **(212) 967-6548**
204 West 35th Street (2nd floor)   btw Seventh/Eighth Ave
NYC 10001 Tues-Fri 10-6

## Earl Jean

Earl Jean was the first of the hip, micro-jeans brands that now include Lucky and Seven and took on the Levi's and Diesels of the world. Devotees like Jennifer Aniston and Cameron Diaz swear by Earl creative director Suzanne Costas Freiwald's super-flattering, leg-lengthening cuts, and her fans grow daily. The look is ultra-sexy, hip bone-revealing jeans in dark denim, slim silhouettes and boot-leg cuts. Epitomizing this look is Earl Jean's most distinctive style #55. There's a world of other jean styles in fabrics like corduroy, chambray, leather and velvet, as well a collection of jean jackets, skirts and tops. Also check out Earl's accessory line of jewelry, handbags, boots and belts. And there's good news for guys: Earl's men's line flatters in the same way as the women's—it includes T-shirts, knits and outerwear, as well as denim in a variety of washes. *earljean.com*

*Moderate* *Amex/MC/V*

**SoHo** **(212) 226-8709**
160 Mercer Street btw Houston/Prince
NYC 10012 Mon-Sat 11-7, Sun 12-6

## Eastern Mountain Sports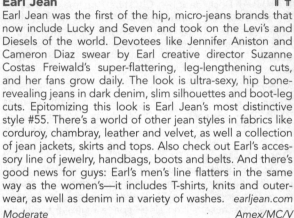

Whether your idea of a great outdoor adventure consists of hiking the Appalachian Trail or just up Fifth Avenue, Eastern Mountain Sports will outfit you for all your wilderness needs—as wild or wimpy as they may be. Specializing in clothing and equipment for mountaineering, backpacking, hiking, skiing and camping, EMS carries the leading nature-loving labels including Columbia, The North Face, Patagonia and their own in-house brand of apparel, gear and goods. 888-463-6367 *ems.com*

*Affordable to moderate* *Amex/MC/V*

**SoHo** **(212) 966-8730**
591 Broadway btw Houston/Prince
NYC 10012 Mon-Fri 10-9, Sat 10-8, Sun 12-6

**Upper West Side** **(212) 397-4860**
20 West 61st Street at Broadway
NYC 10023 (opening hours as above)

## East Side Kids

Cartoons and classic movies play at an earsplitting pitch here in order to entertain the kids while their parents examine a mammoth assortment of dress and athletic shoes—plenty of Nike and Keds ($60), Sam & Libby ($52) and Hush Puppies ($43). And, contrary to the store's name, there are plenty of shoes for grown-ups, too.

*Affordable*                                                     *Amex/MC/V*

**Upper East Side**                                    **(212) 360-5000**
1298 Madison Avenue                                        at 92nd St
NYC 10128                                        Mon-Fri 9:30-6, Sat 9-6

## Easy Spirit
Easy Sprit Shoes have always emphasized comfort, and
the brand commits to continuously advancing shoe construction by incorporating the latest technology. Styles
range from career and fitness to fun and casual. It's
footwear that protects your feet from shock—and your
wallet, too.                                              *eastspirit.com*

*Affordable*                                                     *Amex/MC/V*

**Upper East Side**                                    **(212) 828-9593**
1518 Third Avenue                                      btw 85/86th St
NYC 10028                                Mon-Fri 10-8, Sat 10-7, Sun 11-6

**Upper West Side**                                   **(212) 875-8146**
2251 Broadway                                              at 81st St
NYC 10024                                     Mon-Sat 10-7:15, Sun 11-6

**Midtown East**                                      **(212) 715-0152**
555 Madison Avenue                                    btw 55/56th St
NYC 10022                                Mon-Fri 9-7:30, Sat 10-5, Sun 11-5

**Midtown West**                                      **(212) 398-2761**
1166 Sixth Avenue                                          at 46th St
NYC 10036                                Mon-Fri 9-7, Sat 10-6, Sun 12-4:30

## Eddie Bauer
Classic style for classic Americans should be Eddie Bauer's
motto. Originally a purveyor of innovative, rugged outdoor gear and apparel, Eddie Bauer, having been in business over 80 years, maintain their sporty yet understated
style, providing men and women with perfectly preppy
polos, wrinkle-resistant pleated khakis and ribbed
Henleys, along with parkas, duffles and all the camping
gear and gadgets you need for the perfect weekend getaway.                           800-625-7935  *eddiebauer.com*

*Affordable*                                                     *Amex/MC/V*

**Upper East Side**                                    **(212) 737-0002**
1172 Third Avenue                                          at 68th St
NYC 10021                                        Mon-Sat 10-8, Sun 11-6

**Upper West Side**                                   **(212) 877-7629**
1976 Broadway                                             at 67th St
NYC 10023                             Mon-Thurs 10-8, Fri-Sat 10-9, Sun 11-8

**SoHo**                                              **(212) 925-2179**
578 Broadway                                      btw Houston/Prince
NYC 10012                             Mon-Thurs 10-9, Fri-Sat 10-10, Sun 11-7

## Edmundo Castillo
Edmundo Castillo, former winner of the Council of Fashion
Designers of America's Best Accessories Designer award,
opened what he calls 'the ultimate shoe closet' in Nolita.
The store, inspired by his own living room, lovingly show-
cases Castillo's super-sexy shoes, like metallic stiletto san-

dals that weave seductively around the ankles or bold and bright espadrilles. Prices range from \$350 to a heady \$1,400. *edmundocastillo.com*

*Luxury* *Amex/MC/V*

**Nolita** **(212) 431-5320**
219 Mott Street btw Prince/Spring
NYC 10012 Mon-Sat 11-7, Sun 12-6

## Eileen Fisher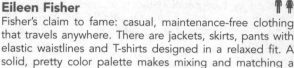

Fisher's claim to fame: casual, maintenance-free clothing that travels anywhere. There are jackets, skirts, pants with elastic waistlines and T-shirts designed in a relaxed fit. A solid, pretty color palette makes mixing and matching a cinch. 800-345-3362 *eileenfisher.com*

*Affordable* *Amex/MC/V*

**Upper East Side** **(212) 879-7799**
1039 Madison Avenue btw 79/80th St
NYC 10021 Mon-Sat 11-7, Sun 12-5

**Upper West Side** **(212) 362-3000**
341 Columbus Avenue btw 76/77th St
NYC 10024 Mon-Sat 10-7, Sun 12-5

**Midtown East** **(212) 759-9888**
521 Madison Avenue btw 53/54th St
NYC 10022 Mon-Sat 10-7, Sun 12-6

**Flatiron** **(212) 924-4777**
166 Fifth Avenue btw 21/22nd St
NYC 10003 Mon-Sat 10-8, Sun 12-6

**SoHo** **(212) 431-4567**
395 West Broadway btw Spring/Broome
NYC 10012 Mon-Thurs 11-7, Fri-Sat 11-8, Sun 12-6

**East Village (outlet)** **(212) 529-5715**
314 East 9th Street btw First/Second Ave
NYC 10003 Daily 12-8 (Sun 12-7)

## Eisenberg & Eisenberg

For over a century this shop has been one of New York's sources for inexpensive formalwear. Don't let the unglamorous façade deter you from venturing inside, where you'll find suits, slacks, sportcoats, blazers, shirts, men's furnishings and a full range of tuxedos. Pay an average price of \$375 for suits and from \$190 to \$650 for tuxedos. Extra for alterations, which are done in the store. *eisenbergandeisenberg.com*

*Moderate* *Amex/MC/V*

**Chelsea** **(212) 627-1290**
16 West 17th Street btw Fifth/Sixth Ave
NYC 10011 Mon-Wed, Fri 9-5:45, Tues 9-5:30
Thurs 9-6:45, Sat 9-5

## Elaine Arsenault

This jaunty accessories store recalls the equally jaunty aesthetic of Kate Spade in a range of clever totes in var-

# Elie Tahari

ious shapes with leather handles, each efficiently displayed like art on the wall. Perfect for taking to Sunday brunch, they come in a variety of prints and are handmade in the store. Also available: make-up bags and clutches. *elainearsenault.com*

*Moderate* *Amex/MC/V*

**East Village** **(212) 228-3251**
305 East 9th Street btw First/Second Ave
NYC 10003 Daily 12-7 (Sun 12-6)

## Eleni Lambros
Consider Eleni Lambros your fashion fairy godmother. She has created couture bridal and eveningwear for over 12 years, and recently launched a ready-to-wear bridal gown collection, which she shows exclusively in a SoHo showroom every bit as decadent as its custom counterpart. From hand-stitched beadwork using Swarovski crystals, to feather trim and braided silk piping, Lambros's creations would make even Cinderella jealous. *elenilambros.com*

*Luxury* *Amex/MC/V*

**SoHo** **(212) 226-1167**
591 Broadway btw Houston/Prince
NYC 10012 (by appointment only)

## Eleven
If Sofia Coppola and Spike Jonze are your style heroes, and the Beastie Boys are your favorite rockers, check out Eleven for downtown-cool vintage clothes, amongst them a collection of striped polo shirts, old baseball shirts, slouchy denim, kitsch shoes and expensive retro logo'd handbags. Best is their rocking collection of sneakers—from old-school Converse Chuck Taylors to Pumas.

*Moderate* *Amex/MC/V*

**Nolita** **(212) 219-1033**
11 Prince Street at Elizabeth
NYC 10012 Daily 1-8

## Elie Tahari
Tahari had runaway success with his Theory sportswear line, and has now refocused attention on his eponymous label. Having cultivated a following at Bergdorf's, Tahari has opened his own beautifully minimalist flagship in SoHo. Sexy, modern, clean pieces are his signature—like his flirty tennis dresses, buckled asymmetrical minis, tweedy skirts, and beautiful double-face wool coats for fall. Tahari's looks are refined, a little glamorous, and great for everything from turning heads at the office to making friends at cocktail hour. *elietahari.com*

*Expensive* *Amex/MC/V*

**SoHo** **(212) 334-4441**
417 West Broadway btw Spring/Prince
NYC 10012 Mon-Fri 10-7, Sat 11-7, Sun 12-6

## Ellen                                                      ♀

Local fashion designers shop at Ellen Koenigsberg's teeny vintage boutique because, the proprietor promises, 'every piece is special'. Eschewing label snobbery in favor of whatever catches her eye, Ellen stocks her limited space with great shoes and hats from the Sixties. Familiar names do crop up, however, in her stash of Pucci shorts in turquoise and yellow, Geoffrey Beene dresses, and the occasional Courrèges floral skirt.

*Expensive*                                              *Amex/MC/V*

**Lower East Side**                             **(212) 471-0080**
122 Ludlow                                btw Rivington/Delancey
NYC 10002                              Daily 1-7 (closed Tuesday)

## Emanuel Ungaro                                            ♀

Ungaro is every girl's guilty pleasure. 'Pink is the institutional color for Ungaro,' says the man himself, and it's more than obvious when you walk into this brilliantly rose-toned store. Ungaro gave up the ready-to-wear reins at his house five years ago to his former design assistant Giambattista Valli, who has started to hit his stride. This store is the perfect showcase for the company's deliciously feminine pieces: flirty dresses in the signature silk jersey, or with floral prints that are regularly sported by seductive celebs like Jennifer Lopez and Cameron Diaz as well as the model set, who often dress the romantic pieces down by wearing them over jeans. Accessories include fabulously flirty shoes (some in, yes, pink), belts, bags and evening shawls.  *ungaro.com*

*Luxury*                                                  *Amex/MC/V*

**Upper East Side**                             **(212) 249-4090**
792 Madison Avenue                                    at 67th St
NYC 10021                                           Mon-Sat 10-6

## Emporio Armani                                         ♂ ♀

Bridging the gap between the perfect Armani power suit and the euro-styled jeans and tees of Armani Exchange is Emporio Armani, where you'll find younger, sportier takes on the restrained elegance of Armani's pant suits, beaded dresses for evenings out, clean lines and fluid cuts. The palette is refined, and the details minimalist—no Hawaiian shirts here. For men, Emporio offers exquisite pinstripe dress shirts and more affordable versions of the classic Armani jackets, pants and suits. Women can head upstairs to try on sporty Italian designs like—and only Armani could make this beautiful—a $500 nylon dress with plastic straps.                                    *emporioarmani.com*

*Expensive*                                              *Amex/MC/V*

**Midtown East**                                **(212) 317-0800**
601 Madison Avenue                           btw 57/58th St
NYC 10022                Mon-Sat 10-7 (Thurs 10-8), Sun 12-7

## Encore                                                    ♀

The idea of the consignment shop began with Encore when it opened in 1954 as a place for uptown ladies to unload last season's digs for cold hard cash. The shop is like taking a trip down memory lane, with all the purchases you never got around to—until now, that is. You'll find Donna Karan dresses, Jil Sander suits, Tod's bags, as well as items from luxe labels like Yohji Yamamoto, Prada, Chloé and Fendi— all deeply discounted from original prices. You, too, can get in on the action by selling your unwanted threads on Tuesdays through Saturdays from 10:30-5. *encoresale.com*

*Moderate*                                                  *Amex/MC/V*

**Upper East Side**                                **(212) 879-2850**
1132 Madison Avenue (2nd floor)              btw 84/85th St
NYC 10028              Mon-Fri 10:30-6:30 (Thurs 10:30-7:30)
Sat 10:30-6, Sun 12-6

### Enerla Lingerie                                          👗
For more than 20 years this East Village shop has been keeping the girls happy with its sexy, romantic lingerie and great basics. The range runs from naughty to nice, and includes sleepwear, robes, foundations, bustiers, swimwear and hosiery from labels like Le Mystère, Claire Pettibone, Chiarugi, Orablu, Eberjey, Mary Green and the ubiquitous Cosabella. Fun accessories, too: don't miss Enerla's massage oils and marabou bedroom slippers.

*Expensive*                                                 *Amex/MC/V*

**East Village**                                   **(212) 473-2454**
48½ East 7th Street                          btw First/Second Ave
NYC 10003                             Daily 12-8 (Fri-Sat 12-9)

### Entre Nous                                               👗
Just between us—or as the French say, entre nous—this shop is one of New York's best kept secrets. It's a sophisticated showcase of luxury European labels—Luciano Barbera's complete collection of pants, classic blazers, cashmeres and tailored shirts; sportswear by Agnona; evening dresses and gowns by Sylvia Heisel.

*Expensive*                                                 *Amex/MC/V*

**Upper East Side**                                **(212) 249-2225**
1124 Third Avenue                               btw 65/66th St
NYC 10021                               Mon-Fri 10-6, Sat 10-5

### Enzo Angiolini                                           👗
Enzo Angiolini is Nine West's better footwear division. Find up-to-the-minute styles that include basic comfort flats, tailored loafers, trendy sandals, platforms, boots and more. It's about fashion-forward shoes that look expensive but aren't.

*Moderate*                                                  *Amex/MC/V*

**Midtown East**                                   **(212) 339-8921**
551 Madison Avenue                                  at 55th St
NYC 10022              Mon-Fri 9:30-7:30, Sat 10-6, Sun 12-5

**Midtown East**                                   **(212) 286-8726**
331 Madison Avenue                                  at 43rd St
NYC 10017                 Mon-Fri 8-8, Sat 10-6, Sun 12-5

**Midtown West** **(212) 695-8903**
901 Sixth Avenue at Manhattan Mall, btw 32/33rd St
NYC 10001 Mon-Sat 10-8, Sun 11-6

## ★ Eres 👤

With boutiques in Paris, Palm Beach and Manhattan, Eres' luxury lingerie draws a sleek-chic clientele (*Vogue* adores it) with its high-quality everyday basics and fabulous, perfect-fitting bra styles. Manufactured in trademark skin tones and featherweight fabrics (trying 'le soufflé' is a must), Eres' natural silhouettes can easily pass for custom lingerie, but at lower prices—panties are $65-$90 and bras $140-$190. Their swimwear is second to none: bikinis, thankfully, are sold as separates, with racy styles like deep V-necks and low-cut backs, and sexy, boy-leg shorts paired with string tops. Pareos and cover-up dresses are also on show, not to mention a seductive line of garter belts, bustiers, pantyhose and tights. *eresparis.com*

*Moderate to expensive* *Amex/MC/V*

**Midtown East** **(212) 223-3550**
621 Madison Avenue btw 58/59th St
NYC 10022 Mon-Sat 10-6

## Erica Tanov 👤👦

This large, clean space is the perfect backdrop for Erica Tanov's collection of sophisticated womenswear, bed linens, baby clothes, lingerie and accessories defined by elegant fabrics, classic styling and careful attention to detail. Her pieces are complemented by knitwear from John Smedley and Brooklyn Handknits, dresses by Megan Park and lingerie by La Cosa. Children can be turned out in Erica Tanov and I Golfini della Nonna's collection of cheerful printed rompers, bloomers and smocks. *ericatanov.com*

*Moderate to expensive* *Amex/MC/V*

**Nolita** **(212) 334-8020**
204 Elizabeth Street btw Prince/Spring
NYC 10012 Mon-Sat 11-7, Sun 12-6

## Eric Shoes 👤

Why ruin your Choos chasing the perfect shoes all over town? Eric Shoes supplies you with all the downtown soles you'll ever need uptown, with brands like Miu Miu, Vanessa Noel, Cynthia Rowley and Mark Swartz, as well as their own label. The store also carries a considerable number of bridal shoes. Prices range from $95-$325.

*Moderate* *Amex/MC/V*

**Upper East Side** **(212) 289-5762**
1222 Madison Avenue at 88th St
NYC 10128 Mon-Fri 10-7, Sat 10-6, Sun 12-6
(except in summer)

**Upper East Side** **(212) 288-8250**
1333 Third Avenue btw 76/77th St
NYC 10021 Mon-Fri 10-7 (Thurs 10-8), Sat 10-6:30
Sun 12-6

## Ermenegildo Zegna

Zegna is, simply, a byword for luxury menswear. Their classic suits range from high-powered tailored styles to deconstructed modern versions at an average price of $1,840 (and much more for custom). Shirts, ties, sportswear, outerwear, shoes and accessories are also available. A first-ever women's line, Agnona, is now in the Zegna boutique. It features hand-finished tailored jackets and knitwear in fine Italian fabrics. *zegna.com*

*Luxury* *Amex/MC/V*

**Fifth Avenue** **(212) 421-4488**
663 Fifth Avenue btw 52/53rd St
NYC 10022 Mon-Fri 10-6:30, Sat 10-6, Sun 12-6

## Escada

German fashion house Escada will color you happy. Opulent fabrics, vibrant prints and lots of embroidery are the trademarks of their three collections: Escada Couture, Escada Ready-to-Wear and Escada Sport. This is the place to find that lime-green skirt suit you've always dreamed of. Looks range from wool suits to glitzy sequined eveningwear. The boutique also offers the Badgley Mischka Bridal and Atelier collections, plus the usual head-turning accessories, handbags, scarves and shoes. *escada.com*

*Expensive* *Amex/MC/V*

**Fifth Avenue** **(212) 755-2200**
715 Fifth Avenue at 56th St
NYC 10022 Mon-Sat 10-6 (Thurs 10-7), Sun 12-5

## Esprit

We hear that your favorite sweet 'n' sexy clothing line is moving into downtown Manhattan, at 110 Fifth Avenue. Expect to find simple casuals with a nice fit, exquisite eveningwear, sportswear, sleepwear, outerwear, shoes, accessories, watches, glasses and great classics for home. They have a great selection of bikinis, too, so you can stock up and be ready for summer's rays. Further details n/a as we went to press—try the website. *esprit.com*

*Moderate* *Amex/MC/V*

## Etro

A luxe Italian label that's perfect for seasoning your wardrobe with color, pattern and texture. Find four floors of ready-to-wear, home furnishings, shoes, accessories, luggage and fragrances, as well as a custom atelier for both men and women. Boldly patterned clothing is distinguished by expert craftsmanship for a look that is both classic in tailoring and rich in design. Stripes and paisleys adorn silks and cashmeres that pair beautifully with sleek pants, jackets and suits. A great place for acquiring urbane uptown style. *etro.it*

*Expensive* *Amex/MC/V*

**Upper East Side**　　　　　　　　　**(212) 317-9096**
720 Madison Avenue　　　　　　　　btw 63/64th St
NYC 10021　　　　　　　　　　　　　Mon-Sat 10-6

★ **Eugenia Kim**　　　　　　　　　　　　　👤

Walk into milliner Eugenia Kim's Rubik's Cube-colored shop to see firsthand her collectible, cool hats that are flaunted at awards shows everywhere by 'look at me!' celebrities like Jennifer Lopez and Nicole Kidman, not to mention the requisite socialites and downtown hipsters. Standouts include simple-chic leather caps, floppy hippy hats with gold chain bands, felt cloches, and fur numbers from rabbit trooper hats and berets to fox toques. Shoes and a couture service (for those who simply can't bear to have the same newsboy as the next celeb) complete the offerings. Prices run from $120 to $500, and you'd be well advised to make an appointment.　　　　　　　　　　*eugeniakim.com*

*Expensive*　　　　　　　　　　　　　　*Amex/MC/V*

**East Village**　　　　　　　　　　　**(212) 673-9787**
203 East 4th Street　　　　　　　　　btw Avenue A/B
NYC 10009　　　　　　　　　　　　　　Daily 10-8

**Express**　　　　　　　　　　　　　　👤👤

This division of the giant fashion conglomerate The Limited is great for younger shoppers who are making the transition from campus to workplace—and who aren't exactly loaded. Dresses, pants, skirts, T-shirts and quick-hit accessories all match the latest color forecasts and trends—from hippy to clubby to relaxed sweats. More than one glam actress-about-town swears by their thongs. In 2001 Express joined forces with its brother store Structure, so men's trendy casual clothes and accessories are now available alongside women's in Express stores.　　877-657-2292　*express.com*

*Affordable*　　　　　　　　　　　　　　*Amex/MC/V*

**Upper West Side (W)**　　　　　　　**(212) 580-5833**
321 Columbus Avenue　　　　　　　　at 75th St
NYC 10023　　　　　　　　　Mon-Sat 10-8, Sun 11-7

**Midtown East**　　　　　　　　　　　**(212) 421-7246**
722-728 Lexington Avenue　　　　　　at 58th St
NYC 10022　　　　　　　　　Mon-Sat 10-9, Sun 11-7

**Midtown East (W)**　　　　　　　　　**(212) 644-4453**
477 Madison Avenue　　　　　　　　　at 51st St
NYC 10021　　　　　　　　　Mon-Sat 10-8, Sun 11-7

**Midtown West (W)**　　　　　　　　　**(212) 629-6838**
7 West 34th Street　　　　　　btw Fifth/Sixth Ave
NYC 10001　　　　Mon-Sat 10-8 (Thurs-Fri 10-9), Sun 12-7

**Midtown West**　　　　　　　　　　　**(212) 971-3280**
901 Sixth Avenue　　　at Manhattan Mall, btw 32/33rd St
NYC 10001　　　　　　　　　Mon-Sat 11-8, Sun 10-6

**Flatiron (W)**　　　　　　　　　　　**(212) 633-9414**
130 Fifth Avenue　　　　　　　　　　at 18th St
NYC 10011　　　　Mon-Sat 10-8 (Thurs-Fri 10-9), Sun 11-7

**SoHo**         **(212) 625-0313**
584 Broadway       btw Houston/Prince
NYC 10012     Mon-Wed 10-8, Thurs-Sat 10-9, Sun 11-7

**Lower Manhattan**       **(212) 693-0096**
89 South Street       at South Street Seaport
NYC 10038       Mon-Sat 10-9, Sun 11-8

## ★ Eye Candy

Eye Candy is a shining jewel of a store, literally...the cute retro baubles in here are bright enough to cause cornea damage. It's also one of the city's top destinations for primo vintage and new accessories, including diamanté and beaded jewelry, hats, sunglasses, a great collection of shoes, and lots of bags (everything from Sixties Gucci to colorful Mexican straw). Owner Ron Caldwell can often be found trying on groovy shades and asking customers for their opinions. The wares aren't cheap, but they're distinctive enough to be worth it.     *eyecandystore.com*

*Moderate to expensive*     *Amex/MC/V*

**NoHo**       **(212) 343-4275**
329 Lafayette Street     btw Bleecker/Houston
NYC 10012       Daily 12-8

## Fabulous Fanny's

A hit with costume designers and vintage aficionados, Fabulous Fanny's antique glasses and 'optical oddities', as they call them, mix the quirky with the cool. Indeed, the carefully organized store lives up to its slogan—'If you have to wear them, make it fun.' Fabulous Fanny's is owned by a pair of serious collectors who outfit many Broadway productions and movies (note the frames in *The Royal Tenenbaums*, for example). They also offer a host of repair services for the old frames you already own. There's an equally great collection of men's and women's vintage clothes, as well as a line of handmade costume jewelry reconfigured from antique and vintage pieces.     *fabulousfannys.com*

*Expensive*     *Amex/MC/V*

**East Village**       **(212) 533-0637**
335 East 9th Street     btw First/Second Ave
NYC 10003       Daily 12-8

## Façonnable

The perfect shop for the well-dressed man has taken up residence in a 21,000-square-foot Rockefeller Center location. It's Façonnable heaven. No wardrobe is complete without a Façonnable tie or spread-collar shirt. Suits come in classic silhouettes, the sportswear is perfect for weekends and the outerwear is a must, including a wide selection of beautiful topcoats as well as the classic parka. It's a stylish French version of Ralph Lauren. Logophobes beware: the Façonnable insignia is everywhere you look. The store also has womenswear and lots of accessories.     *faconnable.com*

*Expensive*     *Amex/MC/V*

**Fifth Avenue**      **(212) 319-0111**
636 Fifth Avenue      at 51st St
NYC 10022      Mon-Sat 10-8, Sun 12-6

## Fame    👤

A pioneering retail effort in the garment district that has fashionistas housed in the glam magazine offices close by especially thankful. They pop into this big, airy space on their lunch breaks to rifle through a groovy sportswear collection including Sharagano, Allen B, Joe's Jeans, Jill Stuart Jeans and the edgy pieces from L.A. label Haley Bob. And where the fashionistas go for a style fix, the curious should definitely follow. *fameny.com*

*Moderate to expensive*      *Amex/MC/V*

**Midtown West**      **(212) 730-4806**
512 Seventh Avenue      btw 37/38th St
NYC 10018      Mon-Fri 9-8, Sun 12-6

## The Family Jewels    👤👤

Have you been searching for a poodle skirt, vintage Pucci or a pair of rounded-toe pumps? This store has a wide range of quirky and fabulous finds for the serious collector. Women will love the Fifties flare dresses reminiscent of many a Doris Day flick, while fellas will enjoy combing through myriad Western shirts, corduroy jackets and striped pants. If you need a breather, take a seat on the couch and check out the record collection in the back. The perfect place to complete any look under the sun. *familyjewelsnyc.com*

*Moderate to expensive*      *Amex/MC/V*

**Chelsea**      **(212) 633-6020**
130 West 23rd Street      btw Sixth/Seventh Ave
NYC 10011      Daily 11-7

## February Eleventh    👤

Women who like their fashion on the arty side will appreciate the tricksy handwork on display here in crocheted dresses, separates and shawls, as well as embroidered, lace and hand-dyed pieces and a new addition: custom bridal gowns. Equally detailed handbags and jewelry are also available. So what's with the store's name? It's the owner's birthday, of course. (You guessed that, really.)

*Expensive*      *Amex/MC/V*

**East Village**      **(212) 529-1175**
315 East 9th Street      btw First/Second Ave
NYC 10003      Tues-Sat 1-8, Sun 1-7

## Fendi    👤

Fendi is the ideal stop for any Roman Goddess. The premier Italian fur and handbag dealer for four generations, Fendi is festooned with gilded objects, only some of which are for sale. The opulent furs in mink and sable practically cry out 'caress me!'—but be prepared to lay out up to

$200,000 for the opportunity to do so. It's no wonder J.Lo commands the spotlight with her Fendi furs and glistening bags. This season, keep an eye out for the Vanity bag, a new baguette that follows in the tradition of Silvia Venturni Fendi's 1997 landmark design. *fendi.com*

*Luxury*                                          *Amex/MC/V*

**Midtown East**                          **(212) 767-0100**
720 Fifth Avenue                              at 56th St
NYC 10019                    Mon-Fri 10-6:30, Sat 10-6, Sun 12-6

## Filene's Basement

One of the country's oldest and most famous discount stores, Filene's has provided higher-end goods at a fraction of the cost since 1908. If you're lucky, you can find a pair of coveted Seven jeans, or an entire outfit by Valentino, Donna Karan, Arnold Scassi or Liz Claiborne. As at all dis-counters, the selection is a little hit or miss, but the store also sells bath products, shoes, clothing, and has a small section for perfume. *filenesbasement.com*

*Affordable*                                      *Amex/MC/V*

**Chelsea**                                 **(212) 620-3100**
620 Avenue of the Americas                   at 18th Street
NYC 10011                        Mon-Sat 9:30-9, Sun 11-7

## Filth Mart

For real rock 'n' roll style, head to Filth Mart. Don't be fooled by the name—the vintage clothes here are anything but filthy. Co-owned by *Sopranos* star Drea de Matteo, this place is the real deal, selling authentic band T-shirts, denim, belt buckles and a large selection of iron-ons. Sadly, the old-school video games are not available for purchase.

*Moderate*                                       *Amex/MC/V*

**East Village**                            **(212) 387-0650**
531 East 13th Street                         btw Avenue A/B
NYC 10009                        Sun-Tues 1-7, Wed-Sat 1-8

## Find Outlet

Imagine the world's smallest sample sale that nevertheless stocks labels like Nili Lotan, Twinkle and Mint. This adorable, well-kept store doesn't have an enormous selec-tion but they do carry Cosabella thongs at $12 a pop, which is significantly less than what you'll pay elsewhere. Everything is always 50-70% off retail, and customers can receive e-mails about weekly arrivals, so get added to their list, quick.

*Affordable to moderate*                          *Amex/MC/V*

**Chelsea**                                 **(212) 243-3177**
361 West 17th Street                      btw Eighth/Ninth Ave
NYC 10011                                   Thurs-Sun 12-7

**Nolita**                                  **(212) 226-5167**
229 Mott Street                           btw Prince/Spring
NYC 10012                                      Daily 12-7

## Fiona Walker

Having grown up studying textiles and fabrics in Ireland, Fiona Walker is a knitter extraordinaire. Best are yarn-fringed tops, popcorn-stitched turtlenecks and tweedy sweaters. A section in the back of the shop is dedicated to Retro Redux—inexpensive, great-condition vintage pieces Walker collects. Custom is also available.

*Moderate*                                    *Amex/MC/V*

**Midtown West**                              **(212) 664-9699**
359 West 54th Street                           at Ninth Ave
NYC 10036                                      Tues-Sat 12-8

## Fisch for the Hip

Anyone in search of a vintage Hermès handbag in perfect condition (and that would be, like, everyone) should hurry down to Fisch for the Hip, a luxe consignment shop. In addition to stocking three display cases with said posh handbags and Louis Vuitton luggage, owner Terin Fischer brings in the best of the best from labels like Gucci, Celine, Helmut Lang, Prada and Dolce & Gabbana. The merchandise is in mint condition and half the price of retail. Also find shoes by Manolo Blahnik, Prada and Chanel.                                  *fischforthehip.com*

*Expensive*                                    *Amex/MC/V*

**Chelsea**                                   **(212) 633-9053**
153 West 18th Street                          btw Sixth/Seventh Ave
NYC 10011                                      Daily 12-7 (Sun 12-6)

## ★ Flight 001

This must be the coolest travel store in New York and maybe anywhere, for that matter. It's all very *Wallpaper\**, with snappy travel gear in cool colors that takes its design straight from the mid-century style celebrated in that interior/travel magazine. From digital watches (which display multiple time zones) to guide books, passport holders, perfectly-proportioned nylon carry-ons, teddy bears that double as in-flight pillows, and de-stress kits, these products are perfect for passengers who insist on being prepared and pampered. The coolest thing? Gift-wrapping is sealed with a sticker that looks like a boarding pass. Book a trip to Flight 001 immediately.                      *flight001.com*

*Moderate*                                    *Amex/MC/V*

**West Village**                              **(212) 691-1001**
96 Greenwich Avenue                           btw West 12th St/Jane
NYC 10011                        Mon-Fri 11-8:30, Sat 11-8, Sun 12-6

## Flirt

Brooklyn loves its own, and Flirt shows its pride by showcasing the work of local designers. Tired of 'Brooklyn' and '718' shirts? With feminine and, you guessed it, flirty dresses just right for a stroll through Prospect Park or a night out on Smith Street, this store provides the perfect alternative to the standard-issue alterna-gear you see in most Brooklyn hoods. Every item in the store is one of a kind, custom is available, and you'll find some steals in Flirt's rummage bin.                                          *flirtbrooklyn.com*

*Affordable*                                              Amex/MC/V

**Cobble Hill**                                    **(718) 858-7931**
252 Smith Street                          btw Douglas/Degraw
Brooklyn 11231                          Wed-Sat 12-8, Sun 12-6

## Flying A                                                    👤👤

Flying A differentiates itself from its peers by offering distinctive styles at affordable prices. The store provides cool sportswear from labels like Fred Perry, brashly colorful T-shirts from Custo Barcelona, girly shirts and skirts from Imperio, folksy tops from Ella Moss and easy-wearing accessories from Sequoia and Loop. They also sell a range of vintage clothes, and with a little digging you can find some choice items.                                    *flyinga.net*

*Affordable*                                              Amex/MC/V

**SoHo**                                             **(212) 965-9090**
169 Spring Street            btw West Broadway/Thompson
NYC 10012                                 Mon-Sat 11-8, Sun 12-7

## FM Allen                                                    👤👤

FM Allen was, according to store lore, 'one of the best great white hunters and safari guides in Africa'. The goods and services bearing his name now tempt gridlocked New Yorkers seeking safari consultants and gear for trips to South Africa, Botswana, Zimbabwe, Kenya and Tanzania. FM Allen offers high quality leather and canvas bush luggage, along with intriguing antique campaign furniture like an elegant early-20th-century English iron-bound leather traveling trunk with leather loop handles. Allen's 'world's best' hot-weather performance clothing has outfitted the likes of Elle Macpherson, Liv Tyler and jungle-lover Tom Selleck.                                          *fmallen.com*

*Luxury*                                                  Amex/MC/V

**Upper East Side**                                **(212) 737-4374**
962 Madison Avenue                            btw 75/76th St
NYC 10021                                 Mon-Sat 10-6, Sun 12-5

## Fogal                                                       👤👤

You can never have enough saucy stockings—so head here for one of the best labels around (alongside Wolford). It's famous for its fabulous colors—at last count, over 80 tempting shades—from sophisticated to downright saucy. They have everything from sheer ($25) and opaque hose ($29.50) to patterned and textured styles like Flamenco, a fishnet, or Petit Points, a sheer style with dots. If you really want to indulge yourself, there are always Fogal's fabulous cashmere-silk tights, which will set you back a mere $295. But think of the joy they'll give you. Other items include luxurious bodysuits in cashmere/silk blends and lingerie. For men, socks and hosiery. Good personalized service. *fogal.com*

*Expensive* *Amex/MC/V*

**Midtown East** **(212) 355-3254**
510 Madison Avenue at 53rd St
NYC 10022 Mon-Sat 10-6:30

★ **Foley + Corinna**

With so many celebrity fans—Gwyneth, Cameron, Liv, Britney (to first-name but a few)—it's hard to believe that this amazing shop is still one of New York's best kept secrets. Co-owned by Dana Foley and Anna Corinna, the store sells Foley's original designs and Corinna's vintage finds. But you will have to look at labels to tell the difference—Foley's creations are so individual they could be vintage and Corinna's treasures are in such great condition they could be brand new. Find anything and everything from sexy chiffon tops to cowboy boots to stylish trench coats Audrey would have loved. There is really no reason to shop anywhere else. Hurry in, before the secret is out... *foleyandcorinna.com*

*Moderate to expensive* *Amex/MC/V*

**Lower East Side** **(212) 529-2338**
108 Stanton Street btw Ludlow/Essex
NYC 10002 Mon-Sat 1-8

**Foley + Corinna Men**

Dana Foley and Anna Corinna know cool. The latest proof is presented by their new men's shop (around the corner from their original boutique), where vintage tees, leather jackets, hip scarves, hats, wallets and a small selection of home furnishings (old-school video games and classy bar sets) rule the roost. A whole hipster lifestyle awaits you— and all you have to do is visit one store. *foleyandcorinna.com*

*Moderate to expensive* *Amex/MC/V*

**Lower East Side** **(212) 529-5043**
143 Ludlow Street btw Stanton/Rivington
NYC 10002 Mon-Fri 1-8, Sat-Sun 12-8

**Foot Locker**

Foot Locker sells athletic wear and footwear for the entire family. There are workout clothes for fitness and basketball and shoes suitable for running, tennis, basketball or cross-training from such brands as Nike, Reebok, Adidas, Fila and New Balance. 800-991-6681 *footlocker.com*

*Affordable to moderate* *Amex/MC/V*

**Upper East Side** **(212) 348-8652**
159 East 86th Street btw Lexington/Third Ave
NYC 10028 Mon-Sat 9-8, Sun 11-6

**Upper West Side** **(212) 280-8562**
2831 Broadway btw 109/110th St
NYC 10025 Mon-Sat 9-8, Sun 11-7

**Midtown East**         **(212) 856-9411**
150 East 42nd Street      btw Lexington/Third Ave
NYC 10017         Mon-Sat 9-8, Sun 11-7

**Midtown West**         **(212) 629-4419**
120 West 34th Street      btw Sixth/Seventh Ave
NYC 10001         Mon-Fri 8-9, Sat 9-9, Sun 11-7

**Midtown West**         **(212) 268-7146**
901 Sixth Ave      at Manhattan Mall, btw 32/33rd St
NYC 10001         Mon-Sat 10-8, Sun 11-6

**Midtown West**         **(212) 971-9449**
43 West 34th Street      btw Fifth/Sixth Ave
NYC 10001         Mon-Fri 8-9, Sat 9-9, Sun 11-7

**Flatiron**         **(212) 673-9749**
853 Broadway      at 14th St
NYC 10003         Mon-Sat 9-9, Sun 11-7

**East Village**         **(212) 254-9187**
252 First Avenue      at 15th St
NYC 10009         Mon-Sat 10-8, Sun 11-6

**Lower East Side**         **(212) 533-8608**
94 Delancey Street      btw Ludlow/Orchard
NYC 10002         Mon-Sat 10-7, Sun 11-6

**NoHo**         **(212) 995-0381**
734 Broadway      at 8th St
NYC 10003         Mon-Sat 9-9, Sun 11-7

**Lower Manhattan**         **(212) 791-5530**
55 Fulton Street      at Gold
NYC 10038      Mon-Fri 9-7, Sat 10-7, Sun 11-6

**Lower Manhattan**         **(212) 608-3640**
89 South Street      at South Street Seaport
NYC 10038         Mon-Sat 10-9, Sun 11-8

## Forman's

This is the place for sportswear, separates and outerwear at terrific discounted prices. Forman's also has extensive petite and plus-size departments, and the merchandise changes constantly. Labels include Jones New York, Evan Picone, Ralph Lauren, Kasper and Liz Claiborne. Prices drop even lower during end-of-season sales.

*Affordable to moderate*      *Amex/MC/V*

**Midtown East**         **(212) 681-9800**
145 East 42nd Street      btw Lexington/Third Ave
NYC 10017      Mon-Thurs 8-8, Fri 8-5:30, Sun 10-6

**Fifth Avenue**         **(212) 719-1000**
560 Fifth Avenue      at 46th St
NYC 10017      Mon-Thurs 8-8, Fri 8-5, Sun 10-7

**Lower Manhattan**         **(212) 791-4100**
59 John Street      at Williams
NYC 10039      Mon-Wed 8-7, Thurs 8-8, Fri 8-5:45

## Forreal

While Forreal Basics targets twentysomethings and teens, Forreal appeals to women in search of dressier looks with a selection of slim-fitted pants, sexy knits, jackets, sweaters and T-shirts from such labels as Juicy Couture, Michael Stars and Petit Bateau. Free delivery in Manhattan.

*Moderate*                                            *Amex/MC/V*

**Upper East Side**                              **(212) 734-2105**
1335 Third Avenue                                 btw 76/77th St
NYC 10021                                    Mon-Sat 11-7, Sun 12-6

## Forreal Basics                                            ♀

Mothers bring their teenage daughters here for the hip assortment of jeans and casual basics, but get sucked in to the vortex and end up buying something for themselves as well. The denim selection includes Diesel, Miss Sixty, Mavi and Buffalo, and there is an abundance of fitted tees from labels like Michael Stars, Three Dots and Petit Bateau. Don't visit after school on a weekday, however, as you'll fear for you life when those teens and moms start fighting over Petit Bateau tanks, James Perse tees and AG jeans. Agoraphobes, take heart: Forreal offers free delivery in Manhattan.

*Moderate*                                            *Amex/MC/V*

**Upper East Side**                              **(212) 396-0563**
1375 Third Avenue                                 btw 78/79th St
NYC 10021                                    Mon-Sat 11-7, Sun 11-6

## ★ Forward                                            ♀

As in 'fashion-forward'. A combination workshop, show-room and retail space for emerging NYC designers, Forward offers handcrafted ballet slippers by La Voleuse, fun tropical print bags and clutches from Alyssa Graves, 'preppy and trashy' jersey shirts by Dina Magnes, and rockin' tops by Phyl Casual Couture. This is the fifth group of young designers the space has sponsored since opening last spring—the inventory changes with each new group, so get what you can while you can.          *forwardnyc.com*

*Expensive*                                           *Amex/MC/V*

**Nolita**                                       **(646) 264-3233**
72 Orchard Street                              btw Broome/Grand
NYC 10002                                                Daily 12-7

## Fossil                                            ♂ ♀

'The American classic, original and genuine,' the nearly 50-year-old Fossil trumpets from the window of this huge colorful store, the first to sell clothing and accessories from the company best known for its funky watches. As far as Fossil gear is concerned, think Quiksilver with a Fifties retro edge. There is a huge range of activewear, including walls of Hawaiian shirts, cheeky tees for the chicks and a signature jeans collection. Great for gifts are, of course, the watches, each one coming in a Fifties tin that the customer chooses.                                        *fossil.com*

*Moderate*                                            *Amex/MC/V*

**SoHo**                                         **(212) 274-9579**
541 Broadway                                   btw Prince/Spring
NYC 10012                                    Mon-Sat 10-9, Sun 11-7

**Flatiron**                 **(212) 243-7296**
103 Fifth Avenue             at 17th St
NYC 10003      Mon-Fri 9:30-8, Sat 9:30-7, Sun 11-7

**Midtown East**             **(212) 997-3978**
530 Fifth Avenue           btw 44/45th St
NYC 10036       Mon-Fri 9:30-8, Sat 10-7, Sun 11-5

## Francis Hendy

Trinidad-born Hendy started as a menswear designer and this is his first New York outpost. The 1,700-square-foot space houses his men's and women's collections, including luxury sportswear, bridge and denim lines. The decor is equally slick: steel and glass fixtures, abstract mirrors and muted lighting. Hendy has positioned himself as one of the industry's most innovative designers, working with silk, linen, wool and Ultrasuede. His efforts have paid off—Wyclef Jean, Missy Elliot, Britney Spears, DMX, Whitney Houston, R.Kelly, L.L.Cool J, and Sean 'Puffy' Combs have all been seen sporting his designs.    *francishendy.com*

*Expensive*                   *Amex/MC/V*

**SoHo**                  **(212) 431-1604**
65 Thompson Street       btw Spring/Broome
NYC 10012                Daily 11-7

## Frank Shattuck

Don't let the long ride in a cramped elevator to the penthouse floor keep you from a Frank Shattuck creation. Frank takes over where his mentor Henry Stewart, one of New York's most distinguished old-world tailors, left off. Each suit is handmade from start to finish, from construction and drafting to the final three-hour pressing process. The handiwork is well worth $4,500—expect to wear it for a lifetime.

*Luxury*                     *Amex/MC/V*

**Midtown East**             **(212) 636-9120**
250 West 57th Street (25th floor)      at Broadway
NYC 10017 (by appointment)

## Frank Stella

Since opening the original Columbus Avenue store in 1976, Frank Stella has been selling updated, no-nonsense classics that range from professional business suits to casual sportswear. He offers many prominent menswear names: Ben Sherman, Ted Baker, Alexander Julian, Tommy Bahama, Nat Nast and more.

*Affordable*                  *Amex/MC/V*

**Upper West Side**         **(212) 877-5566**
440 Columbus Avenue         at 81st St
NYC 10024          Mon-Sat 11-8, Sun 12-6

**Upper East Side**          **(212) 744-5662**
1326 Third Avenue         btw 75/76th St
NYC 10021     Mon-Fri 11-8, Sat 11-6, Sun 12-6

**Midtown**                **(212) 957-1600**
921 Seventh Avenue          at 58th St
NYC 10019     Mon-Fri 10-7, Sat 10-6, Sun 12-5

## Fratelli Rossetti

Italian icon Fratelli Rossetti began making shoes for cyclists and skaters half a century ago and later introduced the first brown loafer to the fashion world. His design mission statement: quality, elegance, comfort and practicality. The classic loafers and lace-ups are best suited for daytime wear. Prices run from $185 to $575 (for leather boots). You'll also find colorful leather bags, belts, and motorcycle jackets. *rossetti.it*

*Moderate*                                      *Amex/MC/V*

**Midtown East**                          **(212) 888-5107**
625 Madison Avenue                            at 58th St
NYC 10022                        Mon-Fri 10-6:30 (Thurs 10-7)
                                      Sat 10-6, Sun 12-5

## ★ Fred Leighton

Fancy a palm-sized rose made entirely of diamonds? Well, if it's 'rare collectible jewels' that you're in the market for, Fred Leighton is the place to be. Huge brooches, jumbo chokers, engagement rings bigger than Jupiter's moons—they're all here in Leighton's impossibly stately showroom, where the pieces are impeccably crafted, ornate in design, and guaranteed to engender envy in all those who lay eyes on them. You'll find Leighton's creations on the pages of fashion magazines (he's a fave of top fashion stylists), on the red carpet at movie premieres and, if you've got the money to spend, on your very lucky fingers and wrists. Bodyguards not included. *fredleighton.com*

*Luxury*                                        *Amex/MC/V*

**Upper East Side**                       **(212) 288-1872**
773 Madison Avenue                            at 66th St
NYC 10021   Mon-Sat 11:30-5 (closed Saturday in summer)

## French Connection

A British company known for sportswear geared toward an under-30 crowd—and for its controversial FCUK logo and advertising campaign. Think Banana Republic or Express with a British edge—suits, jeans, logo'd T-shirts, casualwear, plus accessories and a burgeoning beauty line. Colors lean toward the discreet rather than the adventurous. *frenchconnection.com*

*Moderate*                                      *Amex/MC/V*

**Midtown West**                          **(212) 262-6623**
1270 Sixth Avenue                             at 51st St
NYC 10020                  Mon-Fri 9-9, Sat 10-8, Sun 11-8

**NoHo**                                  **(212) 473-4699**
700 Broadway                       btw Astor Place/4th St
NYC 10003                         Mon-Sat 10-9, Sun 11-8

**SoHo**                                  **(212) 219-1197**
435 West Broadway                             at Prince
NYC 10012                   Sun-Thurs 10-9, Fri-Sat 10-10

## French Sole

If there is a season to shop at French Sole, it will be because flats are back. The store is the size of a rich woman's closet, crammed floor to ceiling with flats, indeed with any kind of flat you can imagine: silver, gold, croc-embossed, quilted, velvet, patent-leather, and ballet shoes. Many designs are the store's own brand, but you'll also see numbers from Delman, Bruno Magli, and Lauretta Reiss. Accessories include satin ribbon wristlets, beaded baguettes, plastic flip-flops and umbrellas. *frenchsoleshoes.com*

*Moderate*                                                  *Amex/MC/V*

**Upper East Side**                              **(212) 737-2859**
985 Lexington Avenue                             btw 71/72nd St
NYC 10021                                    Mon-Fri 10-7, Sat 11-6

## Frida's Closet

Frida Kahlo was a great artist and she doesn't make for a shabby fashion icon, either. Long Mexican peasant skirts, soft feminine blouses and tons of jewelry were signature looks that Kahlo used on canvas and in life, and designer/owner of Frida's Closet, Sandra Paez, is claiming the painter's fashion sensibility as her own. Paez's gorgeous dresses and blouses are custom-made right here in the boutique, and she imports jewelry and handbags direct from Mexico. *fridascloset.com*

*Moderate*                                                  *Amex/MC/V*

**Carroll Gardens**                              **(718) 855-0311**
296 Smith Street                              btw Union/Sackett
Brooklyn 11231                       Wed-Fri 1-8, Sat 11-8, Sun 12-6

## Furla

For less-is-more accessories head to Furla, where you will find the sleek lines, shiny materials, and classic sophistication that one expects from an Italian brand. Find chic, understated handbags designed with crisp, structured lines and minimal hardware. The stylish, minimalist look also characterizes Furla's belts, sunglasses, coin purses and wallets. Quality on par with Prada, but without the jet-setter price tags. *furla.it*

*Expensive*                                                 *Amex/MC/V*

**Upper East Side**                              **(212) 755-8986**
727 Madison Avenue                               btw 63/64th St
NYC 10021                                        Mon-Sat 10-6

## The Fur Salon @ Saks Fifth Avenue

Just what you would expect from the iconic department store—high quality designer furs that will last a lifetime. The Fur Salon provides both classic and trendy styles in fur coats, jackets and accessories. Service is also top-notch. End of the season sales are the time to pick up next year's luxury sable or mink.

*Expensive*                                                 *Amex/MC/V*

**Fifth Avenue**                **(212) 940-4465**
611 Fifth Avenue                          at 49th St
NYC 10022              Mon-Sat 10-7, Sun 12-6

## Gabay's Outlet

An East Village treasure, Gabay's offers high-end design-er fashions at steeply discounted prices. While shoes and handbags are the main attraction, fabulous designer duds can often be scored, too. A recent visit turned up Manolos, Christan Louboutin, Tod's and Chanel shoes with prices far below what these treads go for uptown. As with many outlets, the shopping here is often hit or miss, but those who love high style and good deal (and who doesn't?) check in regularly for new shipments. Excellent staff.                    *gabaysoutlet.com*

*Moderate*                          *Amex/MC/V*

**East Village**                **(212) 254-3180**
225 First Avenue                    btw 13/14th St
NYC 10003              Daily 10-7 (Sun 11-7)

## Gallery of Wearable Art

Although the term 'wearable art' may conjure up night-marish visions of hemp caftans, the one-of-a-kind goods at this boutique are of a decidedly more sumptuous nature. Popular with celebrities such as Whoopi Goldberg and Julie Taymore, the apparel features antique textiles and ornate embroidery. Housed in the ground floor of a brown-stone, the gallery is the perfect atmosphere in which to purchase a richly decorated 'art coat', costume jewelry, bridalwear, daywear, furs and accessories. Rare vintage finds and a new Wearable Art fragrance complete the eclectic offerings.        *galleryofwearableart.com*

*Expensive*                          *Amex/MC/V*

**Upper East Side**                **(212) 570-2252**
34 East 67th Street            btw Madison/Park Ave
NYC 10021                          Tues-Sat 10-6

## Galo

A veteran of Madison Avenue, established shoe label Galo offers a collection of loafers, flats, pumps, sandals and boots. For children (toddler to size 5) there are styles from casual and contemporary basics to dress-up. Prices range from moderate to expensive. The handbag selec-tion includes leather clutches, straw totes and shoulder bags.                          *galoshoes.com*

*Moderate to expensive*                  *Amex/MC/V*

**Upper East Side**                **(212) 288-3448**
1295 Third Avenue                    btw 74/75th St
NYC 10021    Mon-Fri 9:30-7, Sat 9:30-6, Sun 12:30-5:30

**Upper East Side**                **(212) 744-7936**
895 Madison Avenue                    at 72nd St
NYC 10021              (opening hours as above)

**Upper East Side**     **(212) 832-3922**
825 Lexington Avenue                at 63rd St
NYC 10021             (opening hours as above,
                   but closed Sundays in summer)

## Gamine

Walk into this jewel box of a boutique and be darn near over-stimulated by its ultra-feminine collection with an ethnic edge, from flirty daytime dresses by Nanette Lepore to informal eveningwear made up of sari prints, beading and embroidery. Fabulous handbags and colored stone jewelry complete the collection.

*Moderate*                    *Amex/MC/V*

**Upper East Side**     **(212) 472-6918**
1322 Third Avenue            btw 75/76th St
NYC 10021       Mon-Fri 11-8, Sat 11-7, Sun 12-6

## Gant

Gant has traditionally specialized in men's and boys' classic American sportswear. Three floors are devoted to casual basics in categories called 'Ivy University', 'Navigator', 'Key West', 'Park Avenue', 'Adventure' and 'Sport'. Check out jeans, khakis, fleece outfits, rugby shirts, sweatpants, knits, outerwear and polo shirts in all colors. Fleece outerwear is a best bet. A women's line was about to be introduced at the Fifth Avenue store as went to press and will feature rugby sweaters, twinsets, trench coats and flared skirts.                    *gant.com*

*Moderate*                    *Amex/MC/V*

**Fifth Avenue**     **(212) 813-9170**
645 Fifth Avenue            btw 51/52nd St
NYC 10022       Mon-Sat 10-7 (Thurs 10-8), Sun 11-7

**SoHo (M)**     **(212) 431-9610**
77 Wooster Street          btw Spring/Broome
NYC 10012       Mon-Sat 11-7, Sun 12-6

## Gap

While its fashion can be hit-and-miss, Gap remains the source of super staples for everyone, not to mention the unbelievable sales. Fit yourself out with casual weekendwear like khakis for the professional, cool denims and cute T-shirts for twentysomethings and a complete uniform for teenagers. Choose from racks and racks of jeans—from dark to dirty denim—shirts, sweaters, T-shirts, belts and accessories (which have gotten better thanks to former Marc Jacobs designer Emma Hill), all at some of the best prices in town. The GapBody collection features intimates and sleepwear, as well as bath and body products. Try out Gap's new stress-free khakis for men and women which are wrinkle and spill resistant—apparently, they're able to repel coffee, food and oil stains.     800-427-7895  *gap.com*

*Affordable*                    *Amex/MC/V*

**Upper East Side** (212) 794-5781
1511 Third Avenue at 85th St
NYC 10028 Mon-Sat 9-9, Sun 10-8

**Upper East Side** (212) 879-9144
1066 Lexington Avenue at 75th St
NYC 10021 Mon-Fri 10-8, Sat 10-7, Sun 11-6

**Upper East Side** (212) 472-4555
1131-1149 Third Avenue at 66th St
NYC 10021 Mon-Sat 10-8, Sun 11-7

**Upper West Side** (212) 873-1244
2373 Broadway at 86th St
NYC 10024 Mon-Sat 10-9, Sun 11-8

**Upper West Side** (212) 873-9272
335 Columbus Avenue at 76th St
NYC 10023 Mon-Sat 10-8, Sun 11-7

**Upper West Side** (212) 721-5304
1988 Broadway at 67th St
NYC 10023 Mon-Thurs 10-9, Fri-Sat 10-10, Sun 11-8

**Midtown East** (212) 751-1543
734 Lexington Avenue btw 58/59th St
NYC 10022 Mon-Fri 8-9, Sat 10-8, Sun 11-6

**Midtown East** (212) 697-3590
657 Third Avenue at 42nd St
NYC 10017 Mon-Fri 8-9, Sat 10-8, Sun 11-6

**Midtown East** (212) 754-2290
900 Third Avenue at 54th St
NYC 10022 Mon-Sat 9-8, Sun 11-5

**Midtown West** (212) 956-3142
250 West 57th Street btw Broadway/Eighth Ave
NYC 10019 Mon-Thurs 8:30-8:30, Fri 8:30-9
Sat 10-8, Sun 11-7

**Midtown West** (212) 764-0285
1212 Sixth Avenue btw 47/48th St
NYC 10036 Mon-Fri 8-9, Sat 10-8, Sun 11-7

**Midtown West** (212) 382-4500
1466 Broadway at 42nd St
NYC 10036 Mon- Fri 9-9, Sat 10-9, Sun 11-8

**Midtown West** (212) 760-1268
60 West 34th Street at Broadway
NYC 10001 Mon-Fri 9-9:30, Sat 10-9:30, Sun 11-8

**Fifth Avenue** (212) 977-7023
680 Fifth Avenue at 54th St
NYC 10019 Mon-Sat 11-8, Sun 10-7

**Flatiron** (917) 408-5580
122 Fifth Avenue at 18th St
NYC 10011 Mon-Fri 10-9, Sat 10-8, Sun 11-7

**East Village (M)** (212) 674-1877
750 Broadway at 8th St
NYC 10003 Mon-Sat 10-9, Sun 11-8

**East Village (W)** (212) 253-0145
1 Astor Place at Broadway
NYC 10003 Mon-Sat 10-9, Sun 11-8

## Gap Kids & Baby Gap ♦

The ultimate destination for moderately priced—and just trendy enough—children's jeans, T-shirts, overalls, shirts, pants, sweatshirts, sweaters, dresses, pajamas, shoes and accessories. From outdoor play clothes to back-to-school basics, Gap has it all, with great prices and some of the cutest designs around. From newborn to 13 years. *gap.com*

*Affordable*                                          *Amex/MC/V*

**Upper East Side (K/B)**                        **(212) 423-0033**
1535 Third Avenue                                    at 87th St
NYC 10028                              Mon-Sat 9-9, Sun 10-8

**Upper East Side (B)**                          **(212) 327-2614**
1037 Lexington Avenue                                at 74th St
NYC 10021                  Mon-Fri 10-8, Sat 10-7, Sun 11-6

**Upper East Side (B)**                          **(212) 472-4555**
1131-49 Third Avenue                                 at 66th St
NYC 10021                             Mon-Sat 10-8, Sun 11-7

**Upper West Side (K)**                          **(212) 873-2044**
2300 Broadway                                        at 83rd St
NYC 10024                             Mon-Sat 10-9, Sun 11-8

**Upper West Side (K)**                          **(212) 721-5119**
1988 Broadway                                        at 67th St
NYC 10023          Mon-Thurs 10-9, Fri-Sat 10-10, Sun 11-8

**Upper West Side (B)**                          **(212) 875-9196**
341 Columbus Avenue                                  at 76th St
NYC 10023                             Mon-Sat 10-8, Sun 11-6

**Midtown East (K)**                             **(212) 980-2570**
545 Madison Avenue                                   at 55th St
NYC 10022                   Mon-Fri 9-8, Sat 10-8, Sun 11-6

**Midtown East (K)**                             **(212) 697-3590**
657 Third Avenue                                     at 42nd St
NYC 10017                   Mon-Fri 8-9, Sat 10-8, Sun 11-6

**Midtown West (K)**                             **(212) 315-2250**
250 West 57th Street                     btw Broadway/Eighth Ave
NYC 10019                 Mon-Thurs 8:30-8:30, Fri 8:30-9
                                         Sat 10-8, Sun 11-7

**Midtown West (K/B)**                           **(212) 302-1266**
1466 Broadway                                        at 42nd St
NYC 10036    Mon-Wed, Sat 9-9, Thurs 9-9:30, Fri 9-10
                                                     Sun 11-8

**Midtown West (K)**                             **(212) 764-0285**
1212 Sixth Avenue                              btw 47/48th St
NYC 10036                   Mon-Fri 8-9, Sat 10-8, Sun 11-7

**Midtown West (K/B)**                           **(212) 760-1268**
60 West 34th Street                                  at Broadway
NYC 10001         Mon-Fri 9-9:30, Sat 10-9:30, Sun 11-8

**Fifth Avenue (K/B)**                           **(212) 977-7023**
680 Fifth Avenue                                     at 54th St
NYC 10019                   Mon-Fri 10-8, Sat 9-8, Sun 11-7

**Flatiron (K/B)**                               **(917) 408-5580**
122 Fifth Avenue                                     at 18th St
NYC 10011                   Mon-Fri 10-9, Sat 10-8, Sun 11-7

**West Village (K/B)**     **(212) 777-2420**
354 Sixth Avenue     at Washington Place
NYC 10011     Mon-Sat 10-7:30, Sun 11-7

**Lower Manhattan/Tribeca**     **(212) 374-1051**
11 Fulton Street     at John
NYC 10038     Daily 10-9 (Sun 10-8)

## Garde Robe

No walk-in-closet, you say? Space is hard to come by in New York City, but Garde Robe is here to help. This sophisticated service dry-cleans and stores your precious, out-of-season or occasional pieces in their climate-controlled, high-security facility. Don't fear: this is no ordinary storage locker—Garde Robe will photograph each piece so you can view your closet online and request same-day delivery of any one piece, any given day. And if you're lucky enough to have plenty of hanger-space at home, Garde Robe can organize your closet, provide personal shopping and tailoring services, and even help you pack for a trip. Fees start at $225 a month.     *garderobeonline.com*

*Expensive*     *Amex/MC/V*

**Tribeca**     **(212) 227-7554**
137 Duane Street     btw West Broadway/Trimble Place
NYC 10013     (by appointment)

## ★ Gas Bijoux

Fashion girls have been known to make cooing noises while looking in the window of this divine jewelry store in Nolita. The handmade pieces imported from the South of France perfectly mix bohemia with cool—check out how the sales staff dress down their intricately beaded earrings with slouchy jeans and T-shirts. Too-chic-to-speak, and not ridiculously expensive either.

*Moderate to expensive*     *Amex/MC/V*

**Nolita**     **(212) 334-7290**
238 Mott Street     btw Prince/Spring
NYC 10012     Daily 12-8 (Sun 12-7)

## G.C.William

This hip boutique keeps Manhattan's younger uptown crowd outfitted with downtown styles from brands like Puma, Miss Sixty and Juicy Couture. Find great tees from James Perse and Petit Bateau, as well as the de rigueur denim selection.

*Expensive*     *Amex/MC/V*

**Upper East Side**     **(212) 396-3400**
1137 Madison Avenue     btw 84/85th St
NYC 10029     Daily 10-6:30
    (sometimes closed on Sundays)

## Geiger

This established Austrian label is famous for its boiled-wool outerwear. Their jackets and coats come in traditional Alpine colors with embossed silver buttons, their separates are knit with light linen and silk, and they also feature a line of classic sportswear. No burgher's wardrobe is complete without a Geiger jacket. While the store carries items for both *männer* and *frauen*, the men's collection isn't always on display, so be sure to ask if you don't see it. geiger-fashion.com

| *Expensive* | Amex/MC/V |
|---|---|
| **Midtown East** | **(212) 644-3435** |
| 505 Park Avenue | at 59th St |
| NYC 10022 | Mon-Sat 10-6 |

## Geminola

British interior designer Lorraine Kirke's new store will transport you back a century, and make you feel as if you're the belle of the ball. Kirke's West Village shop sells feminine pieces made from reworked and mostly re-dyed vintage and antique fabrics. The lace, silk, tulle and cotton numbers feature a distinctive mix of textures on dresses, tops, skirts, petticoats, slips, gowns, pjs, handbags, bedding, curtains and linens. The store spans a fascinating gap between 1800s decadence and 1950s prom dresses, all updated and redesigned for this year. Also find C+C Brazilian bathing suits, jewelry by Tom Binns and a host of other surprises too sweet to skip over. geminola.com

| *Expensive* | Amex/MC/V |
|---|---|
| **West Village** | **(212) 675-1994** |
| 41 Perry Street | btw Seventh Ave South/West 4th St |
| NYC 10014 | Tues-Wed 11:30-6, Thurs-Fri 11:30-7 |
| | Sat 12-7, Sun 12-6 |

## Geox

Geox is the shoe that breathes. Invented and styled in Italy, Geox has solved the problem of foot odor and exhaustion by creating a perforated rubber outsole containing a microporous membrane which lets sweat out without letting water in, meaning your dogs stay fresh and well insulated. Sound like something perfect for the kids? Check out children's pull-on sneakers and Geox jerseys and shorts. Adults can try laceless sneakers, sport sandals and women's dress shoes. geox.com

| *Moderate* | Amex/MC/V |
|---|---|
| **Midtown East** | **(212) 319-4243** |
| 595 Madison Avenue | at 5/th St |
| NYC 10022 | Mon-Fri 10-6, Sat 10-7, Sun 11-5 |

## Geraldine

This tiny shoe store gives new meaning to the word exclusive. Geraldine's range is small and ruthlessly edited, but nothing short of fabulous. They stock unusual cool looks from about 20 of the world's edgiest designers but never forget that a girl needs a good pair of party shoes, too. Gorgeous footwear from Michel Vivien, Chloé, Pierre Hardy and Veronique Branquinho sits alongside shiny, strappy numbers from Alessandro Dell'Acqua. Oh, they also stock Marc Jacobs, so if his store has sold out of your fave flats or precious pumps, rush on over here.

*Expensive* *Amex/MC/V*

**Nolita** **(212) 219-1620**
246 Mott Street btw Houston/Prince
NYC 10012 Mon-Sat 11:30-7:30, Sun 12-6

## Gerry's

An easy-access clothing store nestled amongst West Village restaurants, Gerry's carries a hip collection of menswear from American and European designers. A variety of Brit-style checked shirts by Ted Baker dominates the racks, and you'll also find sweatshirts by Blue Marlin, sweaters by Nicole Farhi, jeans by Armani, and other threads from Ben Sherman, Henry Cotton's and Masons. If you're feeling a little sportier, Gerry's is a fine spot for Fred Perry tracksuits as well as for cool sneakers by Puma and Camper.

*Expensive* *Amex/MC/V*

**West Village** **(212) 691-0636**
353 Bleecker Street btw West 10th/Charles
NYC 10014 Mon-Sat 11-8, Sun 12-6

**Chelsea** **(212) 243-9141**
110 Eighth Avenue btw 15/16th St
NYC 10011 Mon-Fri 11-8, Sat 11-9, Sun 12-6

**Chelsea (W)** **(212) 691-2188**
112 Eighth Avenue btw 15/16th St
NYC 10011 (opening hours as above)

## Gerry Cosby & Co

Pay attention, sports fans: Gerry Cosby & Co is a great source for pro-level equipment and clothing for your basketball, baseball, hockey and football needs. Shop here for NFL, NBA or NHL jerseys and souvenirs from your favorite team. *cosbysports.com*

*Affordable* *Amex/MC/V*

**Midtown West** **(212) 563-6464**
3 Penn Plaza at Madison Square Garden
NYC 10001 Mon-Fri 9:30-7:30, Sat 9:30-6, Sun 12-5

## Ghost

Float away into British designer Tanya Sarne's world. Ghost is best known for soft, loosely feminine designs in vibrant colors and manufactured in special crinkly rayons which are wrinkle-resistant and machine washable. Sarne's line of light, interchangeable clothing, which some devotees buy in bulk every season, is based on essential pieces like slip dresses, camis and pants that are always available in several colors. Watch for a new denim line and a sale rack (usually to be found to the far right of the store), offering steals at 30-70% off. *ghost.co.uk*

*Expensive* *Amex/MC/V*

**NoHo**        **(646) 602-2891**
28 Bond Street       btw Broadway/Lafayette
NYC 10012       Mon-Sat 11-7, Sun 12-6

# Ghurka

Classic, expertly handcrafted handbags, luggage and accessories perfect for your next African safari. Choose from the exotic Savanna collection of bags in alligator, zebra print or water buffalo—all trimmed with sterling silver accents—or the durable leather-trimmed twill travel bags and handbags (now in new colors such as yellow check and pastel canvas). Be sure to slip your feet into Ghurka's popular moccasins, too.     800-587-1584   ghurka.com

*Luxury*        *Amex/MC/V*

**Midtown East**       **(212) 826-8300**
41 East 57th Street       btw Madison/Park Ave
NYC 10022    Mon-Sat 10-6 (Thurs 10-7), Sun 12-6

# Gianfranco Ferré

Season after season this Italian designer celebrates his über-glam and high-drama muse: the supremely confident woman, unafraid to wear Ferré's deliberately sharp, structured pieces that walk a line between fashion and architecture (he was trained as the latter). Now she can luxuriate in his huge new flagship, where she'll find that Ferré is a master at mixing extremes: hard with soft, tough with feminine. He loves a corset, fur and angular jackets. He is best for sleek pinstriped suits, beautifully detailed blouses, leather pants, fur-lined biker jackets and coats. For evening, Ferré's siren (think Sharon Stone in full diva mode) will conquer all in a clingy cut-out jersey dress. For men, find a slick collection of suits and sportswear.     *gianfrancoferre.com*

*Expensive*        *Amex/MC/V*

**Upper East Side**       **(212) 717-5430**
870 Madison Avenue       btw 70/71st St
NYC 10021       Daily 10-6

# Gi Gi

Gi Gi is Girlie with a capital G. Its collection of sportswear pieces has a deliberately feminine edge, just like the pistachio-colored walls. There are lots of pretty prints, ruffles and flowy chiffons in dresses, blouses and skirts from such labels as Rebecca Beeson, Blue Cult, Myth & Ritual and its own Gi Gi line.

*Moderate*        *Amex/MC/V*

**Nolita**       **(212) 274-1570**
217 Mulberry Street       btw Prince/Spring
NYC 10012       Daily 12-7 (Sun 12-6)

# Giordano's

Women with small feet, rejoice. This store is devoted exclusively to otherwise hard-to-find shoe sizes 4 to 5½. The

great selection includes Charles Jourdan, Via Spiga and
Stuart Weitzman. *petiteshoes.com*

*Expensive* *Amex/MC/V*

**Upper East Side** **(212) 688-7195**
1150 Second Avenue btw 60/61st St
NYC 10021 Mon-Fri 11-7, Sat 11-6

## Giorgio Armani 🕴🏻👩

What else can you say about fashion maestro Giorgio
Armani, who for 30 years has defined understated elegance—dressing everyone who matters in Hollywood from
Richard Gere in *American Gigolo* to Michelle Pfeiffer to
George Clooney and Brad Pitt and Jodie Foster for everything. Armani's pioneering approach to design is a synthe-
sis of opposites: feminine/masculine, simple/complex,
refined/sporty. Women can entrust their femininity to his
well-tailored suits and sculpted jackets. Eveningwear
includes backless dresses, beautiful beaded numbers and
stunning jackets. Armani's menswear—sleek suits, relaxed
jackets, shirts and knee-length coats—is the epitome of
urban modernism. If you're playing dress-up, indulge in
one of his tuxedos as megawatt celebrities do on Oscar
night. *giorgioarmani.com*

*Luxury* *Amex/MC/V*

**Upper East Side** **(212) 988-9191**
760 Madison Avenue at 65th St
NYC 10021 Mon-Sat 10-6 (Thurs 10-7)

## Giraudon 🕴🏻👩

Giraudon's footwear is fit for everyone who digs a chunky
rubber sole. Two lines designed by Alain Guy Giraudon feature everything from rugged boots and sporty loafers with
lug soles to leather-soled dressy lace-ups and slip-ons.
800-278-1552 *giraudonnewyork.com*

*Moderate* *MC/V*

**Chelsea** **(212) 633-0999**
152 Eighth Avenue btw 17/18th St
NYC 10011 Mon-Sat 11:30-11, Sun 1-7

## Girlprops.com 👩

Although the SoHo branch of this shop is below street
level, its zebra-striped interior sucks you right into this 'inexpensive—we never say cheap' (the motto on the canopy
entrance) accessory shop. It's packed to the rafters with an
over-stimulating collection of camouflage belts, rhinestone
jewelry, leather spiked bracelets, handbags, tiaras, sunglasses, beaded bracelets, turquoise and coral jewelry, dangly earrings, purple wigs and boas, all fabulously affordable
and disposable. *girlprops.com*

*Affordable* *Amex/MC/V*

**East Village** **(212) 533-3159**
33 East 8th Street btw Broadway/University Place
NYC 10003 Sun-Thurs 12-8, Fri-Sat 12-9

**SoHo** **(212) 505-7615**
153 Prince Street at West Broadway
NYC 10013 Sun-Thurs 10-9, Fri-Sat 10-11

## Giselle

Please adjust your chronometers, ladies, you are now entering a time warp. Giselle caters to a mature, conservative customer in search of no-nonsense work suits, blouses, sportswear and coordinating accessories, all at 20% below retail. Labels include Bianca, Miss V (Valentino) and Ferré Studio in sizes 4-20. Free shipping.  gisellenewyork.com

*Moderate to expensive* Amex/MC/V

**Lower East Side** **(212) 673-1900**
143 Orchard Street btw Delancey/Rivington
NYC 10002 Sun-Thurs 9-6, Fri 9-4

## Giuseppe Zanotti Design

Giuseppe Zanotti is best known for his jewel-encrusted, high-heeled sandals and stilettos that often feature embroidery, jewel and stone embellishments—which, all up, equals very sexy shoes. The look-at-me designs include closed-toe pumps with mother-of-pearl heels; thigh-high, super-pointy stiletto boots in embroidered leather with encrusted rubies; two- and three-band open-toed flirty sandals, and classic crocodile pumps and slingbacks. Prices run from $285 to $1,300.  giuseppe-zanotti-design.com

*Expensive* Amex/MC/V

**Upper East Side** **(212) 650-0455**
806 Madison Avenue btw 67/68th St
NYC 10021 Mon-Sat 10-6

## Givenchy

The house that Audrey Hepburn built has undergone some renovations, but Givenchy still is the place to go for sleek sophistication. Designer Julien Macdonald has been providing ultra-feminine looks with plenty of wool, silk and tweed, all of which nestle comfortably alongside updated *Breakfast at Tiffany's* icons like the classic belted trench and a dizzying number of variations on the little black dress, many of which catch the light with embedded crystal.  givenchy.com

*Luxury* Amex/MC/V

**Upper East Side** **(212) 688-4338**
710 Madison Avenue at 63rd St
NYC 10021 Daily 10-6 (Thurs 10-7)

## Goffredo Fantini

Goffredo Fantini is a fresco painter turned cobbler (no, we didn't make this up—he's a multi-tasker) and has invented the Fressura, a space-age shoe with a permanent (read: indestructible) sole and changeable elastic tops. You need to see it to believe it. Also, a small collection of urban, chunky heeled shoes. Good for teens.  gfantinishoes.com

*Moderate*                                                      MC/V
**Nolita**                                          **(212) 219-1501**
248 Elizabeth Street                             btw Houston/Prince
NYC 10012                                                 Daily 12-8

## The Good, The Bad and The Ugly

Skateboarding, music, graffiti, hip-hop, art, the can-can…
all are inspirations for designer Judi Rosen, the owner of
this fun, East Village-cute shop. As with all the cool stores
these days, Rosen is inspired by vintage; her quirky
pieces cover the gamut from bright-colored dresses
(she's a brights fanatic) to sweatshirts to adjustable
garters. Basically, the downtown girl can find it all here.
That and the rainbow striped legwarmers she always
wanted…                                  *goodbaduglynewyorkcity.com*

*Moderate*                                               Amex/MC/V
**East Village**                                    **(212) 473-3769**
437 East 9th Street                             btw First/Avenue A
NYC 10002                                                 Daily 1-9

## The Gown Company

Any bride feeling a bit overwhelmed should make The
Gown Company her first and only stop. Find dresses for the
big day from a range of top American and European
designers, such as Lazaro, Peter Langner and Amy
Michelson. Or, save big in the store's sample room, which
sells discontinued styles and excess inventory from those
same top designers at prices from $1,000 to $1,800. Find
accessories in the branch across the street, and ask about
the Gown Co's couture services, custom tailoring, alterations and full-service specialty dry cleaning. The personal
attention is consistent throughout the store, and the
relaxed atmosphere will put anyone with wedding-day jitters at ease.                                      *thegowncompany.com*

*Expensive*                                              Amex/MC/V
**East Village**                                    **(212) 979-9000**
312 East 9th Street                             btw First/Second Ave
NYC 10003                                               Tues-Sat 12-7

## Granny-Made

This shop specializes in handknits from Italy, England and
the U.S. Mothers can choose from a cute-as-pie collection of children's novelty sweaters featuring appliqués,
sweet embroideries, animals and floral motifs. For adults,
there is a similar selection by labels like Christine
Foley, Roni Bis, White and Warren, Susan Bristol and
English Weather. Accessories include socks, hats and
scarves.                                             *granny-made.com*

*Moderate*                                               Amex/MC/V
**Upper West Side**                                 **(212) 496-1222**
381 Amsterdam Avenue                                btw 78/79th St
NYC 10024              Mon-Fri 10:30-7, Sat 10-6, Sun 12-5

## Great Feet
Fashionable feet for kids, featuring brands like Converse, Naturalino, Stride Rite, Elefanten and Primigi. From cute to hipster, any youngster would look ready for recess in these shoes. Sizes range from newborn to 6. *striderite.com*

*Affordable*                                                    *Amex/MC/V*

**Upper East Side**                                    **(212) 249-0551**
1241 Lexington Avenue                                    at 84th St
NYC 10029     Mon-Sat 9:30-6 (Thurs-Fri 9:30-8), Sun 11-5

## Greenstones & Cie
Outfitting children from baby-bottle to lunchbox, Greenstones offer both posh and practical European and American children clothing for fashion-forward kids ages 0-12. In additional to their tiny threads from designers such as Petit Bateau, Jean Bourget and Deux par Deux, Greenstones also carry a large selection of shoes for every occasion, including the Upper West Side favorite and oh-so-cute Kidadorable rain galoshes, ribbons and hair ties galore.

*Moderate to expensive*                                *Amex/MC/V*

**Upper West Side**                                    **(212) 580-4322**
442 Columbus Avenue                                    btw 81/82nd St
NYC 10024                                    Mon-Sat 10-7, Sun 12-6

**Upper East Side**                                    **(212) 427-1665**
1184 Madison Avenue                                    btw 86/87th St
NYC 10128                                    Mon-Sat 10-6:30, Sun 12-5

## ★ Gucci

Shoppers should keep an eye on this space to see what happens now that Tom Ford, long-time creative director of Gucci, has left the company. Snatch up the fall 04/05 pieces—lots of fur-trimmed eveningwear with exquisite details—which are quickly becoming collectors' items. Only Pilates-honed physiques need shop here among the store's hard angles, low benches, chrome and ubiquitous mirrors (all the better for checking yourself out). The looks may be severe, but the ambiance is top-notch, with private dressing-rooms and champagne service. For the logo hounds, please note that double G everything—fragrances, jewelry, bags—is available here. *gucci.com*

*Luxury*                                                    *Amex/MC/V*

**Upper East Side**                                    **(212) 717-2619**
840 Madison Avenue                                    btw 69/70th St
NYC 10021             Mon-Sat 10-6 (Thurs 10-7), Sun 12-5

**Midtown East**                                    **(212) 826-2600**
685 Fifth Avenue                                    at 54th St
NYC 10022                            Mon-Wed, Fri 10-6:30
                                    Thurs-Sat 10-7, Sun 12-6

## Guess?

The store that made Anna Nicole famous (the first time) could probably use a comeback of its own. The label churns out trendy clothes, but still at the slightly inflated prices that evoke the brand's salad days. Still, it's a fine source for flirty casual clothes: fashion jeans, khakis, shirts, T-shirts, outerwear and shoes. Accessories include wallets, watches and sunglasses trademarked with the visible Guess? logo.  *guess.com*

*Moderate*  *Amex/MC/V*

**SoHo**  **(212) 226-9545**
537 Broadway  btw Prince/Spring
NYC 10012  Mon-Sat 10-9, Sun 11-7

**Lower Manhattan**  **(212) 385-0533**
23 Fulton Street  at South Street Seaport
NYC 10038  Mon-Sat 10-9, Sun 11-8

## Gureje

Hailing from Nigeria, Jimi Gureje brings a stylish African sensibility to Brooklyn. Combining African tailoring and tie-dye techniques, Gureje's long denim and cotton dresses for women are natural and cool, while his button-down shirt/jackets for men have a pleasant retro feel. Sexy, comfortable clothes with cross-cultural appeal.  *gureje.com*

*Moderate*  *Amex/MC/V*

**Clinton Hill**  **(718) 857-2522**
886 Pacific Street  at Washington
Brooklyn 11238  Mon-Fri 12-7, Sat 11-8, Sun 11-7

## Gymboree

Gymboree is so big that they offer their own Visa. The store sells great kids' clothes like raglan sweaters, French-inspired outfits complete with berets, and motocross tees for boys. Affordable prices in fun categories from newborn to 'kid boy/girl', plus gifts and toys.  *gymboree.com*

*Affordable*  *Amex/MC/V*

**Upper East Side**  **(212) 717-6702**
1120 Madison Avenue  btw 83/84th St
NYC 10028  Mon-Fri 10-7, Sat 10-6, Sun 12-5

**Upper East Side**  **(212) 517-5548**
1332 Third Avenue  at 76th St
NYC 10021  Mon-Sat 10-7, Sun 11-6

**Upper East Side**  **(212) 688-4044**
1049 Third Avenue  at 62nd St
NYC 10021  Mon-Sat 10-7, Sun 11-6

**Upper West Side**  **(212) 595-9071**
2271 Broadway  btw 81/82nd St
NYC 10024  Mon-Fri 10-9, Sat 10-8, Sun 11-6

**Upper West Side**  **(212) 595-7662**
2015 Broadway  at 69th St
NYC 10023  Mon-Fri 10-8, Sat 10-7, Sun 11-6

## Hable Construction

This jaunty textile company is named after Katharine and Susan Hable's grandfather's road construction business, and their accessories are indeed more than roadworthy. Aiming to 'fuse fabric, art and utility,' their collection of signature print fabrics is turned into colorful canvas totes and baskets, while exaggerated floral designs appear on indispensable shoe bags and cute shoe inserts—perfect for keeping your Jimmy Choos in tip-top order. A great gift stop.

*Moderate*                                            *Amex/MC/V*

**Nolita**                                      **(212) 343-8504**
230 Elizabeth Street                        btw Prince/Houston
NYC 10012                              Mon-Sat 9:30-6, Sun 12-6

## H&M (Hennes & Mauritz)

First things first: H&M rules. This rapidly expanding Swedish retailer continues to break land-speed records by turning out trendy clothes (with many items taking their cues straight from the catwalk) at incredibly low prices. Shop their 35,000-square-foot store on Fifth Avenue and be wowed by the constantly changing inventory. Coats and clubby tops and inexpensive swimwear are H&M's stock in trade. The clothes aren't built to last but at these prices, who cares? Look for kids' clothes (they'll grow out of them soon anyway), at the Broadway and Seventh Avenue locations.                                              *hm.com*

*Affordable*                                          *Amex/MC/V*

**Fifth Avenue**                                **(212) 489-0390**
640 Fifth Avenue                                      at 51st St
NYC 10019                      Mon-Fri 10-8, Sat 10-9, Sun 11-7

**Midtown West**                                **(646) 473-1165**
1328 Broadway                                        at 34th St
NYC 10001                             Mon-Sat 10-9, Sun 11-8

**SoHo**                                        **(212) 343-2722**
588 Broadway                                  btw Prince/Spring
NYC 10012                             (opening hours as above)

**Harlem**                                      **(212) 665-8300**
125 West 125th Street                              at Lenox Ave
NYC 10027                             Mon-Sat 10-8, Sun 11-7

**Midtown West**                                **(212) 643-6955**
435 Seventh Avenue                               at 34th Street
NYC 10001                             Mon-Sat 10-9, Sun 11-8

## Han Feng

Since 1989 when she produced the first of her now-signature pleated scarves, Chinese designer Han Feng has been creating an avant-garde line influenced by the traditional clothes of her homeland. Working mostly in silk, Feng's billowy pants and blouses and hand-embroidered slippers and bags with bamboo hardware accents mix a modern sensibility with eastern elegance.          *hanfeng.com*

*Moderate to expensive*                              *Amex/MC/V*

**Chelsea**                                     **(212) 675-1749**
174 Ninth Avenue                                 btw 20/21st St
NYC 10011                             Mon-Sat 12-8, Sun 11-7

## Handmade NYC
As the name would have it, you'll find handmade personal and home accessories in this lovely small store. Beautiful jewelry by Erica Rosenfeld, Maya Brenner and Kristina Larson (to name a few) mesmerizes, while home accessories like ceramics, hand-blown glass pieces, pillows, bowls and wall hangings will provoke many an 'ooh' and 'aah'. Special orders are available, although chances are you will find the perfect something for yourself the first time stick your head in for a visit. *handmadenyc.com*

*Expensive*                                             *Amex/MC/V*

**West Village**                              **(212) 924-6410**
150 West 10th Street          btw Greenwich/Seventh Ave
NYC 10014                              Mon-Fri 12-8, Sat-Sun 11-7

## Hans Koch
Koch's passion for color drives all his designs in hand-crafted, one-of-a-kind belts, handbags and jewelry. Belts are simple and versatile. His handbag styles, all of which are classic looking, but different, range from soft to constructed.

*Moderate*                                             *Amex/MC/V*

**SoHo**                                       **(212) 226-5385**
174 Prince Street                     btw Sullivan/Thompson
NYC 10012               Mon-Thurs 12-8, Fri-Sat 12-9, Sun 1-8

## Harry Rothman's
A great source for well-priced men's clothing, Rothman's offers discounts of 20-40% on brand names like Canali, Joseph Abboud, Ben Sherman, Kenneth Cole and Hugo Boss. Also find a selection of shirts, ties, underwear, sport jackets, outerwear and shoes. *rothmansny.com*

*Affordable*                                           *Amex/MC/V*

**Flatiron**                                   **(212) 777-7400**
200 Park Avenue South                              at 17th St
NYC 10003                         Mon-Fri 10-7 (Thurs 10-8)
                                          Sat 9:30-6, Sun 12-5:30

## Harry's Shoes
On any given weekend day Harry's is abuzz with families who appreciate the store's enormous selection and full-service approach to shoe buying. While this isn't the spot for sexy stilettos or thigh-high leather boots, Harry's has just about everything else, including sensible styles by Clarks, Rockport and Birkenstock, kids' shoes by Stride Rite and Elefanten, athletic shoes by Puma and New Balance and men's dress shoes by Johnston & Murphy, Cole Haan and Bruno Magli. Those in need of larger or wider sizes will be especially pleased with the extensive offerings available here. *harrys-shoes.com*

*Moderate*                                             *Amex/MC/V*

**Upper West Side**            **(212) 874-2035**
2299 Broadway                    at 83rd St
NYC 10024     Mon, Fri, Sat 10-6:45, Tues-Wed 10:30-6:45
                                 Thurs 10-8, Sun 12-5:30

## ★ Harry Winston                              ♂ ♀

Gems that shine like the sun are the norm at jeweler-to-the-stars (he's dressed more Oscar winners, presenters and nominees than anyone else, ever) Harry Winston's midtown emporium. Once you pass through the heavy iron gates at this Fifth Avenue palace, you'll swoon at the sight of flawlessly cut diamonds, rubies and emeralds adorning watches, rings, tiaras, cufflinks and earrings. If you think you have what it takes to accessorize like Faye Dunaway, Sting, Gwen Stefani, Helena Christensen or any other celeb worth their weight in bling, be prepared to pay half a million dollars for the privilege. Looking like red-carpet royalty comes at a price.                          *harrywinston.com*

*Luxury*                                 *Amex/MC/V*

**Fifth Avenue**                  **(212) 245-2000**
718 Fifth Avenue                     at 56th St
NYC 10019                 Mon-Fri 10-6, Sat 10-5

## The Hat Shop                              ♂ ♀

Enter this tiny milliner and check out up to 30 talented New York designers, including Brenda Lynn, Eric Javits, Jennifer Hoertz and Jennifer Ouellette. Owner Linda Pagan will help you pick out the perfect hat to match your personal style or any occasion. This whimsical world of toppers guarantees the perfect fit for every head and is pretty much a one-stop shop for styles from classic straw boaters to wide-brimmed show-stoppers.                         *thehatshop.com*

*Moderate*                               *Amex/MC/V*

**SoHo**                          **(212) 219-1445**
120 Thompson Street              btw Prince/Spring
NYC 10012                     Daily 12-7 (Sun 1-6)

## Helene Arpels                                 ♀

For over 50 years Helene Arpels has been keeping her loyal, well-heeled customers happy with her unique footwear collection. Her clientele includes royalty and socialites from all over the world, who come for her pumps, loafers, slippers, ornate evening shoes and custom jewelry. The prices are fit for a queen, too—a pair of loafers sells for $595. And for those of us not manor-born, well, we can always look...

*Luxury*                                 *Amex/MC/V*

**Midtown East**                  **(212) 755-1623**
470 Park Avenue                   btw 57/58th St
NYC 10022                      Mon-Sat 10-6:30
                          (closed Saturdays in summer)

## ★ Helen Mariën                                ♀

The fabulously chic bags at Helen Mariën are displayed as works of art, and it suits them. Mariën creates each bag by hand, mostly from lamb, silk and Ultrasuede. Choose from a variety of materials, designs, and 'flavors'. Names for her signature handbags include the Sunday Brunch tote or the Saturday on the Subway shopper. Accessories include belts and jewelry, featuring neckline-adjustable necklaces with magnetic clasps. Modern designs, and superior quality and craftsmanship, set this label apart from the rest. *helenmarien.com*

*Expensive*                                          *Amex/MC/V*

**Nolita**                                  **(212) 680-1911**
250 Mott Street                          btw Prince/Houston
NYC 10012                              Daily 11-7 (Sun 11-6:30)

## Helen Yarmak

After wrapping Russians in sable and chinchilla, this theo-retical-mathematician-turned-fur-designer now dresses celebrity clients like Melanie Griffith and Goldie Hawn. Yarmak's trademarks are her unique pelt processing, which leaves her furs virtually weightless. Find over 350 different pieces, including a line of reversibles, a one-size-fits-all col-lection (there's regular sizing, too) and a kneaded line for the softest possible feel. You'll find mink, fox, rabbit, chin-chilla and, of course, sable—available for a bargain $49,000 and up. Accessories include knit fox scarves, decadent fur-lined handbags and jewelry. *helenyarmak.com*

*Luxury*                                              *Amex/MC/V*

**Fifth Avenue**                            **(212) 245-0777**
730 Fifth Avenue (18th floor)              btw 56/57th St
NYC 10019                                  (by appointment)

## Hello Sari

Find the best in authentic Indian and Pakistani apparel, from beaded and embroidered dresses to cashmere shawls, scarves, saris, mirrored sandals and embroidered shoes. Pair these items with what's already in your wardrobe for a fresh, idiosyncratic look that will have others asking 'Where did you find that?' Best bet: the shalwar kameez, a Pakistani open-front dress with side slits worn over pants (popularized by Jemima Khan).

*Moderate*                                          *Amex/MC/V*

**Lower East Side**                         **(212) 274-0791**
261 Broome Street                        btw Allen/Orchard
NYC 10002                          Daily 12-6 (and by appointment)

## Helmut Lang

From sexy stirrup shirts to nipple-exposing tank tops (for men—no 'wardrobe malfunction' here, ladies), the influen-tial Helmut Lang continues to turn out edgy-looking clothes that boast remarkable tailoring, secretly sensual shapes and hidden luxuries like fur and beading. Find a ready-to-wear collection of his classic-cool trouser suits (unbeatable), shirts, tops, shearlings and beautifully cut coats, all naturally luxe in wools, cashmeres, thick silks and leathers. The minimalist concrete store effectively accents Lang's sober color palettes and clean lines. Check out the cult jeans and slick accessories—and then head across the street to his perfumery to have a complete Helmut Lang conversion. *helmutlang.com*

| | |
|---|---|
| *Luxury* | *Amex/MC/V* |
| **SoHo** | **(212) 925-7214** |
| 80 Greene Street | btw Spring/Broome |
| NYC 10012 | Daily 11-7 (Sunday 12-6) |

## Henri Bendel

Bendel's—fashion lovers use only the last name when addressing their favorite store—is prized by clothes-horses far and wide for its coolly eclectic inventory. One of the store's best features is its manageable size, which makes it perfect for a quick pop in or lunchtime visit. The cosmetics and accessories areas are compact and easy to get around, while the clothing departments are small, well edited and well staffed. Bendel's is the perfect spot to check out new dresses from Peter Som, Sophia Kokosolaki, Shoshanna and Luella Bartley; jeans by Paper Denim & Cloth and Earl; and designs by Lilly Pulitzer, Pout, Sue Wong, Rick Owens, Matthew Williamson and Anna Molinari. The sweater collection is so phenomenal that it warranted additional floor space. Bendel's also boasts a Street of Shops, exclusive in-store boutiques for Diane von Furstenberg, Catherine Malandrino, cult Seventies designer Stephen Burrows, Patricia Field, Agent Provocateur lingerie, Constanca Basto shoes, Flight 001 travel shop and Femme Gems design-your-own gemstone jewelry. Hats, hosiery, casualwear and outerwear departments round out the amazing assortment—while their activewear section (featuring Christy Turlington's Nuala label and Yohji Yamamoto's Y-3) is a hit with sporty types equally concerned with sweat and style. This is a department store that literally outfits you from head to toe—one of New York's top hair stylists, Garren, holds court on the third floor.

800-423-6335  *henribendel.com*

| | |
|---|---|
| *Expensive* | *Amex/MC/V* |
| **Fifth Avenue** | **(212) 247-1100** |
| 712 Fifth Avenue | at 56th St |
| NYC 10019 | Mon-Sat 10-7 (Thurs 10-8), Sun 12-6 |

## Henry Lehr

Henry Lehr carries a fabulous denim selection by the hottest labels in town: Juicy, Paper Denim & Cloth, Seven, Rogan and AG Jeans. Prices run from $97 to $220. The newly consolidated store also features T-shirts in an abundance of styles by Juicy Couture, Jet, Three Dots, Michael Stars, Great Wall of China, Christina Lear and others. A good source for basic, casual tops at reasonable prices. Other items include jean jackets, button-down shirts and hip belts.

*Moderate*   *Amex/MC/V*

**Nolita**   **(212) 274-9921**
11 Prince Street   btw Elizabeth/Bowery
NYC 10012   Daily 11-7

**Nolita (W)**   **(212) 343-0567**
268 Elizabeth Street   btw Prince/Houston
NYC 10012   Daily 11-7

## ★ Hermès   👫

Hermès is the first and last word in classic French accessories. Socialites, celebrities, and the merely very wealthy all flock to this five-story, 20,000-square-foot space to indulge in the brand's distinctive neckties, scarves, handbags, fragrances and leather goods. The lengthy waiting list for the iconic Kelly and Birkin bags seen dangling from many much-photographed arms is a testament to their timeless appeal—they may run $5,000, but they'll last forever. The clothing selection, designed by the deliberately obscure Martin Margiela, provides a world of luxury basics from chic shirts to unbelievably luxe cashmere sweaters. You'll drop a bundle for a slice of this thoroughbred luxury, but it's still a better bet than a punt at the races. *hermes.com*

*Luxury*   *Amex/MC/V*

**Upper East Side**   **(212) 751-3181**
691 Madison Avenue   at 62nd St
NYC 10021   Mon-Sat 10-6 (Thurs 10-7)

## Hervé Léger   👤

Shop in sexy style at Hervé Léger's New York store. On the first floor you'll find a lounge with a large sofa and chairs—the perfect spot for sipping champagne between fittings in the nicely appointed dressing-rooms. On the second level you'll goggle at Leger's famous 'bandage' wrap dresses, delicate silk jersey evening gowns and structured leather tops that leave little to the imagination. Working out certainly seems to be a requirement for wearing these clothes. Perfume, body lotions and shower gels are also available.

*Expensive*   *Amex/MC/V*

**Upper East Side**   **(212) 794-7124**
744 Madison Avenue   btw 64/65th St
NYC 10021   Mon-Sat 10-6, Sun 12-5

## H.Herzfeld   👤

Step in here and you'll find everything the well-heeled gentleman needs: tailored suits, shirts, neckwear, sweaters, sportswear, underwear, pajamas and accessories—all with a classic English flair. Also find shoes by Alden and quality hats. Although the suits are generally custom-made, you will also find a good selection off-the-rack. Hickey Freeman suits are priced from $1,000 to $2,000; custom starts at $2,500. Knowledgeable and courteous staff.

*Luxury*   *Amex/MC/V*

**Midtown East**         **(212) 753-6756**
118 East 57th Street         at Park Ave
NYC 10022         Mon-Sat 9-6

# Hickey Freeman

One of America's premier names in men's tailored clothing, Hickey has been clothing the great and the good for decades—from Colin Powell to numerous chief executives—and is conveniently located next to another iconic American clothier, Brooks Brothers. Suits, jackets and pants in luxurious fabrics and classic cuts are the Hickey Freeman trademark. A perfect place for a father to take his son for his first suit—they can bond over the Bobby Jones golf line.         hickeyfreeman.com

*Expensive*         *Amex/MC/V*

**Fifth Avenue**         **(212) 586-6481**
666 Fifth Avenue         btw 52/53rd St
NYC 10103         Mon-Sat 10-7, Sun 12-6

# Himalayan Crafts

A serene haven from neighborhood hustle and bustle, Himalayan Crafts has been purveying quality artisanal clothes and accessories since 1975. Dharma bums questing for authenticity will dig the trousers in rich silks and linen and the wine- and sea-colored wooly sweaters, slippers and coats. While they do stock plenty of low and moderately priced items, this is not the spot for cheap ethnic novelty— you'll have to go downtown for that.     himalayancrafts.com

*Moderate to expensive*         *Amex/MC/V*

**Upper West Side**         **(212) 787-8500**
2007 Broadway         btw 68/69th St
NYC 10023         Mon-Fri 11-7:30, Sat 11-7

# Hiponica

Hiponica accessorizes downtown hipsters and uptown girls with everything from fabulous handbags for summer to scarves and hats in winter. Japanese owner Jem Filippi is a design perfectionist, and her handbag line is fun, functional and notable for its out-there colors. Most items are unisex, so guys can share in the fun, too. Simple shapes in calfskin and nylon show off playful details like vintage fabrics for linings and leather trimmings. Other accessories include glass-trimmed leather wallets, amusing change purses and fancy fabric briefcases.         hiponica.com

*Moderate*         *Amex/MC/V*

**Nolita**         **(212) 966-4388**
238 Mott Street         btw Prince/Spring
NYC 10012         Daily 12-7

# Hogan

Tired of trudging around town in your battered Nikes? Head for Hogan, sister store to Tod's and the purveyor of a new breed of walking/comfort shoes. Peruse their spacious, minimalist store for rubber soles designed in fabulous solid colors or canvas—these sneakers are hip and edgy. Also check out their sporty, structured handbags in richly hued leather, canvas and suede. All the bags have been designed to be paired with the shoes.

*Moderate*                                                    *Amex/MC/V*

**SoHo**                                              **(212) 343-7905**
134 Spring Street                               btw Greene/Wooster
NYC 10012                                       Mon-Sat 11-7, Sun 12-6

## Hollywould

This shop conjures up a Fifties Hollywood cabana, what with its periwinkle-striped fabric and wicker poolside stools festooned with striped cushions. A fab collection of coordinating shoes and handbags offers looks like chocolate-brown pumps with matching suede shopper's totes. Hollywould's cabana collection includes a number of wicker-handled bags and an array of gorgeous ballet slippers in every color from bronze to electric blue.                     *ilovehollywould.com*

*Expensive*                                                   *Amex/MC/V*

**Nolita**                                           **(212) 343-8344**
198 Elizabeth Street                              btw Prince/Spring
NYC 10012                                       Mon-Sat 11:30-7:30

## Hoofbeats

A delightful miniature store, Hoofbeats has developed a notable following of admirers among au courant shoppers looking for not-so-common gifts. You'll find personalized hooded bath towels ($29), robes ($53), bibs ($25) and mobiles ($45). Small and sweet.

*Affordable*                                                  *Amex/MC/V*

**Upper East Side**                                   **(212) 517-2633**
232 East 78th Street                             btw Second/Third Ave
NYC 10021                                       Mon-Sat 11-6 (Thurs 11-7)

## Hootie Couture

Alison Houtte has been collecting vintage clothing for over 10 years, and her boutique is filled with yesteryear's inexpensive fashion finds. Look for classic floral print dresses or a vintage straw cowboy hat, or dare to wear a pastel lingerie gown as a sweet summer slip dress. New stock arrives daily, so there is always something to add to your wardrobe.

*Affordable*                                                        *MC/V*

**Park Slope**                                       **(718) 857-1977**
321 Flatbush Avenue                                         at 7th Ave
Brooklyn 11217                                  Tues-Sat 11-8, Sun 1-8

## Hotel Venus

Owned by cult stylist Patricia Field (of *Sex and the City* fame), Hotel Venus takes the same deliberately faddish approach as her eponymous downtown store. Shop a daring and colorful selection of vinyl bustiers, sheer fitted shirts, leather halter tops, microminis, hard-core rubberized patent-leather outfits, funky clubwear, boas, lingerie, shoes and accessories from labels like Clutch, Lip Service and, of course, Patricia Field. It's worth a trip just to experience the amusing sales staff. For the camp and fearless. *patriciafield.com*

*Moderate* — *Amex/MC/V*

**SoHo** — **(212) 966-4066**
382 West Broadway — btw Broome/Spring
NYC 10012 — Sun-Wed 11:30-8, Thurs-Sat 11:30-9

## ★ Hot Toddie

Looking for something to make your child stand out during recess? This family-owned children's clothier in Fort Greene stocks hip lines for toddlers such as Petit Bateau, Armani, Diesel and Dolce & Gabbana. Custom-made Rolling Stones and Pink Floyd tour shirts sized for the littlest of rockers are available, too. Hot Toddie hopes that youngsters can learn that it's never too early to be too cool for school. *hottoddieonline.com*

*Moderate* — *Amex/MC/V*

**Fort Greene** — **(718) 858-7292**
741 Fulton Street — btw South Portland/South Elliot
Brooklyn 11217 — Tues-Sat 11-6

## Housing Works

Pretty is as pretty does and no one does it more beautifully than Housing Works. Uptowners who lunch and Midtown hipsters with heart purge their wardrobes by dropping off last year's treasures and this season's impulse buys at one of these chock-a-block thrift shops (store credit for taxi receipts up to $10). Proceeds go toward helping homeless New Yorkers living with HIV and Aids, and the take from all those serendipitous Marc Jacobs and Diane von Furstenberg finds totals over $3m annually. Go early in the day and, if you're lucky enough, you may even spy some do-good designer over-stock. *housingworks.org*

*Affordable* — *Amex/MC/V*

**Upper West Side** — **(212) 579-7566**
306 Columbus Avenue — btw 74/75th St
NYC 10023 — Mon-Fri 11-7, Sat 10-6, Sun 12-5

**Upper East Side** — **(212) 772-8461**
202 East 77th Street — btw Second/Third Ave
NYC 10021 — (opening hours as above)

**Midtown East** — **(212) 529-5955**
157 East 23rd Street — btw Lexington/Third Ave
NYC 10010 — Mon-Sat 10-6, Sun 12-5

**Chelsea** — **(212) 366-0820**
143 West 17th Street — btw Sixth/Seventh Ave
NYC 10011 — (opening hours as above)

131

## Hugo Boss

Having already conquered Europe, this German label landed in New York with a massive four-floor, naturally lit store featuring clean, modern classics for him and her. Such a wealth of floorspace means plenty of room for menswear, accessories, bridge label Hugo and the fitted line Red Label. The Boss man will find a full selection of tailored suits, jackets, pants, shirts, classic trenches, ties, shoes and grooming products. He can also dress down in Boss Sport or play the game in Boss Golf. Boss woman will find a variety of looks, from ultra-tailored blazers and coats to shiny glam eveningwear and vintage-inspired prints. *hugoboss.com*

*Expensive*                                              *Amex/MC/V*

**Fifth Avenue**                                  **(212) 485-1800**
717 Fifth Avenue                                      at 56th St
NYC 10022   Mon-Fri 10-7 (Thurs 10-8), Sat 10-6, Sun 12-6

## Hugo Hugo Boss

Young style-conscious men and women shop Boss's bridge line for unusual and unconventional clothes that won't stretch the wallet. The clothes range from trendy suits and separates in quality fabrics to bubble skirts…think of the hipsters bouncing around in the fragrance ads and you've pretty much got it. *hugoboss.com*

*Expensive*                                              *Amex/MC/V*

**SoHo**                                          **(212) 965-1300**
132 Greene Street                            btw Houston/Prince
NYC 10012                                 Mon-Sat 11-7, Sun 12-6

## Huminska

A milliner who is tired of making hats, Miss Huminska designs dresses, tops and skirts—all with unique designs and described by her as classics with a twist. This allows her to pursue her love affair with fabrics, but among the accessories you'll still find hats (old habits are hard to break) and a sprinkling of bags.

*Expensive*                                              *Amex/MC/V*

**East Village**                                  **(212) 677-3458**
315 East 9th Street                          btw First/Second Ave
NYC 10003            Mon-Fri 1-8, Sat 12-8, Sun 12:30-6:30

## Hunting World

Going on a safari? Then your first stop should be Hunting World. Outfit yourself in the latest safari jackets, pants, vests, silk scarves, hats and shoes. Don't forget to check out their signature travel bags, which range from carryall shoulder bags to canvas duffles. What better way to carry your new gear while stalking big game? *huntingworld.com*

*Moderate*                                               *Amex/MC/V*

**SoHo**                                          **(212) 431-0086**
118 Greene Street                             btw Prince/Spring
NYC 10022                                 Mon-Sat 11-7, Sun 12-6

## Ibiza/Ibiza Kidz

Part hippy-chic boutique for adults filled with long flowing dresses in fun prints and accessories incorporating turquoise and leather; part children's boutique, largely filled with European designers. Be sure to check out the tiny little boots and hats by Elefanten.

*Moderate*                                    *Amex/MC/V*

**West Village**                          **(212) 533-4614**
46 University Place                          btw 9/10th St
NYC 10003                    Mon-Sat 11-8, Sun 12:30-6:30

## If

A SoHo purveyor of avant-garde clothing and accessories, with ready-to-wear from such inspired designers as Comme des Garçons, Ivan Grundahl, Marc Le Bihan, Martin Margiela, Junya Watanabe, Dries Van Noten and Veronique Branquinho. The sales staff are notoriously unfriendly yet knowledgeable, but the truly fashionable consumer neither needs nor wants help in choosing outfits here. Shoes, hats, handbags and accessories are also available.

*Expensive*                                   *Amex/MC/V*

**SoHo**                                  **(212) 334-4964**
94 Grand Street                         btw Mercer/Greene
NYC 10013                      Mon-Sat 11-7, Sun 12-6:30

## Il Bisonte

Come here for durable, handcrafted leather goods embossed with a bison logo and perfect for weekends. The leather may be undyed, vegetable-dyed (which makes things look richer as they age) or colored (black, tan, green, red, brown), and it may have brass and nickel hardware—these are the defining elements of Il Bisonte designs. Choose from a plethora of styles, colors and textures. The store stocks a complete line of handbags, small leather goods, briefcases, agendas and luggage.        *ilbisonte.com*

*Moderate*                                    *Amex/MC/V*

**SoHo**                                  **(212) 966-8773**
120 Sullivan Street                      btw Prince/Spring
NYC 10012                  Sun-Mon 12-6, Tues-Sat 12-6:30

## ★ Ina

Ina's mission: 'To select only what's in fashion from those who are in fashion, for those who want to be in fashion.' This is a truly amazing consignment shop where the fashion cognoscenti part with their designer clothes—including Prada, Gucci, James Perse, Louis Vuitton, Marc Jacobs—and the rest of the fashion cognoscenti scoop them up. Handbags, scarves and shoes by Blahnik, Gucci, Chanel and Hermès round out the brilliantly edited assortment. Ina's secret recipe: her wares are in pristine condition and her prices can't be beat. But as with any consignment store, it takes some digging—or repeated visits—to find the true gems.                                      *inanyc.com*

| | |
|---|---|
| *Moderate to expensive* | *Amex/MC/V* |
| **SoHo** | **(212) 941-4757** |
| 101 Thompson Street | btw Prince/Spring |
| NYC 10012 | Daily 12-7 |
| **Nolita** | **(212) 334-9048** |
| 21 Prince Street | btw Mott/Elizabeth |
| NYC 10012 | Daily 12-7 (Fri-Sat 12-8) |
| **Nolita (M)** | **(212) 334-2210** |
| 262 Mott Street | btw Houston/Prince |
| NYC 10012 | (opening hours as above) |

## Infinity

Maybe they call it Infinity because the piles of T-shirts, pants, skirts and other clothing for tween girls seem like they go on forever. Looks run from bathing suits to strapless dance dresses. You'll also find silly string, temporary hair color, a girl's 'first glitter roll-on deodorant', camp keepsake boxes and soaps in watermelon, peach or lime. Any brand of the moment can be found at Infinity, including Juicy Couture, Miss Sixty and Triple 5 Soul. Prices range from $30-$150. *infinitynyc.com*

| | |
|---|---|
| *Affordable* | *Amex/MC/V* |
| **Upper East Side** | **(212) 517-4232** |
| 1116 Madison Avenue | at 83rd St |
| NYC 10028 | Mon-Sat 10-6 |

## Institut

Institut's party-like atmosphere, colorful interior and selection of trendy European and American designers draw young New Yorkers to its urban street fashions. The clothes are organized by color and arranged against the store's glittering pink walls. Find an assortment of body-hugging pants, leathers, jackets, slinky knits, fitted tops, skirts and accessories that include fun jewelry. Remember that this is hip fashion, not high fashion (although it's priced more toward the latter).

| | |
|---|---|
| *Expensive* | *Amex/MC/Visa* |
| **SoHo** | **(212) 431-5521** |
| 97 Spring Street | btw Mercer/Broadway |
| NYC 10012 | Daily 11-8 |

## ★ Intermix

Ask any dedicated Madison Avenue shopper what her favorite store is, and chances are good that she'll say Intermix. Their bright window displays are like a cosmic force pulling you into the store. Intermix buyers do a brilliant job of bringing you the hottest designers every season, such as Blumarine and C & C California. The accessories include goodies from Marc by Marc Jacobs, Michael Kors and Stella McCartney heels. Everything is conveniently organized by color, so there is no time wasted if you need a pink dress, right now. Prices range from $45 Minnetonka moccasins to $2,500 Chloé dresses. *intermixonline.com*

| *Expensive* | *Amex/MC/V* |
|---|---|

**Upper East Side** (212) 249-7858
1003 Madison Avenue btw 77/78th St
NYC 10021 Mon-Sat 10:30-7, Sun 12-6

**Upper West Side** (212) 769-9116
210 Columbus Avenue at 69th St
NYC 10023 Mon-Wed 11-7, Thurs-Sat 11-7:30, Sun 12-6

**Flatiron** (212) 533-9720
125 Fifth Avenue btw 19/20th St
NYC 10003 Mon-Sat 11-8, Sun 12-6

**West Village** (212) 929-7180
365 Bleecker Street at Charles
NYC 10014 Mon-Sat 11-8, Sun 12-7

## Iramo

Here's an innovative concept in retailing: when you want to open another hip-hop shoe store in the same neighborhood with exactly the same merchandise but want to stay original, simply spell the name of your first store backwards and, voilà, you've created a totally 'new' store. If this makes no sense to you, go to Omari and read all about Iramo. That, and check out the street-cool shoes.

| *Moderate* | *Amex/MC/V* |
|---|---|

**SoHo** (212) 334-9159
89 Spring Street btw Mercer/West Broadway
NYC 10012 Daily 11-8 (Sun 11-7:30)

## ★ Isa

Hands-down, this is one of Brooklyn's brightest shopping highlights. This raw, minimalist store highlights underground labels like Rogan, Noah and Blessed. Politically minded silk-screened tees, Martin Margiela frocks and the latest Nike Trainers all share shelf space in a celebration of street-savvy, hi-lo fashion.

| *Moderate* | *Amex/MC/V* |
|---|---|

**Williamsburg** (718) 387-3363
88 North 6th Street at Wythe
Brooklyn 11211 Mon-Fri 1-9, Sat 12-10, Sun 1-7

## Issey Miyake

Mr Miyake's work is more museum-quality than trendy. A landmark cast-iron building (designed by Frank Gehry, no less), an interior of undulating titanium forms that curve throughout, and the sheer strength of Miyake's aesthetic make for a unique shopping experience. The Japanese designer has shown nearly 100 collections and won almost every fashion award in existence. Long admired for his innovation, Miyake has boiled and melded both natural fibers and synthetic to create groundbreaking fabrics. He has long experimented with pleated fabrics of all kinds...wrinkles have never looked so good. Many of the looks are revealingly sheer and require serious underpinnings. Fabulous bags and accessories in interesting colors and patterns include heavy cotton beach bags with brilliant color stitching and mirroring. *isseymiyake.com*

*Expensive* *Amex/MC/V*

**Tribeca** **(212) 226-0100**
119 Hudson Street at North Moore
NYC 10013 Mon-Sat 11-7, Sun 12-6

**Upper East Side** **(212) 439-7822**
992 Madison Avenue at 77th St
NYC 10021 Mon-Fri 10-6, Sat 11-6, Sun 12-5

## Jacadi 👕

Since the Seventies, Jacadi has been educating children with tasteful, refined clothes. Items are neatly displayed according to size, color and style and include back-to-school basics, casual play clothes, shoes and accessories; looks range from adorable smocked dresses to embroidered and appliquéd overalls. Jacadi has a great sweater and blouse selection, as well as a layette department that sells everything from bumpers to towels. Newborn to age 12. Great sales, too. *jacadiusa.com*

*Moderate* *Amex/MC/V*

**Upper East Side** **(212) 369-1616**
1296 Madison Avenue at 92nd St
NYC 10128 Mon-Sat 10-6 (Thurs 10-7), Sun 12-5

**Upper East Side** **(212) 535-3200**
787 Madison Avenue at 67th St
NYC 10021 (opening hours as above)

## Jack Gomme 👕👚

*C'est tout génial* at this bright and modern Parisian accessory boutique in very eurocentric Nolita. Boasting a selection of colorful leather and polyester goods with the perfect mix of unmistakably French charm and wit, Jack Gomme sells basic bags that still pack a punch with unexpected details like colorful contrasting handles and graphic prints featuring caricatures of the company's designers Paul Droulers and Sophie Renier. Don't forget to check out the small selection of distinctly French clothing, complete with a navy and white striped boat shirt a la Pablo Picasso. *jackgomme.com*

*Moderate* *Amex/MC/V*

**Nolita** **(212) 925-6414**
252 Elizabeth Street btw Houston/Prince
NYC 10012 Daily 11:30-7:30

## Jack Silver Formal Wear 👕

The formalwear 'choice of the stars', Jack Silver has dressed the best in television soap operas, films and major network television shows. Rent or buy, this is the place to find what you need for that black-tie event or gala evening. Labels include Oscar de La Renta, Pierre Cardin, After Six and, of course, Ralph Lauren. Black-tie accessories like shirts, bow ties, cummerbunds, suspenders and shoes are available as well. While you'll find that rentals are in stock, if you plan to purchase you must place your order in advance. *jacksilverformalwear.com*

*Expensive* *Amex/MC/V*

**Midtown West** **(212) 582-0202**
1780 Broadway (suite 303) btw 57/58th St
NYC 10019 Mon-Fri 9-6, Sat 10-3

## Jack Spade
Since 1993 female fashionistas have bought handbags from accessories diva Kate Spade. Good news, gentlemen, it's your turn. Husband Andy Spade has created a collection of snappy, efficient travel bags, day bags, informal briefcases, totes, messenger bags, computer bags, bankers' envelopes and wallets. They fall under the semi-epony-mous Jack Spade label and in fabrications like canvas, nylon, worsted wools and water-repellent, waxed cotton canvas. Lots of extra amenities like pockets for cellphones and pens. Bags start at \$150. *jackspade.com*

*Moderate* *Amex/MC/V*

**SoHo** **(212) 625-1820**
56 Greene Street btw Spring/Broome
NYC 10012 Mon-Sat 11-7, Sun 12-6

## Jaime Mascaro
Jaime Mascaro took over the entire boutique when Kerquelen closed, with impressive results. To cater to SoHo foot traffic Mascaro changes merchandise at least monthly, so there's always a fresh selection of slingbacks, wooden-heeled sandals and satin round-toe flats. *jaimemascaro.com*

*Moderate to expensive* *Amex/MC/V*

**SoHo** **(212) 965-8910**
430 West Broadway btw Prince/Spring
NYC 10012 Mon-Sat 11-7, Sun 12-6

## Jamin Puech
A sophisticated bohemian handbag shop catering to sophisticated bohemian handbag addicts. Intricate bead-ing, exotic feathers and soft, slouchy shapes give these handbags vintage appeal. Find leather and straw bags, del-icate knits, organza floral bags and peacock-trimmed and beaded purses. Each handbag is beautifully made and detailed to perfection. *jaminpuech.com*

*Expensive* *Amex/MC/V*

**Nolita** **(212) 431-5200**
247 Elizabeth Street btw Houston/Prince
NYC 10012 Mon-Sat 11-7, Sun 12-6

## Jane
This petite boutique has been dressing stylish East Side ladies in sophisticated European separates for the past 17

years. Designs range from casual to evening, with an emphasis on luxurious fabrics and chic styling. Poule Vasseur, New York Industry, BluMarine, Philosophy di Alberta Ferretti, Orla Kiely and Les Copains are just a few labels from the eclectic collection. Super-friendly staff will assist you in searching through the overstuffed racks.

*Expensive* *Amex/MC/V*

**Upper East Side** **(212) 772-7710**
1025 Lexington Avenue btw 73/74th St
NYC 10021 Mon-Sat 10-6 (closed Saturdays in summer)

## Janet Russo 👗

Janet Russo's passion is for collecting unusual fabrics, and each year she travels far and wide in search of everything from Indian saris and Chinese silks to Liberty prints from London. Thin materials are used to create sundresses, skirts and tops, all with a subtle sexiness best suited to the curvaceous woman. A selection of cardigans and camisoles by Mary Beth's Design is also available, as are antique purses, earrings and everyday bags. *janetrusso.com*

*Affordable* *Amex/MC/V*

**Nolita** **(212) 625-3297**
262 Mott Street btw Houston/Prince
NYC 10012 Daily 11:30-7 (Sun 12-6:30)

## Jared M 👔

Jared Margolis recently launched Jared M, a high-end, made-to-measure menswear line for Big & Tall clientele. The shop's one-on-one image consultation is a definite plus, and hoops stars like Allan Houston and Kurt Thomas of the NY Knicks are already noted as fans. Livin' large, indeed.

*Expensive* *Amex/MC/V*

**Midtown West** **(212) 868-1400**
252 West 37th Street (suite 1201) btw Seventh/Eighth Ave
NYC 10001 Mon-Fri 9:30-5:30
(appointments highly recommended)

## Jay Kos 👔

Shopping at Jay Kos is like shopping at your own personal club. An intimate atmosphere of beautifully displayed merchandise makes you want to buy it all—classic Italian suits (ready-made or custom), tweed shooting jackets, all-weather coats (including Macintosh jackets and Austrian loden coats), silk-lined cashmere sweaters from Scotland, handmade shirts from one of the oldest workshops in Italy, and English corduroys. In addition, find furnishings and accessories that include fabulous English cufflinks, Swaine Adeney & Brigg umbrellas and hats from Borsalino and James Lock & Co. Kos's appeal is based on traditional styling, luxury fabrics and pure elegance. Expensive—but worth it.

*Luxury* *Amex/MC/V*

**Upper East Side**  (212) 327-2382
986 Lexington Avenue  btw 71/72nd St
NYC 10021  Mon-Thurs 10-7, Fri-Sat 10-6

## J.Crew

J.Crew is where you shop for staples, for work or leisure. There are three options: casual Friday clothes, dressy looks with classic styling, or weekendwear. There is a wide choice of chinos, dress pants, cashmeres, button-down shirts, jeans, T-shirts, dresses, swimsuits, sleepwear and underwear, accessories and shoes. J.Crew has also recently introduced a line of special occasion and bridalwear. The image epitomizes the active all-American lifestyle (even if you don't have one), and every now and then they'll hit the jackpot with a cute striped sweater, say, that looks designer. Great bang for the buck.    800-562-0258  jcrew.com

*Affordable*  *Amex/MC/V*

**Fifth Avenue**  (212) 765-4227
30 Rockefeller Center  at 50th St
NYC 10022  Mon-Sat 10-8, Sun 11-7

**Flatiron**  (212) 255-4848
91 Fifth Avenue  btw 16/17th St
NYC 10003  (opening hours as above)

**SoHo**  (212) 966-2739
99 Prince Street  at Mercer
NYC 10012  (opening hours as above)

**Lower Manhattan**  (212) 385-3500
203 Front Street  at South Street Seaport
NYC 10038  Daily 10-9 (Sun 10-8)

**Midtown East**  (212) 949-0570
347 Madison Avenue  at 45th St
NYC 10017  Mon-Fri 9-8, Sat 10-6, Sun 12-6

## Jean Paul Gaultier

For serious fashion that's a whole lot of fun, take a gander around Jean Paul Gaultier's flagship store. The iconoclastic French designer has for years managed to marry chic and camp like no other: where else could you find his typically ethnic-printed layered pieces alongside snowglobes filled with JPG fragrance, or his striped sailors' T-shirts next to camouflage gym boots? Also, in this surprisingly minimalist store, you will find sunglasses, boxer shorts and cheeky ties emblazoned with the designer's name. Buy up big and make like Cate Blanchett and Nicole Kidman, famous fans of Gaultier's divine couture.    jeanpaulgaultier.com

*Luxury*  *Amex/MC/V*

**Upper East Side**  (212) 249-0235
759 Madison Avenue  btw 65/66th St
NYC 10021  Mon-Wed, Fri 10-6, Thurs, Sat 11-6

## ★ Jeffrey

The Meatpacking District is now fashion central thanks largely to the pioneering efforts of Jeffrey Kalinsky, the

139

impresario of this 18,000-square-foot multi-designer emporium. Kalinsky's unique ability to cull the highlights from each designer's collection sets this mini department store apart from the competition. He has chosen the best pieces from luxe labels like Jil Sander, Helmut Lang, Narciso Rodriguez, Dior, as well as Hedi Slimane's Dior Homme line that women covet as much as men. The best thing about Jeffrey is his fabulous—and dangerously expensive—shoe selection: Gucci, Christian Louboutin, Robert Clergerie, Yves Saint Laurent, Manolo Blahnik and Prada...order a pair of shoes over the phone and have them delivered the same day. The store also has the chicest home furnishings, including objets d'art that also serve as tables. Wonderful.

*Luxury*                                              *Amex/MC/V*

**Meatpacking District**                    **(212) 206-1272**
449 West 14th Street                              btw 9/10th St
NYC 10014        Mon-Fri 10:30-8, Sat 10:30-7, Sun 12:30-6

## Jenne Maag

Texan-born designer Jenne Maag has been making her sig-nature fitted stretch pants for the past 15 years, way before they were the thing. Her boutique carries her line, which comes in matching groups (depending on the season: pants, jackets, halter tops and shirtdresses). Manufactured in her trademark Tarallo fabric, a polyester/Lycra blend sim-ilar to what Prada uses, Maag's designs feature classic cuts and form-fitted shapes and always have a bit of stretch. 'I try to make clothes that fit any shape, from skinny minis to fuller figures, and that make women feel and look great,' she says, which must be why women flock here for her expert tailoring. Sizes run P, S, M and L. Expect to spend between $100 and $400.                          *jennemaag.com*

*Moderate*                                          *Amex/MC/V*

**Nolita**                                      **(212) 625-1700**
29 Spring Street                                       at Mott
NYC 10012                          Mon-Sat 11-7, Sun 12-6

## Jill Anderson

The North Dakota-born designer is a whiz at turning out comfortable clothes with offbeat detail. Design is a kind of yoga, says Anderson, 'where the space of calm content-ment feeds my imagination'. Clean lines and unusual up-to-the-minute fabrics give a modern sensibility to her feminine dresses, including her signature widow dress (loose-fitting, long-sleeved and below-the-knee), skirts, jackets, easy-wearing lace tops and coats. Bonus: free alterations and great sales.                                      *jillanderson.com*

*Expensive*                                          *Amex/MC/V*

**East Village**                                **(212) 253-1747**
331 East 9th Street                        btw First/Second Ave
NYC 10003                                          Daily 12-8

## Jill Stuart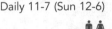

Jill Stuart gets what New York women want to wear: a combination of tasteful and approachable clothes with a deft mix of femininity and urban edge (her perfect-fit jeans are a must). Delicate fabrics and beautiful patterns permeate her collection of dresses, skirts, jackets, cashmeres and tops. Not to be missed is Stuart's basement vintage boutique, a decadent setting housing armoires stuffed with floral print dresses and dramatic, bias-cut evening gowns. *jillstuart.com*

*Expensive*                                  *Amex/MC/V*

**SoHo**                                  **(212) 343-2300**
100 Greene Street                      btw Prince/Spring
NYC 10012                              Daily 11-7 (Sun 12-6)

## Jil Sander

Style-watchers are giddy with Sander's return to the fashion world. Having regained control of her label, the revered designer's labors will bear fruit in her enormous new flagship. There's a lot more space than stuff in the stark black and white store, but that's all the better to appreciate that perfect skirt or structured shirt. A favorite of gallery owners, Sander's look could be called intellectual chic: minimalism with quirky details (a well-placed dot or two, for example) crafted from the best fabrics. Amidst the neighborhood's loud logo madness, Sander's clothes speak to a simpler, quiet luxury. *jilsander.com*

*Expensive*                                  *Amex/MC/V*

**Midtown East**                          **(212) 838-6100**
11 East 57th Street                  btw Fifth/Madison Ave
NYC 10022                          Mon-Sat 10-6 (Thurs 10-7)

## Jimmy Choo

When Madonna searched for the perfect shoes for her wedding and when George W. Bush's daughters Barbara and Jenna twinkle-toed their way to the inaugural ball, which brand did they choo-se? Jimmy Choo, whose shoes have graced the feet of London and New York It-girls (not to mention a movie star or two) for the past nine years. A rival to Manolo Blahnik, Choo causes women to throw logic to the wind and pay up to $1,200 for Tamara Mellon's creations. Narrow toes, high heels and serious femininity define the collection of delicate pumps, slingbacks, demure gingham kitten heels, reptile-skin boots, fanciful stilettos (adorned with fur or seashells), slinky sandals with crystal embroidered straps and towering gold ankle-wrap stilettos. *jimmychoo.com*

*Luxury*                                  *Amex/MC/V*

**Fifth Avenue**                          **(212) 593-0800**
645 Fifth Avenue                              at 51st St
NYC 10022            Mon-Sat 10-6 (Thurs 10-7), Sun 12-5

## Jim Smiley Vintage

'Through the clothing I learn all about history,' says vintage guru Jim Smiley. A second-floor eyrie of exquisite frocks and accessories spanning the Victorian era through the Sixties (many of which are unworn and sporting their original tags), this a shop dedicated to the finest garments of the past. Smiley, who moved his shop from New Orleans to New York two years ago, boasts a client list that includes the Museum of Fine Arts in Boston, movie production houses and A-list actresses who stop by for extraordinary pieces by Dior, Adrian, Trigères and McCardell. While you have to ask to touch some of the rarer dresses, feel free to caress less expensive items like breezy sundresses and embroidered kimonos. *jimsmileyvintageclothing.com*

*Expensive*                                              *Amex/MC/V*

**Chelsea**                                        **(212) 741-1195**
128 West 23rd Street                   btw Sixth/Seventh Ave
NYC 10011                          Mon-Sat 11-7, Sun 12:30-5

## Jivamukti Yoga

The longtime haven of downtown model types seeking inner peace, or at least a body like student Christy Turlington's. The boutique carries an ever-widening selection of yoga pants and tops adorned with Hindu deities, instructional videos, incense sticks and beauty products, including the center's own line of vegan, cruelty-free bath and body treats. Om shanti. *jivamuktiyoga.com*

*Moderate*                                              *Amex/MC/V*

**NoHo**                                           **(212) 353-0214**
404 Lafayette Street                 btw Astor Place/West 4th St
(3rd floor)                           Mon-Thurs 7:30-10, Fri 7:30-8:15
NYC 10003                              Sat 9-4:45, Sun 8:30-7

## J.Lindeberg

The uncommon combination of fashion and golf is what makes Swedish designer Lindeberg tick and his passions coalesce into a contemporary sportswear collection showcased here. This 2,200-square-foot two-level space, equipped with marigold Formica fixtures, houses fashion-forward men's clothing from leathers and three-piece pinstriped suits to staples like black and khaki pants and button-down shirts. Lindeberg's ultra-hip On Course golf collection is appropriate either on and off the links. Women's fashions are sexy and form-fitted, while golf attire for the fellows is preppy chic. *jlindeberg.com*

*Expensive*                                              *Amex/MC/V*

**SoHo**                                           **(212) 625-9403**
126 Spring Street                                    at Greene
NYC 10012                                Mon-Sat 11-7, Sun 12-6

## J.McLaughlin

For over 25 years J.McLaughlin has been putting its mark on classic American sportswear. Men and women shop

Directory

here for a casual, comfortable wardrobe that's appropriate for a relaxed work atmosphere or weekend living. The clothes combine tradition and preppy cool in khakis, corduroys, polo shirts, cable sweaters, button-down shirts and quilted jackets. Accessories include silk headbands and knots, Lucite cufflinks, grosgrain ribbon belts, and handbags. *jmclaughlin.com*

*Moderate to expensive*  Amex/MC/V

**Upper East Side**  **(212) 879-9565**
1343 Third Avenue  at 77th St
NYC 10021  Mon-Fri 10:30-8, Sat 10:30-6, Sun 12-6

**Upper East Side**  **(212) 369-4830**
1311 Madison Avenue  btw 92/93rd St
NYC 10128  Mon-Sat 10-6 (Tues-Thurs 10-7), Sun 12-5

## J.Mendel

PETA activists beware: Fur is in 365 days a year here. This gorgeous fur salon offers the finest ready-to-wear furs and accessories available in mink, chinchilla, sable, fisher and fox, as well as cashmere overcoats and leather handbags. Regular clients include Jennifer Lopez and many Upper East Side It-girls, most of whom are on a first-name basis with the pleasant, accommodating sales staff. *jmendel.com*

*Luxury*  Amex/MC/V

**Upper East Side**  **(212) 832-5830**
723 Madison Avenue  btw 63/64th St
NYC 10021  Mon-Sat 10-6

## J.M.Weston

The handmade shoes offered at this French footwear retailer are classically stylish, and their handstitching ensures they'll last a lifetime. For a slice of this luxury, you'll have to pay anywhere from $400 to $2,500. The company also offers a collection of shoes designed by fashion footwear darling Michel Perry. More good news—you can return your worn shoes and, for a nominal fee, have them resoled and rebuilt. This bright, airy store also sells women's loafers and lace-up golf shoes. Warm sales staff, too.

*Expensive*  Amex/MC/V

**Upper East Side**  **(212) 535-2100**
812 Madison Avenue  at 68th St
NYC 10021  Mon-Fri 9:30-6, Sat 10-6

## John Anthony

Ooh very expensive, but so worth it. John Anthony is the affluent lady's stop for the grandest custom-made attire. High couture and gorgeous gowns can accompany you home—if you have at least $10,000 to spend.

*Luxury*  Amex/MC/V

**Midtown West**  **(212) 245-6069**
130 West 57th Street (suite 11b)  btw Sixth/Seventh Ave
NYC 10019  (by appointment only)

## John Fluevog Shoes  👕👗

Fluevog's shoes may be the wildest footgear in Gotham. With their 6-inch platform heels, they 'will keep you above the urban trash,' says Fluevog (like Patrick Cox, another Canadian shoe maestro). Serious club-hoppers and teen types will find everything from platforms to pedal-pushers, from hand-carved wooden clogs for women to pastel-colored motorcycle boots for men (or women, why not?). Favorites of hip-hoppers Black Eyed Peas, the shoes in general are well made, but you might need both youth and guts to strut the streets in these chunky numbers.                         *fluevog.com*

*Moderate*                                    *Amex/MC/V*

**Nolita**                                **(212) 431-4484**
250 Mulberry Street                            at Prince
NYC 10012                          Daily 12-8 (Sun 12-6)

## John Lobb  👕

Since 1850 John Lobb's handmade shoes have been caressing the feet of distinguished gentlemen and reassuring them with their motto 'Some things are forever'. Now Britain's venerable shoemaker has crossed the pond and is open for business with a selection of straight-cap oxfords, loafers, buckle shoes, Jodhpur boots, evening slip-ons and classic moccasins. Beautiful craftsmanship and traditional styling define the Lobb label. Pay an average price of $800, while custom-made starts at $3,800.

*Expensive to luxury*                          *Amex/MC/V*

**Upper East Side**                       **(212) 888-9797**
680 Madison Avenue                      btw 61/62nd St
NYC 10021                    Mon-Sat 10-6 (Thurs 10-7)

## Johnson  👕

Straightforward attire with a bit of a downtown edge. This small, cozy boutique features Kim Johnson's keyhole dresses, corduroy pants and bow-trim tops. The look is classic with a twist, and you'll find a range of accessories from wrist bags to winter hats.                      *johnsonshop.com*

*Expensive*                                    *Amex/MC/V*

**Lower East Side**                       **(646) 602-8668**
179 Orchard Street                 btw Stanton/Houston
NYC 10002            Mon-Fri 1-7, Sat 12-8, Sun 12-6

## Johnston & Murphy  👕

This American men's footwear retailer has satisfied its customers since 1850 with a full range of styles, from dress and formal to casual and weekend. Johnston & Murphy offer matching accessories, quality shoe care products (including sweet-smelling cedarwood foot trees), and a small casual sportswear selection for the conservative dresser looking to kick back.                 800-424-2854  *johnstonmurphy.com*

*Moderate*                                    *Amex/MC/V*

**Midtown East**                    **(212) 697-9375**
345 Madison Avenue                   btw 44/45th St
NYC 10017              Mon-Fri 9-7, Sat 10-6, Sun 12-5

**Midtown East**                    **(212) 527-2342**
520 Madison Avenue                   btw 44/45th St
NYC 10022              Mon-Fri 9-7, Sat 10-7, Sun 12-5

## John Varvatos
After tours of duty with Calvin Klein and Ralph Lauren, John Varvatos stepped out on his own with this exclusive men's shop. Who is his customer? According to the man himself, 'there's the modern guy who shops at Prada and Gucci, the classic Armani customer and then the guy in the middle—the Varvatos customer, a modern man who wants to look elegant but with a relaxed feel.' Choose from a selection of sophisticated wool suits, luxurious cashmeres, bulky knits, wide-legged pants, shearlings and pea-coats. For a sneak preview, catch Dylan McDermott from *The Practice* wearing Varvatos in court. *Will & Grace*'s Eric McCormick also flaunts Varvatos. Very cool is his collaboration with Converse on designer sneakers, sported by the likes of Jimmy Fallon and Tobey Maguire.                    *johnvarvatos.com*

*Moderate*                              *Amex/MC/V*

**SoHo**                            **(212) 965-0700**
149 Mercer Street                   btw Houston/Prince
NYC 10012               Mon-Sat 11-7, Sun 12-6

## Jonathan Adler
Fashion hounds who favor Jonathan Adler's stylish home accessories—like his signature porcelain aorta vases, or his handmade Beekman sofas—can now take a piece of his to go, thanks to the introduction of a line of luxe handbags. Adler's store is known for its beautiful lighting designs, din-nerware, pottery and furniture (including chic dog beds), and his new purses and totes are marked by the same clean and simple lines (no logos, mercifully) and made of the most supple, luxurious materials. Beautiful.     *jonathanadler.com*

*Expensive*                             *Amex/MC/V*

**SoHo**                            **(212) 941-8950**
47 Greene Street                    btw Broome/Grand
NYC 10013               Daily 11-7, Sun 12-6

## Joovay
A favorite of J.Lo's, this small lingerie boutique is filled with top-of-the-line American and European labels, including Lise Charmel, Marvel, Leigh Bantivoglio, Cosabella, Lejaby and La Perla. Looks run from dainty and sweet to sexy and hot in bras, panties, teddies, nightwear, camisoles and slips. Hosiery by Oroblu and Falke is also available.     *joovay.com*

*Expensive*                             *Amex/MC/V*

**SoHo**                            **(212) 431-6386**
436 West Broadway                          at Prince
NYC 1001                     Daily 12-7 (Sat 11-7)

## Joseph
London retailer Joseph Ettedgui has his customers coming
back for more by sticking to what he knows best: keeping
to the same basic styles, especially his cult pants, which
return every season with updated fabrics, colors and textures. Think Banana Republic or Club Monaco, and then
add a few digits to the price tag. Joseph is all about modern separates in easy-to-wear shapes, including pants,
shirts, jackets, leathers, knitwear and shearlings, as well as
the one drop-dead gorgeous, high-end piece he introduces into each collection.

*Expensive* *Amex/MC/V*

**SoHo** **(212) 343-7071**
106 Greene Street btw Prince/Spring
NYC 10012 Mon-Sat 11-7:30, Sun 12-7

**Upper East Side** **(212) 570-0077**
816 Madison Avenue btw 68/69th St
NYC 10021 Mon-Sat 10-6:30, Sun 12-6

## Joseph A. Bank
A Baltimore retailer featuring tailored career clothing for
the conservative dresser. In keeping with its traditional ori-
gins, Bank offers a comfortable shopping environment for a
complete selection of suits, sportswear, sportswear, ties and
underwear, as well as a Cole Haan shoe department. Even
better: every spring Bank invites you to trade in an old suit
for up to $200 credit towards a new suit (ranging from $300
to $1,600)—now, if only Prada did that…

800-285-2265 *josabank.com*

*Moderate* *Amex/MC/V*

**Midtown East** **(212) 370-0600**
366 Madison Avenue at 46th St
NYC 10017 Mon-Fri 9-7 (Thurs 9-8), Sat 9-6, Sun 12-5

## Joyce Leslie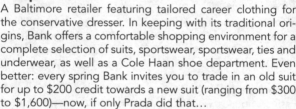
Joyce Leslie's clothes are like Kleenex: so necessary the
day you acquire them, but ultimately disposable. Long
patronized by NYU students on a budget for the cheap, if
slightly slutty, lingerie section in the basement that also
houses a wide selection of sequined bikinis. Upstairs, it
may be worth weeding through a sea of polyester halter
tops for hipster staples such as basic cotton blouses with
Avril Lavignesque ties, plus some surprisingly cute denim
jackets. *joyceleslie.com*

*Moderate* *Amex/MC/V*

**West Village** **(212) 505-5419**
20 University Place at Eighth Ave
NYC 10019 Mon-Wed 10-9, Thurs-Sat 10-10, Sun 10-8

## J.Press
One of the oldest menswear shops in New York, J.Press
prides itself on its selection of traditional suits, sportswear,

formalwear, outerwear and accessories, all in good taste at reasonable prices. A great shop for young career guys. Suit prices start at $475. *jpressonline.com*

*Moderate to expensive*                    *Amex/MC/V*

**Midtown East**                    **(212) 687-7642**
7 East 44th Street          btw Fifth/Madison Ave
NYC 10017                           Mon-Sat 9-6

## Judith Leiber

Accessories legend Judith Leiber has over 500 bags for evening or daytime, from a classic alligator style to an elaborately detailed design for fancy nights out. But true Leiber aficionados shop here for her rhinestone evening bags and tiny jewel-encrusted minaudières. These bags are often seen in the clutches of society types, including Nancy Reagan, oh, and avant-garde darlings like Bjork. See? Versatile. *judiethleiber.com*

*Expensive*                                  *Amex/MC/V*

**Upper East Side**                    **(212) 327-4003**
987 Madison Avenue              btw 76/77th St
NYC 10021                           Mon-Sat 10-6

## Julian and Sara

A cozy shop stocked with children's clothing lines imported from France and Italy. Find back-to-school basics, play clothes and accessories handpicked from top labels like Lili Gaufrette, Arthur, Mona Lisa, Kenzo, Petit Bateau, Clayeux, Mini Man and Elsy. Sizes are aimed mostly at infants, but range from newborn through pre-teen. *julianandsara.com*

*Expensive*                                  *Amex/MC/V*

**SoHo**                    **(212) 226-1989**
103 Mercer Street           btw Prince/Spring
NYC 10012          Mon-Fri 11-7, Sat-Sun 11:30-6

## Julie Artisan's Gallery

Since 1973 this artisan's gallery has showcased techniques like weaving, handpainting, stitching, quilting and knitting. Each piece is a lovingly crafted work of art, either one-of-a-kind or sold in limited editions. Women shop here for loomed and handwoven knitted jackets, colorful sweaters, hand-dyed and painted shirts and more from such labels as Tim Harding and Linda Mendelson. Also find Bakelite and Modernist vintage jewelry, as well as some decorative home accessories. For mature customers into arty dressing, this is your spiritual home. *julieartisans.com*

*Expensive*                                  *Amex/MC/V*

**Upper East Side**                    **(212) 717-5959**
762 Madison Avenue              btw 65/66th St
NYC 10021                           Mon-Sat 11-6

## Jungle Planet

It's a jungle in here, with a thicket of goods spanning the world over, from Nepal to little ol' Gotham. Jungle Planet's

147

global selection of Mandarin dresses, shirts, T-shirts, hand-crafted blazers, scarves, beaded handbags, jewelry, rings and pendants is fun, feminine and full of international flair.

*Moderate*                                               *MC/V*

**West Village**                              **(212) 989-5447**
175 West 4th Street                     btw Sixth/Seventh Ave
NYC 10014                                          Daily 12-8

## Juno
This footwear emporium is all about color—purples, fuchsias, greens and yellows. For shoe addicts who absolutely must have the very latest styles, from casual to sporty to evening, Juno has sexy pumps, boots (a fantastic and well-priced selection—especially in winter), slides and sandals. Men can choose from Prada-esque sneaker/dress shoes, boots and sandals. Great children's shoes, too. 'Buy one pair, get one free,' sales happen frequently, so don't miss out.

*Moderate*                                           *Amex/MC/V*

**SoHo**                                      **(212) 625-2560**
543 Broadway                               btw Prince/Spring
NYC 10012        Mon-Fri 10:30-8, Sat 10:30-8:30, Sun 11-8

## Jussara Lee
This über-hot Brazilian designer known for her custom-made sportswear and eveningwear has opened a super-cool glass and concrete boutique-cum-art-gallery in the Meatpacking District. You'll find Lee's usual assortment of minimalist sheer chiffon dresses and skirts, but people really visit the store for her coats and near-perfect pants. There's a surprise around every corner, including some gorgeous faux-fur wraps and power suits. And if you can't find what you're looking for, get it custom-made for the same price you'd pay if it was on the racks. *caipirinha.com/jussara*

*Expensive*                                          *Amex/MC/V*

**West Village**                              **(212) 242-4128**
11 Little West 12th Street           btw Ninth Ave/Washington
NYC 10014                                   Daily 11-7 (Sun 12-7)

## Just for Tykes
This full-service, high-end children's store sells all the practical essentials and little goodies you'll need for your little ones: clothing, furniture (including cribs), bedding, baby gear, accessories and lots of toys. Drop off your kids in the play space so you can peruse the store quickly, sans distractions. Whether shopping for a new family or the perfect nursery gift, the knowledgeable staff are on hand to make your shopping experience a little easier.    *justfortykes.com*

*Expensive*                                          *Amex/MC/V*

**SoHo**                                      **(212) 274-9121**
83 Mercer Street                           btw Spring/Broome
NYC 10012              Mon-Fri 10-6, Sat 11-7, Sun 12-6

## Jutta Neumann

Hippies and fashion editors (her work has been featured in *Vogue* and *Elle*), two seemingly incompatible groups, nevertheless share a love for Jutta Neumann's traditional craftsmanship and bohemian-chic sandals. Using a variety of skins (cow, calf, suede, snake, stingray, python, alligator), as well as a surfeit of colors (turquoise, bright yellow, orange and traditional browns and blacks, Neumann will create a one-of-a-kind pair just for you. While in the shop, she will also design a handbag to match, or make a coordinating belt or wristband. Everything is lovingly constructed to your specifications. Custom sandals range from $180 to $250 with a five-to-seven week delivery period.                                        *juttaneumann-newyork.com*

*Expensive*                                                            *Amex/MC/V*

**Lower East Side**                                          **(212) 982-7048**
158 Allen Street                                        btw Stanton/Rivington
NYC 10002                                                         Mon-Sat 12-8

## Karikter

Taking a page out of the funny books, this boutique stocks items featuring European characters like Tintin, Asterix, the Little Prince and the Smurfs. Whether the store's unique T-shirts, books, and even housewear designs emblazoned with your favorite cartoons will mark you as a big nerd or a gently eccentric, fashion-forward figure is up to you.                                                          *karikter.com*

*Moderate*                                                            *Amex/MC/V*

**SoHo**                                                        **(212) 274-1966**
19 Prince Street                                     between Elizabeth/Bowery
NYC 10012                                                  Daily 11-7 (Sun 12-6)

## Karen's for People and Pets

Karen Thompson knows that it's almost impossible to look chic with a shabbily turned-out shih tzu at your side. For 29 years she's been keeping our best friends à la mode with canine coats and carriers in to-the-minute styles and colors. Fifi will be one lucky bitch in her camouflage carrier festooned with rhinestones, cotton-candy pink leather handles and leopard lining, and Fido will stay snuggly and dry in a tartan coat or a hot-pink and acid-green rain slicker.                                            *karensforpets.com*

*Moderate*                                                            *Amex/MC/V*

**Upper East Side**                                          **(212) 472-9440**
1195 Lexington Avenue                                      btw 81/82nd St
NYC 10028                                             Mon-Fri 8-6, Sat 9-6

## Karin Alexis

What to do when you've searched high and low and you simply cannot find a decent wardrobe for your newborn? Well, Karin Alexis solved the problem by starting her own line. Reproducing vintage fabric finds, she pairs them with cozy fleece for jackets and 100% cotton flannel for trousers and rompers. The result is an adorable, durable kids' collection with vintage charm and modern practicality. Because Karin's muse is her son, this is one of the few places where the boys actually have more choices—but there's plenty for little girls, too.                    karinalexis.com

*Moderate*                                          *Amex/MC/V*

**Upper West Side**                          **(212) 769-9550**
490 Amsterdam Avenue                        btw 83/84th St
NYC 10024                          Mon-Sat 10:30-6, Sun 12-5

## Kate Spade                                              👤
Fashionistas call her the 'purse queen', and former accessories editor Spade lives up to the name with her classically styled handbags in bold, jaunty colors. Each season she reinvents her signature pieces in fashionable fabrics like glossy satin nylons, silks, bouclé wools, canvas and leathers. Looks run from practical shoulder and tote bags to silk and satin evening bags bright as jelly beans. As for her shoe designs: picture Sophia Loren on the Amalfi coast, wearing a flowered mule during the day and a rhinestone slide at night. Canvas platforms, metallic sandals and a lovely group of heels for walking down the aisle are also available. Spade's accessories include sunglasses, raincoats, pajamas, fragrances and a new assortment of beautiful china (including fine china, casual china, stemware, barware, flatware and giftware). There are even very proper books on etiquette (current titles: *Occasions, Style, Manners*) and an exquisitely detailed bedding collection.          katespade.com

*Expensive*                                         *Amex/MC/V*

**SoHo**                                       **(212) 274-1991**
454 Broome Street                                   at Mercer
NYC 10013                              Mon-Sat 11-7, Sun 12-6

**SoHo (travel store)**                        **(212) 965-8654**
59 Thompson Street                          btw Spring/Broome
NYC 10012                              Tues-Sat 11-7, Sun 12-6

## Kavanagh's Designer Resale Shop                        👤
Owner Mary Kavanagh, former director of personal shopping at Bergdorf Goodman, sells pre-owned but pristine, high-end, designer clothing. Her specialty is Chanel suits priced under a thousand dollars, but you can also find Armani, Ungaro, Jil Sander and Prada. Handbag and shoe labels include Fendi, Hermès, Gucci, Chanel, Tod's and Manolo Blahnik. During the winter, look for sable fur coats from J.Mendel.

*Luxury*                                            *Amex/MC/V*

**Midtown East**                               **(212) 702-0152**
146 East 49th Street                   btw Lexington/Third Ave
NYC 10017                               Tues-Fri 11-6, Sat 11-4

## Kazuyo Nakano                                          👤
Cameron Diaz is said to be one of the many who love the glossy Italian leather of Japanese designer Nakano's femi-

nine yet functional bags. This season finds Nakano flirting with zestier earth tones, large chain-linked straps, tassels, flower adornment and a sexier, sleeker look (yes, that is a cracked-silver finish on that fresh-faced purse) Be sure to slide up to Nakano's new soft-leather Sheila line and her popular Amanda bags.                      *kazuyonakano.com*

*Moderate*                                            *Amex/MC/V*

**Nolita**                                       **(212) 941-7093**
117 Crosby Street                          btw Houston/Prince
NYC 10012                                           Daily 12-7

## K.C.Thompson New York

Jewels, glorious jewels, and a fab store in which to buy them. Designer Kristen Thompson dreamed up a space (in a former nail salon) that she sees as a 'pampered women's dressing-room'. Think vanity mirrors where indulgent customers can try on such pieces as large, vintage-inspired flower earrings, or chunky-chic semi-precious necklaces featuring stones like cornelian, turquoise and coin pearls. Each piece has an 18-karat gold butterfly clasp. Expect to pay from $800 to $1,895 for her jewels—and spend hours more at the mirror at home admiring them.    *kcthompsonny.com*

*Expensive*                                           *Amex/MC/V*

**Upper East Side**                              **(212) 396-0974**
22 East 72nd Street                       btw Fifth/Madison Ave
NYC 10021                                          Mon-Fri 10-5

## KD Dance

Get footloose! KD stands for Kate and David, but it could easily stand for Knitwear and Dance, as that's exactly what you'll find here. Their specialty is dance, fitness and fashion knitwear that moves from yoga and Pilates straight to the streets, all without breaking a sweat. Find great looking tops, cardigans, tanks, yoga pants and stretch cotton/Lycra workout clothes alongside new items like ponchos and shawls. Better yet, almost all items are machine washable. Men and children have to do their shopping online.                                          *kddance.com*

*Moderate*                                            *Amex/MC/V*

**NoHo**                                         **(212) 533-1037**
339 Lafayette Street                                  at Bleecker
NYC 10012                                  Daily 12-8 (Sunday 1-5)

## Keiko

Have you ever wondered where those sexy swimsuits featured in fashion magazines come from? And how do they get such a perfect fit? Well, the answer is Keiko's, which offers a collection of bathing attire in mouth-watering colors. Prices start at $110, and alterations will cost you more. Suits seen in the pages of *Maxim* and *Sports Illustrated* can be mix-matched and paired off with the hottest durable bags and hats. New shady stripes, artsy appliqués and a tantalizing mesh are perfect for draping over basic separates. Customized suits start at $250, and are available for men, women (including more supportive designs) and children (only samples are showcased, ask for assistance). *keikonewyork.com*

*Moderate*                                          *Amex/MC/V*

**SoHo**                                        **(212) 226-6051**
62 Greene Street                            btw Spring/Broome
NYC 10012                                    Daily 12-6 (Sun 1-6)

## Kelly Christy

This eponymous boutique sells chic toppers with a flair for the dramatic: Christy describes her aesthetic as classic with a twist. Shelves of hat molds line the walls, while accessories (jewelry, scarves) sass up the small workshop. Each design highlights her unique use of trim, leather and ribbon on fedoras, boleros, cloches, berets and boaters. Choose off-the-rack or made-to-measure. *kellychristyhats.com*

*Expensive*                                        *Amex/MC/V*

**Nolita**                                       **(212) 965-0686**
235 Elizabeth Street                        btw Houston/Prince
NYC 10012                                   Tues-Sat 12-7, Sun 12-6

## ★ Keni Valenti

Located in the heart of the garment district, this four-room showroom boasts one of the foremost collections of vintage fashions from the Twenties to the Eighties, including beautiful designer dresses, couture eveningwear, shoes, handbags and jewelry. From choice pieces by American sportswear legends like John Kloss and Clovis Ruffin to heavy hitters like Yves Saint Laurent, Halston, Geoffrey Beene, Alaïa and Courrèges, it's all in impeccable condition. Former Fiorucci designer Valenti has also designed his own line, called KV, featuring bias-cut silk jersey evening dresses and luncheon-bound gabardine suits, that the model crew and downtown hipster Chloe Sevigny have been buying up bigtime. Expect to pay high couture designer prices for a little slice of vintage luxury. Also expect to look amazing. *kenivalenti.com*

*Expensive*                                        *Amex/MC/V*

**Midtown West**                                 **(212) 967-7147**
247 West 30th Street (5th floor)     btw Seventh/Eighth Ave
NYC 10001                             Mon-Fri 10-6 (by appointment)

## Kenneth Cole

Socially conscious Kenneth Cole is doing his best to inform minds while covering bodies in clean lines. He started by selling shoes out of a trailer and created a $300 million footwear empire, and he has since become a major force in men's and womenswear. His hallmark: clean, urban functionality at incredible value, and ads that spark political and health awareness. Both sexes can shop for fashionable sportswear, shiny jeans, embracing knits, tailored shirts and coats in buttery leather and shearling. In footwear, find a broad range of styles from career and dress shoes to trendy and casual basics. Accessories include handbags, scarves and sunglasses. Smart designs at smart prices.

800-536-2653 *kennethcole.com*

*Moderate* *Amex/MC/V*

**Fifth Avenue (Rockefeller Center)** **(212) 373-5800**
610 Fifth Avenue at 49th Street
NYC 10020 Mon-Sat 10-8, Sun 11-6

**Midtown East (Grand Central Station)** **(212) 949-8079**
107 East 42nd Street at Park Ave
NYC 10017 Mon-Fri 8-9, Sat 11-9, Sun 11-7

**Midtown East** **(212) 688-1670**
130 East 57th Street at Lexington Ave
NYC 10022 Mon-Sat 10-8, Sun 11-6

## Kids Foot Locker

It has exactly what you expect: a large selection of children's athletic wear, from baseball jerseys and tennis outfits to top-of-the-line sneakers. Brand names include Adidas, Nike and Reebok. From infants to size 6. *footlocker.com*

*Affordable* *Amex/MC/V*

**Midtown West** **(212) 465-9041**
120 West 34th Street btw Sixth/Seventh Ave
NYC 10001 Mon-Fri 8-9, Sat 9-9, Sun 11-7

## Kid Robot

Space monkeys! Mini Satans! Sushi critters! Only Kid Robot would feature such wickedly funny characters as playmates. An excellent place to pick up the best Japanese collectible toys in NYC, Kid Robot is filled with the hottest plastic 12-inch and mini figures (including rare and limited editions) by names and artists such as Michael Lau, Eric So, Toy2R, ITRangers and Mezco—a feast for Far East toy lovers. If you're done playing with the dolls, pick up a signature Kid Robot tee or tank in an assortment of candy colors. Remote controlled cars, books, electronics and a bunch of other accessories add to the fun—be sure to plan ahead, because you'll want plenty of time to browse. *kidrobot.com*

*Affordable* *Amex/MC/V*

**Nolita** **(212) 966-6688**
126 Prince Street btw Greene/Wooster
NYC 10012 Mon-Thurs 11-8, Fri-Sat 11-9, Sun 11-7

## Kinnu

Enter a world of Indian color, fabric and design. Handwoven, iridescent silks and cross-dyed cottons made up into kurta-styled tunics, dresses, asymmetrical wraps and drawstring pants define the collection. Gold brocade trim on hems and cuffs, intricate embroidery, mirror-work and hand-dyeing exemplify the elaborate workmanship that goes into each design. Decorative items like quilted bedspreads, wall-hangings and artwork also available.

*Moderate to expensive*                     *Amex/MC/V*
**Nolita**                                  **(212) 334-4775**
43 Spring Street                            btw Mulberry/Mott
NYC 10012                                   Daily 11:30-7

## ★ Kirna Zabête

Owners Sarah Easley (nicknamed Kirna) and Beth Buccini (nicknamed Zabête) have created a 5,000-square-foot two-level mini department store dedicated to goth, glam, girly but, most importantly, high fashion. The savvy duo buy an eclectic mix of the hottest designers from London, Paris, Belgium and New York, including Bruce, Martine Sitbon, A.F.Vandevorst, DEL, Cacharel, lots of Chloé, Wink and Balenciaga. The lower level is home to funky-chic and sporty looks featuring knits, T-shirts with ironic messages, lingerie, shoes, hats and handbags. Other goodies include lotions and potions, a candy section and a pet section. Accessories include huge numbers of handbags, hats, lingerie and pretty shoes. *kirnazabete.com*

*Expensive*                                 *Amex/MC/V*
**SoHo**                                     **(212) 941-9656**
96 Greene Street                            btw Prince/Spring
NYC 10012                                   Mon-Sat 11-7, Sun 12-6

## Kleinfeld

The baron of designer bridalwear. It may be quite a trek to Kleinfeld's, but the savings alone make it worth the trip. Find over 1,000 gowns in stock at all times from labels including Badgley Mischka, Christian Lacroix and Oscar de la Renta. *kleinfeldbridal.com*

*Expensive*                                 *Amex/MC/V*
**Bay Ridge**                                **(718) 765-8500**
8202 5th Avenue                             at 82nd St
Brooklyn 11209              Tues, Thurs 12:30-9:30, Fri 10-6
                          Sat 9:30-6 (Sundays by appointment)

## Klein's

An Orchard Street institution for over 20 years, Klein's is where savvy shoppers go for luxury European clothing at prices 25% below anywhere else. 'It's a Parisian, Left Bank type of feeling,' owner Eddie Klein says of the store that is as comfortable as your living room. Suits, jackets, pants, cashmere sweaters, blouses and outerwear are from designers like Luciano Barbera, MaxMara, Les Copains, Malo, René Lezard, Gunext and Clara Cottman. Accessories include belts, hats and scarves.

*Expensive*                                 *Amex/MC/V*
**Lower East Side**                          **(212) 966-1453**
105 Orchard Street                          at Delancey
NYC 10002                          Sun-Thurs 10-5, Fri 10-4

## Klurk

Klurk's owner Brian Chik is a former desk clerk-turned-designer whose line of casual menswear is best for the

154

young and adventurous. The collection combines cool urban streetwear with ironic collegiate styles—high-necked sweaters, knits with inside-out seams, funky patterned golf-like pants, dress pants with nylon waistbands and button-down cashmere shirts. Accessories include watches, clever key chains, a few bags and refined wallets.

*Moderate*                                              *Amex/MC/V*

**Nolita**                                          **(212) 966-3617**
360 Broome Street                           btw Mott/Elizabeth
NYC 10012                                  Sun-Fri 1-7 (closed Tues)

## Kmart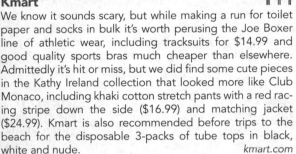

We know it sounds scary, but while making a run for toilet paper and socks in bulk it's worth perusing the Joe Boxer line of athletic wear, including tracksuits for $14.99 and good quality sports bras much cheaper than elsewhere. Admittedly it's hit or miss, but we did find some cute pieces in the Kathy Ireland collection that looked more like Club Monaco, including khaki cotton stretch pants with a red racing stripe down the side ($16.99) and matching jacket ($24.99). Kmart is also recommended before trips to the beach for the disposable 3-packs of tube tops in black, white and nude.                                        *kmart.com*

*Affordable*                                            *Amex/MC/V*

**NoHo**                                            **(212) 673-1540**
770 Broadway                                       at Astor Place
NYC 10003                                             Daily 8-10

**Midtown West**                                    **(212) 760-1188**
250 West 34th Street                      btw Seventh/Eighth Ave
NYC 10019                                 Mon-Fri 7-10, Sat-Sun 8-10

## Knit New York

For seasoned knitters and those who hope to be, Knit New York provides all the accoutrements this timeless pastime requires. Visitors can purchase yarn and needles to take home, or take classes in the store, or sit in the cozy café and find participants for their next quilting bee. *knitnewyork.com*

*Affordable*                                            *Amex/MC/V*

**East Village**                                    **(212) 387-0707**
307 East 14th Street                       btw First/Second Ave
NYC 10003         Daily 10-9 (café Mon-Fri 7-9, Sat-Sun 8-9)

## Koh's Kids

Grace Koh's shop offers hip, offbeat clothing for children (newborn to age 10). Dresses, jackets, shirts and all sorts of dressy and casual attire from American and European labels like Confetti, Flapdoodles, Cherry Tree, Zutano and Petit Bateau are available here; don't miss Koh's handknitted sweaters, either. The shelves of this small store sparkle with seasonal items like snow suits and gloves for winter frolics and shorts, bathing suits and sun hats for those summer beach dates. You'll also find fun toys, shoes and accessories (including hair ornaments and jewelry).

| | |
|---|---|
| *Moderate* | *Amex/MC/V* |
| **Tribeca** | **(212) 791-6915** |
| 311 Greenwich Street | btw Chambers/Reade |
| NYC 10013 | Daily 11-7 (Sun 11-5) |

## Krizia

Krizia designer Mariuccia Mandelli believes clothing is our second skin, so her ready-to-wear designs are body-conscious and comfortable. The collection runs the gamut from a glam $8,000 dress to a simple T-shirt. Other items include sculpted black crepe suits, pants, stretch cashmere twinsets, separates and coats. Her best offering, though, is luxury knitwear, from cling-to-the-body dresses to form-fitted sweaters. Eveningwear includes glamorous beaded chiffon gowns and slinky, black jersey dresses. Fellini fans will purr with delight when they see her signature animal-print sweaters. Her men's fashions border on avant-garde.

| | |
|---|---|
| *Expensive* | *Amex/MC/V* |
| **Upper East Side** | **(212) 879-1211** |
| 769 Madison Avenue | btw 65/66th St |
| NYC 10021 | Mon-Sat 10-6 |

## Label

Store owner Laura Whitcomb was doing Adidas dresses back in 1993 when Hollywood had yet to discover tracksuits, and her funky sportswear boutique is still ahead of the curve with tough yet sexy knitwear for skater chic. Staples like full-length skirts and sweatshirts are given surprise twists like asymmetrical cuts, slashes and zippered collars. Instead of baggy pants, Whitcomb offers full-length skirts with lots of pockets—and major attitude. Also a small selection of menswear.

| | |
|---|---|
| *Moderate* | *Amex/MC/V* |
| **Nolita** | **(212) 966-7736** |
| 265 Lafayette Street | btw Prince/Spring |
| NYC 10012 | Daily 12-7 |

## ★ Lacoste

That little alligator never seems to go out of fashion. Women who love preppy French style tumble over their tennis nets for sexy, striped open-necked tees, pleated minis and beach hats, while men will be immune to unforced errors in those iconic polos and cooler-than-K-Swiss sneaks. Luxuriating in its Fifth Avenue digs, Lacoste tops off its fresh-from-the-Riviera wear with watches, sunglasses and even perfumes. In other words, it's superior sporty gear for people who wouldn't be caught dead breaking a sweat.          800-4-LACOSTE  *lacoste.com*

| | |
|---|---|
| *Expensive* | *Amex/MC/V* |
| **Fifth Avenue** | **(212) 459-2300** |
| 608 Fifth Avenue | at 49th St |
| NYC 10022 | Mon-Sat 10-7:30 (Thurs 10-8), Sun 12-6 |

## Laila Rowe

It's accessories galore at this busy SoHo boutique. Rowe's trendy costume jewelry, handbags and scarves are a great way to update your wardrobe without putting out for an entire new ensemble. The pieces are of-the-moment, but inexpensive enough that you won't kick yourself for following the trend when it passes. Great deals (two scarves for $30) and lots of choice.

*Affordable*                                      *Amex/MC/V*

**SoHo**                                 **(212) 966-9210**
424 West Broadway                        btw Spring/Prince
NYC 10012                                       Daily 11-8

## La Layette et Plus

Attention all doting grandmothers. Exquisite, old-world charm infuses this tiny store, which offers luxurious European children's clothing and a complete layette selection. Appointments are encouraged to ensure customers receive exclusive attention while being shown a large array of receiving blankets, christening gowns, bibs, crib linens and more. Also find luxurious gifts like porcelain piggy banks and satin hangers. Each item is prettier than the next.                                        *lalayette.com*

*Expensive*                                       *Amex/MC/V*

**Upper East Side**                       **(212) 688-7072**
170 East 61st Street               btw Lexington/Third Ave
NYC 10021                          Mon-Fri 11-6, Sat 11-5

## ★ La Perla

Totally gorgeous, fiendishly expensive—the caviar of lingerie. A legendary label of feminine intimates that run from tasteful and elegant to seductive and sexy, La Perla also features a fashion line of bustiers and bodysuits with built-in bra cups, as well as swimwear and sleepwear. Be prepared to pay up to a few hundred dollars for a single item.                                           *laperla.com*

*Luxury*                                          *Amex/MC/V*

**Upper East Side**                       **(212) 570-0050**
777 Madison Avenue                         btw 66/67th St
NYC 10021                          Mon-Sat 10-6, Sun 12-5

**SoHo**                                 **(212) 219-0999**
93 Greene Street                          btw Prince/Spring
NYC 10012                          Mon-Sat 11-7, Sun 12-6

**Meatpacking District**                  **(212) 242-6662**
425 West 14th Street                    btw Ninth/Tenth Ave
NYC 10014                          Mon-Sat 11-7, Sun 12-6

## ★ La Petite Coquette

In business for 25 years, La Petite Coquette remains the in-place for high-end sexy lingerie. Just ask regulars like Julianne Moore, Liv Tyler, Cindy Crawford and Sarah Jessica Parker. Once you've seen the storefront windows, it's impossible to resist stepping into a space that feels more like a boudoir than a shop, with its sweet vanilla smell and hand-painted pin-ups on the wall. There's an incredible selection of private-label silk intimates in a multitude of colors and looks that range from alluring corsets and garters to flirty nighties and feminine basics. Besides the bedroom attire, be sure to check out the swimwear, a new jewelry collection and a small men's collection. Labels include La Perla, Lise Charmel, Ravage, Damaris, Dolce & Gabbana, Andres Sarda, Cotton Club, Naory and Aubade, and prices run from $38 to $1,800. One of the best lingerie shops in the city.                                    *thelittleflirt.com*

*Expensive*                                                  *Amex/MC/V*

**NoHo**                                             **(212) 473-2478**
51 University Place                                     btw 9/10th St
NYC 10003                          Mon-Sat 11-7 (Thurs 11-8), Sun 12-6

## LaCrasia Gloves
In 1973 belt-designer and FIT graduate LaCrasia Lome Duchein had a vision: to reclaim the fame of gloves and bring them back as a women's wardrobe staple. Now, with partner and master glovemaker Jay Ruckel, LaCrasia has brought her dream to life, creating over 60,000 gloves a year for rich and famous folks from the White House to Broadway to Hollywood: Jackie Kennedy, Donna Karan, Michael Jackson, Madonna, Angelica, Gwyneth and Uma are but a few well-known clients. The store sells everything from lacy fingerless styles, white debutante gloves, snakeskin numbers, leather driving gloves and much more. Guess who made Brittany's white leather opera gloves?                                          *wegloveyou.com*

*Moderate*                                                  *Amex/MC/V*

**Midtown West**                                     **(212) 803-1600**
15 West 28th Street (suite 401)                   btw Fifth/Broadway
NYC 10001                          Mon-Fri 10-5 (Sat by appointment)

## Lady Foot Locker
Strictly for the gals, Lady Foot Locker offers a great choice of shoes and athletic apparel for running, tennis, basketball and cross-training. Find all the big names: Nike, Reebok, Adidas, Fila and New Balance.

                                  800-877-5239  *ladyfootlocker.com*

*Affordable*                                                *Amex/MC/V*

**Midtown West**                                     **(212) 629-4626**
120 West 34th Street                                        at Sixth Ave
NYC 10120                                    Mon-Sat 8-9, Sun 11-7

## Laina Jane Lingerie
Slipping into a sound and sexy number is made easy in Laina Jane's great selection of nighties and pajamas from labels like Arianne, Hanky Panky and Sleeping Partners. This is also an excellent West Village destination for some of the top makers of bras and panties such as Eberjay, Le

Mystère, Cosabella and Gemma. Hosiery and a small selection of swimwear also available.

*Moderate to expensive*                                    *Amex/MC/V*

**Upper West Side**                          **(212) 875-9168**
416 Amsterdam Avenue                              at 80th St
NYC 10024                                        Daily 11-7

**West Village**                             **(212) 807-8077**
45 Christopher Street    btw Waverly Place/Seventh Ave
NYC 10014        Sun-Wed 11:30-7:30, Thurs-Sat 11:30-8

## Lana Marks
Handbag aficionados shop here for Lana Marks' exotic skins like alligator, ostrich and lizard. Designs are classic and fashionable and colors run from black to vivid pink. True opulence comes in the form of Lana's $25,000 Cleopatra tote which is embellished with yellow sapphires. Be sure to ask for assistance if you are interested in trying on a bag, as many items are understandably under heavy guard. Don't miss the skinny belts and the limited selection of men's accessories.                                   *lanamarks.com*

*Luxury*                                             *Amex/MC/V*

**Midtown East**                             **(212) 355-6135**
645 Madison Avenue                              btw 59/60th St
NYC 10022              Mon-Fri 9-6:30, Thurs 9-7, Sat 9-6

## Lane Bryant
A name synonymous with plus sizes, but this does not mean that Lane Bryant ain't sexy. Absolutely not—it's getting positively racy: think a curvier Victoria's Secret and you've got it. Size 14-28s will find everything from a fabulous assortment of jeans to sexy intimate apparel, all moderately priced. Although it's quite a trek to visit their only Manhattan store, located in Harlem, it's well worth the trip. The line has embroidered tunics ($49), denim (from $34.50) and special occasion wear from $80. Fabulous knows no size, honey.                                  *lanebryant.com*

*Affordable*                                         *Amex/MC/V*

**Harlem**                                   **(212) 678-0546**
222 West 125th Street            btw Seventh/Eighth Ave
NYC 10027                         Mon-Sat 10-7, Sun 12-5

## Laundry by Shelli Segal
Although she continues to supply major department stores, Segal also has her own store for her softly shaped, reasonably priced pieces, from ruffled dresses and floral shirts to cashmere tops and drawstring pants. A Segal design is feminine, elegantly understated and easy-to-wear.                              *laundrybyshellisegal.com*

*Moderate*                                           *Amex/MC/V*

**SoHo**                                     **(212) 334-9433**
97 Wooster Street                          btw Prince/Spring
NYC 10012                         Mon-Sat 11-7, Sun 12-6

## Laura Biagiotti

Biagiotti has been crowned the Queen of Cashmere by the fashion set because her luxurious, featherweight knitwear is second to none. Biagiotti's designs are versatile and comfortable, with soft tailoring, intricate stitching and a focus on all shades of white from pure to creamy. Every collection includes a series of comfortable baby-doll dresses and pants with elasticated waists. Other looks include soft sweaters paired with chiffon skirts, suits, dresses, separates and coats in cashmere, silk and linen.      *laurabiagiottti.it*

*Expensive*                                      *Amex/MC/V*

**Midtown West**                              **(212) 399-2533**
4 West 57th Street                        btw Fifth/Sixth Ave
NYC 10019                                       Mon-Sat 10-6

## The Leather and Suede Workshop

It's a skins game for owner/tailor Ron Shahar, the go-to man for all your leather needs. Choose from suede, cowhide, leather, and snakeskin in a multitude of colors on, well, pretty much everything: pants, jackets, long and short skirts, dresses, shirts, coats, belts and even hats. Pants start at $395, jackets at $595. Shahar will custom tailor a micromini or a pair of black leather pants that will fit like a glove.

*Expensive*                                      *Amex/MC/V*

**Midtown East**                              **(212) 688-1946**
107 East 59th Street            btw Park/Lexington Ave
NYC 10022            Mon-Fri 10-7, Sat 11-7, Sun 11:30-6:30

## The Leather Man

Okay, so bondage, handcuffs and Crispo masks aren't your thing. How about a pair of five-pocket jeans in motorcycle-weight leather to shake things up a bit? Well, The Leather Man offers custom-fit leather pants, vests and boots that run the gamut from biker to rock star to rough trade. Prices for pants start at $395.      *theleatherman.com*

*Expensive*                                      *Amex/MC/V*

**West Village**                              **(212) 243-5339**
111 Christopher Street               btw Bleecker/Hudson
NYC 10014                           Daily 12-10 (Sunday 12-8)

## Le Chateau

Trendy and ultimately disposable clubwear for teens and twentysomethings who need something cheap for a night out. Hoochie-mama tube tops in bright prints, tight flared bottoms and serious Seventies wedge platforms sit alongside fun accessories, including a wide selection of fake hair.      *le-chateau.com*

*Affordable*                                      *Amex/MC/V*

**NoHo**                                          **(212) 674-5560**
704 Broadway          btw Washington Place/West 4th St
NYC 10003                                  Daily 11-9 (Sun 11-7)

## Le Corset

Ah, le corset! The seductive tool for breathless ladies that has the same (if slightly more forgiving) allure now as it did centuries ago. Owner Selima Salaun is an expert at spotting new trends in lingerie and provides a fabulously enticing selection of new and vintage lingerie that runs from flirty to retro to unabashedly sexy. There are satin and silk corsets, feminine camisoles, demi-cup bras that accentuate cleavage, bodysuits, lacy panties, chemises, garter belts and more from labels that include Selima (Le Corset's house design), Carine Gilson, Khurana, Chantal Thomass, Blumarine, Collette Dinnigan and Roberto Cavalli

*Moderate*                                               *Amex/MC/V*

**SoHo**                                          **(212) 334-4936**
80 Thompson Street                          btw Spring/Broome
NYC 10012                    Mon-Fri 11-7, Sat 11-8, Sun 12-7

## Lederer

In a world dominated by fleeting fashions and trends, this Paris-based bag and accessory maker is only interested in timelessness. Lederer has satisfied five generations of customers and is still going strong. The prices are terrific and the quality and workmanship impressive. Shop for classics like hand-woven leathers, bamboo-handled structured bags, steel or wood-framed investment banker briefcases and their exclusive Angelica bag. Luggage, small leather goods and desk accessories, hunting clothes and Barbour outerwear are also available. There is even a repair shop on the premises.          888-537-6921 *ledererdeparis.com*

*Luxury*                                                 *Amex/MC/V*

**Midtown East**                                  **(212) 355-5515**
457 Madison Avenue                                    at 51st St
NYC 10022                                         Mon-Sat 9:30-6

## Lee Anderson

A haven for the more serious minded New York woman, who orders from Anderson's couture collection of classic suits, separates, daywear and eveningwear. Choose from off-the-rack or order custom-made.

*Expensive*                                              *Amex/MC/V*

**Upper East Side**                               **(212) 772-2463**
23 East 67th Street                      btw Fifth/Madison Ave
NYC 10021                    Mon-Sat 10-6 (and by appointment)

## Legacy

Vintage-inspired clothing without the musty smell or wear and tear of the real thing. Dresses, skirts, blouses, pants and more by a number of underground European designers who all have a retro feel and a distinctive look.    *legacy-nyc.com*

*Moderate*                                               *Amex/MC/V*

**SoHo**                                          **(212) 966-4827**
109 Thompson Street                          btw Prince/Spring
NYC 10012                                              Daily 12-7

## Leggiadro

If you missed out on the resortwear collections at department stores and boutiques, head to this Upper East Side store where sun-ready styles are in season 365 days a year. Clothing and swimwear by Sugar and Leggiadro are perfect for warm-weather destinations from St Tropez to Palm Beach. Expect lots of prints, bright colors and complementary accessories.

*Expensive*                                          *Amex/MC/V*

**Upper East Side**                          **(212) 753-5050**
680 Madison Avenue                          btw 61/62nd St
NYC 10021                                     Daily 10:30-6

## Legs Beautiful

Pretty much what it says—lots of legwear to make the most of your gams. The fabulous hosiery selection includes brand names like DKNY, CK, Hue and Hanes, but there is also sexy lingerie, bodysuits, stretch tops, amusing socks, tights, and flip-flops. Now, if only there were one on every street corner.          1-866-243-1113 *legsbeautiful.com*

*Affordable*                                         *Amex/MC/V*

**Midtown East**                             **(212) 949-2270**
200 Park Avenue                                   at 45th St
NYC 10166                                    Mon-Fri 7:30-8

**Midtown East**                             **(212) 688-9599**
153 East 53rd Street                   btw Lexington/Third Ave
NYC 10022                                  Mon-Sat 8:30-6:30

## Leonard Logsdail

Once a Savile Row tailor, Leonard Logsdail now provides New York bankers, diplomats and high-powered lawyers with his British bespoke tailoring. He takes your measurements, cuts his paper pattern and then ships your order to London to be hand-stitched. Made-to-measure suits of the finest pedigree start at $2,500, custom suits at $4,200. Time is indeed money: expect to wait six to eight weeks for delivery.

*Luxury*                                             *Amex/MC/V*

**Midtown East**                             **(212) 752-5030**
9 East 53rd Street (4th floor)          btw Fifth/Madison Ave
NYC 10022                                    (by appointment)

## Les Copains

This chicly decorated boutique offers a winning mix of classic and avant-garde looks, from suits and tweeds to stylish sweaters and superb coats—highlights include beautiful cashmere pants and great knitwear. Browse the Blue label for more casual finds and Trend for those young pieces perfect for spicing up your wardrobe.          *lescopains.it*

*Expensive*                                          *Amex/MC/V*

**Upper East Side**                          **(212) 327-3014**
807 Madison Avenue                          btw 67/68th St
NYC 10021                                     Mon-Sat 10-6

## Les Petits Chapelais

Packed with whimsical children's clothing, including hand-loomed sweaters, dresses in vintage fabrics, handknit tops, T-shirts, hats and accessories. Wicker baskets, complete with three-piece baby sets (chenille blanket, hat, and toy), make wonderful baby shower gifts.

*Moderate to expensive*                                    *Amex/MC/V*

**SoHo**                                                **(212) 505-1927**
142 Sullivan Street                               btw Houston/Prince
NYC 10012                        Sun-Mon 1-6, Tues-Sat 12-7

## ★ LeSportSac

LeSportSac continues to get better and better. With a more fashion-forward client in mind, LeSportSac take their bags well into the new millennium with modern shapes that reflect a girl-on-the-go lifestyle. With new designs from guest designers like Gwen Stefani, fashionistas will feel no shame in carrying a 100% nylon classic. The white-washed walls, glass tables and friendly staff allow the ultra-personality bags—totes, weekend duffles, cosmetic clutches and handbags, all double-stitched on the inside and machine washable—to hog the spotlight. The price points are mostly under $100, with nothing over $200. With cute names like Rainbow Spectator and Classic Hobo, everyone is bound to find a style that reflects his or her personality.          800-486-BAGS *lesportsac.com*

*Moderate*                                                *Amex/MC/V*

**Upper East Side**                                     **(212) 988-6200**
1065 Madison Avenue                            btw 80/81st St
NYC 10028                          Mon-Sat 10-7, Sun 12-5

**SoHo**                                                **(212) 625-2626**
176 Spring Street              btw West Broadway/Thompson
NYC 10012                          Mon-Sat 11-7, Sun 12-6

## Lester's

A nondescript store that features a good selection of back-to-school basics, casual play clothes and trendy sportswear for hard-to-please juniors from brand names like Juicy, Hard Tail and Quiksilver. There are also full-service layette and shoe departments, as well as accessories. From newborn to size 16 and juniors.

*Affordable*                                              *Amex/MC/V*

**Upper East Side**                                     **(212) 734-9292**
1534 Second Avenue                                   at 80th St
NYC 10021    Mon-Fri 10-7 (Thurs 10-8), Sat 10-6, Sun 12-5

## Liana

This stylish uptown store nods to the trends while keeping things classic with a sizeable selection of casual basics, including sweater sets by Easel, White and Warren, and 525, tanks and tees by Michael Star and pants by Chaiken and Theory. And with the Upper West Side's largest selection of little black dresses, Liana has an ample selection of formalwear, suits, and other tasteful party attire from the likes of Shin Choi, Tahari, Nanette Lepore and Trina Turk.

*Expensive*                                    *Amex/MC/V*

**Upper West Side**                            **(212) 873-8746**
324 Columbus Avenue                            btw 75/76th St
NYC 10023                                      Mon-Sat 11-7, Sun 1-6

## Liberty House                                👫

Originally conceived in 1968 as a co-op that donated profits to the civil rights movement, Liberty House is still known for its large and varied selection of independent designers who work with natural fibers. While there is no shortage of ethnic-inspired prints, they also cram lots of pared-down, urban sophisticate tees, dresses and trousers into this packed, busy space. Check it out for unique jewelry and accessories and charming children's pjs, plus hats by Christine A. Moore Millinery at the 112th Street store.                              *libertyhouseny.com*

*Moderate*                                     *Amex/MC/V*

**Upper West Side**                            **(212) 799-7640**
2466 Broadway                                  at 91st St
NYC 10024                  Tues-Sat 12-6:45, Mon, Thurs 12-7:45
                                               Sun 12-5:45

**Upper West Side**                            **(212) 932-1950**
2878a Broadway                                 at 112th St
NYC 10025                      Mon-Sat 10-6:45, Sun 12-5:45

## Lilliput/SoHo Kids                          👤

Inspired by the Lilliputians in *Gulliver's Travels*, this store carries a soup-to-nuts collection of children's clothing ideal for play, school and dress-up. For boys, choose from jeans, khakis, dress shirts, sweaters, T-shirts and windbreakers, while girls will find looks running from adorable print dress-es to cool, fashionable leather jeans paired with a hip top. And for babies, they've got it all, from onesies in washable silks and cashmeres to a basic Petit Bateau undershirt. Labels include Lili Gaufrette, Marcel & Leon, I Golfini della Nonna, Baby Gordon and Diesel. Shoes, hats, pajamas, bags and toys round out the assortment. From newborn to 18 years old.                              *lilliputsoho.com*
Moderate                                       Amex/MC/V

**SoHo**                                       **(212) 965-9567**
265 Lafayette Street                           btw Prince/Spring
NYC 10012                                      Daily 11-7

**SoHo**                                       **(212) 965-9201**
240 Lafayette Street                           btw Prince/Spring
NYC 10012                              (opening hours as above)

## Lily                                         👩

Imagine that the queen of Palm Beach chic and American design legend Lilly Pulitzer had a daughter who opened her own shop in Brooklyn, and you'll have some idea of what awaits you at Lily. Perhaps younger and hipper (though no less colorful) than Mrs Pulitzer's famous wares, these current takes on sportswear perfectly combine cheekiness with Brooklyn cool. Michael Stars tees and underwear are available, as are cute tops by Free People and Hanky Panky. A neighborhood favorite, Lily is great place to snag a little out-of-the-way style.                    lilybrooklyn.com

*Affordable*                                               *Amex/MC/V*

**Cobble Hill**                              **(718) 858-6261**
209 Court Street                         btw Warren/Wyckoff
Brooklyn 11201            Mon, Wed, Sat 11-7, Thurs-Fri 11-8
                                                    Sun 12-6

## Linda Dresner

Linda Dresner is a legend in fashion-forward retailing, and she continues to lead the pack with her elite collection of cutting-edge designers. John Galliano, Yohji Yamamoto, Marni, Martin Margiela, Dries Van Noten, Chloé and Jil Sander have a regular spot in the store, while hot newcomers such as Zac Posen and Proenza Schouler have also been put into the rotation. High-end shopping for drop-dead chic designer pieces, from knockout evening gowns to urbane suits, in an equally chic retail space. There is a limited range of shoes and accessories.

*Luxury*                                                 *Amex/MC/V*

**Midtown East**                            **(212) 308-3177**
484 Park Avenue                            btw 58/59th St
NYC 10022                                   Mon-Sat 10-6

## Lingerie on Lex

Don't be turned off by the less-than-creative name—this charming store features upscale American and European intimate apparel brands like Hanro, Cosabella and La Perla, to name but a few purveyors of sweet nothings. Customers will appreciate the large variety and good organization. Custom-made pieces are also available.

*Expensive*                                              *Amex/MC/V*

**Upper East Side**                         **(212) 755-3312**
831 Lexington Avenue                        btw 63/64th St
NYC 10021                   Mon-Fri 10-7, Sat 11-6, Sun 12-5

## Lingo

Lingo's teal and red trim facade is hard to miss, as are its fanciful floral window displays. Inside you'll find a heady cross-section of NY fashion: one-of-a-kind handmade, hand-embroidered shoulder bags, dangly silver earrings with semi-precious stones, sassy silk-screened T-shirts and leather clutches in bright colors. Owner Shin Yee Man keeps things current (and wildly eclectic) by featuring a number of different designers, many of whom moonlight as artists and musicians.                          lingonyc.com

*Moderate* *Amex/MC/V*
**Chelsea** **(212) 929-4676**
257 West 19th Street btw Seventh/Eighth Ave
NYC 10011 Tues-Sun 1-8

## Liora Manné

Liora Manné is a true artisan with an incredible eye for detail and color. Employing felt and acrylic, her innovative creations are sewn by hand here in the city using custom-dyed fabrics, and the resulting dresses are exhilarating riots of color. Dazzling handbags, shoes and accessories (including lighting) are also available. *lioramanne.com*

*Moderate* *Amex/MC/V*
**SoHo** **(212) 965-0302**
91 Grand Street btw Mercer/Greene
NYC 10013 Mon-Sat 11-7, Sun 12-6

## Lisa Shaub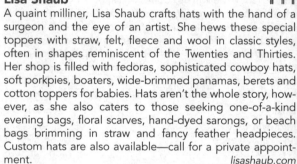

A quaint milliner, Lisa Shaub crafts hats with the hand of a surgeon and the eye of an artist. She hews these special toppers with straw, felt, fleece and wool in classic styles, often in shapes reminiscent of the Twenties and Thirties. Her shop is filled with fedoras, sophisticated cowboy hats, soft porkpies, boaters, wide-brimmed panamas, berets and cotton toppers for babies. Hats aren't the whole story, however, as she also caters to those seeking one-of-a-kind evening bags, floral scarves, hand-dyed sarongs, or beach bags brimming in straw and fancy feather headpieces. Custom hats are also available—call for a private appointment. *lisashaub.com*

*Moderate* *Amex/MC/V*
**Nolita** **(212) 965-9176**
232 Mulberry btw Prince/Spring
NYC 10012 Wed 12-5, Thurs-Sat 12-7, Sun 1-6

## Little Eric Shoes

Fancy some fancy footwear for your kids? Check out this exclusive collection of Italian footwear: casual basics, back-to-school essentials, formal dress shoes and high fashion styles for teenagers. The sales staff claim these shoes will outwear your child. Kids will enjoy the toys inside and the colorful train set painted along the store's ceiling. A good source for all ages, especially for your baby's first walking shoes.

*Expensive* *Amex/MC/V*
**Upper East Side** **(212) 717-1513**
1118 Madison Avenue btw 83/84th St
NYC 10028 Mon-Sat 10-6, Sun 12-5

## ★ Liz Lange Maternity

A former *Vogue* editor, Liz Lange is the reigning queen of maternity chic (no longer an oxymoron) and her stylish store offers one-stop shopping for sportswear, eveningwear and activewear. Her secret: easy, chic clothing you would wear even if you weren't pregnant. Looks include capri pants, cashmere twinsets, sexy halter tops, A-line dresses, shifts, tunics, denim and spaghetti-strap evening dresses. Model mothers like Brooke Shields and Elle Macpherson have compared Lange's designs to Michael Kors and Calvin Klein. *lizlange.com*

*Expensive* *Amex/MC/V*

**Upper East Side** **(212) 879-2191**
958 Madison Avenue btw 75/76th St
NYC 10021 Mon-Fri 10-7, Sat 10-6, Sun 12-5

## Loehmann's

Canny shoppers make this mounting legend their first stop when looking for top brand names at knockout prices. The selection includes men's and women's clothes, a petite section, accessories and shoes but the main attraction is without a doubt the Back Room, a department stocked with designer labels like Calvin Klein, Donna Karan and Armani. A chic Moschino trench for $100? Yes, it is possible here. By the way, if you're not satisfied, Loehmann's has a 14-day, get-your-money-back return policy. *loehmanns.com*

*Moderate* *Amex/MC/V*

**Chelsea** **(212) 352-0856**
101 Seventh Avenue btw 16/17th St
NYC 10011 Mon-Sat 9-9, Sun 11-7

## Loftworks @ Lafayette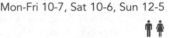

Designed to give folks a marvelous place to shop for designer clothing at discounted prices, Loftworks @ Lafayette draws shoppers to Lower Manhattan for great buys. The large stock includes formal business attire, designer sportswear and casualwear from Hugo Boss, Burberry, Armani, Gucci, DKNY, Abercrombie & Fitch, Fendi, Calvin Klein, Prada and many others—all at slashed down prices. Many of the best bargains can be found on the lower level, where Loftworks keep their close-out items. *loftworkslafayette.com*

*Affordable* *Amex/MC/V*

**Tribeca** **(212) 343-8088**
100 Lafayette Street btw White/Walker
NYC 10013 Daily 10-7

## Longchamp

Longchamp's nylon totes are ubiquitous on the Upper East Side these days, and with good reason. The bags are light, durable, and come in a panoply of colors. Other covetable items at this venerable French boutique include elegant structured handbags in leather, suede and, yes, nylon. Trendier pieces, such as hobo bags, provide some visual punch to Longchamp's otherwise graceful and understated collection. The company's sophisticated sensibility also appears in its briefcases, luggage, raincoats, belts, scarves and gloves. *longchamp.com*

*Expensive*                                    *Amex/MC/V*

**Upper East Side**                            **(212) 223-1500**
713 Madison Avenue                             at 63rd St
NYC 10021                                      Mon-Sat 10-7

## Lord & Taylor

After extensive remodeling, this behemoth department store looks better than ever. The makeover makes it easy to navigate between departments—all of which remain true to the store's mission of providing conservative and affordable clothing for sensible people. The selection is a melting-pot of classic fashion designers like Ralph Lauren, Donna Karan and Calvin Klein. Known for special occasion formalwear and hard-to-find shoe styles, Lord & Taylor also boasts extensive petite, career and sportswear sections. Other departments include cosmetics, accessories, children's, men's, lingerie, outerwear and large sizes. *lordandtaylor.com*

*Moderate*                                     *Amex/MC/V*

**Midtown**                                    **(212) 391-3344**
424 Fifth Avenue                               at 39th Street
NYC 10018                         Daily 10-7 (Wed-Fri 10-8:30)

## Lord of The Fleas

While having little to do with a flea market or the William Golding book of a similar title, this cleverly named boutique sells tight tiny tops, super-short skirts, sassy logo tees and other funky items for juniors, teenagers or anyone willing to show a little skin. If you want to feed the action heroine within by wearing Superwoman skivvies, you're sure to find the perfect piece at Lord of the Fleas.

*Affordable*                                   *Amex/MC/V*

**Upper West Side**                            **(212) 875-8815**
2142 Broadway                                  btw 75/76th St
NYC 10023                       Mon-Sat 11-8:30, Sun 12-6:30

**East Village**                               **(212) 260-9130**
305 East 9th Street                            btw First/Second Ave
NYC 10009                                      Daily 12-8

## Loro Piana

Apparently the higher a goat climbs, the finer its cashmere (impress your friends with this fact). Which means that Loro Piana's goats must have been climbing Everest. The collection features elegant knitwear, outerwear, pants, shirts and jackets in sumptuous fabrics like cashmere, silk and superfine wool. In addition, there is a luxurious assortment of cashmere shawls, scarves, stoles and capes in mouthwatering shades. Prices are sky-high, but then again, so were the goats...

*Luxury*                                       *Amex/MC/V*

**Upper East Side**                            **(212) 980-7961**
821 Madison Avenue                             btw 68/69th St
NYC 10021                          Mon-Sat 10-6 (Thurs 10-7)

## Lost Art

Have a rock star inside you just screaming to get out? Well, follow the lead of Britney Spears, Aerosmith's Steven Tyler and designer Anna Sui and turn to Lost Art's Jordan Betten for rock 'n' roll leather looks in cow, deer, elk, snake, croc and alligator. Intricate handcrafted details include antique beading, unique closures, stones, feathers and fur. Each creation is a one-of-a-kind artwork. Pay from $1,800 for pants and $3,500 for jackets. Best bet: his whip-stitched lace-up leather pants. Kinky. *lostartnyc.com*

| *Expensive* | *Amex/MC/V* |
|---|---|
| **Chelsea** | **(212) 594-5450** |
| 515 West 29th Street | btw Tenth/Eleventh Ave |
| NYC 10001 | Mon-Fri 10-5 (by appointment) |

## Louis Féraud

'Louis Féraud adore les femmes,' and the ladies adore him right back. A scion of the French fashion establishment—young Louis famously dressed Brigitte Bardot in a classic white sundress in the Fifties—the label is better known today for classic designs for an older customer: ladies-who-lunch dresses and beautifully cut suits. Customers can expect a full-bodied cut, tailored looks and sizing that runs from 4 to 16. Their sportswear collection Contraire features versatile, classic basics.

| *Expensive* | *Amex/MC/V* |
|---|---|
| **Midtown West** | **(212) 956-7010** |
| 3 West 56th Street | btw Fifth/Sixth Ave |
| NYC 10019 | Tues-Sat 10-6 (Thurs 10-7) |

## Louis Vuitton

The mere utterance of the name Louis Vuitton conjures up an image of international chic. The often-imitated but never replicated luggage and clothing line, designed by the omnipresent designer of the decade Marc Jacobs, is legendary in its own time. From the classic monogrammed luggage sets that are said to last forever to the limited-edition bags-cum-art-objects customized by Stephen Sprouse and Takashi Murakami, it's clear why people love those little interlocking LVs. Jacob's immensely stylish ready-to-wear collection for Vuitton is here for the taking, too. The new Fifth Avenue flagship is enormous, but for south-of-14th-Street style-seekers, the SoHo branch is also well stocked. 800-847-2956 *vuitton.com*

| *Expensive to luxury* | *Amex/MC/V* |
|---|---|
| **Fifth Avenue** | **(212) 758-8877** |
| 1 East 57th Street | at Fifth Ave |
| NYC 10022 | Mon-Sat 10-7, Thurs 10-8, Sun 12-6 |
| **SoHo** | **(212) 274-9090** |
| 116 Greene Street | btw Prince/Spring |
| NYC 10012 | Mon-Sat 11-7, Sun 12-6 |

## The Lounge

This SoHo boutique sets the scene with a collection of label-loving, super-trendy streetwear from Von Dutch, James Perse, Roberto Cavalli, D&G and Rock and Republic. Complete with a café in the back and a DJ booth spinning (you can buy hot club mixes from Buddha Bar and the Hotel Costes), The Lounge is a fashion destination for those who love the nightlife.

*Expensive*                                           *Amex/MC/V*

**SoHo**                                        **(212) 226-7585**
593 Broadway                                    btw Prince/Houston
NYC 10012                            Mon-Fri 10-9:30, Sat-Sun 12-8:30

## Love Saves the Day

The sign on the door says 'Unattended children will be sold as slaves.' but this crowded labyrinth of cheeky kitsch memorabilia is irresistible to kids and adults alike. Remember the G.I.Joe lunchboxes, Kiss dolls, and Pee Wee Herman collectibles? They're all here. You'll also find vintage clothes and shoes, mostly random pieces like wedding dresses from the Sixties. Some are a bit worse for wear, but you could get lucky—after all, this is where Rosanna Arquette got Madonna's pyramid jacket in *Desperately Seeking Susan*.

*Affordable to moderate*                              *Amex/MC/V*

**East Village**                                 **(212) 228-3802**
119 Second Avenue                                         at 7th St
NYC 10003                                              Daily 12-8

## Love Shine

Describing itself as the 'one-stop shop for bags, muffs and all kinds of stuff,' this crazy East Village store has eclectic ethnic gifts to suit every taste. Examples include a hologram wrist cuff with a Last Supper motif ($18), pink fake-fur hand warmers with plastic flowers ($40), totes adorned with sequined Mexican masks or skull and crossbones, kitschy ashtrays and more skull and crossbones on carryalls.                                      *loveshinenyc.com*

*Affordable*                                          *Amex/MC/V*

**East Village**                                 **(212) 387-0935**
543½ East 6th Street                             btw Avenue A/B
NYC 10009                                        Daily 1-8 (Sun 1-7)

## Luca Luca

Designer Luca Orlandi is a brave man—he's long been known for his bold approach to fashion, involving a strong use of color and bright, eye-popping patterns. And he has range: his silk/linen suits are perfect for an elegant dinner date, while his club-worthy tops look great with jeans. Luca Luca's accessories include t-strap sandals and chain-link leather purses. The store's white walls let the clothes take center stage, from dress suits, bias-cut pleated leather jackets and dresses, to cashmeres, suede shirtdresses, strapless eveningwear and perfectly polished outfits for the lunching set.                                         *lucaluca.com*

*Expensive*                                              *Amex/MC/V*

**Upper East Side**                                  **(212) 288-9285**
1011 Madison Avenue                                      at 78th St
NYC 10011          Mon-Sat 11-6:30 (Thurs 11-8), Sun 12-5

**Upper East Side**                                  **(212) 753-2444**
690 Madison Avenue                                       at 62nd St
NYC 10021                               (opening hours as above)

## Lucien Pellat-Finet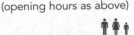

The sweaters on offer from this self-proclaimed 'King Kong of cashmere' are luxurious and come in a range of mouth-watering colors, but they have a decidedly downtown twist. Find the entire irreverent collection (this season's Gangs collection features 'I Hemp NY' sweatshirts, long-sleeved tees with bats, skull and bones bikinis and boss motorcycle jackets) in this exquisitely renovated 19th-century townhouse. Looks for kids eschew the scarier prints in favor of ladybugs and sea creatures. Be sure to see the eclectic interior designs, including vintage Florence Knoll furniture, and inquire about made-to-measure clothing.                    *lucienpellat-finet.com*

*Luxury*                                                  *Amex/MC/V*

**West Village**                                     **(212) 255-8560**
14 Christopher Street                          btw Sixth/Seventh Ave
NYC 10014              Daily 11-7 (closed Sundays in summer)

## Lucky Brand

In the beginning there was Levi's; now there's Lucky Brand, a Californian company that features a floor-to-ceiling selection of jeans, loungewear and everything in between. Pay an average of $70 for a pair of jeans. 'Lucky You' and a four-leaf clover logo mark the lining of every pair. Will they bring you good luck? Who knows…        *luckybrandjeans.com*

*Affordable*                                             *Amex/MC/V*

**Upper West Side**                                  **(212) 579-1760**
218 Columbus Avenue                                      at 70th St
NYC 10023                              Mon-Sat 10-8, Sun 12-7

**Upper East Side**                                  **(646) 422-1192**
1151 Third Avenue                                       at 67th St
NYC 10021                        Mon-Fri 10-8, Sat 11-7, Sun 11-6

**Flatiron**                                         **(917) 606-1418**
172 Fifth Avenue                                       at 22nd St
NYC 10010                        Mon-Fri 10-8, Sat 10-7, Sun 11-6

**SoHo**                                             **(212) 625-0707**
38 Greene Street                                         at Grand
NYC 10013                              Mon-Sat 11-7, Sun 12-6

## Lucy Barnes

Now with two shops in choice spots downtown, Lucy Barnes creates romantic clothing for ladies who demand

171

eclectic elegance. The label offers intricately embroidered and beaded leathers, tailored pants with vintage buttons, lace ruffled tops, and floral chiffon gathered skirts. And the luxurious details are often handcrafted—from crocheting, appliqué, patchwork and knitting, all of which help turn each piece into a treasured possession.    *lucybarnes.com*

*Expensive*                                              *Amex/MC/V*

**West Village**                                    **(212) 647-0149**
117 Perry Street                        btw Hudson/Greenwich
NYC 10011                            Mon-Sat 11:30-7:30, Sun 12-6

**Chelsea**                                          **(212) 255-9502**
320 West 14th Street                    btw Eighth/Ninth Ave
NYC 10014                                          Mon-Sat 11-7

## Luichiny

This footwear retailer is for the fearless, funky—and very well-balanced. Now under new ownership, the artsy, patch-painted store has branched out from its signature platforms into styles slightly more down to earth, but is still the place for sky-high sandals, wedges and even stilettos from Spain, Italy and Brazil.

*Moderate*                                              *Amex/MC/V*

**West Village**                                    **(212) 477-3445**
21 West 8th Street                         btw Fifth/Sixth Ave
NYC 10011                            Mon-Fri 12-9, Sat 11-9, Sun 12-8

## Lulu Guinness

Lulu Guinness handbags are a favorite among celebs like Madonna and Liz Hurley for their whimsical sensibility, and she has proven as widely popular in the States as in her native Great Britain. Instead of logos, find adorable prints (stilettos, dalmatians, gloved hands) and fascinating bags (one comes in the shape of an old rotary phone dial) and cosmetic cases in her new West Village digs. Irreverent and fun.                                              *luluguinness.com*

*Expensive*                                              *Amex/MC/V*

**West Village**                                    **(212) 367-2120**
394 Bleecker Street                          btw 11th/Perry
NYC 10014                                       Daily 11-7, Sun 12-6

## Lunettes et Chocolat

Designer chocolate, sunglasses and prescription eyeglass-es—why didn't someone think of it sooner? French pur-veyor of eclectic eyewear Selima Salaun's spin-off (her main store is at 59 Wooster Street in SoHo) houses a selection of styles from Selima Optique, plus vintage shades by Givenchy, Missoni and St Tropez. This is the perfect pit stop for a marathon shopping session. Grab a gourmet Aztec hot chocolate from the counterperson dressed as Charlie Chaplin at the Cacao bar, and browse the shelves of vintage bags and accessories—you'll find everything from sequined coin purses to chocolate Cuban cigars at $8.50 each.                                       *selimaoptique.com*

*Expensive*                                         *Amex/MC/V*
**Nolita**                                          **(212) 334-8484**
25 Prince Street                              btw Mott/Elizabeth
NYC 10012                                   Daily 12-8 (Sun 12-7)

## Luxury Brand Outlet

With a tag-line that reads 'closeouts of the world's premium brands', LBO makes no bones about the fact that it's
an outlet—with all the slapdash presentation the word
implies. However, bargain lovers are likely to luck into a
feathered Blumarine dress for $169, or a $100 pair of only
slightly scuffed Manolos, or Earl jeans for $50. Never
mind the decor, that sounds like a shopper's paradise to
us.                                            *luxurybrandoutlet.com*

*Moderate*                                          *Amex/MC/V*
**Upper East Side**                                 **(212) 734-2505**
1222 Second Avenue                                       at 64th St
NYC 10021                                     Daily 9-9 (Sun 11-7)

## Lynn Park NY

Downtown darling designer Lynn Park runs this eponymous
boutique, specializing in cutting-edge fashion both from
herself and a great edit of young designers. She offers a
complete collection of individual clothes: roughed up
denim, pop-colored dresses embellished with paillettes
and roses, cute frilly miniskirts and ruched, customized tops
and shirts. Alongside her own funky label, she also stocks
coats by Chan Paul, and hip tops from Mimi Turner and
Ouise. The menswear follows the same hip aesthetic, but
focuses on slouchy-cool denim by Park. A line of fearless
accessories completes the cooler-than-cool collection.

*Expensive*                                         *Amex/MC/V*
**SoHo**                                            **(212) 965-5133**
51 Wooster Street                                        at Broome
NYC 10012                                     Daily 12-6 (Sun 12-5)

## Machine

Finally, one-stop shopping for goth gear has come to the
Lower East Side. Find coffin-shaped carryalls by
Vamperella, latex bodysuits, intricate chain-metal mesh
vests and a wide selection of corsets. Don't forget to check
out the plastic studded bracelets and cute Trailer Trash
tanks on the way out.                              *gothshop.com*

*Moderate*                                          *Amex/MC/V*
**Lower East Side**                                 **(212) 475-4692**
85 Stanton Street                              btw Orchard/Allen
NYC 10002                                            Daily 12-8

## Macy's

Macy's has just about everything under the sun—which
pretty much makes it a parallel universe. There are extensive men's, women's and children's departments, home furnishings and cosmetics, and places to grab a bite to eat.

The end result: the world's largest (and at times messiest) department store, packed to the rafters with aggressive, bargain-hunting shoppers. While designer labels are scarce, you'll find a decent selection of labels like Jones New York, Polo Ralph Lauren and Tommy Hilfiger, and there's a great range of jeans from classic labels like Calvin Klein. For the feet, there's everything from sneakers to dress-up shoes. Another bonus is the vast array of services Macy's provides, such as an International Visitors Center, hair salons, restaurants, post office and jewelry appraising.

800-431-9644  macys.com

*Affordable to expensive*                    *Amex/MC/V*

**Midtown West**                              **(212) 695-4400**
Broadway at Herald Square           btw Broadway/34th St
NYC 10001                         Mon-Sat 10-8:30, Sun 11-7

## Maggie Norris Couture

Maggie Norris knows fashion better than most, having working for Ralph Lauren for 14 years. Her stunning collection is wildly romantic, using fabrics taken from old tapestries and Parisian textile archives, and is marked by intricate beading and vintage Lesage embroidery. You'll gasp when you see breathtaking pieces like her exquisite long evening gowns (for at least $30,000), bespoke shirts and amazing jackets. Private appointments are available at the Midtown Studio.                              *maggienorriscouture.com*

*Luxury*                                     *Amex/MC/V*

**Midtown West**                              **(212) 768-1133**
24 West 39th Street                      btw Fifth/Sixth Ave
NYC 10018                                  (by appointment)

**Fifth Avenue**                              **(212) 872-8957**
754 Fifth Avenue                        at Bergdorf Goodman
NYC 10019                                  (by appointment)

## Magic Shoes

Magic it's not, but you might stumble upon some lucky kicks at this cramped Village store crammed with Doc Martens, cowboy boots, and Converse of every conceivable make (including many hard-to-find or discontinued models). Finding a spot to actually try anything on is a challenge, however, especially if another customer happens to be in Magic Shoes at the same time.

*Moderate*                                   *Amex/MC/V*

**West Village**                              **(212) 673-1633**
178 Bleecker Street                    btw MacDougal/Sullivan
NYC 10012                                        Daily 12-8

## Magic Windows

A full-service shop that gets top marks for putting the, yes, magic back into children's clothing. The assortment is vast, ranging from an incredible layette and baby selection to back-to-school essentials, casual basics, party clothes and special occasion dress (bridesmaids' dresses and christening gowns available in six weeks). The Teen Shop bridges the generation gap with cool casualwear that teens love. Other items include personalized blankets, pillows and robes. Labels include Magil, Arc-en-ciel, Papo d'Anjo, Lilly Pulitzer, Sophie Dess, Petit Bateau, Petit Faune and Florence Eiseman. Newborns to pre-teen. *magic-windows.com*

*Expensive*                                                    *Amex/MC/V*

**Upper East Side**                              **(212) 289-0028**
1186 Madison Avenue                              btw 86/87th St
NYC 10028                                    Mon-Sat 10-6, Sun 11-5

## Magry Knits
Owner Michele Renee whips up a mix of sexy knitwear for a twenty and thirtysomething downtown crowd—think fitted skirts, body-skimming dresses and hats and scarves in every color under the rainbow. But the real draw is the custom knitting supplies, including hand-dyed cashmere, mohair, silk and wool yarn balls. She also hosts weekly knitting classes for all levels. *magryknits.com*

*Moderate*                                                    *Amex/MC/V*

**East Village**                                **(212) 674-6753**
80 East 7th Street                            btw First/Second Ave
NYC 10003                                    Tues-Sat 1:30-6:30, Sun 2-6

## Make 10
Make 10 keeps in step with footwear trends by featuring casual and funky shoes, sandals, and boots from brands like Franco Sarte, Nine West, Anne Klein and Enzo. *make10.com*

*Affordable*                                                  *Amex/MC/V*

**West Village**                                **(212) 254-1132**
49 West 8th Street                            btw Fifth/Sixth Ave
NYC 10011                                    Mon-Sat 11-8, Sun 12-6

**Fifth Avenue**                                **(212) 868-1202**
366 Fifth Avenue                              btw 34/35th St
NYC 10001                                    Mon-Fri 10-7, Sat 11-7, Sun 12-6

**Upper East Side**                             **(212) 472-2775**
1227 Third Avenue                             btw 70/71st St
NYC 10021                                    Mon-Fri 11-7:30, Sat-Sun 12-6

**Midtown West**                                **(212) 956-4739**
1386 Sixth Avenue                             btw 56/57th Street
NYC 10019                                    Mon-Fri 10-7, Sat 11-6, Sun 11-5

## Makie
There is nothing like the joy of a great pair of pajamas. So head to this tiny SoHo store for your happy hit: it's packed with nightwear, including classic-styled pajamas, nightshirts and unisex bathrobes made in France by Bains-Plus. There are solid looks embellished with contrasting piping, jacquards, checks, stripes and florals in top-quality cottons and with the vital elasticized waists. Prices start at $140. Buy kids' pjs for $70 (2-12 years), as well as rompers and cute handmade dresses. Also look out for canvas totes, vintage buttons and other goodies.

*Moderate*                                    *Amex/MC/V*

**SoHo**                                   **(212) 625-3930**
109 Thompson Street                          btw Prince/Spring
NYC 10012                                      Mon-Sat 12-7

# Makola                                                ♀

Venetian designer Ilaria Makola brings New Yorkers the romance and energy of her native country with a collection of ultra-feminine and boldly colored day and evening dresses. Choose from luxurious silks and whimsical, cotton print dresses styled with dainty (code for diet) waistlines and full petticoat skirts. The end result: romantic looks reminiscent of the Fifties. Coordinating accessories include shoes, handbags, jackets and hats. Very Doris Day.

*Expensive*                                    *Amex/MC/V*

**Upper East Side**                        **(212) 772-2272**
1045 Madison Avenue                           btw 79/80th St
NYC 10021                                       Mon-Sat 10-6

# Malatesta                                              ♀

Italian designer Cristina Gitti was so inspired by the jewel-like clothes she saw on a trip to India that she decided to launch a line of clothing built around one simple piece: a shawl/sarong packaged in an exotic floral, embroidered sack. Her one-stop shop contains her signature designs alongside shoes, bags and kurtas (classic Indian shirtdresses). No trip to the beach—or India for that matter—is complete without one of her gorgeous sarongs.

*Moderate*                                    *Amex/MC/V*

**SoHo**                                   **(212) 343-9399**
115 Grand Street                          btw Broadway/Mercer
NYC 10012                                        Daily 12-6

# Malia Mills                                            ♀

Hawaii native Malia Mills believes that all women are beautiful just the way they are—hence her dream bikinis to fit every cut and curve from AA to DD, including maternity. *Vogue* credited Malia with starting a 'veritable body image revolution,' and when you visit this comfy dressing lounge of a store you are applauded for your individuality. A flirty bandeau shows off a small bust, the V-neck 'Sophia' compliments a DD cup, and the cinch bottoms make any hips look like Marilyn Monroe's. For that perfect honeymoon, you can have custom bottoms designed with Swarovski crystals spelling out 'Just Married'.          *maliamills.com*

*Expensive*                                    *Amex/MC/V*

**Nolita**                                 **(212) 625-2311**
199 Mulberry Street                         btw Spring/Kenmare
NYC 10012                                        Daily 12-7

**Upper East Side**                        **(212) 517-7485**
960 Madison Avenue                            btw 75/76th St
NYC 10021                                       Mon-Sat 10-7

## Malo

Malo are the kings of cashmere—theirs coming from the rugged Mongolian goat, which is the world's best source for the material. This is a New York staple for luxury knitwear: crewnecks, cardigans, V-necks, turtlenecks, twinsets and cablestitch pullovers. A ready-to-wear line of coats, jackets and pants fills out the cashmere collection, while Malo's home collection includes pajamas, robes, slippers, pillows and blankets. Items in other fabrics stay true to the brand's luxurious-yet-casual aesthetic. Look for accessories such as raincoats and surprisingly chic handbags.

| *Luxury* | *Amex/MC/V* |
|---|---|
| **Upper East Side** | **(212) 396-4721** |
| 814 Madison Avenue | at 68th St |
| NYC 10021 | Mon-Sat 10-6 |

## Manhattan Portage

Hard-wearing nylon messenger bags are what made this groovy brand's name, and this store carries a full selection of the cult carryalls in a rainbow of bright, colors (from $18 to $105). The line also includes one-strap backpacks, DJ bags for records and the odd-sounding (but very functional) 'urban support system' which is basically a laptop bag-style tote. *manhattanportage.com*

| *Affordable* | *Amex/MC/V* |
|---|---|
| **East Village** | **(212) 995-5490** |
| 333 East 9th Street | btw First/Second Ave |
| NYC 10003 | Daily 12-7 (Wed-Sat 12-8) |
| **SoHo** | **(212) 226-4557** |
| 301 West Broadway | btw Canal/Grand |
| NYC 10013 | Daily 11-7 (Sun 12-7) |

## Mankind

The modern male won't get far in this city looking like a cave dweller. Gentlemen, cast off your practically prehistoric pieces and update your look to the 21st century by wandering over to Mankind. This men's boutique sells the latest in cool casual essential, from Filippa K sailor striped knits and argyle sweaters by Pringle of Scotland to Nicole Farhi leather sandals and bags and accessories by Il Parcel and Ant Industries. If you've taken care of your clothes, that's one less thing to think about when you're on the hunt.

| *Expensive* | *Amex/MC/V* |
|---|---|
| **SoHo** | **(212) 966-5146** |
| 8 Greene Street | btw Grand/Canal |
| NYC 10013 | Mon-Sat 12-6 |

## ★ Manolo Blahnik

Forced to choose between their husbands or their Blahniks, many women might well choose the latter: fans include Faye Dunaway, Madonna, Donatella Versace, Diane von Furstenberg and every fashion magazine editor in the busi-

177

ness. The sultan of the stiletto, Blahnik designs the ultimate in sexy footwear. Each style is feminine, seductive and fabulously comfortable—and achieving this in a pair of sky-high heels is no mean feat. There are more demure offerings, from mules, glittery evening slippers, strappy sandals and chic loafers, and your wedding day will be sadly incomplete without a knockout pair of Manolo's bridal shoes. Prices typically run from $445 to approximately $1,000.

*Expensive*                                          *Amex/MC/V*

**Midtown West**                               **(212) 582-3007**
31 West 54th Street                        btw Fifth/Sixth Ave
NYC 10019                        Mon-Fri 10:30-6, Sat 10:30-5

## Manrico Cascimir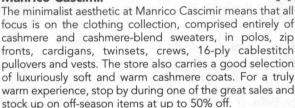
The minimalist aesthetic at Manrico Cascimir means that all focus is on the clothing collection, comprised entirely of cashmere and cashmere-blend sweaters, in polos, zip fronts, cardigans, twinsets, crews, 16-ply cablestitch pullovers and vests. The store also carries a good selection of luxuriously soft and warm cashmere coats. For a truly warm experience, stop by during one of the great sales and stock up on off-season items at up to 50% off.

*Luxury*                                             *Amex/MC/V*

**Upper East Side**                            **(212) 794-4200**
802 Madison Avenue                            btw 67/68th St
NYC 10021                               Mon-Sat 10-6, Sun 12-5

**Upper East Side**                            **(212) 535-6225**
1321 Third Avenue                             btw 75/76th St
NYC 10021                               Mon-Sat 11-8, Sun 1-6

**Upper East Side**                            **(212) 628-5080**
835 Madison Avenue                            btw 69/70th St
NYC 10021                         Mon-Sat 9:30-7, Sun 12:30-5:30

**Upper East Side**                            **(212) 832-8182**
782 Lexington Avenue                          btw 60/61st St
NYC 10021                             Mon-Sat 10-8, Sun 12:30-6

**Upper West Side (outlet)**                   **(212) 787-6550**
131 West 72nd Street          btw Amsterdam/Columbus Ave
NYC 10023                       Mon-Fri 10:30-8, Sat 10-7, Sun 12-6

**Midtown East**                               **(212) 308-8793**
551 Madison Avenue                              at 55th St
NYC 10022                        Mon-Fri 9:30-7, Sat 11-7, Sun 12-6

## ★ Marc Jacobs
Marc Jacobs is the king of New York fashion right now, as well as one of the world's most influential designers. From the Grunge collection 10 years ago to his retro-luxe collections favored by sophisticated downtowners (and every model worth her *Vogue* cover), he can do no fashion wrong. He was the first big-name designer to hit Bleecker Street in the West Village and now everyone else has followed. Visit Jacobs for luxe cashmere sweaters, swingy party dresses and cartoon-cute shoes that all the Hollywood girls like Sofia Coppola wear. His

Marc by Marc Jacobs line, a cheaper version of the luxe label, has been a phenomenal success—style mavens everywhere confess an addiction to his faded, creased jeans, tweedy pants and Sixties-inspired striped shirts. Accessories include his already-classic handbags (around $900), leather goods, and those lovely, lovely shoes (from $250 to $1,000). *marcjacobs.com*

*Luxury* *Amex/MC/V*

**SoHo** **(212) 343-1490**
163 Mercer Street btw Houston/Prince
NYC 10012 Daily 11-7 (Sun 11-6)

### Marc by Marc Jacobs
Ladies love cool Jacobs. Italian leather shoes ($400-$700) and bags ($500-$1,500) are the center of attention in his Bleecker street store, although there is also a limited selection of scarves and perfume. Jacobs' long-time-coming collection of impeccable home furnishings and stunning jewelry point to the designer setting his sights on a larger kingdom than the fashion world he already commands.

*Expensive* *Amex/MC/V*

**West Village** **(212) 924-0026**
403 Bleecker Street at Perry
NYC 10014 Daily 12-8 (Sunday 12-7)

### Mare
Chic shoes on the cutting edge of Italian style can be found at Mare. A sophisticated little shop, Mare offers classic, trendy and very funky footware designs at reasonable prices.

*Moderate* *Amex/MC/V*

**SoHo** **(212) 343-1110**
426 West Broadway btw Prince/Spring
NYC 10012 Mon-Fri 11-8, Sat 11-7, Sun 12-7

### Marianne Novobatzky
Hungarian designer Marianne Novobatzky allows women the opportunity to look stunning for any occasion. Her to-die-for silk ballgowns evoke fairytale princesses, while her floral dresses whisper 'picnic on the lake' and her dressy suits practically conduct haughty luncheons on their own. Chiffon blouses, silk, wool and velvet jackets dripping in terrific color will jolt your too-black wardrobe into today. She will even custom-make a sensual, form-fitting gown (perfect for a wedding day) within a week. Ready to elope?

*Expensive* *Amex/MC/V*

**SoHo** **(212) 431-4120**
65 Mercer Street btw Spring/Broome
NYC 10012 Mon-Fri 12-7

### Mariko
Fancy a bit of glitz? Some costume jewelry to leave the other girls in the dust? Head to this boutique, where the

walls drip with beads and baubles and more beads. Paste diamonds and turquoise are popular here, but look out also for a range of chic silk shirts in jewel-like colors. A tip: put on your sunglasses before entering.

*Affordable*                                              *Amex/MC/V*

**Upper East Side**                              **(212) 472-1176**
998 Madison Avenue                              btw 77/78th St
NYC 10021                                        Mon-Sat 10-6

## Marina Rinaldi

This is the place to shop for upscale, plus-sized fashions (sizes from 10-22). Marina Rinaldi is the sister company of Italian brand MaxMara and shares its sleek look. Find classic, figure-flattering styles in a chic pared-down aesthetic. Neutral colors and wearable fabrics are evident in the high-quality collection that includes everything from outerwear to pants, blouses, sweaters and a small shoe selection.

*Expensive*                                              *Amex/MC/V*

**Upper East Side**                              **(212) 734-4333**
800 Madison Avenue                              btw 67/68th St
NYC 10021                              Mon-Sat 10-6 (Thurs 10-7)

## Marmalade

We hear Sarah Jessica Parker is a fan of this vintage store that stocks pieces from the Seventies and Eighties. Find fabulous handbags, cocktail dresses, tees, great slouchy boots and lots of lace everything, including some Stevie Nicksworthy dresses. Most pieces are under $400. The result? Eighties trash-glam girl meets downtown fashionista.

*Moderate to expensive*                                  *Amex/MC/V*

**Lower East Side**                              **(212) 473-8070**
172 Ludlow Street                              btw Houston/Stanton
NYC 10002                                        Daily 12:30-9

## Marni

Peppered with chic Italian flavor, pure whites, sharp colors and busy prints, Consuela Castiglioni's designs hang from large silver arcs in Marni—a fabulous shop for girls desiring seemingly effortless beauty. Featured are creatively cut pieces that use vintage fabrics to spice up modern styles. Classy jackets, coats and tops (including lovely blouses with puffy three-quarter sleeves) decorated with rainbows and polka dots hang beside breezy skirts. Exquisitely patterned shoes, glorious sunglasses and lovely bags complete Marni's girly-with-an-edge look.

*Expensive*                                              *Amex/MC/V*

**SoHo**                                        **(212) 343-3912**
161 Mercer Street                              btw Houston/Prince
NYC 10012                                    Daily 11-7, Sun 12-6

## Marsha D.D.

If you want a trip to the suburban mall without the car journey, walk over to Marsha D.D. The store features everything teens love: clothes, jewelry and plenty of swag like trucker hats, pencils and mouse pads. The store carries lines like Paul Frank as well as more underground labels like Junk Food. For boys, the clothes are of the surf/skate variety, featuring labels like Quiksilver and The North Face. From 7 to 16 years.

*Affordable*                                          *Amex/MC/V*

**Upper East Side**                    **(212) 831-2422**
1574 Third Avenue                         btw 88/89th St
NYC 10128                            Mon-Sat 10-6, Sun 12-5:30

**Upper East Side (clearance store)**   **(212) 534-9700**
1324 Lexington Avenue                      btw 88/89th St
NYC 10028                            (opening hours as above)

# Martier

At Martier you get two shops rolled into one: upstairs is filled with fashion-forward clothing, while downstairs boasts an abundance of sexy lingerie plus some swimwear. Typical fare includes sexy leather pants, body-hugging tops and print dresses by labels like Anti-Flirt, Vertigo, Parameter, Pinera, Sharagano and Ferré. Downstairs is home to a colorful selection of saucy intimates by La Perla, Lise Charmel and Malizia. Helpful sales staff.

*Expensive*                                          *Amex/MC/V*

**Upper East Side**                    **(212) 758-5370**
1010 Third Avenue                             at 60th St
NYC 10022                            Mon-Sat 10-8, Sun 12-6:30

# ★ Martin

*Harper's Bazaar* once named Martin 'the fashion insiders' closet addiction' and they'd be right on the money. Designer Anne Johnston Albert spins fabulously cool clothes that defy the seasons. Her muses? Jane Birkin, Charlotte Rampling and Brigitte Bardot, whose photos line the walls of her store. Her signature piece is her hip hugging, boot-cut jeans with a distinctive back pocket double M stitching. What to wear with them? Try fitted soft jersey tops, low-slung skirts, delicate silk chiffon blouses, saucy-chic halter dresses or moleskin military jackets. Pay $140 for jeans, $180 for tops and $500 for jackets.

*Expensive*                                          *Amex/MC/V*

**East Village**                       **(212) 358-0011**
206 East 6th Street                     btw Second/Third Ave
NYC 10003                                    Tues-Sun 1-7

# Martinez Valero

A convenient neighborhood shoe shop featuring trendy styles at attractive prices. Shop a selection from classic to trendy and looks that will complement any outfit, whether it's satin evening pumps, boots or summer sandals. Prices run from $125 to $265 for boots.

*Moderate*                                          *Amex/MC/V*

**Upper East Side**                **(212) 753-1822**
1029 Third Avenue              at 61st St
NYC 10021       Mon-Fri 10-8, Sat 11-7, Sun 12-6

## Mary Adams

Because you can-can! Feel like you've stepped into the heart of the Moulin Rouge when you walk through the door of this boutique. The ruffled, lacy dresses would be perfect for a walk through the Left Bank, or to spice up your modern-day Manhattan wardrobe. Her Victorian-inspired designs are festooned with lace, peplums and ruffles and include elaborate corsets, skirts with full petticoats, iridescent silk ballgowns and unconventional wedding dresses. Custom orders also available.

*Expensive*                *Amex/MC/V*

**Lower East Side**            **(212) 473-0237**
138 Ludlow Street         btw Stanton/Rivington
NYC 10002              Wed-Sat 1-6, Sun 1-5

## Mary Efron

Mary Efron is noted for her 'fine and rare antique wearables' from the turn of the century to the Fifties, including silk and embroidered Chinese jackets, dresses from the Twenties and evening and special occasion wear. The beaded, jeweled and painted handbags available here are particularly eye-catching. A mini museum of fashion at your fingertips.

*Moderate*                *Amex/MC/V*

**Upper East Side**            **(212) 288-8809**
308 East 78th Street            at Second Ave
NYC 10021     Tues-Sun 1-7 (or by appointment)

## Mason's Tennis Mart

Mason's is the oldest and most respected tennis retailer in the city. Athletic apparel, including cute tennis dresses, warm-ups, sweaters and shirts, comes from top-of-the-line labels like Ellesse, Polo, Fila, LBH, Nike, Adidas and Lacoste. Equipment brands include Babalot, Gamma, Wilson, Volkl, Head and Prince. Great children's department. Same day stringing for rackets.   *masonstennis.com*

*Moderate to expensive*          *Amex/MC/V*

**Midtown East**             **(212) 755-5805**
56 East 53rd Street       btw Madison/Park Ave
NYC 10022     Mon-Fri 10-7, Sat 11-6, Sun 11-5

## Maternity Work

Maternity Work, the outlet store for Mimi Maternity, A Pea in the Pod and Motherhood Maternity, offers amazing sale items and professional and casualwear for moms-to-be.

*Affordable*                *Amex/MC/V*

**Midtown West**            **(212) 399-9840**
16 West 57th Street (3rd floor)    btw Fifth/Sixth Ave
NYC 10019    Mon-Wed 10-7, Thurs 10-8, Fri-Sat 10-6
                                 Sun 12-6

## Mavi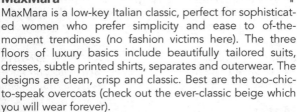

Denim addicts, especially sexy denim addicts, head to Mavi's Union Square store for low-rise, form-fitted, light-weight, stretch or non-stretch and cut-to-fit jeans. Moderately priced, you can expect to pay anything from $50 to $74 from a veritable denim buffet of sizes and lengths. Remember, girls, jeans are your friend… mavi.com

*Affordable*                                              *Amex/MC/V*

**East Village**                              **(917) 289-0520**
832 Broadway                                 btw 12/13th St
NYC 10003                                         Daily 11-9

## MaxMara

MaxMara is a low-key Italian classic, perfect for sophisticat-ed women who prefer simplicity and ease to of-the-moment trendiness (no fashion victims here). The three floors of luxury basics include beautifully tailored suits, dresses, subtle printed shirts, separates and outerwear. The designs are clean, crisp and classic. Best are the too-chic-to-speak overcoats (check out the ever-classic beige which you will wear forever).

*Expensive*                                              *Amex/MC/V*

**Upper East Side**                           **(212) 879-6100**
813 Madison Avenue                                at 68th St
NYC 10021                            Mon-Sat 10-6 (Thurs 10-7)

**SoHo**                                       **(212) 674-1817**
450 West Broadway                          btw Prince/Houston
NYC 10012                              Mon-Sat 11-7, Sun 12-6

## Max Studio

Leon Max's wholesome, pretty designs defy the seasons with simplicity and elegance. Using pastel colors, uncom-plicated designs and soft fabrics, this collection of pretty, feminine clothes includes silk-spun cami tops, flowery georgette skirts, whimsical blouses and dresses, dainty yet warm outerwear and well-cut pants. Accessories include a nice array of belts, shoes, handbags and sun-glasses.                                        maxstudio.com

*Moderate*                                               *Amex/MC/V*

**SoHo**                                       **(212) 941-1141**
415 West Broadway                            btw Prince/Spring
NYC 10012                              Mon-Sat 10-8, Sun 12-7

## Mayle

Jane Mayle's boutique was one of the first to happen in Nolita, and it's a magnet for the Nolita Girl™—think a lacy top and jeans-wearing lass, an ex-model preferably. Her flir-ty tops (around $200) draw in hipsters who love their clothes girly without being precious, and she cuts a lean and mean pair of pants too. Mayle's world is a seductive (and fragrant—she burns beautiful scented candles) place to be. As are her sales.

| | |
|---|---|
| *Moderate* | *Amex/MC/V* |
| **Nolita** | **(212) 625-0406** |
| 242 Elizabeth Street | btw Prince/Houston |
| NYC 10012 | Daily 12-7 (Sun 12-6) |

## ★ Me & Ro

Me & Ro's jewelry has graced the fabbest award ceremonies (The Golden Globes, The Emmys, The Oscars) and there's no secret why. The handcrafted pieces are at once expensive, breathtaking, exotic and extravagant—ready for the red carpet, yet wonderfully simple. This minimalist space showcases designers Michele Quan and Robin Renzi's divine, eastern-inspired pieces, often carved with Sanskrit and Tibetan calligraphy. Be sure to see their line of gorgeous Indian rose cut diamonds set in designs with moons, stars, spheres and crosses.     *meandrojewelry.com*

| | |
|---|---|
| *Expensive* | *Amex/MC/V* |
| **SoHo** | **(917) 237-9215** |
| 241 Elizabeth Street | btw Houston/Prince |
| NYC 10012 | Daily 11-7 (Sun 12-6) |

## Medici

Enter a world of accessories on the Upper West Side, where techno music plays backdrop to a collection of trendy shoes on the Medici label, the youthful CJ Bis by Charles Jourdan, and everything else besides from fringed bags, hats for the races, belts, even birthday cards. Best for men's shoes and summer sandals.

| | |
|---|---|
| *Moderate* | *Amex/MC/V* |
| **Upper West Side** | **(212) 712-9342** |
| 420 Columbus Avenue | btw 80/81st St |
| NYC 10023 | Mon-Fri 10-8, Sat-Sun 10-6 |

## Meg

If you're tired of paying posh uptown prices, get down to Meghan Kinney's East Village store which specializes in polished, multi-purpose sportswear that can be custom-fitted. Separates are key: match pants with a double-knit wool jersey and work it with a jacket or coat. Each season Kinney introduces a new blend of fabric and texture combinations into her dominantly neutral color palette.

| | |
|---|---|
| *Expensive* | *Amex/MC/V* |
| **East Village** | **(212) 260-6329** |
| 312 East 9th Street | btw First/Second Ave |
| NYC 10003 | Daily 12-8, Sun 1-6 |

## Memes

This flava-ful shop sells 'fresh baked gear' to men seeking cool, urban streetwear. Limited-edition clothing from underground brands Mad Anthony and 10 Deep are found alongside more standard fare from Adidas and Nike. Memes' core collection is made up of hip-hop staples like fatigue, track, and nylon pants, lots of denim, hoodies, coats, jackets, funky footwear, as well as a sprinkling of collectibles, sunglasses and CDs. *memes-nyc.com*

*Moderate*                                              *Amex/MC/V*

**NoHo**                                          **(212) 420-9955**
3 Great Jones Street                      btw Lafayette/Broadway
NYC 10012                                  Daily 11-7 (Sunday 11-6)

## Men's Wearhouse

With the addition of names like Armani and Valentino to their regular offerings of Canali, Kenneth Cole Reaction, Oscar De La Renta, Donna Karan and more, Men's Wearhouse can lay claim to having New York's widest selection of suit brands and prices. In addition to the office-ready duds, shop here for outerwear, dress shirts, tuxedos, accessories, casual sportswear, underwear, socks and ties (for print-lovers only, as ties in solid colors are curiously lacking), all for about 25% less than you'd pay elsewhere. Add a complete shoe department with labels such as Florsheim, Bostonian, Cole Haan and Bacco Bucci, tuxedo rentals, a courteous staff and lifetime free pressing on suits, and who can resist?            800-776-7848   *menswearhouse.com*

*Moderate to luxury*                                    *Amex/MC/V*

**Midtown East**                                  **(212) 856-9008**
380 Madison Avenue                                  at 46th St
NYC 10017                      Mon-Fri 8:30-7:30, Sat 10-7, Sun 11-6

**Chelsea**                                       **(212) 243-3517**
655 Sixth Avenue                                    at 20th St
NYC 10010                        Mon-Fri 9-9, Sat 9-8, Sun 11-7

**Lower Manhattan**                               **(212) 233-0675**
115 Broadway                                          at Cedar
NYC 10006                      Mon-Fri 8.30-7:30, Sat 10-7, Sun 11-6

## Metro Bicycle

Metro Bicycle puts service first. Bikes come with a three-year warranty that includes gear and brake adjustments as well as replacement of defective parts. The mountain, road and suspension bikes are from makers such as Trek, Raleigh, Klein, LeMond and Gary Fisher and are all at competitive prices. Bicycles are available for rent by the hour or the day.                                       *metrobicycles.com*

*Expensive*                                             *Amex/MC/V*

**Upper East Side**                               **(212) 427-4450**
1311 Lexington Avenue                               at 88th St
NYC 10128                     Daily 9:30-6:30 (Thurs 9:30-7:30)

**Midtown West**                                  **(212) 581-4500**
360 West 47th Street                               at Ninth Ave
NYC 10036                      Mon-Fri 9:30-6:30, Sat 9:30-6, Sun 10-6

**Chelsea**                                       **(212) 255-5100**
546 Sixth Avenue                                    at 15th St
NYC 10011                                      Daily 9:30-6:30

**East Village**                                  **(212) 228-4344**
332 East 14th Street                          btw First/Second Ave
NYC 10001                                      Daily 9:30-6:30

| **Tribeca** | **(212) 334-8000** |
|---|---|
| 417 Canal Street | at Sixth Ave |
| NYC 10013 | Daily 9:30-6:30 |

## Metropolis 👤

A skip away from NYU, Metropolis is a late-night destination for student hipsters seeking to forget that dull lecture with a shopping hit. It's all quick-fix fashion, with sparkly T-shirts, retro overcoats, multi-pocketed cargos (for your lecture notes, see) and cool denims. Owner Christine Colligan says she plans to open 24/7, so if you need a pair of fuchsia platform maryjanes at 2am, you know where to go.

*Affordable* *Amex/MC/V*

| **East Village** | **(212) 358-0795** |
|---|---|
| 43 Third Avenue | btw 9/10th St |
| NYC 10003 | Sun-Wed 1-10, Thurs-Sat 1-11 |

## MEXX 👤👤👤

Like H&M, only much better. Based in Germany and popular throughout Europe, Mexx has planted its flag on U.S. soil for the first time, offering up its mix of essentials (tees, sweaters, jeans, polos, skirts), sophisticates, sportswear and swimsuits for both sexes. It's more expensive than its European department-store brethren, but the clothes are better made and won't disintegrate weeks after they're purchased. Committed to one-stop shopping, Mexx also offers a kids' line, a shoe line, a cosmetics line, a jewelry line, bags and watches. Word of Mexx's wares spread quickly: the opening of the Union Square flagship last year had NYC hipsters lined up for hours to be cast for the store's inaugural ad campaign. *mexx.com*

*Affordable* *Amex/MC/V*

| **Fifth Avenue** | **(212) 956-6506** |
|---|---|
| 650 Fifth Avenue | at 52nd St |
| NYC 10019 | Mon-Wed 10-8, Thurs-Sat 10-9, Sun 10-7 |

| **East Village** | **(646) 486-7405** |
|---|---|
| 19 Union Square | at 15th St |
| NYC 10016 | Mon-Sat 10-9, Sun 11-8 |

## Miao 👤

A great place for a quick pick-me-up purchase, Miao carries intricate, inexpensive accessories. The beaded purses are cute, and run between $20-30. Costume jewelry includes earrings, necklaces and bracelets that will add some sparkle to your look. Most of the baubles and trinkets are about $10.

*Affordable* *(cash only)*

| **Lower Manhattan** | **(212) 965-9082** |
|---|---|
| 176 Hester Street | btw Mott/Mulberry |
| NYC 10012 | Daily 10:30-11 |

## Michael K 👤👤

Is it a shop, or a party? Lighting plays an important role in Michael K, where an illuminated yellow-brick road (of sorts) allows customers to navigate the fashion and lifestyle products displayed in a disco/nightclub manner. The store takes an ultra-futuristic approach (flat-screen TVs, metal rails, strangely shiny walls) and showcases a DJ booth (with fog machines, natch), creating a theme park atmosphere seemingly more intent on exciting its customers than persuading them to make a purchase. Once you're done being dazzled, though, you'll find a host of shoes and gear by names such as Ben Sherman, Polo Jeans, Nike, Puma, The North Face, Adidas and Lacoste, all set up as a slew of mini boutiques. Get your groove, er, shop, on.

| *Moderate* | *Amex/MC/V* |
|---|---|
| **SoHo** | **(212) 625-9491** |
| 512 Broadway | btw Spring/Broome |
| NYC 10012 | Mon-Sat 9-9 (Sun 10-8) |

## Michael Kors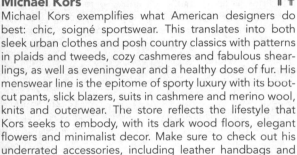

Michael Kors exemplifies what American designers do best: chic, soigné sportswear. This translates into both sleek urban clothes and posh country classics with patterns in plaids and tweeds, cozy cashmeres and fabulous shearlings, as well as eveningwear and a healthy dose of fur. His menswear line is the epitome of sporty luxury with its bootcut pants, slick blazers, suits in cashmere and merino wool, knits and outerwear. The store reflects the lifestyle that Kors seeks to embody, with its dark wood floors, elegant flowers and minimalist decor. Make sure to check out his underrated accessories, including leather handbags and boots. *michaelkors.com*

| *Luxury* | *Amex/MC/V* |
|---|---|
| **Upper East Side** | **(212) 452-4658** |
| 974 Madison Avenue | at 76th St |
| NYC 10021 | Mon-Sat 10-6 |

## Michael's The Consignment Shop for Women

For 45 years Michael's has set the pace in the consignment industry by stocking the ultimate in pre-owned couture clothing and bridalwear. Brides-to-be can select from magnificent dresses by Vera Wang, Arnold Scassi or Dior while non-brides (or bride wannabes) can select from designer frocks and accessories by fashion powerhouses like Prada, Gucci, Manolo Blahnik, Galliano and Hermès. You'll love the great prices, not to mention the thrill of the hunt. *michaelsconsignment.com*

| *Moderate* | *MC/V* |
|---|---|
| **Upper East Side** | **(212) 737-7273** |
| 1041 Madison Avenue (2nd floor) | btw 79/80th St |
| NYC 10021 | Mon-Sat 9:30-6 |

## Michelle Roth New York

Designed, styled and managed by a brother and sister team (Michelle and Henry Roth), Michelle Roth New York specializes in breathtaking European couture wedding dresses. Using interesting colors (like Wedgwood blue and maize) and dramatic silhouettes, they create glamorous styles for lucky ladies' special days. The shop also carries exclusive collections by Elizabeth Emanuel (designer of Princess Diana's wedding dress), Peter Langner, Domo Adami and Max Chaoul ($3,000-$18,000). Lovely mother-of-the-bride outfits and simple evening attire are also good reasons to make an appointment here.   *michelleroth.com*

*Expensive*                                    *Amex/MC/V*

**Midtown West**                         **(212) 245-3390**
24 West 57th Street (suite 203)       btw Fifth/Sixth Ave
NYC 10019                               (by appointment)

## Mika Inatome

For the non-traditional bride, this Tribeca store run by Japanese designer Mika Inatome specializes in slim, form-fitted gowns rather than a romantic—dare we say puffy?—dress. Styles include fashionable column dresses (plain or embroidered), gowns dolled up with magnificent silk chiffon trains, detachable side sarongs, sheath and fringe, and other designs trimmed in lace, pearl and sterling-silver beading. Prices start at $1,700.   *mikainatome.com*

*Expensive*                                    *Amex/MC/V*

**Tribeca**                              **(212) 966-7777**
11 Worth Street (suite 4B)    btw West Broadway /Hudson
NYC 10013                               (by appointment)

## Miks

Sure to please both you and Mom, sweet, smart designs are the rule at this Japanese ex-pat's small and friendly boutique. Find work basics with a twist of cute such as flowered button-downs, bow-trim sweaters and striped skirts. The designs are refreshingly conventional with a whimsical edge.

*Moderate*                                    *Amex/MC/V*

**Lower East Side**                      **(212) 505-1982**
100 Stanton Street                     btw Ludlow/Orchard
NYC 10002                                 Daily 12-730

## Milena Shoes

This neighborhood store stocks footwear that covers the range from work to evening to more relaxed styles. Women will find mules, sandals, boots and evening shoes. For men, there are leather and suede loafers, boots and sandals. Brand names include Cydwoq, Sexy Kiss, Dino Bigioni and Sebastiano Migliore and you will also find purses and a small selection of Italian menswear. Prices run from $150 to $500.   *milenashoes.com*

*Moderate*                                    *Amex/MC/V*

**West Village**                         **(212) 254-5132**
23 West 8th Street                      btw Fifth/Sixth Ave
NYC 10011                             Daily 11-9 (Sun 12-9)

## Mimi Maternity

Don't think being pregnant means having to wear stuff that looks more like your grandma's muumuus than your favorite little black dress. Mimi Maternity offers sophisticated clothing that highlights rather than hides your beautiful body, from fitted tops, A-line skirts and tailored jeans to yoga gear and pant suits, to meet your desire for both style and comfort.

*Affordable*                                          *Amex/MC/V*

**Upper East Side**                          **(212) 737-3784**
1125 Madison Avenue                                at 84th St
NYC 10028              Mon-Fri 10-7, Sat 10-6, Sun 12-6

**Upper East Side**                          **(212) 832-2667**
1021 Third Avenue                            btw 60/61st St
NYC 10021   Mon-Fri 10-7 (Thurs 10-8), Sat 10-6, Sun 11-6

**Upper West Side**                          **(212) 721-1999**
2005 Broadway                                btw 68/69th St
NYC 10023         Mon-Thurs 10-8, Fri-Sat 10-7, Sun 12-6

**Upper West Side**                          **(917) 441-8077**
2384 Broadway                                btw 87/88th St
NYC 10024                      Mon-Sat 10-8, Sun 12-6

## Minette by Blue Bag

Minette is a treasure trove of wonderfully girly accessories from France. High-turnover merchandise that arrives every 15 days makes shopping here a truly excellent adventure. Find fabulous jewelry, great belts, scarves, wallets, hand-crocheted make-up bags that double as evening clutches, a few hats and hair accessories, as well as bathing suits, sandals and sarongs during the summer months. Prices range from $75 to $350.

*Moderate*                                           *Amex/MC/V*

**Nolita**                                   **(212) 334-7290**
238 Mott Street                            btw Prince/Spring
NYC 10012                            Daily 12-8 (Sun 12-7)

## Min-K

Tokyo pop percolates on the iPod at this tiny East Village outpost of Asian fashion. Two racks, one on each side of the narrow store, showcase sharp designs from Japan and Korea. Downtown professionals and trendsetters looking to show off (or show some skin) help themselves to flirty dresses and graphic tees. Fun without being flashy, Min-K shows that a little bit of *shibuya-ku* can go a long way.

*Moderate to expensive*                              *Amex/MC/V*

**East Village**                             **(212) 253-8337**
334 East 11th Street                      btw First/Second Ave
NYC 10003                            Mon-Sat 1-9, Sun 1-8

## Miracle

It might not be truly miraculous, but despite the funky location Miracle's owner and designer Vanessa Lundborg delivers a colorful yet understated collection of dresses, pants, tops and sweaters in quality fabrics. Bridesmaid and special occasion dresses can be custom-ordered in a rainbow of available silks.

*Expensive*                                    *Amex/MC/V*

**East Village**                               **(212) 614-7262**
100 St Mark's Place                      btw First/Avenue A
NYC 10003                              Wed-Sat 12-8, Sun 2-6

## Missbehave                                          👤

The decor at Missbehave—yearbooks, a chalkboard and desk—brings to mind many a naughty schoolday's reverie. Why not stay after class to treat yourself to under-the-radar, super-girly fashions from Leroy's Girl, Kitten and Kim White, or a sweatshirt from Megami Boogie that reads 'I'm in heaven with my boyfriend'? The stylish clothes are sexy, fun, and you won't have to worry about looking good in detention.                                   *missbehavenyc.com*

*Expensive*                                    *Amex/MC/V*

**Lower East Side**                            **(212) 254-9222**
231 Eldridge Street                     btw Stanton/Houston
NYC 10002                                          Daily 12-8

## Miss Sixty                                          👤

Tight, low-ridin', slinky jeans (with plenty of details) punchy sweaters, fiery miniskirts and a multitude of adventurous blouses and halter tops is what you encounter on a Miss Sixty visit. Girlie styles from every era—from the modish Sixties and laid back Seventies to the punk glam of the Eighties—are explored here, with the emphasis on fun, fun, fun. There are hot swimming pieces for the beach, a slew of accessories (including fine sunglasses) and flirty shoes galore. Be sure to check out the netted heels, ribbon-adorned sandals and funky sneakers.         *misssixty.com*

*Moderate*                                     *Amex/MC/V*

**Nolita**                                     **(212) 431-6040**
246 Mulberry Street                         btw Prince/Spring
NYC 10012                               Daily 12-7 (Sun 12-6)

**SoHo**                                       **(212) 334-9772**
386 West Broadway                        btw Spring/Broome
NYC 10012              Mon-Thurs 11-7, Fri-Sat 11-8, Sun 12-6

## Missoni                                           👤👤

For half a century the Missoni family has ruled the fashion world with their distinctive sexy, slinky, stripey knitwear. Angela Missoni is mad for wild, geometric patterns and sharp-edged graphics in bold color combinations...you won't find basic black here. Missoni has turned knitwear into a complete line of women's ready-to-wear that includes pants, halter dresses, skirts, sweaters and swimwear. The style crowd are crazy for the super-long, boho fringed scarves (approx $260), a true fashion classic. The store now features a large home collection as well, with dinnerware, pillows and blankets not available in most department stores, thus giving shoppers one more reason to visit Missoni's only U.S. store. Prices range from $165 for a scarf to $5,300 for a feathered cape. *missoni.it*

*Expensive* *Amex/MC/V*

**Upper East Side** **(212) 517-9339**
1009 Madison Avenue at 78th St
NYC 10021 Mon-Sat 10-6

## Miu Miu

Miu Miu is Prada's cute, playful and slightly mad little sister—a girl who wears floral platform shoes, ragged minidresses and handbags that look like a prop from *Sesame Street*. Uptown girls and downtown hipsters (who can afford the label—this second line sadly comes with first line prices) come here for V-neck cardigans, shrunken sweaters, and vintage-inspired tweeds with a hint of sparkle. You'll also find washed-leather jackets, long-line maxi coats, and slim calf-length dresses. Miu Miu's shoes and fashionable handbags will have you one step ahead of the fashion meter—witness the ever-present crowd of hipper-than-hip Japanese tourists snapping up multiple pairs of girly cartoon shoes. *miumiu.com*

*Expensive* *Amex/MC/V*

**Upper East Side** **(212) 249-9660**
831 Madison Avenue btw 69/70th St
NYC 10021 Mon-Sat 10-6 (Thurs 10-7)

**SoHo** **(212) 334-5156**
100 Prince Street btw Greene/Mercer
NYC 10012 Mon-Sat 11-7, Sun 12-6

## Mixona

This cool Nolita lingerie shop's name is a composite of Korean symbols: mi, beauty; xo, play of opposites; and na, me. Which basically just means that it's a haven for bedroom eyes looking for those intricately patterned bra and panties or camisole brimming in lacy stitches. Unlike Victoria's Secret on nearby Broadway, there's nothing pink or prissy about this shop. Dressing-rooms draped in crimson red silk are spacious enough for husbands/boyfriends to get a private viewing—ooh, saucy. Mixona runs the label gamut, from bold (Undressed, Andres Sarda, Christina Stott) to powdery sweet (Siren, Grazia'Iliani, Kristina Ti). Everyday basics by legends like Hanro and La Cosa, silk sleepwear and daywear are also available. Great sales. *mixona.com*

*Affordable* *Amex/MC/V*

**Nolita** **(646) 613-0100**
262 Mott Street btw Houston/Prince
NYC 10012 Daily 11:30-7:30

## Modell's

Play ball, indeed. Athletes and armchair quarterbacks 'gotta go to Mo's' for everything from basketballs and Mets jerseys to Levi's and running watches. One of America's oldest sporting goods chains, Modell's stocks gear for nearly every kind of recreation, on or off the court, including camping, fishing and swimming. Always a big draw: a huge selection of brand-name sneakers at low prices.

800-275-6633  *modells.com*

*Affordable*                                          *Amex/MC/V*

**Midtown East**                          **(212) 661-4242**
51 East 42nd Street                        at Vanderbilt Ave
NYC 10017                    Mon-Fri 8-9, Sat 9-7, Sun 10-6

**Harlem**                                 **(212) 280-9100**
300 West 125th Street      btw Frederick Douglass Blvd/
NYC 10027                                  St Nicholas Blvd
           Mon-Thurs 9:30-8.30, Fri-Sat 9:30-9, Sun 11-7

**Lower Manhattan**                        **(212) 732-8484**
55 Chambers Street                            at Broadway
NYC 10007           Mon-Fri 8:30-7.30, Sat 10-6, Sun 11-5

**Lower Manhattan**                        **(212) 566-3711**
200 Broadway                               btw Fulton/John
NYC 10038                       (opening hours as above)

**Midtown (Herald Square)**                **(212) 244-4544**
1239 Broadway                              btw 33/34th St
NYC 10001                            Mon-Sat 9-9, Sun 11-7

**Midtown West**                           **(212) 764-7030**
234 West 42nd Street              btw Seventh/Eighth Ave
NYC 10036                     Mon-Fri 10-1, Sat 8-1, Sun 10-10

**Upper East Side**                        **(212) 996-3800**
1535 Third Avenue                              at 86th St
NYC 10028                          Mon-Sat 9-9:30, Sun 10-7

## It's a Mod, Mod World

Feeling down on a rainy Sunday? We dare you to hang onto a bad mood after coming out of this accessories and gifts paradise loaded with completely unnecessary kitsch must-haves. Highlights include a full range of plastic jewelry, including those wafer-thin stackable colored bracelets. Also look for leopard-print light-switch plates, tons of T-shirts and lamps made of plastic dolls and toasters. *modworldnyc.com*

*Affordable*                                          *Amex/MC/V*

**East Village**                           **(212) 460-8004**
85 First Avenue                             btw 5/6th St
NYC 10003         Mon-Thurs 12-10, Fri-Sat 12-11, Sun 12-8

## Mommy Chic

Pregnant with her first child, Angela Chew had trouble finding fashionable maternity clothes and ended up settling for leggings and her husband's sweaters. Her clever solution: Mommy Chic. Her chic (yes, they are what she says) designs run the gamut from casual and business to evening and holidaywear. She favors silks, cashmeres and stretch fabrics with hand crochet, beading and embroidery detailing. Find stretch bootleg jeans, cashmere twinsets, suits, and evening looks like sequined dresses and tops. Check out her children's line, as well as the Marie Chantal label. From newborn to size 6.　　877-973-2864　mommychic.com

*Moderate*　　　　　　　　　　　　　　　　*Amex/MC/V*

**Upper West Side**　　　　　　　　　　**(212) 769-9099**
2449 Broadway　　　　　　　　　　　　　　　　at 90th St
NYC 10012　　　　　　　　　　Mon-Sat 10-7, Sun 12-5

## MoMo FaLana

*Sex and the City* fans saw MoMo FaLana's vintage-inspired, hippy-chic apparel on the tube, and the brand is unwavering in its commitment to taking 'modern-day urban fantasies and making them real'. Now that may or may not be true, but MoMo hand-dyed dresses, embroidered brocade jackets and form-fitting silk tops and skirts certainly will help make your waking hours dreamy.　　momofalana.com

*Expensive*　　　　　　　　　　　　　　　*Amex/MC/V*

**East Village**　　　　　　　　　　　　**(212) 979-9595**
43 Avenue A　　　　　　　　　　　　　　　　at 3rd St
NYC 10009　　　　　　　Daily 12-8 (Thurs-Sat 12-10)

## Mom's Night Out/One Night Out

Mom's Night Out and One Night Out are separate stores located across a hall. The former caters to expectant mothers while the latter is for women who, well, aren't. Both offer an intimate shopping environment filled with glamorous eveningwear and allow you to rent, buy or custom-order. Tricia Shiland started Mom's Night Out because of the lack of sophisticated eveningwear for the woman with child. You'll find that neither store skimps on variety, offering up a multitude of styles, colors and sizes. You'll find bridal, cocktail dresses and evening gowns, as well as accessories—all at reasonable prices.　　　　　　　momsnightout.com

*Moderate*　　　　　　　　　　　　　　　　*Amex/MC/V*

**Upper East Side**　　　　　　　　　　**(212) 744-6667**
147 East 72nd Street (3rd floor)　btw Lexington/Third Ave
NYC 10021　　　　Mon-Fri 11-6 (Tues-Thurs 11-8), Sat 11-5

## Montmartre

These ultimate uptown girl clothing stores dictate Upper West Side style with their selection of C&C California and Michael Star tanks and tees, Milly, Anna Sui, Tibi and Nanette Lepore delicate dresses; plus, the current crop of Seven and Joe's Jeans will keep any girl fashionable every day of the week. The new Shops at Columbus Circle location in the Time Warner Center has a huge selection of work-ready pumps, weekend-off Mella terrycloth flip-flops and plenty of other girly goodies.　　montmartrenyc.com

*Moderate to expensive*　　　　　　　　　　*Amex/MC/V*

| | |
|---|---|
| **Upper West Side** | **(212) 875-8430** |
| 2212 Broadway | btw 78/79th St |
| NYC 10024 | Mon-Sat 11-8, Sun 12-7 |

| | |
|---|---|
| **Upper West Side** | **(212) 721-7760** |
| 247 Columbus Avenue | btw 71/72nd St |
| NYC 10023 | (opening hours as above) |

| | |
|---|---|
| **Midtown West** | **(212) 823-9821** |
| Time Warner Mall | at Columbus Circle |
| NYC 10019 | Mon-Sat 10-9, Sun 12-6 |

| | |
|---|---|
| **Upper East Side** | **(212) 988-8962** |
| 1157 Madison Avenue | btw 85/86th St |
| NYC 10028 | Mon-Sat 11-7, Sun 12-6 |

| | |
|---|---|
| **Lower Manhattan** | **(212) 945-7858** |
| World Financial Center | by West Side Highway/Liberty |
| NYC 10281 | Mon-Sat 11-7, Sun 12-5 |

## Moreschi  � ♀

With an international following at its back, this high-quality Italian footwear brand made a significant step in expanding its consumer base with the opening of its first store in the U.S. in late 2002. While Moreschi offers leather jackets, accessories and, more recently, women's footwear, men's shoes are still the company's true strength. They offer a variety of styles from loafers (from $325) to the Rolls-Royce of footwear, alligator-skin shoes (note the $3,300 price tag). With its handstitching, leather soles and meticulous detailing, Moreschi is sure to please those with an eye for a finely shod foot.

*Expensive to luxury*      *Amex/MC/V*

| | |
|---|---|
| **Midtown East** | **(212) 644-4199** |
| 515 Madison Avenue | at 53rd Street |
| NYC 10022 | Mon-Fri 10-7, Sat 10-6, Sun 12-5 |

## Morgane Le Fay  ♀

Argentinian designer Liliana Casabal expertly translates fantasy into wearable reality with her softly feminine, clean designs in fabrics from silk charmeuse to dreamy chiffon and organza. The collection includes elegant dresses, slacks, coats, cashmeres and the creamiest ecru wedding gowns. This is the perfect place to shop for refined romantic clothing.

*Expensive*      *Amex/MC/V*

| | |
|---|---|
| **Upper East Side** | **(212) 879-9700** |
| 746 Madison Avenue | btw 64/65th St |
| NYC 10021 | Daily 10-6 (Sun 1-6) |

| | |
|---|---|
| **SoHo** | **(212) 219-7672** |
| 67 Wooster Street | btw Spring/Broome |
| NYC 10012 | Daily 11-7 |

## Morris Bros  ♂

This place is such an Upper West Side institution that you half expect to see little Franny and Zooey buying their outfits for *It's a Wise Child* here. Specializing in clothes for summer camp and back-to-school, they keep up with the times with Paul Frank accessories and Saturday togs by Levi's, Dickies and Juicy Couture. Faithful customers love the full-service approach of the staff and the convenience of being able to pick up everything a kid needs—from baseball caps to backpacks to bobby socks. *morrisbrosnyc.com*

*Affordable* *Amex/MC/V*

**Upper West Side** **(212) 724-9000**
2322 Broadway at 84th St
NYC 10024 Mon-Sat 9:30-6:30, Sun 12-5:30

## Moschino

This clever-chic Italian luxury label never takes fashion too seriously. The whimsical interior of the store is dominated by a spiral staircase adorned with wrought-iron question-marks and heart and peace signs are scattered through-out—feel the love. The clothing, meanwhile, manages to marry chic with just the right degree of novelty—strong classics with clever detailing, suits with hand-stitched lapels, fur-trimmed suede bomber jackets, eyelet-trimmed gingham coats and miniskirts with tiers of ruffles. The store also sells the Cheap & Chic line and its Moschino jeans collection. *moschino.it*

*Expensive* *Amex/MC/V*

**Upper East Side** **(212) 639-9600**
803 Madison Avenue btw 67/68th St
NYC 10021 Mon-Sat 10-6

## Moshood

Melding the energies of the African and concrete jungles, Moshood combines African tailoring, bold color, and Afro-centric style to create distinctive, timeless pieces. Following African custom, clothes hang or simply wrap elegantly around the body. Pair pieces like men's flowing shirts or a woman's check wrap skirt with your favorite jeans or tee, and you'll be expressing excellent cross-cultural fashion sense. *africanspirit.com*

*Moderate* *Amex/MC/V*

**Fort Greene** **(718) 243-9433**
698 Fulton Street btw South Oxford/South Portland
Brooklyn 11217 Mon-Sat 10-9, Sun 12-8

## Motherhood Maternity

An affordable alternative to the pricier Manhattan materni-ty boutiques, Motherhood Maternity has everything from suits, casualwear and intimates to jeans, accessories and some swimwear. They also carry a few topical products for expectant mothers, such as anti-stretch mark creams and oils. The styles tend to be very practical, though the newest collection has stepped up the fashion quotient with bright colors and more sophisticated patterns. *motherhood.com*

*Affordable* *Amex/MC/V*

**Upper East Side**                    **(212) 734-5984**
1449 Third Avenue                           at 82nd St
NYC 10028                        Mon-Fri 10-7 (Thurs 10-8)
                                      Sat 10-6, Sun 12-6

**Midtown West**                       **(212) 564-8813**
901 Sixth Avenue       at Manhattan Mall, btw 32/33rd St
NYC 10001                            Mon-Sat 10-8, Sun 11-6

**Midtown West (outlet)**              **(212) 399-9840**
16 West 57th Street (3rd floor)         btw Fifth/Sixth Ave
NYC 10019                        Mon-Wed 10-7, Thurs 10-8
                                      Fri-Sat 10-6, Sun 12-6

**Chelsea**                            **(212) 741-3488**
641 Sixth Avenue                          at 20th Street
NYC 10011                            Mon-Sat 10-7 Sun 11-6

## MZ Wallace

A collection of tote and travel bags in durable materials like leather, Cordura nylon, burlap and printed, laminated cottons. These simply shaped weekend bags come in combinations like navy, floral print and sequins. The creator's goal: 'to create cool bags that have a chic and groovy look.' Good.                                   *mzwallace.com*

*Moderate*                                      *Amex/MC/V*

**SoHo**                               **(212) 431-8252**
93 Crosby Street                         btw Prince/Spring
NYC 10012                 Tues 11-6, Wed-Sat 11-7, Sun 12-6

## Nahbee

Do you get excited by Christian Lacroix, Vera Wang, Sebastian, Jacques Le Corre, L'Autre Chose, Marc by Marc Jacobs and Monique? We're guessing 'yes,' so know that this inviting, Zen-like space is perfect for picking up classic, ultra-feminine shoes for day and evening. Nahbee (Korean for 'butterfly') features many styles from the aforementioned labels, including mules, delicate sandals, boots, ballet flats and beautiful pumps. Prices run from $100 to $600.

*Expensive*                                     *Amex/MC/V*

**Nolita**                             **(646) 613-0860**
262 Mott Street                         btw Houston/Prince
NYC 10012                                        Daily 12-7

## Nalu NYC

Hang ten! Look past the boards at this beach-bum paradise to find some great warm-weather gear that's fashionable enough to wear around town. Come here for Brazilian bikinis, trunks by Billabong and Wet Suit, Havaianas sandals, surf wax, hats and eye-catching sunglasses.   *nalunyc.com*

*Moderate*                                      *Amex/MC/V*

**West Village**                       **(212) 675-7873**
10 Little West 12th Street    btw Seventh Ave/Washington
NYC 10014                                       Daily 12-10

## Nancy & Co

This is one of those hipper-than-traditional neighborhood stores catering to Upper East Side women who want to be fashionable without stepping over the line into trendy. Nothing at all wrong with that, and at Nancy and Co you'll find dresses, cashmere sweaters and the perfect accessories to augment your personal style. Choose from Three Dots tees, Shin Choi silk shells and Jeanne Maag separates.

*Moderate*                                                    *Amex/MC/V*

**Upper East Side**                                    **(212) 427-0770**
1242 Madison Avenue                                    at 89th St
NYC 10128                                                    Daily 10-7

## Nancy Geist

Nancy Geist is one quirky lady—witness her signature shoes in a rainbow of colors and featuring unusual heels that possess an uncompromising femininity. Find leather boots, mules, denim espadrilles with appliqués, strappy sandals, baby-doll flats and evening shoes in looks from flirty to city. Prices run from $185 to $600.    *nancygeist.com*

*Moderate to expensive*                                    *Amex/MC/V*

**SoHo**                                                    **(212) 925-7192**
107 Spring Street                                          at Mercer
NYC 10012                                            Mon-Sat 11-7, Sun 12-6

## Nanette Lepore

Nanette Lepore's clothes have been known to inspire cat fights between rock stars. So there you have it, this is one party-girl label. Her pieces are fabulously sexy and feminine and fearless in color and pattern—all up, it's glam girl meets gypsy. Lepore's SoHo store carries lots of flirty dresses, corsets and suits in luxe fabrics. Accessories include her coveted handbags and select shoe designers. Wonderful sales help.                                        *nanettelepore.com*

*Expensive*                                                    *Amex/MC/V*

**SoHo**                                                    **(212) 219-8265**
423 Broome Street                                    btw Lafayette/Crosby
NYC 10012                                            Mon-Sat 11-7, Sun 12-6

## Naturalizer

Nip into Naturalizer when your Manolos begin to blister or a subway grate claims the heel of your Jimmy Choos, and waltz out in cushiony comfort. Long recognized for their range of sizes, excellent value and, most of all, wearability, Naturalizer have never exactly been considered fashion-forward. Lately they've been trying to vamp up their image and they're making great strides with strappy sandals, classic pumps and, of course, durable flats for those long city treks. You'll probably never spot these babies in the pages of Italian *Vogue*, but when it comes to attractive practicality they've got it in spades.            *naturalizeronline.com*

*Affordable*                                                    *Amex/MC/V*

**Upper West Side**          **(917) 441-0153**
148 Columbus Avenue          btw 66/67th St
NYC 10023          Mon-Sat 9:30-8, Sun 11-6

**Midtown East**          **(212) 759-3094**
712 Lexington Avenue          btw 57/58th St
NYC 10022          Mon-Sat 9-8, Sun 11-6

## Nautica 👫

Known for great casual and outdoor wear—for sailors from Southampton or Fire Island Summer Club—this store features Nautica's huge collection of shirts, sweaters, jeans, shorts, khakis, swimwear and windbreakers in its trademark colors and quality fabrics. Also check out its sportswear collection of dressy pants, hooded cashmeres and smart wool coats. For comfortable workout gear, try the Nautica Competition line.          *nautica.com*

*Moderate*          *Amex/MC/V*

**Fifth Avenue**          **(212) 664-9594**
50 Rockefeller Plaza          at 50th Street btw Fifth/Sixth Ave
NYC 10023          Mon-Fri 10-8, Sat 10-7, Sun 12-7

## Neda 👨

Neda is Persian for 'message', and the point this recently opened store is trying to get across has something to do with embracing a personal style. Culling little-known designers from the Tri-State area, Neda features tops and dresses that are at once edgy and feminine, Western and Middle Eastern, with hand-painted details and contrasting fabrics such as linen and leather. Fabulous ballet flats and leather sandals in matching colors are a real find.

*Moderate*          *Amex/MC/V*

**Park Slope**          **(718) 965-0990/(646) 234-8752**
413a 7th Avenue          btw 13/14th St
Brooklyn 11215          Tues-Fri 12:30-7:30, Sat 12-8, Sun 12-6

## Nellie M Boutique 👨

From the outside Nellie M looks like it should have a sign on the outside that says '$10 or less', but once inside you realize Nellie M is great treat for Upper Eastsiders who do not want to make the trek to the 59th Street department stores. Nellie M features everything from established designers like Anna Sui, Chaiken and Nanette Lepore to fresh labels like Beth Bowley, Jessie Della Femina and Milly. There is also a serious jeans wall (Seven, Citizens of Humanity) in the back of the store that rivals the Co-op.          *nelliemboutique.com*

*Expensive*          *Amex/MC/V*

**Upper East Side**          **(212) 996-4410**
1309 Lexington Avenue          at 88th St
NYC 10128          Mon-Fri 10-8, Sat 11-8, Sun 11-7

## Net-a-Porter

You won't find this shop on any street, not even Madison Avenue or Fifth—it's fashion's unmissable virtual boutique, created by a gang of brilliant alumnae from that stylish and unique London magazine *Tatler*. The original concept was to create an online magazine with fashion features just like the glossies, but which visitors could buy from (see Gisele in a stunning Missoni bikini, double-click and it's yours). Its founder and managing director, Natalie Massenet (born in L.A., raised in Paris, lives in London), is famous for once finding three Hermès Kelly bags in an L.A. thrift store for $10 each, and her idea has been a similar serendipitous triumph (backed by good old-fashioned hard work). Click on runway reporter, bikini boutique, pretty woman, editor's favorites, most wanted, jewel colors, gift shop, sale section (key in your sizes) or The Salon for designer collections. Find out why Jennifer, Gwyneth and Gwen love Maharishi snopants, or who loves Juicy, or what's the next big thing. But why should we tell you any more? This is a fashion superstore which you can browse with your coffee cup—no need even to get dressed, let alone leave home. It's a one-stop shop for those who prefer logging on to trekking about and, like we said, unmissable.      *net-a-porter.com*

## New & Almost New

If you have been searching for this snazzy consignment shop on Mercer, you are on the wrong block—they now have a new home on Elizabeth and a whole new batch of goodies to be snatched up. The rule is: if you see something you fancy, make that purchase, because timing is everything and the pieces are quick to go. Try your luck: dig for designer treasure, like Miu Miu shoes or a Chanel handbag, and there's a good chance that you'll go home happy.

*Affordable*                                          *Amex/MC/V*

**SoHo**                                          **(212) 226-6677**
166 Elizabeth Street                        btw Spring/Kenmare
NYC 10012                                     Mon-Sat 12-6:30

## New Balance New York

Originally a brand primarily targeting runners, New Balance has expanded to offer an impressive selection of quality footwear for running, cross-training, hiking, walking, tennis, golf, basketball…and just sitting around looking cool. The NB apparel line runs from basic shorts and tank tops to microfiber jackets and pants that offer performance, fit and a little fashion too. Men's casual shoes and children's sneakers are also available, as well as assorted paraphernalia which runners are bound to appreciate.

          1-866-521-NBNY  *newbalancenewyork.com*

*Affordable to moderate*                              *Amex/MC/V*

**Midtown East**                                  **(212) 421-4444**
821 Third Avenue                              btw 50/51st St
NYC 10022      Mon-Fri 9-7 (Thurs 9-8), Sat 10-6, Sun 12-5

**Midtown West**                                  **(212) 997-9112**
51 West 42nd Street                          btw Fifth/Sixth Ave
NYC 10036   Mon-Fri 10-7 (Thurs 10-8), Sat 10-6, Sun 11-5

## New York 911

Situated adjacent to the fire station on Lafayette Street, the official outpost of the New York City Police Department's hugely successful mail-order site is the perfect spot to pick up that NYPD T-shirt for out-of-town relatives. Choose from an assortment of hats, patches, sweatshirts, key chains, action videos and special memorial patches from 9/11 from every unit—including the K-9 rescue unit. In addition, you can select an NYC coroner T-shirt or tote bag with chalk out-line. They even have tiny little tees for babies. *ny911.com*

*Affordable* *Amex/MC/V*

**Nolita** **(212) 219-3907**
263 Lafayette Street btw Prince/Spring
NYC 10012 Mon-Sat 10-6, Sun 12-5

## New York Golf Center

Fore! From the driving range to the clubhouse, NYGC has the city's largest selection of equipment for novices and pros. Featuring clubs and clothes from labels like Callaway, Taylor Made, Ping, Nike, Polo, Greg Norman and Titleist, you'll find what you need for smooth swinging on the links. Rainwear, socks, shoes, golf bags, balls, books and acces-sories are available, and be sure to inquire about lessons.

*Moderate* *Amex/MC/V*

**Midtown West** **(212) 564-2255**
131 West 35th Street btw Seventh Ave/Broadway
NYC 10001 Mon-Fri 10-8, Sat 10-7, Sun 11-6

## The New York Look

What does it mean to be fashionable in New York? Local chain store The New York Look is determined to answer that question by providing the latest trends in womenswear including Three Dots and Michael Star tops, Citizens of Humanity and Joe's Jeans, Teen Tahari and Theory work-wear among other sophisticated small brands. And with a great selection of shoes and costume jewelry from little labels, The New York Look is sure to keep you looking sharp from head to toe.

*Moderate to expensive* *Amex/MC/V*

**Upper West Side** **(212) 765-4758**
30 Lincoln Plaza btw 62/63rd St
NYC 10023  Mon-Thurs 10-9, Fri 10-8, Sat 11-9, Sun 12-7

**Upper West Side** **(212) 362-8650**
2030 Broadway btw 69/70th St
NYC 10023 (opening hours as above)

**Midtown West** **(212) 382-2760**
570 Seventh Avenue at 41st St
NYC 10018 Mon-Fri 9-7, Sat 10:30-7

**Fifth Avenue** **(212) 557-0909**
551 Fifth Avenue at 45th St
NYC 10176 Mon-Fri 9-8, Sat 10-8, Sun 10-6

**SoHo** | **(212) 598-9988**
468 West Broadway | btw Houston/Prince
NYC 10012 | Mon-Sat 10-8, Sun 12-7

## New York Om Yoga

Find yoga pants, tops, shoes, mats and more at this small boutique inside Om Yoga studio. All the apparel is from their own label, and is made by American Apparel and Alternative Apparel—sweatshop-free companies—so you can do your Downward Dog without worrying about unfair labor practices. *omyoga.com*

*Moderate* | *Amex/MC/V*
**Union Square** | **(212) 254-9642**
826 Broadway (6th floor) | at 12th St
NYC 10003 | Daily 7:30-8

## Nicole Farhi

British designer Nicole Farhi calls her clothes 'constant friends', but you could also call them instant classics. This three-floor, 16,000-square-foot flagship offers just that with men's and women's ready-to-wear and a home collection. Find racks of pant suits, embroidered skirts, brilliant chunky cashmeres and plenty of leather and suede, as well as classic (but never dull) shoes and accessories. Grab a bite downstairs at Nicole's, her sleek modern restaurant. *nicolefarhi.com*

*Expensive* | *Amex/MC/V*
**Upper East Side** | **(212) 223-8811**
10 East 60th Street | btw Fifth/Madison Ave
NYC 10021 | Mon-Thurs 10-7, Fri 10-6, Sat 11-6

## Nicole Miller

Nicole Miller, from bridalwear to sportswear, has something that appeals to every woman. Designs are an impressive combination of sophistication and whimsy. The formal silk dresses and casual day ensembles will charm with their classic silhouettes and modern details. Look here for solids, prints, basics and eveningwear. Also find an ever-changing line of men's ties, featuring her famously tongue-in-cheek prints. Bridal by appointment. *nicolemiller.com*

*Expensive* | *Amex/MC/V*
**Upper East Side** | **(212) 288-9779**
780 Madison Avenue | btw 66/67th St
NYC 10021 | Mon-Fri 10-7, Sat 10-6, Sun 12-5
**SoHo** | **(212) 343-1362**
134 Prince Street | btw Wooster/West Broadway
NYC 10012 | Mon-Sat 11-7, Sun 12-6

## Niketown

Perhaps a better name for this gigantic shrine to Just Doing It would be Nikecity, or even Nikeworld. Niketown's exterior mimics the facade of a New York high school circa 1950, while its interior is a high-tech atrium.

Enter through a set of turnstiles to find yourself in a five-floor, futuristic environment replete with video screens constantly plugging Nike products. While most of the merchandise is readily accessible, sneakers ascend at high speed from the basement via a series of clear plastic air tubes. All up, 100% pure adrenaline. Look out for a smaller boutique store, rumored to be opening soon in Nolita.          800-806-6453  *nike.com/niketown.com*

*Moderate*                                            *Amex/MC/V*

**Midtown East**                              **(212) 891-6453**
6 East 57th Street                      btw Fifth/Madison Ave
NYC 10022                                  Mon-Sat 10-8, Sun 11-7

## Nine West

This footwear behemoth claims to sell two pair of shoes per second. Nine West carries it all at the most affordable prices in town (even though the service can be downright terrible), from classic flats and loafers to trendy platforms and boots. Keep an eye open, because every so often you'll find a pair of heels that looks like they came straight from Gucci (fool your friends). Accessories include handbags, leather goods, sunglasses and jewelry, as well as a slick outerwear collection in leathers, nylons and shearlings.                          800-260-2227  *ninewest.com*

*Affordable*                                          *Amex/MC/V*

**Upper East Side**                           **(212) 987-9004**
184 East 86th Street                  btw Lexington/Third Ave
NYC 10028          Mon-Fri 10-8:30, Sat 10-7:30, Sun 11-6:30

**Upper West Side**                           **(212) 799-7610**
2305 Broadway                                    btw 83/84th St
NYC 10024                          Mon-Fri 10-8, Sat 10-9, Sun 11-6

**Midtown East**                              **(212) 370-9107**
341 Madison Avenue                                 at 44th St
NYC 10017                            Mon-Fri 8-8, Sat 10-6, Sun 11-5

**Midtown East**                              **(212) 486-8094**
750 Lexington Avenue                           btw 58/59th St
NYC 10022                                  Mon-Sat 10-8, Sun 11-6

**Midtown East**                              **(212) 371-4597**
757 Third Avenue                               btw 47/48th St
NYC 10017                            Mon-Fri 10-8, Sat 10-6, Sun 12-5

**Midtown East**                              **(212) 949-0037**
25 Lexington Avenue                            btw 43/44th St
NYC 10017                            Mon-Fri 10-8, Sat 10-6, Sun 12-5

**Midtown West**                              **(212) 397-0710**
1230 Sixth Avenue                                  at 49th St
NYC 10020                            Mon-Fri 9-8, Sat 10-5, Sun 12-5

**Midtown West**                              **(212) 594-0781**
21 West 34th Street                        btw Fifth/Sixth Ave
NYC 10018                            Mon-Fri 9-8, Sat 10-5, Sun 12-5

**Midtown West**                              **(212) 564-0063**
901 Sixth Avenue          at Manhattan Mall, btw 32/33rd St
NYC 10001                                  Mon-Sat 10-8, Sun 11-6

**Fifth Avenue**         **(212) 319-6893**
675 Fifth Avenue         at 53rd St
NYC 10022         Mon-Sat 10-7, Sun 12-6

**Flatiron**         **(212) 777-1752**
115 Fifth Avenue         at 19th St
NYC 10003         Mon-Sat 10-8, Sun 11-7

**SoHo**         **(212) 941-1597**
577 Broadway         at Prince
NYC 10012         Mon-Sat 10-8, Sun 11-7

**Lower Manhattan**         **(212) 346-0903**
179 Broadway         btw Day/Maiden Lane
NYC 10007         Daily 8-7

## Nocturne

Nocturne imports 100% batiste cotton sleepwear from Brazil with handmade embroideries and lace. You'll find embellished pajamas, feminine nightshirts, luxurious robes worthy of a femme fatale and comfy nightgowns. Adorable children's slippers and cosmetic bags are also available.

*Moderate*         *Amex/MC/V*

**Upper East Side**         **(212) 427-8282**
1744 First Avenue         btw 90/91st St
NYC 10028         Mon-Fri 9-5

## Nom De Guerre

The only thing harder to find than the subtle, minimalist clothes by Nom de Guerre is the store itself. Only the most fashion-hungry know that the black gate and green stairs on the southeast corner of Broadway and Bleecker lead to this below-ground, brick-and-cement shop (though we hear a sign may be in the works). As the name suggests, the shop is characterized by utilitarian, military-inspired clothing in rough, heavy fabrics and dark colors, with a few loud tees ($35-$85) thrown in the mix. Labels include esoteric favorites such as Rogan, Noah, United Bamboo and Habitual, Japan's A Bathing Ape and vintage Nikes.

*Expensive*         *Amex/MC/V*

**NoHo**         **(212) 253-2891**
640 Broadway         at Bleecker
NYC 10012         Daily 12-8 (Sun 12-7)

## Noriko Maeda

Noriko Maeda's aesthetic is ladylike elegance and she achieves it through her superior tailoring of wool, cashmere and silk. There are gorgeous accessories like antique bead-ed chokers ($230) and Russian sable stoles ($3,200) with matching sable-trimmed gloves ($430), and you can nibble from the complimentary tray of chocolate truffles and kiss-es while you think everything over. Sizes run small.

*Luxury*         *Amex/MC/V*

**Upper East Side**         **(212) 717-0330**
985 Madison Avenue         btw 76/77th St
NYC 1002         Mon-Fri 10-6

## Norma Kamali

Norma Kamali provides a superb line of polo jerseys in bright colors that are washable, quick to dry and wrinkle-free. She has been having a resurrection of late, and now sells as many cult vintage pieces as new (singer Mandy Moore is a fan). Her seen-in-*Sports Illustrated* swimwear moves easily from poolside straight to resort lunch, while her everyday pieces like reversible slip dresses, wide-legged or pencil pants and sleeveless tees sit snugly along-side glamorous eveningwear and vintage bridal. One of the first designers to mix vintage with new, Kamali is complete-ly of the moment. Her staff is so dedicated to customer sat-isfaction that they have a 'shop like a celebrity' system, allowing customers to try before they buy—including bathing suits.

*Moderate*                                          *Amex/MC/V*

**Midtown West**                           **(212) 957-9797**
11 West 56th Street                    btw Fifth/Sixth Ave
NYC 10019                                    Mon-Sat 10-6

## Nort 235

A special place for sneaker freaks, Nort sells limited-edition kicks that you can't find anywhere else, like exclusive offer-ings of Nike series that have die-hard enthusiasts lined up around the block. The selection is always hot, and your feet will inspire your friends' envy.

*Expensive*                                            *MC/V*

**Lower East Side**                       **(212) 777-6102**
235 Eldridge Street                    btw Houston/Stanton
NYC 10002                                        Daily 12-7

## N.Peal Cashmere

Ooh, cashmere. The ultimate purveyor of traditional, luxury cashmere, this 200-year-old private label company features a brilliant selection of Scottish knitwear in fabulous colors and textures. Styles include plain or cabled V-necks, round necks, cardigans, twinsets and turtlenecks from single-ply to six-ply. In addition, find skirts, robes, gloves and socks.   npeal.com

*Moderate*                                          *Amex/MC/V*

**Midtown West**                           **(212) 333-3500**
5 West 56th Street                     btw Fifth/Sixth Ave
NYC 10019                                    Mon-Sat 10-6

## No. 436

A real neighborhood jewel, No. 436 carries a quirky range of pieces from underground designers, all with a distinc-tively feminine edge. The colorful space houses a collection heavy on prints, sassy Eva dresses (printed with cartoon foxy ladies), and tube tops with pinwheel appliqués, not to mention a well-stocked shoe selection.

*Moderate*                                          *Amex/MC/V*

**East Village**                           **(212) 529-8231**
436 East 9th Street                    btw First/Avenue A
NYC 10009                                  Daily 1-8 (Sun 12-6)

## Nursery Lines

Nursery Lines specialize in furnishings for, yes, the nursery—whether it's upholstered furniture (choose from over 250 fabrics), window treatments, custom bumpers, linens, monogrammed quilts or interior design for your child's bedroom. Classic blue and pink layette outfits by Bebebo, sailor outfits by LeBonBon de Marquet and Pino cotton pajamas by J.C. de Castelbajac will all help keep your kid cozy. From newborn to size 4.

*Expensive*                                          *Amex/MC/V*

**Upper East Side**                        **(212) 396-4445**
1034 Lexington Avenue                              at 74th St
NYC 10021                              Mon-Fri 10-5, Sat 10-6

## Objets du Desir

Four jewelers—three Swiss and one Japanese—combined forces to open the quaint Objets du Desir gallery. Featuring one-of-a-kind as well as limited-edition pieces, they have set out to provide contemporary rings, bracelets and necklaces in a variety of materials (leather, rubber, bronze, silver, gold) and at a number of different price points (from $50 to $3,000). As might be expected with four creators, the collection is eclectic, but there's an indisputable charm to the boutique's variety, where fanciful insect and plant forms studded with large gems are balanced by simple designs with black and white pearls.                *objetsdudesir.com*

*Moderate to expensive*                              *Amex/MC/V*

**Nolita**                                  **(212) 334-9727**
241 Mulberry Street                       btw Prince/Spring
NYC 10012                          Tues-Sat 12-7, Sun 12-6

## Off Broadway

You just have to stand up and take notice when you hear Barbra belting out 'People' on the overhead system at this outrageous emporium staffed with would-be divas in fabulous head dress. Off Broadway caters to the woman who 'gets a kick out of sculpture and loves making an entrance', with dramatic suits, dresses and accessories in bold colors and realistic sizes for ladies of a certain age. Make no mistake, while Off Broadway is sure to tickle a costume designer's fancy, the clothes here are made and priced for the genuine article. At 30 years, it's the longest running show on the West Side.

*Moderate to expensive*                              *Amex/MC/V*

**Upper West Side**                        **(212) 724-6713**
139 West 72nd Street                 btw Broadway/Columbus
NYC 10023                       Mon-Fri 10-8, Sat 11-7, Sun 1-7

## Oilily

For the Peter Pan in all of us, Oilily is the perfect blend of youthful style and sophisticated silhouettes. The adult line was created for all the hip moms who want to wear their kids' clothes. But don't expect to find children's clothes sized for adults; the Oilily children's aesthetic translates into a bohemian-chic adult look that will appeal to women with or without kids. Find the company's signature prints and bright colors on skirts, dresses, pants, tops and even shoes. As for the famous and funky kids' clothes, prints again adorn almost all the pieces. From dresses to shoes, everything is decorated with energetic, youthful designs that look terrific on kids from newborn to 12 years old. *oililyusa.com*

*Expensive*                                           *Amex/MC/V*

**Upper East Side**                        **(212) 628-0100**
820 Madison Avenue                          btw 68/69th St
NYC 10021              Mon-Sat 10-6 (Thurs 10-7), Sun 12-5

## Old Navy Clothing Company 👨👧👦

Old Navy is the best. Weighing in at 100,000 square feet per location, it is a retail behemoth that gives shoppers maximum buying power for casual clothing that pays perfect homage to designer trends—put it this way, Marc Jacobs would freak out in here. Kids, teens, adults, mothers-to-be and the plus-size set love shopping here for reliable, hip and affordable basics. The store is packed with essentials like jeans, T-shirts, swimwear, shorts, sweatshirts, sweaters and jackets. Best buys: the ribbed tanks for about 10 bucks.                    800-653-6289  *oldnavy.com*

*Affordable*                                          *Amex/MC/V*

**Midtown West**                           **(212) 594-0049**
150 West 34th Street                     btw Sixth/Seventh Ave
NYC 10001                             Mon-Sat 9-10, Sun 10-8

**Chelsea**                                **(212) 645-0663**
610 Sixth Avenue                                 at 18th St
NYC 10011                           Mon-Sat 9-9:30, Sun 11-8

**SoHo**                                   **(212) 226-0865**
503 Broadway                              btw Spring/Broome
NYC 10012                          Mon-Sat 10-9:30, Sun 10-9

**Harlem**                                 **(212) 531-1544**
300 West 125th Street                      at Manhattan Ave
NYC 10027                            Mon-Sat 9-9:30, Sun 10-8

## Olive & Bette's 👩

Best friends and self-proclaimed 'It Girls of the Upper West Side', Olive and Bette opened this series of cheeky boutiques packed with trendy designer staples in order to 'save the world from fashion don'ts'. And just how do they do that? By providing flirtatious females with walls of neatly piled Michael Star and James Perse tanks and tees, rows of Dr. Scholl sandals and Tamara Henriquez rain boots, and racks of Alice & Olivia and Theory pants. And for the on-the-go-girl who just can't get enough must-haves, Olive and Bette even have a monthly e-newsletter. What more could an It Girl want?                    *oliveandbettes.com*

*Moderate to expensive*                               *Amex/MC/V*

**Upper West Side**                        **(212) 579-2178**
252 Columbus Avenue                          btw 71/72nd St
NYC 10023                             Mon-Sat 11-7 Sun 12-6

**West Village/NoHo**                    **212 712 0473**
384 Bleecker Street                          at Perry
NYC 10004                    (opening hours as above)

**SoHo**                                    **(646) 613-8772**
158 Spring Street          btw Wooster/West Broadway
NYC 10012          Mon-Thurs 11-7, Fri-Sat 11-8, Sun 12-6

## Omari

Yet another funky SoHo shoe shop for the young and swinging, with styles that include chunky heeled sandals, sneaker boots, stilettos, combat boots and two-toned leather cowboy boots. Best are the strap shoes evocative of Helmut Lang. All come under the Omari label with prices ranging from $150 to $450.

*Moderate to expensive*                        *Amex/MC/V*

**SoHo**                                    **(212) 219-0619**
68 Spring Street              btw Crosby/Lafayette
NYC 10012                              Daily 11-7:30

## Only Hearts

Helena Stuart opened her Columbus Avenue boutique in 1978 and has created an internationally recognized home for the hopeless romantic. A mecca for all things heart-shaped, from bath beads and paperweights to antiques and candles, Only Hearts sells gifts and intimate apparel for those who want every day to be Valentine's. The store's signature 'inner outwear', a selection of sweet and flirty camisoles, teddies, lace tanks and sexy underwear is so cute that you may be tempted to take them out of the bedroom and into your everyday wardrobe.        *onlyhearts.com*

*Moderate*                                    *Amex/MC/V*

**Upper West Side**                        **(212) 724-5608**
386 Columbus Avenue                  btw 78/79th St
NYC 10024          Mon-Sat 11-7 (Thurs-Fri 11-8), Sun 12-6

**Nolita**                                  **(212) 431-3694**
230 Mott Street                    btw Prince/Spring
NYC 10012                    Mon-Sat 11-7, Sun 12-6

## Onward SoHo

This huge store (well, for SoHo) sells its own ICB brand, featuring pared-down contemporary career and sportswear (similar to Theory) such as relaxed suits, knits, shirts and pants in muted colors, as well as handbags. Look out for the new denim line.        *icb-brand.com*

*Moderate*                                    *Amex/MC/V*

**SoHo**                                    **(212) 274-1255**
172 Mercer Street                        at Houston
NYC 10012                    Mon-Sat 11-7, Sun 12-6

## The Open Door Gallery

Painter-turned-fashion-designer Madani views her work as art, and it looks like it too: movement and color play vital roles in her designs. She uses silks, linens, cottons and interesting prints and mixes them together to create individual pieces finished with raw, zigzagged edges. Her dresses often call for wrapping yourself sarong style. Feminine, flowing and festive, Madani will alter any piece to your exact measurements. Don't miss the unusual array of accessories and jewelry.

*Expensive* *Amex/MC/V*

**East Village** **(212) 982-7859**
77 East 4th Street btw Second/Bowery
NYC 10003 Daily 2-8

## Opening Ceremony
Now this is a cool idea for a boutique: dedicate each year or season to elegant, hard-to-find fashions from a different international hotspot. Started by two Berkeley grads, Opening Ceremony kicked things off last year by selling wares from Hong Kong, before moving on to the sunny glories of Brazil's Sao Paolo. They are now showcasing bold designs from Berlin but the house line (designed by Humberto Leon) is another reason to visit—the unisex collection is filled with smart separates, blazers, coats and more.

*Expensive* *Amex/MC/V*

**SoHo** **(212) 219-2688**
35 Howard Street btw Broadway/Lafayette
NYC 10013 Mon-Sat 11-8, Sun 12-7

## Original Leather
If your looking to complete your *Matrix* look, then Original Leather is your place. Selling mostly their own label, you'll find leather blazers, trenches, skirts, five-pocket 'jeans' as well as a home collection. Fabrics range from suede, fur and shearling to exotic skins—if you can't find it here, you're not going to find it anywhere.

*Moderate* *Amex/MC/V*

**Upper East Side** **(212) 585-4200**
1126 Third Avenue at 66th St
NYC 10021 Mon-Sat 10-6:30, Sun 12-6

**Upper West Side** **(212) 595-7051**
256 Columbus Avenue at 72nd St
NYC 10023 Daily 11-8 (Sun 11-7)

**West Village** **(212) 675-2303**
171 West 4th Street btw Sixth/Seventh Ave
NYC 10014 Mon-Thurs 11-9, Fri 11-12
Sat 11-10, Sun 11-9

**SoHo** **(212) 219-8210**
176 Spring Street btw Thompson/West Broadway
NYC 10012 Mon-Sat 11-7, Sun 12-8

## The Original Levi's Store
The king of the jeans business, Levi's is rising to the challenge of hip brands like Earl and Seven with limited-edition ranges like the twisty Type 1 and the Superlow jeans for girls who still think belly-button flashing is vital. Of course,

there is a huge range of 501s and other classic styles, plus casual basics and accessories. *levis.com*

*Moderate*                                      *Amex/MC/V*

**Midtown East**                          **(212) 826-5957**
750 Lexington Avenue                        btw 59/60th St
NYC 10022                          Mon-Sat 10-8, Sun 11-6

**SoHo**                                  **(646) 613-1847**
536 Broadway                             btw Prince/Spring
NYC 10012                        (opening hours as above)

## Orva
A full-service department store for the price-conscious woman. You could arrive naked (not that we'd advise that) and leave fully dressed in its selection of designer and brand-name sportswear, lingerie, activewear, juniors, hosiery, accessories and shoe department. Labels like Juicy Couture, Von Dutch, Kenneth Cole, Diesel and Calvin Klein are 10-30% below retail prices.

*Moderate*                                      *Amex/MC/V*

**Upper East Side**                       **(212) 369-3448**
155 East 86th Street                 btw Lexington/Third Ave
NYC 10028                          Mon-Sat 10-9, Sun 10-8

## OshKosh B'Gosh
Childrenswear icon OshKosh's claim to fame: the bib over-all, originally worn by farmers and railroad workers in the 1900s, and today worn by toddlers and children world-wide—in smaller sizes, of course. Parents flock here for durable, well-styled clothes that scream pure Americana. It offers everyday essentials like jeans, overalls, corduroys, T-shirts, activewear, swimwear, shoes and accessories, all color-coordinated with the OshKosh B'Gosh logo. Newborn to size 16.     800-282-4674 *oshkoshbgosh.com*

*Affordable*                                    *Amex/MC/V*

**Fifth Avenue**                          **(212) 827-0098**
586 Fifth Avenue                               at 47th St
NYC 10036                     Mon-Fri 10-7, Sat 10-6, Sun 12-5

## Otte
Think of it as an alternative to Scoop—same idea (diverse mix of designers), but not everything in the store costs an arm and a leg. Look for Rebecca Taylor, Juicy Couture, Paper Denim, Mint and Fred Segal among others. Try on a sexy little tank by Fred Segal or check out the necklaces and bracelets, many of which run less than $100 at the West Village outpost (the Williamsburg store is the original). Perfect to weather recessions.

*Moderate*                                      *Amex/MC/V*

**West Village**                          **(212) 229-9424**
121 Greenwich Avenue                           at 13th St
NYC 10014                              Daily 12-8 (Sun 12-7)

**Williamsburg**                          **(718) 302-3007**
132 North 5th Street                        at Bedford Ave
Brooklyn 11211                      Daily 12-8, Sun (12-7)

## The Otter

One of the few West Village shops to sell trendy sports-wear—such a relief for its hipster residents. There are pants, dresses, shirts, sweaters, T-shirts and jeans by hip domestic and imported labels like Seven, Paul & Joe, Burning Torch, Alice & Olivia, Kors, Milly, Vince and Tocca. They also sell Hollywould shoes.

*Moderate*                                                        *Amex/MC/V*

**West Village**                                          **(212) 243-0284**
361 Bleecker Street                        btw Charles/West 10th St
NYC 10014                                        Daily 12-8 (Sun 12-6)

## Ottiva

Here's a genius concept in retailing: when you want to open another trendy shoe store in the same neighborhood selling the same stuff but still want to be 'new', what should you do? Spell the name of your first store backwards, of course. If this makes no sense to you, go to Avitto and read all about Ottiva (Omari and Iramo suffer from the same syndrome). The salespeople may be sick of explaining the whole thing, but you'll still see a very nice selection of leather shoes imported from Italy here, along with some rugged footwear and some trendier numbers and a smattering of handbags and briefcases.

*Moderate*                                                        *Amex/MC/V*

**SoHo**                                                    **(212) 625-0348**
192 Spring Street                              btw Thompson/Sullivan
NYC 10012                                                Daily 11-8:30

## Otto Tootsi Plohound

It's a strange name, and no one knows what it means, but when they see these shoes, no one really cares. This is a fabulous footwear store that straddles the divide between downtown and designer perfectly. Alongside Cynthia Rowley, Nancy Nancy, Miu Miu, Costume National and Prada Sport, you'll find their own label, Otto, that dilutes the trends into super-affordable and distinctive shoes. They have fantastic sales too. A must-visit store for any shoe shopper.

*Affordable to expensive*                                          *Amex/MC/V*

**Midtown East**                                          **(212) 231-3199**
38 East 57th Street                            btw Madison/Park Ave
NYC 10022                            Mon-Fri 11-8, Sat 11-7, Sun 12-6

**Flatiron**                                              **(212) 460-8650**
137 Fifth Avenue                                        btw 20/21st St
NYC 10010                    Mon-Fri 11:30-7:30, Sat 11-8, Sun 12-7

**SoHo**                                                  **(212) 925-8931**
413 West Broadway                                   btw Prince/Spring
NYC 10012                                  Mon-Sat 11:30-8, Sun 12-7

**SoHo**                                                  **(212) 431-7299**
273 Lafayette Street                              btw Houston/Prince
NYC 10012                                  (opening hours as above)

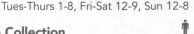
## Outlet 7
Fashion editors in the know seek out high-end designer Showroom Seven's East Village outpost where you can snag last season's designer pieces at wholesale prices. The selection constantly changes, but look for Imitation of Christ dresses, handbags by Pedro Zillia, slinky Whistles dresses and floaty ruffled tops by Holly in the current crop.

*Expensive*                                                *Amex/MC/V*

**East Village**                                      **(212) 529-0766**
117 East 7th Street                             btw First/Avenue A
NYC 10009              Tues-Thurs 1-8, Fri-Sat 12-9, Sun 12-8

## Oxxford Couture Collection
Creative director Jack Simpson, a lover of the classic strong-shouldered American silhouette and a former co-designer of the basketball uniforms for UNC and the Charlotte Hornets, helms this made-to-measure showroom which operates (both literally and figuratively) 'one step above' the classic Oxxford menswear on the ground floor. Fashion-oriented fellas excited by the idea of Sherlock Holmes hitting the runway can rummage through tweedy fabrics for the ultimate fall suit. The tailoring is exquisite, the looks timeless.                    *theoxxfordstore.com*

*Luxury*                                                   *Amex/MC/V*

**Midtown East**                                      **(212) 593-0230**
36 East 57th Street                           btw Madison/Park Ave
NYC 10022                          Daily 10-6 (by appointment)

## Pan American Phoenix
A rare find on the Upper East Side, this cute little store imports the best goods from Mexico. Look for colorful skirts and peasants blouses to satisfy Frida Kahlo or a fashion-forward clientele. The embroidered dresses and gorgeous scarves are winners, too. Also find silver, jewelry, handbags and a great housewares collection. The best part? Prices so reasonable that you might be tempted to break for the border yourself.                              *panamphoenix.com*

*Moderate*                                                 *Amex/MC/V*

**Upper East Side**                                   **(212) 570-0300**
857 Lexington Avenue                              btw 64/65th St
NYC 10021                          Mon-Fri 10:30-6:30, Sat 11-6

## Paragon Sporting Goods
This is truly a sporting goods store for the Noughties: over 100,000 square feet devoted to clothes and gear for every sport imaginable, from racket sports, water sports, skiing and hiking to golf, camping, fitness and fishing. The selection is enormous, but the store is so well organized it makes shopping easy and pleasurable. You might take up a new hobby just to suit yourself in the perfect gear.                              800-961-3030 *paragon.com*

*Moderate*                                                 *Amex/MC/V*

**Chelsea** (212) 255-8036
867 Broadway at 18th St
NYC 10003 Mon-Sat 10-8, Sun 11:30-7

## Parke & Ronen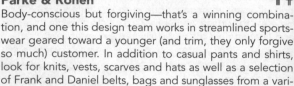

Body-conscious but forgiving—that's a winning combination, and one this design team works in streamlined sportswear geared toward a younger (and trim, they only forgive so much) customer. In addition to casual pants and shirts, look for knits, vests, scarves and hats as well as a selection of Frank and Daniel belts, bags and sunglasses from a variety of European designers. *parkeandronen.com*

*Expensive* *Amex/MC/V*

**Chelsea** (212) 989-4245
176 Ninth Avenue btw 20/21st St
NYC 10011 Mon-Sat 12-8, Sun 1-6

## Patagonia

Patagonia brings an environmentally minded, West Coast attitude to the rough and tough Big Apple. This means cozy fleece pullovers made from recycled plastic bottles, polos and pants made from organic cotton that is grown without the use of any harmful chemicals, and outdoor clothes for every activity from yoga to Alpine mountaineering. Putting consciousness back into cool clothing, the store has a small selection of guides, nature photography, books and novels by the likes of Thoreau and Krakauer, and is happy to provide you with eco-literature at the check-out. A visit to Patagonia makes for a truly fulfilling experience for the mind, body and spirit. 800-638-6464 *patagonia.com*

*Moderate* *Amex/MC/V*

**Upper West Side** (917) 441-0011
426 Columbus Avenue btw 80/81st St
NYC 10024 Mon-Sat 10-7, Sun 11-6

**SoHo** (212) 343-1776
101 Wooster Street btw Prince/Spring
NYC 10012 Mon-Sat 11-7 (Thurs 11-8), Sun 12-6

## Pat Areias

Upon entering this Madison Avenue belt store, face right and select from over 500 hanging belt straps in skins like calf, alligator, crocodile, lizard and ostrich, or horsehair. Decide on a color, from standard neutrals to bold brights and soft pastels. Then admire the sterling-silver buckles in the glass display case. Match a belt strap with a buckle, and voilà—you've just designed your own belt. Straps run from $50 to $450, while buckles go from $80 to $6,000 for an 18-karat gold and diamond number.

*Expensive* *Amex/MC/V*

**Upper East Side** (212) 717-7200
966 Madison Avenue btw 75/76th St
NYC 10021 Mon-Sat 10-6, Sun 11-5

## Patch

Fashionistas have embraced this quirky accessories label and flock to its store, home to the complete Patch NYC by Ross & Carney collection. Each piece is highly individual and looks like your granny might have made it (but in a cool way). It's got handbags, jewelry, stripey hats, cute crochet scarves, tops and home furnishings to boot. Best are their one-of-a-kind handbags with unique detailing (leather flowers, hand-painted cameos, beading, appliqués and vintage fabrics). *patchnyc.com*

*Moderate* Amex/MC/V

**West Village** **(212) 807-1060**
17 Eighth Avenue btw 12th/Jane
NYC 10014 Tues-Sat 12-7

## Patina

A quaint vintage clothing shop, Patina offers a wide choice of vintage clothing, handbags and other goodies like ceramics, decorative glass and period costume jewelry. There are beaded sweater sets, dresses, skirts and handbags from the Forties through the Seventies, all in good condition. As with all vintage shops, timing is everything—repeat visits may be necessary to snag something truly special.

Moderate Amex/MC/V

**SoHo** **(212) 625-3375**
451 Broome Street btw Broadway/Mercer
NYC 10012 Mon-Sat 12-7 (Sun 1-6)

## Paul & Shark

This Italian retailer of yachting attire for, one suspects, the permanently land-locked, fuses urban and nautical influences. The two-level shop sells chic men's and women's sportswear, from sweaters, shirts and warm-up suits to swimwear, lightweight boating jackets, winter-weight coats and a line of polar fleece. It's all specifically fashioned for outdoor living and, best of all, is water-resistant. Some pieces are more hi-tech (don't miss jackets with an interior thermometer that adjusts temperature) than others, but they're all made to withstand the elements—just in case you do get a chance to hit the high seas. Also find golf apparel and boating shoes for men. *paulshark.it*

*Expensive* Amex/MC/V

**Upper East Side** **(212) 452-9868**
772 Madison Avenue btw 66/67th St
NYC 10021 Mon-Sat 10-6, Sun 12-5

## Paul Frank Industries

California designer Paul Frank is a cheeky monkey. Well, sort of. His cartoon chimpanzee Julius has become cult amongst equally cheeky fashion girls who like a bit of kitsch with their cool. Think the Hello Kitty of America. This downtown store carries the full Paul Frank range, from furniture to women's and menswear to handbags and wallets. He recently introduced eyewear too, so, to be franked, this is your place. *paulfrank.com*

*Moderate* *Amex/MC/V*

**Nolita** **(212) 965-5079**
195 Mulberry Street at Kenmare
NYC 10013 Sun-Wed 11-7, Thurs-Sat 11-8

## Paul Smith
One of Britain's most successful designers, and knighted by the Queen to boot, Sir Paul Smith keeps his customers coming back for more. What distinguishes a Paul Smith design: a bold approach to fabric, pattern and color with traditional Old World styling. His classic pieces are never stuffy (more warm and clever, really), and his striped shirts are a must for both sexes. Shop a collection of English tailored menswear that includes suits, at an average price of $1,200, dress and casual shirts, sport jackets and outerwear. Accessories include watches, cufflinks and eyewear. *paulsmith.co.uk*

*Expensive* *Amex/MC/V*

**Flatiron** **(212) 627-9770**
108 Fifth Avenue at 16th St
NYC 10011 Mon-Sat 11-7 (Thurs 11-8), Sun 12-6

## Paul Stuart
With its no-nonsense collection of suits, furnishings, shirts, sportswear and outerwear, as well as English bench-made shoes and accessories, this is the label of choice for high-powered bankers, lawyers, and stockbrokers ready and willing to drop a bundle to look their business best. Corporate men and women will find plenty of straightforward designs to seal the deal. Whether you choose off the rack or opt for made-to-measure, Paul Stuart is a great source for traditional clothing. 800-678-8278 *paulstuart.com*

*Luxury* *Amex/MC/V*

**Midtown East** **(212) 682-0320**
Madison Avenue at 45th St
NYC 10017 Mon-Fri 8-6:30 (Thurs 8-7), Sat 9-6, Sun 12-5

## Peacock NYC
Looking for an outfit that will flaunt your feathers? Peacock carries a variety of downtown interpretations of current popular fashions. Pick out sheer form-fitting separates from Diab'less and Ella Moss to go under a leather jacket, or splurge on accessories like beaded jewelry and heart pendants. All the goods are cool enough for the East Village, but basic enough to carry you well outside the neighborhood.

*Expensive* *Amex/MC/V*

**East Village** **(212) 260-1809**
440 East 9th Street btw First/Avenue A
NYC 10009 Daily 12-8

## A Pea in the Pod

At this flagship store women no longer have to fret about putting together the perfect pregnancy wardrobe. It's 3,300 square feet of selling space offering A Pea in the Pod's private label as well as designs from the maternity lines of Nicole Miller, La Perla, Tahari, Seven and Three Dots. Check out the Yanuk jeans, complete with extra maternity fabric (yes!), and items from Chaiken, jogging suits by Vince, Shoshanna shifts and Lilly Pulitzer swimwear. The clothes are attractive, comfortable and versatile.       *apeainthepod.com*

*Moderate*                                          *Amex/MC/V*

**Upper East Side**                          **(212) 988-8039**
860 Madison Avenue                              at 70th St
NYC 10021               Mon-Fri 10-7, Sat 10-6, Sun 12-6

## Peanutbutter & Jane

Anyone looking for cute and cool childrenswear should head for Peanutbutter & Jane, which carries baby and toddler clothes as well as big kids' sizes up to girls 12/14 and boys 10. The big kids will get a kick out of the printed jeans, beaded tops, surfer shorts, stylish hats and costume shoes. Labels include Ave. Blu, Corky + Co, Cotton Caboodle, Flowers by Zoe, Lipstik, Petit Bateau, Submarine and Wes and Willy. Sadly, no peanut butter sandwich with purchase.

*Moderate*                                          *Amex/MC/V*

**West Village**                             **(212) 620-7952**
617 Hudson Street                        btw Jane/West 12th St
NYC 10014               Mon-Fri 10:30-7, Sat 10-7, Sun 11-6

## Pearl River Mart

They may have moved to new digs—to Broadway from their seedy former location next to the Canal Street subway station—and added a cascading waterfall, but the low prices on everything Asian-inspired remain. You'll find silk jacquard-quilted jackets in bright colors retailing for $80, Japanese silk blouses with hook (or 'frog') closures for $39.50, and a wide assortment of pajamas and kimonos. Check out the housewares section for bamboo blinds and room dividers, ceramics and traditional china, or pick up a rooster alarm clock or dragon-print duvet. There are also green tea beauty products.       *pearlriver.com*

*Affordable*                                      *(cash only)*

**SoHo**                                     **(212) 431-4770**
477 Broadway                              btw Broome/Grand
NYC 10013                                    Daily 10-7:30

## Pelle Via Roma

Want a great bag without a label? Owned by Max Fiorentino, this shop offers a similar selection of handbags and luggage crafted in the Florentine style. The classic designs are in supple and exotic skins like lamb, calf, alligator, lizard and deer, and feature shapes like the Fendi baguette, the Hermès bucket bag and Tod's and Pradaesque designs. Prices run from $250 to $900. Also shop an enormous selection of pashmina shawls retailing at $155.

*Expensive*                                          *Amex/MC/V*

**Upper East Side**                          **(212) 327-3553**
1322 Third Avenue                              btw 75/76th St
NYC 10021                                          Daily 11-8

## A Perfect Day in Paradise
If you want every day to be a Palm Beach day (and who does-n't, really) dive into Denice Summers's collection of brightly colored, Lilly Pulitzeresque print dresses, skirts, tops, pants, silk, corduroys, cashmeres, Mackintosh raincoats and, for the perfect bit of neighborhood pride, polos embroidered with the '10021' zip code. Men will find corduroys, polos and oxford shirts in bold or pastel colors. Pay $140 for a pair of cords, $350 for a cashmere sweater and $1,500 for a custom-made evening frock.          *aperfectdayinparadise.com*

*Moderate to expensive*                             *Amex/MC/V*

**Upper East Side**                          **(212) 639-1414**
153 East 70th Street                   btw Lexington/Third Ave
NYC 10021                             Mon-Fri 10-6, Sat 11-5

## Peter Elliot
An exemplary example of what a men's store should be, this small, dark wood-paneled space gives a nod to Savile Row days of yore. The store stocks business-ready Kiton suits, classic polo shirts, casual knits, dandy Peter Elliot blazers accented by ribbon belts, and Paul Smith polka-dot ties. For a store that is the size of most New York apart-ments, the service is exquisite, with tailors and sales help available at your beck and call, thanks to a 24-hour emer-gency line, a delivery service and free alterations.

*Expensive*                                          *Amex/MC/V*

**Upper East Side**                          **(212) 570-2300**
1070 Madison Avenue                            at 81st St
NYC 10028                          Mon-Fri 10-7, Sat 10-6, Sun 12-5

## ★ Peter Elliot (kids and outlet)
If you want your child to be the chicest kid at his private school, this is your store. Specializing in old-fashioned, well-made clothes, including exquisite French, Italian and English labels as well as their own private line, this is the perfect place to find a seersucker suit from Hickey Freeman or a party dress from Piccano Piccana. Other labels include Due Sorelle, Pears & Bears, Kule, Marie Chantal, Euro Kids and Corgi Cashmere of England. Special amenities include a play area for kids, a changing area for babies, and a photo gallery starring their youthful customers. From 2 to 12 years old.

*Moderate to expensive*                             *Amex/MC/V*

**Upper East Side**                          **(212) 570-5747**
1067 Madison Avenue                            btw 80/81st St
NYC 10028                             Mon-Sat 10-6, Sun 12-5

## Peter Elliot (women)

Fusing masculine tailoring with feminine styling, PE Women offers a great selection of high-end European labels with a chic edge. Highlights include a luxurious Jill Michelle car coat with matching skirt that would be perfect for both town and country; suits and handsome blazers by Isaia and Kiton; hacking jackets by Belvest; traditional men's shirts adapted for women; four-ply cashmere sweater sets from Scotland; double-faced cashmere coats with luxe chinchilla collars and chic alligator shoes.

*Expensive*                                              *Amex/MC/V*

**Upper East Side**                            **(212) 570-1551**
1071 Madison Avenue                                  at 81st St
NYC 10028                        Mon-Fri 10-6, Thurs 10-7, Sun 12-5

## Peter Fox Shoes

Seen on-screen in *Harry Potter* and *Chicago*, Peter Fox shoes are known to be glamorous, practical and comfortable. This is a full-service store specializing in classic styles from Italian leather to satin. Brides-to-be can choose from an extensive selection of bridal shoes.      *peterfoxshoes.com*

*Expensive*                                              *Amex/MC/V*

**SoHo**                                        **(212) 431-7426**
105 Thompson Street                             btw Spring/Prince
NYC 10012                                    Daily 11-7 (Sun12-6)

## Peter Hermann

Hundreds of designer bags are on offer at Peter Hermann. Find a brilliant variety of briefcases, luggage, handbags, knapsacks, totes and wallets from labels like Longchamp, Orla Kiely, Desmo, Jamin Puech and Strenesse. The shop is also the exclusive U.S. retailer of the entire line of Mandarina Duck bags. Sleek eyewear by British spectacle specialists Cutler & Gross is also available.

*Moderate to Expensive*                                  *Amex/MC/V*

**SoHo**                                        **(212) 966-9050**
118 Thompson Street                             btw Spring/Prince
NYC 10012                                   Mon-Sat 12-7, Sun 1-6

## Petit Bateau

Created in 1893 and with over 140 boutiques worldwide, Petit Bateau has been making the best T-shirts in the world (at least for children) for quite some time. This 3,000-square-foot shop has three sections: Les Bébés for 0-24 months, Les Petits for 2-8 year olds and Les Grands for tweens to adults. Find casual daywear, loungewear, sleepwear, underwear and plenty of those classic tees in soft muted colors—each one coming in its own cute lemon-colored box. Prices run from $10 to $150. Petit Bateau's perfume and body products are also available.                          *petitbateau.com*

*Moderate*                                               *Amex/MC/V*

**Upper East Side**                            **(212) 988-8884**
1094 Madison Avenue                                  at 82nd St
NYC 10028                        Mon-Fri 10-7, Sat 10-6, Sun 11-5

## Petit Peton

This upscale shoe store, nominated by both *Vogue* and *Elle* magazines as one of the top three in the U.S., is a sexy shoe lover's dream come true. Find a collection of high fashion footwear from top designers such as Gianfranco Ferré, Casadei, DSquared, Roberto Cavalli and Giuseppe Zanotti. And don't miss the designer sunglasses.     *petitpeton.com*

*Expensive*                                                    *Amex/MC/V*

**NoHo**                                                **(212) 677-3730**
27 West 8th Street                                  btw Fifth/Sixth Ave
NYC 10011                      Mon-Fri 11-9:30, Sat 10-10, Sun 12-9

## Phat Farm

Phat Farm was under renovation as we went to press, but aficionados will hope that impresario Russell Simmons's 'Classic American Flava' label will again live the rap and hip-hop lifestyle full force. The store was known for its denim-based collection, lots of knits and velour, T-shirts, sweatshirts and pants and the signature argyle pieces. Not to mention Simmons's wife Kimora's hot collection for women, Baby Phat, a sassy, sexy mix of oriental and hip-hop style. Alicia Keys, Britney Spears and Destiny's Child are all fans.                                          *phatfarm.com*

*Moderate*                                                    *Amex/MC/V*

**SoHo**                                                **(212) 533-7428**
129 Prince Street                          btw West Broadway/Wooster
NYC 10012                                    Mon-Sat 11-7, Sun 12-8

## Philosophy Di Alberta Ferretti

Her silhouette is romantic without being cloying, wearable without being basic. Her ethereal dresses are perfection, often understated in design and color and distinguished by intricate, weightless folds, smocking and embroidery. Looks run from frothy chiffon skirts and pearly satin tops to velvet dresses and wool coats, all marked by a delicate femininity.                                          *philosophy.it*

*Expensive*                                                    *Amex/MC/V*

**SoHo**                                                **(212) 460-5500**
452 West Broadway                            btw Houston/Prince
NYC 10012                                    Mon-Sat 11-7, Sun 12-6

## Piccione

Is Italy the true home of custom tailoring? A visit to Signor Piccione's workshop will most likely convince you it is. He will graciously make a suit, sportcoat or pair of slacks for men, or a pant and jacket ensemble for women. Choose a fabric from the finest mills such as Zegna, Loro Piana, Holland & Sherry and Scabel. Suits prices start at $3,000 with delivery in five weeks. In addition, Piccione also sells ready-made shirts, cashmere knitwear and ties.

*Expensive*                                                    *Amex/MC/V*

**Midtown East**                                        **(212) 421-2820**
116 East 57th Street (2nd floor)     btw Park/Lexington Ave
NYC 10022                                    Mon-Sat 10-6

## Pieces

The celebrity stylists, trendsetters, and husband and wife fashion duo that run Pieces both have a sharp sense of style and an uncanny knack for what's hip before you do. Picking through colored designs by Petro Zilla, distressed denim pieces by Evisu and underground Parisian imports, you may find yourself shopping beside a local Brooklyn celebrity. Pieces has also been known to carry street-cult classics by such designers as Cedella Marley and the original Not Rational bag. Want to stay a sartorial step ahead? Just let yourself fall to Pieces.

| *Moderate* | *Amex/MC/V* |
|---|---|
| **Clinton Hill** | **(718) 857-7211** |
| 671 Vanderbilt Avenue | at Park Place |
| Brooklyn 11238 | Tues-Thurs 11-8, Fri-Sat 11-9 |
| | Sun 11-6 (Mondays by appointment) |

## Pilar Rossi

For some extra bells and whistles on your big day, check out Pilar Rossi's frilly collection of bridalwear, evening gowns and dressy suits for special occasions. Choose off-the-rack or custom-order your own. Sequins, beads and embroidery are the norm, but subtler, high-glamour styles can also be found. A gown will run at least $3,000, but you will be brilliantly decked out on the way to the altar.

| *Luxury* | *Amex/MC/V* |
|---|---|
| **Upper East Side** | **(212) 288-2469** |
| 784 Madison Avenue | btw 66/67th St |
| NYC 10021 | Mon-Sat 10-6:30 |

## Pipsqueak

Showcasing an international roster of clothing from Portugal, France, Italy, England and Japan, this Nolita boutique provides the new breed of fashionistas with some of the cutest children's clothing on the planet. From T-shirts and playsuits with cheeky slogans such as 'Enjoy Milk,' 'Hell Raiser' and 'Mommy's new man,' to dapper leather loafers by Start-Rite and mod polka-dot bibs by Baroni, Pipsqueak makes each of its petit patrons the coolest kid on their block—even if they don't know it yet. *pipsqueakforkids.com*

| *Affordable* | *Amex/MC/V* |
|---|---|
| **Nolita** | **(212) 226-8824** |
| 248 Mott Street | btw Prince/Houston |
| NYC 10012 | Tues-Sat 11-7, Sun 12 6 |

## Planet Kids

As the name suggests, Planet Kids has just about everything under the sun for little ones. Parents of babies (under age 3) should head to the East Side store for basics and play clothes from Carter's, Zutano, and OshKosh; those with older children will find a better selection at the West Side location. No one's going to stop you on the street and ask you where you bought these outfits, but they're durable, machine-washable classics that will probably be the first thing you reach for on an ordinary day.

*Affordable*                                            *Amex/MC/V*

**Upper West Side**                                  **(212) 864-8705**
2688 Broadway                                             at 103rd St
NYC 10025                                        Mon-Tues 9:30-7:30
                                                  Wed-Sat 9:30-8, Sun 11-6

**Upper East Side**                                  **(212) 426-2040**
247 East 86th Street                            btw Third/Fourth Ave
NYC 10028                                      (opening hours as above)

## Pleats Please, Issey Miyake

Issey Miyake's women's line is practical, light as a feather, hard to wrinkle and perfect to travel with. Inspired by dance (Miyake's perennial source of inspiration) and international influences (from Africa to the Far East), Pleats Please is bursting with smooth, permanently pleated polyester pieces (dresses, pants, T-shirts and coats) primal in shape and painted in mouth-watering colors. Long-lasting, durable and lovely, Pleats Please offers clothing to accompany women for decades.                    *pleatsplease.com*
Moderate                                                *Amex/MC/V*

**SoHo**                                              **(212) 226-3600**
128 Wooster Street                                         at Prince
NYC 10012                                           Daily 11-7, 12-6

## Plein Sud

Celebrities and fashionistas—of slim and sexy figures—come to Plein Sud for French designer Faycal Amor's slinky collection of beautiful knits, curvy leathers and suedes and lots of clingy fabrics. Styles include long dresses cut on the bias, square-shouldered jackets, form-fitted pants, head-turning skirts and a healthy dose of fur.

*Expensive*                                            *Amex/MC/V*

**SoHo**                                              **(212) 431-6500**
70 Greene Street                                  btw Spring/Broome
NYC 10012                                       Mon-Sat 11-7, Sun 11-6

## Plenda

A good store to take your mom, Plenda offers easy pieces for the conservative dresser—and for those with fuller figures. Loose pieces by Flax sit next to pastel knits by Princess, all nestled in a collection of floral print dresses. They also stock a good range of beaded jewelry—very art school teacher chic.

*Moderate*                                             *Amex/MC/V*

**West Village**                                     **(212) 352-2161**
543 Hudson Street                                    btw Perry/Charles
NYC 10014                                          Tues-Sat 12:30-6:30

## Poleci

Johannesburg-by-way-of-Los Angeles designing duo Diane Levin and Janice Levin-Krok take their 15-year-old label

Poleci eastbound with this showroom in the heart of the
Meatpacking District. From delicate silk dresses in punchy
Pucci-inspired prints to rabbit fur stoles in bright indigos
and heather-hued trousers with chartreuse ribbon piping,
this label's quirky pieces are sure to keep even the most
well-traveled jet-setter coming back for Poleci's distinctly
fashion-forward flare.

*Affordable*                                    *Amex/MC/V*
**Meatpacking District**                **(212) 764-0888**
414 West 14th Street                   btw Ninth/Tenth Ave
NYC 10014                               (by appointment)

## ★ Polo Ralph Lauren
Dressier looks may rule at Ralph's mansion, but his Sport
and Black labels take center stage at this location. You'll
find the look for just about any recreational lifestyle here,
whether you're running, cycling, swimming, skiing or simply
sipping cocktails at the club. Polo Golf features the ultimate
in classic golfing attire, while Polo Tennis caters to both
player and spectator with its selection of chic net-ready
duds. Interspersed throughout is Lauren's all-American
sportswear, which includes fabulous suedes and leathers,
cashmere sweaters, shirts, jackets, chinos, shoes and some
vintage pieces. Be sure to see the beautifully embroidered
jackets and pants, and note that the staff are incredibly
helpful if you should have any questions.        *polo.com*

*Expensive*                                     *Amex/MC/V*
**Upper East Side**                      **(212) 434-8000**
888 Madison Avenue                             at 72nd St
NYC 10021                               Mon-Sat 10-6, Sun 12-5

**West Village**                         **(646) 638-0684**
381 Bleecker Street                        btw Perry/Charles
NYC 10014                              Daily 12-8 (Sunday 11-7)

## ★ Pookie & Sebastian
A groovy little store in an unexpected location that sells a
collection of girly (but not too girly) casual pieces. Pink
roses welcome you into a world of paisley and print tops
that sit oh-so-prettily next to Seven jeans, Cosabella lingerie, NY-style T-shirts and an ingenious shelf filled with a
rainbow of well-made tube tops for a great value $28. Staff
are cheerful and friendly—must be the roses…

*Moderate*                                      *Amex/MC/V*
**Upper East Side**                      **(212) 861-0550**
1488 Second Avenue                         btw 77/78th St
NYC 10021                                Daily 11-9 (Sun 11-6)

**Midtown East**                         **(212) 951-7110**
541 Third Avenue                              at 36th St
NYC 10017                                Daily 11-9 (Sun 11-6)

## Poppy
This sweet new Nolita shop offers a bouquet of girly goods
by the finest in ultra-feminine fashions. Selections such as

221

Mint sequined tops, pretty Velvet pastel tanks and tees, not to mention the shimmery slinky imports from Australian designer and Hollywood It-girl favorite Sass & Bride, make Poppy a simply intoxicating find.

*Expensive*                                          *Amex/MC/V*

**Nolita**                                          **(212) 219-8934**
281 Mott Street                              btw Houston/Prince
NYC 10012                        Mon-Wed 12-7, Thurs-Sat 12-8

## Porthault

Long recognized for luxurious bed, bath and tabletop linens, Porthault is also the happy home of a small, enticing sleep-wear department for men and women. Nighties, as they should be, are feminine and romantic, while nightshirts and robes are available in all the Porthault prints. Childrenswear goes from twelve months to six years.      *d-porthault.com*

*Expensive*                                          *Amex/MC/V*

**Upper East Side**                                 **(212) 688-1660**
18 East 69th Street                        btw Fifth/Madison Ave
NYC 10021                            Mon-Fri 10-6, Sat 10-5:30

## Powers Court Tennis

Tennis is in the name, and tennis is what they do. They have the clothes, the footwear, the rackets, the acces-sories…and all at the lowest prices in town. Brand names include Price, Wilson, and Head. Same-day service on racket restringing.                  *powerscourttennis.com*

*Affordable*                                         *Amex/MC/V*

**Chelsea**                                         **(212) 691-3888**
132½ West 24th Street                     btw Sixth/Seventh Ave
NYC 10011                                          Mon-Fri 10-6

## ★ Prada

Even if you can't afford anything in there, you have to check out Italian powerhouse Prada's monolithic, conceptual super-store on Broadway. Designed by avant-garde archi-tect Rem Koolhaas, Miuccia Prada's store aims to transcend basic style constructs. It succeeds grandly, with esoteric murals on the walls and a shoe display area that turns into seating for lectures. She also provides a select range of vin-tage Prada pieces…remember the 'geek chic' wallpaper jackets and 'bourgeoise' chiffon blouses? You can buy them again here. Not to mention the latest beautiful, intelligent Prada clothes—dip-dyed cable knits, buttonless cardigans, nylon handbags, urbane wedges and printed skirts—that have made this label legendary.                  *prada.com*

*Luxury*                                             *Amex/MC/V*

**Upper East Side**                                 **(212) 327-4200**
841 Madison Avenue                                    at 70th St
NYC 10021                            Mon-Sat 10-6 (Thurs 10-7)

**SoHo**                                            **(212) 334-8888**
575 Broadway                                          at Prince
NYC 10012                            Mon-Sat 11-7, Sun 12-6

**Midtown East (shoes only)**
45 East 57th Street
NYC 10022

**(212) 308-2332**
btw Madison/Park Ave
Mon-Sat 10-6 (Thurs 10-7), Sun 12-6

**Fifth Avenue**
724 Fifth Avenue
NYC 10019

**(212) 664-0010**
btw 56/57th St
(opening hours as above)

## Precision

A neighborhood boutique packed with trendy New York, L.A. and European brands. Labels like Theory, Language, Michael Stars, Juicy Couture, Poleci and Earl offer bold and funky styles for the rich and the beautiful (as long as they are a size 10 or under). Accessories include hats and girly bags.

*Expensive*                                          *Amex/MC/V*

**Midtown East**
522 Third Avenue
NYC 10016

**(212) 683-8812**
at 35th Street
Mon-Fri 11:30-8, Sat 11-7, Sun 11-6:30

**Upper East Side**
1310 Third Avenue
NYC 10021

**(212) 879-4272**
at 75th St
Mon-Fri 11-8, Sat 12-7, Sun 12-6:30

## Premium Goods

When in need of the latest and greatest in sneakers, try Premium Goods. Premium Goods rewards kicks enthusiasts with the highest grade of sneakers, stocking limited editions of classic Nikes and Adidas imported from Europe and Japan. Preserved in glass casings, the shoes become museum-ready exhibits: trainers that aren't for sport so much as they are to be seen, on or off your feet.   *premiumgoods.net*

*Moderate*                                           *Amex/MC/V*

**Fort Greene**
694 Fulton Street
Brooklyn 11217

**(718) 403-9348**
at South Portland
Mon-Thurs 1-7, Fri-Sat 12-8, Sun 12-6

## Princeton Ski Shop

Avid skiers, snowboarders and skaters schuss here to scoop up snow-worthy threads from labels like Bogner, Columbia, Obermayer and Burton. The equipment is from equally top-of-the-line manufacturers.        *princetonski.com*

*Expensive*                                          *Amex/MC/V*

**Flatiron**
21 East 22nd Street
NYC 10010

**(212) 228-4400**
btw Broadway/Park Ave South
Mon-Fri 10-10, Sat 10-7, Sun 12-6

## Project 175

Perpetual sample sale is the name of the game at this store. Absent are the pushy mobs and cramped spaces that characterize other such events. They maintain an organized display of regularly rotating merchandise; for example, a recent visit to this large store turned up tons of La Perla lingerie, each piece for $30. Other labels regularly offered are Henry Cotton's and Cerruti.

*Moderate*                                                *MC/V*

**Lower East Side**
175 Orchard Street
NYC 10002

**(212) 505-0500**
at Stanton
Daily 11-7

## ★ Pucci

Pucci has a rich tradition—movie stars on holiday, the luxe resort life—which it retains with its distinctive, knockout printed pieces. Since 1949, Pucci has been famous for its colorful and graphic prints derived from abstract drawings. Now that designer Julio Espada has been replaced by color king Christian Lacroix, expect even more technicolor brilliance. Whoever is at the helm, Pucci's tradition is fabulous enough to make its clothes and accessories eternally desirable. Find a series of dresses, from mini shirtdresses to Sixties shifts, skirts, pants, swimsuits (some of the best around) and accessories. *pucci.com*

*Expensive*                                        *Amex/MC/V*

**Upper East Side**
24 East 64th Street
NYC 10021

**(212) 752-4777**
btw Fifth/Madison Ave
Mon-Sat 10-6

## The Puma Store

No need to be an athlete to sport the Puma brand. A favorite among sporty types and armchair quarterbacks alike, Puma's shoes ooze comfort, color and coolness. Puma's flagship store sells sharp-looking, relaxed-feeling attire to top its sneaks: cute tennis dresses, simple tees (with current and retro themes), tanks, cover-ups, running pants, athletic skirts, shorts, airy mesh pieces and a wide selection of rugged bags. It's a gigantic place and more than just a place to shop—it's a kicks-lover's kick-back universe, with a DJ, groovy people and, best of all, great prices. *puma.com*

*Affordable*                                        *Amex/MC/V*

**SoHo**
521 Broadway
NYC 10012

**(212) 334-7861**
btw Spring/Broome
Mon-Sat 10-8, Sun 11-7

## Pumpkin Maternity

Pumpkin (she was a big baby, it turns out) Wentzel has created a haven for moms-to-be with this cheerful shop dedicated to fierce maternity fashion. With a dazzling array of cozy and pretty dresses, tops and bottoms (including the essential Freebelly skirt, which gives an expectant belly air to breathe), the store allows the lady-with-a-bump to keep her style intact. Along with all the attractive outfits is a great selection of comfortable underwear, special maternity stockings and select workout gear. *pumpkinmaternity.com*

*Moderate*                                        *Amex/MC/V*

**Nolita**
407 Broome Street
NYC 10013

**(212) 334-1809**
btw Lafayette/Center
Daily 12-7 (Sun 12-5)

## Purdy Girl

Girly-girls flock to this apparel and accessories boutique for cute, feminine sundresses by designers including Nanette Lepore, plus shimmery off-the-shoulder numbers and ruffled miniskirts. Corinne Purdy handpicks the merchandise, which might include candy-cane-colored striped handbags, flowered flip-flops and a great selection of intimates by brands such as Loveletters Lingerie, with cheeky tank tops that say 'Naughty' and 'Cranky'.

*Moderate* *Amex/MC/V*

**West Village** **(212) 529-8385**
220 Thompson Street btw Bleecker/West 3rd St
NYC 10012 Mon-Fri 11-8, Sat 10-9, Sun 12-7

**West Village** **(646) 654-6751**
540 LaGuardia Place at Bleecker
NYC 10012 (opening hours as above)

## Push

Owner Karen Karch caters to a hip Nolita crowd with looks that can be layered together for day or big pieces that can stand alone for a big night out. The displays are a mix of semi-precious pieces like a red draped coral necklace or turquoise drop earrings, as well as gold and silver tiaras with diamonds. Also check out the black or blue onyx cross pendants on ribbon—very Madonna. *pushnewyork.com*

*Expensive* *Amex/MC/V*

**Nolita** **(212) 965-9699**
240 Mulberry Street btw Prince/Spring
NYC 10012 Tues-Sat 12-7, Sun 1-6

## Quiksilver

Giant video screens depicting surfer girls and skate dudes enjoying the great outdoors frame this Times Square flagship for gnarly young-person threads. Inside you'll find another large screen, as well as Quiksilver logo tees, bathing suits, very large shorts and hooded sweatshirts. Tourists who would rather catch a wave or launch an Ollie than be in Midtown will find much to love here. *quiksilver.com*

*Affordable* *Amex/MC/V*

**Midtown West** **(212) 840-8111**
3 Times Square at 42nd St/Seventh Ave
NYC 10036 Sun-Mon 10-11, Tues-Sat 10-12

**SoHo** **(212) 334-4500**
109 Spring Street btw Mercer/Greene
NYC 10012 Daily 10-8 (Fri-Sat 10-9)

## Rachel Ashwell Shabby Chic

Designs for home that can be 'lived in' but remain lovely. England's Ashwell has converted huge numbers of people to her Shabby Chic aesthetic, which includes country-tinged furniture, easily washable bedding, quaint accessories, books on decorating and everything that your baby might need. She recently introduced a modest line of sleepwear/loungewear in coordinated separates, making it easier than ever to feel comfortably cool in your home without spending a fortune. *shabbychic.com*

*Moderate*                                                    *Amex/MC/V*

**SoHo**                                              **(212) 274-9842**
83 Wooster Street                            btw Broome/Spring
NYC 10012                                    Daily 10-7 (Sun 12-7)

## Rafé New York

When celebs are snapping up your beauteous bags, you know you're onto a good thing. Cameron Diaz bought a Rafé multicolored wooden bead bag, Sandra Bullock a lacquered straw tote, and Kristen Davis a, well, Kristen bag. Rafé specializes in simple shapes in sleek leathers, including totes, messenger bags, briefcases with vacchetta trim, and evening purse knockoffs in a rainbow of fabrics. As if that wasn't enough, Rafé also stocks a winning collection of shoes and jewelry. *rafe.com*

*Expensive*                                                   *Amex/MC/V*

**NoHo**                                              **(212) 780-9739**
1 Bleecker Street                                        at Bowery
NYC 10012                                                Daily 12-7

## Rags A Go Go

Situated alongside many under par used-clothing stores, this vintage emporium distinguishes itself by the sheer mass of choice, spanning the Fifties to the Nineties, and by its bargain basement prices. They have everything, from sport jerseys, shoes, jackets and dresses to an entire wall of vintage jeans, as well as unusual accessories like Seventies watchbands. They also offer rentals for up to four days. *ragsagogo.com*

*Affordable*                                                        *MC/V*

**West Village**                                     **(646) 486-4011**
218 West 14th Street                      btw Seventh/Eighth Ave
NYC 10011                                               Mon-Sat 11-7

## ★ Ralph Lauren

'The romance, the beauty, the world of Ralph Lauren' say the fragrance advertisements, and don't we all want a piece of it. Ralph Lauren is the king of the American fashion establishment, who has earned his title over the past 35 years by delivering a luxe interpretation of classic American sportswear. His clothes embody the aspirational American lifestyle, one of leisure, privilege…and polo. And Ralph is on form—following a highly imitated prairie-themed collection he segued effortlessly into Victoriana, all the while retaining the quintessential Lauren look. Think Penelope Cruz in an evening dress in the rain, and dream… As for men, Ralph is your man. He has cultivated the preppy look for years, and it works a charm. Enter Lauren's anglophile world, where you'll find everything from ready-to-wear and Oscar-caliber eveningwear to sports and casualwear. Looks include tissue-thin leathers and suedes, luxurious cashmeres paired with tweed jackets, checked ponchos and strapless evening gowns. *polo.com*

*Luxury*                                      *Amex/MC/V*

**Upper East Side**                      **(212) 434-8000**
888 Madison Avenue                         at 72nd St
NYC 10021                         Mon-Sat 10-6, Sun 12-5

**SoHo**                                 **(212) 625-1660**
381 West Broadway                     btw Broome/Spring
NYC 10012                           Daily 11-7 (Sun 11-6)

## Ralph Lauren Baby
A testament to the idea of branding from birth, this outlet for pint-size versions of Ralph Lauren staples—like incredibly soft cashmere sweaters and sturdy polos—retains the trademark deep wood and white walls of its parent flagship store up the block. Outfitting newborns through size 4, the collection also includes such kid-centric items as cuddly crib blankets and 'Sunday best' girls' dresses in navy with matching white stockings. *polo.com*

*Luxury*                                      *Amex/MC/V*

**Upper East Side**                      **(212) 434-8099**
872 Madison Avenue                     btw 71/72nd St
NYC 10021                         Mon-Sat 10-6, Sun 12-5

## Rampage
Seasonal, but fun. Rampage tackles the latest trends and packages them in affordable ensembles for youthful shoppers. Flying off the racks as soon as they are hung, Rampage pieces are constantly refreshed according to popular taste. Pleated minis, clingy sweaters (like a ribbed, off-the-shoulder zippered number), stretch cord cargos, jeans (with sashes) and puckered tops—the selection is huge, basic and delicious. Handbags and hats top off that new (for now) look. *rampage.com*

*Affordable*                                  *Amex/MC/V*

**SoHo**                                 **(212) 995-9569**
127 Prince Street                         at Wooster
NYC 10012                         Mon-Fri 11-8, Sun 11-7

## Rapax
A good neighborhood shoe store that carries a large selection of fashionable classics, including simply styled flats, mules, sandals and evening pumps by Rapax, Roberto Peruzzini and Nadine.

*Moderate*                                         *MC/V*

**Upper East Side**                      **(212) 734-5171**
1100 Madison Avenue                     btw 82/83rd St
NYC 10028                         Mon-Sat 10-7, Sun 11-5

## R by 45rpm

An extremely trendy shop, R by 45rpm is home to one of the hottest Japanese jean collections around. Noted for wickedly detailed clothes (skirts, jackets, T-shirts, accessories) and hand-stressed denim, this place has great atmosphere and beautiful decor (floor-to-ceiling columns made from Japanese chestnut trees). It's the ultimate destination for denim fanatics who want their jeans aged just so, because each pair is worn-in by hand and then personally stamped on the inside pocket by the employee who 'distressed' it. Prices range from $150-$600.

*Expensive*                                          *Amex/MC/V*

**SoHo**                                        **(917) 237-0045**
169 Mercer Street                                     at Houston
NYC 10012                              Tues-Sat 11-7, Sun 12-7

## Really Great Things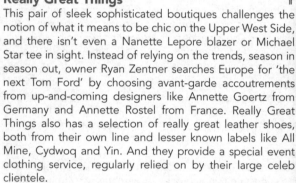

This pair of sleek sophisticated boutiques challenges the notion of what it means to be chic on the Upper West Side, and there isn't even a Nanette Lepore blazer or Michael Star tee in sight. Instead of relying on the trends, season in season out, owner Ryan Zentner searches Europe for 'the next Tom Ford' by choosing avant-garde accoutrements from up-and-coming designers like Annette Goertz from Germany and Annette Rostel from France. Really Great Things also has a selection of really great leather shoes, both from their own line and lesser known labels like All Mine, Cydwoq and Yin. And they provide a special event clothing service, regularly relied on by their large celeb clientele.

*Expensive*                                              *MC/V*

**Upper West Side**                             **(212) 787-5354**
284 Columbus Avenue                          btw 73/74th St
NYC 10023                                Mon-Sat 11-7, Sun 1-6

**Upper West Side**                             **(212) 787-5868**
300 Columbus Avenue                               at 74th St
NYC 10023                            (opening hours as above)

## Rebecca Norman

Rebecca Norman's jewelry is arty, sleek and progressive looking. The silver and vermeil earrings, bangles and necklaces tantalize with sharp, modern designs; groovy bohemian jewelry features diamonds with suede or gold with rubies. Norman also fashions exquisite custom-made leather cuffs adorned with onyx, mother-of-pearl, carnelian, jade, tiger-eye or blue chalcedony. Many pieces are one-of-a-kind and very special indeed.   *rebeccanormanjewelry.com*

*Moderate*                                          *Amex/MC/V*

**SoHo**                                          **888-420-7327**
35 Crosby Street                             btw Broome/Grand
NYC 10013                                          Daily 12-6

## Rebecca Taylor

Delicate and edgy without losing their feminine quality, New Zealand designer Taylor's clothes include silk skirts, sheer shirts and form-fitting dresses that enhance the women who wear them. Taylor's passion for the smallest detail keeps celebrities like Cameron Diaz, Anna Paquin, Ashley Judd and Minnie Driver coming back for more. Also find a collection of wallets and shoes. The beautiful courtyard in the back makes this a lovely place to shop.                *rebeccataylor.com*

*Expensive*                                                        *Amex/MC/V*

**SoHo**                                                    **(212) 966-0406**
260 Mott Street                                       btw Houston/Prince
NYC 10012                                            Daily 11-7 (Sun 12-6)

## Recon

Owned by downtown graffiti artist legends Futura 2000 and Stash, this Lower East Side storefront is packed with street gear and accessories by Subware and Silas among others. Highlights include the almost-impossible-to-find shirts and camouflage bags by The Bathing Ape (BAPE), a line designed by Tokyo DJ Nigo.

*Affordable*                                                      *Amex/MC/V*

**Lower East Side**                                        **(212) 614-8502**
237 Eldridge Street                                  btw Houston/Stanton
NYC 10002                                                        Daily 12-7

## Redberi

Add something sweet to your wardrobe. Redberi sells fun, frisky clothing that includes frilly bikinis, cozy loungewear, sexy fitted tees by James Perse, traditional moccasins and Lulu Guinness handbags. A welcome fashion addition to Flatbush Avenue.

*Affordable*                                                      *Amex/MC/V*

**Park Slope**                                             **(718) 622-1964**
339 Flatbush Avenue                                    btw Park/Prospect
Brooklyn 11217                         Tues-Fri 12-8, Sat 11-8, Sun 11-7

## Red Wong

Owner Suzy Wong never has a dull (retail) moment. Her Red Wong line is big on dresses—in colorful silk styles, with charmeuse cowl-neck and bateau-neck designs. Her super-short one-shoulder blousons and bias-cut dresses are truly lovely, and custom-made designs are also available. In addition, find beautiful chiffon coats alongside knits and chunky sweaters by Zoli and Smith & Home, lingerie from Juana De Arco and reconstructed vintage by Hillary Moore. There are some carefully chosen vintage accessories and a small but nice selection of shoes.

*Expensive*                                                      *Amex/MC/V*

**Nolita**                                                 **(212) 625-1638**
181 Mulberry Street                               btw Kenmare/Broome
NYC 10012                                            Daily 12-8 (Sun 12-6)

## Reebok
Here is a large, futuristic showplace for Reebok's fitness, tennis, running and cycling gear. The clothes are practical, good-looking and well priced. Reebok's sneaker selection is outstanding, even for kids. *reebok.com*

*Affordable*                                                    *Amex/MC/V*

**Upper West Side**                              **(212) 595-1480**
160 Columbus Avenue                          btw 67/68th St
NYC 10023                              Mon-Sat 10-8, Sun 12-6

## ★ Reem Acra
You know you're in for something special when the frosted glass wall slides back to reveal a row of stunning bridal designs and eye-popping eveningwear. Pink strapless bejeweled gowns fit for a princess and a Deco-inspired, beaded, plunging crepe gown (with matching headband) out of a Fitzgerald novel are outdone only by wedding dresses that mix Empire waists with daring black embroidery or crystal and silver-accented Chantilly lace. The A-line cuts that have to be seen to be believed, and Acra's tiaras and hair jewels add to the fantasy. Plan ahead though, because these couture creations can only be viewed by appointment. *reemacra.com*

*Luxury*                                                         *Amex/MC/V*

**Upper East Side**                              **(212) 308-8760**
14 East 60th Street                        btw Fifth/Madison Ave
NYC 10022                                   (by appointment)

## Rejoice
It's a-thrifting you will go at this modest downtown hang, which encourages customers to 'buy, sell, and trade' vintage clothing and accessories. The selection is fairly standard thrift-store fare, but it's reasonably well priced for the neighborhood and offers a nice assortment of western shirts, old belts and buckles and dresses. Be sure to take a look at the well-edited bin of vinyl records resting near the front of the store.

*Moderate*                                                      *Amex/MC/V*

**Lower East Side**                              **(212) 777-6606**
182 Orchard Street                    btw East Houston/Stanton
NYC 10002                             Daily 12:30-8, Sun 12:30-6:30

## Reminiscence
A big draw for younger types who want a bit of retro grooviness in their wardrobe. Find fun and affordable Hawaiian T-shirts, baggy tie-string overalls, tube tops, halter tops, bike jackets, wrap skirts, vintage lingerie and boas, as well as military-style clothing. Accessories include handbags, body glitter, bikini headbands, Betty Boop lunch boxes and more. *reminiscence.com*

*Affordable*                                                    *Amex/MC/V*

**Chelsea**                                      **(212) 243-2292**
50 West 23rd Street                         btw Fifth/Sixth Ave
NYC 10010                              Mon-Sat 11-7:30, Sun 12-7

## René Collections

Iconic designer handbags get knocked off in style at this shop, which carries all shapes, sizes and colors at great prices. From an Hermès Kelly bag to Gucci's Hobo, it's hard to tell the copies from the originals. Costume jewelry and belts also available.

*Moderate*                                              *Amex/MC/V*

**Upper East Side**                            **(212) 987-4558**
1325 Madison Avenue                           btw 93/94th St
NYC 10128                                      Mon-Sat 9:30-6:30

**Upper East Side**                            **(212) 327-3912**
1007 Madison Avenue                           btw 77/78th St
NYC 10021                          (opening hours as above)

## René Mancini

Refined, elegant shoes that are meticulously crafted in France. A signature Mancini design comes with perfect cap toes and delicate small heels, although he also gets adventurous with, for instance, clear plastic stilettos. Although expensive, they are worth every dollar. It's best to stock up during the semi-annual sales.                *renemancini.fr*

*Luxury*                                                *Amex/MC/V*

**Midtown East**                               **(212) 308-7644**
470 Park Avenue                                      at 58th St
NYC 10022                                        Mon-Sat 9:30-6

## Replay

Replay's location in SoHo offers casual threads bearing the Italian company's label, including T-shirts, jeans, khakis, underwear and shoes. Not trendy, but fashionable enough to be current and you can find all sorts of sportswear and durable outdoor clothing for everyone in the family.

*Moderate*                                              *Amex/MC/V*

**SoHo**                                       **(212) 673-6300**
109 Prince Street                                    at Greene
NYC 10012                               Daily 11-7 (Sun 11-6)

## ★ Resurrection Vintage

In a city teeming with vintage clothing stores, Resurrection is one of the best. It's packed with well-chosen, mint-condition clothing from the Sixties to the Eighties, edited to reflect the current movements in fashion (which, of course, often looks backward for inspiration). It's a retro designer universe from Sixties Courrèges to Seventies Cacharel and Chloé, to Valentino, Yves Saint Laurent, Pucci, Ferragamo, Gucci…you name it. This is the store where the designers shop—Chloé's Phoebe Philo has been known to pick up Chloé originals here.              *resurrectionvintage.com*

*Expensive*                                             *Amex/MC/V*

**Nolita**                                     **(212) 625-1374**
217 Mott Street                             btw Prince/Spring
NYC 10009                               Daily 11-7 (Sun 12-7)

## Richard Metzger ⚥

This designer has made it his mission to dress plus-size women sumptuously with body-conscious, sexy designs, and a lot of plus-size women are very grateful. By appointment only, he will show you his looks for the season (everything from tailored casual to drop-dead-entrance-making eveningwear) and tailor them just for your body. With curvaceous celebrity devotees such as Oprah Winfrey, Queen Latifah and Emme, Metzger is well on his way to being *the* couturier for plus-size women.

*Expensive*                                              *Amex/MC/V*

**Midtown West**                                    **877-METZGER**
325 West 38th Street (suite 1504)      btw Eighth/Ninth Ave
NYC 10018                                     (by appointment only)

## Ricky's ⚥⚥⚥

This is possibly the world's best one-stop shop for sexy costumes and kitscherie. Whether tramping up for the office Halloween party or vamping up for a night on the town, Ricky's has your number with wild wigs, a psychedelic rainbow of make-up and nail polish colors and novelty hosiery that would make the naughtiest nurse blush crimson. Complete your alter ego's ensemble with the unlimited array of funky bags, costume jewelry and hair and body accessories.                                              *rickys-nyc.com*

*Affordable*                                              *Amex/MC/V*

**Upper West Side**                              **(212) 769-3678**
112 West 72nd Street           btw Broadway/Columbus Ave
NYC 10024                      Mon-Fri 9-10, Sat 10-10, Sun 10-8

**Upper East Side**                              **(212) 879-8361**
1189 First Avenue                                        at 64th St
NYC 10021                            Mon-Sat 9-11, Sun 10-10

**Midtown West**                                  **(212) 957-8343**
988 Eighth Avenue                                       at 58th St
NYC 10019                            (call for opening hours)

**Fifth Avenue**                                    **(212) 949-7230**
509 Fifth Avenue                                     btw 42/43rd St
NYC 10017                      Mon-Fri 8-9, Sat 10-8, Sun 10-7

**Chelsea**                                          **(212) 206-0234**
267 West 23rd Street                    btw Seventh/Eighth Ave
NYC 10011                             Daily 10-11 (Sun 10-10)

**West Village**                                    **(212) 924-3401**
466 Sixth Avenue                                    btw 11/12th St
NYC 10011   Mon-Thurs 8-11, Fri 8-12, Sat 9-12, Sun 10-11

**NoHo**                                            **(212) 979-5232**
718 Broadway                           btw Astor Place/4th St
NYC 10003     Mon-Thurs 9-9, Fri 9-10, Sat 10-10, Sun 11-9

**NoHo**                                            **(212) 254-5247**
44 East 8th Street                                       at Greene
NYC 10003                             Daily 9-9 (Fri-Sat 9-10)

**SoHo**                                            **(212) 226-5552**
590 Broadway                              btw Houston/Prince
NYC 10012                      Mon-Thurs 9-9, Fri-Sun 10-10

## Ripplu

A firm bod without surgery—or a life in the gym? 'Yeah right, whatever', you say. Well, speak to the folks at Ripplu, who will fit you with a series of custom bras and panties that will lift and reshape those critical anatomical parts. If you find this hard to believe, just look at the sales helps' hourglass figures (incidentally, they are also courteous and helpful). Bra sizes run from 30A to 40G. Custom fittings and free alterations are available, too.                    *ripplu.com*

*Expensive*                                                          *Amex/MC/V*

**Fifth Avenue**                                          **(212) 599-2223**
575 Fifth Avenue (2nd floor)                              btw 46/47th St
NYC 10017                                                   Mon-Sat 11-7

## Ritz Furs

Foxy ladies come here for new and 'gently' pre-owned furs. For years, Ritz has been a destination for a fine selection of used mink, lynx, fox, sable and more—all of which the store expertly restores to like-new condition. In addition, find shearlings, fur-trimmed and lined outerwear, fur hats and stoles. An attentive, polite sales staff and great prices are the keys to Ritz's 70 successful years in the biz.  *ritzfurs.com*

*Moderate*                                                          *Amex/MC/V*

**Midtown West**                                          **(212) 265-4559**
107 West 57th Street                                  btw Sixth/Seventh Ave
NYC 10019                                                   Mon-Sat 9-6

## Robert Clergerie

Fashionistas crave Clergerie's footwear for his chic combination of comfort and style. Heels, ballet slippers, and loafers are fashionable and easy to wear. Trendier numbers can be found in the selection of boots and sandals. All designs come in great colors and serious quality leathers, and there is a small selection for men.

*Expensive*                                                          *Amex/MC/V*

**Upper East Side**                                        **(212) 207-8600**
681 Madison Avenue                                          btw 61/62nd St
NYC 10021                                          Mon-Sat 10-6 (Thurs 10-7)

## Roberta Freymann

Chic retailer (and former hand-knitter) Roberta Freymann sells 'a little bit of everything'. This translates to a fabulously eclectic range of ethnic-inspired women's and children's clothing and home accessories. Freymann travels the world to source clothing and fabrics from India, Argentina, Bolivia, Vietnam and Thailand. She will take home furnishing fabric from Thailand, for example, and fashion it into an elegant ready-to-wear collection of separates. Her focus is on distinctive eveningwear in jewel-like colors. These clothes are a trip worth taking.

*Moderate to expensive*                                                    *MC/V*

**Upper East Side**                                        **(212) 794-2031**
23 East 73rd Street                                   btw Fifth/Madison Ave
NYC 10021                                                   Mon-Fri 11-6

## Roberto Cavalli

Ladeez, Roberto Cavalli thinks you are booty-licious. To wit, the sex-o-matic Italian designer offers high-energy, sultry fashions that will do something debilitating to any helpless man in their path. From glam rock to glam chic, Cavalli has built his reputation around his larger-than-life approach to fashion: unusual prints, bright colors and luxuries like suede, leather and fur. Oh, and skin, skin, skin! There are lots of printed stretch denim, tapestry ensembles, sexy knits, sheer blouses, deer and eagle printed dresses, enormous shearlings, lush lynxes, sensuous chiffon evening dresses and va-va-voom lingerie. Shrinking violets, stay home. *robertocavalli.com*

*Luxury* *Amex/MC/V*

**Upper East Side** **(212) 755-7722**
711 Madison Avenue at 63rd St
NYC 10021 Mon-Sat 10-6 (Thurs 10-7), Sun 12-4

## Robert Talbott

A fashionable California-based shirt shop that allows you to choose from 40 ready-made styles or custom-order from a selection of over 200 fabric swatches. Dress shirts are tailored in a full cut and made in top quality cottons and broadcloths. Ties, cufflinks, cummerbunds and pocket squares make perfect accessories. Shirt prices average $150. And don't miss the lovely women's shirts, sweaters and outerwear. *roberttalbott.com*

*Expensive* *Amex/MC/V*

**Upper East Side** **(212) 751-1200**
680 Madison Avenue btw 61/62nd St
NYC 10021 Mon-Sat 10-6

## Roberto Vascon

What do you do when you've searched the city for a handbag and cannot find one that is perfectly 'you'? Custom-order one, of course. Brazilian leather designer Roberto Vascon has got all your handbag fantasies covered, working with 30 shapes and around 200 different hides from ostrich to pony. And with your creation completed in a matter of weeks, you can take your name off that long waiting list for the bag of the moment that'll be *so* last season before you even lay your hands on it. *robertovascon.com*

*Luxury* *Amex/MC/V*

**Upper West Side** **(212) 787-9050**
140 West 72nd Street btw Broadway/Columbus Ave
NYC 10023 Mon-Sat 11-7, Sun 1-6

## Rochester Big & Tall Clothing

Welcome to America's number one source for the discriminating man in need of larger and lengthier sizes. This is a full-service shop running the gamut from underwear to designer suits with labels like Zegna, Canali, Donna Karan and Versace. Sportswear, casual and activewear and acces-

sories complete the collection. Shoes are by Allen
Edmonds, Cole Haan and Ferragamo.        800-282-8200

*Moderate to expensive*                          *Amex/MC/V*

**Midtown West**                            **(212) 247-7500**
1301 Sixth Avenue                               at 52nd St
NYC 10019             Mon-Sat 9:30-6:30 (Thurs 9:30-8)

## Rockport
Rockport's mission is 'to make the world more comfortable',
and they do. Their comfy hiking boots look rugged but feel
splendid, and the same goes for their sneakers, loafers,
sandals, lace-ups, sturdy pumps and trendy golf shoes.
Foot-soothing massage products and sprays are also available to ease your precious tootsies.            *rockport.com*

*Moderate*                                      *Amex/MC/V*

**Upper West Side**                         **(212) 579-1301**
160 Columbus Avenue                          btw 67/68th St
NYC 10023                          Mon-Sat 10-8, Sun 12-6

## Rosa Custom Ties
Globetrotting executives visit Rosa's while in New York to
custom-order luxurious cravats. Choose from over 5,000
Italian silk prints, stripes, wovens and solids, then wait two
weeks for your tie to be hand-stitched and interlined to
perfection. Prices range from $95 to $125. No minimum
order required.

*Moderate*                                      *Amex/MC/V*

**Midtown West**                            **(212) 245-2191**
30 West 57th Street (6th floor)             btw Fifth/Sixth Ave
NYC 10019                               Mon-Fri 9:30-5:30
                                    (Saturdays by appointment)

## Roslyn
Style-savvy uptowners who demand the sophistication of
always-in-vogue virtuoso Steven Alan's SoHo boutique but
don't want to brave the subway to the bottom of the island
finally have a shop in their hood: Roslyn, an accessories
store on the Upper West Side run by, you guessed it, Alan's
mother of the same name. Proving that good taste is in the
genes, this specialty shop is the stop for the latest in hip
hats, from cloches to berets and back again. Not to mention handbags in all imaginable shapes, sizes and shades by
the likes of Cammie Hill, Un Après Midi de Chien and Hervé
Chapelier, plus a huge selection of new and re-worked
antique diamond and semi-precious stone jewelry.

*Expensive*                                     *Amex/MC/V*

**Upper West Side**                         **(212) 496-5050**
276 Columbus Avenue                             at 73rd St
NYC 10023                                        Daily 11-7

## Ruco Line
This store specializes in chunky footwear, similar in style to
Spain's cult and quirky Camper. Think solid sneakers in

earthy colors, some covered with the company logo, and a healthy selection of walking sandals. They also carry a number of 'R' embossed shoulder bags.                    *rucoline.it*

*Moderate*                                                        *Amex/MC/V*

**Upper East Side**                                          **(212) 861-3020**
794 Madison Avenue                                               at 67th St
NYC 10021                                                        Daily 10-6

## Rue St Denis

A longtime East Village staple—Jennifer Esposito and Drea de Matteo are regulars—this shop is revered for the quality of its merchandise, including unused European vintage from the Forties to the Eighties. Everything is clean and well organized—vintage jeans including Levi's 501s and Jordaches in one section; shirts, sports T-shirts and slacks in the room marked 'Vintage'. And its assortment of men's and women's restored leather jackets is unbeatable—everything from leather bombers to zippered black Eighties numbers and belted trench coats.

*Moderate*                                                        *Amex/MC/V*

**East Village**                                             **(212) 260-3388**
174 Avenue B                                                     at 11th St
NYC 10009                                           Daily 12-8 (Sat-Sun 12-7:30)

## ★ Rugby North America

This friendly, two-floor store does what the Canadians (see Club Monaco) do so well—chic basics for Americans. Leather is a focus here, from a huge range of coats and jackets (the mens' are a standout) to matching accessories like sleek handbags, briefcases and purses all stamped with the subtle Rugby logo. But look out for the brilliant selection of high-quality viscose T-shirts, polo shirts and simple cotton skirts, in a rainbow of colors and all at easy-access prices.

*Moderate*                                                        *Amex/MC/V*

**SoHo**                                                     **(212) 431-3069**
115 Mercer Street                                            btw Prince/Spring
NYC 10012                                                Mon-Sat 11-7, Sun 12-6

## Runway

Personalized and attentive service is the watchword at Runway, a boutique that celebrates the beauty of all ages with a collection of lifestyle-friendly separates in tactile techno fabrics that are appropriate for work, cocktails or dinner.

*Moderate*                                                        *Amex/MC/V*

**Flatiron**                                                 **(212) 807-1708**
12 West 23rd Street                                          btw Fifth/Sixth Ave
NYC 10010                                       Mon-Fri 12-8, Sat 11-7, Sun 12-6

**SoHo**                                                     **(212) 925-9817**
450 Broome Street                                                at Mercer
NYC 10013                                                        Daily 11-7

## Saada

Downtown goes uptown at this groovy Upper East Side boutique. Its eclectic collection of pieces from up-and-coming designers is well worth checking out. You'll find cute dresses, pants, tops and accessories like fun hats and cool handbags from some of the hottest labels in town, including Tracey Reese, Nanette Lepore, Rene Bardo, Kablan, Paper Denim & Cloth jeans and Pierre Urbach bags.

*Moderate*                                                          *Amex/MC/V*

**Upper East Side**                                        **(212) 223-3505**
1159 Second Avenue                                        btw 60/61st St
NYC 10021                                          Mon-Sat 11-8, Sun 12-6

## Sac Boutique

Multitasking is the m.o. at Vietnamese-born Calvin Tran's small two-story shop. Tran designs with utility in mind: many of his pieces can be worn two, three, even four different ways. Take his matte jersey dresses, for example, which can transform into ponchos or skirts, or tie-tops that can be rearranged as off-the-shoulder or halter numbers. And if you're looking for stay-the-same items, more conventional goods are to be found in Sac's classic wool coats and workplace-ready suits.

*Moderate*                                                          *Amex/MC/V*

**SoHo**                                                      **(212) 431-2576**
115 Grand Street                                      btw Mercer/Broadway
NYC 10013                                          Mon-Sat 11-7, Sun 12-6

## Sacco

Sacco is a footwear chain that makes the girls happy, because there truly is something for everyone. There are mules, pumps, loafers, maryjanes, platforms, slingbacks, sandals, great boots and more from such labels as Cynthia Rowley, Audley, Lisa Nading and Sacco's own line. The average price is $150 and they have great sales, too. Also, check out a jaunty selection of handbags, from floral prints to basic black.                                     *saccoshoes.com*

*Moderate*                                                          *Amex/MC/V*

**Flatiron**                                                  **(212) 243-2070**
14 East 17th Street                          btw Fifth/Union Square West
NYC 10003                          Mon-Fri 11-8, Sat 11-7, Sun 12-7

**Upper West Side**                                        **(212) 799-5229**
324 Columbus Avenue                                        btw 75/76th St
NYC 10023                                      (opening hours as above)

**Chelsea**                                                   **(212) 675-5180**
94 Seventh Avenue                                          btw 15/16th St
NYC 10011                                      (opening hours as above)

**SoHo**                                                      **(212) 925-8010**
111 Thompson Street                                    btw Prince/Spring
NYC 10012                          Mon-Fri 11-8, Sat 11-7, Sun 12-7

## Saigoniste

This funky houseware and accessories shop is the brainchild of two Canadian friends with a serious love for everything Vietnamese. Each item—think slick staples like gorgeous hot-pink bamboo vases, flatware, and a yoga mat carrier made entirely of plastic buttons—is accompanied by a card by Ho Chi Mama, a cheeky tour guide with advice about each product. Price points range from $2 for a chopstick rest to $950 for a bamboo bicycle. For summer, check out the plastic tote bags and gorgeous silk kimono shawls. Also a small selection of books by Vietnamese authors.

*Moderate to expensive*                                    *Amex/MC/V*

**Nolita**                                          **(212) 925-4610**
186 Spring Street                          btw Sullivan/Thompson
NYC 10012                                   Mon-Sat 11-7, Sun 12-6

## St John

Power dressing lives on at St John. This knitwear company sells head to-toe outfits perfect for executives, ladies who lunch, and more than a few politicians. St John's signature Santana fabric is wrinkle-resistant (and thus ideal for travel, to lunch or that political meeting), and they're not shy of color and other decorative touches like shiny buttons, silk flowers, paillettes and serious sequins. Looks include suits and elegant chiffon evening pants, classic black jackets with colorful underpinnings, sporty leathers and long knit gowns dusted with crystals and sequins. Also find a full range of accessories. Sizes from 2 to 16. Suits start at $1,200, evening couture at $3,000.

*Expensive*                                               *Amex/MC/V*

**Fifth Avenue**                                    **(212) 755-5252**
665 Fifth Avenue                                         at 53rd St
NYC 10022                     Mon-Sat 10-6 (Thurs 10-7), Sun 12-6

## Saint Laurie Merchant Tailors

A reliable supplier of traditional made-to-measure suits, jackets and shirts for the man about town. Choose from a great selection of fabrics and let Saint Laurie's tailors get to work with their 3D body-scanner, which ensures the accuracy of all measurements. Custom suits start at $1,200, dress shirts at $175. The super-attentive staff make shopping here a pleasure. Need more convincing? Hollywood heavyweights such as Al Pacino, John Goodman and Steve Buscemi will be happy to put in a good word.                      *saintlaurie.com*

*Luxury*                                                  *Amex/MC/V*

**Midtown West**                                    **(212) 643-1916**
22 West 32nd Street                       btw Broadway/Fifth Ave
NYC 10001                                   Mon-Fri 9-6, Sat 9-5:30

## Saks Fifth Avenue

Set in a gorgeous landmark building, this icon of New York fashion is in the midst of a five-year renovation to improve

display and augment the selection of designer labels.
There's no reason to wait for the plaster to dry, however:
Saks remains an au courant stop for any serious shopper.
Cosmetics, handbags, hosiery and accessories occupy the
frenzied main floor, but women's fashions take center stage
over four floors devoted to ready-to-wear, eveningwear and
sportswear from a stellar line-up of designers: Gucci, Dolce
& Gabbana, Burberry, Escada, Jean Paul Gaultier, Marc
Jacobs, Alexander McQueen and more. Don't miss out on
the lingerie, the extensive shoe department, the newly
opened, full-service bridal department, the wonderful
selection of furs and plenty of clothes for kids. Men have
two complete floors devoted to American and European
designers, which include suits by Armani and Zegna, casualwear by Hugo Boss and John Varvatos and exquisite
Ferragamo ties. Factor in a café, exclusive beauty treatments at the Elizabeth Arden Spa and the complete La Mer
line of anti-ageing wonder creams, and you'll understand
why Saks makes for the perfect all-in-one shopping experience.                     800-345-3454  *saksfifthavenue.com*

*Moderate to expensive*                     *Amex/MC/V*

**Fifth Avenue**                     **(212) 753-4000**
611 Fifth Avenue                     at 50th St
NYC 10022          Mon-Sat 10-7 (Thurs 10-8), Sun 12-6

## Salvatore Ferragamo

Ferragamo's expansion of the Fifth Avenue flagship store
allows more room than ever for luxurious suits, scarves,
dresses, sportswear and home furnishings. But it's the little
things, like the standard-setting ties (note the little animal
prints and the über-rich colors) and those unbelievably well-
made shoes (from the snappiest stilettos to the coolest
sneakers) that make return shoppers out of discerning busi-
nessmen and fashionable women alike. Fashion influence is
strongest in the rich, whimsical neckwear (buy up those
ties!) and the shoes, which run from business and formal to
casual and sporty.                     *ferragamo.com*

*Expensive*                     *Amex/MC/V*

**Fifth Avenue**                     **(212) 759-3822**
661 Fifth Avenue                     btw 52/53rd St
NYC 10022                     Mon-Sat 11-7, Sun 12-6

**SoHo**                     **(212) 226-4330**
124 Spring Street                     at Greene
NYC 10012                     (opening hours as above)

## Sample

This tiny boutique carries a signature collection of
knitwear in special yarns from Italy. There is a good color
range featuring silk/cotton/rayon blends in sensuous
designs, including half-turtlenecks, ruffle-edged cardigans, roll-neck tops and zip-front cardigans perfect over
Sample's own zip-up skirts. Also available: great oversized
printed totes, towels, bath products and semi-precious
and precious jewelry.                     *samplestudio.com*

*Expensive* *Amex/MC/V*
**Nolita** (212) 431-7866
268 Elizabeth Street btw Houston/Prince
NYC 10012 Daily 12-7

## Samuel's Hats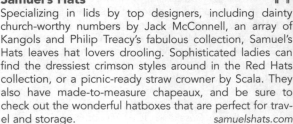
Specializing in lids by top designers, including dainty church-worthy numbers by Jack McConnell, an array of Kangols and Philip Treacy's fabulous collection, Samuel's Hats leaves hat lovers drooling. Sophisticated ladies can find the dressiest crimson styles around in the Red Hats collection, or a picnic-ready straw crowner by Scala. They also have made-to-measure chapeaux, and be sure to check out the wonderful hatboxes that are perfect for travel and storage. *samuelshats.com*

*Expensive* *Amex/MC/V*
**Lower Manhattan** (212) 513-7322
74 Nassau Street btw Fulton/John
NYC 10038 Mon-Fri 9-7, Sat 10-5

## Samurai
Samurai is an eclectic discount store (of the 99-cent variety) jam-packed with unexpected goodies. Find wildly inexpensive treasures and necessity items ranging from stationery to make-up to home decor accents and accessories (great bags—no, really). If you are willing to make the trip to Queens, Samurai will not disappoint. Great deals for little money.

*Affordable* *Amex/MC/V*
**Astoria** (718) 278-1433
31-08 Steinway Street at 31st Ave
Queens 11103 Daily 10-8:15 (Sat 10-8:30)

## Santoni
Santoni will supply you with those $4,800 crocodile shoes you've been looking for. This is a small and intimate store with friendly service, specializing in men and women's fine shoes, for Wall Streeter or soccer mom. The intoxicating smell whisks you inside to peruse the woven leather loafers, driving moccasins and boat shoes.

*Luxury* *Amex/MC/V*
**Upper East Side** (212) 794-3820
864 Madison Avenue btw 70/71st St
NYC 10021 Mon-Sat 10-6, Sun 12-5

## Sari-Sari Store
A soundtrack of Latin drums has you rolling your hips and fluttering your hands over pareos and scarves in tropical bird colors. Culling most of their stock from the Philippines, Sari-Sari has a large, well-displayed selection of handmade accessories, bags and jewelry as well as separates by Flax and Corozo. The staff are sincere and helpful—and can tell you the unique history of each item you select.

*Moderate*                                    *Amex/MC/V*
**Upper West Side**                      **(212) 579-3422**
111 West 72nd Street     btw Columbus/Amsterdam Ave
NYC 10023                              Daily 11-7 (Sun 11-6)

## Scandinavian Ski Shop
A convenient Midtown source for ski and winter sports apparel and equipment by Bogner, Helly Hansen, Obermeyer, RLX and Killy. When the snow melts, Scandinavian's incredibly knowledgeable staff outfits the customers with gear for tennis, hiking and competition swimming.                                *skishop.com*

*Moderate*                                    *Amex/MC/V*
**Midtown West**                         **(212) 757-8524**
40 West 57th Street                    btw Fifth/Sixth Ave
NYC 10019             Mon-Fri 10-6:30, Sat 10-6, Sun 11-5

## Scarpe Diem
Deep in the jungle of chains and children's stores that make up the Upper West Side, Scarpe Diem can only be a blessing to the neighborhood's hip young singles. The racks on the wall are neatly lined with sexy, urban shoes and bags from the likes of Francesco Biasia, Jack Gomme, Hervé Chapelier and Cynthia Rowley. Prices and styles are well suited to high-earners who spend most of their salaries on rent.

*Expensive*                                   *Amex/MC/V*
**Upper West Side**                      **(212) 362-5070**
2286 Broadway                            btw 82/83rd St
NYC 10024                      Mon-Sat 11-11, Sun 12-7:30

## ★ Scoop
Scoop makes trends—everyone else just follows. After all, this was the first store in town to stock the famous Marc by Marc Jacobs line. The four NYC locations continue to carry cult classics such as Juicy Couture, Seven and Theory while keeping their eye on the trends from coast to coast, including new acquisitions from California labels RH Vintage, Love Nature Life and C&C California. The jean collection alone is worth the trip—they stock the most up-to-date and extensive collection of designer jeans around, including, but never limited to, Joe's, Yanuk, and Paper Denim & Cloth.                                   *scoopnyc.com*

*Moderate to expensive*                       *Amex/MC/V*
**Upper East Side**                      **(212) 535-5577**
1275 Third Avenue                        btw 73/74th St
NYC 10021             Mon-Fri 11-8, Sat 11-7, Sun 12-6

**West Village**                         **(212) 929-1244**
873 Washington Street                        at 14th St
NYC 10014                      (opening hours as above)

**SoHo**                                 **(212) 925-2886**
532 Broadway                          btw Prince/Spring
NYC 10012                             Daily 11-8 (Sun 11-7)

**Meatpacking District**       **(212) 929-1244**
873 Washington Street       btw 13/14th St
NYC 10014       (opening hours as above)

## Screaming Mimi's

Although this store already had a cult following among downtown cognoscenti, the women of *Sex and the City* made it famous. Carrie and Co were often decked out in vintage garb (from the Forties to the Eighties) from Mimi's. Although the clothing is from previous eras, the collection is refreshingly well edited. Come here to rifle through girly dresses (including some real finds by Pucci and Yves Saint Laurent), vintage bustiers, skirts, tops, assorted shoes and an array of accessories. Girls don't get to have all the fun, though—the store stocks a nice selection of men's duds from days past, too.    *screamingmimis.com*

*Moderate*       *Amex/MC/V*

**NoHo**       **(212) 677-6464**
382 Lafayette Street       btw 4th/Great Jones
NYC 10003       Mon-Sat 12-8, Sunday 1-7

## Sean

Upper-crust menswear with a look that is Ralph Lauren meets agnès b. Find designer Emil Lafaurie's collection of well-made wool suits, silk ties, fabulous shirts in solid shades, cotton and corduroy pants, casual painter's jackets and Italian parkas. All up, just cool enough.

*Moderate*       *Amex/MC/V*

**Upper West Side**       **(212) 769-1489**
224 Columbus Avenue       btw 70/71st St
NYC 10023       Mon-Sat 11-8, Sun 12-7

**SoHo**       **(212) 598-5980**
132 Thompson Street       btw Houston/Prince
NYC 10012       (opening hours as above)

## Searle

What happens when you begin as a sportswear company but then start making fantastic coats? You get pigeon-holed as an outerwear company. Well, that was then—Searle is going back to where it started. Although there's still plenty of outerwear (shearlings, cashmeres, trench coats and the coveted Moncler goose down jackets), the real focus now is on contemporary sportswear. Find over 60 trendy labels like Milly, Shoshanna, Lacoste and Trina Turk, as well as shoes, Puma sneakers and stylish accessories. Great service.

*Expensive*       *Amex/MC/V*

**Upper East Side (W)**       **(212) 988-7318**
1124 Madison Avenue       at 84th St
NYC 10028       Mon-Sat 10-6 (Thurs 10-7), Sun 12-5

**Upper East Side (W)**       **(212) 717-4022**
1035 Madison Avenue       at 79th St
NYC 10021       (opening hours as above)

| Upper East Side | (212) 628-6665 |
| 805 Madison Avenue | btw 67/68th St |
| NYC 10021 | Mon-Fri 10-7, Sat 10-6, Sun 12-6 |

| Upper East Side | (212) 717-5200 |
| 1296 Third Avenue | at 74th St |
| NYC 10021 | (opening hours as above) |

| Upper East Side (W) | (212) 838-5990 |
| 1051 Third Avenue | at 62nd St |
| NYC 10021 | Mon-Sat 10-6 (Thurs 10-7), Sun 12-5 |

| Midtown East | (212) 753-9021 |
| 609 Madison Avenue | btw 57/58th St |
| NYC 10021 | Mon-Fri 10-7, Sat 10-6, Sun 12-6 |

| Flatiron | (212) 924-4330 |
| 156 Fifth Avenue | at 20th St |
| NYC 10010 | Mon-Sat 11-8, Sun 12-6 |

## Seigo

Tie one on. Seigo sells limited-edition, 100% handmade silk ties using the same mills that manufacture Japan's traditional kimonos. The selection ranges from intricately colored ties to simple patterned ones, plus a large assortment of bow ties in vibrant colors. Bow ties start at $45, neckties at $80.

*Affordable*                                          *Amex/MC/V*

| Upper East Side | (212) 987-0191 |
| 1248 Madison Avenue | btw 89/90th St |
| NYC 10128 | Mon-Sat 10-6:30, Sun 11:30-5:30 |

## ★ Seize sur Vingt (16/20)

Luxury ready-to-wear and custom-made clothes for both sexes, and now children too. Choose from their specialty, impeccably tailored Italian cotton shirts, cashmere sweaters, pants, jackets and suits, as well as handmade boxers—ooh, fancy!—and accessories. While Seize sur Vingt has given itself the French school grade of 16/20 (equivalent to an A-), we'll give them a 20/20. Great men's-styled collar shirts for women, too.          *16sur20.com*

*Expensive*                                          *Amex/MC/V*

| Nolita | (212) 343-0476 |
| 243 Elizabeth Street | btw Houston/Prince |
| NYC 10012 | Mon-Sat 11-7, Sun 12-6 |

## Selia Yang

Finally, a beaded gown that says elegance, not high-school prom. Find this, as well as safely feminine fashions like dresses in simple hourglass silhouettes, skirts, shirts and knits that are perfect for cocktails at this high-end boutique. Yang's favorite fabrics are silk organza and beaded satin. Great coordinating accessories include handbags, tiaras and jewelry. The bridal boutique is next door at #328, (212) 254-9073.          *seliayang.com*

*Luxury*                                          *Amex/MC/V*

| **East Village** | **(212) 254-8980** |
|---|---|
| 324 East 9th Street | btw First/Second Ave |
| NYC 10003 | Tues-Fri 12-7, Sat-Sun 12-6 |

## Selima Optique 👤

Want to see the world through rose-tinted glasses? Check out the destination of choice for celebrities desperately seeking eyewear. French optician Selima Salaun's flagship New York store (she also has locations in Paris and Beverly Hills) showcases hundreds of styles in every shape and color imaginable: everything from the rhinestone-encased variety favored by P.Diddy to simple metal-rimmed styles for under $30. Cat's eye, aviator, Jackie O…you name it, she's got it. *selimaoptique.com*

*Moderate to expensive*                          *Amex/MC/V*

| **Upper East Side** | **(212) 988-6690** |
|---|---|
| 899 Madison Avenue | btw 72/73rd St |
| NYC 10028 | Mon-Sat 10-7, Sun 12-6 |

| **SoHo** | **(212) 343-2715** |
|---|---|
| 59 Wooster Street | btw Spring/Broome |
| NYC 10012 | Mon-Sat 11-8, Sun 12-7 |

| **East Village** | **(212) 677-8487** |
|---|---|
| 7 Bond Street | btw Broadway/Lafayette |
| NYC 10003 | (opening hours as above) |

| **East Village** | **(212) 260-2495** |
|---|---|
| 84 East 7th Street | btw First/Second Ave |
| NYC 10003 | Daily 12-7:30 |

## Selma and Sid 👤

Adorable clothes made for grown women. This small, friendly store sells innocent, whimsical styles—think lots of polka dots, stripes and candy-colored hues. Sound too sugary? The fresh-looking handbags are the perfect complement to any New York woman's otherwise all-black wardrobe.

*Expensive*                                      *Amex/MC/V*

| **Upper East Side** | **(212) 486-1992** |
|---|---|
| 220 East 60th Street | btw Second/Third Ave |
| NYC 10022    Mon-Sat 11-6:30, Thurs 11-7:30, Sun 11-5:30 | |

## Selvedge 👤👤

Art meets cutting-edge fashion at this tiny Levi's-owned boutique whose red floors and minimalism make it look like a SoHo gallery. They are deliberately elusive (they don't want just anyone to have it), but here you will find Levi's Vintage, Premium and Red collections, many indeed displayed like art on the walls. Most of the merchandise is limited-edition and notable for its special wash or conceptual cut. Men will also find, a tad surprisingly, motorcycle boots.

*Moderate*                                       *Amex/MC/V*

| **Nolita** | **(212) 219-0994** |
|---|---|
| 250 Mulberry Street | btw Prince/Spring |
| NYC 10012    Mon-Fri 11-7 (Thurs 11-8), Sat 11-8, Sun 12-6 | |

# Sergio Rossi

Ooh, Mr Rossi! You are very, very bad—but so, so good. Mr Rossi's designs are so fabulous that women have been known to buy an outfit just to match a pair of his shoes. Rossi's look-at-me numbers are for glamour girls who aren't afraid of pointy, sky-high heels and who love anything metallic, beaded and knockout sexy. Find classic pointy-toe pumps with curved heels, beaded satin mules, platforms, wedges and more. An expanded line of men's casual and dressy shoes also available.                  *sergiorossi.it*

*Expensive*                                    *Amex/MC/V*

**Upper East Side**                        **(212) 327-4288**
772 Madison Avenue                              at 66th St
NYC 10021                            Mon-Sat 10-6, Sun 12-5

# Seven New York

Seven is one of the most progressive stores in New York, and is helping establish the Lower East Side as a vital fashion destination. Its mission statement is 'a perfect combination of art and fashion where one foot is in retailing and the other in the art world'. Cult bags from As Four are stocked next to Tess Giberson's handmade arty T-shirts and Bernard Willhelm sweaters. Then there's Preen, the feminine designer with an edge, and Marjan Pejoski's eclectic designs—she did Björk's swan dress for the Oscars.

*Expensive*                                    *Amex/MC/V*

**Lower East Side**                        **(646) 654-0156**
180 Orchard Street                      btw Houston/Stanton
NYC 10002                       Daily 12-7 (Thurs-Sat 12-9)

# Shack Inc

Of all the shops that have migrated south from retail-choked SoHo to laid-back Tribeca, Shack is a highlight. Designer J.Morgan Puett takes her inspiration from nature, history and daily events to create unisex clothing that women will 'feel utterly at ease in'. Most of her clothing is made in the shop and her fabrics of choice are silk, linen and cotton gauze in soft shades. On offer: coordinating separates like dresses, skirts, shirts, drawstring pants, tops and easy-wearing jackets.

*Moderate*                                     *Amex/MC/V*

**Tribeca**                                **(212) 267-8004**
137 West Broadway                        btw Thomas/Duane
NYC 10013                 Mon-Fri 11-7, Sat 11-6, Sun 12-5

# Shanghai Tang

Despite its moody, mysterious decor, there is a blaze of brilliant color from Tang's Asian-inspired fashions and accessories. Everyone should experience this vibrant fusion of East meets West at least once. Shop a full range of Shanghai Tang's signature silky clothing, accessories and home products (great oriental lamps), from traditional Mao jackets and long cheongsam dresses to modern reproductions in lush velvets, silks, linens and printed cottons. Best bet: their silk Coolie and Tang jackets. Custom also available.                                                                    *shanghaitang.com*

*Expensive*                                                                                 *MC/V*

**Upper East Side**                                            **(212) 888-0111**
714 Madison Avenue                                         btw 63/64th St
NYC 10021                                                Daily 10-6 (Sun 12-6)

## Sharagano                                                                              👤
Wondering where to get those hotpants you love so much? Well, fear not, the flashy Sharagano will have your booty (barely) covered. This is a flaunt-it kind of store, for sassy girls who must have the very latest in clothing trends from military to denim to peasant to prints…and who will probably ditch them tomorrow. Find dresses, frilly blouses, sweaters, pants and coats—but dominant is their range of super-tight jeans. Good prices.                             *sharagano.com*

*Moderate*                                                                      *Amex/MC/V*

**SoHo**                                                          **(212) 941-7086**
529 Broadway                                                  btw Prince/Spring
NYC 10012                                                   Mon-Sat 10-9, Sun 11-8

## Shelly Steffee                                                                         👤
Sleek, pared down, with playful details, newcomer Shelly Steffee's line comes across like a mix of Costume National and Chloé—think structured leather, jersey dresses, silky skirts, motorcycle boots and heavily seamed coats. All in all, a winning combination that indicates Shelly Steffee will soon stand for a style all her own.

*Expensive*                                                                      *Amex/MC/V*

**West Village**                                               **(917) 408-0408**
34 Gansevoort Street                                              at Hudson
NYC 10014                                                   Tues-Sat 12-9, Sun 12-6

## Shen                                                                                   👤
If you like a layer or two or three in your look, get yourself to Shen immediately. Sample their gossamer-weight chiffon pieces, stretch gabardine pants, jersey jackets with coordinating round-neck tops, silk skirts, tunic tops, comfortable pants and sweaters. FYI: They make it a rule not to carry dresses. We don't know why.

*Moderate*                                                                      *Amex/MC/V*

**Upper East Side**                                            **(212) 717-1185**
1005 Madison Avenue                                          btw 77/78th St
NYC 10021                                                Mon-Fri 10-6:30, Sat 10-6

## Shin Choi                                                                              👤
Practical and pretty, Korean designer Shin Choi's basics are sophisticated, classic and available for bridge prices. Adorable ribbed skirts with ribbons, silk chiffon trimmed tops, satin skirts, sheath dresses and three-quarter length

jackets are staples of her smart, lovely collection. Strong separates in black and white are intermingled with Choi's brilliant color scheme. Spring lines are filled with fresh pink, mauve, light blue and flowery prints while the winter line warms up in shades of plum, chocolate, red and rose. Quality fabrics, clean lines, and all-around wearability define Choi's timeless and tasteful designs.    *shinchoi.com*

*Moderate*                                          *Amex/MC/V*

**SoHo**                                    **(212) 625-9202**
119 Mercer Street                          btw Prince/Spring
NYC 10012                                    Mon-Sat 11-7

## The Shirt Store

The stars of *Thoroughly Modern Millie* got their stage shirts here, so why shouldn't you? At least you'll know a shirt will last through a song-and-dance number (so important). Request off-the-rack, made-to-measure or custom. Each shirt is finely tailored in Sea Island cotton and reasonably priced (from $50 to $250). Request any alteration, whether adding a pocket or shortening a sleeve. Custom shirts run from $120 to $300 with a six-to-eight-week delivery. Ties, cufflinks and suspenders are also available.            800-buy-a-shirt  *shirtstore.com*

*Moderate*                                          *Amex/MC/V*

**Midtown East**                            **(212) 557-8040**
51 East 44th Street                         at Vanderbilt Ave
NYC 10017                              Mon-Fri 8-6:30, Sat 10-5

## Shoe

Men are particular fans of this store for L.A. designer Balouzin's Cydwoq collection, a line of deconstructed, handmade shoes that combine form, function and pure comfort. It also carries an assortment of select footwear labels with styles that include dainty mules, pumps, boots and sandals, especially great beaded sandals. Complement your feet with Shoe's accessory collection of totes and leather handbags, beaded evening purses and kidskin gloves in luscious colors.

*Moderate*                                          *Amex/MC/V*

**Nolita**                                  **(212) 941-0205**
197 Mulberry Street                        btw Spring/Kenmare
NYC 10012                                      Daily 12-7

## The Shoe Box

You'll find a great selection of popular shoe brands at this clean, unimposing shop—from mid-priced, unfussy, casual shoes by Cole Haan, Stuart Weitzman, Lilly Pulitzer and Giuseppe Zanotti to snappy dress-up numbers from Chloé, D&G, Emilio Pucci, Ernesto Esposito, Givenchy, Jill Sander, Lambertson Truex, Kate Spade, Kors, Marc Jacobs and Sigerson Morrison. This is a footwear shop for grandmothers, their granddaughters, and everyone in between.

*Expensive*                                         *Amex/MC/V*

**Upper East Side**                         **(212) 535-9615**
1349 Third Avenue                                    at 77th St
NYC 10021                    Mon-Fri 9:30-8, Sat 9:30-7, Sun 12-7

# Shoofly

A stylish, well-priced footwear store for your small fry. Find European labels like Aster, Mod 8, Minibel, Venetinni and Babybotte, newborn to size 9. Great accessories like wild-print tights, summer and winter hats, jewelry and cute beaded and faux-fur bags.                    *shooflynyc.com*

*Moderate*                                          *Amex/MC/V*

**Tribeca**                                  **(212) 406-3270**
42 Hudson Street                            btw Thomas/Duane
NYC 10013                            Mon-Sat 10-7, Sun 12-6

**Upper West Side**                         **(212) 580-4390**
465 Amsterdam Avenue                                 at 82nd St
NYC 10024                            Mon-Sat 11-7, Sun 12-6

# Shop

The clothes at Shop are as cool as the sales staff's attitude, so instead of waiting for a friendly hello just dive right into the great selection. Find trendy pieces from designers such as Development and Mint, hip-hugging jeans, cute skirts, T-shirts, separates and select vintage pieces. Also find Jill Stuart shoes, Underglam underwear and the ubiquitous Juicy Couture.

*Expensive*                                         *Amex/MC/V*

**Lower East Side**                         **(212) 375-0304**
105 Stanton Street                                   at Ludlow
NYC 10002                                          Daily 12-7

# Sigerson Morrison (shoes)

Many swear that shoes make the outfit, and Sigerson Morrison's always steal the show. Dazzling colors, metallic and suede textures, all sorts of heel and toe designs—these shoes are knockouts. Although Morrison's shoes are highly fashionable, they are never seasonal (i.e. they don't date—yes!). Be sure to check out the new Belle collection, a more affordable line. The gumdrop-colored 1½-inch heel flip-flops are lovely and the patent-leather heels (in black, orange and gold) are a must.                    *sigersonmorrison.com*

*Expensive*                                         *Amex/MC/V*

**Nolita**                                   **(212) 219-3893**
28 Prince Street                            btw Mott/Elizabeth
NYC 10012                            Mon-Sat 11-7, Sun 12-6

# Sigerson Morrison (handbags)

Here is Sigerson Morrison's gorgeously fashionable and cunningly functional handbag store. Styles include ideal boxy day totes, triangular-shaped bags with metal handles, canvas beach totes and the popular hobo bags. Prices run from $160 to $700.

*Expensive*                                         *Amex/MC/V*

**Nolita**     **(212) 941-5239**
242 Mott Street     btw Houston/Prince
NYC 10012     Mon-Sat 11-7, Sun 12-6

## Silverado

Unsurprisingly, you'll find only leather here. Pants, jackets, shearling outerwear, western boots, briefcases, handbags and accessories are manufactured in lambskin, cowhide, leather and suede. Pay $500 for jackets and $550 for pants. Allow three to four weeks for custom-made.

*Expensive*     *Amex/MC/V*

**SoHo**     **(212) 966-4470**
542 Broadway     btw Prince/Spring
NYC 10012     Daily 11-8

## Sisley

This is Benetton's higher-end label, packed with up-to-date basics and fun pieces for a fashion fix. They've added a new NoHo location, where you'll find suits, dresses, pants, sweaters, tops and outerwear that give you a head-to-toe look. While the clothes are hardly as saucy as Sisley's naughty advertising would have you believe, the prices are still hot enough to excite anyone.     sisley.com

*Moderate*     *Amex/MC/V*

**Midtown West**     **(212) 823-9567**
Time Warner Mall     at Columbus Circle
NYC 10019     Mon-Sat 10-9, Sun 12-6

**Fifth Avenue**     **(212) 420-5700**
133 Fifth Avenue     at 20th St
NYC 10013     Mon-Sat 10-8, Sun 11-6

**NoHo/West Village**     **(212) 979-2537**
753 Broadway     at 8th St
NYC 10003     Mon-Thurs 10-9
    Fri-Sat 10-9:30, Sun 12-8

## Skechers USA

This California-based company, born by the water in Manhattan Beach, sells easy breezy footwear for the easy breezy crowd. Choose from a selection of men's, women's and children's shoes loaded with hip-hop attitude and ranging from utility rugged to casual basics, sport joggers and sneakers.     800-shoe-411  skechers.com

*Affordable*     *Amex/MC/V*

**Upper West Side**     **(212) 712-0539**
2169 Broadway     btw 76/77th St
NYC 10024     Mon-Sat 10-8, Sun 11-6

**Midtown East**     **(212) 869-9550**
3 Times Square     at 42nd/Seventh Avenue
NYC 10036     Daily 10-10 (Fri-Sat 10-12)

**Midtown West**     **(646) 473-0490**
140 West 34th Street     btw Sixth/Seventh Ave
NYC 10011     Mon-Sat 9-10, Sun 11-8

**Flatiron**             **(212) 627-9420**
150 Fifth Avenue             btw 19/20th St
NYC 10011             Mon-Sat 10-8, Sun 11-6

**SoHo**             **(212) 431-8803**
530 Broadway             at Spring
NYC 10012             Mon-Fri 11-9, Sat 10-9, Sun 11-8

## Skella

Looking for a bustle skirt? Find completely feminine, modern versions of the 19th-century style classic at Skella, in denim, linen, silk and cashmere. Prices start at $400 and escalate from there, depending on the material used. Skella's separates and dresses are equally feminine and pretty, as are the shop's wedding dresses.

*Expensive*             *Amex/MC/V*

**Lower East Side**             **(212) 505-0115**
156 Orchard Street             btw Stanton/Rivington
NYC 10002             Tues-Sat 12-6, Sun 12-5
            (Mondays by appointment)

## Slang Betty

An excellent stop for rockers and bohemians alike, Slang Betty serves up vintage gear with plenty of attitude. Accessories like silver jewelry and watches are located in the front; clothes, like colorful wrap dresses and printed skirts with travel scenarios, are filed in the back. The latter are similar to last year's Prada collection, but cost half as much. Don't miss the collection of funky tights and colorful socks that add the perfect twist to any dull wardrobe.

*Affordable*             *Amex/MC/V*

**Park Slope**             **(718) 638-1725**
172 5th Avenue             btw Lincoln/Berkeley
Brooklyn 11217             Tues-Sat 12-7:30, Sun 12-7

## Smaak

Swedish caterer and store owner Susannah Gaterud-Mack not only knows the special ingredients needed for delicious dishes, she knows how to spice up NYC fashion as well. Her delightful shop Smaak (Swedish for 'good taste') features special pieces by some of the best Scandinavian and Dutch designers, including the vibrant, decorative duds of Anna Holtblad, the hip bohemian collection of Munthe + Simonsen and the clean lines of Filippa K. A distinctive selection of pretty basics, chunky sweaters, quilted tops, intricate long skirts, scarves, shawls and coats offers something for every shoppper.        sma2k.com

*Expensive*             *Amex/MC/V*

**Nolita**             **(212) 219-0504**
219 Mulberry Street             btw Prince/Spring
NYC 10012             Wed 11-7, Thurs-Sat 11-8, Sun 12-7

## Small Change

Having recently relocated to a much larger space, this well-edited boutique specializing in beautiful European kids' clothing for parents with decidedly uptown tastes is better than ever. Brands carried here include Lacoste, Simonetta, Ralph Lauren and adorable Lili Gaufrette (just as cute for boys as it is for girls). The store's window display showcases bright accessories housed in old apothecary jars.

*Moderate*                                    *Amex/MC/V*

**Upper East Side**                        **(212) 772-6455**
1196 Lexington Avenue                      btw 80/81st St
NYC 10021                        Mon-Fri 10-5:30, Sat 10-4:45

## Soda Fine

Refurbishing vintage duds with handmade details, Soda Fine brings whimsy to fashion lovers. Owned by two young female entrepreneurs and featuring clothes, accessories and even a few fanzines, Soda Fine is host to several local designers and artists. Pretty vintage beaded clutches lie next to fabric satchels made by talented new designer Roxy Marj, while the innovative apparel from Feral Child employs traditional sewing techniques and fabric treatments to make must-see pieces.                        *sodafine.com*

*Affordable*                                  *Amex/MC/V*

**Clinton Hill**                          **719-230-3060**
246 DeKalb Avenue                  btw Clermont/Vanderbilt
Brooklyn 11205                       Tues-Sat 12-8, Sun 1-6

## SoHo Baby

Dorothy Shu grew so frustrated buying clothes for her baby, she decided to take matters into her own hands. Her store is brimming with layettes, casual clothing, special occasion dresses, flotation swimsuits, sleepwear, raincoats and accessories, all fit for newborn to 8 years. Along with the best in babywear from Jean Bourget, Berlingot, Alphabets and Baby Steps is a collection of stuffed animals, framed pictures and all the bedding baby needs. Gift baskets are also available.

*Moderate*                                    *Amex/MC/V*

**Nolita**                                **(212) 625-8538**
251 Elizabeth Street                    btw Houston/Prince
NYC 10012                            Mon-Sat 11-7, Sun 12-6

## SoHo Woman

Exquisite fabrics in simple silhouettes for sizes 10 through 28, including 100% cotton, linen, matte jersey, wool, crepe and silks. There are mandarin-styled tops in great colors, washable silks by URU and year-round merchandise from labels like Flax and Coco and Juan. A good source for easy-to-wear clothing perfect for travel.

*Moderate*                                    *Amex/MC/V*

**Midtown West**                          **(212) 391-7263**
32 West 40th Street                     btw Fifth/Sixth Ave
NYC 10018                             Mon-Fri 11-7, Sat 12-5

## Sol

Sexy swimwear from Brazil (and it's not just thongs) fills this tiny SoHo boutique. Find all you need for the beach including suits, coverups, tops, skirts and dresses. Labels include Rio-ready Rosa Chá, Linda de Morrer and Havaianas. *solnewyork.com*

*Expensive* *Amex/MC/V*

**Nolita** (212) 966-0002
6 Prince Street btw Bowery/Elizabeth
NYC 10012 Mon-Thurs 11-7, Fri, Sat 11-8, Sun 12-6

## ★ Some Odd Rubies

Not content with being just another vintage boutique on the Lower East Side, Some Odd Rubies' owners Summer Phoenix (actress and Joaquin's sister) and Odessa Whitmire go that extra style mile by customizing slightly worn cotton dresses, T-shirts or cast-off sweaters with new hems, new cuts, new seams or even a new ribbon—utterly transforming each to your exact specifications. Their small shop also stocks newer designers and a little jewelry, and has homey touches like a leafy terrace and a couch for weary trend-hunters (or their weary boyfriends).

*Expensive* *Amex/MC/V*

**Lower East Side** (212) 353-1736
151 Ludlow Street btw Stanton/Rivington
NYC 10002 Mon-Fri 1-8, Sat-Sun 12-8

## Somethin' Else

A record store/clothing boutique, Somethin' Else looks more like a teenager's bedroom than your typical boutique. The vinyl selection is a music snob's dream—lots of rare funk and post-punk are here for the playing. Take a few minutes to flip through hyperbolic British mags from the Eighties highlighting cult bands like the Cocteau Twins and Aztec Camera before heading up to the second floor, which is lined with antique black velvet dresses and mod black and white striped button-downs, all priced under $50. One-stop hipster shopping has never been easier. *somethinelse.com*

*Affordable* *Amex/MC/V*

**Park Slope** (718) 768-5131
294 5th Avenue btw 1st/2nd St
Brooklyn 11215 Mon-Fri 1-8, Sat 12- 9, Sun 11- 6

## Sonia Rykiel

Sonia Rykiel is known as the queen of knits and she has never strayed from her quintessentially luxe French style. Also known for her use of fluid jersey, wide trousers and black hose, Rykiel's tiny hotpants, hound's-tooth check jackets and flirty lace dresses will delight style seekers. Chic is evidently a family affair, as Rykiel's daughter Nathalie has created a line called Modern Vintage which reissues versions of Rykiel classics. And don't forget Mama Rykiel's superlative accessories, include punky bags with multicolored cats-eye snaps, satin caps and fabulous satin shoes with a rhinestone heel. *soniarykiel.fr*

*Luxury* *Amex/MC/V*

**Upper East Side**
849 Madison Avenue
NYC 10021

**(212) 396-3060**
btw 70/71st St
Mon-Sat 10-6

## Sorelle Firenze

Sorelle Firenze is Italian for 'sisters of Florence,' and is a fitting name for a store owned and operated by—you guessed it—two Italian sisters, Barbara and Monica Abbatemaggio. They sell a sexy, feminine line designed by themselves and their mother back in Florence. Along with treasures like delicate bikinis, silk and cashmere sweaters, flared dresses, stylish jewelry and hot denim, you'll find clothes from small, independent designers, including the fresh, angular designs of Heike Jarrick.   sorellefirenze.com

*Expensive*                                          *Amex/MC/V*

**Tribeca**
139½ Reade Street
NYC 10013

**(212) 528-7816**
btw Hudson/Greenwich
Mon-Sat 11-7

## Space Kiddets

Everything for hip children or, should we say, hip parents who want their child to be the belle of the blackboard. It's all about jeans, print lace dresses and kid-and-teen-friendly labels like Juicy, Paul Frank, Riley, Diesel and Lili Gaufrette.

*Moderate*                                          *Amex/MC/V*

**Flatiron**
46 East 21st Street
NYC 10010

**(212) 420-9878**
btw Broadway/Park Ave South
Mon-Sat 10:30-6 (Wed-Thurs 10:30-7)

## Spence-Chapin Thrift Shops

If you're looking for posh designer cast-offs that make you feel good about you, Spence-Chapin should be one of your first stops. The well-heeled like to unload their gently used (so gently used, in fact, that the staff sometimes have to remove the original price tag) goodies here so that the proceeds can benefit the Spence-Chapin Adoption Services. Go early on Mondays and Fridays to take advantage of newly reduced prices.            spence-chapin.org

*Affordable*                                          *Amex/MC/V*

**Upper East Side**
1850 Second Avenue
NYC 10128

**(212) 426-7643**
btw 95/96th St
Daily 11-6

**Upper East Side**
1473 Third Avenue
NYC 10128

**(212) 737-8448**
btw 83/84th St
Mon-Fri 11-6, Sat 11-5:30, Sun 12-5

## Sports Authority

Sports Authority caters to everyone's sports needs with apparel and equipment for skiing, skating, rollerblading, biking, tennis and football and more.   *sportsauthority.com*

*Affordable*                                          *Amex/MC/V*

**Midtown East**
845 Third Avenue
NYC 10022

**(212) 355-9725**
at 51st St
Mon-Sat 10-8, Sun 11-6

**Midtown West**         **(212) 355-6430**
57 West 57th Street         at Sixth Ave
NYC 10019         Mon-Fri 9-8, Sat 10-7, Sun 11-6

**Chelsea**         **(212) 929-8971**
636 Sixth Avenue         at 19th St
NYC 10001         Mon-Fri 10-8, Sat 10-7, Sun 11-6

## Spring Flowers

A large selection of European kids' clothes, including Burberry, Cacharel, G.C by Detomasso, Magil and Petit Bateau for boys, girls and layette. Plenty of dresses for birthday parties and church suits for boys. Spring Flowers is how you remember childhood—sweet, innocent and charming.

*Expensive*         *Amex/MC/V*

**Upper East Side**         **(212) 717-8182**
905 Madison Avenue         btw 72/73rd St
NYC 10021         Mon-Sat 10-6

**Upper East Side**         **(212) 758-2669**
1050 Third Avenue         at 62nd St
NYC 10021         Mon-Sat 10-6

## Stackhouse

One of the better streetwear stores on this streetwear block of Lafayette Street, Stackhouse has an easy access selection of hip clothes for, er, hip-hoppers. Hurley jeans, Hummel track jackets, hoodies and 2K T-shirts are offered among sneakers (such as Etnies and Quick), shoes and bags. Other brands such as Volcom, Roial, Mooks, Obey, 55DSL and Mato are also represented on the racks. An assortment of accessories, including bandanas and jewelry, is here as well, ready to add a bit of bling to any outfit.

*Moderate*         *Amex/MC/V*

**SoHo**         **(212) 925-6931**
276 Lafayette Street         btw Houston/Prince
NYC 10012         Mon-Fri 12-7:30
        Sat 11:30-7:30, Sun 12-6:30

## Stella McCartney

Stella McCartney shot out of nowhere to head Chloé seven years ago, and quickly quintupled its sales with her cheeky rock 'n' roll aesthetic—remember those naughty slogan T-shirts and diamanté sunglasses? Stella continues to cultivate her strength by tailoring suits and spaghetti-strapped numbers to accentuate the most beautiful parts of the female form, and remains current by making delicate pieces that highlight rather than hug the figure. She still loves a wacky T-shirt, but has added sculpted jackets, no-mess mules, and wonderful leg-elongating jeans. In keeping with her vegetarian principles, the store sells accessories made from non-leather materials—which is ironic in a neighborhood synonymous with meat. *stellamccartney.com*

*Luxury*         *Amex/MC/V*

**Meatpacking District**                    **(212) 255-1556**
429 West 14th Street            btw Washington/Ninth Ave
NYC 10014                              Daily 12-7 (Sun 12:30-6)

## Stephane Kélian

An elite footwear designer who made his glossy reputation in the Eighties, Stephane Kélian is the master of handwoven leather shoes. His slick collection includes platforms, wedges, boots, open-toed slings, two-tone woven pumps, sandals and loafers. Best bets: stretch leather knee-length boots, sandals and perfect black stilettos. His comfort line, a sneaker/loafer hybrid, is available in textured leathers and suedes.

*Expensive*                                         *Amex/MC/V*

**Upper East Side**                          **(212) 980-1919**
717 Madison Avenue                          btw 63/64th St
NYC 10021                            Mon-Sat 10-7, Sun 12-6

**SoHo**                                      **(212) 925-3077**
158 Mercer                            btw Houston/Prince
NYC 10012                            Mon-Sat 11-7, Sun 12-6

## ★ Steven Alan

Steven Alan carries progressive fashion at its best—for women who love edgy up 'n' coming designers. The store carries the coolest labels around, like Olga Kapustina, Preen, Bruce, Twinkle, Lauren Moffat, A.P.C, United Bamboo and 6 by Martin Margiela, plus the Steven Alan house label. It's a serious fashion destination for serious fashion lovers—or not so serious: check out their naughty slogan tanks.

*Expensive*                                         *Amex/MC/V*

**SoHo (W)**                                  **(212) 334-6354**
60 Wooster Street                      btw Spring/Broome
NYC 10012              Mon-Sat 11-7 (Thurs 12-8), Sun 12-7

**Tribeca (M)**                               **(212) 343-0692**
103 Franklin Street          btw West Broadway/Church
NYC 10013                            Daily 12-7 (Thurs 12-8)

## Steve Madden

Over-the-top, right-price shoes for young hipsters in search of the latest trends. If Madden is going to feature, say, leopard one season, he'll do 10 times more of it than anyone else. The collection includes platform-based styles like open-backed mules, platform boots, bumped-toe mary-janes, high wooden-stacked sandals (a summer staple) and sneakers.           800-747-6233 *stevemadden.com*

*Affordable*                                        *Amex/MC/V*

**Upper East Side**                          **(212) 426-0538**
150 East 86th Street          btw Lexington/Third Ave
NYC 10028                               Mon-Thurs 11-8:30
                                       Fri-Sat 11-9, Sun 11-7:30

**Midtown West**　　　　　　　　**(212) 736-3283**
41 West 34th Street　　　　　　btw Fifth/Sixth Ave
NYC 10001　　　　　　Mon-Sat 10-9, Sun 11-7

**SoHo**　　　　　　　　　　　**(212) 343-1800**
540 Broadway　　　　　　　btw Prince/Spring
NYC 10012　　　　　Daily 11-9 (Sun 11-7:30)

## Steven　　　　　　　　　　　　　　　♀

Steven (formerly David Aaron, still the higher end line designed by the Steve Madden team) will satisfy anyone in search of Prada looks without Prada prices, with stilettos, flats, mules, driving moccasins, fun sandals, slip-ons and boots. Pay anywhere from $79 to $249 and have everyone think you're wearing designer when you're not.

*Moderate*　　　　　　　　　　　　　　*Amex/MC/V*

**SoHo**　　　　　　　　　　　**(212) 431-6022**
529 Broadway　　　　　　　btw Prince/Spring
NYC 10012　　　　　　　Mon-Thurs 11-8:30
　　　　　　　　　　　　Fri-Sat 11-9, Sun 11-7:30

## Strawberry　　　　　　　　　　　♂ ♀

Whether you just spilled something on your shirt or are doing a walk of shame home after a night out, join the throngs of teenyboppers searching the ever-changing selection of cheap junior fashions including lots of rayon and polyester halter tops, platform shoes and piles of funky hair accessories and socks. There are no fewer than 16 other locations in Manhattan, all on the website.　　*strawberrystores.com*

*Affordable*　　　　　　　　　　　　*Amex/MC/V*

**West Village**　　　　　　　　**(212) 353-2700**
38 East 14th Street　　　btw University Place/Broadway
NYC 10003　　　　　　　Daily 10-8 (Sun 10-6)

## Stuart Weitzman　　　　　　　　　♀

Women shop at this sensible store knowing that Weitzman has a shoe for every foot, small or large (sizes 4 to 12), narrow or wide (from AAAA to C). Styles run from casual, slip-on mules, wood-stacked heel slides and sporty golf shoes to dress pumps, spindly boots (OK, not so sensible), crystal sandals and made-to-order rhinestone pumps. Walking down the aisle soon? Choose from over 40 bridal shoes. Rest assured that your Stuart Weitzman shoes are constructed with care: the brand boasts 80 craftsmen who will work on each pair of shoes over the six to seven weeks it takes to make them.　　　　*stuartweitzman.com*

*Expensive*　　　　　　　　　　　　*Amex/MC/V*

**Midtown East**　　　　　　　　**(212) 750-2555**
625 Madison Avenue　　　　　　btw 58/59th St
NYC 10022　　　　Mon-Fri 10-6:30, Sat 10-6, Sun 12-5

## Stüssy　　　　　　　　　　　　　♂

In 1980 Sean Stüssy was surfing California's Laguna Beach and selling his T-shirts to his surf buddies. Today, he runs an empire that covers the globe, selling streetwise clothing like checked shirts, tees, sweatshirts and caps, all covered with Stüssy's scrawling signature logo. Head to this coolly minimalist store—complete with graffiti wall—and also check out Head Porter's line of industrial-strength nylon bags including backpacks, messenger bags and briefcases, located on the second floor. *stussy.com*

*Expensive*                                         *Amex/MC/V*

**SoHo**                                    **(212) 995-8787**
140 Wooster Street                       btw Houston/Prince
NYC 10012                                      Mon-Thurs 12-7
                                            Fri-Sat 11-7, Sun 12-6


## Suarez Handbags
Since 1938 the Suarez family has been selling fine Italian-made handbags and shoes by designers like Roberta di Camerino and Desmo. Belts, scarves and small leather goods are also available.

*Moderate*                                         *Amex/MC/V*

**Midtown East**                            **(212) 753-3758**
450 Park Avenue                                    at 57th St
NYC 10022                                          Mon-Sat 10-6


## Super Runners Shop
The best specialized running shop in Manhattan sells shoes, clothing and accessories from brand names like Nike, New Balance, Asics, Adidas, In Sport and Moving Comfort for the super-athletic and super-chic alike. The staff are all runners, too, so you'll get firsthand advice while you browse. Try Saucony's Shadow 6000 for a splash of color to compliment your laps around Prospect Park, or look super-cute while huffing and puffing around The Jackie Onassis Reservoir in new Asics DS Trainers. The store also offers watches by Timex and Nike.        *super-runnersshop.com*

*Moderate*                                         *Amex/MC/V*

**Upper East Side**                         **(212) 369-6010**
1337 Lexington Avenue                              at 89th St
NYC 10028   Mon-Fri 10-7 (Thurs 10-9), Sat 10-6, Sun 12-5

**Upper East Side**                         **(212) 249-2133**
1244 Third Avenue                            btw 71/72nd St
NYC 10021                         (opening hours as above)

**Upper West Side**                         **(212) 787-7665**
360 Amsterdam Avenue                         btw 77/78th St
NYC 10024   Mon-Fri 10-7, Thurs 10-9, Sat 10-6, Sun 11-5


## Supreme
Urban skaters love Supreme for its video wall sporting tricky skateboard maneuvers, racks overflowing with logo-driven threads, sneakers (Gravis, Axion) and skateboards and wheels. There's a slew of brands here, along with Supreme's own line of clothing and accessories, including Rookie, Lakai and DC. Perfect for the pro-skater, DJ dude or athletic hipster in your life.

*Moderate*                                         *Amex/MC/V*

**Nolita**  (212) 966-7799
274 Lafayette Street  btw Houston/Prince
NYC 10012  Daily 12-7 (Sun 12-6)

## Suzanne Couture Millinery

Squeeze into this tiny millinery shop stuffed with every hat imaginable. It's a great source for fancy dress or special occasion hats, like her natural straw Cannes number. If you're off to the Saratoga races, visit Suzanne for a memorable topper. Her bridal range is also excellent.

*Expensive*  *Amex/MC/V*

**Upper East Side**  (212) 593-3232
27 East 61st Street  btw Madison/Park Ave
NYC 10021  Mon-Sat 11-6 (and by appointment)

## Swiss Army

You might not think it, but this store carries much more than all-in-one blade/screwdriver/scissors/toothpick utility tools. In addition to those world-famous knives, Swiss Army features a range of menswear, from good-looking, high-performance sportswear to simple blazers and jackets. Casual, everyday pieces such as button-down shirts and rough and tumble trousers offer a winning combination of function and fashion. But the real attraction in this large, airy store are the accessories. Find durable luggage, high-tech writing utensils, watches and, of course, a multitude of signature Swiss Army knives in a range of colors and options.

*Expensive*  *Amex/MC/V*

**SoHo**  (212) 965-5714
136 Prince Street  btw West Broadway/Wooster
NYC 10012  Mon-Sat 11-7, Sun 12-6

## Tani

Long an unassuming fixture on the Upper West Side, Tani has had an interior facelift and the result is a clean, bright store that effectively showcases a great, colorful selection of shoes. There's everything from chunky and funky to sleek and feminine from such labels as Kors, Cynthia Rowley, Via Spiga, BCBG, Donald Pliner and more.

*Moderate*  *Amex/MC/V*

**Upper West Side**  (212) 873-4361
2020 Broadway  btw 69/70th St
NYC 10023  Mon-Sat 10-8, Sun 12-7

## T.Anthony

In 1946 T.Anthony's collection of sophisticated luggage catered to the world's social elite, including the Duke and Duchess of Windsor. The tradition continues today with briefcases, handbags, small leather goods, desk sets, photo albums, jewelry boxes and, of course, the signature leather and canvas luggage. Up there in the prestige stakes with the estimable Louis Vuitton.  tanthony.com

*Expensive*  *Amex/MC/V*

**Midtown East**                          **(212) 750-9797**
445 Park Avenue                               at 56th St
NYC 10022                            Mon-Fri 9:30-6, Sat 10-6

★ **Takashimaya**

What a breathtaking break from Fifth Avenue's stifling, nose-in-the-air, pristine path—Takashimaya is a clean, minimalist piece of Tokyo on Fifth Avenue. There are wonderful clothes here, exotic but wearable, the sort you'll never find anywhere else, and much more besides. The first floor includes a floral boutique, while the upper levels include a travel shop that sells everything from totes and carry-ons to rainwear and travel journals. Explore the store's exquisite home collection of unique tabletop items and giftware, and be sure to stop by the sixth floor for Takashimaya's unrivalled beauty and skincare department, featuring an array of treatments and essences from around the world.

*Expensive*                                  *Amex/MC/V*
**Fifth Avenue**                          **(212) 350-0100**
693 Fifth Avenue                           btw 54/55th St
NYC 10022                            Mon-Sat 10-7, Sun 12-5

## Talbots

Talbots was founded in 1947 in a 17th-century colonial frame house in Hingham, Massachusetts. Who knew? Their mail-order business and nationwide chain of stores took off, and these days you'll find great career and casual clothing like preppy knits, pant suits, and comfy dresses that never go out of style (in certain circles, at least). Classics such as five-pocket jeans ($38) and wrinkle-resistant cotton shirts ($58) can be found all year round. Reliability can be a woman's best friend.          800-992-9010  *talbots.com*

*Moderate*                                   *Amex/MC/V*
**Upper East Side**                        **(212) 988-8585**
1251 Lexington Avenue                         at 72nd St
NYC 10021                     Mon-Fri 10-8, Sat 10-7, Sun 12-6

**Upper West Side**                        **(212) 875-8754**
2289-2291 Broadway                         btw 82/83rd St
NYC 10024                     Mon-Fri 10-9, Sat 10-8, Sun 12-6

**Lower Manhattan**                        **(212) 425-0166**
189-191 Front Street                at South Street Seaport
NYC 10038                            Mon-Sat 10-9, Sun 11-8

**Midtown East**                           **(212) 838-8811**
525 Madison Avenue                         btw 53/54th St
NYC 10022                     Mon-Fri 10-7, Sat 10-6, Sun 12-5

## Talbot Kids

Talbots Kids caters to your wee ones' everyday needs. Unlike the conservative women's collection, Talbot's children's looks are pure fun, and include pants, dresses, blazers, ties, skirts, dress shirts, T-shirts, sweatshirts, sleepwear and even underwear. And their prices aren't too bad, either. With all the cutesy kids' boutiques in this neighborhood charging $50 for a T-shirt, Talbot Kids is a welcome break, providing real kiddie clothes that don't have to be treated as if they were precious artifacts.

*Moderate*  *Amex/MC/V*

**Upper East Side** **(212) 570-1630**
1523 Second Avenue at 79th St
NYC 10021 Mon-Sat 9:30-7 (Thurs 9:30-8), Sun 12-5

## Tanino Crisci  👕 👗

Tanino Crisci offers conservative, handmade shoes in a range of styles from alligator pumps to loafers, from boots to classic wing-tips. Top-of-the-line leathers and expert craftsmanship set Tanino Crisci apart from other cobblers (and justify the prices). Jackets, ties, belts and wallets are also available.

*Expensive*  *Amex/MC/V*

**Upper East Side** **(212) 535-1014**
795 Madison Avenue btw 67/68th St
NYC 10021 Mon-Sat 10-6

## Taryn Rose  👕 👗

Designer Taryn Rose is an L.A.-based, shoe-crazed orthopedic surgeon. Her shoes are conservative enough for the office but fashion-forward enough to set you apart from the other worker drones, and all models are designed with acute attention to comfort. 877-440-7673 *tarynrose.com*

*Luxury*  *Amex/MC/V*

**Midtown East** **(212) 753-3939**
30 East 60th Street btw Madison/Park Ave
NYC 10022 Mon-Sat 10-6

## Ted Baker London  👕

Ted Baker shirts are a favorite of youthful British guys everywhere who swear by their relaxed cut and cool colors. Some have been known to claim that donning a Ted Baker shirt is like wearing lingerie (not that they would know, we hope). Manufactured in high-tech fabrics, these silky, soft shirts come long and short-sleeved in adventurous shades like lavender, pink and yellow. Contemporary-styled suits, knitwear and pants are also available. Baker's Endurance line includes wrinkle-free wool suits ideal for travel, mosquito-repellant shirts, as well as sun-resistant and anti-stain shirts. *tedbaker.co.uk*

*Moderate*  *Amex/MC/V*

**SoHo** **(212) 343-8989**
107 Grand Street btw Mercer/Broadway
NYC 10012 Mon-Sat 11:30-7, Sun 12-6

## Tees.com  👕 👗

Ever had a hankering for a customized iron-on T-shirt? We thought so, so head to this boutique filled with a mix of local designers including Bouncy Wear, Itsus and Glamhead. The perfect spot to find tees with slogans like

'Jesus is My Homeboy', 'Drama Queen' and 'Touch My Monkey'—or use your imagination to create a one-of-a-kind heat transfer at the 10th Street store. While waiting for the iron-on, check out the line of bath products from the Sonoma Bath Company including Slut, Kinky, and Lesbian soaps. *tees.com*

*Affordable* *Amex/MC/V*

**Lower East Side** **(212) 529-1030**
124 Ludlow Street at Rivington
NYC 10002 Daily 12-7

**East Village** **(212) 254-5400**
280 East 10th Street btw First/Avenue A
NYC 10009 Daily 12-7

## ★ Temperley

London fashion phenom Alice Temperley brings some Old World charm to her Stateside store, decking the halls with vintage furniture from Italy and France, romantic columns and floor-to-ceiling windows. Loved by the likes of Renée Zellweger, Elizabeth Hurley and J.Lo, Temperley is known for her delicate sequined chiffon and silk tops and cashmere knits, while beading and Egyptian prints mark her undeniably chic ready-to-wear collection, which includes fur hats and grand wool coats (with interesting straps and edging). In addition to the lovely threads, she also features luggage designed by the British model Laura Bailey, as well as shoes. *temperleyxxii.com*

*Expensive* *Amex/MC/V*

**SoHo** **(212) 219-2929**
453 Broome Street (2nd floor) at Mercer
NYC 10013 (by appointment only)

## TG-170

Shop at TG-170 to be the first to know tomorrow's trends. A neighborhood mainstay, this LES store has been supporting downtown designers since 1992. Fashion followers come here to be the first to wear new collections by under-the-radar labels like Lauren Moffitt and Living Doll. Note the assortment of sturdy Freitag messenger bags ringing the upper shelves, perfect for carting off tomorrow's styles today. *tg170.com*

*Expensive* *Amex/MC/V*

**Lower East Side** **(212) 995-8660**
170 Ludlow Street btw East Houston/Stanton
NYC 10002 Daily 12-8

## Theory

World famous for their straight-cut tailored pants that are casual enough for a stroll in the park but dressy enough for a night out on the town, Theory has mastered classic looks with understated chic. Their signature combination of soft and slightly stretchy sumptuous textiles lends an easy elegance to their mix-and-match wardrobe staples, from cotton button-downs, cashmere sweaters, jersey tanks and tees to basic blazers. *theory.com*

*Moderate* *Amex/MC/V*

**Upper West Side** **(212) 362-3676**
230 Columbus Avenue btw 70/71st St
NYC 10023 Mon-Fri 11-7, Sun 12-5

## Thomas Pink

Don't let the name fool you: not every shirt at this distinguished UK clothier is the same hue as its rosy surname. Also, do not be deceived by the brand's historically masculine image—LVMH-owned Thomas Pink is fully unisex these days. The company occupies a spacious store filled with an extraordinarily colorful selection of elegant shirts and ties, aimed at satisfying the British dandy in all of us. Find ready-made shirts in quality fabrics, traditional British tailoring and wonderful patterns, with prices starting at $130. Pay $10 for sleeve alterations and $12 for monogramming. Accessories include ties, cashmere sweaters, cufflinks, suspenders, pocket squares and scarves. In London, Thomas Pink began on Jermyn Street, elegant home of British shirtmaking for men, but now struts other über-fashionable locales as well such as Sloane Street, which even has a dedicated women's store. 888-336-1192 *thomaspink.com*

*Expensive* *Amex/MC/V*

**Midtown East** **(212) 838-1928**
520 Madison Avenue at 53rd St
NYC 10022 Mon-Sat 10-6, Sun 11-5

**Midtown West** **(212) 840-9663**
1155 Sixth Avenue at 44th St
NYC 10036 Mon-Fri 10-7 (Thurs 10-8), Sat 10-6, Sun 12-5

**Midtown West** **(212) 823-9650**
Time Warner Mall at Columbus Circle
NYC 10019 Mon-Sat 10-9, Sun 12-6

## 30 Vandam

Like being the only kid on your block with the flashiest new threads? Well, you aren't truly running with the in crowd if you haven't heard of 30 Vandam. This new SoHo boutique, practically a stone's throw from the Holland tunnel, showcases 50 handpicked designers that it foresees being the next batch of fashion big shots. Names like Colleen Quen Couture, Pure Ginger, Ashley Dearborn and Mle Hagen may not mean anything to you now, but remember: you saw it here first. *30vandam.com*

*Expensive* *Amex/MC/V*

**SoHo** **(212) 929-6454**
30 Vandam Street btw Sixth/Varick
NYC 10013 Daily 12-8 (Sun 12-6)

## Thread

Even if you never get to be a bride, you'd be thrilled to be a bridesmaid dressed by Thread. Eschewing the dowdy, the frumpy and everything taffeta in favor of hip colorful numbers in organza, duchesse satin, bengaline and chiffon, these wedding outfits could easily double as cocktail dresses. You'll hear rock 'n' roll in Thread's light and airy showroom while the fit-and-color-conscious staff do a great deal to defuse tying-the-knot jitters. Delivery takes 10-12 weeks and don't miss Thread's cute little extras, like 'Just Married' panties and bikinis. *threaddesign.com*

*Moderate*     Amex/MC/V

**Chelsea**     **(212) 414-8844**
26 West 17th Street (suite 301)     btw Fifth/Sixth Ave
NYC 10011     Mon-Sat (by appointment)

## Tibet Arts & Crafts

This tiny boutique encapsulates the distinctive charm of Tibetan style. Best pieces include raw silk shirts at around $75 (a favorite of Cameron Diaz), reversible pashmina scarves and shawls in a dazzling array of colors, silk shirts ($38 for short sleeves, $60 for long), antique patched and brocaded bags at a mere $12, beaded slippers at $18-28, plus traditional ceremonial hats and jewelry.

*Affordable*     Amex/MC/V

**West Village**     **(212) 260-5880**
197 Bleecker Street     btw Sixth/MacDougal
NYC 10012     Mon-Thurs 10-9, Fri-Sun 12-10

## Tibet Bazaar

Begin your search for enlightenment at Tibet Bazaar, a specialty boutique offering unique clothing, with beaded fabrics, accessories and gifts direct from the Himalayas. Adorn yourself in luxurious apparel from slippers to jackets and faux fur-trimmed hats. Or choose from their wide variety of ritual items including singing bowls, CD recordings of Tibetan mantras and, of course, incense.

*Moderate*     Amex/MC/V

**Upper West Side**     **(212) 595-8487**
473 Amsterdam Avenue     btw 82/83rd St
NYC 10024     Daily 10:30-7

## Timberland

Although Timberland made its reputation on its functional, outdoor footwear and accessories, lately the brand has gained popularity as a ubiquitous urban style. But whether you choose to wear their shoes on the street or in the country, rest assured that they will withstand the elements and the rigors of time. Styles run from casual shoes to rugged boots and include hiking boots, driving moccasins, boating shoes and weatherbucks. Men's outdoor

apparel is also available. Children's from size 5 toddler
and up. *timberland.com*

*Moderate* *Amex/MC/V*

**Upper East Side** **(212) 754-0434**
709 Madison Avenue at 63rd St
NYC 10021 Mon-Fri 9:30-7, Sat 10-6, Sun 12-6

## Tina Tang

Tina Tang left a successful career at an investment bank to
pursue a dream of designing jewelry. Two stores later, each
filled with precious metals and stones, from chandelier earrings and monogram necklaces to custom-made charm
bracelets and hair clips, Tina Tang's dream has become a
glittering reality. Choose from an array of pieces made with
gold, sterling silver, freshwater pearls and semi-precious
stones. *tinatang.com*

*Affordable* *Amex/MC/V*

**Nolita** **(212) 226-3369**
230 Mulberry Street btw Prince/Spring
NYC 10012 Tues-Sat 12-7, Sun 12-6

## Tip Top Kids

If your tiny tots demand the snazziest sneakers in the
schoolyard, this shoe store is sure to put them in tip-top
shape. With their large selection of casual and athletic
shoes for infants and children (up to size 7), Tip Top Kids will
keep your little ones' toes covered in smart styles from in
demand brands such as Ecco, Ugg, Diesel, Puma, Adidas
and Converse.

*Moderate to expensive* *Amex/MC/V*

**Upper West Side** **(212) 874-1004**
149 West 72nd Street btw Broadway/Columbus Ave
NYC 10023 Mon-Sat 9-6:45 (Thurs 9-7:45), Sun 12-5

## T.J.Maxx

Off-price merchandise for the entire family, as well as a
large selection of accessories for home, bed and bath. If
you're lucky, you might find a designer name like Polo,
DKNY or Tahari. *tjmaxx.com*

*Affordable* *Amex/MC/V*

**Chelsea** **(212) 229-0875**
620 Sixth Avenue btw 18/19th St
NYC 10011 Mon-Sat 9:30-9, Sun 11-7

## Tod's

Tod's shoes enjoy a cult following among Hollywood
actresses and society types who swear by their signature
pebble driving shoes—available in a rainbow of colors—
priced around $325. Other guaranteed chic styles include
smart-looking mules, classic loafers, stylish pumps and sexy
black boots with contrasting heels. Check out the status-

symbol bags, as well as new sporty leather jackets that you're sure to see on the red carpet.

800-457-TODS  *tods.com*

*Luxury*                                           *Amex/MC/V*

**Midtown East**                              **(212) 644-5945**
650 Madison Avenue                        btw 59/60th St
NYC 10022           Mon-Sat 10-6 (Thurs 10-7), Sun 12-5

## Togs

Urban streetwear and European chic are happily married in Togs's collection of imported Italian clothing. Contemporary separates, tops, knitwear, leather pants and a large selection of jeans are all surprisingly affordable. Low-key labels include Anima, Cristina Gavioli, Blu Sand and Esempio. Perfect for the resort.

*Moderate*                                        *Amex/MC/V*

**SoHo**                                         **(917) 237-1882**
68 Spring Street (W)                       btw Crosby/Lafayette
NYC 10012                                    Daily 11-8 (Sun 11-7)

**SoHo**                                         **(212) 343-9311**
93 Spring Street (M)                       btw Mercer/Broadway
NYC 10012                              (opening hours as above)

## Tokio 7

Don't let this consignment shop's dingy interior deter you, because you'll find everything here from old-school vintage to this season's hand-me-downs. Recent sightings include a studded Chloé dress, Ungaro pants and scores of Marc by Marc Jacobs—all under $100 dollars. Never-been-worn items garner higher prices, but all the pieces are covetable and, most importantly, attainable. The ever-rotating selection is worth checking out often.

*Moderate to expensive*                           *Amex/MC/V*

**East Village**                               **(212) 353-8443**
64 East 7th Street                         btw First/Second Ave
NYC 10003                                  Daily 12-8:30 (Sun 12-8)

## Tokyo Joe

A cramped, overstocked consignment shop featuring hip designer labels at accessible prices. The merchandise changes each day, so scoop something up when you see it because it ain't gonna be there tomorrow. The goods include designer clothing, shoes, bags and accessories by labels like Gucci, Marc Jacobs, Prada, Comme des Garçons, Miu Miu and Donna Karan. Items are generally in good condition and the prices can't be beat. Current season shoes from top designers have been known to turn up, worn only once.

*Moderate*                                        *Amex/MC/V*

**East Village**                               **(212) 473-0724**
334 East 11th Street                       btw First/Second Ave
NYC 10003                                         Daily 12-9

## Tommy Hilfiger

The American idol of fashion designers, Tommy Hilfiger is known for his bold line of sportswear and legion of celebrity endorsers (including David Bowie, who lives nearby). Tommy Hilfiger's three-floor, 11,000-square-foot specialty store in SoHo caters to ladies and lads with sportswear, denim (emphasis on juniors) and accessories. Striped polos for preppy looks, worker-washed utility jeans for blue-collar kids, stitched denim jackets for the rockers and the jeans and tees that will carry you from street to club to beach. *tommy.com*

*Moderate*                                                  *Amex/MC/V*

**SoHo**                                        **(917) 237-0983**
372 West Broadway                        btw Spring/Broome
NYC 10012                            Mon-Sat 11-7, Sun 12-6

## ★ Tory by TRB

Behind the bright orange doors of this Nolita hideaway lies a high-end haven for those who believe that more really is more. Society girl around town turned style surveyor Tory Burch launched her namesake label in 2004 with clothing fit for a jaunt on the jitney or some playtime in Palm Beach. Lush cashmere tennis sweater, cotton canvas espadrilles, and terrycloth beach towels, all available in Tory's signature 4T Op-art print, go hand in hand with rhinestone-encrusted caftans and other savory separates. Fabulous. *toryltd.com*

*Moderate to expensive*                           *Amex/MC/V*

**Nolita**                                      **(212) 334-3000**
257 Elizabeth Street                     btw Prince/Houston
NYC 10012                            Mon-Sat 11-7, Sun 12-6

## Tracy Feith

Hot Australian surfer-dude-turned-designer Tracy Feith is one smart man. Not only does he know what the girls want to wear, he knows what their boyfriends want them to wear, too. His collection of romantic corset tops, pretty silk skirts, dolled-up dresses, fancy fabric totes and sultry printed pants will help any missy snag second glances. One peek into this island resort of a shop will have girls dreaming up steamy tropical encounters. *tracyfeith.com*

*Moderate*                                                  *Amex/MC/V*

**Nolita**                                      **(212) 334-3097**
209 Mulberry Street                      btw Spring/Kenmare
NYC 10012                                Daily 11-7 (Sun 12-7)

## Training Camp

'Footwear is my addiction; the only thing I like more than footwear is my wife,' says Udi Avshalom. Now that is love. Training Camp followers like P. Diddy shop here for the latest in brand-name sneakers, including Nike Air Jordans and Bo Jacksons, and streety looks by Avirex, Phat Farm and the cool Aussie import Royal Elastics. Prices run from $30 to $160.

*Affordable*                                                 *Amex/MC/V*

**Midtown West**          **(212) 840-7842**
25 West 45th Street       btw Fifth/Sixth Ave
NYC 10036          Mon-Sat 9-7:30

**Midtown West**          **(212) 921-4430**
1079 Sixth Avenue         at 41st St
NYC 10036   Mon-Sat 9-7:30, Sun 10-6:30

## Transit

One-stop shopping for sneaker enthusiasts (and those who just need a great pair of kicks). This two-floor emporium offers a healthy selection of New Balance, Nike, Puma, Adidas, Fred Perry and more, in a wide range of styles, colors and sizes. Chances are the large selection will satisfy any shoe connoisseur, but the staff are happy to order a specific item if they don't have it in stock.

*Expensive*          *Amex/MC/V*

**NoHo**          **(212) 358-8726**
665 Broadway         at Bond
NYC 10012       Mon-Sat 9-9, Sun 10-8

## Trash and Vaudeville

Trash and Vaudeville, the destination of choice for punk gear for decades, is actually two stores in one. The upstairs Vaudeville is full of rock T-shirts, skirt/tie combos, apron-front pants, safety-pinned tops and plaids reminiscent of Vivienne Westwood. There's also an amazing selection of shoes from Doc Martens to spiked stilettos, some in hard-to-find sizes. The Trash underground is dedicated to goth: the front section has piercing jewelry, studded bracelets and belts and vintage lunchboxes, while the back is packed with fetish gear (think PVC corsets and rubber dresses).

*Moderate*          *Amex/MC/V*

**East Village**          **(212) 982-3590**
4 St Mark's Place     btw Second/Third Ave
NYC 10003   Mon-Thurs 12-8, Fri 11:30-8:30
         Sat 11:30-9, Sun 1-7:30

## Tribeca Luggage

Ever find yourself downtown, looking for that perfect piece of carry-on luggage? Even if you haven't, you should make the trip to Tribeca Luggage to peruse their selection of luggage, including oh-so-handy triple bag combos, all sorts of handbags, straw totes, leather treats, crocheted and beaded pieces, briefcases, knapsacks, carry-ons and more. There is also a cornucopia of accessories like umbrellas, wallets and photo albums. Known for its discounted prices and for carrying great labels like including Longchamp, Rafé, Francesco Biasia, Kazuyo Nakano and Isabella Fiore, this is the place to stop before boarding your next flight.

*Moderate*          *Amex/MC/V*

**Tribeca**          **(212) 343-8159**
90 Hudson Street         at Harrison
NYC 10013   Mon-Fri 10-7:30, Sat 11-6, Sun 12-5

## Triple Five Soul

Sweet street style is Triple Five Soul's stock in trade. It's all about pairing low-rise jeans with a hot terry tank to help you get down on the dance floor later on. Just step to Triple Five Soul's selection of cargos, logo-heavy hoodies, shirts, tanks (screaming such important messages as 'Brooklyn' and 'Survival'), and record cases (for DJs and wannabes) for hip-hop wear *par excellence*.        triple5soul.com

*Moderate*                                                    *Amex/MC/V*

**Nolita**                                                   **(212) 431-2404**
290 Lafayette Street                               btw Houston/Prince
NYC 10012                              Daily 11-7 (Fri-Sat 11-7:30)

## Tristan & America

A Canadian import that caters to the young professional woman and man in search of career and casual clothing at reasonable prices. Styles are simple, classic and sporty and include an ample selection of suits. Women's jackets run $100-$150 and skirts average $58.        *tristan-america.com*

*Affordable*                                                 *Amex/MC/V*

**Midtown West**                                         **(212) 246-2354**
1230 Sixth Avenue                                          at 49th St
NYC 10020                                    Mon-Sat 10-8, Sun 12-6

## ★ Tse

The revolution continues at Tse, formerly Tse Cashmere. The luxe label is obviously best known for its cashmere and a brief design stint by London conceptualist Hussein Chalayan but it's now being helmed by Annette Ishida who has been with the company for years. Check out the brand's new diffusion line, TseSay, for sumptuous quality but with an of-the-moment sensibility and seriously more affordable prices.

*Luxury*                                                     *Amex/MC/V*

**Upper East Side**                                      **(212) 472-7790**
827 Madison Avenue                                         at 69th St
NYC 10021                                Mon-Sat 10-6 (Thurs 10-7)

## Tumi

Specializing in bags that will last just about forever, Tumi offers everything from purses, briefcases, and messenger bags to garment bags, full-sized luggage and golf bags. While some pieces are offered in leather, most are constructed in the highly durable woven nylon for which Tumi is famous.        800-322-8864 *tumi.com*

*Expensive*                                                  *Amex/MC/V*

**Midtown East**                                         **(212) 973-0015**
64 Grand Central Terminal                    (Lexington Passage)
NYC 10017             Mon-Fri 8:30-7:30, Sat 10-7, Sun 11-6

**Midtown East**                                         **(212) 813-0545**
520 Madison Avenue                                         at 54th St
NYC 10022                                    Mon-Sat 10-7, Sun 11-6

## Turnbull & Asser

Turnbull & Asser has dressed England's aristocrats, moguls and movie stars since 1855. This New York outpost of London's finest haberdasher offers traditional suits, formal-wear, sportswear, outerwear, sleepwear and accessories for both men and women. The best reason to shop here remains their bespoke shirt selection, which boasts over 600 fabrics and styles from bold stripes to checks to patterns. Rely on the remarkably friendly and helpful service to help you find the perfect fit.

877-887-6285   turnbullandasser.com

*Luxury*                                    *Amex/MC/V*

**Midtown East**                          **(212) 752-5700**
42 East 57th Street              btw Madison/Park Ave
NYC 10022                    Mon-Fri 10-6:30, Sat 9:30-6

## Uncle Sam's Army and Navy Outfitters

Since the military trend shows no sign of abating, buy all that you can at this army outpost that offers a mixture of vintage men's and women's pieces with seas of brand-new khaki and green. The amiable and mellow staff will help you navigate the cute camouflage tees, cargo pants, military motif lighters and cheap leather belts. Be sure to check out the vintage leather jackets.

*Affordable*                                      *MC/V*

**West Village**                          **(212) 674-2222**
37 West 8th Street              btw MacDougal/Sixth Ave
NYC 10011        Mon-Wed 10-9, Thurs-Sat 10-10, Sun 12-9

## Union

This small men's boutique is select, edgy and on the verge. Filled with the latest in street and skate clothing by cool, visionary designers (Duffer of St George, Mhi, Goodenough, Pam, Gimme 5, Kingston 12, Tao), this place has its collective finger on the pulse of hip NYC. Be sure to check out the T-shirts by local artists, sweaters, jackets, jeans and graphic pieces.

*Moderate*                                  *Amex/MC/V*

**SoHo**                                 **(212) 226-8493**
172 Spring Street             btw Thompson/West Broadway
NYC 10012                            Daily 11-7 (Sun 12-7)

## Unis

Best known for making very cool (but never fey) looks for men—think softer-than-expected military jackets, slim Sixties trenches, classic jeans—former DKNY designer Eunice Lee (the store's name is a play on 'unisex' and her first name) started making clothes for women last year. The results? Well, now Lee ranks Kirsten Dunst and Maggie Gyllenhaal as fans alongside regular customers Mos Def and the Chemical Brothers. Hipsters delight in the silks and chiffons lending sexy texture to tops with plunging neck-lines, and applaud cargos with belted ankles and tight

motorcycle jackets, demonstrating the feminine flipside to
Lee's traditional male styles. *unisnewyork.com*

*Moderate* *Amex/MC/V*

**Nolita** **(212) 431-5533**
226 Elizabeth Street btw Houston/Prince
NYC 10013 Mon-Fri 12-7, Sat 12-8, Sun 12-6:30

## Unisa ♀

Unisa offers simple, fashionable footwear at truly fabulous
prices (almost everything is under $100). The shoes tend to
stay on the safer side of current trends, but are cute
enough to keep you walking in style. Find colorful sandals,
feminine stilettos, and neutral mules, loafers and slingbacks, all under the Unisa label. Although the handbags
do break the $100 rule (running about $75 to $175), they
appeal to both those in and outside of Madison Avenue
tax brackets. *unisa.com*

*Affordable* *Amex/MC/V*

**Upper East Side** **(212) 753-7474**
701 Madison Avenue btw 62/63rd St
NYC 10021 Mon-Sat 10-7 (Thurs 10-8), Sun 12-5

## ★ United Nude Terra Plana ♀

An offshoot of the Terra Plana footwear line, United Nude
features ultra-modern sandals (available in 2½ and 3½-inch
heels), with an open toe and an open space where you'd
normally find a wedge. The brainchild of Dutch architect
Rem D. Koolhaas, nephew of even more famous Rem
Koolhaas (who designed the Prada flagship store), the not-
quite wedges are modeled after Mies van der Rohe's iconic Barcelona chair. These exquisitely minimalist shoes
deserve to be placed on a pedestal, and look even cooler
spinning atop the turntables in the boutique's window.
Over a dozen variations, in suede and leather, prints and
solid colors, and a new closed-toe model, can be found
inside. *terraplana.com*

*Moderate* *Amex/MC/V*

**Nolita** **(212) 274-9000**
260 Elizabeth Street btw Houston/Prince
NYC 10012 Mon-Tues 12-7, Wed-Sat 12-8, Sun 12-6

## Untitled ♂♀

Regardless of the store's sign, you find plenty of major-
name designers here. Downstairs, peruse the array of sexy,
tight-fitting sportswear for women, featuring labels like
Juicy Couture and Follies, an excellent selection of denim
and hats by Philip Treacy. Scoot upstairs to see how
Untitled ups the men's fashion ante with Moschino, Class by
Cavalli, Dirk Bikkemberg and Jean Paul Gaultier. Everything
you need to cover you from head to toe can be found
here—even a small shoe selection.

*Expensive* *Amex/MC/V*

| West Village | (212) 505-9725 |
|---|---|
| 26 West Eighth Street | btw Fifth/Sixth Ave |
| NYC 10011 | Daily 11:30-9 (Sunday 12-9) |

## Urban Outfitters

Urban Outfitters is the perfect location for a quick fashion fix. Its collegiate-cool clothing and cute pick-me-up accessories (let alone its funky housewares and CD collection) make it worth a pilgrimage. Fast becoming an American classic, the labels here include Bulldog, Lux, Bella Dahl, Lee, Free People, Mooks and Urban Outfitters themselves. Tip 1: if something you like is a little pricey, wait a week or so—it will go on sale for sure. Tip 2: buy, buy, buy the cool printed tank tops—often as low as $4.99.          *urbn.com*

*Affordable*                                              *Amex/MC/V*

| Upper West Side | (212) 579-3912 |
|---|---|
| 2081 Broadway | at 72nd St |
| NYC 10023 | Mon-Thurs 10-9, Fri-Sat 9-10, Sun 11-8 |

| Chelsea | (646) 638-1646 |
|---|---|
| 526 Sixth Avenue | at 14th St |
| NYC 10011 | Mon-Sat 10-10, Sun 11-8 |

| East Village | (212) 375-1277 |
|---|---|
| 162 Second Avenue | btw 10/11th St |
| NYC 10002 | Mon-Wed 11-10, Thurs-Sat 11-11, Sun 12-9 |

| West Village | (212) 677-9350 |
|---|---|
| 374 Sixth Avenue | btw Waverly/Washington Place |
| NYC 10011 | Mon-Sat 10-10, Sun 12-8 |

| NoHo | (212) 475-0009 |
|---|---|
| 628 Broadway | btw Bleecker/Houston |
| NYC 10012 | (opening hours as above) |

## Utility Canvas

Canvas lovers will be beside themselves at this store's collection of practical, versatile all-American clothing manufactured in canvas, from heavy-duty industrial weights to light-as-air soft-brushed textures. There are canvas-lined wool jackets, shirts, pants and shorts, as well as a few non-canvas pieces like anoraks and nylon jackets by the Artist in Orbit label. Best bet is the line of canvas bags, from a $60 binocular bag to a $98 bucket tote.          *utilitycanvas.com*

*Affordable*                                              *Amex/MC/V*

| SoHo | 800-680-9290 |
|---|---|
| 146 Sullivan Street | btw Houston/Prince |
| NYC 10012 | Daily 11-7 (Sun 11-6) |

## Utowa

It means 'universal unity' in Japanese, and Utowa's ideal customer is looking for 'physical and spiritual balance focusing on health and the health of the environment'. If that's you, head on down. The store lets 'the feelings of the season' dictate current design of their products, like army-inspired shirt-jackets and chic button-front minis infused with a trace of Far East style. Utowa also carries a lovely array of beauty products and funky jewelry. *utowa.com*

*Moderate* *Amex/MC/V*

**Chelsea** **(212) 929-4800**
17 West 18th Street btw Fifth/Sixth Ave
NYC 10011 Mon-Fri 11-7, Sat 11-6

# Valentino

Valentino is the master of old-school glamour that even the new girls want to wear. He is king of meticulous detailing and beautiful embroidery that is never ostentatious, yet remains fabulously luxurious. And his favorite color? Racy red, of course. For day, Valentino women will find beautiful suits, ruffled and pleated silk shirts paired with simple black pants, mink-edged cashmere cardigans, delicate lace blouses worn with long tweed skirts and saucy leathers. Eveningwear is Oscar-caliber and ranges from black crepe column dresses to jewel-encrusted evening gowns. Men will find smart-looking suits, shirts and Oscar night tuxedos. Prices are over the top, but that's Valentino—and we wouldn't have him any other way. *valentino.it*

*Luxury* *Amex/MC/V*

**Upper East Side** **(212) 772-6969**
747 Madison Avenue at 65th St
NYC 10021 Mon-Sat 10-6 (Thurs 10-7), Sun 12-5

# Varda

Italian handmade shoes in one-width sizing and classic designs that make the transition from day to evening as easy as one-two-three. Although the sales staff claim the neutral-colored shoes will fit narrow or wide feet, you will have to be the judge. Prices run from $200 to $550.

*Moderate to expensive* *Amex/MC/V*

**Upper East Side** **(212) 472-7552**
786 Madison Avenue btw 66/67th St
NYC 10021 Mon-Sat 10-7

**Upper West Side** **(212) 873-6910**
2080 Broadway btw 71/72nd St
NYC 10023 Mon-Sat 10-7:30, Sun 12-7

**SoHo** **(212) 941-4990**
147 Spring Street btw West Broadway/Wooster
NYC 10012 Daily 11-7:30

# Variazioni

Fashionistas who crave the look of Cameron Diaz and Britney Spears will love this chain store for the huge selection of sassy skirts, skimpy tops, hip-hugging jeans and bold accessories from the likes of Diane von Furstenberg, Anna Argiolera, Red Engine and Von Dutch. And with their large and frequently rotating selection of sales items with up to 50% mark downs, Variazioni is sure to keep every girl happy, even those who don't have Justin

Timberlake backing the bill. Cameron has her own money, surely?

*Moderate*                                          *Amex/MC/V*

**Upper East Side**                              **(212) 744-9200**
1376 Third Avenue                                   at 78th Street
NYC                                        Mon-Sat 11-8, Sun 12-7

**Chelsea**                                      **(212) 627-4444**
156 Fifth Avenue                                        at 20th St
NYC 10011                               Mon-Sat 10:30-8, Sun 12-7

**Upper West Side**                              **(212) 874-7474**
309 Columbus Avenue                                btw 74/75th St
NYC 10023                               Mon-Sat 10:30-8, Sun 11-7

## VBH Gallery
The enormous Warhol hanging in the foyer will be the first thing to catch your eye at this new Rome-based emporium of leather goods, 20th-century collectible furnishings and myriad objets d'art, but it certainly won't be the last. Housed in a magnificent three-story engraved concrete building (it used to be a bank), the luxe interior is nearly as impressive as the Whitney Museum down the street. The basement level is even more refined, featuring evening bags and fine jewelry, including signature 18k white gold bands and 'orchid' rings with rubies and black diamonds, which will only set you back $65,000.

*Luxury*                                            *Amex/MC/V*

**Upper East Side**                              **(212) 717-9800**
940 Madison Avenue                                 btw 74/75th St
NYC 10021                               Mon-Fri 11-7, Sat 11-6

## ★ Vera Wang Bridal Salon
Vera Wang has revolutionized the wedding dress, and that has made her collections renowned throughout the world. This heavenly salon will have the bride even more luminous than usual—just ask customers like Sharon Stone and Karena Gore. Sheer elegance, sophisticated styling and beautiful craftsmanship define a Wang design, from the simple to the elaborate. Also find gorgeous eveningwear, like long beaded column dresses, bias-cut chiffon gowns with hand-sewn details and the perfect amount of beading and ruffles—just like her wedding dresses. Wang also has a complete ready-to-wear collection, featuring skirts and trousers with tidy, narrow waistbands, delicate blouses, chiffon tops, and fine cashmere sweaters. Be sure to check out her new forward-looking jewelry line, too. The flagship salon, located next to the Carlyle Hotel, is truly focused on the individual's needs—a welcome respite for anyone experiencing wedding-bell butterflies.          verawang.com

*Luxury*                                            *Amex/MC/V*

**Upper East Side**                              **(212) 628-3400**
991 Madison Avenue                                      at 77th St
NYC 10021                          Mon-Sat 9-6 (by appointment)

## ★ Vera Wang Maids on Madison

Across the street from Wang's bridal salon is this store dedicated entirely to bridesmaids. 'The entire bridal party should be as beautiful as the bride,' Wang says. The whole wedding world is here, from dresses, skirts, separates and camisoles, to blouses and sweaters in wonderful shades of champagne, lilac, maize, soft pink and navy. You'll want your friends to get married over and over again.

*Luxury* — *Amex/MC/V*

**Upper East Side** — **(212) 628-9898**
980 Madison Avenue (3rd floor) — btw 76/77th St
NYC 10021 — Mon-Sat (Thurs 10-7)
(by appointment)

## Veronique Maternity

Veronique's expectant-mommy mission: 'To design clothes like the ones you're used to wearing when you're not pregnant.' Now there's an idea. The exclusive collections are imported from Paris and Milan and emphasize comfort, fit and fashionability. Looks include flat-front pants and Ultrasuede jackets by labels like Chaiken, Seven and Cadeau. Expensive, but worth it. *veroniquematernity.com*

*Expensive* — *Amex/MC/V*

**Upper East Side** — **(212) 831-7800**
1321 Madison Avenue — at 77th St
NYC 10021 — Mon-Sat 9:30-6 (Tues-Thurs 11-7)

## Versace

Viva Versace! Flashy and fearless, the Milanese label—from Gianni to Donatella—takes sex by the horns (or was that the heels?). The powerhouse that is Versace continues to fuse the worlds of fashion, royalty and music, earning Donatella the sobriquet 'rock 'n' roll designer'. These clothes are for vixens (or Elizabeth Hurley) who want to feel young, sexy and be noticed—kinetic, kaleidoscope prints, biker leathers and skinny silhouettes. Find ready-to-wear, sportswear, glam-slam couture, racy eveningwear, a collection of home furnishings fit for Cleopatra, and a world of accessories (Medusa-head bathrobe, anyone?). Sin is in. *versace.com*

*Luxury* — *Amex/MC/V*

**Fifth Avenue** — **(212) 317-0224**
647 Fifth Avenue — btw 51/52nd St
NYC 10022 — Mon-Sat 10-6:30, Sun 12-6

## Verve Shoes

A West Village accessories shop that includes extras from Cynthia Rowley, Kazuyo Nakano, Santi, Hollywould, Lola, Nancy Nancy and IXOS. There are over 125 different lines in this tiny shop, from handbag and hat styles to sunglasses, jewelry and watches. Handbags include leather day bags and beaded purses, while the hat selection stretches all the way from the street to the beach.

*Expensive* — *Amex/MC/V*

**West Village**                       **(212) 675-6693**
338 Bleecker Street     btw Christopher/West 10th St
NYC 10014                  Daily 11-8 (Sunday 12-6)

## Via Spiga

Offering just about every shoe for every occasion, this Italian footwear company steps from knee-high suede boots with very high heels to the most sensible of slip-ons. Lucite slingbacks and open-toed pastel polka-dot numbers rest easily alongside more modest beige clogs and espadrilles. Via Spiga also offers a small sampling of men's shoes, as well as watches, sunglasses and playful bags with bow-tie handles.

*Moderate*                            *Amex/MC/V*

**Upper East Side**               **(212) 871-9955**
692 Madison Avenue            btw 62/63rd St
NYC 10021           Mon-Sat 10-7, Sun 12-6

**SoHo**                          **(212) 431-7007**
390 West Broadway          btw Spring/Broome
NYC 10013           Mon-Sat 11-7, Sun 12-6

## Vice

This hip outpost, an offshoot of the Canadian music magazine of the same name, carries a mix of American and British designers for men and women. Look for unique one-offs like ruffled tank sundresses, zippered minidresses and windbreakers with shark designs on the back by You Must Create (YMC), and tops by Putsch. Also very cool athletic-inspired looks, like a pink tracksuit skirt with ruffles and 'Religion' stitched on the side.

*Moderate*                            *Amex/MC/V*

**Nolita**                       **(212) 219-7788**
252 Lafayette Street          btw Prince/Spring
NYC 10012             Daily 12-8 (Sun 12-6)

## Victoria Keen

By handpainting and silk-screening vibrant, abstract, psychedelic patterns onto her clothing, accessories, and home furnishings, Victoria Keen extends her craft into wearable art. Tops, skirts, dresses, bags, sofas, chairs—each piece is unique and made from fine fabrics. Explore the store's three levels, with home furnishings in the basement and an art gallery in the sub-basement. Coming soon: menswear.          *victoriakeen.com*

*Moderate*                            *Amex/MC/V*

**Nolita**                       **(212) 473-1412**
357 Lafayette Street          btw Bond/Bleecker
NYC 10012                 Daily 11-7

## Victoria's Secret

All you can see is curves, don't you know. Well, Gisele's curves mostly, but there's hope here for the rest of us mortals too. Kudos to this lingerie power brand, which markets romance and allure at totally reasonable prices. Find short, sexy, baby-doll teddies, racy black garters and stockings, bustiers, lots of bras (plain or lacy and embellished), the best seamless thongs and sleepwear and slinky accessories in bright colors and soft feminine prints. Visit the new mega-mega store on Herald Square and thank God Victoria shared her secret.    800-888-1500  *victoriassecret.com*

*Affordable*                                      *Amex/MC/V*

**Upper East Side**               **(212) 717-7035**
1240 Third Avenue                     at 72nd St
NYC 10021                   Mon-Sat 10-8, Sun 12-6

**Upper West Side**             **(646) 505-2280**
1981 Broadway                     at 67th St
NYC 10023         (opening hours as above)

**Midtown East**                **(212) 758-5592**
34 East 57th Street        btw Madison/Park Ave
NYC 10022    Mon-Fri 10-8, Sat 10-7, Sun 12-6

**Midtown West**               **(646) 473-0950**
901 Sixth Avenue              btw 32/33rd St
NYC 10001                 Mon-Sat 10-8, Sun 11-6

**Herald Square**               **(212) 356-8380**
1328 Broadway                    at 35th St
NYC 10001                 Mon-Sat 10-9, Sun 11-7

**Flatiron**                       **(212) 477-4118**
115 Fifth Avenue               btw 18/19th St
NYC 10011                 Mon-Sat 10-8, Sun 12-6

**SoHo**                         **(212) 274-9519**
565 Broadway                      at Prince
NYC 10012                    10-8:30, Sun 11-7

**Lower Manhattan**            **(212) 962-8122**
19 Fulton Street    Pier 17, South Street Seaport
NYC 10038                 Mon-Sat 10-9, Sun 11-8

## Vilebrequin                    �♂ ♂

Who knew you could make an entire store around men's swimsuits? This French store sells cute father-son swim trunks in snappy prints like butterflies and pears—perfect for that Kodak moment. Suits come in four lengths with a variety of manly accessories such as towels, sarongs, sunglasses and baseball hats. From classic drawstring styles to surfer trunks, you and your little buddy will own the beaches. Pay $75-125 for men's or boys. From six months to adult.                    *vilebrequin.com*

*Moderate to expensive*            *Amex/MC/V*

**Upper East Side**               **(212) 546-9220**
1070 Madison Avenue           at 82nd St
NYC 10028            Daily 10-7 (Sun 10-6)

## Village Scandal                   ♂ ♀

Hedda Hopper rising? Perhaps not, but vintage addicts will love the selection of retro pieces at this cool East Village store. Boxes of hats are artfully arranged along the top shelves—from pleather rain hats in a floppy old-school

Hollywood style to currently trendy newsboys and bucket caps. Though it's really a hat store, there is also a fab selection of look-at-me handbags. The best bits? It's open until midnight, and it offers 10% off to students. Scandalous.

*Moderate* *Amex/MC/V*

**East Village** **(212) 460-9358**
19 East 7th Street btw Second/Third Ave
NYC 10003 Daily 12-12 (Sun 1-12)

## Vincent and Edgar

There is Lobb, there is Cleverley—and then there is Vincent and Edgar. V & E is New York's finest custom-made shoe establishment. Shoemaker Roman Vaingauz can labor for 40 hours to produce a single pair of his bespoke shoes. Men's shoes start at $1,700 and women's at $1,300, with an additional $575 for a pair of wooden shoe lasts. Four to five months for delivery.

*Luxury* *Amex/MC/V*

**Upper East Side** **(212) 753-3461**
972 Lexington Avenue at 71st St
NYC 10021 (by appointment only)

## Vincent Nicolosi

A high-end tailor of classic bespoke suits for chairman-of-the-board types. Expect six-to-eight-week delivery, but they will rush an order if necessary. What they will not do is quote you prices over the phone—it's better that you make an appointment, and see for yourself.

*Luxury* *(cash only)*

**Midtown East** **(212) 486-6214**
510 Madison Avenue at 53rd St
NYC 10022 Mon-Fri 10-6, Sat 10-5

## Vitraux

Better than your average bling. Vitraux by Alejandra's jewelry designs are sold in high-end department stores like Bendel's and Barneys, and pictures of celebs like Beyoncé and Christina wearing her pieces line the walls of this SoHo boutique. It's easy to understand the appeal of pieces like her turquoise and sterling-silver lariat choker—it's elegant, full of color, and brimming with personality and versatility...jewelry that perfectly compliments any outfit, no matter how casual or dressy. 877-388-2907 *vitrauxstore.com*

*Expensive* *Amex/MC/V*

**SoHo** **(212) 925-8259**
72 Thompson Street btw Spring/Broome
NYC 10012 Daily 11-7

## Vivienne Tam

New York style stalwart Vivienne Tam says her pieces take on a new feeling with each person. 'Once I put an idea on cloth, that cloth becomes a garment,' she says, 'and when somebody wears it, the garment comes to life.' She applies her signature arty, crafty, East-meets-West style to her collection of sheer floral dresses, embroidered skirts, jackets, printed nylon mesh tops and separates, many with delicate beading (reminiscent of Chinese art) and embroidery. *viviennetam.com*

*Moderate*                                                    *Amex/MC/V*

**SoHo**                                              **(212) 966-2398**
99 Greene Street                                      btw Prince/Spring
NYC 10012              Mon-Fri 12-7, Sat 11:30-7:30, Sun 12-6

## Viv Pickle 👤
DIY design at its best—you dream up the handbag, they do all the work, and everything is under $100. At Viv Pickle, choose a shape, pick out fabric, handle and lining, and the staff will custom-create your handbag on the premises. You can be as creative or conservative as you like—the look is all your own. If you can't make it to the store, shop online or gather all your friends and have a Pickle Party in your own home. Really. *vivpickle.com*

*Moderate*                                                    *Amex/MC/V*

**West Village**                                     **(212) 924-0444**
238 West 10th Street                                 at Bleecker/Hudson
NYC 10014                                            Wed-Sun 12-7

## Vlada 👤
Vlada has done stints at both Donna Karan and Chanel, but her own clothing passions have a vintage bent—from the Sixties to the Eighties, especially. For rock 'n' roll style (especially of the Studio 54 bent) start here, where the eclectic items range from sheer ponchos (think Halston) to the hipster-requisite military-inspired jackets. Also find flowing jersey dresses, silk-screened tops and a great shoe selection.

*Expensive*                                                   *Amex/MC/V*

**Lower East Side**                                  **(212) 387-7767**
101 Stanton Street                                          at Ludlow
NYC 10002                                            Daily 12-8 (Sun 12-7)

## Walter Steiger 👤👤
Walter Steiger is one of the founding members of the shoe establishment: in a word, quality. Known for unusual heel shapes, Steiger offers a range of feminine styles, including sexy stilettos, mid-heeled pumps, platforms, sandals, loafers and even a treaded walking shoe (best, though, are their two-toned golf shoes). Men's shoes feature pointy or round-toed loafers, boots and sleek sneakers. *walter-steiger.com*

*Expensive*                                                   *Amex/MC/V*

**Midtown East**                                     **(212) 826-7171**
417 Park Avenue                                            at 55th St
NYC 10022                                            Mon-Sat 10-6

## Warehouse 👤
Trendy and seasonal, Warehouse is Britain's street label known for hot gear for the 18-35 crowd (leaning more

towards the younger end, though). Stylish and very 'today', but not necessarily 'next week', the store is filled with basic tops, jeans, skirts, jackets, pants, suits and fun accessories.

*Moderate*                                     *Amex/MC/V*

**SoHo**                                      **(212) 941-0910**
581 Broadway                              btw Houston/Prince
NYC 10012                 Mon-Fri 11-8, Sat 10-9, Sun 12-7

**East Village**                               **(212) 228-5960**
55 East 8th Street         btw University Place/Broadway
NYC 10003            Mon-Thurs 11-8, Fri-Sat 11-9, Sun 12-7

## Warren Edwards

Great, stylish footwear from hand-stitched suede loafers and buttery leather boots to glamorous evening pumps and comfortable, plush moccasins. All the looks are feminine and attractive and the sales staff are pleasant.

*warrenedwards.com*

*Expensive*                                    *Amex/MC/V*

**Upper East Side**                            **(212) 223-4374**
107 East 60th Street            btw Park/Lexington Ave
NYC 10022                                    Mon-Sat 10-5:45

## Watts

Watts specializes in contemporary and vintage apparel and accessories for men. Already host to labels such as Ben Sherman, Fred Perry and Penguin, Watts earns even more cool points by decorating their shop with Seventies memorabilia like lunchboxes. At Watts, dressing up doesn't mean taking oneself too seriously. Mixing chic sportswear with outlandish ties (check out the cravat decorated with a picture of an Uzi), Watts presents preppy looks with a laugh.                                     *wattsonsmith.com*

*Moderate*                                     *Amex/MC/V*

**Cobble Hill**                                **(718) 596-2359**
248 Smith Street                     btw Douglass/Degraw
Brooklyn 11231                      Tues-Sat 12-7, Sun 12-6

## Western Spirit

Yee Haw! One does not need to be a Texan to dress like a cowboy, as the staff at New York's largest western store would be the first to tell you. Rustle up some gear—boots and moccasins galore, sharp hats, belt buckles and pearl-buttoned shirts are just some of the items to be found here. Men, women, and children can troll through three stories of clothing from Montana, Stetson, Akubra, Renegade and Charlie 1 Horse. Saddle up.

*Moderate*                                     *Amex/MC/V*

**SoHo**                                      **(212) 343-1476**
486 Broadway                                    at Broome
NYC 10013                                      Daily 10:30-8

## Wet Seal

This California-based clothing company markets inexpensive, ultra-hip clothing for the junior set, and now that the store's layout has been overhauled it is easier to shop for everything from jeans, T-shirts and clubwear to underwear, sleepwear and accessories. Wet seal also carries plenty of sexy, tight-fitting little numbers for girls looking to grin-and-bare it.                                    wetseal.com

*Affordable*                                        *Amex/MC/V*

**NoHo**                                        **(212) 253-2470**
670 Broadway                                            at Bond
NYC 10012                              Mon-Sat 10-9, Sun 12-7

**Nolita**                                      **(212) 228-6188**
65 East 8th Street                        btw Broadway/Mercer
NYC 10009                              Mon-Sat 10-9, Sun 12-7

## What Comes Around Goes Around

...and indeed it does, about every five years. This vintage boutique sells its recycled wares to stylists, celebs and fashionistas citywide. The collection includes everything from Victorian tops to Thirties ballgowns, Sixties Pucci, Seventies Cacharel...you get the idea. Also head here for Hawaiian shirts, retro shoes and must-have military jackets. Sales staff are knowledgeable and eager to please.      nyvintage.com

*Moderate*                                          *Amex/MC/V*

**SoHo**                                        **(212) 343-9303**
351 West Broadway                           btw Broome/Grand
NYC 10013                              Mon-Sat 11-8, Sun 12-7

## Whiskey Dust

Willie Nelson plays softly in this emporium with a huge selection of just about everything western (apart from whiskey and a poker game): bandanas, badges, barrels, belts, bolo ties, boots, buckles, bull whips—not to mention cowboy clothes not starting with 'b' are available for sale, or even rent. 'Go west without leaving New York' is Whiskey Dust's promise, and with an impressive collection of T-shirts, chaps and holsters, you'll be the John Wayne of the West Village, cowboy.                            whiskeydust.com

*Moderate*                                          *Amex/MC/V*

**West Village**                                **(212) 691-5576**
526 Hudson Street                        btw West 10th/Charles
NYC 10014                              Mon-Sat 12:30-7, Sun 1-6

## The Wicker Garden

If you ever have a craving to see a perfectly decorated nursery, indulge it with a trip to Pamela Scurry's Wicker Garden. You'll find spotless white wicker bookcases and hampers, crystal-knobbed, handpainted dressers, and sterling-silver frames and crocheted pillows for those shoppers carrying a black Amex. Rocking gliders start at $1,195, with matching ottomans for $650, and you can have custom upholstery made from 1,000 different fabrics. Don't miss the beautifully kitschy handpainted, nearly seven-feet-tall dollhouse armoire, which retails for $3,950 and seems straight out of *Mommy Dearest*. And what's all this to do with a fashion directory? They also have the most adorable children's clothes.

*Luxury*                                    *Amex/MC/V*

**Upper East Side**                         **(212) 410-7001**
1327 Madison Avenue                         btw 93/94th St
NYC 10128                                   Mon-Sat 10-6

## William Fioravanti

Descended from a long line of Neapolitan tailors, Fioravanti
sets the standard for custom-made clothes. He has a waiting list just to get an appointment, but once you've got a
foot in the door you're in for a sartorial treat. Choose from
luxurious English and Italian fabrics and customize a suit,
shirt or topcoat. Suits start at $5,000, and you should
expect a two-month delivery.          *williamfioravanti.com*

*Luxury*                                    *Amex/MC/V*

**Midtown West**                            **(212) 355-1540**
45 West 57th Street                         btw Fifth/Sixth Avenue
NYC 10019                                   Mon-Fri 9-5 (by appointment)

## Wolford Boutique

Long considered the Rolls-Royce of hosiery, Wolford is the
ultimate provider of novelty hose, sheers, thigh-highs,
opaques and knee-highs in colors running from cute to
kinky. For the silkiest sheers, ask for the Aura 5 Collection
and for a great run-resistant microfiber hose ask for their
best-selling Individual 10. It's also the place for killer bodysuits, swimwear and, surprisingly, men's socks. *wolford.com*

*Luxury*                                    *Amex/MC/V*

**Upper East Side**                         **(212) 327-1000**
996 Madison Avenue                          btw 77/78th St
NYC 10021                                   Mon-Sat 10-6

**Midtown East**                            **(212) 688-4850**
619 Madison Avenue                          btw 58/59th St
NYC 10022                                   Mon-Sat 10-6

**SoHo**                                     **(212) 343-0808**
122 Greene Street                           at Prince
NYC 10012                                   Mon-Sat 11-7, Sun 12-6

## Work In Progress

Regardless of its name, Work In Progress seems to have
reached its goal of stocking its shelves with every hot little
number a sexy girl could desire. Boasting a large jean section, tasty skirts, fabulous tops and hip T-shirts, the clothing
selection is fierce and varied. Hip-hop and dance beats
blare as young shoppers sort through all the hot gear,
which includes a wide selection of Miss Sixty apparel. Shoes
are displayed in the middle of the shop, surrounded by a
cheeky selection of accessories, books, gifts and other fun
goodies.

*Moderate*                                  *Amex/MC/V*

**SoHo**                                     **(212) 343-2577**
513 Broadway                                btw Broome/Spring
NYC 10012          Mon-Wed 10-8, Thurs-Sat 10-9, Sun 11-8

## The World of Golf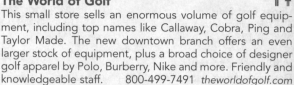

This small store sells an enormous volume of golf equipment, including top names like Callaway, Cobra, Ping and Taylor Made. The new downtown branch offers an even larger stock of equipment, plus a broad choice of designer golf apparel by Polo, Burberry, Nike and more. Friendly and knowledgeable staff. 800-499-7491 *theworldofgolf.com*

*Moderate* *Amex/MC/V*

**Midtown East** **(212) 755-9398**
147 East 47th Street btw Lexington/Third Ave
NYC 10017 Mon-Sat 9-7, Sun 11-5

## X Girl

Kim Gordon of Sonic Youth fame knows a thing or two about clothes for riot grrrrls. She started this streetwear line for trendy rockers, who feast on Gordon's groovy selection of T-shirts, snazzy pants, swimwear, embroidered tops and glorious accessories like studded vinyl belts. Be sure to pick up the newest addition to X Girl's inventory—too-cute Me, Myself & I pieces by German designer Katrin Wiens. *xgirlusa.com*

*Moderate* *Amex/MC/V*

**Nolita** **(212) 343-245**
265 Lafayette Street btw Prince/Spring
NYC 10012 Daily 12-7 (Sun 12-6)

## Y & Kei Water The Earth

Yes, it is a spectacularly odd name, but these designers' intentions are pure; if not exactly watering the earth, they do a fine job of dressing its inhabitants. The husband and wife team of Y (Hanii Y) and Kei (Gene Kei) spirit up feminine pieces like ruffled shirts with tulle detail in all colors from lemon to black, also deconstructed denim jeans, shoes and boho belts. Best bets in this bright, airy store are the pant suits, knockout flapper dresses and accessories.

*Expensive* *Amex/MC/V*

**SoHo** **(212) 477-7778**
125 Greene Street btw Prince/Spring
NYC 10012 Mon-Sat 11-7, Sun 12-6

## Yaso

Turkish owner Janan Tomko is very proactive, launching the careers of many design talents from Europe and L.A.. The large selection here includes labels like Punch, Ines Raspoort, Claudette, Michael Stars, Belgium's Just in Case and the Yaso Pazo vintage private label. Then there are belts by Paolo Angeluc, hats by Eric Javits and Louise Green and the absolutely, positively vital dog carriers for your pooch by Emre NY.

*Expensive* *Amex/MC/V*

**SoHo** **(212) 941-8506**
62 Grand Street btw West Broadway/Wooster
NYC 10012 Daily 11-7

# Yellow Rat Bastard

Since causing an animal rights frenzy when it opened in 1996 by placing scurrying rats in the display window, this men's boutique has morphed into an urban legend that now houses a women's collection, dormwear and a quarterly magazine. YRB's key to longevity is its innate sense of what's right now, which means that cargo pants by Liv-N-Large and crocheted skullcaps can be found next to smart dress shirts by Ben Sherman. *yellowratbastard.com*

*Amex/MC/V*                                                    *Affordable*

**SoHo**                                          **1-877-YELL-RAT**
478 Broadway                                btw Broome/Grand
NYC 10013                              Daily 10-8:30 (Sun 10-7:30)

# Yigal Azrouel

Theatrical lighting, black-gray concrete floors, deep red brick walls and a single Victorian-style antique couch create the dramatic effect in Azrouel's store, all the better to highlight the Israel-born, French-Moroccan designer's gauzy floral skirts, sexy clingy tops in dusty pinks, electric blues and yellows and stop-in-your tracks eveningwear. Azrouel has managed to attract downtown types while catering to a more mature crowd who won't flinch at the site of a $300 shirt. The store also has a few candles, bath beads and room sprays to add to the allure. *yigal-azrouel.com*

*Luxury*                                                      *Amex/MC/V*

**Chelsea**                                          **(212) 929 7525**
408 West 14th Street                                    at Ninth Ave
NYC 10014                              Mon-Sat 11-7, Sun 12:30-6

# Yohji Yamamoto

Yohji Yamamoto's designs are complex (he frequently uses tricky draping, ruching and folding), his color palette strong and stark, and his collections inventive, never trendy. Known for his sexy gabardine suits and sharp dresses, Yamamoto has also been innovative with sportswear (those polyester jogging pants are wonderful), pairing dressed-down designs with more sophisticated pieces. Loose-fitting yet wildly creative, his new collection for men demands attention with its integration of historical and modern looks (the emperor's new clothes apparently include leather), while the women's line uses layers, angles and roomy twists and turns with fabric to create truly breathtaking clothes. *yohjiyamamoto.co.jp*

*Expensive*                                                  *Amex/MC/V*

**SoHo**                                            **(212) 966-9066**
103 Grand Street                                          at Mercer
NYC 10013                                Mon-Sat 11-7, Sun 12-6

# ⭐ Yona Lee

At last, a vintage clothing store in the East Village where you don't have to rummage through baskets of old shirts and scarves. Yona Lee made sure her space was shopping-friendly, and it houses a well-chosen collection of retro somethings, mostly from the Sixties and the Seventies, plus gently used denim. Everything is arranged by color and nothing is over $100. She also stocks beaded jewelry in turquoise and coral, Sixties bangles and a few pieces of imported Indian jewelry.

*Affordable*                                        *Amex/MC/V*

**East Village**                          **(212) 253-2121**
412 East 9th Street                    btw First/Avenue A
NYC 10003                                        Daily 12-8

## Young's Hat Corner

Gentlemen (and younger), look no further than Young's Hat Corner for casual and dressy styles. This shop has plenty of haberdashery history under its belt, having catered to male hat lovers since 1890, and offers a grand selection of fancy toppers, English caps, baseball and straw hats. A warning: call on Friday afternoon to make sure they'll be open on Saturday.

*Moderate*                                          *Amex/MC/V*

**Lower Manhattan**                      **(212) 964-5693**
139 Nassau Street                              at Beekman
NYC 10038                    Mon-Fri 9-5:30, Sat 10-3:30

## ★ Yoya

Only the best for baby at this tiny West Village boutique: kid-friendly organic bath products, extra-soft North African blankets that can be worn as a wrap by Mom, Yoya's own cool crocheted sweaters, boys' check shirts and India-inspired embroidered pullover tops. Brands include European designers like Quincy, Petit Bateau and Bonpoint. The two fashionable matrons who own and run Yoya even had the forethought to provide a sliding-panel changing-room with a diaper table in the back. *yoyashop.coms*

*Moderate*                                          *Amex/MC/V*

**West Village**                          **(646) 336-6844**
636 Hudson Street                              at Horatio
NYC 10014                                      Mon-Sat 11-7

## Yumi Katsura

An upscale bridal salon with an extensive selection of 'marry me' gowns. Erisa, who designs for Yumi Katsura and The Erisa Collection, wants 'to shatter the mold of tradi-tional bridal dressing'. That she does: from simple chic to elaborate embroideries, her pieces are never less than modern. Four to six months delivery time; prices start at $3,200.                                        *yumikatsura.com*

*Luxury*                                                  *MC/V*

**Upper East Side**                      **(212) 722-3760**
907 Madison Avenue                      btw 72/73rd St
NYC 10021          Mon-Fri 11-6, Sat 10-5 (by appointment)

Directory

## Yves Saint Laurent Rive Gauche

Dozens of surprisingly friendly black-suited staff are ready to serve at the sleekest YSL store, where you'll find chic sunglasses, perfumes, watches and handbags amidst two floors of Tom Ford's dazzling designs. Shiny black walls and shelves show off sexy black leather gear for fashion-forward guys, while au courant women take notice of satin-tied velvet blazers and sheer ruffled dresses. A word to the wise: snag an item from Tom Ford's final collection, it'll be worth a fortune in years to come. *ysl.com*

*Luxury*                                    *Amex/MC/V*

**Midtown East**                            **(212) 980-2970**
3 East 57th Street                btw Fifth/Madison Ave
NYC 10022             Mon-Fri 10-7, Sat 10-6, Sun 12-5

**Upper East Side**                         **(212) 988-3821**
855 Madison Avenue                        btw 70/71st St
NYC 10021                                    Mon-Sat 10-6

## Yvone Christa

Hollywood's It-girls are big fans of the cool handbags and ethnic-inspired jewelry from this girly, white-curtained store. Bags come in all shapes, colors, sizes and textures—the tapestry sewing bags are particularly cute—but are primarily for evening; priced from $50 to $500. There also is a vast selection of delicate, flirty jewelry for L.A. babes (or their East Coast sisters).

*Moderate*                                  *Amex/MC/V*

**SoHo**                                    **(212) 965-1001**
107 Mercer Street                      btw Prince/Spring
NYC 10012              Mon-Fri 12-7, Sat 12-8, Sun 1-6

## Zabari

Zabari will take a trend and run with it—translation, it's perfect for teenagers. This bright, cavernous store stocks all the latest looks, from capri pants and skimpy tops to slip dresses, jeans and jackets. Zabari's bright fabrics look great from a distance but feel a leetle flimsy up close. Best buys are their hip, colorful knickers and fun handbags. Labels include Alice & Trixie, Zabari, Plenty and Anna Kuan.

*Affordable*                                *Amex/MC/V*

**SoHo**                                    **(212) 431-7502**
506 Broadway                          btw Spring/Broome
NYC 10012                                      Daily 11-8

## Zan

These spacious boutiques with their stark white shop fittings and diverse collections including suiting, sportswear, leather pieces and formalwear, would be right at home in an upscale suburban mall. Flirty pieces by Cynthia Steffe, Trina Turk and Cultura attract the younger, time-share set, while women with more classic tastes appreciate the well-made, affordable careerwear by French label Tehen.

*Moderate*                                  *Amex/MC/V*

**Midtown West** **(212) 582-5580**
1666 Broadway btw 51/52nd St
NYC 10019 Mon-Sat 9:30-8:30, Sun 11-7:30

**Upper West Side** **(212) 877-4853**
2394 Broadway btw 87/88th St
NYC 10024 Mon-Sat 10-8:30, Sun 11-6:30

##  Zara

This super-cool Spanish chain is taking over the globe with strikingly accurate interpretations of current designer looks. Find everything from Marc Jacobs-inspired tops and skirts to near-replications of Chanel's tweed suits and bags. Young professionals head here for smart suits, basic shirts, sweaters and coats (some for a bargain $160) for work, while clubbier types can indulge themselves with colored Lycra halters and super-tight jeans. The company has recently added footwear: Prada Sport-meets-Diesel sneaks for men and strappy *Sex and the City* stilettos for women; the quality of materials and construction, however, leaves something to be desired. *zara.com*

*Moderate* *Amex/MC/V*

**Midtown East** **(212) 754-1120**
750 Lexington Avenue at 59th St
NYC 10022 Mon-Sat 10-8, Sun 12-7

**Midtown West** **(212) 868-6551**
39 West 34th Street btw Fifth/Sixth Ave
NYC 10001 Mon-Sat 10-8:30, Sun 12-7:30

**Flatiron** **(212) 741-0555**
101 Fifth Avenue btw 17/18th St
NYC 10003 Mon-Sat 10-8, Sun 12-7

**SoHo** **(212) 343-1725**
580 Broadway at Prince
NYC 10012 Mon-Sat 10-8, Sun 12-7

## Z'baby

The sign behind the cash register says 'Your husband called… he said buy anything you want', and you'll want to when you see the European and domestic duds from Magill B. Kids, Valeria Blue, Blumarine and D&G. Just as cool for boys as it's cute for girls. *zbabycompany.com*

*Moderate* *Amex/MC/V*

**Upper East Side** **(212) 472-2229**
996 Lexington Avenue at 72nd St
NYC 10021 Mon-Sat 10-7, Sun 11:30-5

**Upper West Side** **(212) 579-2229**
100 West 72nd Street at Columbus Ave
NYC 10023 Mon-Sat 10:30-7:30, Sun 11-6

## Zeller Tuxedo

Rent or purchase men's formalwear here from a good selection of designer names. Oscar de la Renta and Loro Piana are available for rentals, and you can buy such well-known high-profile lines as Calvin Klein and Joseph Abboud, as well as less expensive brands. Rental prices start at $135, while buying runs from $400 to $1,000. Shirts and black tie accessories available. *zellertuxedo.com*

*Moderate to expensive*                                    *Amex/MC/V*

**Upper East Side**                              **(212) 688-0100**
1010 Third Avenue (2nd floor)              btw 60/61st St
NYC 10021          Mon-Fri 9-6:30, Sat 10-5:30, Sun 11-4:30

**Midtown East**                                **(212) 286-9786**
459 Lexington Avenue                          at 45th St
NYC 10017                    Mon-Fri 9-6:30, Sat 10-5:30

**Midtown West**                                **(212) 290-0217**
421 Seventh Avenue                            at 33rd St
NYC 10001                    Mon-Fri 9-6:30, Sat 10-5:30

## Zero / Maria Cornejo

Actresses, models (lots of models), 20-year-olds and, yes, 60-year-olds are all among the women who shop here. Designer Maria Cornejo's strength is in subtle, geometric clothes: her signature piece is 'the circle top', a circle of fabric that drapes over the shoulder with holes for the head and arms. Other looks include dresses cut in one piece without seams and shirts that twist provocatively around the body.

*Moderate*                                              *Amex/MC/V*

**Nolita**                                      **(212) 925-3849**
225 Mott Street                             btw Prince/Spring
NYC 10012          Daily 12:30-7:30 (Sat-Sun 12:30-6:30)

## Zion

Sylvia Lee Zion's wonderful little shop is filled with sophisticated apparel for women, including a wide range of sharp suits and dresses. Attentive shoppers will appreciate the delicate tailoring, colors and patterns helping to build Zion's burgeoning following.

*Moderate*                                              *Amex/MC/V*

**SoHo**                                        **(212) 226-7917**
93 Grand Street                             btw Greene/Mercer
NYC 10013                                    Mon-Sat 11-7

## ★ Zitomer

A mini department store—with crazy themed windows—boasting three floors of shopping for everything from beauty to toys. The main floor is home to every beauty, bath and health product imaginable. The second and third have the children's clothing and the toy department. And they will even cater to your pet's needs with their pet shop one door down.

*Affordable to expensive*                               *Amex/MC/V*

**Upper East Side**                             **(212) 737-4480**
969 Madison Avenue                            btw 75/76th St
NYC 10021                    Mon-Fri 9-8, Sat 9-7, Sun 10-6

## Zora

Zora's owner Bushra Gill has been many things: sculptor, museum educator and, finally, clothing designer. She now specializes in bridal clothing, her sculptural edge apparent in her elegant, non-conformist pieces. The made-to-order collection runs $1,400-$4,000; accessories include jewelry, handbags and sandals. *zoraonline.com*

*Expensive*                                          *Amex/MC/V*

**Midtown West**                              **(212) 840-7040**
55 West 45th Street (4th floor)        btw Fifth/Sixth Ave
NYC 10036                                      (by appointment)

# Stores by Neighborhood

# Harlem

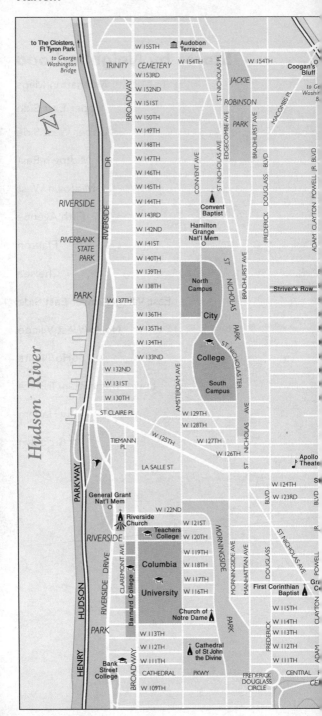

# East Harlem, Spanish Harlem

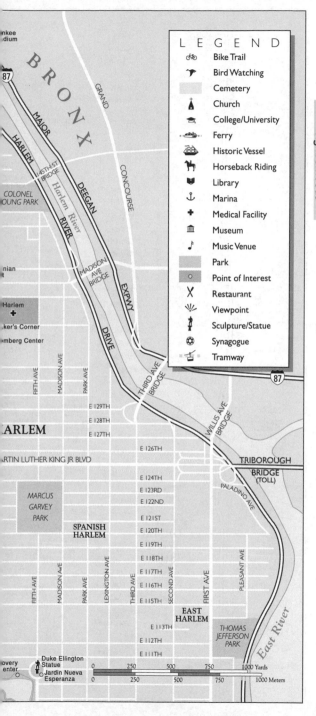

**LEGEND**

| | |
|---|---|
| 🚲 | Bike Trail |
| 🐦 | Bird Watching |
| | Cemetery |
| ⛪ | Church |
| 🎓 | College/University |
| ⛴ | Ferry |
| 🚢 | Historic Vessel |
| 🐎 | Horseback Riding |
| 📖 | Library |
| ⚓ | Marina |
| ✚ | Medical Facility |
| 🏛 | Museum |
| 🎵 | Music Venue |
| | Park |
| ○ | Point of Interest |
| ✕ | Restaurant |
| ☼ | Viewpoint |
| 🗿 | Sculpture/Statue |
| ✡ | Synagogue |
| | Tramway |

Neighborhoods

## Upper West Side

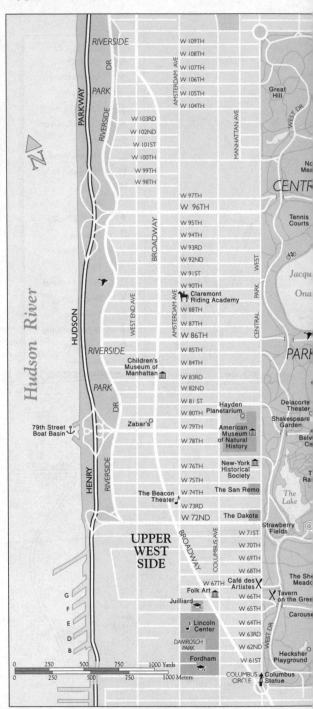

Neighborhoods

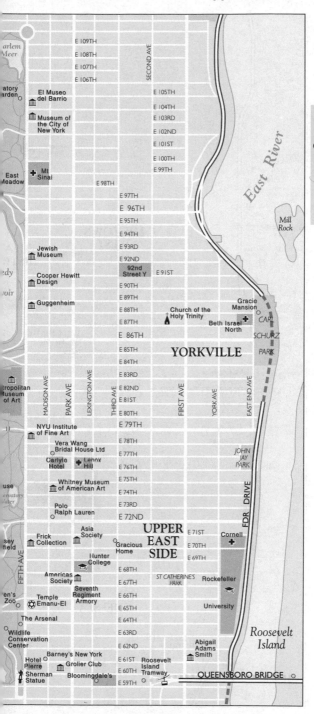

E 109TH
E 108TH
E 107TH
E 106TH

SECOND AVE

arlem
Meer

atory
arden

El Museo
del Barrio

Museum of
the City of
New York

E 105TH
E 104TH
E 103RD
E 102ND
E 101ST
E 100TH
E 99TH

East River

East
Meadow

Mt
Sinai

E 98TH

E 97TH

E 96TH

E 95TH

E 94TH

Mill
Rock

Jewish
Museum

E 93RD

E 92ND

edy
voir

Cooper Hewitt
Design

Guggenheim

92nd
Street Y

E 91ST

E 90TH

E 89TH

E 88TH

E 87TH

Church of the
Holy Trinity

Gracie
Mansion

Beth Israel
North

CARL

SCHURZ

E 86TH

PARK

E 85TH

YORKVILLE

E 84TH

ropolitan
useum
of Art

MADISON AVE
PARK AVE
LEXINGTON AVE

E 83RD

THIRD AVE

E 82ND

FIRST AVE

E 81ST

YORK AVE

E 80TH

EAST END AVE

NYU Institute
of Fine Art

E 79TH

E 78TH

Vera Wang
Bridal House Ltd

Carlyle
Hotel

Lenox
Hill

E 77TH

E 76TH

JOHN
JAY
PARK

Whitney Museum
of American Art

E 75TH

E 74TH

Polo
Ralph Lauren

E 73RD

E 72ND

FDR DRIVE

use
ervatory
/ater

Frick
Collection

Asia
Society

UPPER
EAST
SIDE

E 71ST

Hunter
College

Gracious
Home

E 70TH

Cornell

E 69TH

sey
field

FIFTH AVE

Americas
Society

E 68TH

Seventh
Regiment
Armory

E 67TH

ST CATHERINE'S
PARK

Rockefeller

en's
Zoo

Temple
Emanu-El

E 66TH

E 65TH

University

The Arsenal

E 64TH

Wildlife
Conservation
Center

E 63RD

E 62ND

Abigail
Adams
Smith

Roosevelt
Island

Hotel
Pierre

Sherman
Statue

Barney's New York

Grolier Club

Bloomingdale's

E 61ST

E 60TH

Roosevelt
Island
Tramway

E 59TH

QUEENSBORO BRIDGE

## Midtown West, Chelsea

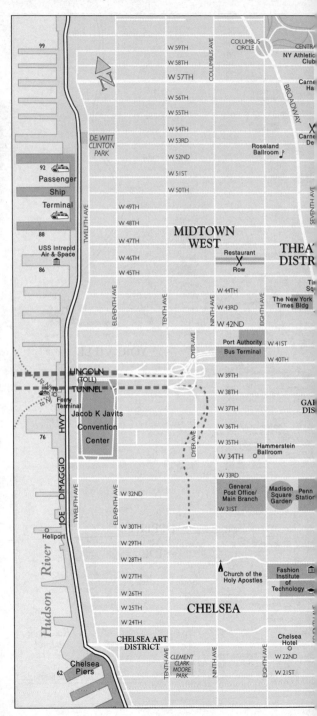

# Midtown East, Fifth Avenue

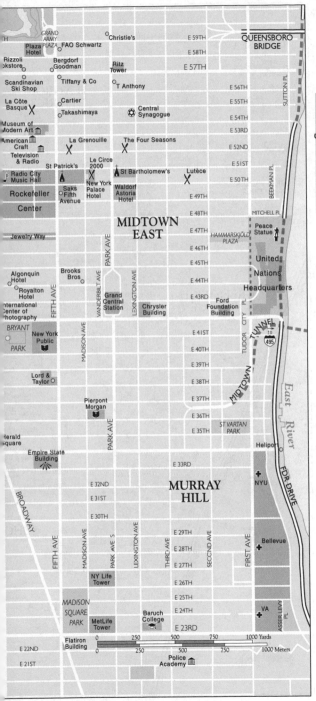

Map labels:

Plaza Hotel · GRAND ARMY PLAZA · FAO Schwartz · Christie's · E 59TH · QUEENSBORO BRIDGE
E 58TH
Rizzoli Bookstore · Bergdorf Goodman · Ritz Tower · E 57TH
Scandinavian Ski Shop · Tiffany & Co · E 56TH · SUTTON PL
La Côte Basque · Cartier · T Anthony · E 55TH
Takashimaya · Central Synagogue · E 54TH
Museum of Modern Art · E 53RD
American Craft · La Grenouille · The Four Seasons · E 52ND
Television & Radio · St Patrick's · Le Circe 2000 · St Bartholomew's · Lutèce · E 51ST
Radio City Music Hall · Saks Fifth Avenue · New York Palace Hotel · Waldorf Astoria Hotel · E 50TH · BEEKMAN PL
Rockefeller Center · E 49TH · MITCHELL PL
E 48TH · Peace Statue
Jewelry Way · MIDTOWN EAST · E 47TH · HAMMARSKJÖLD PLAZA
E 46TH · United
PARK AVE · E 45TH · Nations
Algonquin Hotel · Brooks Bros · E 44TH · Headquarters
Royalton Hotel · VANDERBILT AVE · LEXINGTON AVE · E 43RD · Ford Foundation Building
International Center of Photography · FIFTH AVE · Grand Central Station · Chrysler Building · TUDOR CITY PL
BRYANT PARK · New York Public · E 41ST · TUNNEL · 495
MADISON AVE · E 40TH
E 39TH · MIDTOWN
Lord & Taylor · E 38TH · East River
Pierpont Morgan · E 37TH
E 36TH
Herald Square · PARK AVE · E 35TH · ST VARTAN PARK · Heliport
Empire State Building · E 33RD · NYU
BROADWAY · E 32ND · MURRAY HILL
E 31ST
FIFTH AVE · MADISON AVE · PARK AVE S · E 30TH
E 29TH · Bellevue
LEXINGTON AVE · THIRD AVE · SECOND AVE · E 28TH · FIRST AVE
E 27TH
NY Life Tower · E 26TH
E 25TH · VA · ASSER LEVY PL
MADISON SQUARE PARK · MetLife Tower · Baruch College · E 24TH
E 23RD
Flatiron Building · 0 250 500 750 1000 Yards · 0 250 500 750 1000 Meters
E 22ND · Police Academy
E 21ST

# Chelsea, Flatiron, West Village, SoHo

# East Village, NoHo, NoLiTa, Lower East Side

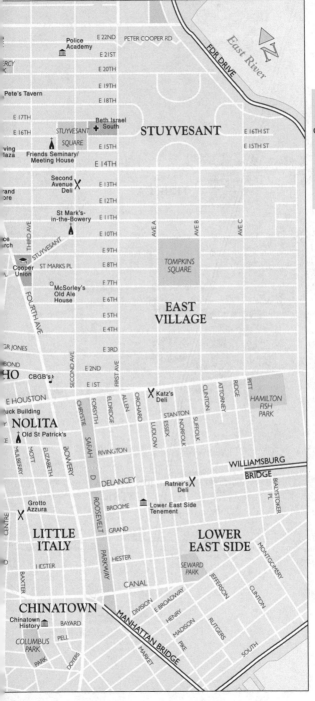

297

## TriBeCa

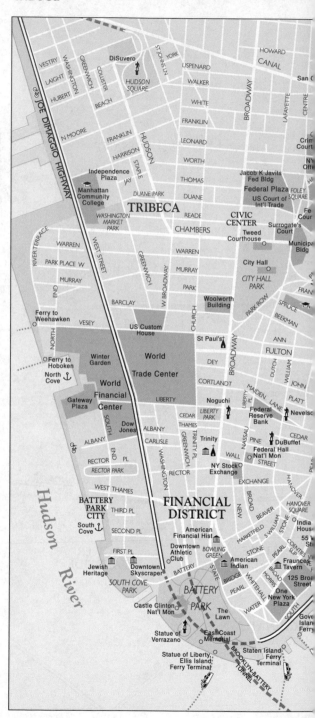

# Lower Manhattan

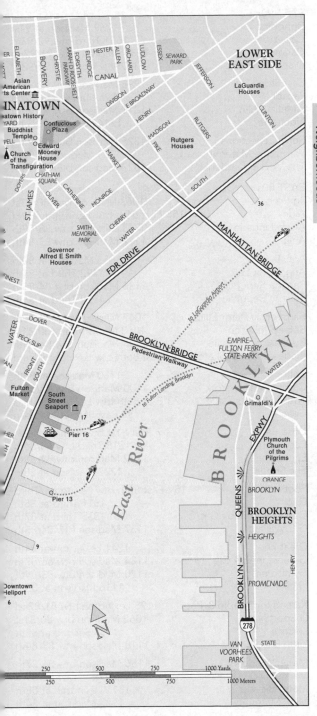

299

## Upper East Side  *See map page 293*

**EAST 90s**

| | |
|---|---|
| Bonpoint | 1269 Madison at 91st |
| Capezio | 1651 Third btw 92/93rd |
| Catimini | 1284 Madison btw 91/92nd |
| Diana & Jeffries | 1310 Madison btw 92/93rd |
| East Side Kids | 1298 Madison btw 92/93rd |
| Jacadi | 1296 Madison at 92nd |
| J.McLaughlin | 1311 Madison btw 92/93rd |
| Nocturne | 1744 First btw 90/91st |
| René Collections | 1325 Madison btw 93/94th |
| Veronique Maternity | 1321 Madison at 93rd |
| The Wicker Garden | 1327 Madison btw 93/94th |

**EAST 80s**

| | |
|---|---|
| agnès b. | 1063 Madison btw 80/81st |
| Aldo | 157 East 86th btw Lexington/Third |
| Allure Lingerie | 1324 Lexington btw 88/89th |
| Anik | 1122 Madison btw 83/84th |
| Ann Taylor | 1055 Madison at 80th |
| Ann Taylor Loft | 1492 Third at 84th |
| Banana Republic | 1136 Madison btw 84/85th |
| Banana Republic | 1529 Third at 86th |
| Barbour by Peter Elliot | 1047 Madison btw 79/80th |
| Betsey Johnson | 1060 Madison btw 80/81st |
| Bis Designer Resale | 1134 Madison btw 84/85th |
| Blades Board & Skate | 160 East 86th btw Lexington/Third |
| Bolton's | 1180 Madison at 86th |
| Cashmere New York | 1100 Madison btw 82/83rd |
| The Children's Place | 173 East 86th btw Lexington/Third |
| Coach | 35 East 85th at Madison |
| Cose Belle | 7 East 81st btw Fifth/Madison |
| Easy Spirit | 1518 Third btw 85/86th |
| Encore | 1132 Madison btw 84/85th |
| Eric Shoes | 1222 Madison at 88th |
| Foot Locker | 159 East 86th btw Lexington/Third |
| Gap | 1511 Third at 85th |
| Gap Kids & Baby Gap | 1535 Third at 87th |
| G.C.William | 1137 Madison btw 84/85th |
| Great Feet | 1241 Lexington at 84th |
| Greenstones & Cie | 1184 Madison btw 86/87th |
| Gymboree | 1120 Madison btw 83/84th |
| Infinity | 1116 Madison at 83rd |
| Karen's for People & Pets | 1195 Lexington btw 81/82nd |
| LeSportSac | 1065 Madison btw 80/81st |
| Lester's | 1534 Second at 80th |
| Little Eric Shoes | 1118 Madison btw 83/84th |
| Magic Windows | 1186 Madison btw 86/87th |
| Marsha D.D. | 342 Lexington btw 88/89th |
| Metro Bicycle | 1311 Lexington at 88th |
| Mimi Maternity | 1125 Madison at 84th |

| | |
|---|---|
| Modell's | 1535 Third btw 86/87th |
| Montmarte | 1157 Madison btw 85/86th |
| Motherhood Maternity | 1449 Third at 82nd |
| Nancy & Co | 1242 Madison at 89th |
| Nellie M. Boutique | 1309 Lexington at 88th |
| Nine West | 184 East 86th btw Lexington/Third |
| Original Leather | 1100 Madison btw 82/83rd |
| Orva | 155 East 86th btw Lexington/Third |
| Peter Elliot | 1070 Madison at 81st |
| Peter Elliot (kids & outlet) | 1067 Madison btw 80/81st |
| Peter Elliot Women | 1071 Madison btw 80/81st |
| Petit Bateau | 1100 Madison at 82nd |
| Planet Kids | 247 East 86th btw Third/Fourth |
| Rapax | 1100 Madison btw 82/83rd |
| Searle | 1124 Madison at 84th |
| Seigo | 1248 Madison btw 89/90th |
| Spence-Chapin Thrift Shops | 1850 Second btw 95/96th |
| Spence-Chapin Thrift Shops | 1473 Third btw 83/84th |
| Steve Madden | 150 East 86th btw Lexington/Third |
| Super Runners Shop | 1337 Lexington at 89th |
| Vilebrequin | 1070 Madison at 81st |

EAST 70s

| | |
|---|---|
| A Pea in the Pod | 860 Madison at 70th |
| ABH Design | 401 East 76th at First |
| Alexandre de Paris | 971 Madison btw 75/76th |
| Alicia Mugetti | 999 Madison btw 77/78th |
| Anik | 1355 Third btw 77/78th |
| Ann Taylor | 1320 Third btw 75/76th |
| Annika Inez | 243 East 78th btw Second/Third |
| Antoin | 1110 Lexington btw 77/78th |
| A Perfect Day In Paradise | 153 East 70th btw Lexington/Third |
| Arche | 995 Madison at 77th |
| Baby Gap | 1037 Lexington at 74th |
| Ballantyne Cashmere | 965 Madison btw 75/76th |
| Bambini | 1367 Third at 78th |
| Barami | 1404 Second at 73rd |
| Betsey Bunky Nini | 980 Lexington btw 71/72nd |
| Big Drop | 1321 Third btw 75/76th |
| Bra Smyth | 905 Madison btw 72/73rd |
| Calypso St Barths | 935 Madison btw 74/75th |
| Cantaloup | 1036 Lexington at 74th |
| Carolina Herrera | 954 Madison at 75th |
| Cashmere New York | 1052 Lexington at 75th |
| Che Che | 1045a Lexington btw 73/74th |
| Chloé | 850 Madison at 70th |
| Christian Louboutin | 941 Madison btw 74/75th |
| Clea Colet 960 Madison | at 71st |
| Delfino | 1351a Third btw 77/78th |
| Eileen Fisher | 1039 Madison btw 79/80th |

| | |
|---|---|
| Eric Shoes | 1333 Third btw 76/77th |
| FM Allen 962 Madison | btw 75/76th |
| Forreal | 1335 Third btw 76/77th |
| Forreal Basics | 1375 Third btw 78/79th |
| French Sole | 985 Lexington btw 71/72nd |
| Galo | 895 Madison at 72nd |
| Gamine | 1322 Third btw 75/76th |
| Gap | 1066 Lexington at 75th |
| Gianfranco Ferré | 845 Madison btw 70/71st |
| Gymboree | 1332 Third at 76th |
| Hoofbeats | 232 East 78th btw Second/Third |
| Intermix | 1003 Madison btw 77/78th |
| Issey Miyake | 992 Madison at 77th |
| Jane | 1025 Lexington btw 73/74th |
| Jay Kos | 986 Lexington btw 71/72nd |
| J.McLaughlin | 1343 Third at 77th |
| Judith Leiber | 987 Madison btw 76/77th |
| K.C.Thompson | 22 East 72nd btw Fifth/Madison |
| Liz Lange Maternity | 958 Madison btw 75/76th |
| Luca Luca | 1011 Madison at 78th |
| Make 10 | 1227 Third btw 70/71st |
| Makola | 1045 Madison btw 79/80th |
| Malia Mills | 960 Madison btw 75/76th |
| Mariko | 998 Madison btw 77/78th |
| Mary Efron | 308 East 78th at Second |
| Michael Kors | 974 Madison at 76th |
| Michael's The Consignment Shop for Women | |
| | 1041 Madison btw 79/80th |
| Missoni | 1009 Madison at 78th |
| Miu Miu | 831 Madison btw 69/70th |
| Mom's Night Out/One Night Out | 147 East 72nd |
| | btw Lexington/Third |
| Noriko Maeda | 985 Madison btw 76/77th |
| Nursery Lines | 1034 Lexington at 74th |
| Pat Areias | 966 Madison btw 75/76th |
| Pelle Via Roma | 1322 Third btw 75/76th |
| Pookie & Sebastian | 249 East 77th btw Second/Third |
| Prada | 841 Madison at 70th |
| Precision | 1310 Third at 75th |
| Ralph Lauren | 867 Madison at 72nd |
| Ralph Lauren | 888 Madison at 72nd |
| Ralph Lauren Baby | 872 Madison btw 71/72nd |
| René Collections | 1007 Madison btw 77/78th |
| Roberta Freymann | 23 East 73rd btw Fifth/Madison |
| Santoni | 864 Madison btw 70/71st |
| Scoop | 1275 Third btw 73/74th |
| Searle | 1296 Third at 74th |
| Searle | 1035 Madison at 79th |
| Selima Optique | 899 Madison btw 72/73rd |

| | |
|---|---|
| Shen | 1005 Madison btw 77/78th |
| The Shoe Box | 1349 Third at 77th |
| Small Change | 964 Lexington btw 70/71st |
| Sonia Rykiel | 849 Madison btw 70/71st |
| Spring Flowers | 905 Madison btw 72/73rd |
| Super Runners Shop | 1244 Third btw 71/72nd |
| Talbots | 1251 Third at 72nd |
| Talbots Kids | 1523 Second at 79th |
| VBH Gallery | 940 Madison btw 74/75th |
| Vera Wang Bridal Salon | 991 Madison at 77th |
| Vera Wang Maids on Madison | 980 Madison btw 76/77th |
| Victoria's Secret | 1240 Third at 72nd |
| Vincent & Edgar | 972 Lexington at 71st |
| Wolford Boutique | 996 Madison btw 77/78th |
| Yumi Katsura | 907 Madison btw 72/73rd |
| Yves Saint Laurent Rive Gauche | 855 Madison btw 70/71st |
| Z' Baby | 996 Lexington at 72nd |
| Zitomer | 969 Madison btw 75/76th |

**EAST 60s**

| | |
|---|---|
| Aerosoles | 1555 Second at 61st |
| Anne Fontaine | 687 Madison btw 61/62nd |
| Ann Taylor | 645 Madison at 60th |
| Ann Taylor Loft | 1155 Third btw 67/68th |
| Anya Hindmarch | 29 East 60th btw Madison/Park |
| Arche | 1045 Third btw 61/62nd |
| Athlete's Foot | 1031 Third at 61st |
| Baby Gap | 1131-49 Third at 66th |
| Banana Republic | 1110 Third at 65th |
| Barneys New York | 660 Madison at 61st |
| Bati | 1052 Third btw 62/63rd |
| BCBG by Max Azria | 770 Madison at 66th |
| Bebe | 1127 Third at 66th |
| Beretta | 718 Madison btw 63/64th |
| Betsey Johnson | 251 East 60th btw Second/Third |
| Billy Martins | 220 East 60th btw Second/Third |
| Bonpoint | 811 Madison at 68th |
| Borrelli | 16 East 60th btw Fifth/Madison |
| Boyds Madison | 655 Madison btw 60/61st |
| Brioni | 57 & 67 East 57th btw Madison/Park |
| Calvin Klein | 654 Madison at 60th |
| Canyon Beachwear | 1136 Third btw 66/67th |
| Capezio | 136 East 61st btw Park/Lexington |
| Celine | 667 Madison at 61st |
| Cesare Paciotti | 833 Madison btw 69/70th |
| Chuckies | 1073 Third btw 63/64th |
| Church's English Shoes | 689 Madison at 62nd |
| Clifford Michael Design | 45 East 60th btw Madison/Park |
| Club Monaco | 1111 Third at 65th |
| Cole Haan | 667 Madison at 61st |

Neighborhoods

| | |
|---|---|
| Davide Cenci | 801 Madison btw 67/68th |
| Diesel | 770 Lexington at 60th |
| DKNY | 655 Madison at 60th |
| Dolce & Gabbana | 825 Madison btw 68/69th |
| Donna Karan New York | 819 Madison btw 68/69th |
| Dooney & Bourke | 28 East 60th btw Madison/Park |
| Eddie Bauer | 1172 Third at 68th |
| Emanuel Ungaro | 792 Madison at 67th |
| Entre Nous | 1124 Third btw 65/66th |
| Etro | 720 Madison btw 63/64th |
| Furla | 727 Madison btw 63/64th |
| Gallery of Wearable Art | 34 East 67th btw Madison/Park |
| Galo | 825 Lexington at 63rd |
| Gap | 1131-49 Third at 66th |
| Giordano's | 1150 Second btw 60/61st |
| Giorgio Armani | 760 Madison at 65th |
| Giuseppe Zanotti Design | 806 Madison btw 67/68th |
| Givenchy | 710 Madison at 63rd |
| Gymboree | 1049 Third at 62nd |
| Hermès | 691 Madison at 62nd |
| Hervé Léger | 744 Madison btw 64/65th |
| Jacadi | 787 Madison at 67th |
| Jean Paul Gaultier | 759 Madison btw 65/66th |
| J.Mendel | 723 Madison btw 63/64th |
| J.M.Weston | 812 Madison at 68th |
| John Lobb | 680 Madison btw 61/62nd |
| Joseph | 816 Madison btw 68/69th |
| Julie Artisan's Gallery | 762 Madison btw 65/66th |
| Krizia | 769 Madison btw 65/66th |
| La Layette et Plus | 170 East 61st btw Lexington/Third |
| La Perla | 777 Madison btw 66/67th |
| Lee Anderson | 23 East 67th btw Fifth/Madison |
| Leggiadro | 680 Madison btw 61/62nd |
| Legs Beautiful | 1025 Third at 61st |
| Les Copains | 807 Madison btw 67/68th |
| Lingerie on Lex | 831 Lexington btw 63/64th |
| Longchamp | 713 Madison at 63rd |
| Loro Piana | 821 Madison btw 68/69th |
| Luca Luca | 690 Madison at 62nd |
| Lucky Brand Jeans | 1151 Third at 67th |
| Luxury Brand Outlet | 1222 Second at 64th |
| Malo | 814 Madison at 68th |
| Manrico Cascimir | 802 Madison btw 67/68th |
| Marina Rinaldi | 800 Madison btw 67/68th |
| Martier | 1010 Third at 60th |
| Martinez Valero | 1029 Third at 61st |
| MaxMara | 813 Madison at 68th |
| Morgane Le Fay | 746 Madison btw 64/65th |

| | |
|---|---|
| Moschino | 803 Madison btw 67/68th |
| Nicole Farhi | 10 East 60th btw Fifth/Madison |
| Nicole Miller | 780 Madison btw 66/67th |
| Oilily | 820 Madison btw 68/69th |
| Oilily For Women | 820 Madison btw 68/69th |
| Olive & Bette's | 1070 Madison btw 80/81st |
| Pan American Phoenix | 857 Lexington btw 64/65th |
| Paul & Shark | 772 Madison btw 66/67th |
| Pilar Rossi | 784 Madison btw 66/67th |
| Porthault | 11 East 69th btw Fifth/Madison |
| Pucci | 24 East 64th btw Fifth/Madison |
| Reem Acra | 14 East 60th btw Fifth/Madison |
| Ricky's | 1189 First at 64th |
| Robert Clergerie | 681 Madison btw 61/62nd |
| Roberto Cavalli | 711 Madison at 63rd |
| Robert Talbott | 680 Madison btw 61/62nd |
| Ruco Line | 794 Madison at 67th |
| Saada | 1159 Second btw 60/61st |
| Searle | 805 Madison btw 67/68th |
| Searle | 1051 Third at 62nd |
| Selma & Sid | 220 East 60th btw Second/Third |
| Sergio Rossi | 772 Madison at 66th |
| Shanghai Tang | 714 Madison btw 63/64th |
| Spring Flowers | 1050 Third at 62nd |
| Stephane Kélian | 717 Madison btw 63/64th |
| Suzanne Couture Millinery | 27 East 61st btw Madison/Park |
| Tanino Crisci | 795 Madison btw 67/68th |
| Timberland | 709 Madison at 63rd |
| Tse | 827 Madison at 69th |
| Unisa | 701 Madison btw 62/63rd |
| Valentino | 747 Madison at 65th |
| Varda | 786 Madison btw 66/67th |
| Versace | 815 Madison at 68th |
| Via Spiga | 692 Madison btw 62/63rd |
| Warren Edwards | 107 East 60th btw Park/Lexington |
| Zeller Tuxedo | 1010 Third btw 60/61st |

## Upper West Side    *See map page 292*

| | |
|---|---|
| Aerosoles | 310 Columbus btw 74/75th |
| Allan & Suzi | 416 Amsterdam at 80th |
| Alskling | 228 Columbus btw 70/71st |
| Ann Taylor | 2380 Broadway at 87th |
| Ann Taylor | 2015-17 Broadway at 69th |
| April Cornell | 487 Columbus btw 83/84th |
| Assets London | 464 Columbus btw 82/83rd |
| A.Tempo | 290 Columbus btw 73/74th |
| Athlete's Foot | 2265 Broadway btw 81/82nd |
| Athlete's Foot | 2563 Broadway at 96th |
| Baby Gap | 341 Columbus at 76th |

| | |
|---|---|
| Banana Republic | 215 Columbus btw 69/70th |
| Banana Republic | 2360 Broadway at 86th |
| Bati | 2151 Broadway btw 75/76th |
| Betsey Johnson | 248 Columbus btw 71/72nd |
| Blades Board & Skate | 120 West 72nd btw Amsterdam/Columbus |
| Bloch | 304 Columbus btw 74/75th |
| Brief Encounters | 239 Columbus at 71st |
| The Children's Place | 2187 Broadway btw 77/78th |
| The Children's Place | 2039 Broadway btw 70th/Amsterdam |
| Club Monaco | 2376 Broadway at 87th |
| CPW | 495 Amsterdam at 84th |
| Crunch | 162 West 83rd btw Amsterdam/Columbus |
| Danskin | 159 Columbus btw 67/68th |
| Daphne | 467 Amsterdam btw 82/83rd |
| Darryl's | 492 Amsterdam btw 83/84th |
| Diana & Jeffries | 2062 Broadway btw 70/71st |
| Eastern Mountain Sports | 20 West 61st at Broadway |
| Easy Spirit | 2251 Broadway at 81st |
| Eddie Bauer | 1976 Broadway at 67th |
| Eileen Fisher | 341 Columbus btw 76/77th |
| Express | 321 Columbus at 75th |
| Filene's Basement | 2222 Broadway at 79th |
| Frank Stella | 440 Columbus at 81st |
| French Connection | 304 Columbus btw 74/75th |
| Gap | 1988 Broadway at 67th |
| Gap | 2373 Broadway at 86th |
| Gap | 335 Columbus at 76th |
| Gap Kids | 1988 Broadway at 67th |
| Gap Kids | 2300 Broadway at 83rd |
| Granny-Made | 381 Amsterdam btw 78/79th |
| Greenstones & Cie | 442 Columbus btw 81/82nd |
| Gymboree | 2271 Broadway at 81/82nd |
| Gymboree | 2015 Broadway btw 68/69th |
| Intermix | 210 Columbus at 69th |
| Karen Alexis | 490 Amsterdam btw 83/84th |
| Kenneth Cole | 353 Columbus at 77th |
| Laina Jane Lingerie | 416 Amsterdam at 80th |
| Liana | 324 Columbus btw 75/76th |
| Liberty House | 2389 Broadway btw 87/88th |
| Liberty House | 2878 Broadway at 112th |
| Lord of the Fleas | 2142 Broadway btw 75/76th |
| Lucky Brand Jeans | 218 Columbus at 70th |
| Medici | 420 Columbus btw 80/81st |
| Mimi Maternity | 2005 Broadway btw 68/69th |
| Mommy Chic | 2449 at 90th |
| Montmartre | 247 Columbus btw 71/72nd |
| Montmartre | 2212 Broadway btw 78/79th |

Morris Bros                    2322 Broadway at 84th
Naturalizer                   148 Columbus btw 66/67th
The New York Look          30 Lincoln Plaza btw 62/63rd

The New York Look          2030 Broadway btw 69/70th
Nine West                     2305 Broadway btw 83/84th
Off Broadway   139 West 72nd btw Broadway/Columbus

Olive & Bette's              252 Columbus btw 71/72nd
Only Hearts                  386 Columbus btw 78/79th
Original Leather                 256 Columbus at 72nd

Patagonia                    426 Columbus btw 80/81st
Planet Kids                  2688 Broadway at 103rd
Really Great Things          284a Columbus btw 73/74th

Really Great Things           300 Columbus at 74th
Reebok                       160 Columbus btw 67/68th
Ricky's        112 West 72nd btw Broadway/Columbus

Roberto Vascon   140 West 72nd btw Broadway/Columbus
Rockport                     160 Columbus btw 67/68th
Roslyn                           276 Columbus at 73rd

Sacco                        324 Columbus btw 75/76th
Sari-Sari Store   111 West 72nd btw Amsterdam/Columbus
Scarpe Diem                  2286 Broadway btw 81/82nd

Sean                         224 Columbus btw 70/71st
Skechers                     2169 Broadway btw 76/77th
Super Runners Shop           360 Amsterdam btw 77/78th
Talbots          2289-2291 Broadway btw 82/83rd

Tani                         2020 Broadway btw 69/70th
Theory                       230 Columbus btw 70/71st
Tibet Bazaar                 473 Amsterdam btw 82/83rd

Tip Top Kids   149 West 72nd btw Broadway/Columbus
Varda                        2080 Broadway btw 71/72nd
Variazioni                   309 Columbus btw 74/75th

Victoria's Secret            1981 Broadway at 67th
Z' Baby                      100 West 72nd at Columbus
Zan                          2394 Broadway btw 87/88th

## Midtown East               See map page 295

Addison On Madison         29 West 57th btw Fifth/Sixth
Aldo                       730 Lexington btw 58/59th
Alexandros Furs            5 East 59th btw Fifth/Madison

Alfred Dunhill                   711 Fifth btw 55/56th
Allen Edmonds              551 Madison btw 55/56th
Allen Edmonds        24 East 44th btw Fifth/Madison

Amsale                           625 Madison at 58th
Ann Taylor                        850 Third at 52nd
Ann Taylor                      330 Madison at 43rd

Ann Taylor Loft            150 East 42nd at Lexington
Ann Taylor Loft                 488 Madison at 52nd
A.T.Harris Formalwear   11 East 44th btw Fifth/Madison

307

| | |
|---|---|
| Athlete's Foot | 41 East 42nd at Madison |
| Athlete's Foot | 655 Lexington at 55th |
| Bally | 628 Madison at 59th |
| Banana Republic | 130 East 59th at Lexington |
| Barami | 136 East 57th at Lexington |
| Barami | 375 Lexington at 41st |
| Bebe | 805 Third at 50th |
| Belgian Shoes | 110 East 55th btw Park/Lexington |
| Benetton | 666 Third at 42nd |
| Bloomingdale's | 1000 Third btw 59/60th |
| Bolton's | 4 East 34th btw Fifth/Madison |
| Bolton's | 109 East 42nd btw Vanderbilt/Lexington |
| Bottega Veneta | 635 Madison btw 59/60th |
| Bridal Atelier | 127 East 56th btw Park/Lexington |
| Brioni | 57 East 57th btw Madison/Park |
| Brioni | 55 East 52nd btw Madison/Park |
| Brooks Brothers | 346 Madison btw 44/45th |
| Caché | 805 Third btw 49/50th |
| Chanel | 15 East 57th btw Fifth/Madison |
| Charles Tyrwhitt | 377 Madison btw 46/47th |
| Christian Dior | 21 East 57th btw Fifth/Madison |
| Citishoes | 445 Park btw 56/57th |
| Clarks/Bostonian | 363 Madison at 45th |
| Coach | 342 Madison at 44th |
| Coach | 595 Madison at 57th |
| Conrad's Bike Shop | 25 Tudor City Place at 41st |
| Crouch & Fitzgerald | 400 Madison btw 47/48th |
| Crunch | 1109 Second btw 58/59th |
| Daffy's | 335 Madison at 44th |
| Daffy's | 125 East 57th btw Park/Lexington |
| Dana Buchman | 65 East 57th btw Madison/Park |
| Denimaxx | 444 Madison btw 49/50th |
| Designer Loft | 260 West 39th btw Seventh/Eighth |
| Dior Homme | 19 East 57th btw Fifth/Madison |
| Domenico Spano | 611 Fifth at 50th |
| Easy Spirit | 555 Madison btw 55/56th |
| Eddie Bauer | 711 Third at 45th |
| Eileen Fisher | 521 Madison btw 53/54th |
| Emporio Armani | 601 Madison btw 57/58th |
| Enzo Angiolini | 551 Madison at 55th |
| Enzo Angiolini | 331 Madison at 43rd |
| Eres | 621 Madison btw 58/59th |
| Express | 477 Madison at 51st |
| Express | 722-728 Lexington at 58th |
| Fogal | 510 Madison at 53rd |
| Forman's | 145 East 42nd btw Lexington/Third |
| Frank Shattuck | 250 West 57th at Broadway |
| Fratelli Rossetti | 625 Madison at 58th |
| Gap | 657 Third at 42nd |
| Gap | 900 Third at 54th |

| | |
|---|---|
| Gap | 734 Lexington btw 58/59th |
| Gap Kids | 545 Madison at 55th |
| Gap Kids | 657 Third at 42nd |
| Geiger | 505 Park at 59th |
| Geox | 595 Madison at 57th |
| Ghurka | 41 East 57th btw Madison/Park |
| Helene Arpels | 470 Park btw 57/58th |
| H.Herzfeld | 507 Madison btw 52/53rd |
| Johnston & Murphy | 520 Madison at 54th |
| Johnston & Murphy | 345 Madison btw 44/45th |
| Jos. A. Bank | 366 Madison at 45th |
| J.Press | 7 East 44th btw Fifth/Madison |
| Kavanagh's Designer Resale Shop | 146 East 49th btw Lexington/Third |
| Kenneth Cole | 107 East 42nd at Park |
| Kenneth Cole | 130 East 57th at Lexington |
| Lana Marks | 645 Madison btw 59/60th |
| The Leather & Suede Workshop | 107 East 59th btw Park/Lexington |
| Lederer | 457 Madison at 51st |
| Legs Beautiful | 153 East 53rd at Lexington |
| Legs Beautiful | 200 Park btw 44/45th |
| Leonard Logsdail | 9 East 53rd btw Fifth/Madison |
| Linda Dresner | 484 Park btw 58/59th |
| Mason's Tennis Mart | 56 East 53rd btw Madison/Park |
| Men's Wearhouse | 380 Madison at 46th |
| Modell's | 51 East 42nd btw Madison/Vanderbilt |
| Moreschi | 515 Madison at 53rd |
| Naturalizer | 712 Lexington btw 57/58th |
| New Balance New York | 821 Third btw 50/51st |
| Niketown | 6 East 57th btw Fifth/Madison |
| Nine West | 750 Lexington btw 58/59th |
| Nine West | 757 Third btw 47/48th |
| The Original Levi's Store | 750 Lexington btw 59/60th |
| Otto Tootsi Plohound | 38 East 57th btw Madison/Park |
| Oxxford Couture Collection | 36 East 57th btw Madison/Park |
| Paul Stuart | Madison at 45th |
| Pookie & Sebastian | 541 Third at 36th |
| Prada (shoes only) | 45 East 57th btw Madison/Park |
| Precision | 522 Third at 35th |
| René Mancini | 470 Park at 58th |
| Richard Metzger | 325 West 38th btw Eighth/Ninth |
| Ricky's | 509 Fifth btw 42/43rd |
| Saint Laurie Merchant Tailors | 22 West 32nd btw Broadway/Fifth |
| Searle | 609 Madison btw 57/58th |
| The Shirt Store | 51 East 44th at Vanderbilt |
| Skechers USA | 3 Times Square at 42nd/Seventh |

| | |
|---|---|
| Sports Authority | 845 Third at 51st |
| Stuart Weitzman | 625 Madison btw 58/59th |
| Suarez | 450 Park btw 56/57th |
| Talbots | 525 Madison btw 53/54th |
| T.Anthony | 445 Park at 56th |
| Taryn Rose | 30 East 60th btw Madison/Park |
| Thomas Pink | 520 Madison at 53rd |
| Tod's | 650 Madison btw 59/60th |
| Tumi | 64 Grand Central Terminal (Lexington Passage) |
| Tumi | 520 Madison at 54th |
| Turnbull & Asser | 42 East 57th btw Madison/Park |
| Victoria's Secret | 34 East 57th btw Madison/Park |
| Vincent Nicolosi | 510 Madison at 53rd |
| Walter Steiger | 417 Park at 55th |
| Wolford Boutique | 619 Madison btw 58/59th |
| World of Golf | 147 East 47th btw Lexington/Third |
| Yves Saint Laurent Rive Gauche | 3 East 57th btw Fifth/Madison |
| Zara International | 750 Lexington at 59th |

## Midtown West    *See map page 294*

| | |
|---|---|
| Aldo | 15 West 34th btw Fifth/Sixth |
| Alixandre | 150 West 30th btw Sixth/Seventh |
| Ann Taylor | 1166 Sixth at 46th |
| Ann Taylor Loft | 1290 Sixth at 52nd |
| Arche | 128 West 57th btw Sixth/Seventh |
| Arthur Gluck Shirtmakers | 47 West 57th btw Fifth/Sixth |
| Ascot Chang | 7 West 57th btw Fifth/Sixth |
| Athlete's Foot | 46 West 34 at Sixth |
| Athlete's Foot | 1568 Broadway at 47th |
| Baldwin Formalwear | 1156 Sixth at 45th |
| Banana Republic | 17 West 34th btw Fifth/Sixth |
| Barami | 485 Seventh btw 36/37th |
| Behrle | 440 West 34th btw Ninth/Tenth |
| Blades Board & Skate | at Manhattan Mall, 901 Sixth at 32nd |
| Blair Delmonico | Time Warner Mall at Columbus Circle |
| Bolton's | 27 West 57th btw Fifth/Sixth |
| Bolton's | 1700 Broadway at 54th |
| Burberry | 9 East 57th btw Fifth/Madison |
| Capezio | 1776 Broadway at 57th |
| Capezio | 1650 Broadway at 51st |
| Champs | 1381-1399 Sixth at 56th |
| The Children's Place | 1460 Broadway btw 41/42nd |
| The Children's Place | at Manhattan Mall 901 Sixth btw 32/33rd |
| Christie Brothers Furs | 150 West 30th btw Sixth/Seventh |
| Club Monaco | 8 West 57th btw Fifth/Sixth |
| Crunch | 144 West 38th btw Broadway/Seventh |
| Crunch | 555 West 42nd at Eleventh |

| | |
|---|---|
| Daffy's | 1311 Broadway btw 33/34th |
| Delfino | 56 West 50th at Rockefeller Center |
| Duty Free Apparel | 204 West 35th at Seventh |
| Easy Spirit | 1166 Sixth at 46th |
| Enzo Angiolini | at Manhattan Mall, 901 Sixth btw Broadway/33rd |
| Express | 7 West 34th btw Fifth/Sixth |
| Express | at Manhattan Mall, 901 Sixth btw Broadway/33rd |
| Fame | 512 Seventh btw 37/38th |
| Fiona Walker | 359 West 54th at Ninth |
| Foot Locker | at Manhattan Mall, 901 Sixth at 33rd |
| Foot Locker | 120 West 34th btw Sixth/Seventh |
| Foot Locker | 43 West 34th btw Fifth/Sixth |
| Frank Stella | 921 Seventh at 58th |
| French Connection | 1270 Sixth at 51st |
| Gap | 60 West 34th at Broadway |
| Gap | 1212 Sixth btw 47/48th |
| Gap | 1466 Broadway at 42nd |
| Gap | 250 West 57th btw Broadway/Eighth |
| Gap Kids | 1212 Sixth btw 47/48th |
| Gap Kids & Baby Gap | 1466 Broadway at 42nd |
| Gerry Cosby & Co | 3 Penn Plaza at MSG |
| H&M | 1328 Broadway at 34th |
| Jack Silver Formal Wear | 1780 Broadway btw 57/58th |
| John Anthony | 130 West 57th btw Sixth/Seventh |
| Keni Valenti | 247 West 30th btw Seventh/Eighth |
| Kmart | 250 West 34th btw Seventh/Eighth |
| Lady Foot Locker | 120 West 34th at Sixth |
| Laura Biagiotti | 4 West 57th btw Fifth/Sixth |
| Louis Féraud | 3 West 56th btw Fifth/Sixth |
| Macy's | Broadway at 34th |
| Maggie Norris Couture | 24 West 40th btw Fifth/Sixth |
| Make 10 | 1386 Sixth btw 56/57th |
| Manolo Blahnik | 31 West 54th btw Fifth/Sixth |
| Maternity Work | 16 West 57th btw Fifth/Sixth |
| Metro Bicycle | 360 West 47th at Ninth |
| Michelle Roth & Co | 24 West 57th btw Fifth/Sixth |
| Modell's | 1293 Broadway at 34th |
| Montmartre | Time Warner Mall at Columbus Circle |
| Motherhood Maternity | at Manhattan Mall, 901 Sixth at 33rd |
| Motherhood Maternity (outlet) | 16 West 57th btw Fifth/Sixth |
| New Balance | 51 West 42nd btw Fifth/Sixth |
| New York Golf Center | 131 West 35th btw Broadway/Seventh |
| The New York Look | 570 Seventh at 41st |
| Nine West | 1230 Sixth at 49th |
| Norma Kamali | 11 West 56th btw Fifth/Sixth |
| N.Peal | 5 West 56th btw Fifth/Sixth |
| Old Navy Clothing Co | 150 West 34th btw Sixth/Seventh |
| Piccione | 7 West 56th btw Fifth/Sixth |
| Quiksilver | 3 Times Square at 42nd/Seventh |

Neighborhoods

311

| | |
|---|---|
| Ricky's | 988 Eighth at 58th |
| Ritz Furs | 107 West 57th btw Sixth/Seventh |
| Rochester Big & Tall | 1301 Sixth at 52nd |
| Rosa Custom Ties | 30 West 57th btw Fifth/Sixth |
| Scandinavian Ski Shop | 40 West 57th btw Fifth/Sixth |
| Sisley | Time Warner Mall at Columbus Circle |
| Skechers | 140 West 34th btw Sixth/Seventh |
| Soho Woman | 32 West 40th btw Fifth/Sixth |
| Sports Authority | 57 West 57th at Sixth |
| Steve Madden | 41 West 34th btw Fifth/Sixth |
| Thomas Pink | 1155 Sixth at 44th |
| Thomas Pink | Time Warner Mall at Columbus Circle |
| Training Camp | 25 West 45th btw Fifth/Sixth |
| Training Camp | 1079 Sixth at 41st |
| Tristan & America | 1230 Sixth at 49th |
| Victoria's Secret | at Manhattan Mall, 901 Sixth at 33rd |
| Victoria's Secret | Herald Square at 34th |
| Wet Seal | at Manhattan Mall, 901 Sixth at 33rd |
| William Fioravanti | 45 West 57th btw Fifth/Sixth |
| Zan 1666 | Broadway btw 51/52nd |
| Zara International | 39 West 34th btw Fifth/Sixth |
| Zora | 55 West 45th btw Fifth/Sixth |

## Fifth Avenue
*See map page 295*

| | |
|---|---|
| Alfred Dunhill | 711 Fifth btw 55/56th |
| American Girl Place | 609 Fifth at 49th |
| Ann Taylor | 575 Fifth btw 46/47th |
| Asprey | 723 Fifth at 56th |
| A.Testoni | 665 Fifth btw 52/53rd |
| A/X Armani Exchange | 645 Fifth at 51st |
| Banana Republic | 626 Fifth at Rockefeller Center |
| Barami | 535 Fifth at 45th |
| Benetton | 597 Fifth btw 48/49th |
| Bergdorf Goodman | 754 Fifth at 58th |
| Bergdorf Goodman The Men's Store | 745 Fifth at 58th |
| Best of Scotland | 581 Fifth btw 47/48th |
| Botticelli | 666 Fifth btw Fifth/Sixth (enter on 53rd) |
| Botticelli | 522 Fifth btw 43/44th |
| Botticelli (women) | 620 Fifth at Rockefeller Center |
| Brooks Brothers | 666 Fifth btw 52/53rd |
| Coach | 620 Fifth at Rockefeller Center |
| Cole Haan | 620 Fifth at 50th |
| Domenico Spano | 611 Fifth at 50th |
| Domenico Vacca | 781 Fifth btw 59/60th |
| Ermenegildo Zegna | 743 Fifth btw 57/58th |
| Escada | 715 Fifth at 56th |
| Façonnable | 689 Fifth at Rockefeller Center |
| Fendi | 720 Fifth at 56th |
| Forman's | 560 Fifth at 46th |
| The Fur Salon at Saks Fifth Avenue | 611 Fifth at 49th |

| | |
|---|---|
| Gant | 645 Fifth btw 51/52nd |
| Gap | 680 Fifth at 54th |
| Gucci | 685 Fifth at 54th |
| H&M | 640 Fifth at 51st |
| Helen Yarmak | 730 Fifth btw 56/57th |
| Henri Bendel | 712 Fifth btw 55/56th |
| Hickey Freeman | 666 Fifth btw 52/53rd |
| Hugo Boss | 717 Fifth at 56th |
| Jimmy Choo | 645 Fifth at 51st |
| Kenneth Cole | 610 Fifth at Rockefeller Center |
| Lacoste | 608 Fifth at 49th |
| Lord & Taylor | 424 Fifth btw 38/39th |
| Louis Vuitton | 1 East 57th at Fifth |
| Maggie Norris Couture | 754 Fifth at Bergdorf Goodman |
| Make 10 | 366 Fifth btw 34/35th |
| MEXX | 650 Fifth btw 51/52nd |
| Nautica | 50 Rockefeller Center btw Fifth/Sixth |
| The New York Look | 551 Fifth at 45th |
| Nine West | 675 Fifth at 53rd |
| Oshkosh B'Gosh | 586 Fifth btw 47/48th |
| Prada | 724 Fifth btw 56/57th |
| Ripplu | 575 Fifth btw 46/47th |
| Saks Fifth Avenue | 611 Fifth btw 49/50th |
| Salvatore Ferragamo | 661 Fifth btw 52/53rd |
| Sisley | 133 Fifth at 20th |
| St John | 665 Fifth at 53rd |
| Takashimaya | 693 Fifth btw 54/55th |
| Versace | 647 Fifth btw 51/52nd |

**Flatiron** *See map pages 296–297*

| | |
|---|---|
| agnès b. | 13 East 16th btw Fifth/Union Square West |
| Ann Taylor | 149 Fifth at 21st |
| Anthropologie | 85 Fifth at 16th |
| Banana Republic (women) | 89 Fifth at 16th |
| Banana Republic (men) | 114 Fifth at 17th |
| Bebe | 100 Fifth at 15th |
| The Children's Place | 36 Union Square East at 16th |
| Club Monaco | 160 Fifth at 21st |
| Copperfields New York | 117 East 24th btw Park/Lexington |
| Couture by Jennifer Dule | 89 Fifth at 16th |
| Crunch | 54 East 13th btw Broadway/University Place |
| Daffy's | 111 Fifth at 18th |
| Eileen Fisher | 116 Fifth btw 21/22nd |
| Emporio Armani | 110 Fifth at 16th |
| Express | 130 Fifth at 18th |
| Foot Locker | 853 Broadway at 14th |
| Gap | 122 Fifth at 18th |
| Gap Kids & Baby Gap | 122 Fifth at 18th |
| Harry Rothman's | 200 Park South at 17th |
| Intermix | 125 Fifth btw 19/20th |

| | |
|---|---|
| J.Crew | 91 Fifth btw 16/17th |
| Kenneth Cole | 95 Fifth at 17th |
| Lucky Brand Jeans | 172 Fifth at 22nd |
| Nine West | 115 Fifth at 19th |
| | |
| Otto Tootsi Plohound | 137 Fifth btw 20/21st |
| Paragon Sporting Goods | 867 Broadway at 18th |
| Paul Smith | 108 Fifth at 16th |
| Princeton Ski Shop | 21 East 22nd btw Broadway/Park South |
| | |
| Runway | 12 West 23rd btw Fifth/Sixth |
| Sacco | 14 East 17th |
| | btw Fifth/Union Square West |
| | |
| Scoop | 156 Fifth at 20th |
| Skechers | 150 Fifth btw 19/20th |
| Space Kiddets | 46 East 21st btw Broadway/Park |
| | |
| Thread | 26 West 17th btw Fifth/Sixth |
| Victoria's Secret | 115 Fifth btw 18/19th |
| Zara International | 101 Fifth btw 17/18th |

## Chelsea                       *See map pages 294, 296*

| | |
|---|---|
| Alexander McQueen | 417 West 14th btw Ninth/Washington |
| Alexandros Furs | 213 West 28th btw Seventh/Eighth |
| Balenciaga | 542 West 22nd btw Tenth/Eleventh |
| Banana Republic | 111 Eighth btw 15/16th |
| | |
| Benetton | 120 Seventh at 17th |
| Ben Thylan Furs | 150 West 30th btw Sixth/Seventh |
| Blades Board & Skate | 23rd and West Side Highway |
| | at Chelsea Pier 62 |
| | |
| Burlington Coat Factory | 707 Sixth at 23rd |
| Camouflage | 139/141 Eighth at 17th |
| Carlos Miele | 408 West 14th btw Ninth/Tenth |
| Comme des Garçons | 520 West 22nd btw Tenth/Eleventh |
| | |
| Destination | 32-36 Little West 12th btw Washington/Ninth |
| Eisenberg & Eisenberg | 16 West 17th btw Fifth/Sixth |
| The Family Jewels | 130 West 23rd btw Sixth/Seventh |
| Filene's Basement | 620 Sixth at 18th |
| | |
| Find Outlet | 361 West 17th btw Eighth/Ninth |
| Fisch for the Hip | 153 West 18th btw Sixth/Seventh |
| Gerry's | 110 & 112 Eighth btw 15/16th |
| Giraudon | 152 Eighth btw 17/18th |
| | |
| Han Feng | 174 Ninth btw 20/21st |
| Jeffrey | 449 West 14th btw Ninth/Tenth |
| Jim Smiley Vintage | 128 West 23rd btw Sixth/Seventh |
| LaCrasia Gloves | 15 West 28th btw Fifth/Broadway |
| | |
| La Perla | 425 West 14th btw Ninth/Tenth |
| Lingo | 257 West 19th btw Seventh/Eighth |
| Loehmann's | 101 Seventh btw 16/17th |
| | |
| Lost Art | 515 West 29th btw Tenth/Eleventh |
| Lucy Barnes | 320 West 14th btw Eighth/Ninth |
| Men's Wearhouse | 655 Sixth at 20th |

| Metro Bicycle | 546 Sixth at 15th |
| Motherhood Maternity | 641 Sixth at 20th |
| Old Navy Clothing Co | 610 Sixth btw 17/18th |
| Parke & Ronen | 176 Ninth btw 20/21st |

| Poleci | 414 West 14th btw Ninth/Tenth |
| Powers Court Tennis Outlet | 132½ West 24th btw Sixth/Seventh |
| Reminiscence | 50 West 23rd btw Fifth/Sixth |

| Ricky's | 267 West 23rd btw Seventh/Eighth |
| Sacco | 94 Seventh btw 15/16th |
| Selima Optique | 888 Broadway at 19th |
| Shelly Steffee | 34 Gansevoort at Hudson |

| Sports Authority | 636 Sixth at 19th |
| Stella McCartney | 429 West 14th btw Ninth/Washington |
| T.J.Maxx | 620 Sixth btw 18/19th |

| Urban Outfitters | 526 Sixth at 14th |
| Utowa | 17 West 18th btw Fifth/Sixth |
| Yigal Azrouel | 408 West 14th btw Ninth/Tenth |

## East Village/Lower East Side  *See map page 297*

| 99X | 84 East 10th btw Third/Fourth |
| A.Cheng | 443 East 9th btw First/Avenue A |
| Alife | 178 Orchard btw Houston/Stanton |
| Alife Rivington Club | 158 Rivington btw Clinton/Suffolk |

| Alpana Bawa (outlet) | 70 East 1st btw First/Second |
| Amarcord Vintage Fashion | 84 East 7th btw First/Second |
| American Apparel | 183 East Houston at Orchard |
| Amy Downs Hats at YU | 151 Ludlow btw Stanton/Rivington |

| Angelo Lambrou | 96 East 7th btw First/Avenue A |
| Anna | 150 East 3rd btw Avenue A/B |
| Atomic Passion | 430 East 9th btw First/Avenue A |
| Azaleas | 223 East 10th btw First/Second |

| Barbara Feinman Millinery | 66 East 7th btw First/Second |
| Barbara Shaum | 60 East 4th btw Bowery/Second |
| DDC Lab | 180 Orchard btw Stanton/Houston |
| D/L Cerney | 13 East 7th btw Second/Third |

| Do Kham | 304 East 5th btw First/Second |
| Doyle & Doyle | 189 Orchard btw Houston/Stanton |
| Eileen Fisher (outlet) | 314 East 9th btw First/Second |
| Ellen | 122 Ludlow btw Rivington/Delancey |

| Enerla Lingerie | 18½ East 7th btw First/Second |
| Eugenia Kim | 203 East 4th btw Avenue A/B |
| Fabulous Fanny's | 335 East 9th btw First/Second |
| February Eleventh | 315 East 9th btw First/Second |

| Filth Mart | 531 East 13th btw Avenue A/B |
| Foley & Corinna | 108 Stanton btw Ludlow/Essex |
| Foley & Corinna (men) | 143 Ludlow btw Stanton/Rivington |

| Foot Locker | 252 First at 15th |
| Foot Locker | 94 Delancey btw Ludlow/Orchard |
| Forman's | 82 Orchard btw Broome/Grand |

Neighborhoods

| | |
|---|---|
| Gabay's Outlet | 225 First btw 13/14th |
| Gap (men) | 750 Broadway at 8th |
| Gap (women) | 1 Astor Place at Broadway |
| The Gown Company | 312 East 9th btw First/Second |
| Hello Sari | 261 Broome btw Allen/Orchard |
| Huminska New York | 315 East 9th btw First/Second |
| Jill Anderson | 331 East 9th btw First/Second |
| Johnson | 179 Orchard btw Houston/Stanton |
| Jutta Neumann | 158 Allen btw Stanton/Rivington |
| Klein's | 105 Orchard at Delancey |
| Knit New York | 307 East 14th btw First/Second |
| Lord of the Fleas | 305 East 9th btw First/Second |
| Love Saves the Day | 119 Second at 7th |
| Love Shine | 543½ East 6th btw Avenue A/B |
| Machine | 85 Stanton btw Orchard/Allen |
| Magry Knits | 80 East 7th btw First/Second |
| Manhattan Portage | 333 East 9th btw First/Second |
| Marmalade | 172 Ludlow btw Houston/Stanton |
| Martin | 206 East 6th btw Second/Third |
| Mary Adams | 138 Ludlow btw Stanton/Rivington |
| Mavi | 832 Broadway btw 12/13th |
| Meg | 312 East 9th btw First/Second |
| Metro Bicycle | 332 East 14th btw First/Second |
| Metropolis | 43 Third btw 9/10th |
| miks | 100 Stanton btw Ludlow/Orchard |
| Min-K | 334 East 11th btw First/Second |
| Miracle | 100 Mark's Place btw First/Avenue A |
| Missbehave | 231 Eldridge btw Stanton/Houston |
| Mod World | 85 First btw 5/6th |
| MoMo FaLana | 43 Avenue A at 3rd |
| New York Om Yoga | 826 Broadway at 12th |
| No. 436 | 436 East 9th btw First/Avenue A |
| Nort 235 | 235 Eldridge btw Houston/Stanton |
| The Open Door Gallery | 77 East 4th btw Second/Bowery |
| Outlet 7 | 117 East 7th btw First/Avenue A |
| Peacock NYC | 440 East 9th btw First/Avenue A |
| Project | 175 Orchard at Stanton |
| Recon | 237 Eldridge btw Houston/Stanton |
| Rejoice | 182 Orchard btw East Houston/Stanton |
| Rue St Denis | 174 Avenue B at 11th |
| Selia Yang | 328 East 9th btw First/Second |
| Selima Optique | 7 Bond btw Broadway/Lafayette |
| Selima Optique | 84 East 7th btw First/Second |
| Skella | 156 Orchard btw Stanton/Rivington |
| Shop | 105 Stanton at Ludlow |
| Some Odd Rubies | 151 Ludlow btw Stanton/Rivington |
| Tees.com | 124 Ludlow btw Rivington/Delancey |
| Tees.com | 280 East 10th btw First/Avenue A |
| TG-170 | 170 Ludlow btw Houston/Stanton |
| Tokio 7 | 64 East 7th btw First/Second |
| Tokyo Joe | 334 East 11th btw First/Second |

| | |
|---|---|
| Urban Outfitters | 162 Second btw 10/11th |
| The Village Scandal | 19 East 7th btw Second/Third |
| Vlada | 101 Stanton at Ludlow |
| Yona Lee | 412 East 9th btw First/Avenue A |

## NoHo/West Village    *See map pages 296–297*

| | |
|---|---|
| Aerosoles | 63 East 8th btw Broadway/University Place |
| Aldo | 700 Broadway at East 4th |
| American Apparel | 712 Broadway at Washington Place |
| American Apparel | 373 Sixth at Waverly |
| | |
| Andy's Chee Pees | 691 Broadway btw 3/4th |
| Annelore | 636 Hudson at Horatio |
| Ann Taylor Loft | 770 Broadway btw 8/9th |
| Arche | 10 Astor Place btw Lafayette/Broadway |
| | |
| Arleen Bowman | 353 Bleecker btw West 10th/Charles |
| Athlete's Foot | 60 East 8th at Broadway |
| Atrium | 644 Broadway at Bleecker |
| Banana Republic | 205 Bleecker at Sixth |
| | |
| Basic Basic | 710 Broadway btw Washington Place/4th |
| Benetton | 749 Broadway btw 8th/Astor Place |
| Betwixt | 245 West 10th btw Bleecker/Hudson |
| Blades Board & Skate | 659 Broadway btw West 3rd/Bleecker |
| | |
| Bond 07 | 7 Bond btw Broadway/Lafayette |
| Calypso | 654 Hudson at 14th |
| Cherry | 19 Eighth btw West 12th/Jane |
| Classic Kicks | 298 Elizabeth btw Houston/Bleecker |
| Constanca Basto | 573 Hudson btw West 11th/Bank |
| | |
| Crunch | 404 Lafayette btw Astor Place/East 4th |
| Crunch | 152 Christopher at Greenwich |
| Crunch | 623 Broadway at Houston |
| Darling | 1 Horatio at Eighth |
| | |
| Decollage | 23 Eighth btw 12th/Jane |
| Diane von Furstenberg The Shop | 385 West 12th btw Washington/West Side Highway |
| Diesel | 1 Union Square West at 14th |
| Eye Candy | 329 Lafayette btw Bleecker/Houston |
| Flight 001 | 96 Greenwich btw West 12th/Jane |
| Foot Locker | 734 Broadway at 8th |
| French Connection | 700 Broadway btw Astor Place/4th |
| | |
| Gap Kids & Baby Gap | 354 Sixth at Washington Place |
| Geminola | 41 Perry btw Seventh Ave South/West 4th |
| Gerry's | 353 Bleecker btw West 10th/Charles |
| Ghost | 28 Bond btw Lafayette/Bowery |
| | |
| Handmade NYC | 150 West 10th btw Greenwich/Seventh |
| Joyce Leslie | 20 University Place at Eighth |
| Jungle Planet | 175 West 4th btw Sixth/Seventh |
| KD Dance | 339 Lafayette at Bleecker |
| | |
| Kmart | 770 Broadway at Astor Place |
| Laina Jane Lingerie | 45 Christopher btw Waverly Place/Seventh |

*Neighborhoods*

317

La Petite Coquette    51 University Place btw Ninth/Tenth
The Leather Man    111 Christopher btw Bleecker/Hudson
Le Chateau   704 Broadway btw Washington Place/West 4th
Lucien Pellat-Finet    14 Christopher btw Sixth/Seventh

Lucy Barnes    117 Perry btw Hudson/Greenwich
Luichiny    21 West 8th btw Fifth/Sixth
Lulu Guinness    394 Bleecker btw 11th/Perry
Magic Shoes    178 Bleecker btw MacDougal/Sullivan

Make 10    49 West 8th btw Fifth/Sixth
Marc Jacobs    403 Bleecker btw West 11th/Hudson
Marc Jacobs (accessories)    385 Bleecker
btw West 11th/Perry

Memes    3 Great Jones btw Lafayette/Broadway
Milena Shoes    23 West 8th btw Fifth/Sixth
Nalu NYC    10 Little West 12th btw Seventh/Washington
Nom De Guerre    640 Broadway at Bleecker

Olive & Bette's    384 Bleecker at Perry
Otte    121 Greenwich at 13th
The Otter    361 Bleecker btw Charles/West 10th
Patch NYC    17 Eighth btw 12th/Jane

Peanutbutter & Jane    617 Hudson btw Jane/12th
Petit Peton    27 West 8th btw Fifth/Sixth
Plenda    543 Hudson btw Perry/Charles
Polo Ralph Lauren    381 Bleecker btw Perry/Charles

Purdy Girl    220 Thompson btw Bleecker/West 3rd
Purdy Girl    540 LaGuardia Pl at Bleecker
Rafé New York    1 Bleecker at Bowery
Rags A Go Go    218 West 14th btw Seventh/Eighth

Ricky's    718 Broadway btw Astor Place/4th
Ricky's    44 East Eighth at Greene
Scoop    873 Washington at 14th
Screaming Mimi's    382 Lafayette btw Great Jones/4th

Sisley    753 Broadway at 8th
Strawberry    38 East 14th btw University Place/Broadway
Tibet Arts & Crafts    197 Bleecker btw MacDougal/Sixth
Transit    665 Broadway at Bond

Untitled    26 West 8th btw Fifth/Sixth
Urban Outfitters    374 6th btw Waverly/Washington Place
Urban Outfitters    628 Broadway btw Houston/Bleecker
Verve Shoes    105 Christopher btw Bleecker/Hudson

Viv Pickle    238 West 10th btw Bleecker/Hudson
Wet Seal    670 Broadway at Bond
Whiskey Dust    526 Hudson btw 10th/Charles
Yoya    636 Hudson at Horatio

## SoHo/Nolita    *See map pages 296–297*

37=1    37 Crosby btw Broome/Grand
30 Vandam    30 Vandam btw Sixth/Varick
Active Wearhouse    580 Broadway btw Broome/Spring
Add accessories   461 West Broadway btw Houston/Prince

| | |
|---|---|
| A Atelier | 125 Crosby at Prince |
| A Détacher | 262 Mott btw Houston/Prince |
| Adidas | 136 Wooster btw Houston/Prince |
| agnès b. | 103 Greene btw Prince/Spring |
| agnès b. homme | 79 Greene btw Spring/Broome |
| Alex | 268 Elizabeth btw Houston/Prince |
| Alpana Bawa | 41 Grand btw West Broadway/Thompson |
| Amy Chan | 247 Mulberry btw Prince/Spring |
| Anna Sui | 113 Greene btw Prince/Spring |
| Anne Fontaine | 93 Greene btw Prince/Spring |
| Anne Klein | 417 West Broadway btw Prince/Spring |
| Anthropologie | 375 West Broadway btw Spring/Broome |
| A.P.C. | 131 Mercer btw Prince/Spring |
| Arden B | 532 Broadway btw Prince/Spring |
| Art Fiend Foundation | 123 Ludlow btw Rivington/Delancey |
| Ash Francomb | 35 Crosby btw Grand/Broome |
| Avirex | 652 Broadway btw Bleecker/Bond |
| A/X Armani Exchange | 568 Broadway at Prince |
| Bagutta Life | 76 Greene btw Broome/Spring |
| Banana Republic (men) | 528 Broadway at Spring |
| Banana Republic (women) | 550 Broadway btw Prince/Spring |
| Barbara Bui | 117 Wooster btw Prince/Spring |
| Barneys Co-op | 116 Wooster btw Prince/Spring |
| Barry Kieselstein Cord | 454 West Broadway btw Houston/Prince |
| BBL (Baby Blue Line) | 238 Mott btw Prince/Spring |
| Benetton | 555 Broadway btw Prince/Spring |
| Betsey Johnson | 138 Wooster btw Houston/Prince |
| Big Drop | 174 Spring btw Thompson/West Broadway |
| Big Drop | 425 West Broadway btw Prince/Spring |
| Bio | 29 Prince btw Elizabeth/Mott |
| Bisou-Bisou | 474 West Broadway btw Houston/Prince |
| Bloomingdale's SoHo | 504 Broadway btw Spring/Broome |
| Blue Bag | 266 Elizabeth btw Houston/Prince |
| Bodyhints | 462 West Broadway btw Prince/Houston |
| Brooklyn Industries | 286 Lafayette btw Prince/Houston |
| Buffalo Chips USA | 355 West Broadway btw Broome/Grand |
| Built by Wendy | 7 Center Market Place btw Broome/Grand |
| Cadeau | 254 Elizabeth btw Houston/Prince |
| Calvin Klein Underwear | 104 Prince btw Greene/Mercer |
| Calypso Bijoux | 252 Mott btw Houston/Prince |
| Calypso | 280 Mott btw Houston/Prince |
| Calypso | 424 Broome btw Crosby/Lafayette |
| Calypso Enfant | 426 Broome btw Crosby/Lafayette |
| Calypso Homme | 405 Broome btw Centre/Lafayette |
| Cat Girl | 167 Elizabeth btw Spring/Kenmare |
| Catherine Malandrino | 468 Broome at Greene |
| Cath Kidston | 201 Mulberry btw Spring/Kenmare |
| Chanel | 139 Spring at Wooster |

Neighborhoods

| | |
|---|---|
| Chelsea Girl | 63 Thompson btw Spring/Broome |
| Christopher Totman | 262 Mott btw Houston/Prince |
| Club Monaco | 121 Prince btw Wooster/Greene |
| Club Monaco | 520 Broadway btw Spring/Broome |
| Coach | 143 Prince at West Broadway |
| C.P.Shades | 154 Spring btw Wooster/West Broadway |
| C.Ronson | 269 Elizabeth btw Houston/Prince |
| Cynthia Rowley | 112 Wooster btw Prince/Spring |
| D&G | 434 West Broadway btw Prince/Spring |
| Deco Jewels | 131 Thompson btw Houston/Prince |
| Design in Textiles by Mary Jaeger | 51 Spring btw Lafayette/Mulberry |
| Detour | 472 West Broadway btw Houston/Prince |
| Detour | 154 Prince btw West Broadway/Thompson |
| Detour | 425 West Broadway btw Prince/Spring |
| Dinosaur Designs | 250 Mott btw Houston/Prince |
| DKNY | 420 West Broadway btw Prince/Spring |
| Dosa | 107 Thompson btw Prince/Spring |
| Dusica Dusica | 4 Prince btw Bowery/Elizabeth |
| Earl Jean | 160 Mercer btw Houston/Prince |
| Eastern Mountain Sports | 591 Broadway btw Houston/Prince |
| Eddie Bauer | 578 Broadway btw Houston/Prince |
| Edmundo Castillo | 219 Mott btw Prince/Spring |
| Eleni Lambros | 591 Broadway btw Houston/Prince |
| Elie Tahari | 417 West Broadway btw Prince/Spring |
| Emporio Armani | 410 West Broadway btw Prince/Spring |
| Eres | 98 Wooster at Spring |
| Flying A | 169 Spring btw West Broadway/Thompson |
| Fossil | 541 Broadway btw Prince/Spring |
| Francis Hendy | 65 Thompson btw Spring/Broome |
| French Connection | 435 West Broadway at Prince |
| Gas Bijoux | 238 Mott btw Prince/Spring |
| Geraldine | 246 Mott btw Houston/Prince |
| Gi Gi | 217 Mulberry btw Prince/Spring |
| Girlprops.com | 153 Prince at West Broadway |
| Guess? | 537 Broadway btw Prince/Spring |
| H&M | 588 Broadway btw Prince/Spring |
| Hans Koch | 174 Prince btw Sullivan/Thompson |
| The Hat Shop | 120 Thompson btw Prince/Spring |
| Helen Mariën | 250 Mott btw Houston/Prince |
| Helmut Lang | 80 Greene btw Spring/Broome |
| Henry Lehr | 232 Elizabeth btw Prince/Lafayette |
| Henry Lehr | 268 Elizabeth btw Houston/Prince |
| Hiponica | 238 Mott btw Prince/Spring |
| Hogan | 134 Spring btw Greene/Wooster |
| Hollywould | 198 Elizabeth btw Prince/Spring |
| Hotel Venus | 382 West Broadway btw Spring/Broome |
| Hugo Boss | 132 Greene btw Houston/Prince |
| Hunting World | 118 Greene btw Prince/Spring |
| If | 94 Grand btw Mercer/Greene |

| | |
|---|---|
| Il Bisonte | 120 Sullivan btw Prince/Spring |
| Ina | 101 Thompson btw Prince/Spring |
| Institut | 97 Spring btw Mercer/Broadway |
| Jack Gomme | 252 Elizabeth btw Houston/Prince |
| Janet Russo | 262 Mott btw Houston/Prince |
| J.Crew | 99 Prince at Mercer |
| Jenne Maag | 29 Spring at Mott |
| Jill Stuart | 100 Greene btw Prince/Spring |
| J.Lindeberg | 126 Spring at Greene |
| John Fluevog Shoes | 250 Mulberry at Prince |
| Jonathan Adler | 130 West 57th btw Sixth/Seventh |
| Joovay | 436 West Broadway at Prince |
| Joseph | 106 Greene btw Prince/Spring |
| Julian & Sara | 103 Mercer btw Prince/Spring |
| Juno | 543 Broadway btw Prince/Spring |
| Just for Tykes | 83 Mercer btw Spring/Broome |
| Karikter | 19 Prince btw Elizabeth/Bowery |
| Kate Spade | 454 Broome at Mercer |
| Kate Spade (travel store) | 59 Thompson btw Spring/Broome |
| Kazuyo Nakano | 117 Crosby btw Houston/Prince |
| Keiko | 62 Greene btw Spring/Broome |
| Kelly Christy | 235 Elizabeth btw Houston/Prince |
| Kenneth Cole | 597 Broadway btw Houston/Prince |
| Kid Robot | 126 Prince btw Greene/Wooster |
| Kinnu | 43 Spring btw Mulberry/Mott |
| Kirna Zabête | 96 Greene btw Prince/Spring |
| Klurk | 360 Broome btw Mott/Elizabeth |
| Label | 265 Lafayette btw Houston/Prince |
| Laila Rowe | 424 West Broadway btw Prince/Spring |
| La Perla | 93 Greene btw Prince/Spring |
| Laundry by Shelli Segal | 97 Wooster btw Prince/Spring |
| Le Corset | 80 Thompson btw Spring/Broome |
| Legacy | 109 Thompson btw Prince/Spring |
| Les Petits Chapelais | 142 Sullivan btw Houston/Prince |
| LeSportSac | 176 Spring btw West Broadway/Thompson |
| Lilliput/SoHo Kids | 265 Lafayette btw Prince/Spring |
| Lilliput/SoHo Kids | 240 Lafayette btw Prince/Spring |
| Liora Manné | 91 Grand btw Mercer/Greene |
| Lisa Shaub | 232 Mulberry btw Prince/Spring |
| Living Doll | 280 Lafayette btw Houston/Prince |
| Louis Vuitton | 116 Greene btw Prince/Spring |
| The Lounge | 593 Broadway btw Prince/Houston |
| Lucky Brand Jeans | 38 Greene at Grand |
| Lunettes et Chocolat | 25 Prince btw Mott/Elizabeth |
| Lynn Park NY | 51 Wooster at Broome |
| Makie | 109 Thompson btw Prince/Spring |
| Malatesta | 115 Grand btw Broadway/Mercer |
| Malia Mills | 199 Mulberry btw Spring/Kenmare |
| Malo | 125 Wooster btw Prince/Spring |
| Manhattan Portage | 301 West Broadway btw Canal/Grand |

Neighborhoods

321

| | |
|---|---|
| Mankind | 8 Greene btw Grand/Canal |
| Marc Jacobs | 163 Mercer btw Houston/Prince |
| Mare | 426 West Broadway btw Prince/Spring |
| Marianne Novobatzky | 65 Mercer btw Spring/Broome |
| Marni | 161 Mercer btw Houston/Prince |
| Mary Efron | 68 Thompson btw Spring/Broome |
| Mat Mercer | 49 Mercer btw Grand/Broome |
| Mavi | 510 Broome btw Thompson/West Broadway |
| MaxMara | 450 West Broadway btw Prince/Houston |
| Max Studio | 415 West Broadway btw Prince/Spring |
| Mayle | 242 Elizabeth btw Prince/Houston |
| Me & Ro | 241 Elizabeth btw Houston/Prince |
| Michael K | 512 Broadway btw Spring/Broome |
| Miss Sixty | 246 Mulberry btw Prince/Spring |
| Miss Sixty | 386 West Broadway btw Spring/Broome |
| Miu Miu | 100 Prince btw Greene/Mercer |
| Mixona | 262 Mott btw Houston/Prince |
| Morgane Le Fay | 67 Wooster btw Spring/Broome |
| MZ Wallace | 93 Crosby btw Prince/Spring |
| Nahbee | 262 Mott btw Houston/Prince |
| Nancy Geist | 107 Spring at Mercer |
| Nanette Lepore | 423 Broome btw Lafayette/Crosby |
| New & Almost New | 65 Mercer btw Spring/Kenmare |
| New York 911 | 263 Lafayette btw Prince/Spring |
| Nicole Miller | 134 Prince btw Wooster/West Broadway |
| Nine West | 577 Broadway at Prince |
| Objets du Desir | 241 Mulberry btw Prince/Spring |
| Old Navy Clothing Co | 503 Broadway btw Spring/Broome |
| Olive & Bette's | 158 Spring btw Wooster/West Broadway |
| Omari | 68 Spring btw Crosby/Lafayette |
| Only Hearts | 230 Mott btw Prince/Spring |
| Onward Soho | 172 Mercer at Houston |
| Opening Ceremony | 35 Howard btw Broadway/Lafayette |
| The Original Levi's Store | 536 Broadway btw Prince/Spring |
| Ottiva | 192 Spring btw Thompson/Sullivan |
| Otto Tootsi Plohound | 413 West Broadway btw Prince/Spring |
| Otto Tootsi Plohound | 273 Lafayette btw Houston/Prince |
| Patagonia | 101 Wooster btw Prince/Spring |
| Patina | 451 Broome btw Broadway/Mercer |
| Pearl River Mart | 477 Broadway btw Broome/Grand |
| Peter Fox Shoes | 105 Thompson btw Prince/Spring |
| Peter Hermann | 118 Thompson btw Prince/Spring |
| Phat Farm | 129 Prince btw West Broadway/Wooster |
| Philosophy di Alberta Ferretti | 452 West Broadway btw Houston/Prince |
| Pipsqueak | 248 Mott btw Houston/Prince |
| Pleats Please, Issey Miyake | 128 Wooster at Prince |
| Plein Sud | 70 Greene btw Spring/Broome |
| Poppy W | 281 Mott btw Houston/Prince |

| | |
|---|---|
| Push | 240 Mulberry btw Prince/Spring |
| Prada | 575 Broadway at Prince |
| The Puma Store | 521 Broadway btw Spring/Broome |
| Pumpkin Maternity | 407 Broome btw Lafayette/Centre |
| | |
| Quiksilver | 109 Spring btw Mercer/Greene |
| Rachel Ashwell Shabby Chic | 83 Wooster btw Broome/Spring |
| Ralph Lauren | 381 West Broadway btw Broome/Spring |
| | |
| Rampage | 127 Prince at Wooster |
| R by 45rpm | 169 Mercer at Houston |
| Rebecca Norman | 35 Crosby btw Broome/Grand |
| Rebecca Taylor | 260 Mott btw Houston/Prince |
| | |
| Red Wong | 181 Mulberry btw Kenmare/Broome |
| Replay Store | 109 Prince at Greene |
| Resurrection Vintage | 217 Mott btw Prince/Spring |
| Ricky's | 590 Broadway btw Houston/Prince |
| | |
| Rugby North America | 115 Mercer btw Prince/Spring |
| Sac Boutique | 115 Grand btw Mercer/Broadway |
| Sacco | 111 Thompson btw Prince/Spring |
| Saigoniste | 239 Mulberry btw Prince/Spring |
| | |
| Salvatore Ferragamo | 124 Spring at Greene |
| Sample | 268 Elizabeth btw Houston/Prince |
| Scoop | 532 Broadway btw Prince/Spring |
| Sean | 132 Thompson btw Houston/Prince |
| | |
| Seize sur Vingt | 243 Elizabeth btw Houston/Prince |
| Selvedge | 250 Mulberry btw Prince/Spring |
| Sharagano | 529 Broadway btw Prince/Spring |
| Shin Choi | 119 Mercer btw Prince/Spring |
| | |
| Shoe | 197 Mulberry btw Spring/Kenmare |
| Sigerson Morrison | 242 Mott btw Houston/Prince |
| Sigerson Morrison | 28 Prince btw Mott/Elizabeth |
| Silverado | 542 Broadway btw Prince/Spring |
| | |
| Skechers | 530 Broadway at Spring |
| Smaak | 219 Mulberry btw Prince/Spring |
| SoHo Baby | 247 Elizabeth btw Houston/Prince |
| Sol | 6 Prince btw Bowery/Elizabeth |
| | |
| Stackhouse | 276 Lafayette btw Houston/Prince |
| Stephane Kélian | 158 Mercer btw Houston/Prince |
| Steve Madden | 540 Broadway btw Prince/Spring |
| Steven | 529 Broadway btw Prince/Spring |
| | |
| Steven Alan | 60 Wooster btw Spring/Broome |
| Stüssy | 140 Wooster btw Houston/Prince |
| Supreme | 274 Lafayette btw Houston/Prince |
| Swiss Army | 136 Prince btw West Broadway/Wooster |
| | |
| Ted Baker London | 107 Grand btw Mercer/Broadway |
| Temperley | 453-455 Broome at Mercer |
| Tina Tang | 230 Mulberry btw Prince/Spring |
| | |
| Togs | 68 Spring btw Crosby/Lafayette |
| Tommy Hilfiger | 372 West Broadway btw Spring/Broome |
| Tory by TRB | 257 Elizabeth btw Houston/Prince |

Neighborhoods

| | |
|---|---|
| Tracy Feith | 209 Mulberry btw Spring/Kenmare |
| Triple Five Soul | 290 Lafayette btw Houston/Prince |
| Union | 172 Spring btw West Broadway/Thompson |
| Unis | 226 Elizabeth btw Houston/Prince |
| United Nude Terra Plana | 260 Elizabeth btw Houston/Prince |
| Utility Canvas | 146 Sullivan btw Houston/Prince |
| Varda | 147 Spring btw Wooster/West Broadway |
| Vice | 252 Lafayette btw Prince/Spring |
| Victoria Keen | 357 Lafayette btw Bond/Bleecker |
| Victoria's Secret | 565 Broadway at Prince |
| Vitraux | 72 Thompson btw Spring/Broome |
| Vivienne Tam | 99 Greene btw Prince/Spring |
| Warehouse | 581 Broadway btw Houston/Prince |
| Western Spirit | 486 Broadway at Broome |
| Wet Seal | 65 East 8th btw Broadway/Mercer |
| What Comes Around Goes Around | 351 West Broadway btw Broome/Grand |
| Wolford Boutique | 122 Greene at Prince |
| Work in Progress | 513 Broadway btw Broome/Spring |
| X Girl | 265 Lafayette btw Prince/Spring |
| Y & Kei water the earth | 125 Greene btw Prince/Spring |
| Yaso | 62 Grand btw West Broadway/Wooster |
| Yellow Rat Bastard | 478 Broadway btw Broome/Grand |
| Yohji Yamamoto | 103 Grand at Mercer |
| Yvone Christa | 107 Mercer btw Prince/Spring |
| Zabari | 506 Broadway btw Spring/Broome |
| Zara International | 580 Broadway at Prince |
| Zero/Maria Cornejo | 225 Mott btw Prince/Spring |
| Zion | 93 Grand btw Greene/Mercer |

## Lower Manhattan/Tribeca  *See map pages 298–299*

| | |
|---|---|
| Abercrombie & Fitch | 119 Water at S.S.S. |
| Aerosoles | 18 John btw Broadway/Nassau |
| Assets London | 152 Franklin btw Hudson/Varick |
| Banana Republic | 200 Vesley at the World Financial Center |
| Benetton | 10 Fulton at S.S.S. |
| Century 21 | 22 Cortland btw Church/Broadway |
| Champs | 89 South at S.S.S. |
| Foot Locker | 89 South at S.S.S. |
| Gap Kids & Baby Gap | 11 Fulton at S.S.S. |
| Garde Robe | 137 Duane btw West Broadway/Trimble Place |
| Guess? | 23-25 Fulton at S.S.S. |
| Issey Miyake | 119 Hudson at North Moore |
| J.Crew | 203 Front at S.S.S. |
| Koh's Kids | 311 Greenwich btw Chambers/Reade |
| Loftworks@Lafayette | 100 Lafayette btw White/Walker |
| Men's Wearhouse | 115 Broadway at Cedar |
| Metro Bicycle | 417 Canal at Sixth |
| Miao | 176 Hester btw Mott/Mulberry |

| | |
|---|---|
| Mika Inatome | 11 Worth btw West Broadway/Hudson |
| Modell's | 200 Broadway btw Fulton/John |
| Modell's | 55 Chambers at Broadway |
| Montmartre | at the World Financial Center |
| Nikki B | 20 Harrison btw Greenwich/Hudson |
| Samuel's Hats | 74 Nassau btw Fulton/John |
| Shack Inc | 137 West Broadway btw Thomas/Duane |
| Shoofly | 42 Hudson btw Duane/Thomas |
| Sorelle Firenze | 139½ Reade btw Hudson/Greenwich |
| Steven Alan | 103 Franklin btw West Broadway/Church |
| Talbots | 189-191 Front at S.S.S. |
| Tribeca Luggage & Leather | 90 Hudson at Harrison |
| Victoria's Secret | 19 Fulton at S.S.S. |
| Young's Hat Corner | 139 Nassau at Beekman |

## Harlem
*See map pages 290–291*

| | |
|---|---|
| Aerosoles | 2913 Broadway btw 113/114th |
| Champs | 208 West 125th at Seventh |
| The Children's Place | 428 West 125th btw Seventh/Eighth |
| Cole Hann | 208 West 125th at Seventh |
| H&M | 125 West 125th at Lenox |
| Lane Bryant | 222 West 125th btw Seventh/Eighth |
| Modell's | 300 West 125th btw Frederick Douglass Blvd/ St Nicholas Blvd |

## Brooklyn

| | |
|---|---|
| Amarcord Vintage Fashion | 223 Bedford Ave btw North 4th/North 5th |
| B2Gear | 777 Fulton btw South Oxford/South Portland |
| Baby Bird | 428 7th Ave btw 14/15th |
| Beacon's Closet | 220 5th Ave btw President/Union |
| Beacon's Closet | 88 North 11th btw Berry/Wythe |
| Brooklyn Industries | 152 5th Ave btw Lincoln/St John |
| Brooklyn Industries | 162 Bedford Ave at North 8th St |
| Castor & Pollux | 67½ 6th Ave at Bergen |
| Diana Kane | 229b 5th Ave btw Carroll/President |
| Domseys | 1609 Palmetto btw Wycoff/Myrtle |
| Domseys | 431 Broadway at Hewes |
| Domseys | 90 Smith at King |
| Flirt | 252 Smith btw Douglas/DeGraw |
| Frida's Closet | 296 Smith btw Union/Sackett |
| Gureje | 886 Pacific at Washington |
| Hootie Couture | 321 Flatbush Ave at 7th |
| Hot Toddie | 741 Fulton btw South Portland/South Elliot |
| Isa | 88 North 6th at Wythe |
| Kleinfeld | 8202 5th Ave at 82nd |
| Lily | 209 Court btw Warren/Wyckoff |
| Moshood | 698 Fulton btw South Oxford/South Portland |
| Neda | 413a 7th Ave btw 13/14th |

| | |
|---|---|
| Otte | 132 North 5th at Bedford Ave |
| Pieces | 671 Vanderbilt Ave at Park Place |
| Premium Goods | 694 Fulton at South Portland |
| Redberi | 339 Flatbush Ave btw Park/Prospect |
| Slang Betty | 172 5th Ave btw Lincoln/Berkeley |
| Soda Fine | 246 DeKalb Ave btw Clermont/Vanderbilt |
| Somethin' Else | 294 5th Ave btw 1/2nd |
| Watts | 248 Smith btw Douglass/Degraw |

## Queens

| | |
|---|---|
| Samurai | 31-08 Steinway at 31st Ave |

# Stores by Category

## Women's Accessories

AB Apollo Braun
Add Accessories
Alexandre de Paris
Alexia Crawford Accessories

Amy Chan
Annika Inez
Anthropologie
Azaleas

Barneys New York
Barry Kieselstein Cord
Bergdorf Goodman
Bess

Blair Delmonico
Bloomingdale's
Borealis
Boucher Jewelry

Boyd's Pharmacy
Calypso St Barths
Castor & Pollux
Cat Girl

Catherine
Chanel
Che Che
Decollage

Destination
Dinosaur Designs
Doo.ri
Doyle & Doyle

Dressing Room
En Soie
Eye Candy
Fabulous Fanny's

Flight 001
Gamine
Gas
Girlprops.com

The Good, The Bad
  & The Ugly
Handmade NYC

Helen Mariën
Henri Bendel
Hermès

Hiponica
Hollywould
Kors Michael Kors

LaCrasia Gloves
Laila Rowe
Lingo
Lord & Taylor

Love Shine
Lunettes et Chocolat
Lynn Park
Macy's

Marc Jacobs
Max Studio
Me & Ro
Miao

Miss Sixty
Mod World
Objets du Desir
Orva

Pat Areias
Patch NYC
Peacock
Pearl Daddy

Pearl River
Precision
The Puma Store
Purdy Girl

Push
Rampage
Reminiscence
Roslyn

Saigoniste
Sari-Sari Store
Scarpe Diem
Selima Optique

Slang Betty
Soda Fine
Sonia Rykiel
Steven Vaughan

Tommy Hilfiger
Toto
Variazioni

VBH Gallery
Verve
Vitraux

XGirl
Yvone Christa
Zitomer

## Women's Ballet, Dance & Work-Out

Adidas
Athlete's Foot
Bloch
Capezio

Champs
Crunch
Daffy's

Danskin
KD Dance
Kmart
Lady Foot Locker

New York Om Yoga
Niketown
The Puma Store

## Bridal

Amsale
Angelo Lambrou
Barneys New York
Bergdorf Goodman

Blair Delmonico
Blue
Bridal Atelier
Carolina Herrera

Clea Colet
Cose Belle
Couture by Jennifer Dule
Eleni Lambros

Escada
February Eleventh
The Gown Company
Jimmy Choo (shoes only)

Kenneth Cole (shoes only)
Kleinfeld
Lucy Barnes
Manolo Blahnik (shoes only)

Mary Adams
Michael's, The Consignment
  Shop for Women

Michelle Roth & Co
Mika Inatome
Morgane Le Fay
Nicole Miller

Norma Kamali
Peter Fox (shoes only)
Pierre Garroudi
Pilar Rossi

Reem Acra
Reva Mivasagar
Robert Danes
Saks Fifth Avenue

Selia Yang
Skella
Stuart Weitzman (shoes only)
Thread (bridesmaids only)

Vanessa Noel (shoes only)
Vera Wang
Vera Wang Maids on
  Madison

Yumi Katsura
Zora

## Women's Cashmere / Knitwear

Anik
Ballantyne Cashmere
Banana Republic
Bergdorf Goodman

Berk
Best of Scotland
Blair Delmonico
Bloomingdale's

Calypso St Barth's
Camouflage
Cashmere New York
Dosa

Hello Sari
J.Crew
Klein's

Laura Biagiotti
Loro Piana
Lucien Pellat-Finet
Malo

Manrico Cascimir
N.Peal
Ralph Lauren
Saks Fifth Avenue

Sample
Seize sur Vingt
Temperley
Theory

Tibet Bazaar
Tse
Vera Wang

Categories

## Women's Career

| | |
|---|---|
| A.Cheng | Giselle |
| Anik | J.Crew |
| Anne Klein | J.McLaughlin |
| Ann Taylor | Lord & Taylor |
| Barami | Montmartre |
| Barneys New York | The New York Look |
| Benetton | Onward Soho |
| Bergdorf Goodman | Paul Stuart |
| Bloomingdale's | Runway |
| Brooks Brothers | Saks Fifth Avenue |
| Burlington Coat Factory | St.John |
| Club Monaco | Talbots |
| Dana Buchman | Tristan & America |
| Darryl's | Vertigo |
| Express | Zan |
| Filene's Basement | Zara International |

## Women's Casual

| | |
|---|---|
| Abercrombie & Fitch | Granny-Made |
| Active Wearhouse | Guess? |
| Adidas | Henry Lehr |
| Alex | J.Crew |
| American Apparel | Lacoste |
| American Colors | Leggiadro |
| American Eagle Outfitters | Lord & Taylor |
| Ann Taylor Loft | Lucky Brand Dungarees |
| Anthropologie | Macy's |
| April Cornell | Nautica |
| A/X Armani Exchange | Nicole Miller |
| Banana Republic | Old Navy Clothing Co |
| Barneys New York | The Original Levi's Store |
| Basic Basic | Otte |
| Benetton | A Perfect Day in Paradise |
| Bloomingdale's | Petit Bateau |
| Bloomingdale's SoHo | Phat Farm |
| Brooklyn Industries | The Puma Store |
| C.J.Laing | Quiksilver |
| Diesel | Replay Store |
| Eddie Bauer | Rugby North America |
| Express | Saks Fifth Avenue |
| Forreal Basics | Talbot's |
| Fossil | Tommy Hilfiger |
| Gap | Utility Canvas |

## Women's Classic

Arleen Bowman
Beretta
Borrelli
Bottega Veneta

Brioni
Burberry
Cose Belle
Davide Cenci

Entre Nous
Etro
Geiger
Hermès

Holland & Holland
Hunting World
Jane
Jil Sander

J.McLaughlin
Klein's
Loro Piana
Luca Luca

Noriko Maeda
Paul & Shark
Peter Elliot Women
Ralph Lauren

Saks Fifth Avenue
San Francisco Clothing
Shen
Steven Stolman

St John
Sylvia Heisel
Ventilo

## Women's Consignment

Alice Underground
Allan & Suzi
Bis Designer Resale
Encore

Fisch for the Hip
Ina
Kavanagh's Designer
  Resale

Michael's, The Consignment
  Shop for Women
New & Almost New
  (NAAN)

Project
Tehen (jewelry only)
Tokio 7
Tokyo Joe

Categories

## Women's Contemporary

AB Apollo Braun
ABH Design
A.Cheng
A Détacher

agnès b.
Alpana Bawa
Alskling
American Apparel

Amy Chan
Anastasia Holland
Anik
Anna

Anthropologie
The Apartment
A.P.C.
Arden B

Assets London
Atrium
BBL (Baby Blue Line)
Bagutta

Barneys New York
Basiques
BCBG by Max Azria
Bebe

Believe It
Bergdorf Goodman
Berkley Girl
Betsey Bunky Nini

Big Drop
Bisou Bisou
Bloomingdale's
Bond 07

Boudoir
Brooklyn Industries
Calypso St. Barths
Cantaloup

Carlos Miele
Catherine Malandrino
Christopher Totman
Club Monaco

C.P.Shades
CPW
C.Ronson
Crush

Darling
Darryl's
Decollage
Detour

Diana & Jeffries
Diesel Style Lab
DKNY
D/L Cerney

Doo.ri
Dosa
Dressing Room
Eileen Fisher

Emporio Armani
Epperson Studio
Erica Tanov
Fame

February Eleventh
Find Outlet
Fiona Walker
Flirt

Foley & Corinna
Forreal
French Connection
Galo

Gamine
Ghost
Gi Gi
Henri Bendel

Hiponica
H&M
Hugo Boss
Huminska New York

If
Institut
Intermix
Jeffrey New York

Jenne Maag
J.Lindeberg
Jill Anderson
Johnson

Joseph
Kirna Zabête
Label
La La

Language
Laundry by Shelli Segal
Le Chateau
Liana

Lily
Linda Dresner
Loftworks @ Lafayette
Lucy Barnes

Lynn Park NY
Magry Knits
Mark Montano
Marni

Martier
Martin
Max Studio
Mayle

Meg
Miks
Min-K
Min Lee

Miracle
Missbehave
Miss Sixty
MoMo FaLana

Montmartre
Mshop
Nalu NYC
Nancy & Co

Nanette Lepore
Nellie M
No. 436
Oilily for Women

Olive & Bette's
Onward Soho
The Open Door Gallery
Opening Ceremony

The Original Levi's Store
Otte
The Otter
Outlet 7

Parke & Ronen
Peacock NYC
Pleats Please, Issey Miyake
Plein Sud

Pookie & Sebastian
Precision
Purdy Girl
Quiksilver

Rampage
Really Great Things
Recon
Redberri

Red Wong
Roberta Freymann
Robert Danes
Runway

Saada
Sac Boutique
Saks Fifth Avenue
Scoop

Searle
Selia Yang
Shack Inc
Shanghai Tang

Sharagano
Shin Choi
Shop
Sisley

Skella
Smaak
Sorelle Firenze
Steven Alan

Strawberry
Tees.com
Tehen
TG-170

Theory
Togs
Tracy Feith
Trash & Vaudeville

Untitled
Variazioni
Vertigo
Vice

Vlada
Warehouse
Xgirl
Yaso

Yellow Rat Bastard
Yigal Azrouel
Zabari
Zan

Zara International
Zero/Maria Cornejo
Zora

Categories

## Women's Custom Tailoring

A Perfect Day in Paradise
Arthur Gluck Shirtmakers
Couture by Jennifer Dule
Domenico Spana

Domenico Vacca
Frank Shattuck
Frida's Closet
John Anthony

Jussara Lee
Keiko (swimwear)
The Leather & Suede
  Workshop

Lee Anderson
Lucy Barnes
Maggie Norris

Mary Adams
Meg

Mika Inatome (bridal)
Miracle
Mom's Night Out/One
  Night Out

New York City Custom
  Leather
Piccione
Pierre Garroudi

Pilar Rossi
Reva Mivasagar
Ripplu (undergarments)
Seize sur Vingt

Silverado
Skella
Sylvia Heisel

Thread
Vincent Nicolosi

## Women's Discount

Bolton's
Burlington Coat Factory
Century 21

Daffy's
Filene's Basement
Find Outlet

Forman's
Gabay's Outlet
Loehmann's

Loftworks @ Lafayette
Samurai
TJ Maxx

## Women's Ethnic

Bokhee
Christopher Totman
Craft Caravan
Do Kham

Frida's Closet
Gureje
Hello Sari
Himalayan Crafts

Jungle Planet
Kenzo
Kinnu

Love Shine
Moshood
Malatesta
Neda

Pan American Phoenix
Pearl River Mart
Roberta Freymann
Tibet Arts & Crafts

Tibet Bazaar
Toto

## Women's Designer

Alexander McQueen
Anna Sui
Anne Klein
Balenciaga

Barbara Bui
Betsey Johnson
Blair Delmonico
Calvin Klein

Carolina Herrera
Catherine Malandrino
Celine
Chanel

Chloé
Christian Dior
Comme des Garçons
Costume National

Cynthia Rowley
D&G
Diane von Furstenberg
Dolce & Gabbana

Donna Karan New York
Eleni Lambros
Elie Tahari
Emanuel Ungaro

Escada
Fendi
Francis Hendy
Geoffrey Beene

Gianfranco Ferré
Giorgio Armani
Givenchy
Gucci

Helmut Lang
Hervé Léger
Hugo Boss
Issey Miyake

Jean Paul Gaultier
Jill Stuart
Kenzo
Kors Michael Kors

Krizia
Laura Biagiotti
Les Copains
Louis Féraud

Louis Vuitton
Lucien Pellat-Finet
Lucy Barnes
Maggie Norris Couture

Marc Jacobs
MaxMara
Michael Kors
Missoni

Miu Miu
Morgane Le Fay
Moschino
Net-a-Porter

Nicole Farhi
Nicole Miller
Norma Kamali
Philosophy by Alberta
   Ferretti

Poleci
Prada
Pucci

Ralph Lauren
Roberto Cavalli
Salvatore Ferragamo
Shelly Steffee

Sonia Rykiel
Stella McCartney
Temperley
Tory by TRB

Valentino
Vera Wang
Versace
Vivienne Tam

Y & Kei water the earth
Yohji Yamamoto
Yves Saint Laurent Rive
   Gauche

Categories

335

## Women's Evening & Special Occasion

37=1
Alicia Mugetti
Amsale
Angelo Lambrou

Ann Taylor
A Perfect Day in Paradise
A.Tempo
BBL (Baby Blue Line)

BCBG Max Azria
Betsey Bunky Nini
Betsey Johnson
Bergdorf Goodman

Bloomingdale's
Caché
Calvin Klein
Carolina Herrera

Cashmere New York
Celine
Chanel
Cheap Jack's

Christian Dior
Circle
Clea Colet
Clifford Michael Design

Cose Belle
Costume National
Couture by Jennifer Dule
D&G

Darryl's
DKNY
Donna Karan New York
Eleni Lambros

Emporio Armani
Entre Nous
Escada
Eva

Fendi
Gallery of Wearable Art
Geoffrey Beene
Gianfranco Ferré

Giorgio Armani
Gucci
Hervé Léger
Jane

Janet Russo
Jill Stuart
John Anthony
Jussara Lee

Keni Valenti
Krizia
Lee Anderson
Liana

Linda Dresner
Liz Lange Maternity
Lord & Taylor
Luca Luca

Lucy Barnes
Maggie Norris Couture
Makola
Marianne Novobatzky

Mary Adams
Mary Efron
Max Studio
Michael Kors

Michelle Roth & Co
Mommy Chic
Mom's Night Out/
　One Night Out

Montmartre
Morgane Le Fay
Nellie M.
Net-a-Porter

The New York Look
Nicole Miller
Norma Kamali
Pierre Garroudi

Pilar Rossi
Ralph Lauren
Reva Mivasagar
Richard Metzger

Roberta Freymann
Robert Danes
Roberto Cavalli
Saks Fifth Avenue

San Francisco Clothing
Steven Stolman
St John
Sylvia Heisel

Thread
Untitled
Valentino
Variazioni

Vera Wang Bridal Salon
Versace
Vivaldi Boutique
Yigal Azrouel

## Women's Furriers

Alexandros Furs
Alixandre
Basso Furs
Ben Thylan Furs

Bergdorf Goodman
Bloomingdale's
Christie Brothers Furs
Denimax

Fendi
The Fur Salon
   at Saks Fifth Avenue
Helen Yarmak

J.Mendel
Ritz Furs
Saks Fifth Avenue

## Women's Handbags & Leather Goods

Add Accessories
A Détacher
Alexia Crawford
Amy Chan

Anya Hindmarch
A.Testoni
Baghouse
Barneys New York

Bergdorf Goodman
Bloomingdale's
Blue Bag
Bond 07

Bottega Veneta
Brooklyn Industries
Bruno Magli
Burberry

Calypso St Barths
Castor & Pollux
Cat Girl
Celine

Chanel
Che Che
Christian Dior
Coach

Cole Haan
Crouch & Fitzgerald
Crush
Cynthia Rowley

Davide Cenci
Deco Jewels
Delfino
Denimaxx

Dernier Cri
Destination
Dior

Dolce & Gabbana
Dooney & Bourke
Doo.ri

Dressing Room
Edmundo Castillo
Elaine Arsanault
Eye Candy

Fendi
Fisch for the Hip
Forward
Frida's Closet

Furla
Gabay's Outlet
Gap
Ghurka

Gucci
Guess?
Hans Koch
Helen Mariën

Helen Yarmak
Henri Bendel
Hermès
Hiponica

Hogan
Hollywould
Hunting World
Il Bisonte

Ina
Issey Miyake
Jack Gomme
Jamin Puech

Jonathan Adler
Judith Lieber
Jutta Neumann
Kate Spade

Kazuyo Nakano
Kenneth Cole
Laila Rowe

Lana Marks
Lederer
LeSportSac

## Women's Handbags & Leather Goods *(continued)*

Lingo
Longchamp
Lord & Taylor
Louis Vuitton

Love Shine
Lulu Guinness
Lunettes et Chocolat
Lynn Park

Macy's
Manhattan Portage
Marc Jacobs
Max Studio

Minette by Blue Bag
Miss Sixty
MZ Wallace
Patch NYC

Peacock NYC
Pelle Via Roma
Peter Hermann

Prada
Rafé New York
René Collections
Roberto Vascon

Roslyn
Rugby North America
Saks Fifth Avenue
Salvatore Ferragamo

Scarpe Diem
Scoop
Sigerson Morrison
Suarez

T.Anthony
Tod's
Tribeca Luggage & Leather
Utility Canvas

Verve
Viv Pickle
Yvone Christa

## Women's Hats

Add Accessories
Amy Downs Hats at YU
Barbara Feinman Millinery

Barneys New York
Bergdorf Goodman
Bloomingdale's

Bond 07
Calypso St. Barths
Cheap Jack's

Denimaxx
Destination
Doo.ri

Eugenia Kim
Forward
The Hat Shop

Henri Bendel
Huminska New York

Kelly Christy
Kirna Zabête
Lisa Shaub

Lord & Taylor
Macy's
Magry Knits

Patch NYC
Precision
Rampage

Roslyn
Saks Fifth Avenue
Samuel's Hats

Shoo Fly
Suzanne Couture Millinery
Temperley

Verve
Village Scandal

## Women's Hosiery

Allure Lingerie
Ann Taylor Loft
Assets London
Barneys New York

Bergdorf Goodman
Bloomingdale's
Capezio
Enerla Lingerie

Eres
Fogal
Henri Bendel

Joovay
Laina Jane Lingerie
Legs Beautiful
Lingerie on Lex

Lord & Taylor
Macy's
Orva
Ricky's

Saks Fifth Avenue
Victoria's Secret
Wolford Boutique

## Women's Juniors

Abercrombie & Fitch
American Apparel
American Eagle Outfitters
A.Tempo

B2Gear
Basic Basic
Betwixt
Bloomingdale's

Century 21
Crush
Express
Forreal Basics

Gap
H&M
Infinity
Le Chateau

Lester's
Lord of the Fleas
Luxury Brand Outlet
Macy's

Magic Windows
Marsha D.D.
Miss Sixty
The New York Look

Old Navy Clothing Co
The Original Levi's Store
Orva
Peter Elliot Junior

Quiksilver
Ralph Lauren
Reminiscence
Space Kiddets

Strawberry
Tommy Hilfiger
Wet Seal
X Girl

XLarge
Zabari
Z' Girl

## Women's Leather

Avriex
Behrle
Buffalo Chips USA

Chanel
Chrome Hearts
Clifford Michael Design

Denimaxx
Dior
Fendi
Gucci

Jack Gomme
Kenneth Cole
Leather Corner

The Leather & Suede
  Workshop
Lost Art

New York City Custom
  Leather
Rugby North America
Silverado

## Women's Lingerie & Sleepwear

37=1
Agent Provocateur
Allure Lingerie
Azaleas

Barneys New York
Bergdorf Goodman
Bloomers
Bloomingdale's

Bodyhints
Bolton's
Bonne Nuit
Bra Smyth

Brief Encounters
Darling
Diane Kane
Enerla Lingerie

Eres
Erica Tanov
Fogal
Gap

Henri Bendel
Hotel Venus
J.Crew

Joovay
Joyce Leslie

Laina Jane Lingerie
La Perla
La Petite Coquette
Le Corset

Legs Beautiful
Lingerie on Lex
Lord & Taylor
Macy's

Makie
Martier
Mixona
Motherhood Maternity

Nocturne
Old Navy Clothing Co
Only Hearts
Petit Bateau

Porthault
Purdy Girl
Rachel Ashwell Shabby Chic
Ripplu

Roberto Cavalli
Saks Fifth Avenue
Takashimaya

Victoria's Secret
Wet Seal

## Maternity

A Pea in the Pod
Barneys New York
Burlington Coat Factory
Cadeau

Liz Lange Maternity
Lucy Barnes
Maternity Work

Mimi Maternity
Mommy Chic
Mom's Night Out/One
   Night Out

Motherhood Maternity
Pumpkin Maternity
Veronique Maternity

## Women's Petite Size

Ann Taylor
Bloomingdale's
Dana Buchman
Forman's
Loehmann's

Lord & Taylor
Macy's
Saks Fifth Avenue
Talbots

## Women's Plus Size

Bloomingdale's
Burlington Coat Factory
Daphne

Forman's
H&M
Lane Bryant
Lord & Taylor

Macy's
Marina Rinaldi
Old Navy Clothing Co

Richard Metzger
Saks Fifth Avenue
SoHo Woman

## Women's Shirts

A.Cheng
agnès b.
Anne Fontaine
Ann Taylor

A.P.C.
Banana Republic
Barami
Barneys New York

Basiques
Bergdorf Goodman
Bloomingdale's
Borrelli

Brioni
Brooks Brothers
Charles Tyrwhitt
Davide Cenci

D/L Cerney
Elie Tahari
Gap

J.Crew
J.Lindeberg
J.McLaughlin
Joseph

Leggiadro
Miks
Paul Smith
Paul Stuart

Peter Elliot Women
Ralph Lauren
Saks Fifth Avenue
Scoop

Seize sur Vingt
Shin Choi
Talbots
Temperley

Theory
Thomas Pink
Turnbull & Asser

## Women's Shoes

Aerosoles
Aldo
Anthony T. Kirby
Antoin

Arche
A.Testoni
Avitto
Banana Republic

Barbara Shaum
Barneys Co-op
Barneys New York
Bati

Belgian Shoes
Bergdorf Goodman
Bloomingdale's
Bottega Veneta

Botticelli
Bruno Magli
Camper
Capezio

Cat Girl
Celine
Cesare Paciotti
Chanel

Charles Jourdan
Cherry
Chloé
Christian Louboutin

Chuckies
Cole Haan
Constanca Basto
Costume National

## Women's Shoes *(continued)*

Dusica Dusica
East Side Kids
Easy Spirit
Edmundo Castillo

Emanuel Ungaro
Enzo Angiolini
Eric Shoes
Fratelli Rossetti

French Sole
Gabay's Outlet
Galo
Geraldine

Giordano's
Giraudon
Giuseppe Zanotti Design
Goffredo Fantini

Gucci
Harry's Shoes
Helene Arpels
Hogan

Hollywould
Iramo
Jaime Mascaro
Jeffrey New York

Jimmy Choo
J.M.Weston
John Fluevog Shoes
Juno

Jutta Neumann
Kenneth Cole
Lord & Taylor
Luichiny

Macy's
Magic Shoes
Make 10
Manolo Blahnik

Marc Jacobs
Mare
Martinez Valero
Maud Frizon

Medici
Michel Perry
Milena Shoes
Miss Sixty

Miu Miu
Nahbee

Nancy Geist
New York Look
Nine West
Omari

Orva
Ottiva
Otto Tootsi Plohound
Peter Fox Shoes

Petit Peton
Prada
Rapax
Really Great Things

René Mancini
Robert Clergerie
Rockport
Ruco Line

Sacco
Saks Fifth Avenue
Salvatore Ferragamo
Santoni

Scarpe Diem
Sergio Rossi
Shoe
The Shoe Box

Sigerson Morrison
Skechers
Sonia Rykiel
Stephane Kélian

Steve Madden
Stuart Weitzman
Stubbs & Wootton
Tani

Tanino Crisci
Timberland
Tod's
Trash & Vaudeville

Unisa
United Nude Terra Plana
Vanessa Noel
Varda

Verve Shoes
Via Spiga
Vincent & Edgar
  (custom only)

Walter Steiger
Warren Edwards

## Women's Swimwear

Azaleas
Barneys New York
BCBG Max Azria
Believe It NYC

Benetton
Bergdorf Goodman
Bloomingdale's
Blue Bag

Bodyhints
Bra Smyth
Calypso St Barths
Canyon Beachwear

Enerla Lingerie
Eres
J.Crew
Keiko

La Perla
Leggiadro
Lord & Taylor

Macy's
Malia Mills
Martier
Missoni

Miss Sixty
Modell's
Nautica
Norma Kamali

Old Navy Clothing Co
Paul & Shark
Pucci
Quiksilver

Ralph Lauren
Saks Fifth Avenue
Scandinavian Ski Shop
Sol

Sonia Rykiel
Speedo Authentic Fitness
Wolford Boutique

## Women's Tweens

Abercrombie & Fitch
Berkley Girl
Betwixt

Bloomingdale's
Crush
Gap

Infinity
Lester's
Le Petit Bateau

Lord of the Fleas
Macy's
Magic Windows

Marsha D.D.
Old Navy Clothing Co
Petit Bateau

Space Kiddets
Wet Seal

## Women's Wearable Art

Design in Textiles by Mary
  Jaeger

Gallery of Wearable Art
Julie Artisan's Gallery

## Women's Vintage & Retro

99X
Alice Underground
Allan & Suzi
Amarcord Vintage Fashion

Andy's Chee-pees
Anna
Atomic Passion
Barneys New York

Beacon's Closet
Bond 07
Cheap Jack's
Chelsea Girl

Cherry
Crush
Decollage
DKNY

Dressing Room
Eleven
Ellen
Eye Candy

Fabulous Fanny's
The Family Jewels
Filth Mart
Fiona Walker

Fisch for the Hip
Flying A
Foley & Corinna

Gabay's Outlet
Hootie Couture
Jill Stuart
Jim Smiley Vintage

Keni Valenti
Le Corset
Legacy
Love Saves the Day

Lunettes et Chocolat
Marmalade
Mary Efron
Norma Kamali

Patina
Rags A Go Go
Rejoice
Reminiscence

Resurrection Vintage
Rue St Denis
Screaming Mimi's
Slang Betty

Soda Fine
Some Odd Rubies
Tokio 7
The Village Scandal

What Comes Around
   Goes Around
Yona Lee

## Women's Young & Trendy

99X
Alife
Assets London
B2 Gear

Barney's Co-op
Barneys New York
Beacon's Closet
Berkley Girl

Big Drop
Bloomingdale's
Bloomingdale's SoHo
Built by Wendy

DDC Lab
Detour
Diesel

Forward
French Connection
G.C.William

H&M
Hotel Venus
Le Chateau
Lily

Lord of the Fleas
Luca Luca
Macy's
Otte

Rampage
Scoop
Soda Fine
Steven Alan

TG-170
Unis
Urban Outfitters

Warehouse
Zara International
Z' Girl

## Men's Business Apparel—European

agnes b. Homme
Barneys New York
Bergdorf Goodman (men)
Bloomingdale's

Borrelli
Brioni
Davide Cenci
Domenico Spanno

Domenico Vacca
Emporio Armani
Ermenegildo Zegna

Etro
Façonnable
Frank Stella

Giorgio Armani
Helmut Lang
Hugo Boss
Jay Kos

Jeffrey New York
Leonard Logsdail
Paul Smith
Rochester Big & Tall

Saks Fifth Avenue
Salvatore Ferragamo
Sean

Seize sur Vingt
Thomas Pink

## Men's Business Apparel—Discount

Century 21
Eisenberg & Eisenberg
Harry Rothman's

Loftworks @ Lafayette
Men's Wearhouse

## Men's Business Apparel—Traditional

Addison on Madison
Alfred Dunhill
Anthony T. Kirby
Barneys New York

Bergdorf Goodman (men)
Bloomingdale's
Brooks Brothers

Burberry
H.Herzfeld
Hickey Freeman

Jay Kos
Jos. A. Bank
J.Press
Oxxford Clothes

Paul Stuart
Peter Elliot
Ralph Lauren

Saint Laurie
Saks Fifth Avenue
Turnbull & Asser

## Men's Cashmere/Knitwear

Ballantyne Cashmere
Barneys New York
Bergdorf Goodman (men)

Berk
Best of Scotland
Bloomingdale's

Borrelli
Cashmere New York
Loro Piana

Lucien Pellat-Finet
Malo
Manrico Cascimir

Micheal Kors
N.Peal
Ralph Lauren

Saks Fifth Avenue
Tse

## Men's Casual

Abercrombie & Fitch
American Apparel
American Eagle Outfitters
A Perfect Day In Paradise

Avirex
A/X Armani Exchange
Banana Republic
Barneys New York

Benetton
Bloomingdale's
Diesel
Eddie Bauer

Fossil
Gant
Gap

Guess?
H&M
J.Crew

Lacoste
Lord & Taylor
Lucky Brand Dungarees
Macy's

Mexx
Nautica
Old Navy Clothing Co
The Original Levi's Store

Original Penguin
Phat Farm
Quiksilver
Ralph Lauren

Replay Store
Rugby North America
Tommy Hilfiger

Utility Canvas
Watts
Yellow Rat Bastard

## Men's Custom Tailoring

Addison on Madison
Anthony T. Kirby
Arthur Gluck Shirtmakers

Ascot Chang
Bironi
Borrelli

Domenico Spano
Domenico Vacca
Etro

Frank Shattuck
H.Herzfeld
Hickey Freeman

Jay Kos
Leonard Logsdail
Rosa Custom Ties

Vincent Nicolosi
William Fioravanti

## Men's Designer

Burberry
Calvin Klein
Comme des Garçons
Costume National

D&G
Dior Homme
Dolce & Gabbana
Donna Karan

Fendi
Francis Hendy
Gianfranco Ferré
Giorgio Armani

Gucci
Helmut Lang
Hugo Boss
Issey Miyake
Jean Paul Gaultier

Kenzo
Krizia
Louis Vuitton
Marc Jacobs

Missoni
Moschino
Nicole Farhi
Prada

Paul Smith
Roberto Cavalli
Ralph Lauren
Salvatore Ferragamo

Valentino
Versace
Yohji Yamamoto
Yves Saint Laurent

## Men's Discount

Burlington Coat Factory
Century 21
Daffy's
Filene's Basement

Forman's
Loehman's
TJ Maxx

## Men's Ethnic

Men's Wearhouse
Pan American Phoenix
Shanghai Tang

## Men's Formal Wear & Tuxedos

A.T.Harris Formalwear
Baldwin Formalwear
Barney's New York
Bloomingdale's

Hickey Freeman
J.Press
Jack Silver Formal Wear
Turnbull & Asser

Domenico Spano
Eisenberg & Eisenberg
Giorgio Armani

Valentino
Zeller Tuxedo

## Men's Hats

Barneys New York
Bergdorf Goodman
Bloomingdale's
Brooks Brothers

Jay Kos
Kelly Christy
Lisa Shaub
Macy's

Cheap Jacks
Foley & Corrina Men
The Hat Shop
H.Herzfeld
Lord & Taylor

Paul Stuart
Saks Fifth Avenue
Samuel's Hats
Young's Hat Corner

## Men's Juniors

Abercrombie & Fitch
American Apparel
American Eagle Outfitters
Blades Board & Skate

Lester's
Lord & Taylor
Lord of the Fleas
Macy's

Bloomingdale's
Brooks Brothers
Century 21
Diesel

Old Navy Clothing Co
The Original Levi's Store
Patagonia
Peter Elliot

Gant
Gap
H&M

Quiksilver
XLarge

## Men's Large Sizes

Harry's Shoes
Rochester Big & Tall

## Men's Leather

Averix
Behrle
Buffalo Chips USA
Burberry

Chrome Hearts
Denimaxx
Leather Corner

The Leather Man
Lost Art
New York City Custom
 Leather

Rugby North America
Silverado

## Men's Leathergoods

Bally
Barneys New York
Bergdorf Goodman (men)
Bloomingdale's

Bottega Veneta
Coach
Crouch & Fitzgerald
Dooney & Burke

Fendi
Ghurka
Gucci

Hermès
Hunting World
Il Bisonte

Jack Gomme
Jack Spade
Lederer
Longchamp

Lord & Taylor
Louis Vuitton
Macy's
Peter Hermann

Prada
Rugby North America
Saks Fifth Avenue

Salvatore Ferragamo
T.Anthony
Tribeca Luggage & Leather

## Men's Shirts

Addison On Madison
Alfred Dunhill
Ascot Chang
Barneys New York

Bergdorf Goodman (men)
Bloomingdale's
Borrelli
Brooks Brothers

Burberry
Charles Tyrwhitt
Davide Cenci
Domenico Vacca

Façonnable
Frank Stella
H.Herzfeld

Hickey Freeman
Hugo Boss
Jay Kos
Lord & Taylor

Macy's
Men's Wearhouse
Paul Stuart
Robert Talbott

Saks Fifth Avenue
Sean
Seize sur Vingt
The Shirt Store

Thomas Pink
Turnbull & Asser

## Men's Shoes

99X
Aerosoles
Aldo
Alife Rivington Club

Allen Edmonds
Anthony Kirby
A.Testoni
Avitto

Bally
Barbara Shaum
Barneys New York
Belgian Shoes

Bergdorf Goodman (men)
Bloomingdale's
Bottega Veneta
Botticelli

Bruno Magli
Camper
Cesare Paciotti
Church's English Shoes

Citishoes
Clarks/Bostonian
Classic Kicks
Cole Haan

Fratelli Rossetti
Gabay's Outlet
Giraudon
Goffredo Fantini

Gucci
Hogan
Iramo
Jaime Mascaro

J.M.Weston
John Fluevog
John Lobb
Johnston & Murphy

Juno
Jutta Neumann

Kenneth Cole
Lord & Taylor
Macy's
Magic Shoes

Make 10
Mare
Milena Shoes
Nort 235

Omari
Ottiva
Otto Tootsi Plohound
Petit Peton

Prada
Premium Goods
Robert Clergerie
Rockport

Ruco Line
Saks Fifth Avenue
Salvatore Ferragamo
Santoni

Sergio Rossi
Shoe
Sigerson Morrison
Skechers

Stephane Kélian
Steve Madden
Stubbs & Wootton
Tanino Crisci

Timberland
Training Camp
Tod's
United Nude Terra Plana

Varda
Via Spiga
Vincent & Edgar
  (custom only)

Walter Steiger
Warren Edwards

Categories

## Men's Sportswear—Contemporary

Adidas
agnès b. homme
A.P.C.
Atrium

Banana Republic
Camouflage
Club Monaco
Diesel Style Lab

Dior Homme
DKNY
D/L Cerney

Emporio Armani
Flying A
French Connection

H&M
Helmut Lang
Hugo Boss

If
J.Lindeberg
Joseph
Lynn Park NY

Mankind
Parke & Ronen
Rugby North America
Sisley

Swiss Army
Ted Baker London
Tommy Hilfiger

Triple Five Soul
Tristan & America
Union

Untitled
Unis
Zara International

## Men's Sportswear—Traditional

Bally
Barneys New York
Bergdorf Goodman (men)
Beretta

Borrelli
Brioni
Brooks Brothers
Burberry

Davide Cenci
Domenico Vacca
Dunhill
Ermenegildo Zegna

Etro
H.Herzfeld
Hermès

Hickey Freeman
Holland & Holland
Hunting World
Jay Kos

J.McLaughlin
Joseph A. Bank
Lord & Taylor
Loro Piana

Paul & Shark
Paul Stuart
Peter Elliot
Ralph Lauren

Saks Fifth Avenue
Turnbull & Asser

## Men's Swimwear

Barneys New York
Bergdorf Goodman
Bloomingdale's

J.Crew
Lord & Taylor
Macy's

Polo Sport
Prada Sport
Quiksilver

Saks Fifth Avenue
Speedo Authentic Fitness
Vilebrequin

## Men's Ties

Addison on Madison
Anthony T. Kirby
Alfred Dunhill
Barneys New York

Bergdorf Goodman
Bloomingdale's
Borrelli
Brioni

Brooks Brothers
Burberry
Charles Tyrwhitt

Domenico Vacca
Ermenegildo Zegna
Etro

Façonnable
Hermès
Hugo Boss

Jay Kos
Jos. A. Bank
J.Press
Lord & Taylor

Macy's
Men's Wearhouse
Paul Stuart
Ralph Lauren

Robert Talbott
Rosa Custom Ties
Saks Fifth Avenue

Salvatore Ferragamo
Seigo
Thomas Pink

Today's Man
Turnbull & Asser

## Men's Vintage & Retro (& consignment)

99X
Alice Underground
Amarcord Vintage Fashion
Andy's Chee Pees

Atomic Passion
Beacon's Closet
Cherry
The Family Jewels

Filth Mart
Fisch for the Hip
Foley & Corinna Men
Ina

Jim Smiley's Vintage
Original Penguin
Rejoice
Reminiscence

Resurrection Vintage
Screaming Mimi's
Tokio 7
Tokyo Joe

The Village Scandal
What Comes Around
  Goes Around

## Men's Young & Trendy

99X
Alife
American Apparel
Amarcord Vintage Fashion

Beacon's Closet
Bloomingdale's
Brooklyn Industries
DDC Lab

Diesel
Foley & Corinna Men
H&M
Hotel Venus
Isa

Klurk
Lord of the Fleas
Macy's
Mexx

Original Penguin
Stackhouse
Stüssy
Supreme

Transit
Union
Unis
Urban Outfitters
Watts

351

## Unisex Athletic

Adidas
Athlete's Foot
Blades Board & Skate
Champs

Crunch
Foot Locker
Modell's
New Balance

Niketown
Paragon
The Puma Store
Reebok

Speedo Authentic Fitness
Sports Authority
Super Runners Shop
Training Camp

## Unisex Department Stores

Barneys New York
Bergdorf Goodman
Bergdorf Goodman (men)

Bloomingdale's
Brooks Brothers

Loftworks @ Lafayette
Lord & Taylor
Macy's

Saks Fifth Avenue
Takashimaya

## Unisex Golf

Champs
Hugo Boss
J.Lindeberg

Lacoste
New York Golf Center

Niketown
Paragon
Ralph Lauren

Walter Steiger (shoes only)
World of Golf

## Unisex Jeans

Abercrombie & Fitch
A/X Armani Exchange
Barneys New York
Bloomingdale's

Diesel
Earl Jean
Gap
Guess?

Henry Lehr
Lucky Brand Dungarees
Old Navy Clothing Co
The Original Levi's Store

R by 45rpm
Replay Store
Selvedge

## Unisex Outdoor Sports (clothes & equipment)

Adidas
Athlete's Foot (shoes only)
Blades Board & Skate
Champs

Conrad's Bike Shop
Copperfields New York
Diesel
Eastern Mountain Sports

Gerry Cosby & Co
Lacoste
Lady Foot Locker
Mason's Tennis Mart
Metro Bicycle

Modell's
Niketown
Orvis
Paragon Sporting Goods

Patagonia
Powers Court Tennis Outlet
Princeton Ski Shop
The Puma Store

Reebok
Scandinavian Ski Shop
Speedo Authentic Fitness
Sports Authority
Training Camp

## Unisex Outerwear

Barneys New York
Bergdorf Goodman
Bloomingdale's

Brooks Brothers
Burberry
Davide Cenci

Denimaxx
Lord & Taylor
Macy's

Paul Stuart
Saks Fifth Avenue
Searle

## Unisex Tennis

Champs
Foot Locker
Lacoste

Mason's Tennis Mart
Modell's
New Balance

Niketown
Paragon Sporting Goods
Powers Court Tennis Outlet

Ralph Lauren
Reebok
Sports Authority

## Unisex Western

Billy Martins
Buffalo Chips USA

Western Spirit
Whiskey Dust

## Children's Clothing

April Cornell
Baby Bird
Bambini
Barneys New York

Basiques
Bebe Thompson
Bloomingdale's
Bombalulus

Bonpoint
Bu & the Duck
Calypso Enfant
Catimini

C.J.Laing
The Children's Place
City Cricket

Design in Textiles
  by Mary Jaeger
Erica Tanov
Gap Kids & Baby Gap

Granny-Made
Greenstones & Cie
Gymboree
Hoofbeats

Hot Toddie
Jacadi
Julian & Sara
Just for Tykes

Koh's Kids
La Layette et Plus
La Petite Etoile

Lester's
Lilliput/SoHo Kids
Lord & Taylor
Macy's

Magic Windows
Morris Bros
Nursery Lines
Oilily

Old Navy Clothing Co
OshKosh B'Gosh
Patagonia
Peanutbutter & Jane

Peter Elliot Kids
Petit Bateau
Pipsqueak

Quiksilver
Ralph Lauren Baby
Saks Fifth Avenue
San Francisco Clothing

Shanghai Tang
Small Change
SoHo Baby
Space Kiddets

Spring Flowers
Talbots Kids
Vilebrequin
Yoya

Z' Baby Company
Zitomer

## Children's Discount

Century 21
Daffy's

TJ Maxx

## Children's Shoes

Bambini
East Side Kids
Galo
Great Feet

Hogan
Jacadi
Juno
Kids Foot Locker
Lester's

Little Eric Shoes
Shoofly
Skechers
Spring Flowers

Timberland
Tip Top Kids
Tod's
Training Camp

# Restaurants

## In-Store Restaurants

**American Café @ Lord & Taylor**   (212) 391-3344 (ext 5068)
424 Fifth Avenue                                  btw 38/39th St

**Au Bon Pain @ Macy's**                        (212) 494-3959
Broadway @ Herald Square        btw Broadway/34th St

**Auntie Anne's @ Macy's**                      (212) 695-4400
Broadway @ Herald Square        btw Broadway/34th St

**Blanche's Organic Café @ DKNY**          (212) 223-3569
655 Madison Avenue                               at 60th St

**Café @ The Lounge**                           (212) 431-5696
593 Broadway                          btw Prince/Houston

**Café SFA @ Saks Fifth Avenue**   (212) 753-4000 (ext 4080)
611 Fifth Avenue                                  btw 49/50th St

**745 Café @ Bergdorf Goodman**            (212) 339-3326
The Men's Store 745 Fifth Avenue       btw 57/58th St

**Café On Five @ Bergdorf Goodman**       (212) 872-8843
754 Fifth Avenue                              btw 57/58th St

**40 Carrots @ Bloomingdale's**              (212) 705-3085
1000 Third Avenue                             btw 59/60th St

**Cucina & Co @ Macy's**                        (212) 695-4400
Broadway @ Herald Square        btw Broadway/34th St

**Fred's @ Barneys**                             (212) 833-2200
10 East 61st Street                    btw Fifth/Madison Ave

**Jimmy's Pizza @ Macy's**                      (212) 695-4400
Broadway @ Herald Square        btw Broadway/34th St

**Le Train Bleu @ Bloomingdale's**          (212) 705-2100
1000 Third Avenue                             btw 59/60th St

**Macy's Cellar Bar & Grill @ Macy's**       (212) 695-4400
Broadway @ Herald Square        btw Broadway/34th St

**Nicole's @ Nicole Farhi**                     (212) 223-2288
10 East 60th Street                    btw Fifth/Madison Ave

**Showtime Café @ Bloomingdale's**        (212) 705-2155
1000 Third Avenue                             btw 59/60th St

**The Tea Box @ Takashimaya**               (212) 350-0180
693 Fifth Avenue                              btw 54/55th St

## Restaurants

Shop till you drop…then drop into a comfortable chair for lunch. Here is a select list of restaurants perfect for your shopping spree.

**UPPER EAST SIDE (61st-96th)**

EAST 60S

**Aureole** (New American)
34 East 61st Street
**(212) 319-1660**
btw Madison/Park Ave

**Ferrier** (French bistro)
29 East 65th Street
**(212) 772-9000**
btw Madison/Park Ave

**Jackson Hole** (hamburgers)
232 East 64th Street
**(212) 371-7187**
btw Second/Third Ave

**La Goulue** (French bistro)
746 Madison Avenue
**(212) 988-8169**
btw 64/65th St

**Le Bilboquet** (French bistro)
25 East 63rd Street
**(212) 751-3036**
btw Madison/Park Ave

**Le Charlot** (French bistro)
19 East 69th Street
**(212) 794-1628**
btw Madison/Park Ave

**Lexington R.S.V.P. Café** (American)
1012 Lexington Avenue
**(212) 861-5350**
btw 72/73rd St

**Maya** (haute Mexican)
1191 First Avenue
**(212) 585-1818**
btw 64/65th St

**Nello** (Italian bistro)
696 Madison Avenue
**(212) 980-9099**
btw 62/63rd St

**Park Avenue Café** (New American)
100 East 63rd Street
**(212) 644-1900**
at Park Ave

**Serafina** (Italian pizzeria)
29 East 61st Street
**(212) 702-9898**
btw Madison/Park Ave

EAST 70S

**Atlantic Grill** (Asian)
1341 Third Avenue
**(212) 988-9200**
btw 76/77th St

**Bid** (American)
1334 York Avenue
**(212) 988-7730**
at 71st St

**Cafe Boulud** (French)
20 East 76th Street
**(212) 772-2600**
btw Fifth/Madison Ave

**Carvao** (Brazilian)
1477 Second Avenue
**(212) 879-4707**
at 77th St

**EJ's Luncheonette** (glorified diner)
1271 Third Avenue
**(212) 472-0600**
at 73rd St

**The Gallery @ the Carlyle Hotel**
(omelettes, salads, sandwiches)
35 East 76th Street
**(212) 744-1600**
at Madison Ave

**Ikeno Hana** (Japanese)
1016 Lexington Avenue
**(212) 737-6639**
btw 72/73rd St

**J.G.Melon** *(hamburgers)*     **(212) 744-0585**
1291 Third Avenue     at 74th St

**Mezzaluna** *(pizzas, pasta)*     **(212) 535-9600**
1295 Third Avenue     btw 74/75th St

**Orsay** *(bistro)*     **(212) 517-6400**
1057 Lexington Avenue     at 75th St

**The Sultan** *(Turkish)*     **(212) 861-0200**
1435 Second Avenue     btw 74/75th St

**Swifty's** *(American bistro)*     **(212) 535-6000**
1007 Lexington Avenue     btw 72/73rd St

**Via Quadronno** *(Italian)*     **(212) 650-9880**
25 East 73rd Street     btw Fifth/Madison Ave

## EAST 80S & 90S

**Brasserie Julien** *(French)*     **(212) 744-6327**
1422 Third Avenue     btw 80/81st St

**Cafe Sabarsky** *(Austrian)*     **(212) 288-0665**
1048 Fifth Avenue     at 86th St

**E.A.T.** *(gourmet sandwiches and salads)*     **(212) 772-0022**
1064 Madison Avenue     btw 80/81st St

**Island** *(Italian bistro)*     **(212) 996-1200**
1305 Madison Avenue     btw 92/93rd St

**Jackson Hole** *(hamburgers)*     **(212) 427-2820**
1270 Madison Avenue     at 91st St

**Luca** *(Italian)*     **(212) 987-9260**
1712 First Avenue     btw 88/89th St

**Pio Pio** *(South American)*     **(212) 426-5800**
1746 First Avenue     btw 90/91st St

**Sarabeth's** *(tea room)*     **(212) 410-7335**
1295 Madison Avenue     btw 92/93rd St

**Taste** *(American)*     **(212) 717-8100**
1411 Third Avenue     btw 80/81st St

## UPPER WEST SIDE

**Café Arte** *(Italian)*     **(212) 501-7014**
106 West 73rd Street     btw Amsterdam/Columbus Ave

**Café Luxembourg** *(French bistro)*     **(212) 873-7411**
200 West 70th Street     btw Amsterdam/West End Ave

**The Great Burrito** *(Mexican)*     **(212) 724-5151**
405 Amsterdam Avenue     btw 79/80th St

**Isabella's** *(Mediterranean)*     **(212) 724-2100**
359 Columbus Avenue     at 77th St

**Jean Georges** *(French)*     **(212) 299-3900**
1 Central Park West     at 60th

**Nick & Toni's** *(Mediterranean)*     **(212) 496-4000**
100 West 67th Street     btw Broadway/Columbus Ave

**O-I-Shi-I Sushi @ Ivy Café** *(Japanese)*      **(212) 787-0165**
154 West 72nd Street      btw Columbus Ave/Broadway

**Ouest** *(French)*      **(212) 580-8700**
2315 Broadway      at 84th St

**Ruby Foo's** *(Chinese)*      **(212) 724-6700**
2182 Broadway      at 77th St

**Sarabeth's** *(tea room)*      **(212) 496-6280**
423 Amsterdam Avenue      btw 80/81st St

**Shun Lee Café** *(Chinese)*      **(212) 769-3888**
43 West 65th Street  btw Columbus Ave/Central Park West

**Time Café** *(brunch, salads, sandwiches)*      **(212) 579-5100**
2330 Broadway      at 85th St

**Vince and Eddie's** *(American bistro)*      **(212) 721-0068**
70 West 68th Street  btw Columbus Ave/Central Park West

## MIDTOWN / FIFTH AVENUE (42nd-61st)

**Atelier** *(French)*      **(212) 521-6125**
50 Central Park South      btw Fifth/Sixth Ave

**Azaza** *(Chinese)*      **(212) 751-0700**
891 First Avenue      at 50th St

**Bice** *(northern Italian)*      **(212) 688-1999**
7 East 54th Street      btw Fifth/Madison Ave

**Blue Fin** *(seafood)*      **(212) 918-1400**
1567 Broadway      btw 46/47th St

**Bricco** *(Italian)*      **(212) 245-7160**
304 West 56th Street      btw Eighth/Ninth Ave

**Burger Joint** (@ the Parker Meridien hotel)   **(212) 245-5000**
118 West 57th Street      btw Sixth/Seventh Ave

**California Pizza Kitchen** *(pizza, pasta, salads)* **(212) 755-7773**
201 East 60th Street      btw Second/Third Ave

**Carnegie Deli**      **(212) 757-2245**
854 Seventh Avenue      at 55th St

**Chola** *(Indian)*      **(212) 688-4619**
232 East 58th Street      btw Second/Third Ave

**DB Bistro Moderne** *(French bistro)*      **(212) 391-2400**
55 West 44th Street      btw Fifth/Sixth Ave

**The Four Seasons** *(New American)*      **(212) 754-9494**
99 East 52nd Street      btw Park/Lexington Ave

**Fresco by Scotto on the Go** *(Italian)*      **(212) 754-2700**
40 East 52nd Street      btw Madison/Park Ave

**Le Bernardin** *(French)*      **(212) 489-1515**
155 West 51st Street      btw Sixth/Seventh Ave

**Norma's** *(breakfast)*      **(212) 708-7460**
18 West 57th Street      at Sixth Ave

Restaurants

**Per Se** *(New American)*     **(212) 823-9335**
10 Columbus Circus     btw 58/59th St

**Rue 57 Brasserie** *(French bistro)*     **(212) 307-5656**
60 West 57th Street     at Sixth Ave

**San Domenico** *(Italian)*     **(212) 265-5959**
240 Central Park South     btw Broadway/Seventh Ave

## FLATIRON/NOHO/CENTRAL VILLAGE

**Artisanal** *(cheese)*     **(212) 725-8585**
2 Park Avenue     at 32nd St

**Blue Smoke** *(BBQ)*     **(212) 447-7733**
116 East 27th Street     btw Park/Lexington Ave

**Borgo Antico** *(Tuscan)*     **(212) 807-1313**
22 East 13th Street     btw Fifth/University Place

**Cosi Sandwich Bar** *(great sandwiches)*     **(212) 414-8469**
3 East 17th Street     btw Broadway/Fifth Ave

**Craft** *(American)*     **(212) 780-0880**
43 East 19th Street     btw Broadway/Park Ave

**Gramercy Tavern** *(American)*     **(212) 477-0777**
42 East 20th Street     btw Broadway/Park Ave South

**Indochine** *(French/Vietnamese)*     **(212) 505-5111**
430 Lafayette Street     btw Astor Place/4th St

**Marquet Patisserie** *(bistro)*     **(212) 229-9313**
15 East 12th Street     btw Fifth/University Place

**Thé Adore** *(pastries, salads, sandwiches)*     **(212) 243-8742**
17 East 13th Street     btw Fifth/University Place

**Time Café** *(brunch, salads, sandwiches)*     **(212) 533-7000**
380 Lafayette Street     at Great Jones

**T Salon** *(soups, salads, sandwiches)*     **(212) 358-0506**
11 East 20th Street     btw Broadway/Fifth Ave

**Union Square Café** *(New American)*     **(212) 243-4020**
21 East 16th Street     btw Fifth/Union Square West

**Wichcraft** *(American, sandwiches)*     **(212) 780-0577**
49 East 19th Street     btw Broadway/Park Ave

## CHELSEA/WEST VILLAGE

**Amy's Bread** *(sandwiches)*     **(212) 462-4338**
75 Ninth Avenue     btw 15/16th St (Chelsea Market)

**Barbuto** *(Italian)*     **(212) 924-9700**
775 Washington Street     btw West 12th/Jane

**Blue Ribbon Bakery** *(American)*     **(212) 337-0404**
35 Downing Street     at Bedford

**Chelsea Bistro & Bar** *(French bistro)*     **(212) 727-2026**
358 West 23rd Street     btw Eighth/Ninth Ave

**Corner Bistro** *(hamburgers)*     **(212) 242-9502**
331 West 4th Street     at Jane

**Diner 24**
102 Eighth Avenue
**(212) 242-7773**
at 15th St

**EJ's Luncheonette** *(diner)*
432 Sixth Avenue
**(212) 473-5555**
btw 9/10th St

**Florent** *(diner)*
69 Gansevoort Street
**(212) 989-5779**
btw Washington/Greenwich

**Havana Chelsea Restaurant** *(Cuban)*
190 Eighth Avenue
**(212) 243-9421**
btw 19/20th St

**'ino** *(panini)*
21 Bedford Street
**(212) 989-5769**
btw Sixth Ave/Downing

**La Bottega** *(Italian)*
88 Ninth Avenue
**(212) 243-8400**
at 16th St

**Le Madri** *(Italian)*
168 West 18th Street
**(212) 727-8022**
btw Sixth/Seventh Ave

**Markt** *(Belgian brasserie)*
401 West 14th Street
**(212) 727-3314**
at Ninth Ave

**Otto Enoteca Pizzeria**
1 Fifth Avenue
**(212) 995-9559**
at 8th St

**Pastis** *(French bistro)*
9 Ninth Avenue
**(212) 929-4844**
at Little West 12th St

**The Park** *(American/lounge)*
118 Tenth Avenue
**(212) 352-3313**
btw 17/18th St

**Petite Abeille** *(soups, waffles, sandwiches)*
107 West 18th Street
**(212) 604-9350**
btw Sixth/Seventh Ave

**Pintxos** *(tapas)*
510 Greenwich Street
**(212) 343-9923**
btw Canal/Spring

**Snackbar** *(American)*
111 West 17th Street
**(212) 627-3700**
btw Sixth/Seventh Ave

**Son Cubano** *(Cuban)*
405 West 14th Street
**(212) 366-1640**
btw Ninth/Tenth Ave

**Spice Market** *(Asian)*
29-35 Ninth Avenue
**(212) 675-2322**
at 13th St

**Tartine** *(French bistro)*
253 West 11th Street
**(212) 229-2611**
at West 4th St

**Vento** *(Italian)*
675 Hudson Street
**(212) 699-2400**
at 13th St

**Washington Park** *(American)*
24 Fifth Avenue
**(212) 529-4400**
btw 9/10th St

## SOHO/NOLITA/LOWER EAST SIDE

**AKA Café** *(American)*
49 Clinton Street
**(212) 979-6096**
btw Stanton/Rivington

**Balthazar** *(French bistro)*
80 Spring Street
**(212) 965-1414**
btw Broadway/Crosby

**Boom** *(Italian)*
152 Spring Street
**(212) 431-3663**
btw Wooster/West Broadway

## Restaurants

**Butter** (New American)
415 Lafayette Street
**(212) 253-2828**
btw West 4th St/Astor Place

**Café Gitane** (French bistro)
242 Mott Street
**(212) 334-9552**
btw Houston/Prince

**Café Habana** (Cuban)
17 Prince Street
**(212) 625-2001**
at Elizabeth

**Cipriani Downtown** (Italian)
376 West Broadway
**(212) 343-0999**
btw Spring/Broome

**Congee Village** (Chinese)
100 Allen Street
**(212) 941-1818**
at Delancey

**Cornershop** (sandwiches)
643 Broadway
**(212) 253-7467**
at Bleecker

**Fanelli's Café** (hamburgers)
94 Prince Street
**(212) 226-9412**
at Mercer

**Felix** (French bistro)
340 West Broadway
**(212) 431-0021**
at Grand

**Hampton Chutney Company** (Indian)
68 Prince Street
**(212) 226-9996**
at Crosby

**Inoteca** (panini)
98 Rivington Street
**(212) 614-0473**
at Ludlow

**Katz's Deli**
205 East Houston Street
**(212) 254-2246**
at Ludlow

**Kuma Inn** (Asian small plates)
113 Ludlow Street (2nd floor)
**(212) 353-8866**
btw Rivington/Delancey

**Lil' Frankie's Pizza**
19 First Avenue
**(212) 420-4900**
btw East 1/2nd St

**Lombardi's** (pizza)
32 Spring Street
**(212) 941-7994**
btw Mulberry/Mott

**Mercer Kitchen** (French/Mediterranean)
99 Prince Street
**(212) 966-5454**
at Mercer

**Mezzogiorno** (Italian)
195 Spring Street
**(212) 334-2112**
at Sullivan

**Pink Pony** (sandwiches)
178 Ludlow Street
**(212) 253-1922**
btw Houston/Stanton

**Rialto** (French American)
265 Elizabeth Street
**(212) 334-7900**
btw Houston/Prince

**Rice** (Thai/Asian)
227 Mott Street
**(212) 226-5775**
btw Prince/Spring

**Schiller's Liquor Bar** (American traditional)
131 Rivington Street
**(212) 375-0010**
at Norfolk

**Teany** (vegetarian)
90 Rivington Street
**(212) 475-9190**
btw Orchard/Ludlow

**Thom @ the Thompson Hotel**
(modern American)
60 Thompson Street
**(212) 219-2000**
btw Spring/Broome

**Vine** *(Chinese)*     **(212) 344-8463**
25 Broad Street     at Exchange Place

## TRIBECA / LOWER MANHATTAN

**Bouley** *(modern French)*     **(212) 964-2525**
120 West Broadway     at Duane

**Bubby's** *(soups, burgers, salads, sandwiches)*   **(212) 219-0666**
120 Hudson Street     at North Moore

**Franklin Station Café** *(Malaysian)*     **(212) 274-8525**
222 West Broadway     btw West Broadway/Varick

**Next Door Nobu** *(Japanese)*     **(212) 334-4445**
105 Hudson Street     btw Franklin/North Moore

**The Odeon** *(bistro)*     **(212) 233-0507**
145 West Broadway     btw Duane/Thomas

**66** *(Chinese)*     **(212) 925-0202**
241 Church Street     btw Worth/Leonard

**Tribeca Grill** *(modern American)*     **(212) 941-3900**
375 Greenwich Street     at Franklin

## BROOKLYN

**Allioli** *(tapas)*     **(718) 218-7338**
Grand Street     btw Roebling/Havemeyer

**Bacchus** *(French)*     **(718) 852-1572**
409 Atlantic Avenue     btw Nevins/Bond

**Bar Tabac** *(bistro)*     **(718) 923-0918**
128 Smith Street     at Dean

**Biscuit** *(BBQ)*     **(718) 398-2227**
367 Flatbush Avenue     btw Sterling Place/Carlton Ave

**ChipShop** *(fish and chips)*     **(718) 244-7746**
383 5th Avenue     at 6th St

**Diner**     **(718) 486-3077**
85 Broadway     at Berry

**D.O.C. Wine Bar** *(small plates)*     **(718) 963-1925**
83 North 7th Street     at Wythe Ave

**Faan** *(Pan-Asian)*     **(718) 694-2277**
209 Smith Street     btw Baltic/Butler

**Peter Luger** *(steakhouse)*     **(718) 387-7400**
178 Broadway     btw Bedford/Driggs

**Schnäck** *(hamburgers, hot dogs)*     **(718) 855-2879**
122 Union Street     near Columbia

**Thai Sky**     **(718) 788-7889**
386 5th Avenue     at 7th St

**Verb Café**     **(718) 599-0977**
218 Bedford Avenue     btw North 4/5th St

Restaurants

# Health & Beauty

## Barbers

**Chelsea Barbers**
465 West 23rd Street
NYC 10011

**(212) 741-2254**
btw Ninth/Tenth
Mon-Fri 9-7, Sat 9-6

**Delta Men's Hairstylists**
992 Lexington Avenue
NYC 10021

**(212) 628-5723/650-9055**
btw 71/72nd
Mon-Sat 8-6:30

**La Boite a Coupe**
18 West 55th Street
NYC 10019

**(212) 246-2097**
btw Fifth/Sixth
Daily 9-7

**Paul Mole Barber Shop**
1031 Lexington Avenue
NYC 10021

**(212) 535-8461**
btw 73/74th
Mon-Fri 7:30-6:30
Sat 7:30-5:30, Sun 9-3:30

**York Barber**
981 Lexington Avenue
NYC 10021

**(212) 988-6136**
btw 70/71st
Mon-Fri 8-7, Sat 8-6

## Haircuts—Unisex

**Astor Place Hair**
2 Astor Place
NYC 10003

**(212) 475-9854**
at Broadway
Mon-Sat 8-8, Sun 9-6

**Jean Louis David**
2146 Broadway
NYC 10023

**(212) 873-1850**
at 75th
Mon-Sat 10-7 (Thurs 10-8), Sun 11-5

**Jean Louis David**
783 Lexington Avenue
NYC 10021

**(212) 838-7372**
at 61st
Mon-Fri 10-7 (Thurs 10-7:30)
Sat 9-7, Sun 11-5

**Jean Louis David**
1180 Sixth Avenue
NYC 10011

**(212) 944-7389**
at 46th
Mon-Sat 10-7 (Thurs 10-8)

## Haircuts—Children

**Cozy's Cuts for Kids**
1125 Madison Avenue
NYC 10028

**(212) 744-1716**
at 84/85th
Mon-Fri 10-6, Sat 9-5

**Cozy's Cuts for Kids**
448 Amsterdam Avenue
NYC 10024

**(212) 579-2600**
btw 81/82nd
Mon-Sat 10-6

**Kids Cuts**
201 East 31st Street
NYC 10016

**(212) 684-5252**
btw Second/Third
Mon-Sat 10-6

**Lulu's Cuts and Toys**
310 Fifth Avenue
Brooklyn 11215
www.luluscuts.com

**(718) 832-3732**
btw 2nd/3rd St
Mon-Sat 10-6, Sun 11-5

## Hair Salons

**Salon A.K.S.**   **(212) 888-0707**
694 Madison Avenue   btw 62/63rd
NYC 10021   Mon-Sat 9-6 (Wed-Thurs 9-8)

**Antonio Prieto Salon**   **(212) 255-3741**
25 West 19th Street   btw Fifth/Sixth
NYC 10011   Mon-Fri 12-8, Sat 10-6

**April Barton's Suite 303**   **(212) 633-1011**
**@ the Chelsea Hotel**   btw Seventh/Eighth
222 West 23rd Street   Tues-Fri 12-7, Sat 12-5
NYC 10011

**Armando Corral Salon**   **(212) 206-7712**
12 Little West 12th Street   btw Ninth/Washington
NYC 10014   Tues-Sat 11:30-8

**Bollei**   **(212) 759-7985**
115 East 57th Street   btw Park/Lexington
NYC 10022   Mon-Sat 9-6:30

**Bumble & Bumble**   **(212) 521-6500**
146 East 56th Street   btw Lexington/Third
NYC 10022   Tues-Fri 9:30-7, Sat 9-5

**Charles Worthington Salon**   **(212) 941-9696**
568 Broadway (suite 101)   at Prince
NYC 10012   Mon-Wed 10-7, Thurs-Fri 10-8, Sat 9:30-6

**Devachan Hair Salon**   **(212) 274-8686**
560 Broadway   btw Spring/Prince
NYC 10012   Tues-Fri 11-7, Sat 10-5

**Donsuki**   **(212) 826-3397**
19 East 62nd Street   btw Fifth/Madison
NYC 10021   Tues-Sat 9-6 (Thurs 9-6:30)

**Dop Dop Salon**   **(212) 965-9540**
170 Mercer Street   btw Houston/Prince
NYC 10012   Mon 12-6, Tues, Thurs-Sat 11-7:30
Wed 11-5, Sun 11-6

**Eiji**   **(212) 570-1151**
768 Madison Avenue (2nd floor)   btw 65/66th
NYC 10021   Tues-Sat 9-6 (Wed 9-4:30)

**Frédéric Fekkai**   **(212) 753-9500**
15 East 57th Street   btw Fifth/Madison
NYC 10022   Mon-Tues, Sat 8:30-6
Wed, Fri 8:30-7, Thurs 8:30-8

**Garren New York @ Henri Bendel**   **(212) 841-9400**
712 Fifth Avenue (3rd floor)   btw 55/56th
NYC 10019   Mon-Sat 9-7 (Thurs 9-8)

**Gemini Salon & Spa**   **(212) 675-4546**
547 Hudson Street   btw Charles/Perry
NYC 10014   Mon-Fri 10-9, Sat 9:30-7

**John Barrett Salon**     **(212) 872-2700**
754 Fifth Avenue (9th floor)     @ Bergdorf Goodman
NYC 10019     Mon-Sat 10-7 (Thurs 10-8), Sun 12-6

**John Frieda**     **(212) 879-1000**
797 Madison Avenue (2nd floor)     btw 67/68th
NYC 10021     Mon-Sat 8:30-6:30 (Thurs 8:30-7:30)

**John Masters Organic Haircare**     **(212) 343-9590**
77 Sullivan Street     btw Spring/Broome
NYC 10012     Mon-Fri 11-6:30, Sat 11-6:30

**John Sahag**     **(212) 750-7772**
425 Madison Avenue (2nd floor)     at 49th
NYC 10017     Mon 8:30-5:30, Tues-Sat 8:30-7:30

**Joseph Valery**     **(212) 517-2333**
1044 Madison Avenue     btw 79/80th
NYC 10021     Mon-Sat 9-6 (Tues, Thurs 9-7)
    Sun 12-5

**Joseph Valery**     **(212) 517-7377**
820 Madison Avenue     btw 68/69th
NYC 10021     (opening hours as above)

**Josephine Beauty Retreat**     **(212) 223-7157**
200 East 62nd Street     btw Second/Third
NYC 10021     Mon-Fri 10-7, Sat 10-4

**Julien Farel**     **(212) 888-8988**
605 Madison Avenue     btw 57-58th
NYC 10022     Mon-Sat 9-6 (Thurs 9-7)

**Julius Caruso Salon**     **(212) 759-7574**
22 East 62nd Street     btw Fifth/Madison
NYC 10021     Mon-Sat 9-5

**Kenneth Salon**     **(212) 752-1800**
301 Park Avenue     @ the Waldorf Astoria Hotel
NYC 10022     Mon-Sat 9-6 (Wed 9-7)

**Louis Licari Color Group**     **(212) 758-2090**
693 Fifth Avenue     @ Takashimaya btw 53/54th
NYC 10021     Mon-Tues 7:30-7, Wed, Sat 7:30-5:30
    Thurs-Fri 7:30-8

**Miano Viel**     **(212) 980-3222**
16 East 52nd Street     btw Fifth/Madison
NYC 10022     Tues 9-6, Wed 9-5
    Sat 9-5, Thurs-Fri 9-7

**Minardi Salon**     **(212) 308-1711**
29 East 61st Street (5th floor)     btw Madison/Park
NYC 10021     Tues-Thurs 9-9, Fri-Sat 9-7

**Mudhoney**     **(212) 533-1160**
148 Sullivan Street     btw Houston/Prince
NYC 10012     Tues-Fri 12-8, Sat 12-6

**Oscar Blandi**     **(212) 593-7930**
768 Fifth Avenue     @ the Plaza Hotel at 58th
NYC 10019     Mon-Fri 9-5

**Oscar Bond**
42 Wooster Street
NYC 10013

**(212) 334-3777**
btw Broome/Grand
Tues-Wed 10-8, Thurs-Fri 11-9
Sat 10-6, Sun 11-6

**Peter Coppola**
746 Madison Avenue
NYC 10021

**(212) 988-9404**
btw 64/65th
Mon-Sat 9-6

**Pierre Michel**
131 East 57th Street
NYC 10022

**(212) 593-1460**
btw Park/Lexington
Mon-Sat 10-6

**Prive @ the Soho Grand**
310 West Broadway
NYC 10013

**(212) 274-8888**
btw Grand/Canal
Mon 11-5, Tues-Wed, Fri 10-8
Thurs 10-10, Sat 10-6, Sun 12-6

**Q Hair**
19 Bleecker Street
NYC 10012

**(212) 614 8729**
at Elizabeth
Tues-Sat 11-8

**Red Salon**
323 West 11th Street
NYC 10014

**(212) 924-1444**
btw Greenwich/Washington
Tues-Fri 12-8, Sat 11-5

**Robert Kree Salon**
375 Bleecker Street
NYC 10014

**(212) 989-9547**
btw Charles/Perry
Sun-Mon 12-7, Tues-Fri 11-8
Sat 10-6:30

**Salon AKS**
694 Madison Avenue
NYC 10021

**(212) 888-0707**
btw 62/63rd
Mon-Sat 9-6 (Thurs 9-8)

**Salon Ishi**
70 East 55th Street
NYC 10022

**(212) 888-4744**
btw Park/Madison
Mon-Wed 9-5, Thurs-Fri 8-7, Sat 8-5

**Sally Hersehberger**
423 West 14th Street
NYC 10014

**(212) 206-8700**
btw Ninth/Tenth
Mon-Sat 9-5

**Simon**
22 East 66th Street
NYC 10021

**(212) 517-4566**
btw Fifth/Madison
Mon-Sat 10-5 (Thurs-Fri 10-6:30)

**Soon Beauty Lab**
318 East 11th Street
NYC 10003

**(212) 260-4423**
btw First/Second
Mon-Fri 11-9, Sat-Sun 10-6

**Space**
155 Sixth Avenue
NYC 10013

**(212) 647-8588**
at Spring
Mon-Fri 10-8, Sat 9-7

**Sparkle Beauty Studio**
3 Charles Street
NYC 10014

**(212) 645-4745**
at Greenwich
Tues-Fri 12-8, Sat 10-5

**Thomas Morrissey Salon**
787 Madison Avenue
NYC 10021

**(212) 772-1111**
btw 66/67th
Mon-Fri 9-5 (Thurs 9-7), Sat 9-4

Health & Beauty

**Ultra** (212) 677-4380
233 East 4th Street btw Avenue A/B
NYC 10009 Tues-Wed, Fri 11-8, Thurs 12-9, Sat 10-5

**Yann Varin** (212) 734-9055
142 East 73rd Street btw Park/Lexington
NYC 10021 Mon-Fri 10-7, Sat 9-6

**Younghee Salon** (212) 334-3770
64 North Moore Street btw Hudson/Greenwich
NYC 10013 Tues-Fri 10:30-6:30, Sat 9-4:30

## Hair Removal

**Bernice Electrolysis & Beauty Center** (212) 355-7055
29 East 61st Street (2nd floor) btw Madison/Park
NYC 10021 Mon-Sat 8-6

**Completely Bare** (212) 717-9300
764 Madison Avenue btw 65/66th
NYC 10021 Mon-Thurs 10-9, Fri 10-7, Sat-Sun 10-5

**Expert Electrolysis Inc** (212) 755-0671
57 West 57th Street (suite 810) btw Fifth/Sixth
NYC 10022 (by appointment)

**Isabella Electrolysis** (212) 832-0431
794 Lexington Avenue btw 61/62nd
NYC 10021 Mon-Fri 9-7 (Thurs 10-8), Sat 9-6

**Miriam Vasicka** (212) 734-1017
895 Park Avenue at 79th
NYC 10021 Mon-Fri 8-8 (by appointment)

**Smooth** (212) 759-6997
133 East 58th Street (suite 507) btw Park/Lexington
NYC 10022 Mon-Fri 12-7, Sat 1-4

**Victor Orris Dermatology** (212) 249-3050
30 East 76th Street (suite 6) btw Madison/Park
NYC 10021 (by appointment)

## Beauty Treatments

**Beauty Basics** (212) 288-7781
1166 Lexington Avenue at 80th
NYC 10028 (by appointment)

**Bernice Electrolysis & Beauty Center** (212) 355-7055
29 East 61st Street (2nd floor) btw Madison/Park
NYC 10021 Mon-Sat 8-6 (Wed-Thurs 8-8)

**Carlos Araque Essential Therapy** (212) 777-2325
36 East 23rd Street btw Park Ave South/Broadway
NYC 10010 (by appointment)

**Cornelia Zicu** (212) 759 9375
680 Madison Avenue at 62nd
NYC 10021 Mon-Fri 9-9, Sat 10-6

**Dashing Diva Nail Spa & Boutique**   **(212) 673-9000**
41 East 8th Street            at Broadway
NYC 10003      Mon-Fri 10-8, Sat 9-9, Sun 9-7

**Diane Young Anti-Aging Salon**   **(212) 753-1200**
38 East 57th Street (8th floor)     btw Madison/Park
NYC 10022     Mon-Thurs 10-8, Fri 10-6, Sat 9-5

**Eastside Massage Therapy Center**   **(212) 249-2927**
351 East 78th Street      btw First/Second
NYC 10021     Mon-Fri 10-9:30, Sat-Sun 10-8

**Norclaire Spa**   **(212) 754-9866**
815 Fifth Avenue      btw 62/63rd
NYC 10021     Tues-Sat 9-5 (by appointment)

**Elizabeth Arden**   **(212) 546-0200**
691 Fifth Avenue      btw 54/55th
NYC 10022     Mon-Tues, Sat 8-6:30
Wed 8-7:30, Thurs-Fri 8-8, Sun 9-6

**Erbe**   **(212) 966-1445**
196 Prince Street     btw MacDougal/Sullivan
NYC 10012      Daily 11-7

**Firozé**   **(212) 249-5445**
*manicure/pedicure/house calls*   (by appointment)

**Gemayel Salon**   **(212) 787-5555**
2030 Broadway      at 70th
NYC 10023     Mon-Fri 10-8, Sat-Sun 9-6

**Janet Sartin**   **(212) 751-5858**
500 Park Avenue      btw 58/59th
NYC 10022     Mon-Fri 10-7, Sat 10-6

**Lia Schorr Skin Care**   **(212) 486-9670**
686 Lexington Avenue (4th floor)     btw 56/57th
NYC 10022     Mon-Fri 9-8, Sat-Sun 9-5

**Ling Skin Care**   **(212) 989-8833**
12 East 16th Street     btw Fifth/Union Square
NYC 10003    Mon-Thurs 10-9, Fri-Sun 11-7 (Sat 9:30-8)

**Mario Badescu**   **(212) 758-1065**
320 East 52nd Street     btw First/Second
NYC 10022     Mon-Tues, Fri 8:30-6
Wed-Thurs 8:30-8:30, Sat 9-5, Sun 10-5:30

**The Mezzanine Spa**   **(212) 431-1600**
**@ SoHo Integrated Health**   btw Spring/Broome
62 Crosby Street   Tues-Wed 12-8, Thurs-Fri 9-8
NYC 10012     Sat-Sun 10-6

**Miano Viel**   **(212) 980-3222**
16 East 52nd Street     btw Fifth/Madison
NYC 10022   Tues 9-6, Wed, Sat 9-3, Thurs-Fri 9-7

**Oasis Day Spa**   **(212) 254-7722**
108 East 16th Street     btw Irving Place/
(2nd floor)      Union Square
NYC 10003     Mon-Fri 10-10, Sat-Sun 9-9

Health & Beauty

**Skinklinic** (212) 521-3100
800b Fifth Avenue at 61st
NYC 10021 Mon-Tues 1-7, Tues-Thurs 8-8
Fri 8-7, Sat 9-3

**Soho Sanctuary** (212) 334-5550
119 Mercer Street (3rd floor) btw Prince/Spring
NYC 10012 Mon 3-9, Tues-Fri 10-9, Sat 10-6, Sun 12-6

**Simi Fazeli @ the Steven Knoll Salon** (212) 421-0100
625 Madison Avenue btw 58/59th
NYC 10022 Tues-Fri, some Sat—call for hours

**Tracie Martyn** (212) 206-9333
59 Fifth Avenue btw 12/13th
NYC 10003 Mon-Sat 8:30-6 (by appointment)

**The Wellpath** (212) 737-9604
1100 Madison Avenue at 83rd
NYC 10028 (by appointment)

**Yasmine Djerradine** (212) 588-1771
30 East 60th Street btw Madison/Park
NYC 10022 Mon-Sat 8:30-8

## Eyebrow Grooming

**Ramy Beauty Therapy** (212) 684-9500
30 East 31st Street btw Madison/Park
NYC 10016 Tues-Sat 10-7

**Eliza's Eyes @ Avon Salon & Spa** (212) 755-2866
725 Fifth Avenue btw 56/57th
NYC 10022 Mon, Sat 8-6, Tues-Fri 7:30-8, Sun 11-6

**Oama @ Pierre Michel** (212) 593-1460
131 East 57th Street btw Park/Lexington
NYC 10022 Mon-Sat 8:30-7

## Manicures/Pedicures

**Acqua Beauty Bar** (212) 620-4329
7 East 14th Street btw Fifth/Union Square
NYC 10003 Mon, Thurs 10-9, Tues-Wed
Fri 10-8, Sat-Sun 10-7

**Buff Spa @ Bergdorf Goodman** (212) 872-8624
754 Fifth Avenue at 58th
NYC 10019 Mon-Sat 10-7 (Thurs 10-8), Sun 12-6

**Ellegee Nail Salon** (212) 472-5063
22 East 66th Street btw Fifth/Madison
NYC 10021 Mon-Fri 9-6:30, Sat 8:30-6:30

**Four Seasons** (212) 350-6420
57 East 57th Street btw Madison/Park
NYC 10022 Mon-Sat 8-9

**Josephine Beauty Treatment** (212) 223-7157
200 East 62nd Street btw Second/Third
NYC 10021 Mon-Fri 10-6 (Thurs 10-8), Sat 10-5

**Just Calm Down** (212) 337-0032
32 West 22nd Street btw Fifth/Sixth
NYC 10010 Mon-Wed 11-8, Thurs-Fri 12-9
Sat 10:30-6, Sun 11-6

**Paul Lebrecque @ Reebok Sports Club/NY** (212) 595-0099
160 Columbus Avenue btw 68/69th
NYC 10023 Mon-Fri 8-11, Sat 9-8, Sun 10-8

**Ramy Spa** (212) 684-9500
39 East 31st Street btw Madison/Park
NYC 10016 (by appointment)

**Rescue Beauty Lounge** (212) 431-0449
8 Center Market Place btw Broome/Grand
NYC 10012 Tues-Fri 11-8, Sat-Sun 10-6

**Rescue Nail Spa** (212) 431-3805
21 Cleveland Place btw Spring/Kenmare
NYC 10012 Mon-Fri 11-8, Sat-10-6

**Robin Narvaez @ Borja Color Studio** (212) 308-3232
118 East 57th Street btw Park/Lexington
NYC 10022 Tues-Fri 10-8, Sat 10-6

**Shobha** (212) 931-8363
594 Broadway (suite 403) btw Houston/Prince
NYC 10012 Tues-Fri 11-7 (Thurs 11-8), Sat 10-6

**Shobha** (212) 223-2872
595 Madison (suite 1403) at 57th
NYC 10022 (opening hours as above)

**Warren-Tricomi** (212) 262-8899
16 West 57th Street (4th floor) btw Fifth/Sixth
NYC 10019 Mon-Sat 9-7

## Day Spas—Women

**Ajune** (212) 628-0044
1294 Third Avenue at 74/75th
NYC 10021 Mon 9-6, Tues-Fri 9-8, Sat 9-6, Sun 11-6

**Allure Day Spa** (212) 644-5500
139 East 55th Street btw Third/Lexington
NYC 10022 Mon-Fri 10:30-7:30, Sat-Sun 10-6

**Amorepacific** (212) 966-0400
114 Spring Street btw Greene/Mercer
NYC 10012 Tues-Sat 11-7, Sun 12-6

**Anushka Day Spa & Cellulite Clinic** (212) 355-6404
501 Madison Avenue btw 52/53rd
NYC 10022 Mon, Sat 10-6, Tues, Thurs 10-8
Wed, Fri 10-7

**The Avon Center** (212) 755-2866
725 Fifth Avenue btw 56/57th
NYC 10022 Mon, Sat 8-6, Tues-Fri 8-8, Sun 11-6

**be mini spa** (212) 253-5665
173 Ludlow Street btw Houston/Stanton
NYC 10002 Daily 12:30-8:30

**Bliss Spa @ the W Hotel**                 **(212) 407-2970**
541 Lexington Avenue                         btw 49/50th
NYC 10022                  (opening hours n/a at press time)

**Bliss Spa**                               **(212) 219-8970**
19 East 57th Street (3rd floor)            btw Fifth/Madison
NYC 10022                            Mon-Fri 9:30-8:30
                          (Wed 12:30-8:30), Sat 9:30-6:30

**Bliss Spa**                               **(212) 219-8970**
568 Broadway (2nd floor)                         at Prince
NYC 10012                    (opening hours as above)

**Body Central**                            **(212) 677-5633**
9 University Place (5th floor)                   btw 11/12th
NYC 10003              Mon-Thurs 4-9, Fri 10-3, Sat 11-3:45

**Buff Spa in Bergdorf Goodman**            **(212) 872-8624**
754 Fifth Avenue                                  at 57th
NYC 10019                                   Mon-Fri 10-7

**Butterfly Studio**                        **(212) 253-2100**
149 Fifth Avenue                                 at 21st
NYC 10010          Mon-Fri 10-6 (Thurs 10-8), Sat 9-5

**D'Mai Urban Spa**                         **(718) 398-2100**
157 Fifth Avenue              btw Lincoln/St John's Place
NYC 11217      Tues-Fri 11-7 (Thurs 11-9:30), Sat-Sun 10-6

**Dorit Baxter Day Spa**                    **(212) 371-4542**
47 West 57th Street (3rd floor)             btw Fifth/Sixth
NYC 10019                         Mon-Sat 9-8, Sun 10-6

**Eden Day Spa**                            **(212) 226-0515**
388 Broadway                             btw Walker/White
NYC 10013                        Mon-Sat 9:30-9, Sun 9-7

**Exhale**                                  **(212) 249-3000**
150 Central Park South                   btw Sixth/Seventh
NYC 10019                        Daily 6:30-9:30 (Sun 8-8)

**Faina European Spa**                      **(212) 245-6557**
315 West 57th Street                       btw Eighth/Ninth
NYC 10019              Mon-Fri 10-8, Sat 9-8, Sun 10-7

**Gemayel Salon & Spa**                     **(212) 787-5555**
2030 Broadway                                    at 70th
NYC 10023                       Mon-Fri 10-8, Sat-Sun 9-6

**Georgette Klinger**                       **(212) 838-3200**
501 Madison Avenue                            btw 52/53rd
NYC 10022          Mon-Thurs 9-8, Fri, Sun 9-6, Sat 8:30-6

**Glow Skin Spa**                           **(212) 319-6654**
41 East 57th Street (suite 1206)          btw Madison/Park
NYC 10022                           (by appointment)

**Gloss Day Spa**                           **(212) 249-2100**
51 East 73rd Street                       btw Madison/Park
NYC 10021              Mon-Fri 10-7, Sat 11-5, Sun 12-5

**The Greenhouse Day Spa**                  **(212) 644-4449**
127 East 57th Street                     btw Park/Lexington
NYC 10022        Mon-Fri 9-8 (Thurs 9-9), Sat 10-6, Sun 12-6

**Hair Fashion East**      **(212) 686-7524**
411 Park Avenue South      btw 28/29th
NYC 10016      Tues-Fri 10-7:30, Sat 9:30-3

**Haven**      **(212) 343-3515**
150 Mercer Street      btw Prince/Houston
NYC 10012      Mon-Fri 11-7, Sat 10-6, Sun 12-7

**Jin Soon Natural Hand & Foot Spa**      **(212) 473-2047**
56 East 4th Street      btw Bowery/Second
NYC 10003      Daily 11-8

**Karen Wu Beauty & Wellness Spa**      **(212) 585-2044**
1377 Third Avenue      btw 78/79th
NYC 10021      Mon-Fri 10:30-9, Sat 10:30-8, Sun 10:30-7

**La Prairie Spa @ the Ritz-Carlton**      **(212) 521-6135**
50 Central Park South (2nd floor)      at Sixth
NYC 10022      Daily 8-9

**Lush Essential Hand & Foot Spa**      **(212) 625-1839**
98 Thompson Street      btw Prince/Spring
NYC 10012      Mon-Fri 11-8, Sat-Sun 12-7

**Maximus**      **(212) 431-3333**
15 Mercer Street      btw Grand/Canal
NYC 10013      Tues-Wed, Fri 10-7, Thurs 11-9, Sat 10-6

**The Mezzanine Spa**      **(212) 431-1600**
**@ SoHo Integrated Health**      btw Spring/Broome
62 Crosby Street      Tues-Wed 12-8, Thurs-Fri 9-8
NYC 10012      Sat-Sun 10-6

**Oasis Day Spa**      **(212) 254-7722**
108 East 16th Street      btw Irving Place/Union Square East
NYC 10003      Mon-Fri 10-10, Sat-Sun 9-9

**The Peninsula Spa**      **(212) 903-3910**
700 Fifth Avenue (21st floor)      at 55th
NYC 10022      Mon-Fri 8:30-10, Sat 8:45-8

**Repechage Spa de Beaute**      **(212) 751-2500**
115 East 57th Street      btw Park/Lexington
NYC 10022      Mon, Thurs 10-8
     Tues-Wed, Fri 10-6:30, Sat 10-6

**Shija Day Spa**      **(212) 366-0706**
37 Union Square West      btw 16/17th
NYC 10003      Daily 10-8

**Shiseido Studio**      **(212) 625-8821**
155 Spring Street      btw Wooster/West Broadway
NYC 10012      Tues 11-6, Wed-Sat 11-7, Sun 12-6

**Silk Day Spa**      **(212) 255-6457**
47 West 13th Street      btw Fifth/Sixth
NYC 10011      Mon-Sat 10-9:30, Sun 11-7

**Skin Care Lab**      **(212) 334-3142**
568 Broadway      btw Prince/Houston
NYC 10012      Mon-Fri 11-8, Sat 10-7, Sun 12-6

**Sole**      **(212) 420-SOLE**
227 East 14th Street      btw Second/Third
NYC 10003      Wed-Fri 12-7, Sat-Sun 10-7

**Spa 64**       **(212) 753-1064**
154 East 64th Street       at Lexington
NYC 10021       Mon-Sat 10-9, Sun 11-7

**Stone Spa**       **(212) 254-3045**
125 Fourth Avenue       btw 12/13th
NYC 10003       Mon-Fri 10-9, Sat-Sun 10-6

**Susan Ciminelli Day Spa**       **(212) 872-2650**
754 Fifth Avenue @ Bergdorf Goodman       btw 57/58th
NYC 10019       Mon-Sat (Thurs 10-8), Sun 11:30-6

**Ula Day Spa**       **(212) 343-2376**
8 Harrison Street       btw Greenwich/Hudson
NYC 10013       Tues-Fri 11-7, Sat 10-6, Sun 12-6

## Day Spas—Men

**Aveda**       **(212) 473-0280**
456 West Broadway       btw Houston/Prince
NYC 10012       Mon-Fri 10-9, Sat 9-8, Sun 10-6

**Bliss Spa**       **(212) 219-8970**
19 East 57th Street (3rd floor)       btw Fifth/Madison
NYC 10022       Mon-Fri 9:30-8:30
      (Wed 12:30-8:30), Sat 9:30-6:30

**Bliss Spa**       **(212) 219-8970**
568 Broadway (2nd floor)       at Prince
NYC 10012       (opening hours as above)

**Carapan Spa**       **(212) 633-6220**
5 West 16th Street       at Fifth
NYC 10011       Daily 10-19

**Eden Day Spa**       **(212) 226-0515**
388 Broadway       btw Walker/White
NYC 10013       Daily 9:30-9 (Sun 9:30-6:30)

**Equinox Spa**       **(212) 396-9611**
205 East 85th Street       at Third
NYC 10028       Mon-Tues 9-10, Wed-Fri 9-9, Sat-Sun 9-8

**Equinox Spa**       **(212) 750-4671**
140 East 63rd Street       at Lexington
NYC 10021       Mon-Thurs 9-8, Fri-Sun 9-7

**Glow Skin Spa**       **(212) 319-6654**
41 East 57th Street (suite 1206)       btw Madison/Park
NYC 10022       (by appointment)

**John Allan's Club**       **(212) 922-0361**
46 East 46th Street       btw Madison/Park
NYC 10017       Mon-Fri 11-7

**Nickel Day Spa**       **(212) 242-3203**
77 Eighth Avenue       at 14th
NYC 10014       Sun, Mon 1-9, Tues-Sat 11-9

**Paul Lebrecque @ Reebok Sports Club/NY**       **(212) 595-0099**
160 Columbus Avenue       btw 68/69th
NYC 10023       Mon-Fri 8-11, Sat 9-8, Sun 10-8

**Qiora Spa**                          **(212) 527-0400**
535 Madison Avenue                          btw 54/55th
NYC 10022          Tues-Fri 11-6 (Thurs 11-7), Sat 12-6

**SkinCareLab**                        **(212) 334-3142**
568 Broadway                       btw Prince/Houston
NYC 10012          Mon-Fri 11-8, Sat 10-7, Sun 12-6

## Gyms

**Casa Fitness (personal training only)**   **(212) 717-1998**
48 East 73rd Street                   btw Madison/Park
NYC 10021                           (by appointment)

**Classic Bodies**                     **(212) 737-8440**
189 East 79th Street                btw Second/Third
NYC 10021                         (call for class hours)

**Crunch**                             **(212) 875-1902**
162 West 83rd Street        btw Amsterdam/Columbus
NYC 10024               Mon-Fri 5:30-10, Sat-Sun 8-9

**Crunch**                             **(212) 758-3434**
1109 Second Avenue                         btw 58/59th
NYC 10022                              Mon-Thurs 5-11
                                  Fri 5-10, Sat-Sun 8-9

**Crunch**                             **(212) 594-8050**
555 West 42nd Street                       at Eleventh
NYC 10036                 Mon-Fri 6-10, Sat-Sun 7-7

**Crunch**                             **(212) 869-7788**
144 West 38th Street           btw Broadway/Seventh
NYC 10018                  Mon-Fri 6-10, Sat-Sun 8-6

**Crunch**                             **(212) 475-2018**
54 East 13th Street     btw Broadway/University Place
NYC 10003                  Mon-Fri 6-10, Sat-Sun 8-8

**Crunch**                             **(212) 614-0120**
404 Lafayette Street       btw Astor Place/East 4th
NYC 10003         Mon-Fri open 24 hrs, Sat-Sun 9-8

**Crunch**                             **(212) 420-0507**
623 Broadway                   btw Houston/Bleecker
NYC 10012            Mon-Fri 6-11, Sat 8-8, Sun 9-8

**Crunch**                             **(212) 366-3725**
152 Christopher Street   btw Washington/Greenwich
NYC 10014                  Mon-Fri 6-11, Sat-Sun 8-9

**David Barton Gym**                   **(212) 517-7577**
30 East 85th Street                    btw Fifth/Madison
NYC 10028                Mon-Fri 5:30-11, Sat-Sun 8-9

**David Barton Gym**                   **(212) 727-0004**
552 Sixth Avenue                           btw 15/16th
NYC 10011            Mon-Fri 6-12, Sat 9-9, Sun 10-11

**The Equinox**                        **(212) 799-1818**
2465 Broadway                              btw 91/92nd
NYC 10025      Mon-Thurs 6-11, Fri 6-10, Sat-Sun 8-9

**The Equinox**                                    **(212) 721-4200**
344 Amsterdam Avenue                                        at 76th
NYC 10024                              (opening hours as above)

**The Equinox**                                    **(212) 780-9300**
897 Broadway                                           btw 19/20th
NYC 10003                              (opening hours as above)

**The Equinox**                                    **(212) 620-0103**
97 Greenwich Avenue                              at West 12th
NYC 10012                              (opening hours as above)

**The Equinox**                                    **(212) 750-4900**
140 East 63rd Street                               at Lexington
NYC 10021                              (opening hours as above)

**The Equinox**                                    **(212) 439-8500**
205 East 85th Street                            btw Second/Third
NYC 10028                              Mon-Thurs 5:30-10:30
                                                Fri 5:30-10, Sat-Sun 8-9

**The Equinox**                                    **(212) 277-5400**
250 East 54th Street                                at Second
NYC 10022                              Mon-Thurs 5:30-11
                              Fri 5:30-9, Sat 8-9, Sun 8-8

**Lotte Berk Method**                              **(212) 288-6613**
23 East 67th Street                           btw Fifth/Madison
NYC 10021                              Mon-Fri 7-7, Sat-Sun 8-2

**Radu**                                           **(212) 581-1995**
24 West 57th Street (2nd floor)                       at Fifth
NYC 10019                              (call for opening hours)

**Reebok Sports Club/NY**                          **(212) 362-6800**
160 Columbus Avenue                                    at 67th
NYC 10023          Mon-Thurs 5-11, Fri 5-10, Sat-Sun 7-9

**The Sports Center @ Chelsea Piers**              **(212) 336-6000**
Pier 60, West Side Highway                       at West 23rd
NYC 10011                              Mon-Fri 6-11, Sat-Sun 8-9

**Studio Uma**                                     **(212) 249-7979**
20 East 68th Street                           btw Fifth/Madison
NYC 10021                              Mon-Fri 6-9, Sat 7-9, Sun 9-6

**Synergy Fitness Center**                         **(212) 879-6013**
1438 Third Avenue                                  btw 81/82nd
NYC 10028                              Mon-Fri 5:30-11, Sat-Sun 8-8

**Synergy Fitness Center**                         **(212) 545-9590**
4 Park Avenue                                         btw 33/34th
NYC 10016                              Mon-Fri 5:30-11, Sat-Sun 8-7

**Threshold**                                      **(212) 868-2837**
521 West 26th Street                         btw Tenth/Eleventh
NYC 10001                              (by appointment only)

## Pilates/Mat Classes

**Pilates on Fifth**                               **(212) 687-8885**
501 Fifth Avenue (suite 22)                          at 42nd
NYC 10017                              Mon-Fri 7-9, Sat-Sun 10-2

**Drago's Gymnasium** **(212) 757-0724**
50 West 57th Street (6th floor) btw Fifth/Sixth
NYC 10019 Mon-Fri 7-8, Sat 8-2

**InForm Fitness** **(212) 755-9895**
201 East 56th Street btw Second/Third
NYC 10022 (by appointment)

**The Kane School of Core Integration** **(212) 463-8308**
7 East 17th Street (5th floor) btw Fifth/Broadway
NYC 10003 Mon-Fri 9-8 (by appointment)

**Power Pilates** **(212) 627-5852**
49 West 23rd Street (10th floor) btw Fifth/Sixth
NYC 10011 Mon-Fri 7-8, Sat 9-6, Sun 9-3

**re:AB** **(212) 420-9111**
33 Bleecker Street at Mott
NYC 10012 Mon-Fri 7-8, Sat 9-2, Sun 10-4

**Real Pilates** **(212) 625-0777**
177 Duane Street btw Greenwich/Hudson
NYC 10013 Mon-Thurs 7-9, Fri 7-8, Sat 9-4, Sun 10-6

## Yoga

**Integral Yoga Institute** **(212) 721-4000**
200 West 72nd Street at Broadway
NYC 10023 (call for class hours)

**Integral Yoga Institute** **(212) 929-0586**
227 West 13th Street btw Seventh/Eighth
NYC 10011 (call for class hours)

**Jivamukti Yoga Center** **(212) 353-0214**
404 Lafayette Street btw West 4th/Astor Place
NYC 10003 Mon-Fri 8-9, Sat 10-5, Sun 9-5:30

**Pantajali Yoga Shala** **(212) 431-3738**
430 Broome Street at Crosby
NYC 10012 (call for class hours)

**Soho Sanctuary** **(212) 334-5550**
119 Mercer Street (3rd floor) btw Prince/Spring
NYC 10012 Mon 3-9, Tues-Fri 10-9
Sat 10-6, Sun 12-6

## Massage Therapists *(office & home visits)*

Lisa Smith **(212) 969-8718**

Massage Massage **(212) 696-9069**

Marcelo Countinho **(212) 924-3741**

Osaka **(212) 956-3422**
50 West 56th Street (2nd floor) btw Fifth/Sixth
NYC 10019 Daily 10-1

Physical Advantage **(212) 460-1879**

New York Massage Company **(212) 427-8175**

**Salon de Tokyo**
200 West 57th Street (suite 1308)
NYC 10019

**(212) 757-2187**
at Seventh
Mon-Sat 11-12

**Tui Na**

**(212) 387-0733**

## Tanning Salons

**Portofino Sun Center**
1300 Third Avenue
NYC 10021

**(212) 988-6300**
at 75th
Mon-Fri 9-8, Sat 9-7, Sun 10-6

**Portofino Sun Center**
104 West 73rd Street
NYC 10023

**(212) 769-0200**
at Columbus
Mon-Sat 9-9:930, Sun 9-8:30

**Portofino Sun Center**
38 East 58th Street
NYC 10022

**(212) 355-2772**
at Madison
Mon-Tues, Fri 9-9
Wed-Thurs 9-10, Sat 9-8, Sun 10-7

**Portofino Sun Center**
462 West Broadway
NYC 10012

**(212) 473-7600**
btw Houston/Prince
Mon-Sat 9-8:15, Sun 11-5:15

**Portofino Sun Center**
64 Greenwich Avenue
NYC 10011

**(212) 627-4775**
at Seventh
Mon-Fri 9-10, Sat 9-9, Sun 11-7

## Self-tanning

**Completely Bare Downtown**
103 Fifth Avenue
NYC 10003

**(212) 366-6060**
btw 17/18th
Tues-Wed 12-8, Thurs 12-9
Fri 10-7, Sat 10-6

**Completely Bare @ Barneys**
660 Madison Avenue
NYC 10021

**(212) 366-6060**
btw 60/61st
Mon-Sat 10-7, Sun 11-6

**Paul Lebrecque @ Reebok Sports Club/NY**
171 East 65th Street
NYC 10021

**(212) 595-0099**
btw Lexington/Third
Mon-Fri 8-9, Sat 9-8, Sun 10-8

## Bridal Consultants

**Ober, Onet & Associates**
9 East 97th Street
NYC 10128

**(212) 876-6775**
btw Fifth/Madison
*Contact: Polly Onet*

**Marcy Blum Associates**
259 West 11th Street
NYC 10014

**(212) 929-9814**
at Fourth
*Contact: Marcy Blum*

**Saved by the Bell**
11 Riverside Drive
NYC 10023

**(212) 874-5457**
btw 73/74th
*Contact: Susan Bell*

## Make-up Artists

**Carlos Solano** **(917) 447-5197**

**Kimara Ahnert** **(212) 452-4252**
1113 Madison Avenue btw 83/84th
NYC 10028 (by appointment)

**Rochelle Weithorn** **(212) 472-8668**
431 East 73rd Street btw York/First
NYC 10021 (also does hair; by appointment)

## Personal Shoppers

**Barneys New York** **(212) 826-8900**
660 Madison Avenue (3rd floor) btw 60/61st
NYC 10021 Mon-Sat 10-6

**Bergdorf Goodman** **(212) 872-8772**
754 Fifth Avenue btw 57/58th
NYC 10019 Mon-Fri 9:30-5:30
*Contact: "Solutions" by Betty Halbreich*

**Bloomingdale's** **(212) 705-2000**
1000 Third Avenue at 59/60th
NYC 10022 Mon-Fri 10-8:30, Sat 10-7, Sun 11-7

**Dorian May** **(212) 249-8378**
(by appointment)

**Go Lightly** **(212) 352-1153**
95 Horatio Street (suite 432) at Washington
NYC 10014 *Contact: Jenny Gerin*
*golight@go-lightly.com*

**Lord & Taylor** **(212) 391-3344**
424 Fifth Avenue btw 38/39th
NYC 10018 Mon-Sat 10-8:30, Sun 11-7

**Macy's** **(212) 494-4181**
151 West 34th Street at Herald Square
NYC 10001 Mon-Sat 10-7:30, Sun 11-6
*Contact: Linda Lee*

**Paul Stuart** **(212) 682-0320**
Madison Avenue at 45th
NYC 10017 Tues-Sat 8:30-5:30 (by appointment)

**One on One @ Saks Fifth Avenue** **(212) 940-4145**
611 Fifth Avenue btw 49/50th
NYC 10022 Mon-Sat 10-7 (Thurs 10-8), Sun 11-7

**Visual Therapy** **(212) 315-2233**
24 West 57th Street (suite 502) btw Fifth/Sixth
NYC 10019 Mon-Fri 9-5:30
*Contact: Jesse Garza, Joe Lupo, Lani Rosenstock*

# Repairs & Services

Dry Cleaners

Mending & Alterations

Custom Tailoring

Boutique Clothing Storage

Shoe Repair

Leather Repair (handbags & luggage)

Trimmings (ribbons, buttons, etc.)

Thrift Shops

## Dry Cleaners—Haute Couture & Bridal

**Dunrite**                                    **(212) 221-9297**
141 West 38th Street                     btw Broadway/Seventh
NYC 10018                                    Mon-Fri 7:30-5:20

**Fashion Award Cleaners**              **(212) 289-5623**
1462 Lexington Avenue                          btw 94/95th
NYC 10128                                    Mon-Fri 7:30-6:30
                                    Sat 9-3 (except in summer)

**Hallak Cleaners**                       **(212) 879-4694**
1232 Second Avenue                            btw 64/65th
NYC 10021                                Mon-Fri 7-6:30, Sat 8-3

**Jeeves of Belgravia**                   **(212) 570-9130**
39 East 65th Street                        btw Madison/Park
NYC 10021                                  Mon-Fri 8-6, Sat 10-2

**Madame Paulette**                       **(212) 838-6827**
1255 Second Avenue                            btw 65/66th
NYC 10021                                   Mon-Fri 7:30-7, Sat 8-5

**Montclair**                             **(212) 289-2070**
1331 Lexington Avenue                          btw 88/89th
NYC 10128                                   Mon-Fri 7-7, Sat 8-5

## Dry Cleaners—All-Purpose

**Anita Cleaners**                        **(212) 717-6602**
1380 First Avenue                             btw 73/74th
NYC 10021                                       Mon-Fri 8-6

**Meurice Garment Care**                  **(212) 475-2778**
31 University Place                             btw 8/9th
NYC 10003            Mon-Fri 7:30-7, Sat 9-3, Sun 9:30-3

**Meurice Garment Care & Tiecrafters**    **(212) 759-9057**
245 East 57th Street                       btw Second/Third
NYC 10022                                 Mon-Fri 8-6:30, Sat 9-3

**Montclair**                             **(212) 289-2070**
1331 Lexington Avenue                          btw 88/89th
NYC 10128                                   Mon-Fri 7-7, Sat 8-5

**New York's Finest French Cleaners**     **(212) 431-4010**
154 Reade Street                      btw Hudson/Greenwich
NYC 10013                                 Mon-Fri 8-6:30, Sat 8-5

**Tiecrafters**                           **(212) 629-5800**
252 West 29th Street                      btw Seventh/Eighth
NYC 10001                                  Mon-Fri 9-5, Sat 10-2

**Young's Cleaners and Launderers**       **(212) 473-6154**
188 Third Avenue                                at 17th
NYC 10003                                  Mon-Fri 7-7, Sat 8-5

## Mending & Alterations

**Alfonso Sciortino Custom Alteration**    **(212) 888-2846**

**Bhambi Custom Tailors**    **(212) 935-5379**
14 East 60th Street (room 610)    btw Fifth/Madison
NYC 10022    Mon-Sat 10-7

**Eddie Ugras**    **(212) 595-1596**
125 West 72nd Street (3rd floor)   btw Columbus/Broadway
NYC 10023    Mon-Fri 9:30-7, Sat 10-5

**Fine Alterations & Sewing**    **(212) 253-2022**
240 East 6th Street    at Second
NYC 10003    (by appointment)

**French American Weaving Co**    **(212) 765-4670**
119 West 57th Street (room 1406)    btw Sixth/Seventh
NYC 10019    Mon-Fri 10:30-5:30

**John's European Boutique & Tailoring**    **(212) 752-2239**
118 East 59th Street (2nd floor)    btw Park/Lexington
NYC 10022    Mon-Fri 9-6:30
Sat 10-1 (by appointment)

**Nelson Ferri**    **(212) 988-5085**
766 Madison Avenue (4th floor)    btw 65/66th
NYC 10021    Mon-Fri 9-6, Sat 10-5

**Sebastian Tailors**    **(212) 688-1244**
767 Lexington Avenue    btw 60/61st
NYC 10021    Tues-Fri 8:30-5, Sat 9-4:30

**Superior Repair Center (leather)**    **(212) 889-7211**
7 West 30th Street (9th floor)    btw Fifth/Broadway
NYC 10016    Mon-Fri 10-6, Sat 10-3 (winter only)

**Three Star Leather Custom Tailors**    **(212) 879-4200**
790 Madison Avenue (room 507)    at 67th
NYC 10021    Mon-Sat 10-6

## Custom Tailoring

**Albert Sakhai**    **(212) 397-7883**
144 West 19th Street    btw Sixth/Seventh
NYC 10011    (by appointment; closed July and August)

**Dynasty Custom Tailoring**    **(212) 679-1075**
6 East 38th Street    btw Madison/Fifth
NYC 10016    Mon-Fri 9-6:30, Sat 10-3

**Guillermo Couture**    **(212) 366-6965**
153 West 27th Street, suite 301    btw Sixth/Seventh
NYC 10001    by appointment

**Hong Kong Tailor Jack**    **(212) 675-0818**
136 Waverly Place    at Sixth
NYC 10014    Mon-Sat 10-7

**Mr Ned**    **(212) 924-5042**
137 Fifth Avenue    at 20th
NYC 10010    Mon-Fri 8-5, Sat 8-1

## Boutique Clothing Storage

**Garde Robe**                                   **(212) 227-7554**
137 Duane Street                              btw Church/West
NYC 10013                                      by (appointment)
*www.garderobeonline.com*


## Shoe Repair

**Andrade Boot and Shoe Repair**                **(212) 787-0465**
379 Amsterdam Avenue                              btw 78/79th
NYC 10024                                    Mon-Fri 8-7, Sat 9-6

**Andrade Shoe Repair**                         **(212) 529-3541**
103 University Place                               btw 12/13th
NYC 10003                                   Mon-Fri 7:30-6, Sat 9-6:30

**Angelo Shoe Repair**                          **(212) 757-6364**
666 Fifth Avenue (lower level)                        at 51st
NYC 10136                                   Mon-Fri 7:30-6:30, Sat 10-5

**B.Nelson**                                    **(212) 869-3552**
1221 Sixth Avenue                                  btw 48/49th
NYC 10020 (level C2)                            Mon-Fri 7:30-5

**Hector's Shoe Repair**                        **212 727 1237**
11 Greenwich Avenue                        btw Christopher/11th
NYC 10014                                    Mon-Fri 7-7, Sat 9-6

**Jim's Shoe Repair**                           **(212) 355-8259**
50 East 59th Street                           btw Madison/Park
NYC 10022                                        Mon-Fri 8-6

**Shoe Service Plus**                           **(212) 262-4823**
15 West 55th Street                              btw Fifth/Sixth
NYC 10019                                    Mon-Fri 7-7, Sat 10-5

**Top Service**                                 **(212) 765-3190**
845 Seventh Avenue                                 btw 54/55th
NYC 10019                                    Mon-Fri 8-6, Sat 9-3


## Leather Repair *(handbags & luggage)*

**Modern Leather**                              **(212) 947-7770**
2 West 32nd Street (4th floor)               btw Fifth/Broadway
NYC 10001                                        Mon-Fri 8:30-5
                                            Sat 8:30-1 (winter only)

**Superior Repair Center**                      **(212) 889-7211**
141 Lexington Avenue                                  at 29th
NYC 10016                          Mon-Fri 10-6, Sat 10-3 (winter only)


## Trimmings *(ribbons, buttons, feathers, odds & ends)*

**Greenberg & Hammer**                          **(212) 246-2836**
24 West 57th Street                              btw Fifth/Sixth
NYC 10019                                    Mon-Fri 9-6, Sat 10-5
*(trims, notions, buttons, zippers etc)*

**Hyman Hendler & Sons**    **(212) 840-8393**
67 West 38th Street    btw Fifth/Sixth
NYC 10018    Mon-Fri 9-5
*(the highest quality ribbons from around the world)*

**M&J Trimming Co**    **(212) 391-9072**
1000-1008 Sixth Avenue    btw 37/38th
NYC 10018    Mon-Fri 9-6, Sat 10-5
*(ribbons, trimmings, buttons, rhinestones etc)*

**Margola**    **(212) 564-2929**
48 West 37th Street    btw Fifth/Sixth
NYC 10018    Mon-Fri 8:30-6, Sat 10-4
*(feather trimmings, silk flowers, ribbons,
veiling and netting, beading and stones)*

**Mokuba**    **(212) 869-8900**
55 West 39th Street    btw Fifth/Sixth
NYC 10018    Mon-Fri 9-5
*(super-fancy ribbons in silk, velvet, chiffon, fake fur)*

**Tender Buttons**    **(212) 758-7004**
143 East 62nd Street    btw Lexington/Third
NYC 10021    Mon-Fri 10:30-6, Sat 10:30-5:30
*(an exquisite collection of buttons, modern and antique)*

**Tinsel Trading**    **(212) 730-1030**
47 West 38th Street    btw Fifth/Sixth
NYC 10018    Mon-Fri 10-5:30
*(flowers, fringes, ribbons, cords, tassels;
specialist in 1920s metallics)*

## Thrift Shops

**Cancer Care Thrift Shop**    **(212) 879-9868**
1480 Third Avenue    btw 83/84th
NYC 10028    (call for opening hours)

**Housing Works Thrift Shop**    **(212) 772-8461**
202 East 77th Street    btw Second/Third
NYC 10021    Mon-Fri 11-7, Sat 10-6, Sun 12-5

**Housing Works Thrift Shop**    **(212) 579-7566**
306 Columbus Avenue    btw 74/75th
NYC 10023    (opening hours as above)

**Housing Works Thrift Shop**    **(212) 529-5955**
157 East 23rd Street    btw Third/Lexington
NYC 10004    Mon-Sat 10-6, Sun 12-5

**Housing Works Thrift Shop**    **(212) 366-0820**
143 West 17th Street    btw Sixth/Seventh
NYC 10004    (opening hours as above)

**Memorial Sloan-Kettering**    **(212) 535-1250**
Cancer Center Thrift Shop    btw 81/82nd
1440 Third Avenue    Mon-Fri 10-5:30, Sat 11-5
NYC 10028

**Spence-Chapin Thrift Shop**    **(212) 737-8448**
1473 Third Avenue    at 83rd
NYC 10028    Mon-Fri 11-6, Sat 11-5, Sun 12-4:45